# STRATEGIC
# MANAGEMENT

# STRATEGIC MANAGEMENT

**GARTH SALONER**
*Stanford University*
*Graduate School of Business*

**ANDREA SHEPARD**
*Stanford University*
*Graduate School of Business*

**JOEL PODOLNY**
*Stanford University*
*Graduate School of Business*

**JOHN WILEY & SONS, INC.**
*New York / Chichester / Weinheim / Brisbane / Singapore / Toronto*

| | |
|---|---|
| *Executive Editor* | Brent Gordon |
| *Editor* | Jeff Marshall |
| *Developmental Editor* | Johnna Barto |
| *Marketing Manager* | Jessica Garcia |
| *Production Editor* | Sandra Russell |
| *Cover Illustrator* | Mick Wiggins |
| *Designer* | Madelyn Lesure |
| *Illustration Editor* | Anna Melhorn |
| *Production Management Services* | Hermitage Publishing Services |

This book was typeset in Janson by Hermitage Publishing Services and printed and bound by Courier Companies. The cover was printed by Lehigh Press, Inc.

The paper in this book was manufactured by a mill whose forest management programs include sustained yield harvesting of its timberlands. Sustained yield harvesting principles ensure that the number of trees cut each year does not exceed the amount of new growth.

This book is printed on acid-free paper. ∞

*Library of Congress Cataloging in Publication Data*

Saloner, Garth.
    Strategic management/Garth Saloner, Andrea Shepard, Joel Podolny.
        p. cm.
    Includes bibliographical references and index.
    ISBN 0-471-38071-7 (cloth: alk. paper)
    1. Strategic planning. I. Shepard, Andrea. II. Podolny, Joel M. (Joel Marc) III. Title.
HD30.28.S25 2001
658.4'021–dc21

                                                00-043275

ISBN 0-471-38071-7

Printed in the United States of America.

10  9  8  7  6  5  4  3  2

*To*
*Marlene, Amber, Romy, and Kim*
*Diane, Anna, and Colin*
*Tamara, Aaron, and Asa*
*for this book and so much more*

# PREFACE

We have each taught the Strategic Management MBA core course at Stanford University's Graduate School of Business at various times over the past decade. Like many strategic management courses, ours is case-based, but we typically end our classes with a lecture summarizing the teaching points of the day. Over the years those lessons evolved from single slides to lengthy class notes. At some point we decided it would be easy and fruitful to pull this material together into a book. We were wrong about the former; we hope we were right about the latter.

We have written this book for current and future general managers who have or will have overall responsibility for a business. These managers have what can be the most rewarding of managerial jobs: to craft a strategy that will guide their business, to build an organization that can achieve their strategic goals, and to make the fundamental strategic decisions to navigate a changing world. *The essential ability for this job is a well-developed capability for strategic thinking.* We have tried to provide a set of frameworks, tools, and concepts to build this capability. We have drawn from research in the disciplines that surround and support strategic management with an inevitable emphasis on our own disciplinary backgrounds: theoretical and empirical microeconomics (especially industrial organization) and organization theory. While these disciplines have guided our writing, our steadfast focus has been on strategic management. Our goal has been to provide insights into organizations and strategy that will help general managers make strategic thinking in their firms pervasive, effective, and rewarding.

In writing a book about strategy from the perspective of the disciplines we have tried to achieve several things:

- We have tried to meld the various approaches rather than to pit them against one another. Consequently economic and organizational ideas are presented side-by-side.

- We have tried to focus on insights and concepts without bringing the full formal machinery of the related research to bear. As a result, we have written a book that is frugal in its use of footnotes to the literature, trusting that instructors will recognize and expand upon the underlying research as they see fit.

- Finally, we have chosen our material based on what we think is important for strategic thinking and have not, therefore, provided complete coverage of underlying disciplinary topics.

A number of colleagues have taught the course with us over the years and have contributed to our thinking. These colleagues are Bill Barnett, Thomas Hellmann, Rebecca Henderson (on leave from MIT), Fiona Scott Morton, Kevin Murdock, and Ezra Zuckerman. Undoubtedly many of their ideas have found their way into the text.

Fiona and Rebecca also generously read and provided feedback on many of the chapters as we went along. Special thanks are due to Robert Burgelman who developed the predecessor course from which our course and book inherit a number of ideas and to Julio Rotemberg who helped develop some of the basic themes in the book. Thousands of Stanford MBA, Sloan, and executive education students have patiently endured many rough drafts of this material. Their feedback—and sometimes pushback—have molded and improved the book.

The course and book were developed during the decade in which Mike Spence presided as Dean of the Stanford GSB. His commitment to the strategy area was absolute, and his support for our efforts was unwavering. A number of other colleagues at the Stanford GSB and elsewhere have been influential in our thinking about this material and have helped us in various ways. We are grateful to David Baron, Jim Baron, Severin Borenstein, Tim Bresnahan, Mike Hannan, Paul Joskow, Jeffrey Pfeffer, David Kreps, Peter Reiss, John Roberts, Nancy Rose, Bob Wilson, and Mark Wolfson. We are also thankful to other colleagues who have read draft chapters or "beta tested" them in their own classrooms, including Judy Chevalier, Luis Garicano, Rob Gertner, Marvin Lieberman, and Peter Zemsky.

We have had the privilege of working with many outstanding general managers. These interactions have greatly influenced our understanding of what general managers need to know. We are especially grateful to managers and fellow board members at all the companies with whom we have worked. Special thanks are due to Peter Johnson, Chairman of QRS, for his wisdom over several years.

Our publisher, John Wiley & Sons, also solicited feedback from many reviewers to whom we are grateful. Some have been mentioned above and some have chosen to remain anonymous. We thank them all, including Duncan Angwin, Brian Boyd, Mason Carpenter, Kenneth Corts, James Davis, Derrick D'Souza, Arthur Francis, Philip Gibbs, Ari Ginsberg, Bruce Kogut, Julia Porter Liebeskind, John McGee, Mark Meckler, William Mitchell, Peter Moran, Atul Nerkar, John Prescott, Michael D. Ryall, Anju Seth, Richard A. Spinello, John Stanbury, Rod White, and Robert Wiseman.

The editors and staff at John Wiley have been wonderful partners. Joe Heider began working with us on this project before we had even decided to do it! Brent Gordon patiently managed the editorial process, Gerald Lombardi improved every sentence, and Johnna Barto ably managed development. At Stanford, Sandra Berg poured hours into correcting draft after draft, and Linda Bethel provided assistance with the illustrations.

Our greatest debt is to our parents, partners, and children for their love and support. For all the times this book took precedence over more important things, the dedication comes from the bottom of our hearts. At last we can say with certainty— and no small measure of relief—that the answer to the persistent question "When *will* the book be finished?" is "Now."

*Garth Saloner*
*Andrea Shepard*
*Joel Podolny*

*Stanford, California*

# BRIEF CONTENTS

1 INTRODUCTION  1

2 BUSINESS STRATEGY  19

3 COMPETITIVE ADVANTAGE  39

4 INTERNAL CONTEXT: ORGANIZATION DESIGN  65

5 ORGANIZATION AND COMPETITIVE ADVANTAGE  93

6 EXTERNAL CONTEXT: INDUSTRY ANALYSIS  119

7 THE SPECTRUM OF COMPETITION AND NICHE MARKETS  149

8 COMPETITION IN CONCENTRATED MARKETS  185

9 ENTRY AND THE ADVANTAGE OF INCUMBENCY  215

10 CREATING AND CAPTURING VALUE IN THE VALUE CHAIN  239

11 STRATEGIC MANAGEMENT IN A CHANGING ENVIRONMENT  271

12 STRATEGY IN MARKETS WITH DEMAND-SIDE INCREASING
RETURNS  305

13 GLOBALIZATION AND STRATEGY  329

14 CORPORATE STRATEGY: MANAGING FOR VALUE IN
A MULTIBUSINESS COMPANY  351

15 THE STRATEGY PROCESS  381

Appendix  APPLYING GAME THEORY TO STRATEGIC
MANAGEMENT  405

Credits  427

Index  429

# CONTENTS

**1  INTRODUCTION**  1
  1.1  Strategic Management  1
  1.2  The Role of Business Strategy  2
       Examples: Dell Computer and Compaq Computer  4
       The Dynamics of Business Strategy  6
       Strategic Planning versus Strategic Thinking  8
  1.3  The Organization and Its Objectives  10
       Performance: Overarching Objectives  10
       Firms and Managers  12
  1.4  Perspectives on the Impact of the General Manager  14
  1.5  Organization of the Book  16

**2  BUSINESS STRATEGY**  19
  2.1  Introduction  19
  2.2  Describing Business Strategy  19
       Goals  20
       Scope  21
       Competitive Advantage  21
       Logic  22
  2.3  Relationship of Strategy to Mission, Purpose, Values, and Vision  24
       Mission, Purpose, and Values  24
       Vision  27
  2.4  The Strategy Statement  28
       Benefits of an Explicit Strategy Statement  29
       The Form and Use of the Strategy Statement  30
       An Example: Borders Books  31
  2.5  Developing Strategy: The Strategy Process  33
       Strategy Identification  34
       Strategy Evaluation: Testing the Logic  35
       Strategy Process and Strategic Change  36
  2.6  Summary  38

**3  COMPETITIVE ADVANTAGE**  39
  3.1  Introduction  39

**3.2**  Value and Competitive Advantage   39

**3.3**  Two Main Routes to Competitive Advantage   41
Position   43
Capabilities   46

**3.4**  Sustainable Competitive Advantage   48
Capability as Sustainable Competitive Advantage   49
Position as Sustainable Competitive Advantage   50

**3.5**  The Relationship of Position to Capabilities   51

**3.6**  Position, Capabilities, and "The Resource-Based View of the Firm"   53

**3.7**  The Cost-Quality Frontier and Competitive Advantage   55
Product Quality and Cost   56
A Cost-Quality Framework   58
Using the Cost-Quality Frontier to Illustrate Competitive Advantage:
An Example   59

**3.8**  Summary   63

**4   INTERNAL CONTEXT: ORGANIZATION DESIGN   65**

**4.1**  Introduction   65

**4.2**  Organization Design and Competitive Advantage   65

**4.3**  Strategy and Organization at Southwest Airlines   67
Southwest's Strategy and Performance   67
Southwest's Organization   68
Comparisons to Other Airlines   70
Summary: Consistency and Alignment   71

**4.4**  The Challenge of Organization Design   71
The Coordination Problem   72
The Incentive Problem   73

**4.5**  Meeting the Challenge   75
Architecture: Structure   76
Architecture: Compensation and Rewards   82
Routines   86
Culture   88

**4.6**  ARC Analysis   89

**4.7**  Summary   90

**5   ORGANIZATION AND COMPETITIVE ADVANTAGE   93**

**5.1**  Introduction   93

**5.2**  Aligning Strategy and Organization   95
Applying ARC Analysis to Assess Strategic Alignment: Southwest
Airlines Revisited   97
Other Examples: Sony, Apple Computer, and Silicon Graphics   101

**5.3**  Building and Creating Competitive Advantage   102

Explorers and Exploiters    103
Interdependence and Tight-Coupling    106
Organizational Slack    109
Central Direction    110
The ARC of Explorers and Exploiters    111

5.4    Combining Exploration and Exploitation    114
5.5    Costs of Organizational Change    117
5.6    Summary    117

6    EXTERNAL CONTEXT: INDUSTRY ANALYSIS    119
6.1    Introduction    119
6.2    The Effects of Industry Characteristics on Firm Performance    120
6.3    Organizing Industry Analysis    123
6.4    A Framework for Industry Analysis    127
Value Creation: Potential Industry Earnings (PIE)    129
Determinants of PIE    130
An Example of Value Creation: Lobster PIE    133
Capturing Value: Dividing PIE    136
Competition    136
Entry and Incumbency Advantage    138
An Example of the Effects of Competition and Entry    139
Vertical Power: Buyer or Supplier Power    140
Dividing the Lobster PIE    142
6.5    Industry Definition    144
Industry Definition Based on "Close" Substitutes    145
Industry Definitions for Systems of Complementary Products    146
6.6    Summary    147

7    THE SPECTRUM OF COMPETITION AND NICHE
MARKETS    149
7.1    Introduction    149
7.2    The Spectrum of Competition    150
Structure and Behavior    153
7.3    Niche Markets and Product Differentiation    154
Building, Defending, and Exploiting a Market Niche: Benetton and
the Gap    155
7.4    Consumer Preferences and Product Differentiation    157
Preferences and Products    157
Horizontal and Vertical Product Differentiation    161
7.5    Differentiation and Competition    162
Niches and Neighbors    163
Differentiation Softens Competition    165
Price Competition and Market Share    168

**7.6**  Product Positioning    **170**

**7.7**  Summary    **172**

**Appendix**  Monopoly, Competition, and Niche Markets    **172**

Monopoly    **173**

Perfect Competition    **176**

Niche Markets    **178**

**8**  COMPETITION IN CONCENTRATED MARKETS    **185**

**8.1**  Introduction    **185**

**8.2**  Oligopoly: The Elements of Strategic Interaction    **186**

Differences in Actions    **189**

Timing    **197**

Players    **199**

Information    **200**

Repetition    **202**

Summary    **208**

**8.3**  Dominant Firms    **209**

**8.4**  Antitrust    **211**

Collusion and Antitrust    **211**

**8.5**  Summary    **213**

**9**  ENTRY AND THE ADVANTAGE OF INCUMBENCY    **215**

**9.1**  Introduction    **215**

**9.2**  Types of Incumbency Advantage    **217**

Scale Advantages    **217**

Incumbency Advantage from Cumulative Investment    **222**

Incumbency Advantage from Consumer Loyalty    **226**

Incumbency Advantage from Switching Costs and Demand-Side
Increasing Returns    **227**

Incumbency Advantage from Sunk Costs    **228**

Firm Scope    **229**

**9.3**  Entry Barriers at Work    **231**

**9.4**  Strategically Creating Incumbency Advantage    **232**

Packing the Product Space    **232**

Blocking Entry through Contract or Vertical Integration    **235**

Signaling to Prevent Entry    **235**

Entry Barriers and Antitrust    **236**

**9.5**  Summary    **237**

**10**  CREATING AND CAPTURING VALUE IN THE VALUE
CHAIN    **239**

**10.1**  Introduction    **239**

**10.2**  Value Creation and Value Capture    **239**

10.3  The Value Chain and Buyer or Supply Power  242

10.4  Capturing Value  244

    Value Capture without Buyer or Supplier Power  245

    Value Capture by a Single Powerful Supplier (or Buyer)  247

    Value Capture When Buyers and Suppliers Are Powerful  249

    Reducing Power in Other Segments  254

10.5  Creating Value  255

    Opportunities for Creating Value: The Coordination Problem  257

    Contracting to Create Value: The Incentive Problem  260

10.6  Summary  263

Appendix  Price Discrimination  264


11  STRATEGIC MANAGEMENT IN A CHANGING ENVIRONMENT  271

11.1  Introduction  271

11.2  The Evolution of the U.S. Automobile Industry  272

11.3  Change and Competitive Advantage  274

11.4  Industry Life Cycle  277

    Emergence  278

    Growth  283

    Maturity and Decline  284

11.5  The Evolution of Industry Organization  287

    Horizontal vs. Vertical Organization  287

    Organizational Implications of Industry Structure  292

11.6  Managing Strategic Change  294

    Overcoming the Barriers to Strategic Change  294

    Managing Under Uncertainty: Scenario Analysis  301

    Strategic Change: An Example  302

11.7  Summary  304


12  STRATEGY IN MARKETS WITH DEMAND-SIDE INCREASING RETURNS  305

12.1  Introduction  305

12.2  Sources of Demand-Side Increasing Returns (DSIR)  306

    Compatibility Benefits  306

    Network Benefits  308

12.3  Competition in Markets with Demand-Side Increasing Returns  311

    Installed Base and Tipping  311

    Competitive Strategies for Building DSIR  315

12.4  Systems of Components  317

    System Compatibility  317

    Leveraging Market Position  318

**12.5**  Technology Adoption  321
**12.6**  Managing the Adoption Process  323
    Marketing to Create Momentum  324
    Leveraging Reputation  324
    Committing to "Open" Standards  325
    Winning Over An Influential Buyer  325
    Advance Sign-Ups  325
    Winks at Pirates  325
    Leasing  326
    Price Commitments  326
**12.7**  Standards-Setting Processes  326
**12.8**  Summary  328

**13  GLOBALIZATION AND STRATEGY  329**
**13.1**  Introduction  329
**13.2**  Implications for Managers  330
**13.3**  Strategic Gains from Globalization  332
**13.4**  Globalization of Industries and Economies  334
**13.5**  Strategic Challenges  335
    The Challenge of Local Responsiveness  336
    The Challenge of Global Efficiency  340
    The Challenge of Learning  341
**13.6**  Organizing to Meet the Challenge  344
    Federated vs. Centralized  344
    Building the Middle Ground  345
    The Regional Organization  346
    Locational Advantage  346
    The Transnational Corporation  348
**13.7**  Summary  349

**14  CORPORATE STRATEGY: MANAGING FOR VALUE IN A
MULTIBUSINESS COMPANY  351**
**14.1**  Introduction  351
**14.2**  A Framework for Corporate Strategy  352
    Managing Strategic Spillovers  354
    A Framework for Corporate Strategy  356
**14.3**  Does Corporate Add Value?  358
    The Performance of Diversified Firms  359
**14.4**  Strategic Spillovers and Competitive Advantage  361
    Identifying and Managing Spillovers  362
    Sources of Spillovers  363
**14.5**  Levers: Resource Allocation and Organization Design  366
    Resource Allocation  367

Organization Design    371
Corporate Direction    377

**14.6** Summary    379

**15 THE STRATEGY PROCESS    381**

**15.1** Introduction    381
**15.2** Some Principles of the Strategy Process    382
**15.3** Business Strategy Process    383
Strategy Identification    384
Strategy Evaluation    385
Developing and Evaluating Strategic Options    387
Selecting and Communicating the Strategy    388
Strategy Process in a Rapidly Changing Environment    389
**15.4** Strategic Plans    390
**15.5** The Evolution of Strategy    393
Autonomous and Intentional Strategic Changes    395
**15.6** Corporate Strategic Processes    397
Corporate Strategy Processes for Strategically Independent Businesses    397
Corporate Strategy for Strategically Interdependent Businesses    401
The Role of General Managers    402
**15.7** Concluding Remarks    403

**APPENDIX   APPLYING GAME THEORY TO STRATEGIC MANAGEMENT    405**

**A.1** Introduction    405
**A.2** A Famous Example: The Prisoners' Dilemma    406
**A.3** Nash Equilibrium and Duopoly    410
**A.4** The Effect of Repetition    414
**A.5** Credibility, Commitment, and Flexibility    416
The Value of Flexibility: Real Options    417
Commitment and Credibility    418
**A.6** Strategic Behavior in the Presence of Asymmetric Information    422
**A.7** Summary    425

**CREDITS    427**

**INDEX    429**

# STRATEGIC MANAGEMENT

# CHAPTER

# 1

# INTRODUCTION

## 1.1 STRATEGIC MANAGEMENT

Some firms experience meteoric growth, achieving industry leadership, while others falter, stagnate, or fail. Some firms seem to seize every opportunity, while others seem always to move too late or not at all. Consider, for example, the performance of Coca-Cola relative to its contemporaries. One dollar invested in the Coca-Cola Company at its initial public offering in 1919 would have been worth over $200,000 in 2000, while a dollar invested in a portfolio of representative large U.S. stocks over the same period would have been worth less than $4200![1] Moreover, for every successful company started when Coca-Cola was founded, many more have long gone out of business.

A manager who is keenly aware of this tremendous range of firm performance naturally looks for some pattern that distinguishes success from failure. However, a review of the history of successful firms suggests a broad range of ways to achieve superior performance. Some firms have succeeded by innovating, and others by eschewing innovation in favor of operational efficiency. Some successful firms have sought to grow as quickly as possible, while others have pursued modest growth. Some dominate their market, while others prosper by concentrating on a small market segment.

Variation in firm performance and in the strategies successful firms pursue is not surprising given the vast differences in the industries in which firm participate, the regulatory environments they face, and the human, financial, and physical assets they can bring to bear. But the variation is perplexing for a manager who must navigate the firm's external environment in a way that makes the most of the firm's assets. Strategic management is fundamentally about helping the manager in that quest. It is about developing a set of tools and conceptual maps for uncovering the systematic relationships between the choices the manager makes and the performance the firm realizes.

---

[1] *Source: Stocks, Bonds, Bills, and Inflation: 1997 Yearbook* (Chicago: Ibbotson Associates, 1997) and authors' calculations.

Having a set of tools and frameworks is essential because a manager faces a bewildering array of choices every day. This array includes deciding which products or services to pursue, which investments to make, which human resource management policies to implement, and which organizational structures to adopt. Furthermore, in an organization of even modest size, strategic choices are made by multiple decision makers and implemented by many employees in different functional areas and geographies.

There is the danger, then, that the course the firm takes will be determined by the buffeting it receives from its competitive environment and by the aggregation of uncoordinated decisions made by independent actors within the firm. Its performance will be haphazard, opportunities will be lost, and threats will loom uncountered. The alternative is for the firm's managers to develop a common, overall sense of what they want the business to achieve and to formulate a strategy that they believe will enable it to achieve those goals. Developing and implementing a strategy that allows managers to exercise more control over the firm's direction and to chart a course that enhances the firm's performance are the objectives of strategic management.

## 1.2   THE ROLE OF BUSINESS STRATEGY

Firm performance depends both on the actions the firm takes and on the context in which those actions are taken. By "action" we mean the acquisition and deployment of the firm's assets. Each firm has some existing set of assets including know-how, business processes, plant and equipment, brand equity, formal and informal organizational structure, financial resources, and so forth. Action consists of deploying existing assets and acquiring new ones. Although many of these decisions are routine and incremental, some asset acquisition and deployment decisions can profoundly affect the firm.[2] For example, in an attempt to improve its performance in the small car segment of the automobile industry, General Motors (GM) decided in the early 1980s to invest more than a *billion* dollars in a new, small car division it named "Saturn." Saturn represented a sharp break with the product development, manufacturing, distribution, and human resources management processes common to GM's other divisions. The shift represented by Saturn was embodied in significant redeployment of GM's human resources, a change in its fundamental business practices, and a major investment of its financial assets in a new plant.

Although the firm chooses the actions it takes, factors that are immutable, at least in the short run, also affect its performance. These factors represent the "context" in which the firm acts. As our discussion of "action" suggests, some of these factors are internal. The firm's *internal context* consists of the assets it owns and the way it is organized.[3] Other factors are external to the firm. The firm's *external environment* includes

---

[2] This perspective is consistent with the focus of Pankaj Ghemawat who describes the firm's major resource *commitments* as its major strategic assets. (*Source:* Pankaj Ghemawat, *Commitment: The Dynamics of Strategy*, New York: Free Press, 1991.)

[3] It is tempting to include the way the firm is organized as an asset rather than as a separate feature of its internal context. Instead we choose to preserve organization as a separate category to highlight the complex and important role it plays in affecting firm performance. Because organization determines the way people interact, the activities they choose to pursue, and the policies and routines the firm employs to get things done, we believe that the organizational attributes of the firm deserve separate mention.

both industry characteristics—such as actual and potential competitors, buyers, and suppliers—as well as nonmarket factors, such as the regulatory, political, and social environment in which the firm operates.

The firm's actions and the context in which they are taken *together* determine performance as Figure 1-1 illustrates. Note that, instead of separate arrows from context and action to performance, the arrows in the figure merge to represent this codetermination of performance. Context and action can combine to determine performance in several ways. Typically, the actions that managers take are importantly conditioned by the context they face. For example, the stance that government regulators take toward mergers and acquisitions affects a firm's ability to change its scope. Or the product development behavior of rival firms might affect the performance of a firm that has decided to delay its new product line. Sometimes the actions the firm takes contribute to shaping its context, as when a firm completes an acquisition that alters its rivals' market behavior. In either case, the performance the firm achieves is a product of both its context and its action.

There is no simple prescription for action that will work in most situations because the relationship between action and context is complex. Actions that are stunningly effective in one context may fail abysmally in another. As a result, managers need to understand how context mediates the effect of action on performance. This understanding allows the manager to assess how a competitor's introduction of new products or repositioning of its existing product line will affect the firm's own competitive position, for example, or to determine what new capabilities the business needs to acquire to take advantage of new market opportunities, the kinds of financial returns the firm should expect from expanding capacity, or whether it is worth investing in that new technology the engineers have been recommending.

More generally, understanding these interactions enables general managers to assess whether the kinds of actions the firm has been taking, and currently contemplates taking, are likely to result in the performance management would like to achieve. One goal of strategic management is to provide the conceptual frameworks that will help a manager understand the key relationships among actions, context, and performance. These frameworks are designed to answer the question "What actions will be most likely to achieve the organization's goals given its internal and external context?"

Answering this question is essential to formulating a potentially successful strategy, but it is not enough. It is not enough for the manager to know what kinds of

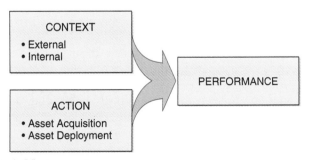

**FIGURE 1-1**   Strategic Management

actions are likely to lead to success. The general manager must also have some way to communicate that understanding to the rest of the organization. Because the general manager does not make the thousands of decisions that, in aggregate, determine the success or failure of the firm, he or she must articulate a framework, plan, or approach for the firm to guide the many specific decisions that must be made as the business goes forward. This is the role of strategy. A strategy reflects the manager's understanding of the key relationships among actions, context, and performance and is crafted to guide the firm's many decision makers to take actions that are consistent with that understanding. Helping managers formulate and implement such a strategy is central to strategic management as a normative field.

We want to stress that a strategy, as the term is used here, may not (in general, does not) specify any particular action. A strategy will not specify the tactics that should be used to implement it. A manager generally cannot describe all the possible contextual elements that the firm might encounter and all the relevant actions that it might consider taking. Even if this were feasible, a lengthy, detailed analysis would be difficult to communicate to all the relevant decision makers within the firm and not terribly useful for those who must implement a consistent plan of action.

Rather, the strategy defines a framework for guiding the choice of actions. It is a broad articulation of the kinds of products the organization will produce, the basis on which its products will compete with those of its competitors, and the types of resources and capabilities the firm must have or develop to implement the strategy successfully. A strategy in this sense is the starting point for developing a detailed action plan, but it transcends the specifics of any particular plan.

We stress this particular interpretation of strategy to distinguish it from the many different ways the word "strategy" frequently is used in business settings. For example, it is common usage to pose questions such as "What was Jim's strategy in negotiating the new contract with his client?" or "What was Kodak's strategy in addressing the threat from Fuji?" Although these are legitimate uses of the word "strategy" (and indeed, we will sometimes slip into this usage in later chapters), they do not correspond to the way we are using the term here. These uses refer to the means for achieving a limited objective. We are using the term to encompass an overall approach to a business.

## Examples: Dell Computer and Compaq Computer

To illustrate how strategy can frame a firm's actions, compare the strategies of Dell and Compaq at the turn of the century. Both firms are leading manufacturers of personal computers, but they have very different strategies. Dell focuses primarily on direct sales of customized, personal computers to end-users. By selling directly to the end-user, Dell can have very low distribution costs. It can customize computers at low cost because it produces to order, avoiding a large inventory of finished goods. As a complement to production-to-order, Dell has established a supply chain management system that enables it to order components shortly before they are actually needed rather than carrying them in inventory. Because the cost of computer components often declines with time, just-in-time component acquisition enables Dell to keep its manufacturing costs low.

Because Dell can keep its manufacturing and distribution costs low while rapidly producing customized computers, it can offer customers an attractive product and service at very competitive prices. The high demand that this creates enables Dell to reap manufacturing and distribution scale efficiencies, driving unit costs lower still. To summarize, the essence of Dell's strategy has been selling customized computers directly to end-users, minimizing the time from placement of customer order to ultimate fulfillment, while offering attractive prices supported by low manufacturing and distribution costs. This strategy is reflected in Dell's advertising message: "At Dell, we believe nothing should stand between you and us. Want a clear path to success?"[4]

Another leading personal computer manufacturer, Compaq Computer, has adopted a quite different strategy. Two of Compaq's acquisitions exemplify the difference between Compaq and Dell. The first was Compaq's purchase of Tandem Computer, a manufacturer of "fault-tolerant" computers for firms, such as financial institutions and insurance companies, for whom business interruptions caused by the computer "going down" are particularly costly. The other was Compaq's acquisition of Digital Equipment Corporation (DEC), one of the most significant producers of midrange computers in the pre-PC era. One of the key assets that DEC brought to Compaq was its services and support organization. Through its history of selling to large corporate customers, DEC has developed significant know-how in helping its customers use information technology to solve their business problems. With these acquisitions, Compaq has positioned itself as a computer company with a broad range of computer products and the know-how to help its business customers deploy those products to meet their business needs. Consistent with this strategy, Compaq's advertising sends a different message from Dell's, rhetorically posing the question: "Who's at the hub of today's most important strategic IT partnerships?"[5]

Each of these quite different strategies provides the management of Dell and Compaq with a *framework* to guide their future choice of actions. In Dell's case, for example, one expects to see actions directed toward cost-cutting and ensuring that end-users' points of contact with the company, such as its Web site, are robust, user-friendly, and efficient. In Compaq's case, one expects to see efforts aimed at producing robust technologies that interact in networks suitable for deployment by large corporate customers. Although it would be virtually impossible for the firms' managers to describe fully the actions these firms should take as a function of all the contextual elements they might face, their strategies outline an overall approach to the personal computer business that is a valuable guide to decision making.

These two companies are pursuing different strategies, even though they face many common contextual factors. Because both manufacture computers, both are susceptible to trends in demand for computing as well as to changes in computer technology. They also face many of the same competitors and potential competitors. Both are affected by a common nonmarket environment.

Despite these similarities, there are also differences in their contexts that provide some hints as to why they might be pursuing different strategies. For one, each faces

---

[4] *Time,* July 6, 1998, p. 57.

[5] *Fortune,* July 20, 1998, p. 13.

the other as a competitor, so their competitive environments differ! As we will emphasize later, firms can sometimes enhance performance by differentiating their products
and services from those of their major competitors. More importantly perhaps,
through their years in business, Dell and Compaq have developed different internal
contexts: different workforces, areas of technical expertise, corporate cultures, brand
awareness, abilities to adapt to changing market and technological conditions, financial positions, and so on. Their different internal contexts suggest that they might successfully pursue different strategies.

Although it is not possible to assess the likelihood that these strategies will be successful without more analysis, some features of their contexts can be identified that
may be key determinants of success or failure. Compaq, for example, is responding to
a void created by the failure of many of the large vertically integrated computer companies of the mainframe era, which had previously helped large companies solve their
information technology problems. Its success will depend on the demand for these
services and the extent to which it can meet that demand. Compaq is also betting that
it has the organizational ability to integrate its merger partners successfully. For its
part, Dell is relying both on having a first-mover advantage with this strategy, so that
it faces no immediate serious competition from rivals pursuing similar strategies, and
on its ability to stay ahead of emerging competitors as they learn from Dell's success.

Although we have only scratched the surface of these companies' strategies, these
examples give a glimpse of what fuller descriptions might entail and what the utility of
a comprehensive strategy would be. A strategy describes a framework for charting a
course of action. It explicates an approach for the company that builds on its strengths
and is a good fit with the firm's external environment. Because the strategy is succinct,
it is easy to communicate within and outside the firm and is a good guide for the managers who have to implement it. Moreover, by explaining how the firm intends to succeed given the context it faces, the strategy alerts management to the assumptions
about the firm's context that are essential for the strategy's success. This information
enables them to interpret contextual changes, anticipating how these changes might
affect the firm's performance.

## The Dynamics of Business Strategy

Because the firm's internal and environmental context changes over time, so too does
the efficacy of a given strategy. Consequently, the idea that strategy is dynamic is
inherent in our conception of strategic management. Indeed, the impetus for a change
in the firm's deployment and acquisition of its assets is frequently a change in the context in which it operates. In a stable environment, strategic analysis tends to take a
back seat to efficient, effective implementation. When simply "doing more of the
same" is clearly insufficient, however, strategy and strategic change quickly become a
focus of managerial attention.

The GM example introduced earlier illustrates this idea. The development of the
Saturn division was motivated in part by a growing view inside GM that its current
methods of designing, producing, and selling cars were causing it to lose ground
against other, primarily Japanese, auto manufacturers. Organizational structures in

which design, manufacturing, and marketing were largely separate and independent processes led to very long cycle times (the time from conception of a vehicle to the production of the first car) and final products that were unresponsive to customer preferences. Adversarial relations between management and the United Auto Workers union resulted in high labor costs and inflexible manufacturing processes. The organization and incentive structure of the dealer network led to adversarial customer–dealer relations. The company's top management viewed the resulting loss of competitive advantage as a major strategic issue. They recognized that the set of actions appropriate in the old context was no longer effective.

Many forces for change act on the firm's external environment. Some of these are fairly predictable, such as the changes that typically occur as an industry goes through a life cycle from inception through growth, maturity, and decline. Other changes are less predictable and result from underlying changes in the demand and supply conditions facing the industry. For example, globalization may change the nature of competition in a previously domestic industry as foreign firms enter the market. The entry of Asian and European automobile manufacturers into the United States dramatically affected GM's competitive position. Or the industry may consolidate as rival companies merge, thereby changing the nature of competition. The current wave of mergers in telecommunications, for example, is restructuring competition in the global telecom market. Technological change may affect the firm's strategic situation as when the Internet makes it possible for individuals to trade stocks and book airline tickets at low cost from home, thereby threatening the cherished relationships between brokers and customers and travel agents and clients. Changes in the nonmarket environment, such as deregulation of financial institutions in the United States, alter the strategic context of existing industry participants as well as potential entrants. As Figure 1-2 illustrates, all such changes affect the efficacy of the firm's strategy. To be able to react in a timely manner, firms have to understand the potential impact of these changes.

The firm's strategic and environmental context can also change as a result of its own actions. Figure 1-2 shows change initiated by the company as the arrow from action to context. Sometimes a firm *deliberately* acts to change its context. A company, for example, may decide to acquire new resources to address a new business objective, thereby changing the firm's strategic assets. Compaq's acquisition of Tandem Computer is a good example of this. Similarly, a firm can take actions to change its external environment. Kodak, for example, has invested heavily in seeking the intervention of U.S. trade policy to enhance its competitive position in camera film in Japan. Around 1900, huge corporations like Standard Oil and U.S. Steel were formed by managers intent on concentrating control of whole industries under a single management. Software firms engage in alliances intended to influence the emergence of industry standards and, therefore, their stature as standard bearers.

Sometimes, however, the changes created by the firms are *unanticipated*. Companies may find an opportunity to exploit new technologies produced as unintended byproducts of their R&D programs. Or strategic alliances may open new, unexpected opportunities for the firm to pursue new markets. Some firms are adept at exploiting these opportunities as they arise, while others allow them to slip away. 3-M, for example, is renowned for its ability to move effectively to develop a wide range of innova-

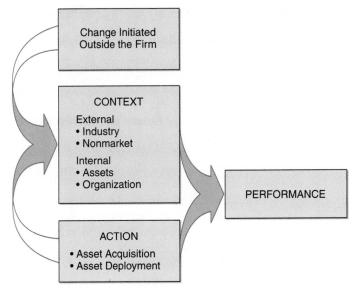

**FIGURE 1-2**   Dynamics of Business Strategy

tions. In contrast, IBM and Xerox suffer from a legacy of failing to capture value from the ancillary innovations created in their research labs. In some particularly dramatic cases, the changes wrought by incumbent firms have unexpectedly swept the incumbents aside. The Swiss watch industry, for example, developed quartz technology only to discover that the industry as it was organized—with many specialist producers of individual components—was ill-suited to commercializing the technology. As a result, Swiss leadership of the industry was (temporarily) ceded to Japanese firms. Intentionally or not, firms can be agents of change.

### Strategic Planning versus Strategic Thinking

As already asserted, formulating and implementing strategy require that a general manager have a cognitive map of the relationships among actions, context, and performance. The manager must understand current sources of performance, the threats and opportunities presented by changes inside and outside the firm, and how to change course in response to them. How the firm obtains the necessary information to develop and maintain that map, formulate and change strategy, and communicate the strategy within the organization is termed *strategy process*.

Most mature companies have a systematic, formal *strategic planning* routine as their strategy process. Although there is substantial variation in who is involved in such a process and how it is carried out, we can describe the general features of a typical formal strategic planning process. Strategic planning is discussed in more detail later in the book, but it is useful to provide a rough sketch here to distinguish between strategic *planning* and the kind of strategic *thinking* that is the focus of this book.

A strategic planning process in a mature company is typically conducted on an annual cycle and often involves the development of an annual and, perhaps, multiyear business plan. In firms with multiple business units, each unit is asked to develop a plan for itself, and those plans get reviewed, revised, and aggregated by more senior managers as the plan "moves up" the organization. The content of a strategic plan is typically some combination of the strategic analysis described here and an operating plan and budget. For example, a strategic plan for a business unit at General Electric (GE), a company renowned for its strategic planning processes, was described as having the following elements in the early 1980s:

- Identification and formulation of environmental assumptions of strategic importance,
- Identification and in-depth analysis of competitors, including assumptions about their probable strategies,
- Analysis of the [unit's] own resources,
- Development and evaluation of strategy alternatives,
- Preparation of the [unit's] strategic plan, including estimates of capital spending for the next five years,
- Preparation of the [unit's] operating plan, which detailed the next year of the [unit's] strategic plan.[6]

This list sensibly covers many issues that should be thought about in formulating business unit strategy. But the strategic planning process in many companies also has several characteristics that make it an ineffective tool for strategic thinking. First, there is often a mismatch between the timing of the planning process and the dynamics of strategic change. In many cases, the firm's strategy is more durable than any specific business or strategic plan. Although the strategy may be "tweaked" now and then in response to critical changes in the elements of Figure 1-2, it is not uncommon for its essential characteristics to survive many planning periods and, hence, many annual plans. In other cases, environmental change is so rapid that the formulation of static annual plans to which managers must adhere impedes the firm's ability to respond in time.

A second type of problem firms encounter is the nature of the review process. We will have much more to say about this later, but participants in these processes typically report that the review process is cumbersome and replete with incentives for playing company politics. The timing and review problems together have prompted many companies, particularly new, high-technology firms, to eschew formal strategic planning processes in favor of a more fluid and dynamic approach to strategy formulation.

A final, and critical, problem that many companies have encountered in implementing a formal planning process is that most of the emphasis tends to be placed on

---

[6] Francis J. Aguilar and Richard Hamermesh, "General Electric: Strategic Position—1981," Harvard Business School Case, 381–174.

the budget and operating plans. In GE's process, for example, the budget and operating plan are only two of the six basic elements. In practice, however, GE and other companies have found that these elements, particularly the capital budget, consume the bulk of managerial attention. The other elements are at the heart of strategic thinking but get short shrift. The reason for this is that the strategic plan is as much a part of the political process of resource allocation within the firm as it is an attempt to think creatively about business unit strategy. Indeed, GE later amended its strategic planning process to provide much more emphasis on coherent explication of strategy and less on preparing detailed plans and budgets.

In this book we are more concerned with discussing tools and ideas for rigorously formulating strategy than with the planning process *per se*. We are concerned with general managers' ability to develop and maintain a conceptual map of their businesses that ties together the elements of Figure 1-2, to conceptualize a strategy, and then to think through, "on their feet," the impact of changes in their internal and external environment. We call this *strategic thinking* rather than strategic planning, and it is our main focus.

One reason for our focus on strategic thinking is that many general managers do not have the luxury of spending long periods of time in reflective, detailed, strategic planning. A more compelling reason, however, is that we believe strategic thinking is critical to achieving the firm's objectives and that embedding it in a formal planning process too often obscures rather than enhances strategic thought. We also believe that boards of directors and senior management are increasingly demanding that their general managers think strategically. They want their managers to have a mental model of the business they run that consists of a comprehensive understanding of the forces at work in Figure 1-2 as well as a strategy that provides a framework for translating that understanding into action. Most of the book is therefore devoted to providing such a manager with the tools and frameworks necessary for building a mental model and developing a strategy. We do, however, return to the subject of strategic planning in Chapter 15, where we discuss integrating strategic thinking with a strategic planning process.

## 1.3   THE ORGANIZATION AND ITS OBJECTIVES

So far, we have talked about "firms," "performance," and "managers" as if these concepts were clearly defined. Before proceeding, however, we need to clarify what we mean by performance, the kinds of organizations to which strategic management can be applied, and the managers who might most benefit from understanding strategic management.

### Performance: Overarching Objectives

Figures 1-1 and 1-2 describe the outcome of the firm's action plan as "performance." There are many possible measures of firm performance, including market share, reputation, innovation, brand image, profitability, employee satisfaction, and so on. In striving to formulate strategy to improve firm performance, managers need to be clear about which of these performance dimensions they hope to affect. Often a firm's strategy is couched in terms of excelling on a particular dimension. For example, the firm may have a stated objective of achieving a dominant position in the market in which it competes or of being the highest quality producer, or the most innovative firm in the industry. Under the leadership of Jack Welch, for example, one of GE's stated goals was to be "number one or two" in every market in which it competed.

Yet a goal like being "number one or number two" or the most innovative is typically not the ultimate goal of the firm. The ultimate goal is profitability. The directors of for-profit firms have a fiduciary responsibility to the firm's shareholders, and these investors are interested primarily in receiving as high a return as possible. Dominating the industry or producing the highest quality product can be a useful description of how the firm's managers hope to maximize the firm's profit, but it should not be confused with the firm's ultimate goal. Apple Computer, for example, discovered that producing the highest quality computer hardware possible was not the way for it to maximize profit. The firm's managers were slow to come to this conclusion because they confused the strategic goal—great hardware products—with the firm's overarching objective: maximize profit. When the strategic goal no longer enhances profits, it should be changed. In what follows, therefore, we assume that profit-maximization is the firm's overarching objective.

We take this to be a reasonable description of reality in many, but certainly not all, for-profit organizations. In practice there are two main sets of reasons why behavior may deviate from the pursuit of this goal. The first is that even a for-profit firm may have been established with a social goal as an explicit objective. Shareholders may have invested (and continue to invest) knowing that they are sacrificing some monetary gain in exchange for progress on the social objective. Patagonia, for example, is a California-based company devoted to producing outdoor hiking, climbing, and camping equipment that is environmentally friendly. The company's devotion to the environment may well make it a less profitable enterprise, since it devotes resources to activities that other companies without those concerns might not.

The second reason the firm might not pursue wealth-maximization is that the goals of managers at for-profit organizations are not necessarily the same as those of the owners. Self-interested managers may pursue activities that are in their own, but not necessarily the shareholders', best interests. For example, a manager may be inclined to take actions that boost short-run at the expense of long run profitability if that could lead to a promotion. Or managers may pursue personal power and influence at the expense of organizational performance. For a variety of reasons explored later in this book, shareholders have problems preventing this kind of self-serving behavior.

To the extent that organizations can and do define their overarching goals differently from profit-maximization, they must recognize those differences in formulating and implementing strategy. To the extent that firms define their overarching goal in terms of profit-maximization but deviate from that pursuit because of the personal agendas of the actors within the firm, strategy formulation and implementation must be sensitive to issues of politics, influence, and incentives inside the firm. For example, managers who want to direct the firm's resources toward a new product position may encounter resistance from engineers whose compensation depends on patent output and the rate of new product development. Redirection may be good for the firm but bad for the productivity of key engineers. We will return to the issue of designing the organization to account for incentive problems and internal conflict in Chapter 4.

The view that profit-maximization is the appropriate overall objective is clearly inappropriate for private nonprofit and public organizations. For these organizations, strategic thinking often involves defining their overall objective. Private nonprofit and public organizations are "owned" by their customers and/or the larger community, and the organizations' objectives must reflect those interests. Once ownership is established and the interests of the owners are defined, however, the role of management—as in the for-profit environment—is to promote those objectives as effectively as possible. For this endeavor, the same principles that guide strategy formulation in the for-profit world are also appropriate for these organizations.

## Firms and Managers

We have been speaking about devising a strategy that could enhance the performance of the "firm." In doing so, we have glossed over the tremendous variation in the scope and complexity of businesses. Some firms operate (almost exclusively) in a single business: Genentech is a pharmaceutical firm, Dell is a computer firm, Coca-Cola was, for much of its history, a purveyor of Coke. For these companies, there is a good match between what we have been calling a firm and a business. For these firms it makes sense to talk about an external context, internal assets, and the interaction that leads to performance. But many companies consist of a number of disparate lines of business, each of which has a distinct external context and set of strategic assets. How can one strategy be appropriate for this entire set of businesses? How can one talk about a mental map of the relationship among external context, internal context, and performance for a firm like ABB whose products range from financial services to railroad rolling stock to large power generators? Or a Hewlett-Packard that makes Unix servers, laser printers, and ink jet printers?

The answer, of course, is that one cannot. Strategic thinking requires you to describe the industry and the internal assets to which the strategy applies. For example, Hewlett-Packard has a Unix server business, an ink jet printer business, a laser printer business, and so on. Each of those businesses includes a number of products in a product line that is logically grouped together and constitutes a business unit. One can think about formulating a strategy for Hewlett-Packard's ink jet printer business or its Unix server business. But no single strategy will apply to both of these business units. Each unit has distinct assets that it brings to its business, and each has a distinct market environment in which it competes. If we were to detail the characteristics of the internal and external environments for each unit, we would describe two different "firms" that are part of a single company. For this reason, the strategy literature traditionally distinguishes between "business unit strategy" and "corporate strategy." This distinction is not important for the many small firms who operate in a single line of business, but it is important for companies competing in more than one industry. We will turn to the topic of corporate strategy in Chapter 14, but most of this book will be about business unit strategy.

Because we are focusing on business unit strategy, the "manager" we have in mind as our strategic thinker is the individual (or team) with responsibility for setting the direction for the business unit as a whole. This general manager sets the strategic direction and goals of the business, typically with input from subordinates, and integrates and coordinates the functional areas within it to achieve those goals. To do this effectively, the general manager needs to understand the functional areas for the business he or she manages. However, the general manager's role is not simply to oversee those functional areas but rather to set the strategic direction and goals for the business that serve as a guide for functional area policies.

Most companies have many general managers. Among the most senior management of the firm's business units are those who have ultimate responsibility for their overall strategic direction and who therefore, by definition, are general managers. However, it is incorrect to equate "senior" and "general." There are many senior managers (e.g., the chief financial officer) whose responsibilities do not include strategic responsibility for a business unit. On the other hand, managers much lower in the hierarchy often do have general management responsibilities. The principles of strategic management examined in this book are relevant to all general managers, regardless of their position in the firm.

This view of the strategic responsibility of general managers does not imply that strategic thinking consumes their day-to-day lives. Nor does it imply that strategic thinking is the activity on which general managers spend the most time. Indeed, it is not. As documented convincingly by Mintzberg,[7] the general manager fulfills a variety of roles, including performing ceremonial duties, acting as a company spokesperson, allocating resources, and dealing with day-to-day crises. However, even if one would not describe general managers primarily as strategic thinkers from observing their day-to-day activities, their decision making can drive the strategy of their organizations. A firm's strategy is in fact determined, consciously or unconsciously, by the decisions made by its general managers.

Implicit in this general management perspective is the idea that general managers can make a difference in firm performance. Indeed, the underlying premise of this book is that the deliberate coordination of the organization's acquisition and deployment activities can have a significant, positive effect on the probability that the organization will achieve its objectives. This may seem like a logical position for a strategic management text, and, ultimately, we believe that it is. But it is not uncontroversial, and some elements of the controversy suggest important limitations of this underlying premise. We will take these limitations seriously in later chapters and so briefly describe the source of them here.

---

[7] Henry Mintzberg, "The Manager's Job: Folklore and Fact," *Harvard Business Review* (July–August 1975), 49–61.

## 1.4 PERSPECTIVES ON THE IMPACT OF THE GENERAL MANAGER

The view of general manager as strategist evokes the image of the "captain of the ship" selecting the business unit's destination, setting its course, guiding it through unexpected storms, and shouting commands to the crew. Several criticisms of this view have been proposed, and, indeed, this view of management seems much too simplistic. Here, we review some of the primary perspectives on how managers affect performance and then summarize the perspective we adopt.

One clear problem with the "captain of the ship" view of strategy is that there is tremendous variety in who is involved in the strategy process. Small firms and those in rapidly changing high-technology markets often have quite centralized strategic decision making. Many other organizations have more participatory strategy-setting processes in which several layers of management are involved in gathering, analyzing, and drawing strategic conclusions from relevant data. This process helps build a common knowledge base and goals among the many managers in a complex organization. However, even though the process resembles the "captain of the ship" imagery much less in these organizations than it does in a small organization because the process is more participatory, ultimate responsibility for strategy typically rests with the senior general management of the business unit.

A more radical criticism is that the "captain of the ship" view ascribes far too large a role for managers in the fortunes of the organizations they lead and presents too rational and organized a view of how strategic change occurs. In this view, even a manager with a clear idea about where the firm should go has only limited ability to determine the firm's direction. The limitation arises through some combination of inertia and limited rationality. Inertia implies that the firm's internal context is difficult to change. Limited rationality means that it is hard for managers to have a clear, precise view of the path the firm should follow.

The strongest form of this criticism is associated with evolutionary economics and organizational ecology, where, it is argued, firms engage in behavior that is largely routine rather than purposive or strategic.[8] In a stable environment, an industry is populated by firms with routines that are well adapted to the environment. The surviving firms are all well adapted because firms that were not have failed. If the environment changes, the performance of the existing firms will be determined by how well their routines fit with the new environment. Existing organizations that happen to have routines that are also well adapted to the new environment do well. Others suffer and fail because their existing routines are not effective in the new environment, and they are unable to adapt. In this view, adaptation means mimicking the routines of the (accidentally) well-adapted firms, a process that is extremely risky and impeded by the existence of well-entrenched, tacit routines. As older, less-well adapted firms fail, new, better-adapted firms, born without the baggage of the old routines, replace them. In the most extreme interpretation of this evolutionary view, general managers deserve little of the credit for

---

[8] See, for example, Michael Hannan and John Freeman, *Organizational Ecology* (Cambridge, MA: Harvard University Press, 1989).

success or failure. Success is determined not by the firm purposively developing a strategy that fits its internal and external context but by the incidental fit of fairly inert firms to their environments.

Some scholars have argued for an intermediate approach. For example, Brian Quinn[9] argues that "the processes used to arrive at the total strategy are typically fragmented, evolutionary, and largely intuitive." He argues that strategy processes are best described by "logical incrementalism" in which relatively minor changes in strategy are made in response to changes in external conditions in an evolutionary and adaptive manner. Thus his view accommodates both an evolutionary view of strategic change and a role for senior management in incremental change. Similarly, Nelson and Winter[10] have argued that firms can be seen as a collection of routines that are largely tacit knowledge. When a routine fails, the firm searches for a modification or a substitute, but this search will not, in general, lead to an optimal change and may fail completely.

Robert Burgelman propounds another intermediate view.[11] Like Quinn, he emphasizes evolutionary change. However, he ascribes a more activist, explicit, and effective role for senior managers in setting the strategic direction of the firm. He argues that reasonably complex organizations (a category that includes most firms) are subject to both evolutionary and planned processes. In his view, at any point in time, senior management is responsible for articulating a strategy that is consistent with the strategic context the firm faces. Over time, however, other managers in the organization take actions that change the internal strategic context. For example, they may discover new product opportunities, improve manufacturing processes, or invent new technologies. If the internal changes are profound, the actual strategy the firm is implementing may be changed. The responsibility of senior managers is to recognize that the change has affected or might affect the firm's strategy, determine whether the change should be encouraged or resisted, and, if embraced, alter the firm's official strategy to accommodate the change.

These different views suggest quite different roles for general managers in the formulation of strategy and for strategy itself. We lean more towards a view of the world in which general managers and the strategies they formulate can and do make a difference. This book reflects that bias. At the same time, we see merit in the criticisms posed by these other perspectives and attempt to incorporate relevant insights from those views in our approach. We recognize, for example, that there are limits to how much management can control the fate of the firm. Environmental change cannot be fully foreseen and, even when recognized, cannot be fully offset by the actions/decisions of management. In short, luck matters. The best strategy cannot *guarantee* good performance.

---

[9] James Brian Quinn, "Strategic Change: 'Logical Incrementalism,'" *Sloan Management Review* 20 (Fall 1978), 7–21.

[10] R. R. Nelson and S. Winter, *An Evolutionary Theory of Economic Change* (Cambridge, MA: Harvard University Press, 1982).

[11] Robert A. Burgelman, "A Model of the Interaction of Strategic Behavior, Corporate Context, and the Concept of Strategy," *Academy of Management Review* 8 (1983), 61–70.

Moreover, we recognize that being well adapted frequently carries a cost: Adaptation is a two-edged sword. In a stable environment, a firm takes actions over time that make it well adapted to its current environment but limit its ability to change should the need arise. Consequently, a firm that is the best at some narrowly defined task may find itself suddenly at a competitive disadvantage when the environment no longer rewards excellence in that task. Sometimes this creeps up on firms as they incrementally adapt to their environment; sometimes it is part of a conscious tradeoff between being efficient at what the firm is currently doing and being organized to foresee and manage change well.

Fundamental change is difficult. One reason for this is that firms develop routines that are spread throughout the organization and are difficult to change. In addition to the inertia from routines, change is difficult because there are always constituencies within the firm for whom the change is not beneficial and who will resist it. As a result, top management's declaration that the firm will change does not make change happen. To return to our captain of the ship metaphor, shouting orders has little effect if the crew is not listening.

Not only does the "top" of the organization often find it difficult to mandate change, but the unauthorized and unanticipated actions of lower management and/or operational personnel may profoundly affect the performance of the firm. As a consequence, strategy process is complex. An approach to strategic management that envisions strategy as simply a decision problem undertaken by a few analysts neglects the complex processes through which strategy is formulated, evaluated, and modified in organizations.

In short, it is a mistake to assume that strategy is a simple process in which a decision maker analyzes the situation, chooses the best course of action, and implements it. Although dispassionate analysis is crucial, so too is understanding the organizational context within which, and the process by which, strategy evolves. In this book we attempt to balance an analytical "top-down" approach to strategy with one that recognizes the complexities of the strategy process in practice. Strategic thinkers must appreciate that they cannot control fully the future of the organization. However, management does get to place bets in the deployment and acquisition of its assets. Understanding the strategic determinants of performance will help management place better bets but will not eliminate all the uncertainties the organization faces. Moreover, since the locus of strategy is often dispersed through the organization, the strategic thinker must understand the constraints on strategic change that the organization of the firm imposes. To maximize the likelihood of success as the firm's strategy evolves, managers must also understand how to alter the way the firm is organized and behaves. The alternative is to relegate strategic thinking to crisis management. Discovering in the middle of a typhoon that the crew has redesigned the navigation systems is not conducive to setting and following an optimal course.

## 1.5 ORGANIZATION OF THE BOOK

The first five chapters of this book are about strategy and the internal context of the firm. In Chapter 2 we define what we mean by "strategy" and describe the essential elements a strategy should have. We also discuss some related concepts, such as mission, vision, purpose, values, and so on. In Chapter 3, we turn to the issue of creating competitive advantage by leveraging the firm's capabilities or achieving an advantageous position. We also discuss the problem of sustaining competitive advantage in the face of competition and imitation by rivals.

With this basic understanding of strategy and competitive advantage established, we turn to the organization of the firm. Competitive advantage is achieved when a firm has a strategy that draws on the strengths of the firm's internal context. Although many views of strategy depict this context primarily as the firm's assets (its human and physical capital), we believe that the way these assets are organized is at least as important. In Chapters 4 and 5, therefore, we focus on the role of organization in firm performance and the relationship of organization design to strategy and strategic change. We begin by defining the fundamental problems of coordination and incentives that the organization design must resolve and how the solution achieved by the firm must align with its strategy. We then turn to a more dynamic view of organization design, exploring the tension between organization design that is well suited to taking advantage of the firm's current environment and a design that is appropriate for responding to and creating change in the firm's environment.

In Chapters 6–9, we examine the "environmental context" part of Figure 1-2. In particular, we examine the impact that the characteristics of the firm's industry have on its performance. Chapter 6 introduces our framework for analyzing the characteristics of a firm's external context that affect its ability to create and capture value. Chapter 7 provides an overview of the effects of competition on performance and explores the opportunities for mitigating competition through product differentiation. Chapter 8 examines competition in markets where the nature of competition is determined by the behavior of the major players in the industry and provides a framework for thinking about competitive interaction. Since the number and size distribution of firms are critical factors in determining the strength of competition, Chapter 9 discusses entry and barriers to entry.

Chapter 10 discusses the firm's position within its value chain, exploring how the structure of the value chain affects its relationships with buyers and suppliers and how it can create and capture value. Chapter 10 also provides a bridge to Chapters 11–13 where we move to an examination of the "change arrows" in Figure 1-2. In particular, in Chapter 11 we look at issues that arise as industries evolve and firms undertake strategic actions to alter their external context. In Chapter 12 we apply these ideas to industries like electronic commerce, telecommunications, and others that are characterized by network effects or demand-side increasing returns. We then discuss globalization. Increasingly, the fact that they compete in a global economy is a crucial aspect of many firms' strategic context. In Chapter 13, we examine the challenges and opportunities of developing and implementing strategy in a global context.

In Chapter 14 we turn our attention to strategy in large multibusiness firms, the subject known as corporate strategy. This chapter discusses how the corporate office might add value to the firm's constituent businesses. We discuss the difference between corporate and business strategy and the avenues available for enhancing business unit performance.

Finally, in Chapter 15, we turn our attention to the process by which strategy is, and should be, formulated and implemented. Remembering that our focus throughout is on strategic thinking rather than formal strategic planning, we discuss the relationship between the concepts and approach advocated in this book and sensible strategic planning processes in firms.

# 2

# BUSINESS STRATEGY

## 2.1 INTRODUCTION

The core of strategic management as a practical endeavor is formulating a successful strategy for the firm. In Chapter 1, we asserted that strategic thinking is about understanding the relationships among the firm's internal and external contexts, its actions and its performance (as illustrated in Figure 1-2 and reproduced here as Figure 2-1). In this chapter, we describe how a manager who has a mental map of these relationships can define a strategy that acts as a guide to decision making for all members of the organization. To make the concept of strategy more concrete, we begin by describing the components a strategy should have. We also want to distinguish strategy from other terms that are related to it, such as vision, mission, values, and purpose. These are useful complements to strategy, but they are generally different from and imperfect substitutes for it.

Having described what we mean by strategy, we will discuss how to identify a strategy in practice and then how to evaluate it. We round out the chapter by outlining the steps beyond strategy identification and evaluation that a business unit typically goes through when it tries to change its strategy. Since the goal of subsequent chapters is to provide the building blocks for developing and implementing a strategy, we need to know the steps involved in doing that before we proceed.

## 2.2 DESCRIBING BUSINESS STRATEGY

To be a useful guide for decision making, a strategy must have elements that clearly define the firm's goals and the direction it will take to achieve them. Although there are many ways a manager might choose to accomplish this, any coherent strategy should have four components. First, it should include a clear set of long-term goals. Second, it should define the scope of the firm, the kinds of products the firm will offer, the markets it will pursue, and the broad areas of activity it will undertake. Third, a strategy should have a clear statement of what competitive advantage it will achieve and sustain. Finally, the strategy must present the essential logic that is suggested in Figure 2-1; what is it about the firm's internal context that will allow it to achieve a competitive advantage in

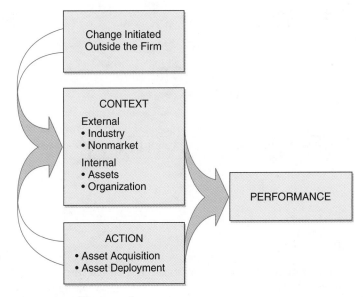

**FIGURE 2-1**    Dynamics of Business Strategy

the environment in which it has chosen to compete? We will define each of these components and describe how the final component, logic, ties them together.

## Goals

The first element of a coherent strategy is a clear set of long-term goals toward which strategy is directed. These long-term goals typically refer to the market position or status that the firm hopes to achieve through its strategy. For example, long-term goals might be to "dominate the market," to be "the technology leader," or to be "the premium quality firm." By "long term" we mean that these goals are enduring. They are different from the specific targets that a firm might set for a particular planning period. A long-term goal, such as having the highest quality products in the industry, is not one that can be achieved and then checked off a list. Rather, it is a goal that may take a long time to attain and once achieved, it must be actively maintained.

By including long-term goals within the strategy, we may seem to be confusing ends (long-term goals) with means (strategy). But the two are closely intertwined. "Market dominance" is a goal because it states what the firm hopes to achieve. Yet it is also part of the strategy because it has implications for the plan of action the firm should pursue. A strategy designed to support market dominance will usually imply a different set of activities from a strategy intended to support being one of many equal competitors. Being the "lowest price" producer, for example, is consistent with market dominance. Setting a price that matches competitors' prices is more likely to be consistent with a strategy of sharing the market.

The goals should be clearly directional. Goals can be thought of as the "where" of the strategy: Where do the managers of the firm want it to be? To be directional, goals must be more specific than the overarching edict of "maximize profit." A long-term goal like profit-maximization is too broad to have much strategic content. In some circumstances, dominating the market might maximize a firm's profits; in others, a firm will maximize its profit by being a niche player in an industry dominated by another firm. In sum, long-term goals should provide guidance for what actions the firm should take.

Beyond the primary purpose of helping to explicate the strategy, incorporating goals within it can serve at least two other purposes. The first is motivational. Providing a common target can give employees a sense of purpose as well as the knowledge that they and their fellow workers are working towards a common goal. The second is competitive. By clearly staking out a desired competitive position, the firm may be able to persuade rivals to focus their efforts elsewhere. For example, GE's commitment to being "number one or two" in the markets it serves is not lost on its competitors!

## Scope

The scope of a business defines the activities in which it will engage. This includes a definition of the products, markets, geographies, technologies, and processes with which it will be involved. The scope nearly always defines the products and services the firm will provide and the markets (demographic, sectoral, or geographic) it targets. An online retailer of baby products, for example, might define its scope as advice and products for expectant and new mothers in the United States. It may also define which of the activities in the value chain for these products and services it will do in-house. Will development of the Web site be conducted in-house to ensure the desired interface or outsourced to a Web development specialist that can reduce cost by achieving economies of scale? As we shall see, for some companies the scope may also include a definition of what technological capabilities the firm intends to master. Scope is the "what" of the strategy: *What* kinds of products will the firm produce, *what* activities will it carry out in-house, and *what* markets will it target?

The scope also defines (implicitly) the activities the firm will *not* undertake. Much of the bite of the strategy comes from this feature. Companies are bombarded with opportunities to venture out of their current scope of activities and with arguments from line managers about the merits of bringing currently outsourced activities in-house. Some business advisors argue that firms will be better off if they sharply focus their activity, while others emphasize the importance of expanding the firm's scope to embrace new opportunities. The statement of scope defines the firm's position with respect to these broad and controversial strategic issues. The scope of the firm's strategy minimizes time-consuming confusion about what activities the firm should pursue and allows it to focus on performing well within that scope.

## Competitive Advantage

Competitive advantage is the "how" of strategy. It defines *how* the firm intends to achieve its long-term goals within its chosen scope. Since the firm faces actual or potential competitors, it must have a compelling reason to expect that it will be able to compete effectively against them. As the phrase "competitive advantage" suggests, a high-performance firm must achieve advantage over its competitors. To be successful, a firm does not need to have an advantage over *all* of its competitors. Many markets have room for several firms that have parity in their ability to compete. Generally speaking, however, a firm will do better if its source of competitive advantage is unique.

There is great variety in the potential sources of competitive advantage. These include lower manufacturing costs than one's competitors, higher quality products, greater customer loyalty, the capacity to innovate more quickly, a superior service capability, a better business location, an information technology system that enables the firm to replenish inventory more quickly and efficiently than rivals, and so on. While the list is long, most forms of competitive advantage mean either that a firm can produce some service or product that its customers value more than those produced by competitors or that it can produce its service or product at a lower cost than its competitors.

A firm that is better at something than most of its actual or potential competitors has an advantage in that activity. But this can be a *competitive* advantage only if being better at that activity contributes to the firm's ability to meet its long-term goals. A firm that is best in its industry at filing documents has an advantage in document filing. This will not provide it a competitive advantage, however, unless document filing speed is somehow linked to the basis on which firms compete. For a hospital, document filing speed might be related to service quality; the more rapidly patient records are re-filed, the more likely they will be available the next time the patient comes in for treatment. For a mining company, it is hard to imagine that the speed at which it files its documents will have much effect on its ability to compete effectively.

## Logic

Perhaps the most important element of a strategy is the logic by which the firm intends to achieve its goals. To see why, consider the following (simplistic) example:

> Our strategy is to dominate the U.S. market for inexpensive coffee mugs by being the low-cost, mass-market producer.

This strategy contains a long-term goal and a simple description of both scope and competitive advantage. The goal is to dominate the coffee mug market. The scope is to produce inexpensive mugs for the U.S. mass market. The competitive advantage is the firm's low cost. Yet the example omits a crucial element of any strategy: an explanation of why this strategy will work. Why will this product scope and this competitive advantage result in high performance for this particular firm in this particular industry? The "why" is the logic of the strategy.

To see what logic contributes to a strategy, consider the following expanded strategy:

> Our strategy is to dominate the U.S. market for inexpensive coffee mugs by being the low-priced manufacturer selling through mass-market channels. Our low price in these channels will generate high volume and, because there are economies of scale in the production of mugs, will make us the low-cost producer enabling us to achieve favorable margins even with a low price.

This more complete strategy does two things. First, it answers the "why" question. In particular, it explains the linkage among the "low cost," the "low prices," and the goal of "dominating the market." Low costs enable the firm to charge low prices, which generate large volumes. Economies of scale in production imply that the large volumes enable the firm to produce at low costs. If the firm has the largest market share (which it will if it "dominates the market") and if economies of scale persist at these very large volumes, the firm has a competitive advantage over its rivals. This is what enables it to charge lower prices than its competitors. Figure 2-2 represents the mutually reinforcing elements of this logic.

Second, the more complete strategy makes explicit some of the assumptions about the firm and its environment that must be true if the strategy is to succeed. For example, it must be true that economies of scale are sufficient to give the firm the cost advantage it believes it will have over smaller competitors.

Obviously, even this "more complete" strategy is a simplified example. In practice, the firm's strategic goals are often more complex, its scope is more detailed, its sources of competitive advantage are more numerous and specific, and its logic is more intricate. Our purpose here has been to describe the components of a strategy rather than to provide a complete or realistic one. Later in the chapter, we provide a more richly textured example. More important than the details and specificity, however, is the idea of what the logic does: the notion that *the logic contains the core argument for why the firm will succeed.* Until one is able to articulate how the goals, scope, and competitive advantage come together to provide a coherent and convincing case for firm success, you have only a list of elements, not a strategy.

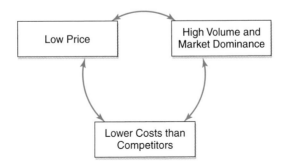

**FIGURE 2-2**    The Logic of the More Complete Strategy

## 2.3  RELATIONSHIP OF STRATEGY TO MISSION, PURPOSE, VALUES, AND VISION

The purpose of strategy is to guide the decisions the firm makes, but it is not the only guide that firms use. The choices they make are also affected by the values endorsed by the firm, the vision embraced by its leaders, and the mission it pursues. Indeed, words such as "values," "mission," "purpose," and "vision" are often used interchangeably with "strategy." In our view, values, vision, and mission are often complements to a strategy, but they also serve distinct purposes and should not be confused with strategy.

### Mission, Purpose, and Values

Firms often commit their major goals and corporate philosophy to writing in a Mission Statement or a Statement of Purpose. Though varied in its structure and form, the statement typically describes the firm's *raison d'etre*, its reason for existing. [1] It also sometimes outlines the "core values" on which the company is based and to which it expects corporate behavior to conform. The statement of Sunrise Medical reproduced in Figure 2-3 is an example of the kind of statement we have in mind. This company (which uses the term "charter" for "scope") prominently posts its statement in its annual reports and on its Web page. The way in which it emphasizes the statement suggests that its managers believe it is important.

The mission or purpose parts of these statements seldom contain the essential elements of a strategy. In particular, although they sometimes define product scope and may refer to competitive advantage, they almost never clearly state the logic supporting the firm's strategy. The Sunrise statement is more detailed than many. It informs the reader that the firm produces rehabilitation aids, and it suggests that product superiority is a potential competitive advantage for Sunrise. Other statements lack even these rudimentary clues to a firm's strategy. Consider, for example, the mission statement in Figure 2-4.

This statement clearly fails what might be referred to as the "person on the bus test." If a person on a bus read it without the company name attached to it, he or she would have little hope of identifying the company, much less of discerning what its strategy might be. The scope of the company is almost a complete mystery. (Is this a TV station? the Disney Corporation?) Moreover, while (1) and (2) list some purported sources of competitive advantage, they are short on specifics (How, for example, will the company "understand the entertainment interests of the consumer better than anyone else"?), and the logic is not explained. Told that this is the Mission Statement of the Blockbuster Entertainment Group (a division of Viacom Inc.) that operates a chain of video rental stores, the bus rider might wonder how Blockbuster will deliver "unique products."

[1] See Jeffrey Abrahams, *The Mission Statement Book* (Berkeley, CA: Ten Speed Press, 1995), for a number of examples.

**Sunrise Charter:** Sunrise Medical designs, manufactures and markets products used in institutional and homecare settings that address the recovery, rehabilitation and respiratory needs of the patient.

**Sunrise Mission:** To improve people's lives by creating innovative, high quality products.

**Sunrise Values:**

1. *Product Superiority:* We are a product-driven company: We are only as good as the products we make. We are committed as a corporation to offering products with genuine superiority in quality, innovation and value, but the most important of these is quality. Our quality standard is: do it right the first time.

2. *Service to Customers:* In our company, the customer comes first. Our customer service goal is to Exceed Customer Expectations Every Day: EXCEED. We must outperform our competitors in demonstrating sensitivity and responsiveness to our customers' needs.

3. *Respect for Associates:* We value the diversity of our Associates and believe in the dignity and worth of every individual. We will treat our Associates with fairness and respect, while empowering them to think independently and act resourcefully. Every job is important and must be performed well if we are to succeed. Our company provides equal opportunity worldwide for all Associates to achieve personal growth and fulfillment in their careers.

4. *Teamwork:* All of us together are stronger and wiser than any of us is individually. We will foster within our company the attitude of a championship team: a spirit of enthusiasm, dedication and fun while working together in the pursuit of common goals. We will be known as people who care about our customers, our products, our company and one another.

5. *Performance:* We must earn an attractive return for our stockholders, which in turn ensures our corporate future and permits us to reinvest in growth. The key to corporate performance is achieving continuous improvement in every area of our business. To do this we must develop our core competencies, operate with the latest methods and technologies, and invest in education to improve our critical skills.

6. *Social Responsibility:* Through our commitment to corporate excellence, we will improve the welfare of those who use our products and advance the progress of society. We will respect and help protect the environment. We will also be good citizens of every community and every country in which we operate, thereby contributing to global prosperity and harmony.

7. *Integrity:* We are committed as an organization to acting with integrity and character. When faced with moral choices, we will do the right thing. We will bring professionalism and proper business conduct to everything we do. Above all, we are dedicated to being a company with integrity.

**FIGURE 2-3**    Charter, Mission, and Values Statement of Sunrise Medical

The statement of company values is usually even less like a strategy. Some are simply a list of unexceptional virtues (integrity, customer service, treating employees well, and so forth). These routine lists include many statements that could not reasonably be contradicted. Could a firm, for example, state that it believes in treating employees badly or in providing shoddy service? Other statements have less routine

"[Our] mission is to be the best provider of entertainment options that meet consumer needs. We will accomplish this by:

1. Understanding the entertainment interests of the consumer better than anyone else.
2. Delivering unique products with the highest level of customer service.

Our resolve to consistently provide the best customer entertainment experience will result in exciting opportunities for our employees and an exceptional return for our investors."

**FIGURE 2-4**   A Mission Statement

content. The statement from Sunrise Medical, for example, contains a paragraph on "social responsibility" that, if adhered to, might distinguish Sunrise from its competitors. Even when the value statement has substance, it usually has little in common with what we have called strategy. Consider, for example, the values statement of a leading company listed in Figure 2-5. Which company's values are these? Apart from the hint provided by the word "technology," you would be hard-pressed to guess which of many thousands of companies that might aspire to these values actually produced this statement.[2]

If they have little strategic value, why do firms formulate and publicize these kinds of statements? A cynical view is that they are largely public relations statements; indeed, the wide publicity given to them seems to indicate that managers believe they will enhance the firm's image. But in fact, mission and values statements can serve several positive functions:

- First, the mission statement can clarify the firm's goals, reducing the tendency for people to work at cross-purposes. Some strategic management scholars, for example, stress the importance of consistency between the views of the company's leaders and the company's strategy. A mission statement may help promote this congruence.

- Second, in not-for-profit organizations, the mission statement can serve to inform the organizations' external constituency (including potential donors) about the overarching goals of the organization. Because not-for-profit organizations tend to have more varied overarching goals than for-profits, this kind of statement may be critical to defining the organization's goals.

- Third, to the extent that the firm can commit itself to a distinctive set of values, these may have positive effects on suppliers, customers, and employees. The device that enables the firm to commit to these values is its reputation. We will return to the role of values and reputation later in this book.

Our main point, however, is that whatever merit these statements have, they should not be confused with a statement of the firm's strategy.

---

[2] In fact, this is the values statement of Applied Materials, a leading producer of semiconductor manufacturing equipment (Abrahams, *The Mission Statement Book*, p. 97).

*Close to Customer*
   More than technology, customers define our accomplishments.
*Achievement Oriented*
   Aggressive goals and meeting commitments drive our success.
*Respect for the Individual*
   Mutual trust and respect are shared by all.
*Honesty and Integrity*
   Honesty and integrity are essential for building trust.
*Teamwork*
   Effectiveness increases when we exchange ideas and share responsibilities.
*Performance and Rewards*
   Commitment and performance ensure growth.
*Professional Management*
   Professional managers lead employees to translate values into action.
*Excellence and Quality*
   Every task can be continually improved.
*Global Awareness*
   Embracing different perspectives leads to a wealth of opportunities.
*Obligations to Stockholders*
   Return long-term value to our investors.
*Positive Social Contribution*
   Make a meaningful contribution in our communities.

**FIGURE 2-5**  A Statement of Values

## Vision

To develop a strategy with a coherent internal logic, the strategist needs to understand where the firm and the industry are headed. The general manager must have some sense about technological trajectories, competitors' likely actions, and developing market opportunities. Because these cannot be precisely and definitively described, the manager has to make some assumptions about them, about the way they interact, and about what outcomes are likely. Forecasting how this related set of events will unfold requires foresight because the current situation often provides few hints about what the future holds. Because of the foresight that is required to imagine how events might unfold and the role the firm might play in shaping that future to the firm's advantage, the term "vision" is often used to describe the strategist's plan for closing the gap between current reality and a potential future. For example, Bennis and Nanus describe the role of vision as follows:

> To choose a direction, a leader must first have developed a mental image of a possible and desirable future state of the organization … which we call a *vision*. [A] vision articulates a view of a realistic, credible, attractive future for the organization. … With a vision, the leader provides the all-important bridge from the present to the future of the organization.[3]

[3] Warren Bennis and Burt Nanus, *Leaders: The Strategies for Taking Charge* (New York: Harper and Row, 1985).

Having a vision of the future might (and often does) contribute to formulating a good strategy and motivating the firm's employees to achieve it. Indeed, as we saw, it is difficult to articulate a strategy without also indicating the long-term goals at which it is aimed.

Developing and communicating an envisioned future for a firm in a rapidly changing and uncertain world is a leadership function of general managers. The strategist's, and even the firm's, value added can sometimes depend on the creativity and innovation of the vision. Especially for a new organization or a firm involved in fundamentally changing its strategic direction, a clear (and clearly articulated) vision of where the strategy is intended to take the company and why it has a chance for success is important to attract and motivate employees and investors. Managers themselves believe that vision is a key role of senior management. For example, one survey indicates that 98 percent of international senior managers believe that conveying a strong sense of vision is the most important role for a CEO, and that strategy formulation to achieve a vision is the CEO's most important skill.[4]

At the same time, a vision is not always necessary for strategy, and, more importantly, it is never sufficient. Some very boring strategies that require little creativity to formulate are successful. Particularly in industries in which change is slow and incremental, a successful strategy may require little vision. Conversely, a great vision without a supporting strategy is unlikely to succeed. Hundreds of companies have been built on the founder's vision of how consumers would use the Internet, and most have failed. Some have failed because the vision was wrong. Others have failed because they had no strategy enabling them to succeed. There was no strategy to guide the firm in its acquisition and deployment of assets that would provide it with competitive advantage *given* the vision. At its best, vision can guide the formulation of strategy, but it is not a substitute for it.

## 2.4   THE STRATEGY STATEMENT

Even when a firm is pursuing a clear, logical strategy, the firm may never have publicly articulated it. Typically, the company's annual report and its other public disclosures describe some elements of the strategy. In the United States, for example, a publicly held firm's annual report and its other filings with the Securities and Exchange Commission usually say something about the scope of the firm and its competitive advantage. However, those documents generally do not lay out long-term goals (except perhaps in a vague and not strategically meaningful way), and, more importantly, they do not explain how the firm intends to tie the pieces together to outperform its competition. The absence of a public, explicit strategy statement is in sharp contrast to the mission statement, which the firm often takes pains to disseminate widely. The reason for this difference is, of course, that the firm often wishes to keep its strategic intentions hidden from its rivals, whereas the mission statement is intended to communi-

---

[4] Results of Korn/Ferry International survey as quoted in Joseph Quigley, *Vision: How Leaders Develop It, Share It, and Sustain It* (New York: McGraw-Hill, 1993).

cate core values, purpose, and mission to employees, investors, suppliers, customers, and the general public.

While it is understandable that a firm would refrain from publishing its strategy, some firms do not even explicitly articulate their strategy *privately*. Perhaps the most common reason for not articulating a strategy is that the senior general managers have a mutual understanding of what the strategy is and need not bother to formulate an explicit strategy statement.

A second reason is that the firm may be pursuing its strategy un-self-consciously. That is, it may be operating within a clear scope and successfully outperforming its rivals with a clear source of competitive advantage without ever having analyzed why it is successful or what the logic of its actions and policies might be. Whether the firm originally embarked on its strategy by following a grand design or stumbled on it through a process of incremental change or pure chance, the key to its competitive advantage may long ago have become embodied in its routines, policies, and organizational structure.

Once a firm has hit (or stumbled) on a recipe for success, it can replicate its success without even analyzing why it is successful, provided its environment does not change. In such an organization, each part plays its role as shaped by the firm's history. When individuals within those roles leave, others who continue that function replace them. The various parts work together, like a well-oiled machine, similarly ignorant of how the pieces fit together or how the whole functions. In such cases it is sometimes easier for an outsider to divine what the firm's strategy actually is than it is for an insider who is blinded or biased by the idiosyncratic nature of the role he or she performs.

The third reason for a firm not to have an explicit, articulated strategy is that the firm is confused about its strategy or has a strategy that has no compelling logic. Since the process of precisely articulating the strategy reveals these inconsistencies, often accompanied by disagreement and conflict among senior management, such firms often prefer to focus on the details of the next year's business plan rather than to confront the fundamentals of their strategy.

## Benefits of an Explicit Strategy Statement

Firms can sometimes function well without an explicit strategy statement, but it is generally good practice to be explicit about the strategy. Articulating and communicating to the relevant decision makers a strategy for the business have several benefits:

- *Clarity:* Even if all senior managers believe they know the strategy, the failure to write it down allows for ambiguity that can lead to lack of focus. Moreover, even if the senior management does have a consensus about the strategy, differences in how it is articulated to those who must implement it often lead to unnecessary confusion and conflict. Strategy can be a framework for choosing actions only if those who make the choices know what the strategy is.

- *Coordination:* If the strategy is explicit and well-communicated, people throughout the organization can "pull" in the same direction without having to check constantly that their actions are coordinated with each other. That is, an explicit strategy is a coordinating mechanism. This can also occur with an implicit strategy that the entire organization understands, but creating a common understanding is easier when the strategy is made explicit.

- *Incentives:* If an organization can commit to a specific strategy, employees will have some assurance that the activities the organization values today are the same ones it will value in the future. Therefore, to the extent that rewards for today's effort depend on the fruits of that effort tomorrow, it is easier to provide incentives for that effort. Aguilar expresses this view as follows:

  > Consistency of word and deed on the leader's part is absolutely necessary if others are to commit themselves to the personal and business risks associated with new and unproven courses of action. The general manager who runs hot and cold will fail to encourage confidence in others … Nobody wants to go out on a limb and risk being abandoned at the first sound of cracking wood."[5]

- *Efficiency:* Day-to-day decisions can be evaluated in terms of whether they "fit" the existing strategy. This is considerably less expensive in terms of management time than doing a full-scale evaluation of the merits of all possibilities.

- *Evaluation/Adaptation:* It is usually possible to articulate the performance goals the firm should achieve from following the stated strategy. This is useful in tracking how well the strategy is performing. Having an explicit strategy based on clearly understood assumptions may also make it easier to change the strategy when circumstances require change.

- *Change:* A significant change in the firm's strategy almost always requires a clear articulation of the proposed new strategy, so that all relevant parts of the firm can implement it.

These benefits of being explicit about strategy must be weighed against some potentially adverse effects. The most important of these effects is that being explicit about the strategy can reinforce rigidity and inertia. Even worthwhile experimentation beyond the boundaries of the current strategy may be blocked by middle managers on the grounds that it falls outside the current strategy. The issue of balancing focus on the current strategy with exploration into new areas is taken up in Chapter 5 and discussed more fully in Chapter 15. In most circumstances, however, we believe that the benefits of being explicit about strategy far outweigh any potential costs.

## The Form and Use of the Strategy Statement

When a firm decides to be explicit about its strategy, we call the vehicle that the firm uses to describe its strategy a "strategy statement." Earlier we gave an example of a

---

[5] Francis Aguilar, *General Managers in Action* (New York: Oxford University Press, 1985), p. 71.

complete one-sentence statement of strategy. Most firms will not be able to boil their strategy down to a single sentence. The long-term goals, scope, and sources of competitive advantage may each involve a number of points, and the logic that binds them may take several paragraphs to explain. The statement needs to be detailed enough to do justice to its components; yet it must be concise enough to be succinctly communicated. Most people who have experience with attempting to communicate strategy stress the need for simplicity and brevity. Think of the strategy statement as an "elevator pitch": a statement of the firm's strategy that is sufficiently detailed to be useful to the functional managers who must implement the strategy, yet concise enough to be delivered in an elevator ride.

## An Example: Borders Books

We present a strategy statement for Borders, Inc., a book distributor employing a superstore format.[6] Borders distributes both through its traditional offline "bricks and mortar" stores and through a newer online division, Borders.com. In Figure 2-6 we have presented the strategy for Borders before its adoption of online distribution. We have done this both to focus on a somewhat simpler strategy, but also to show later in the chapter how Borders should think about adapting to external change with the advent of online bookstores.

Note, first, that the entire statement is only about a page long. Note, too, that while the strategy statement may change a little in its details over time, this basic strategy is likely to be enduring. In particular, the long-term goals will take some time to achieve and will take significant effort to maintain once they have been achieved. The scope is clear about which activities in the value chain the firm will provide itself and which it will not. Finally, observe that while the purported sources of competitive advantage are outlined, the competitive advantages themselves are vacuous without a statement of the logic that ties those competitive advantages to the company's goals and scope.

This strategy statement illustrates several of the advantages of being explicit about strategy that we discussed above. First, clarity about the scope of the strategy can help to focus management's efforts on growth by emphasizing the kinds of stores and geographic areas that the firm has chosen for expansion. Second, the logic of the strategy makes it clear that the firm ought to be interested in cost-saving innovations that will enable it to reduce unit costs while maintaining or increasing service levels. Understanding the logic of the firm's strategy will provide employees with the right incentives to suggest improvements that advance the logic of the business. Third, the in-store employees are a key part of the strategy as outlined in this statement. Helping them to see the important role they play in the company's strategy may also motivate them.

---

[6] Since the details of firms' strategies are typically highly confidential, the strategy statement in Figure 2-6 has been inferred by the authors from publicly available information. The example is meant only to be illustrative of the components of a strategy statement, rather than a description of Borders' actual strategy.

---

## BORDERS' STRATEGY STATEMENT

*Long-term goals:* Borders will be the leading retail distribution outlet for books in the United States measured by the number of books sold and revenue market share. We will have the greatest revenue per square foot of any book retailer and the highest margin per book. Our customers will have the most satisfying book purchasing experience in terms of variety of books offered, in-store availability of desired titles, and helpfulness of staff. We will expand from our base in the United States to Australia, New Zealand, Singapore and the United Kingdom.

*Scope:* Borders will run a chain of large (in excess of 20,000-sq. ft.) bookstores carrying a wide variety of titles (in excess of 80,000) in each store. We will be located in all major metropolitan areas in the United States and Canada. Our facilities will be leased rather than purchased, and, while designed to fit into the local architecture, they will share a common layout and common information systems. Most stores will have a coffee bar, the operation of which will be outsourced. We have developed and continue to maintain and improve a proprietary information technology system for tracking and managing inventory. We are not vertically integrated into the production of books.

*Competitive Advantages:* We believe that the following are key sources of competitive advantage:

- Our large scale
- Our proprietary inventory system
- Our highly trained in-store staff
- Customer awareness of our name and reputation for service and value
- Our prime locations of existing stores
- Perception of our stores among real estate developers as valuable "anchor tenants."

*Logic:* Our wide variety of titles, low prices, highly trained staff, and attractive stores provide an attractive shopping experience for our customers, making us their first choice in bookstores. The high volumes this generates in each store coupled with the size of the chain give us significant purchasing power that enables us to procure books at favorable prices. Furthermore, our proprietary inventory management gives us superior knowledge of what to stock and minimizes "out of stock" occurrences, optimizes inventory on hand, and minimizes returns of books to suppliers. Our unit costs are therefore the lowest in the industry, allowing us to have the highest margins despite having below average prices. While we have significant expenses in terms of creating and maintaining our proprietary information systems, training, brand advertising, and administration, our ability to spread those expenses over many stores enables us to keep our operating expenses a low fraction of revenue. Our current store locations give us a first-mover location advantage, and our reputation for attracting traffic makes us an attractive anchor tenant in new locations, facilitating growth through new stores, allowing us to leverage our competitive advantages into new locations.

**FIGURE 2-6**   Strategy Statement for Borders, Inc.

## 2.5  DEVELOPING STRATEGY: THE STRATEGY PROCESS

So far we have discussed what a strategy should do and what components it should have. In the rest of this chapter, we offer some comments on the process of developing a strategy. Formulating a strategy that is an effective guide to action is both an art that individual managers must develop and a process that a well-managed firm must implement. The individual manager must first have the tools she or he needs to analyze the firm's internal and external context. Much of this text is devoted to providing the essential tools. She or he must also understand what role strategy plays within the firm and the elements that a strategy should contain. This has been the topic of this chapter.

It is also important, however, to recognize that strategy is developed within a firm. The final product will necessarily be shaped by the history of that firm, the processes it has in place for making fundamental business decisions, and the interests and perspectives of its senior managers. Typically, these factors come together in a "strategy process," a (sometimes formal) process through which strategy is defined and evaluated by the firm's managers. The issue of strategy process will be discussed in the final chapter of this book, but we want to complete our current discussion by sketching the major steps such a process might involve. The conceptual steps are illustrated in Figure 2-7.

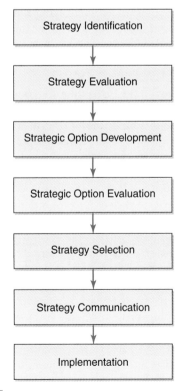

**FIGURE 2-7**  Steps in Setting Strategy

For our current purpose, the steps of strategy identification and evaluation are most relevant, and we will focus on them. The remaining steps are particularly important when the firm is changing its strategy or, in the case of a new firm, establishing an initial strategy.

## Strategy Identification

It might seem strange to start with the notion that the manager needs to identify the firm's strategy. After all, it may seem obvious that he or she will know what the strategy is. However, this is not always the case. Previously, we described a firm for which strategy is embodied in its routines but has never been articulated. Managers at this type of firm who want to develop a strategy statement will first have to "reverse engineer" the firm's routines. They will have to look at what the firm does and try to figure out what strategy might be consistent with that set of activities. Managers also have to identify the firm's strategy when some of the firm's actions have diverged from its formal strategy. If, for example, the firm's external environment has changed significantly, the managers may have responded by taking appropriate actions. If these actions are inconsistent with the old strategy, the strategy has *de facto* been changed, perhaps without the managers' recognition of how it has changed. Over time, small changes can cumulate to produce a *de facto* strategy that bears little resemblance to the official strategy. In these circumstances, identifying the existing strategy is necessary to crafting an accurate and useful strategy statement. But creating a strategy statement is not the only reason for identifying a firm's strategy. Identifying a firm's current strategy is also the starting point for the general managers responsible for developing and overseeing strategy implementation.

Outsiders who are analyzing the firm either for competitive or investment reasons or with an eye to a merger or acquisition also want to identify the firm's strategy. For them, it is tempting simply to examine what the firm may have said its strategy is. Such statements can often be found in its financial reports, annual reports, Web pages, investor information kits, and so on. However, as we have noted above, such statements are rarely coherent and comprehensive articulations of strategy. To understand a firm's strategy, one also needs to look at the firm's actual policies and what the firm actually does: that is, its pattern of decisions. Sometimes what the firm claims as its strategy is in conflict with what the firm does. More often, what the firm does provides additional information about its strategy.

To return to the example of Borders, a key component of its strategy is to provide superior customer service. If this is the reality of Borders' strategy rather than wishful thinking on its part, we would expect it to have a set of human resources management policies that are aligned with this strategy. We would look for personnel recruiting and selection policies, training programs, and compensation schemes that are well suited to developing a workforce that delivers high-quality customer service.

Thus the starting point for strategy identification is an examination of the firm's approach to business in each of its key areas of operation: finance, sales and marketing, manufacturing, procurement, R&D, marketing, distribution, product line, pricing, formal and informal organization structure, human resources management policies, and so on. From an examination of the firm's practices in each of these areas, we can generally determine the key elements of the scope of the strategy as well as the areas in which the firm might have competitive advantage. The final step is to attempt to infer what logic ties the pieces together. That is basically an inductive exercise in which one attempts to build a coherent argument for how the firm's actions and policies combine to form a cohesive strategy. As we discuss in the following section, it is easiest to infer the logic of the strategy when the strategy is in fact compelling. When what the firm is doing doesn't make much sense, there may be no logic to infer.

## Strategy Evaluation: Testing the Logic

Logic is the component of strategy that brings the other elements together. The logic of the strategy contains the argument for how the scope and competitive advantage identified in the strategy will enable the firm to reach its goals given its internal assets and its external environment. Strategy evaluation is testing whether that logic is compelling.

To evaluate the logic, the managers want to ask: "What must be true about this firm and about the environment in which we compete if this strategy is to be successful?" If the strategy calls for the firm to offer the most advanced products, the managers want to ask whether the firm's internal context has the strategic assets it needs to produce more advanced products than its competitors and whether its buyers want more advanced products enough to pay the cost of developing them. Or, to return to our one-sentence example on page 23, a strategy might depend on costs declining with output. If the firm's technology has only negligible economies of scale, the logic of the strategy is flawed. It might be true that a low-cost position would be advantageous given the firm's external environment, but the firm's internal context—its technology in this case—is inconsistent with achieving a low-cost position.

Because testing the logic requires looking at both the firm's internal and external environments, practitioners commonly speak of "opportunity analysis" and "asset analysis." An opportunity analysis looks at whether there is, in fact, an attractive opportunity in the external context that this strategy can exploit. Does the world really want a better mousetrap? An asset analysis examines the firm's internal context: Does this firm have the human and physical capital necessary to build a better mousetrap, and are those assets organized in a way that allows the firm to be better than its competitors at building mousetraps? Although it is convenient to separate the analysis this way, it is important to remember that the pieces all have to fit together for the logic to work.

Our description of strategy evaluation has some common language with a tool known as *SWOT Analysis*, an acronym for the firm's Strengths, Weaknesses, Opportunities, and Threats. SWOT Analysis encourages managers to identify the firm's strengths and weaknesses. The strengths and weaknesses component is similar to our asset analysis, and the threats and opportunities component is similar to our opportunities analysis. However, there are some key differences between the SWOT approach and a test of strategic logic. An application of the SWOT framework will produce an organized inventory of factors that are potentially relevant to the firm's strategic situation. This, however, is not enough. A firm's assets and opportunities must be appraised in terms of its strategy.

Suppose, for example, that we were to determine that Borders was weak in its financial controls and in understanding wide-area networking technology. Its weakness in financial controls might be of some concern, but since networking is critical to the proprietary inventory system on which its strategy depends, its networking weakness has much larger strategic significance. The threats and opportunities facing the firm must also be assessed in terms of its strategy. A book superstore must evaluate the opportunity to augment its scope by offering music CDs within its superstores versus, say, the chance to open small bookstores in addition to large superstores, in terms of how each possibility fits with the overall logic of its strategy. What implications does adding CDs have for staff training or for the quality of the "shopping experience," both of which might be important parts of the firm's competitive advantage in its current strategy? What implications does adding small bookstores have for the cost structure of the firm, and how will these stores compete with the existing small, independent bookstores that already offer this business format? Because there may be demand for a CD superstore and for small bookstores, these options represent opportunities for the firm. But deciding which opportunities to pursue requires analyzing them with respect to the firm's strategy and, specifically, the logic of the strategy.

## Strategy Process and Strategic Change

Our primary goals in this chapter were to define the concept of strategy, compare it to related concepts such as mission and vision, and describe how a strategy statement might capture the essence of a firm's strategy. We also described how to identify a business unit's strategy in practice and outlined the criteria used to evaluate the strategy once it has been identified. In the process, we also have begun to develop the steps that are typically involved in strategic change and that we discuss in greater detail later in the book. As illustrated in Figure 2-7, strategy identification and evaluation are the initial steps in formulating and implementing a new strategy. The remaining steps are:

- *Developing Strategic Options:* If the strategy evaluation reveals problems with the firm's current strategy, the next step is to determine what other strategic options the firm has. A strategic option should be a coherent, self-contained strategy with the four elements of long-term goals, scope, competitive advantage, and logic.

- *Evaluating the Strategic Options:* Evaluating the strategic options raises issues similar to those discussed in evaluating the current strategy. The chosen strategy should exploit opportunities presented by the external environment for which the firm's strategic assets are well suited. But one does not generally expect the firm's *current* organization and assets to be consistent with that option. If a strategic option represents a departure from the previous strategy, the firm's internal context will likely have to be changed. The issue in evaluating an option is whether the firm can make the required changes.

- *Selecting a Strategy:* With the options clearly laid out, the firm has to select among them. The temptation at this stage is to attempt to combine the bits and pieces of various options that are most appealing to the managers. This amalgamation is particularly appealing when the firm has many constituencies, each of which has a stake in some piece of its strategy. Marketing, for example, might resist reducing the number of products the firm offers even if the change will benefit the firm as a whole. Or the R&D group might resist a movement from leading-edge to consumer-friendly products even though there is little demand for the "technically superior" product. If, however, the options are carefully developed, combining their elements will produce an incoherent strategy that may be ill-suited to any possible environment. It is because the temptation to waffle or merge elements of disparate strategies is so strong that we include a separate step for *selecting* a strategy.

- *Communicating a Strategy:* If a strategy is to guide the firm's actions, its employees must understand what the strategy is. Because it is difficult to get even a simple message about the firm's strategy across to everyone in the organization, clarity and brevity are crucial. Moreover, managers with experience in communicating strategy stress the importance of repetition and retaining the same strategy statement unless the firm has indeed made a fundamental change in its strategy.

- *Implementing a Strategy:* Strategy implementation is the process of executing the strategy. From a process point of view, it is conceptually attractive to draw a bright line between formulation and implementation. First you decide what to do, and then you do it. However, the starting conditions for developing and evaluating strategy are formed by prior implementation actions. For example, formulating a new product strategy might be necessary only because implementing the current strategy resulted in a major product innovation. Similarly, the development of a culture of trust and respect may provide the basis for a high-quality service orientation that may be a potential source of competitive advantage later on. It is therefore misleading to think of implementation as merely the mechanical carrying out of a plan of action. There is a strong feedback loop from implementation to formulation.

To illustrate the kind of analysis required for the steps listed in Figure 2-7, let's go back to Borders at the time when online sales of books were just beginning. Strategy evaluation might reveal that the company's offline ("bricks and mortar") strategy is not well designed to counter the threat posed by retailing books over the Internet. The early success of Amazon.com is an example of the kind of contextual change that should trigger a full strategy reevaluation. This alternative channel reduces the demand for bookstore services and changes the kind of services potential customers value in book retailing. How do buyers make the tradeoff between ambiance—where Borders' stores have a purported advantage—and convenience which is Amazon.com's strength? What is the value of easy access to book reviews and customized recommendation lists that are provided on-line? How does this compare with the knowledge and helpfulness of Borders' sales staff? Answering these kinds of questions gives Borders a start on evaluating its current strategy given this new threat.

Once the nature of the external change is identified and the firm has some idea about how well its current strategy can respond to it, the firm can develop strategic options. One obvious option would be the one Borders has in fact pursued—to expand the scope of its strategy to include online retailing. To evaluate this option it would need to think about which of its assets could be leveraged in this endeavor and what assets it would need to acquire. For example, while it has some information technology know-how, it may need to acquire some Web development capabilities. It would also need to understand enough about online retailing to assess whether it could reasonably match Amazon.com's strengths and overcome any first-mover advantage Amazon.com might have. Borders might also need to expand its product line to include video and music to compete with the expanding product line at Amazon.com. Borders should also consider the history of losses at Amazon given its dominance of online book retailing. What will enable several competing firms to make a profit when Amazon.com could not when it had the market to itself?

To implement the online option, Borders must develop a clear strategy for that part of the business as a stand-alone venture as well as for the integrated business. For example, a potential competitive advantage that Borders has from having both an online presence and traditional stores is that it can arrange to handle returns of online purchases through the stores. Because the launch of the online operation represents a sharp strategic change for the company, the importance of clearly communicating this shift inside the company cannot be overestimated. Current employees need to know what changes they should make in their decision making and orientation. They also need to know that the company continues to support (if indeed it does) the prior strategy in its stores.

## 2.6  SUMMARY

In this chapter we have described the components of strategy as goals, competitive advantage, and logic. We have emphasized the logic component because it is the one so often overlooked. It is much easier to imagine some competitive advantage than to carefully describe how this firm has a distinctive ability to create that advantage and why this market environment will reward the "advantage" the firm can create. We have also tried to distinguish strategy from some commonly used and related approaches to directing the efforts of the firm, such as mission and vision, that typically do not have a logic. We have described the form of the strategy statement, discussed the benefits of having such a statement, and provided a detailed example of Borders books to illustrate what one should look like. Finally, we introduced the process by which strategy is formulated and implemented, focusing for now on the strategy identification and evaluation steps of the process. We return to the strategy process in greater detail in Chapter 15. We turn next to a more detailed exploration of competitive advantage.

# CHAPTER

# 3

# COMPETITIVE ADVANTAGE

## 3.1 INTRODUCTION

A firm achieves superior performance only if it can provide products or services that customers will pay more for than it costs the firm to provide them. That is, the firm must be able to *create value*. Value creation is at the heart of any successful strategy. However value creation is not enough. In order to prosper, the firm must also be able to *capture* the value it creates. In order to create *and* capture value the firm must have a sustainable competitive advantage.

We first describe why it is important to think about capturing value and not just about creating value. Then we discuss competitive advantage and what makes some competitive advantages transitory while others are enduring. Lastly, we develop an extended example of competitive advantage from product quality or low cost, and introduce the cost-quality frontier, a framework used throughout the book.

## 3.2 VALUE AND COMPETITIVE ADVANTAGE

Scholars of strategic management often stop with an analysis of value creation, simply advising firms to maximize the value they create. But that advice is inadequate because it assumes that an increase in value created will translate into an increase in profit. This need not be true. Indeed, a firm usually cannot retain all the value it generates. For example, competition may allow the firm's customers to capture some of the value the firm creates. The firm's employees may also capture some of that value. It is not unusual for a firm to substantially increase the value it creates without gaining a commensurate increase in profits. A famous example of this unhappy phenomenon is the invention of the CT (computed tomography) scanner.[1] EMI invented this technology

---

[1] Introduced by EMI in 1972, the CT scanner was initially used for brain scans. Innovations by EMI in 1974 alone are estimated to have added approximately $7 billion (1980 dollars) in value. EMI's profits from the technology were modest at best. See Manual Trajtenberg. *Economic Analysis of Product Innovation: The Case of CT Scanners* (Cambridge, MA: Harvard University Press, 1990).

and brought the first products to a market where demand was high. But EMI earned little of the tremendous value it created. While it initially dominated this market, EMI abandoned it seven years after it sold its first scanner. EMI found that it could not compete with firms like General Electric which rapidly copied the innovation and had the complementary resources for on-going product development, marketing, service, and distribution.

Sometimes a firm can capture value other firms create. In the CT scanner example, General Electric probably captured some of the value created by EMI. Or consider the case of America Online (AOL). Because of its premier status as the leading on-line content gateway, AOL has been able to capture much of the value generated by the content providers featured on its site.

To create and capture value consistently, there must be something special about the firm. Otherwise, a rival could replicate what the firm does, and the ensuing competition would sharply limit the firm's ability to capture value. The search for the underlying sources of such "specialness" is an obsession in strategic management; it is the field's version of the search for the Holy Grail. Every now and then a book appears with the claim that the author has found it, or at least its primary source, and a rush to exploit the fad *du jour* ensues. For example, recent candidates for the fundamental source of superior performance include quality, customer focus, and superior management of human resources. Firms have been told to redesign their business processes, get close to their customers, and empower their workers to enhance profitability.

The very notion that there could be a universal key to success is misguided: If the source of superior firm performance could so easily be identified and replicated, it would quickly cease to be a source of competitive advantage at all! Many firms create and capture value consistently, but the reasons for their success are extremely varied. It is not that customer focus, for example, is unimportant, but rather that there is no magic elixir good for all business problems. We believe instead that the way firms have been able to create and capture value varies because there is enormous heterogeneity among firms and industries. In this book we do not attempt to provide a checklist of universal keys to success or recipes for greatness. Instead, we examine how competitive advantage works in general. Our goal is to provide a method for assessing a firm's current competitive advantage, formulating a strategy to sustain it and creating additional advantage. We mention many specific forms of competitive advantages firms have developed, but our goal is to help managers understand competitive advantage.

We start from the position that any specific competitive advantage derives from the firm's context. By context we mean a firm's assets, its organization, its industry, and its nonmarket environment. As Figure 3-1 illustrates, competitive advantage is a characteristic of both the firm and its relationship to its environment. The firm has an asset—the ability to provide customer service efficiently, for example—and because that asset is superior to that of its competitors and is valued by its customers, it is a competitive advantage for the firm. Any such advantage the firm can exploit through its activity contributes to superior performance.

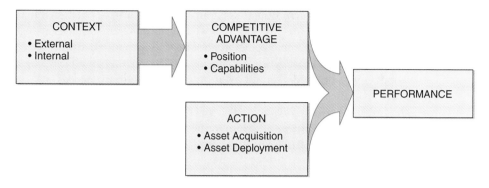

**FIGURE 3-1**    Sources of Competitive Advantage

## 3.3    TWO MAIN ROUTES TO COMPETITIVE ADVANTAGE

There are many kinds of competitive advantage, and they can be divided into two categories: advantages based on the firm's *position* and advantages based on the firm's *capabilities.*

To provide concrete examples of these kinds of competitive advantage, consider two hypothetical firms: Positions Inc. and Global Capabilities. They operate in different industries, but both earn returns on shareholders' equity that are well above average.

- *Positions Inc.* was founded in 1802 to provide a secure way to send cash over long distances. In the early days, a person wanting to send money deposited the funds (plus a healthy commission) at a nearby Position Inc. branch office. Positions Inc. would then send a message to its branch that was closest to the intended recipient of the money authorizing it to pay the sum deposited. Messages were initially sent by stagecoach, then by telegraph, and, ultimately, by a computer network. Although the communications technology has changed, Positions Inc. has never faced serious competition because potential rivals found setting up a competitive branch network prohibitively costly (especially because whenever they opened a branch, Positions Inc. mysteriously dropped the commission it charged in that location). Today, detractors describe Position Inc.'s computer system as "archaic," but managers at Positions Inc. say it works well enough. Customers sometimes complain about shoddy service (relative to, say, the local branch bank), but management responds that it is in the business of providing money transfer services, not entertainment.

- *Global Capabilities* is a Japanese firm that produces a broad range of consumer electronics products as a supplier for major electronics firms. Its customers, who themselves manufacture and sell electronic products, outsource the design and manufacture of selected products to Global Capabilities because Global can transform customer requirements into designs that are light, compact, and easy to manufacture. Its customers and rivals have long marveled at its competence in miniaturization and manufacturing, but have been unable to figure out how Global Capabilities can do what it does. There is some disagreement among Global's management about precisely why the firm is so adept. Certainly no single individual or team in the company has all the knowledge required to understand how it functions so well. Instead Global has complicated routines that bring together the expertise of its teams and coordinates the firm's activities. Outsiders observe how fluid and automatic this process appears to be, with each person knowing exactly whom to contact for help, when and how to participate, and when to hand off to someone else. A sophisticated, computerized project management system supports this human system, but other companies have had little success using similar information technology systems.

These (admittedly colorful) descriptions illustrate the two different kinds of competitive advantage and the futility of searching for the Holy Grail of unique and universal success factors. Whereas Global Capabilities takes prides in its world-class design capabilities and outstanding customer relations, Positions Inc. is weak in the former and atrocious in the latter. Positions Inc. enjoys a dominant position in its industry, but Global Capabilities has many rivals, including its primary customers.

Not only is Positions Inc. weak in customer relations, it does not appear to perform *any* particular function very well. Indeed, nothing about its internal context—neither its tangible and intangible assets nor how they are organized—is a source of strength for the company. For example, its information systems are central to the service it offers but are far from state of the art, and it has no proprietary know-how enabling it to distinguish its service from competitors Instead, the main source of Positions Inc.'s superior performance is that it was the first to enter the industry and build a network of branch offices. It yields extraordinary value to consumers because it provides the only way they can send money to almost anywhere from wherever they happen to be. No other firm has been able to duplicate Position Inc.'s pervasiveness. *Positions Inc.'s competitive advantage is its position as the dominant incumbent firm.* This position alone enables it to earn superior returns, even though it has no remarkable capabilities.

Compare its position to Global Capabilities'. *The essence of Global Capabilities' competitive advantage is its ability to miniaturize and its skill in design-for-manufacturing.* Nothing in its position distinguishes it from its rivals; it is not larger, it has no early-mover advantage, and it provides no valuable asset on which its performance depends. It has competitive advantage because Global is particularly good, indeed better than most of its competitors, at performing certain activities. Global earns its superior returns by exercising these capabilities over and over again for its customers. Since it would cost the customers more to perform these same functions themselves—if indeed they can do them themselves—or to outsource them to another firm, Global Capabilities earns a high return on its capabilities.

These two attributes of a firm and its relationship to its external environment—its *position* in its competitive environment and the *capabilities* that enable it to perform certain functions better than its rivals can—are the two main kinds of competitive advantage that firms can have. Each type of advantage can take a number of specific forms as we describe below, but a firm's competitive advantage can usually be traced to a positional or capability-based strength.

It is tempting to think of a capability as being primarily rooted in the firm's internal context and of position as being rooted primarily in the firm's external context. And indeed, this distinction has some bite. The analysis of positional advantage, for example, has been developed primarily by scholars focusing on the challenges and opportunities posed by the external environment. They tend to treat the firm's internal context as unimportant. From this perspective, the way for a firm to achieve superior performance is to find an advantageous and defensible position within its industry.

By contrast, scholars who primarily focus on the firm's internal context have been responsible for developing the analysis of capabilities-based advantage. They have explored ways the firm can acquire and organize tangible and intangible assets to outperform its competitors. From this perspective, a firm can achieve superior performance by exploiting the firm's assets and organizational structure and protecting them from imitation by rival firms. This view is discussed later in this chapter in the section on the "resource-based" view of the firm. The contributions made by scholars from the positional advantage school of thought are covered in Chapter 6.

Both sources of advantage, however, depend on the firm's internal *and* external context. A superior capability arises in the firm's internal context but is advantageous to the firm only if competing firms cannot mimic it and customers value what it allows the firm to offer them. Advantage is always measured relative to competitors as assessed by potential customers. In another industry, the capability on which the firm's competitive advantage is based might not provide any advantage. Similarly, although superior position is necessarily relative to competitors and sometimes attained by historical accident, it is often the outgrowth of some internal asset. Perceiving the need for money transfer services and organizing a system to deliver them, for example, suggests some capability. Furthermore, the firm's internal assets must be used to defend the position. A dominant firm, for example, will not remain dominant unless it can undercut potential competitors by upgrading service offerings or pricing aggressively. Positions Inc. and Global Capabilities each had only *one* kind of competitive advantage. We made this sharp distinction between positions and capabilities to highlight the differences between these two types of advantage. Most firms, however, have some advantages of both types, and each type reinforces the other. For now, to explain what we mean by each, we will discuss them separately. Later in this chapter we return to how they tend to be interrelated.

## Position

A firm can have many specific kinds of positional advantage, but any positional advantage takes one of three main forms:

- *Positional advantage from an attractive industry structure.* Sometimes all the firms in an industry benefit from the industry's structure. For example, a duopoly, an industry with just two firms, is typically more profitable than an industry with many competing firms. In a duopoly, each firm has somehow managed to achieve a position as one of two incumbents and is likely to be profitable because it has that position. Airbus and Boeing, for example, are the only two manufacturers of large, commercial aircraft in the world, and each benefits from that position.

- *Positional advantage from heterogeneity within the industry.* Often positions within an industry create advantage for the firms occupying them. For example, a firm that has a dominant position in an otherwise fragmented industry usually does better than other industry incumbents. Large fast-food chains have been able to leverage scale economies in production and advertising that give them a competitive advantage over the competing, independent fast-food outlets. The smaller firms have higher costs and less brand equity than their dominant rivals.

- *Positional advantage from a network of relationships.* A firm may derive positional advantage from its relationships with buyers, suppliers, or competitors. For example, venture capital firms compete based on their ability to identify good investment opportunities, create pools of investment capital, and manage their investment portfolios. Within the venture capital community, a few firms have achieved a central position in the network that makes up the "deal flow." Because these firms are well-connected to other venture capitalists, investors, and entrepreneurs, they are well positioned to broker deals among them and to be compensated for their services.

### Examples of Positional Advantage

There are many specific positional advantages, some of which can easily be assigned to one category. Others, however, are more complex and are derived from more than one category. The following list provides some sense of the rich variety of positional advantage.

- *Brand name:* A firm with a widely recognized and appreciated brand name has positional advantage over other firms in its industry whose brands are weaker. A strong brand lets the firm command premium shelf space, wider customer attention, and higher prices. Nike, for example, developed a very powerful global brand in sports shoes and has recently leveraged this positional advantage in shoes into related consumer products.

- *Customer relationships:* A firm with an established reputation for "fair dealing" has a positional advantage over competitors whose customers are concerned about opportunistic behavior. For example, Marks and Spencer in the United Kingdom and Nordstrom in the United States are companies that have developed strong customer relationships based in part on their reputations for no-questions-asked return policies and consistent product quality.

- *Government protection and support:* A firm can derive positional advantage from government intervention in many ways. For example, a firm may gain advantage from being the sole domestic producer in a country where the government's commercial policies favor domestic firms. Dominion Engineering Works benefited for many years from its position as Canada's national champion in the manufacture of paper-making machinery. Its favored position gained it various subsidies and shelter from some forms of competition.

- *Status:* Investment banks that compete with one another to underwrite commercial debt issues can gain positional advantage from their status within the banking community. Banks recognized as "high status" get more opportunities to underwrite lucrative issues on better terms. When they are the lead bank of the underwriting syndicate, other banks are happy to be junior partners in the syndicate, and banks forming syndicates seek them out as syndicate partners. In both cases, the other banks are willing to make concessions to the high-status bank to gain the benefit of being associated with it.

- *Distribution channels:* A firm may have a dominant position with the major firms in its distribution channels. Procter and Gamble makes many leading consumer products that are sold through supermarkets. Because it owns many of the products that draw retail traffic, it is in a better position to persuade its channel partners to devote valuable shelf space to its new products than is a firm with a more limited product scope.

- *Geographic incumbency:* Sometimes the geographic location of a firm is a source of advantage. Wal-Mart, for example, was the first mass merchant to locate its outlets in small towns. It located its stores in areas with too few customers to support more than one large discount store. It also blanketed regions with its stores, leaving no geographic niche for a competitor to enter.

- *Installed base and de facto standards:* In markets where product compatibility is important, firms with a large installed base have a positional advantage. For example, a consumer choosing a word processing package will probably prefer one that makes her files compatible with her co-workers' files. If they use Microsoft Word®, she will probably use Microsoft Word®.

- *Gatekeepers in the flow of goods or information:* Sometimes a firm gains positional advantage from controlling a key connection between other firms or consumers. For example, consider the owner of the only bridges across a river. The need to transport goods across the river gives the bridge owner significant positional advantage. Similarly, search engines (such as Yahoo, Lycos, and others) control major points of access to information on the Internet, giving them a positional advantage they can exploit by charging advertisers for the right to be featured on their sites.

Some general characteristics of positional advantage are exemplified in this list. First, many positional advantages accrue to firms that "move first." Wal-Mart moved into small towns first, preempting an opportunity for other firms. The first venture capital firms in Silicon Valley to achieve great success became the central firms. The observation that moving early to exploit an opportunity can be advantageous is the source of the expression "first-mover advantage." Second, positional advantage is only defined *relative* to actual and potential competitors. If Procter and Gamble were one of a thousand detergent manufacturers with equal scope, it would have no positional advantage within its channels. Similarly, a firm's position in a network is only advantageous relative to the other actors (competitors, customers or suppliers) who are also members of the network.

## Capabilities

Firms, like individuals, differ in their abilities. Consider a firm's ability to manufacture products at low cost. Some might be able to do this because they have special access to low-cost inputs, such as raw materials or labor, or because they are the favored recipients of government subsidies. These firms' low costs are due to positional advantages. Other firms, however, are low-cost producers because they have learned how to combine their inputs more efficiently than do other firms. Through on-going experimentation, learning, and experience, they develop methods that others lack. Their ability to process and combine inputs efficiently is a capability.

Firms possess many different kinds of capabilities. Some, like the Sony Corporation, are renowned for their ability to miniaturize consumer electronics. Indeed, Sony is the model for the fictional firm Global Capabilities. Another capability that has become increasingly important is an ability to minimize "time to market": designing and producing products quickly. For example, in the 1980s Toyota was able to design and produce a car in just three years, while the typical U.S. car manufacturer took five years. Not all capabilities, of course, relate to design and manufacturing. Merck, for example, is a leading pharmaceutical company with a capability for extraordinarily productive research and development, and LL Bean is a mail-order retailer known for its ability to provide a focused range of consumer products through an efficient and effective customer interface.

Sometimes a firm's capability is exercised repetitively for a specific process, whereas in other cases the capability has more general applications. Compare, for example, the following statements: "Sony knows how to miniaturize," and "Georgia-Pacific (GP) knows how to make high-quality check-writing paper." Georgia-Pacific's know-how refers to a specific process it has mastered to produce a particular kind of paper. Because only a handful of firms in the United States have mastered this production process, GP has a capabilities-based competitive advantage. But this ability does not, by itself, give it a competitive advantage in other products, even other kinds of paper. Indeed, this ability is so specific that GP has successfully produced check paper on only a few of its paper-making machines and has had difficulty transferring this ability to other machines even when using the same operators. In contrast, Sony's miniaturization skills enable it to miniaturize within a broad class of electronics applications (computers, stereos, televisions, etc.). This capability, for example, allowed Sony to solve the manufacturing problems associated with producing a laptop computer for Apple Computer quickly enough to satisfy intense time-to-market pressure. Sony accomplished this even though it had never before produced a laptop computer. Its success in this venture was an application of its general capability in designing and manufacturing electronic products.

Often it does not matter whether the firm's capability is specific know-how related to a given process or a more general capability. Sometimes, however, it matters a lot. To understand why, consider what will happen to Georgia Pacific and Sony if some change in their environment makes their current products obsolete. If Georgia Pacific no longer has a market for check paper, its check paper know-how will be worthless because it cannot be used for other products. In contrast, Sony's capability gives it an ability to compete in a broad range of products; it is therefore less vulnerable to environmental changes and better able to take advantage of new opportunities. If the market is no longer interested in miniaturized mobile tape players, it may still be interested in miniaturized computers.

Often, the firm's most valuable capabilities are an attribute of the firm as an organization; that is, it is not possible to separate the capability from the firm. Expertise is dispersed through many parts of the firm, and the organization has routines that access and coordinate that information. In this case, we can say that the capability is an attribute *of the organization*. As an example, consider a fire department's firefighting capability. When an emergency call comes in, the dispatcher decides which fire stations to alert based on the location and severity of the blaze. At each alerted station, the firefighters automatically fill a variety of roles, often with no need to communicate among themselves. Based on the information received, various teams assemble in their preassigned positions on specific equipment that is appropriate to the circumstance. On reaching the fire, the firefighters again perform many tasks habitually and without explicit direction from others. When unexpected or particularly complex contingencies require on-site evaluation, a chain of command and routines for making and carrying out decisions governs the team's behavior.

In this example, as in most cases of organizational capabilities, elements of individual know-how and ability play a role. More important, however, are the organizational routines, the hierarchy that determines formal authority, and the formal procedures and informal rules that the team has developed to enable it to carry out its complex tasks almost automatically. A firefighter who leaves the team is relatively easy to replace; the team only suffers a temporary loss of efficiency before the replacement can take up where his predecessor left off. The capability survives the individual members because the organizational glue that embodies the capability does not depend on any individual.

Although latent capabilities may provide a *potentially* rich source of competitive advantage, they are not in themselves a competitive advantage. The firm needs to apply the capability in a specific setting to realize the competitive advantage. It must also be able to exercise them in a market where they are superior to the capabilities of most of the actual and potential competitors it faces there. Even the most impressive capabilities are not a source of competitive advantage if most competing firms can match them. When a firm has actually demonstrated its competitive prowess by performing a set of activities better than its rivals can, the specific application of the capability is sometimes called a *distinctive competence*.

Examining a firm's distinctive competences is a good starting point for identifying what capabilities the firm possesses. This is useful, generally speaking, because it is harder to recognize competitive advantages based on capabilities than those based on position. Often positional advantages are fairly easy to identify and well known to the decision makers in the firm. The firm's capabilities tend to be harder to identify. Moreover, the strategy literature is more divided over what the important classes of capabilities are and how one should catalog and measure them. Thus it is usually easiest to identify valuable capabilities by starting with the areas in which the firm has already demonstrated success, and then to uncover the capabilities underlying them. For example, starting with Sony's distinctive competence in the design and manufacture of consumer electronics, one would go on to uncover its underlying capabilities in miniaturization and design-for-manufacture.

A serious pitfall in assessing capabilities is maintaining objectivity. In a study of the simpler task of assessing a firm's current competitive strengths and weaknesses, Stevenson[2] found that managers had widely differing views of their distinctive competencies. As Grant[3] has observed, "Organizations frequently fall victim to past glories, hopes for the future, and wishful thinking. Among the failed industrial companies of both America and Britain are many which believed themselves world leaders with superior products and customer loyalty." As he notes, systematically comparing the firm's capabilities with those of its competitors is one way to guard against this kind of misperception.

## 3.4 SUSTAINABLE COMPETITIVE ADVANTAGE

We will have more to say about position and capabilities and their relationship to one another shortly. First, however, we should note that *competitive advantage is not necessarily enduring:* A firm's competitive advantages may erode over time. It is in the very nature of competition that rivals attempt to duplicate or eliminate a firm's competitive advantage. For example, once outsiders recognize that its capabilities earn Global Capabilities superior returns, existing rivals or new entrants will attempt to understand and reproduce those capabilities, or find new miniaturization and design-for-manufacturing techniques that give *them* competitive advantage over Global Capabilities.

When the sources of competitive advantage resist competition, the competitive advantage is said to be *sustainable.*[4] The major threat to the sustainability of an advantage based on capabilities is the possibility that a rival can diagnose and duplicate or make obsolete your competitive advantage. A firm can lose positional advantage because some other firm moves into the same position or because the value of the position itself is destroyed.

---

[2] Howard H. Stevenson, "Defining Corporate Strengths and Weaknesses," *Sloan Management Review* (1976), 51–68.

[3] Robert M. Grant, "The Resource-Based Theory of Competitive Advantage: Implications for Strategy Formulation," *California Management Review* (Spring 1991), 114–135.

[4] For more on sustainable advantage, see Pankaj Ghemawat, "Sustainable Advantage," *Harvard Business Review* (September-October 1986), pp. 53–58.

## Capability as Sustainable Competitive Advantage

If a firm's competitive advantage is based on its capabilities, a sustainable advantage requires either that imitation is difficult or that the firm can improve its capabilities (learn) before its rivals catch up. In the former case, the source of the competitive advantage must be difficult for others to understand or duplicate. In the latter case, competitors may always be imitating the leader, but the leader is always moving ahead. These kinds of learning advantages are a good example of a competitive advantage based on both capability and position. The firm's initial advantage may have arisen because it was an early entrant to the industry. To sustain this initial positional advantage, however, the firm has to learn at a competitive rate.

Some capability-based competitive advantages are difficult to imitate even when rivals know that a firm possesses them. The problem is one of *causal ambiguity:* the difficulty for those outside (or even those inside) the organization to identify exactly what leads the organization to have the capability-based advantage. The difficulty of imitating Sony's capability in miniaturization is illustrative. It is relatively easy to see that Sony has a competitive advantage in creating compact consumer goods. It is also relatively easy to surmise that this advantage is based on design and manufacturing capabilities. But what are these capabilities? More precisely, what elements or combination of elements of Sony's internal context generate these capabilities? A competitor could adopt Sony's mission and vision statements, hire away some of Sony's key engineers, adopt its organizational and human resource policies, and imitate its plant and equipment. But the competitor could probably not duplicate Sony's capability in miniaturization.

As illustrated in Figure 3-2, causal ambiguity has at least two underlying determinants. The first is the complexity of structures, routines, and individual attributes that combine to produce the capability-based advantage. It is not enough to copy some of the elements of the firm's context in isolation. And it is difficult to know which ones must be adopted together to achieve the desired ends because it is difficult to identify how the elements interact. We noted this problem in the description of Global Capabilities. Rivals had adopted its information technology system but had been unable to match its capabilities.

In addition to complexity, causal ambiguity also arises because much of the knowledge underlying a capability-based advantage is often *tacit.* Tacit knowledge is knowledge that is uncodified. Tacit knowledge is not written down. Moreover, in general, it is extremely difficult to communicate if only because those possessing it typically do not rationalize their behavior. A classic example of tacit knowledge is a ship captain's knowing where and how to fish in the deep sea. A passenger aboard the captain's ship may imitate every behavior he sees the captain undertake and still be unable to match the captain's yield. Even the captain may not be able to articulate completely all the behaviors that give him or her a superior capability in finding and catching fish, at least partly because those behaviors are internalized. They are taken-for-granted. The captain simply does not need to think about each and every behavior that enhances his or her fishing ability. Organizations renowned for superior customer service also find that their capability is grounded as much in tacit as in overt knowledge.

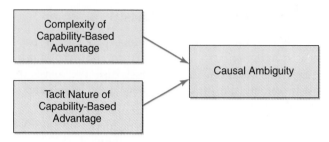

**FIGURE 3-2**    Sources of Causal Ambiguity

Their employees simply take a strong customer orientation for granted and do not dissect every individual behavior that sustains that advantage.

To provide sustainable competitive advantage, a capability must not be "owned" by a small group of employees, or it can literally walk away from the firm. If a firm's ability to design microprocessors depends only on the knowledge and skill of key people, that capability can leave the firm with those people. If a fishing vessel's catch depends on the ability of the ships' captain, the owner of the boat does not own the ability to catch fish.

Even if the valuable asset doesn't leave the firm, those who control it may be able to extract much of the value it creates because they can *threaten* to walk away. For example, movie stars can extract much of the value that is created when a syndicate is formed to make a film in which they star even if they do not explicitly own a share of the syndicate. A substantial share of the value of the film can be attributed to the brand name and ability of its leading actors, and they will bargain to capture as much of that value as possible. One reason for the Disney Corporation's success might be that its animated stars cannot leave: Mickey Mouse extracts none of the value he creates for Disney! The creative staff responsible for creating and extending Mickey can leave, but the capability of creating animated films depends on many people and on a set of organizational routines and structures that are embedded in the organization itself. It is an attribute of the organization, not of individual know-how.

## Position as Sustainable Competitive Advantage

An advantageous position can be sustainable, but frequently it is not. Positions Inc.'s advantage seems to be sustainable because its network of offices has given it an enduring advantage relative to potential entrants. Although the industry is attractive for the established firm, it appears to be unattractive for a second firm to enter. To offer a competing network, a rival must open branches in many cities. Thus the entry costs are significant. At the same time, entry would trigger fierce competition with Positions Inc. because Positions Inc. strategically prices to discourage entry.

AT&T's data transmission network or IBM's installed base in mainframe computers might be other examples of sustainable positional advantage. An installed base can be a durable advantage because overcoming it requires that customers be at a disadvantage while the firm "catches up." Suppose I want to start a firm that will compete with IBM. Even if the first customer who buys from me gets hardware as good as IBM's central processing unit, she will have no established base of peripheral manufacturers or software application developers from whom to buy products. These third parties will not design products compatible with my mainframe until I sell enough of them to make their investment in product development worthwhile. But I can't sell enough until they make the investment. This chicken-and-egg problem presents a formidable barrier to anyone interested in challenging IBM.

In contrast, many domestic firms that depended on trade barriers found their positional advantage disappeared when trade barriers were dropped. With high trade barriers blocking direct investment by foreign firms, the domestic banks in Korea exploited their position as domestic firms to earn attractive returns. As the trade barriers were lowered, these firms found they had no capability-based advantage to protect them once their positional advantage was lost. The value of the domestic banks' position was destroyed when entry became feasible.

In other cases, the position retains its value, but *the firm occupying it changes.* In the 1990s, the only firm licensed to provide direct satellite broadcasting (DSB) to televisions in the United Kingdom was unexpectedly challenged by a new entrant using an unregulated technology. The system costs for DSB are so high that only one firm could profitably serve the market. This is a market structure known as a "natural monopoly." The two firms struggled to win the monopoly position, incurring huge operating losses. In the end, the first firm was forced to give in and was purchased by its competitor. This kind of battle can occur only because it is the *position itself* that is valuable. Similarly, in the case of IBM's dominant position in mainframe computers, IBM's status as the industry standard was valuable. Because all third-party suppliers of complementary hardware and software want to support the dominant design and all consumers want to buy it, smaller players struggled to survive. In this situation, it may not be possible to be a successful niche player; the only way to compete successfully might be to replace IBM as the standard.

## 3.5  THE RELATIONSHIP OF POSITION TO CAPABILITIES

Although we have found it useful to describe position and capabilities as though they are distinct sources of competitive advantage and, indeed, have illustrated them largely through examples in which they *are* distinct, position and capabilities usually interact to produce competitive advantage for the firm as illustrated in Figure 3-3.

Cisco Systems, for example, is the dominant supplier of computer networking hardware. It has capabilities in the underlying technologies that helped it attain its dominant position, but it has also leveraged its position to obtain complementary technologies developed at other firms through an aggressive acquisitions program. The fact that it was an early mover in network infrastructure also allowed it to build a position that would have been more difficult for it to attain later. Looking at the firm now, we find it very difficult to decide exactly how much of its advantage is positional and how much is based on its capabilities.

Nonetheless, it is frequently useful for managers to understand whether their firm's competitive advantage is based primarily on position or on capabilities. A pri-

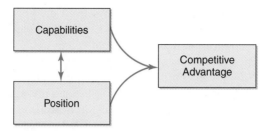

**FIGURE 3-3**  Capabilities and Position Interact

mary reason to identify the firm's sources of competitive advantage is to alert its management to those attributes that must be protected and exploited if the firm is to succeed. Consider, for example, the owner of a coffee shop that is successful only because it happens to have a prime location. If its manager mistakenly believes she has some particular facility at management or a strong brand name and opens new stores based on that belief, she is likely to be disappointed. If the managers of Global Capabilities had not recognized that its design and manufacturing success with its first products was the result of a capability that could be widely applied, it might never have expanded beyond its initial base as a maker of electronic calculators. If the managers of Positions Inc. decide to compete in electronic fund transfer over the Internet using their brand name and technological expertise, they will make a serious mistake.

Some analysts go further, arguing that whether a firm conceives of its competitive advantage in terms of position or capabilities fundamentally affects how it perceives the opportunities it faces. This line of argument is perhaps made most forcefully in an article by Prahalad and Hamel[5] in which they suggest that managers should think of their firm as defined by its capabilities rather than by its products. Xerox, for example, has recently tried to recast its public image from a manufacturer of copiers to a firm that manages documents. A firm that views itself in terms of positional advantage will tend to view its opportunities relative to its existing product line. For example, it may think about ways to reposition its current products, to enhance them, or to extend the existing family of products incrementally. A firm that conceives of itself in terms of capabilities, however, may be inclined to think more broadly about ways to leverage its existing capabilities into products it has not previously considered. For example, a natural way for the Boeing Corporation to conceive of itself is in terms of its product line, predominantly aircraft. An alternative conception might focus on Boeing's extraordinary capabilities in managing complex, large-scale projects (of which aircraft manufacture is one). Such a conception might usefully open the door to opportunities Boeing might not otherwise have considered.

Although the idea that a firm should be defined as a bundle of capabilities is useful for managers developing the firm's strategies, it is also easy to abuse. It is tempting to define these capabilities too broadly. For example, it is currently popular to describe

[5] C. K. Prahalad and Gary Hamel, "The Core Competence of the Corporation," *Harvard Business Review* (May–June 1990), pp. 79–91.

firms as providers of "business solutions." The intent seems to be to emphasize that the firm has the capability to solve a broad spectrum of business problems. But the term is used so widely that it hardly has any content. Truck manufacturers, financial institutions, maintenance companies, and information technology outsourcing firms have all described themselves as providers of business solutions. In addition, a view of the firm's capabilities as its sole or major source of competitive advantage neglects the fact that any existing positional advantage that the firm has achieved through those capabilities may be more valuable than the potential advantage the capabilities might yield elsewhere. Positions Inc. may have had an unusual capability for organizing a geographically dispersed firm when it was first established. But by now, that capability is common, and only the firm's position is valuable.

## 3.6  POSITION, CAPABILITIES, AND "THE RESOURCE-BASED VIEW OF THE FIRM"

Despite the importance of understanding competitive advantage, most early treatments of the determinants of firm performance simply distinguished between "internal" and "environmental" factors. Moreover, the treatment was typically superficial, consisting of a listing of strengths and weaknesses. This changed with the publication of Michael Porter's *Competitive Strategy* in 1980. Drawing on a rich body of theoretical and empirical research in the subfield of economics known as Industrial Organization, Porter demonstrated the importance of thoroughly understanding the firm's *industry and its competitive position within it*. That book in turn helped fuel a flurry of research activity and writing on analyzing the firm's external context. At the same time, economists were using the tools of applied game theory to develop a more systematic understanding of a firm's interactions with its rivals and with other participants in the value chain. As a consequence, the 1980s was a period in which researchers focused predominantly on the external environment. This research has produced an important body of knowledge to which we shall return in later chapters. But its success contributed to the neglect of the internal and organizational determinants of firm performance.

By the early 1990s, however, a series of articles in strategic management had reasserted the importance of considering factors internal to the firm when searching for the source of heterogeneous firm performance. Articles by Wernerfeld, Barney, and Montgomery,[6] for example, revived the ideas of Edith Penrose[7] stressing a "resource-based" view of the firm. As the name suggests, the resource-based view of the firm emphasizes the firm's internal resources as a source of potential competitive advantage. To the extent that a firm's capabilities are based on its resources—its routines and organization, for example—the resource-based view certainly encompasses capabilities. To the extent that a firm's positional advantage is based on its tangible and

---

[6] See, for example, Birger Wernerfeld, "A Resource Based View of the Firm," *Strategic Management Journal* 5 (1984) 171–180; Jay B. Barney, "Strategic Factor Markets: Expectations, Luck, and Business Strategy," *Management Science* 42 (1986) 1231–1241; and Cynthia Montgomery and Birger Wernerfeld, "Diversification, Ricardian Rents, and Tobin's q," *Rand Journal of Economics* 19 (1988) 623–632.

[7] Edith T. Penrose, *The Theory of the Growth of the Firm* (New York: Wiley, 1958).

intangible assets, the resource-based view can also be interpreted as pushing for a deeper understanding of the underlying internal sources of the firm's positional advantage. And this has created a more balanced view of competitive advantage as arising from a combination of internal and external factors.

However, using the resource-based view to justify a focus *on the firm's assets in and of themselves* is a mistake. The resources are a source of competitive advantage only if they create positional advantage or advantageous capabilities. To see what we mean consider a third hypothetical company which, like Positions Inc. and Global Capabilities, also has superior performance:

*Resources Associates* is a medical device manufacturer. The founder and current CEO, a former university professor, patented a process for producing a specialized medical instrument. Convinced that the founder's knowledge of the process provides it with a competitive advantage in manufacturing, Resources Associates makes all its own devices, selling them through sales agents to medical equipment distributors. Industry sources say that Resources Associates' cost of goods sold is slightly lower than its competitors'. Resources Associates has refused several offers to buy the company (offers the founder viewed as attempts to rob him of the value of his invention). The firm has also consistently refused to license its patented technology, fearing it would sacrifice the firm's competitive advantage if it did.

In contrast to Global Capabilities, Resources Associates does not seem to be particularly good at manufacturing (since it has only a slight cost advantage in production despite proprietary ownership of a superior, patented manufacturing process). In fact, it does not seem to have any identifiable capabilities. For example, it has none in the sales and distribution areas (it outsources these functions). Rather, the key determinant of Resources Associates' success is its patent for producing a particular piece of medical equipment. Without that patent, Resources Associates' financial performance would likely be mediocre, or worse. In this case, the firm's competitive advantage derives from its possession of an asset that no other firm can acquire without its consent. Its proprietary technology enables the firm to be low-cost, thereby creating a positional advantage over its rivals. The patent ensures that a competitor cannot simply acquire the technology.

Although scarce and proprietary assets like Resource Associates' patent are valuable, owning them is not a sufficient basis for building a high-performance organization. Resources Associates' value is derived solely from its asset, and that asset is separable from the firm and tradable. Because Resources Associates has no complementary manufacturing and distribution abilities, the founder could probably do better by selling the patent to a firm that does have these capabilities. The firm that purchased the patent would then have the positional advantage, and Resources Associates would have none. If strategy is about guiding action to maximize performance given the firm's context, the only strategic choice that makes sense for Resources Associates is to sell its asset to the highest bidder. In other cases, the firm owning the asset may have *other* capabilities or a positional advantage that makes it the organization best able to take advantage of this asset. Even in this case, however, these additional assets by themselves might not provide the firm with a competitive advantage *absent* ownership of the scarce resource. Even if Positions

Inc. also owned an efficient manufacturing operation, for example, it might be unable to distinguish itself among other device manufacturers without the patented process.

Economists call the value that the owner can capture from a scarce asset the *rent* from the asset. It is useful, where possible, to identify which component of a firm's superior performance is simply a rent to a scarce asset that it owns. For Resources Associates, the value that the firm is able to create and capture is simply the rent from its patent. Similarly, to return to the example of the coffee shop, a proprietor of a coffee shop who owns the land on which it is located may have a spectacular rate of return compared to the many other shops with which he competes. Yet, that return is appropriately attributed to the value of the land not to the shop, and the superior financial performance of the coffee shop would likely disappear if, as landowner, she charged herself an appropriate rent for the land.

These examples are introduced to make two distinct points about resources as a source of competitive advantage. First, it is important to recognize when a firm's superior performance is simply due to a rent earned on some asset. It is dangerous, for example, for a firm to attribute its superior performance to its superior manufacturing or marketing capabilities if indeed those capabilities are ordinary and its superior performance is the rent earned from its location, patent, or brand name. Second, it is a mistake to think of a firm as simply a bundle of resources or assets, ignoring the external context. It is this narrow focus that encouraged the founder of Resource Associates to create a firm with a meager competitive advantage rather than selling the asset to another owner to whom it would be more valuable. An organization creates value when it can deploy its assets so that they are more valuable under its control than they would be elsewhere. Often, as many of our previous examples have suggested, this is because the firm has some capability that enables it to use those assets in ways others cannot replicate.

## 3.7 THE COST–QUALITY FRONTIER AND COMPETITIVE ADVANTAGE

We have emphasized that competitive advantage flows from superior capabilities or position or from some combination of the two. We have taken this approach because we believe that it is vital for an organization to understand the source of its competitive advantage if it is to build on and defend it. To make our point, we have talked about many specific forms of positional and capability-based advantages. Having done so, we can now explore two general dimensions in which competitive advantage often can be summarized: cost and quality. A firm may have lower costs than other firms producing similar products or more valuable products than firms with similar costs. In either case, its superior performance flows from being well positioned in cost and quality dimensions.

Inasmuch as superior performance is based on a firm's ability to create and capture value, it is not surprising that a firm's competitive advantage frequently can be represented by its cost–quality position. A firm creates value only when there is a difference (preferably large) between what customers are willing to pay for its products or services and what the firm must pay to provide them.[8] What customers are willing to pay is related to the quality of the firm's products. What the firm must pay to provide the product is the firm's cost. Since creating value is about generating a gap between customer valuation and the cost of providing the product, quality and cost are often useful ways to describe competitive advantage.

Because cost and quality are so commonly the dimensions in which competitive advantage can be described, it is useful to have a framework for examining competitive advantage in those terms. The framework developed in this section will be used in subsequent chapters to discuss how changes in rivals' positions can pose a competitive threat, to determine how a firm can make strategic investments in capabilities and position in order to change its competitive advantage, and to examine the relationship between organizational structure and competitive advantage. We begin by defining what we mean by "high quality" and "low cost" and then present a framework that captures the basic tradeoff between these advantages.

Remember, however, that the advantage represented by these dimensions is itself derived from some combination of capability and position. For quality, for example, it may be the firm's reputation for reliability, durability, or after-sales service (positional advantages) that makes its offerings more attractive than those of other firms in the industry. Or the firm may have superior capabilities in quickly bringing new products to market, so that its products are more advanced than its rivals'. On the cost side, the firm may have superior access to raw materials or the ability to share costs with another part of the company (positional advantages), or, like Global Capabilities, it may have developed a set of routines that lowers its overall development costs. In short, although cost and quality are a useful shorthand for thinking about a firm's competitive position, they usually derive from some asset that the firm must nurture and protect.

## Product Quality and Cost

Think of two products within a well-defined product category. If all customers buy one of them when the two are offered at identical prices, the chosen product has a higher perceived quality.[9] To use a more concrete example, consider pens. BIC and Mont Blanc are both well-known brand names in the pen market with clear and distinct images. BIC pens are reliable, inexpensive, functional writing instruments. Mont Blanc pens are made with more costly materials, are designed to be durable, are engineered to write more smoothly, and are associated with higher socioeconomic status. Mont Blanc's advertising uses words like "elegant" and "distinctive." Most consumers would agree that Mont Blanc pens are higher quality than BIC pens. More people buy

---

[8] If one thinks of this in income statement terms, operating margin can be increased only by increasing revenue for given costs, or decreasing costs for given revenue. In economic terms, profit can only be increased by increasing the distance between the demand and cost curves for the firm's products.

[9] As we will see in Chapter 6, products about which consumers agree on quality rankings are referred to as "vertically" differentiated. We discuss product differentiation in Chapter 7.

BIC because they are unwilling to pay the price premium Mont Blanc charges for its pens, but even these people would usually agree that BIC is lower quality. Put slightly differently, if most of us were offered the choice of a Mont Blanc pen or a BIC pen as a gift, we would choose the Mont Blanc.

Many other products or services also have this characteristic. Manufacturers who buy ball bearings rank quality in terms of delivery times and defect rates. Travelers prefer airlines with better on-time departure records. Computer users prefer faster hard drive access to slower hard drive access. Sprint, a long-distance carrier, advertises itself as having better sound quality ("You can hear a pin drop"). Thinking carefully about these examples suggests that the quality ranking may be a composite of many characteristics: Travelers care about on-time departures, safety, comfort, and other dimensions of product quality, for example. It is nonetheless helpful to think about combining these dimensions into a single measure of perceived quality.[10]

Note the importance of the modifier "perceived" here. It is often tempting to think of quality as determined by the physical characteristics of the product as an engineer might define them. Thinking of quality in this way, however, misses the point. Higher quality can confer a competitive advantage on a product only if potential buyers *perceive* it to have higher quality. If a clever brand manager can convince consumers that water from springs in the Alps is better than water from springs in the Rockies, he will create a quality advantage for his product. If consumers cannot perceive a quality difference between audio systems despite the fact that electronic testing reveals that one is clearly superior at sound reproduction, the two systems have the same quality.

Just as product quality can differ in many ways, any student of cost accounting knows that the way costs are measured is open to interpretation and depends ultimately on the purpose for which the measurement is done. For our purposes, we have in mind a measure of average cost, which includes the typical expenses that go into cost of goods sold (production labor costs, materials, etc.), *and* design and marketing costs, appropriately amortized over the products sold. The reason for this, as will become clear shortly, is that in order to differentiate one's product or service offerings it may be necessary to make substantial, fixed investments in advertising, product development, and so forth. Because these costs are essential to attaining the firm's quality position, we want them reflected in our measure of cost.

Before we became enmeshed in the details of how we were defining "low cost" and "perceived quality," we claimed that these two factors could summarize competitive advantage. It is obvious why having low cost can be advantageous. A firm with lower costs for the same product will be able to price lower than its rivals, thereby capturing a larger market share while earning a margin at least as attractive as theirs. Alternatively, a low-cost firm can charge the same price as its rivals and earn a substantially higher margin on what it sells. Although the benefit of lower cost typically is realized through its impact on price, it is important to understand that it is the low

---

[10] Careful thought also suggests that not all products are well characterized in this way. Sometimes consumers don't agree about quality rankings. Some people prefer Coke to Pepsi, others Pepsi to Coke. We will return to this type of differentiation in Chapter 7 and discuss how the framework we develop here would apply to that case.

cost that is the competitive advantage and not the low price per se. Quality can be a competitive advantage because a product perceived to be higher quality can command a price premium. If the products have the same cost, the higher quality product has a clear competitive advantage. The higher quality firm has the choice of charging the same price as its rival and capturing a very large market share or charging more and making a higher margin on its sales.

If both lower cost and higher quality can be competitive advantages, it is tempting to conclude that the best overall position is to be a high-quality, low-cost firm. In principle, this is correct. In fact, it is usually not possible. The Rolls Royce managers would be overjoyed to produce its cars for a cost lower than that achieved by Chevrolet. And any four-star restaurant owner would be delighted to produce its meals at the same cost as McDonald's. The problem, of course, is that high quality and low cost are frequently in conflict. A handcrafted walnut and leather automobile interior is more costly to produce than a vinyl and molded plastic interior. Paté and arugula cost more than chopped beef and french fries. Firms that are operating efficiently face an inevitable tradeoff between cost and quality.

## A Cost–Quality Framework

Figure 3-4 illustrates what we mean when we say there is an inevitable tradeoff between cost and quality. In this diagram, quality is measured on the vertical axis and cost on the horizontal. Note that cost *decreases* along the horizontal axis; that is, the farther we move to the right, the lower the cost. Cost is represented in this way so that the firm is better off in both quality and cost the farther it is positioned from the origin.

The shaded region of this diagram indicates all the quality and cost combinations that are feasible given currently available technology. By technologically available, we mean not just to the firm but to the industry more generally. It is easy to produce at any point near the origin, well in the interior of the shaded region. Any such point represents a combination of low quality and high costs—not a difficult position to

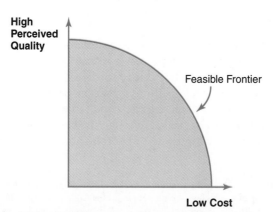

**FIGURE 3-4**   The Cost and Perceived Quality Framework

attain. As one moves away from the origin, however, the cost–quality combinations become increasingly challenging to attain because they involve lower costs and/or higher levels of quality.

The curved edge of the shaded region represents the limits of what is available with current technology. This line identifies the highest quality that can be provided for a given cost. Conversely, it identifies the lowest cost at which a product of a given quality can be provided. We therefore call this line the "cost–quality frontier." Points beyond the frontier are simply not achievable given the current technology at the disposal of the firms in the industry. Any firm would like to be able to go boldly where no firm has gone before, but this is simply not possible with the best available technology.

The frontier is a downward-sloping curve because along it there is a tradeoff between perceived quality and low cost: Higher-quality products (produced as efficiently as possible) cost more to produce than lower-quality ones (produced as efficiently as possible). Starting at any given point on the frontier, perceived quality can only be increased by expending additional effort and resources, that is, by increasing costs. For some readers, this assertion flies in the face of examples in which firms have been able to increase perceived quality while holding cost constant or even reducing them. This is possible in two circumstances. Most commonly, it means the firm was not initially operating on the frontier. As noted above, a firm located near the origin has lots of room to improve quality without increasing its cost.[11] Less commonly, the firm achieves some technological breakthrough that changes the frontier. We will return to this possibility later in the book. Here we assume that the frontier is fixed.

The concave shape of the frontier we've drawn reflects an assumption that additional cost has a diminishing effect. That is, at the point the frontier intersects with the cost axis, it is relatively inexpensive to increase perceived quality, but as you move in a northwesterly direction, any given quality improvement becomes increasingly costly. Imagine, for example, what it costs to substantially improve the quality of a premier bordeaux wine compared to improving the quality of a mass-produced jug wine! While we think that this is a reasonable assumption for many products, it is not essential to the framework. What is essential is that the frontier be downward sloping.

## Using the Cost–Quality Frontier to Illustrate Competitive Advantage: An Example

Suppose we are analyzing the hotel industry in the United States and have data that suggest that the hotels are situated at points A, B, and C in Figure 3-5. Point A might represent a hotel like the Ritz Carlton that prides itself on its luxurious accommodation and service. Point C might represent a budget chain of hotels, such as the Travelodge or Quality Inn, that prides itself on providing affordable, if basic, accommodations with little service. Point B might represent an intermediate chain, such as the Sheraton. As suggested by their relationship to the vertical axis, most con-

---

[11] We do not mean to minimize the managerial and organizational commitment necessary to be on the frontier. Indeed, few firms are so efficient that they are clearly on the frontier. It is nonetheless important to recognize that improving quality and reducing cost are usually conflicting objectives for *reasonably* efficient firms.

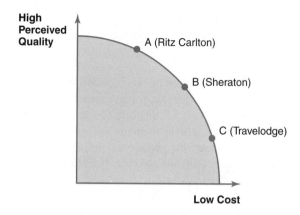

**FIGURE 3-5**   Using the Cost-Quality Framework to Map Competition

sumers would rank the perceived quality of the hotels as the Ritz, followed by the Sheraton, followed by the Travelodge.

There is nothing disparaging about positioning the Travelodge in this way. Indeed, putting any hotel on the frontier is a compliment because it says that it is being as efficient as possible in providing its level of perceived quality.

Conversely, there is nothing disparaging about observing that the Ritz has higher costs than the Travelodge. It is simply a fact of life in the hotel industry that creating and sustaining a perceived quality of the kind associated with the Ritz is more costly. The furnishings and decor, hotel locations, hours of room service availability, promotional materials, and so on, are all more expensive for an exclusive hotel than for a budget hotel. If it were possible to create a Ritz Carlton experience for the cost of a Travelodge experience, this quality diversity would not exist in the marketplace: Every hotel would be like the Ritz and price like the Travelodge. Quality diversity exists precisely because there is a tradeoff between perceived quality and cost, as assumed in the figure.

Since the Ritz Carlton and the Travelodge are at the extremes of the frontier (at least in our example), it is tempting to articulate their strategies in terms of just the dimension at which they excel—that is, to represent the Ritz's strategy as being one of high perceived quality and the Travelodge's as one of low cost. Indeed, some strategic management texts follow Michael Porter's lead and argue that high quality and low cost are distinct and generic strategies.[12] This treatment, however, glosses over an important point about the competitive advantage of firms on the frontier. Yes, the Ritz is higher quality than Travelodge and, by necessity, has higher cost than the Travelodge. But the Ritz in our example is as low cost as possible *given* that it produces a high-quality product. The Travelodge produces a product that is as high quality as possible *given* that it has low cost.

[12] Michael E. Porter, *Competitive Strategy* (New York: Free Press, 1980).

An even more important problem with claiming that "high quality" and "low cost" are the clear positions of competitive advantage is that these polar cases need not provide performance superior to an intermediate position. Consider the Sheraton's position. The strategy represented by the Sheraton in the figure is an intermediate one. It is neither as high quality as the Ritz Carlton nor as low cost as the Travelodge. At the same time, its costs are not as high as the Ritz Carlton nor its quality as low as the Travelodge. This enables the Sheraton to position itself on the frontier "between" its more extreme rivals. The fact that its costs are lower than the Ritz enables it to price lower, attracting customers who want higher perceived quality than the Travelodge offers at a price lower than that of the Ritz. If this position appeals to enough hotel visitors, it could be the most profitable position on the frontier. More generally, there is a continuum of cost and quality positions on the frontier, and there is no reason to believe that occupying either the high-quality or the low-cost position is the only possible way to achieve competitive advantage.

On the other hand, contrast the Sheraton's position with that of Hotel D (which we will not name because to do so *would be* disparaging!) in Figure 3-6. Hotel D is in an unfavorable position. Although its perceived quality is higher than that of the Travelodge and its costs are lower than the Ritz Carlton, it is in an inferior position on both dimensions to a hotel like the Sheraton. In a reasonably competitive industry, such a firm would not be expected to last very long. Given its superior positioning, the Sheraton would be expected to offer a superior experience at a lower price than Hotel D could. As consumers learn of this fact, Hotel D will steadily lose market share to the Sheraton and finally be driven out of business. The Sheraton's position on the frontier gives it competitive advantage in both cost and quality over Hotel D. A hotel located at any point in the cross-hatched region in Figure 3-6 is at a competitive disadvantage to the Sheraton.

Although firms on the frontier have a competitive advantage over firms in the interior, these latter firms may be viable. If, for example, D is in an industry with high barriers to entry and faces only a few competitors, such as A and C, it may be able to

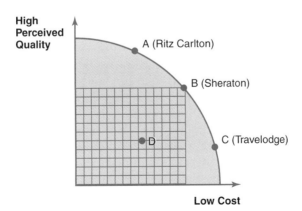

**FIGURE 3-6**   Firm B Has a Competitive Advantage over Firm D

survive thanks to the lack of competition from a firm like B. Nonetheless, such a position is precarious. If a firm manages to surmount the entry barriers and adopts a position like B, or if firm A or C decides to move toward B and can do so while remaining on the frontier, firm D will be in an untenable competitive position.

The strategy literature sometimes characterizes a firm in Hotel D's position as being "stuck in the middle." This phrase is used to describe a firm that is disadvantaged relative to its rivals in terms of cost–quality positioning and certainly applies to Hotel D. Unfortunately, the term "stuck in the middle" is also sometimes applied to any firm that does not occupy an extreme position on the frontier, that is, is not at position A or C. This usage is inappropriate. As argued above, an intermediate position on the frontier is not necessarily disadvantageous. There is nothing "stuck" about the Sheraton's position. A more appropriate, but less mellifluous, phrase to describe firms that are mired in a disadvantageous cost–quality position might be "stuck inside the frontier."

Constructing a map like the one shown in Figure 3-4 is useful for several reasons. Suppose, for example, your firm is firm D. This map tells you that you have a competitive disadvantage relative to your competitors. It also tells you that you are most directly threatened by hotels represented by points B and C. Product C has much lower cost and a quality that is only slightly lower than yours. Because your products are nearly identical to theirs, competition with the hotels at C will be based primarily on price, the very dimension in which you are least well positioned to compete with them. With respect to hotels located at B, you are disadvantaged in both dimensions. Hotels at B can charge a price higher than your cost (and even higher than theirs) and force you to charge a price less than your cost to capture any market share. With respect to those hotels, firm D is in the unenviable position of a local bar that resorted to advertising "Warm beer, bad service, moderate prices" to compete with its more fortunate rivals.

Maps like these can also provide some guidance about where the attractive openings in an industry might be. As will be argued in more detail in Chapter 7, firms that can differentiate their products from those of their competitors may benefit from reduced price competition. Suppose, for example, that no firms were located on the frontier between A and C. Then, the position denoted by B might be attractive for a new entrant or for a firm located at A or C who wanted to move away from its competitors at those locations. The firm that first recognizes this underserved part of the market may gain an important first-mover advantage by being the first to develop a product well suited to this segment.

Note, however, that such a map provides only an incomplete description of competitive advantage because it does not contain information on the distribution of demand. For example, incumbent firms may have avoided some segment of the cost–quality frontier because there is little demand for a product of that quality at a price that would cover the cost of providing it. Being on the frontier ensures that no other firm will be able to provide a higher-quality product at lower cost, but it does not ensure that buyers want to pay the cost necessary to produce a product of that quality. We will return to the topic of thinking about product positioning and the distribution of demand in Chapter 7.

## 3.8  SUMMARY

In this chapter we explored how the firm's capabilities and position can enable it to create and capture value, and we discussed the conditions under which the competitive advantage will be sustainable in the long run. We examined how its capabilities and position can give it competitive advantage in the form of lower costs than its rivals or the ability to differentiate its product and service offerings from theirs. Finally, we developed a cost–quality framework to illustrate a firm's competitive advantage with respect to its competitors, which will be used in later chapters.

We turn now to a discussion of how the firm is organized. We do this at this juncture because a firm's competitive advantage—especially when it derives from its capabilities—often resides in the way it is organized. In Chapter 4 we explore the components of organization and the factors that shape them. In Chapter 5 we examine the relationship of organization design to strategy and strategic change.

# 4

# INTERNAL CONTEXT: ORGANIZATION DESIGN

## 4.1 INTRODUCTION

A firm's competitive advantage is rooted in its context. Whether its strategic advantage is based on position or capabilities, the advantage derives from both its environment and its internal context. An advantage based on design capability, for example, is sustained by the assets and organization of the company (internal context) and by the perception of the firm's customers that its product provides better value than the products of its competitors (external context). Managers who want to create and sustain competitive advantage need, therefore, to have a deep understanding of both the internal and external context of the firm. This chapter and the next explore the firm's internal context before turning to its external context in Chapter 6. We begin with an overview of the relationship between organization design and competitive advantage before turning to a detailed examination of that relationship at Southwest Airlines. We then examine the main classes of problems organization design must address and the levers the firm has for doing so. Finally, we provide a framework, ARC analysis, for designing a high performance organization.

## 4.2 ORGANIZATION DESIGN AND COMPETITIVE ADVANTAGE

As illustrated in Figure 4-1, the firm's internal context is defined as its assets and the way those assets are organized. Chapter 3 provided many examples of how a firm's assets might be a source of competitive advantage. Here the focus is on achieving competitive advantage through the organization of those assets because organization is central to whether the assets are able to create competitive advantage. The importance of the organization design problem is frequently underestimated. Managers sometimes believe that having the best engineers or the best salespeople is enough to make a firm effective. Although the quality of the assets—human or physical—clearly is important to achieving competitive advantage, how those assets are organized can

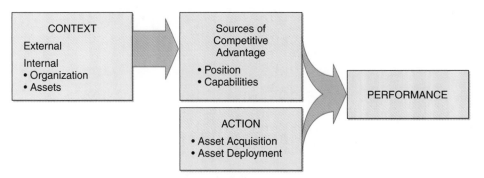

**FIGURE 4-1** Sources of Competitive Advantage

be equally important. The best engineer, for example, cannot be productive if she doesn't have access to the information she needs to design products consumers value.

We have already taken issue with the claim that there is a single source of competitive advantage. We are equally skeptical about some of the popular claims that any single organization design is "best." The best design for a firm actually depends on the strategy it is pursuing. As a simple example, consider the relationship between the organization of a photo processing firm and its strategy. Most photo processing firms compete on the basis of low-cost, mass production. Boutique firms offering high-quality custom processing at correspondingly high prices occupy a different segment of the market. A typical mass-production firm is organized differently than a typical high-quality firm. Among the mass producers, the sales divisions are usually separate from the production divisions. Salespeople basically function as order-takers for a standardized product that the production unit attempts to produce as efficiently as possible. At the boutique firms, the salespeople must work much more closely with those in production to translate customer needs and to communicate the feedback from production to the customer. These firms therefore hire salespeople who know more about photography than the salespeople at the mass-production firms. But high-quality firms also establish consultation routines within the firm that facilitate communication between production and sales and supply resources for building customer relationships. The mass producers have no need for these routines or for spending resources to get to know specific customers. Furthermore, incentives at the mass producers are geared to keeping volumes high (at acceptable quality levels), while at the boutique firms, rewards are tightly tied to customer satisfaction.

This chapter provides a way to think systematically about the problem of organization design and the levers managers have to address it. Our approach is illustrated in Figure 4-2 where the internal context box is expanded to summarize the organization design challenge and the tools managers have to grapple with it. The first step in achieving competitive advantage through organization is to understand the problem that organization is supposed to solve. This overarching problem has two parts: the *coordination* problem and the *incentive* problem. Once a clear picture emerges of what the organization design should achieve, we can turn to the tools the manager has for meeting the challenge. As illustrated in Figure 4-2, a manager can work with three

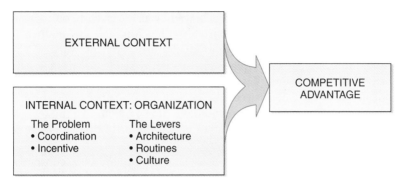

**FIGURE 4-2**   Organization and Competitive Advantage

levers: architecture, routines, and culture (or ARC). Before these levers and how they can be applied to address incentive and coordination problems are described, we first provide a detailed example.

## 4.3  STRATEGY AND ORGANIZATION AT SOUTHWEST AIRLINES

In exploring organization design, taking issues one at a time may help us understand each issue, but it sacrifices the richness of the problem managers actually face. Before proceeding with the analysis then, let's start with how one firm, Southwest Airlines, built an organization that has contributed to its competitive advantage. This example illustrates how the elements of organization design can interact and how organization and strategy can be linked.

### Southwest's Strategy and Performance

By almost any measure, Southwest has been one of the most successful airlines in the United States. It is the only one to have earned a profit every year since 1973, its net margins have been the highest in the airline industry in many years, and for 20 years it had the highest stock return of *any* publicly traded firm in the United States. Southwest also stands out from its competitors in the strategy it has pursued and the organization it has created to support that strategy.

Southwest Airlines offers its customers low-cost, convenient service on selected routes. It primarily serves short-haul routes on which many of the travelers are frequent users and business travelers. The Houston-San Antonio and San Jose-Orange County (Los Angeles) markets are typical of the routes it serves. Unlike most major airlines that build their offerings around a hub-and-spoke design, Southwest offers nonstop, origin-destination flights. A hub-and-spoke system is designed to have planes from many origination points converge on the same "hub" airport at roughly the same time so that passengers can be reassigned to flights that fan out to multiple destinations. A great virtue of this system is that it tends to increase passenger loads on each flight and is therefore much more cost efficient than one in which passengers are routed nonstop from each origination point to each destination.

Bucking the trend, Southwest has achieved even lower costs on its routes. One source of its cost advantage is its high aircraft utilization rate: the number of hours a day each plane is in the air. Since its flights are not linked to a network of other flights by a common hub, any particular plane has less unavoidable downtime while it waits for the arrival of other planes. This leaves Southwest free to work on reducing the time the plane sits at the gate between flights. The airline is respected throughout the industry for consistently achieving a turnaround time of about 15 minutes. As a result, Southwest has been able to increase aircraft utilization to 11 hours per day compared to an industry average of 8 hours per day.

Part of the secret to Southwest's quick plane turnaround is its constant drive for simplicity and its success in "training" its customers to adapt to its systems. For example, unlike its competitors, Southwest has abandoned the use of tickets, does not reserve specific seats, serves peanuts instead of meals, and uses only one kind of airplane. In addition to enabling rapid turnaround, these deviations from traditional industry procedures also directly contribute to lower costs. Peanuts are cheaper than (even bad) meals. Using a single aircraft model reduces maintenance and training costs. Despite its "no frills" policy, Southwest has managed to achieve very high levels of customer satisfaction. It is the only U.S. carrier to have achieved the record of "best" in three key areas in a given month: best baggage handling, fewest customer complaints, and best on-time performance. By 1998, it had won this coveted "triple crown" 24 times.

Southwest's costs also are lower than the industry average because it has lower than average employee costs. For example, pilots often earn half as much at Southwest as at other airlines, even though they fly up to 40 percent more hours per month. Despite lower salaries, Southwest is famous for its high employee morale and the lowest employee turnover in the industry. Its route structure, simplified service, and low labor costs have given Southwest a clear cost advantage over its competitors: in the early 1990s it boasted costs of 7.1 cents per mile, compared to 10 cents or more for its larger rivals. Lower costs have translated into lower prices. As a result, Southwest typically dominates the markets it serves; it has a market share of 60 percent or more in the vast majority of the nonstop markets it serves.

## Southwest's Organization

Much has been written about Southwest and the secrets to its success.[1] Although its success is in part attributed to its atypical market positioning and a classic low-cost strategy, analysts have also focused on Southwest's unique organization and the tight fit between how it is organized and how it achieves competitive advantage. For example, at the heart of Southwest's ability to turn its planes around quickly *and* keep its

---

[1] For more detailed examinations see Kevin and Jackie Frieber, *Nuts* (Bard Press, 1996): Fred Wiersema, *Customer Service* (New York: Harper Business, 1998), and Charles O'Reilly and Jeffrey Pfeffer, *Southwest Airlines,* a Stanford Graduate School of Business teaching case on which we have drawn for much of the detail here.

customers happy in the process is the cross-functional team that it assigns to each route. Many airlines strictly limit the discretion of ground crews, flight attendants, and pilots, and tightly define what employees assigned to each role can and cannot do. In contrast, Southwest encourages its teams to use discretion and to get the job done. So, for example, although Southwest's standard policy is that a plane is not to return to the gate simply because a passenger has boarded the wrong plane, the pilot can override that policy if she deems it worthwhile in a particular case. Southwest allows teams to define their members' roles and to cross these role boundaries where appropriate. It is not unusual, for example, to see flight attendants and pilots stowing bags. The airline also cross-trains managers to enable them to take on multiple tasks and to develop an overall understanding of the organization. This information allows them to understand the ramifications of the decisions they make and to communicate with all the groups in the organization.

Underlying Southwest's approach to business is a corporate culture that emphasizes having fun on the job and acting a little "zany." Recruiting favors people who are extroverts and team players and who lack industry experience. Southwest reaps advantage from the fact that its human resources policy contributes to a culture in which employees are rewarded for having fun on the job. The people who find the Southwest atmosphere appealing enjoy their jobs enough that they are willing to work for less than other airlines must pay. This policy, in conjunction with how teams are assigned to routes, also means that crews often get to know their passengers well. In part, this is because of employees' outgoing natures, but it is also because teams stick to the same routes, and many passengers fly those routes frequently. The employee selection and retention policies that favor extroverted employees and the "fun" culture that the company promotes lead to close customer relationships that are much more important in a repeat-business setting than they are in a larger network characterized by more anonymity. It is not unusual for regular customers to get birthday cards from their flight crews!

Employee discretion is also more important in a setting where employees put on a "friendly face" because flight attendants who crack jokes and sing are also expected to be more responsive to customers' problems. Stories are told and retold throughout the firm about employees who have gone far out of their way to help customers, including, in one case, flying a passenger in the employee's private plane. The fact that most Southwest employees do not have much industry background facilitates their inculcation into the firm's culture. They are more likely to adopt the Southwest way of providing customer service than are veterans of other airlines who would first have to "unlearn" their standard operating procedures.

Employees are encouraged to act like owners rather than employees, both by a corporate profit-sharing plan and by a corporate culture that encourages sharing ideas throughout the company. Stories abound about how employee suggestions have been implemented. To facilitate the transmission of ideas, the organization is very "flat" (i.e., it has few levels in its hierarchy) and informal. Senior managers are renowned for the time they spend in casual conversation with employees at all levels. Trust of senior management is extraordinarily high, and matters often resolved through contract negotiations at other firms are settled with a handshake at Southwest.

## Comparisons to Other Airlines

Some observers argue that Southwest's internal context is simply better than those of its rivals and that other airlines should learn from—and replicate—what Southwest has done. Other high-performance customer service organizations often do, in fact, share many of the characteristics of Southwest's organization. For example, they are often very flat, informal organizations that have a high degree of trust among employees. These characteristics empower employees to exercise discretion to keep customers satisfied and encourage employees to pass their ideas and suggestions up to senior management who can then disseminate best practice across the firm. However, even though many firms with these characteristics are successful, it is important to recognize that not all firms, and, in particular, not all airlines, would be successful if they followed Southwest's example.

Several of Southwest's competitors have attempted to imitate some of the features of its organization but with only limited success. One problem has been that competitors have attempted to copy just some of the pieces. Thus, for example, competitors have formed cross-functional teams to improve plane turnaround times, but they have not copied other features of Southwest's organizational design that make the cross-functional teams an effective contributor to competitive advantage. They have not, for example, given these teams as much discretion in how to implement standard procedures or allowed them to make many exceptions to standard operating procedures. One reason they may not have copied all the important pieces is that it is difficult to tell which pieces *are* important. Another reason, however, is that Southwest's strategy is strikingly different from that of its competitors.

Southwest's strategy is based on point-to-point routes rather than on a hub-and-spoke network of routes. Each route in Southwest's system is therefore largely independent of the other routes. In the hub-and-spoke system used by most major airlines, any breakdown in performance on one route has repercussions that are felt throughout the system. If a Southwest flight is late on the Oakland-Los Angeles route, that might affect some other flights on that route until the time can be made up. When a flight is late arriving at a hub, the airlines faces a choice of holding all the planes the customers on the late flight are scheduled to take or leaving a plane load of customers stranded at the hub for several hours. Allowing a team responsible for one spoke to make a choice to delay a flight, then, can be costly for a hub-and-spoke system. Furthermore, an airline operating a complex hub-and-spoke network is more likely to experience unexpected and complex scheduling problems (such as when a snow storm somewhere in the system causes delays across the entire system). These problems are more efficiently resolved through standardized routines than by allowing employees responsible for single routes to make idiosyncratic decisions. In short, the discretion Southwest grants its flight teams is probably inappropriate for the route structure used by many of its competitors.

Because Southwest's routes are independent, a flight team can also control most of the variables that affect its performance. The team is not at the mercy of some large group of other employees who operate an entire network. If its flights are late, the team bears the cost of delay. The members not only must bear the ire of the passengers waiting to depart on the delayed flight, but they also must face the annoyance of the passengers who board that flight for its return trip and for its subsequent flights that day. In hub-and-spoke networks, flight teams have less control over the experience of their customers who typically fly on more than one flight to complete a trip. And their angry passengers are passed onto other, large groups of employees at a hub.

There is less interdependence among different teams at Southwest, and so monitoring team performance is more straightforward. Because every team understands that it is judged by its performance, its members have a strong incentive to pitch in and help. Some of this incentive is nonpecuniary; team members come to know and depend on each other. But Southwest also ties compensation to team performance. Pilots, for example, are paid per flight rather than per hour as is the practice at most other major airlines. They are happy to help board a flight and stow bags because it helps their team make performance goals and because it increases their compensation. At airlines where the airplane turnaround is affected by many other flights, this kind of compensation scheme is less appropriate.

### Summary: Consistency and Alignment

This example emphasizes that organizations are composed of many elements, and the effect of one element may depend on the characteristics of another. Organizations have both structure and process; they are made up of ways of doing things and rewards for doing them; they have formal rules and structures and informal routines and norms. Many of these elements are interactive. The firm's informal behavioral norms modify the effect of its compensation scheme. The effectiveness of its decision making is influenced by the design of its processes for acquiring and diffusing information. Changing how activities are organized alters the incentives for cooperation across groups. It is essential, then, for the various elements to be *consistent*; they must work together. The remainder of this chapter explores the elements of organization design and how they might interact to affect performance.

Equally important, the effect of a particular organization design on firm performance depends on the strategy the firm is pursuing. Not only must the elements of the organization fit with one another, they must also fit with the strategy of the firm. We turn to the question of aligning strategy and organization in the next chapter.

## 4.4  THE CHALLENGE OF ORGANIZATION DESIGN

Every organization must face two main classes of problems: the coordination problem, and the incentive problem. The *coordination problem* is the challenge of designing an optimal organization even when everyone in the firm fully internalizes its goals and puts self-interest aside in helping it to pursue those goals.[2] Many coordination problems are familiar to students of operations where the focus is on designing systems

---

[2] Economists call this the "team problem" under the hypothesis that all members of a team share the same objectives.

that meet specified objectives. In our context, we use the term more broadly to mean the way the firm acquires and deploys the many assets it controls. The *incentive problem* is the challenge of inducing people whose private goals might diverge from the firm's to take actions that are consistent with achieving the firm's goals. The coordination problem encompasses the issues those managers charged with designing an organization would face if there were no incentive problem. The incentive problem encompasses the additional issues that arise because actors inside the firm typically have their own agendas and will, if the incentive problem is not solved, take actions that are not in the best interest of the firm no matter how well the organization design solves the coordination problem.

## The Coordination Problem

The coordination problem is fundamental to any organization. If there were no gain to coordination, there would be no reason for firms to exist. Individuals could perform all activity by buying inputs they needed from other individuals and selling their output to those who needed it. All transactions would be handled by market exchanges, with none of the hierarchical control and coordination associated with firms. That this vision of individuals interacting only through the market is so foreign to our experience is a testament to the value of coordination. Firms exist because activity coordinated by organizations can be more efficient than activity coordinated by the market.[3]

The activity of coordination is the acquisition and allocation of the firm's assets. Assets, whether they are tangible (e.g., work-in-progress inventory, machines, or buildings) or intangible (e.g., expertise or information) need to be available in the right types and amounts in the right places for the organization to operate efficiently. Think, for example, of the huge number of resources and activities that must be coordinated to produce a typical car. A car has thousands of parts that must be combined in a specific pattern. Assembly must be coordinated to bring the desired combination together efficiently. The production process must also be responsive to the requirements of the design and sales processes if the final product is to meet customers' needs. Establishing an organization design that accomplishes the flow of assets within the firm so that it can achieve its objectives as efficiently as possible is what we mean by the coordination problem.

A central coordination problem is to balance the gains from specialization and the gains from integration. Assembly-line production in which each worker repetitively performs a very narrow task illustrates the gains from specialization. When firms with assembly-line production competed with firms that produced using skilled workers performing multiple tasks, the productivity advantage of assembly-line production gave firms using this approach a large cost advantage. In effect, each worker became incredibly proficient at a narrow set of activities, and the assembly line aggregated the efforts of the specialists. Even in the assembly-line story, however, there are gains to

---

[3] The "can be" in this sentence is important. There is a large literature on when activities should be coordinated within a firm and when they should be left to the market. Within a single firm, this problem is often encountered in the form of decisions about outsourcing. We will discuss these issues in Chapter 10.

integration. The flow of work must be managed to coordinate the work of the specialists efficiently. "Integration" here is reduced to a set of routines built into the workflow. In other examples, integration is more complex and requires that workers and units within the organization consciously work together. One unit may need to modify its output to make the other unit more productive, for example. The units may need to share information and make joint decisions to achieve the competitive advantage on which the firm depends. It may, for example, be important for the design engineers to work closely with sales managers to meet the customers' needs.

How decision-making processes are designed is another central coordination problem. In some organizations, senior managers make most strategic decisions centrally, and in others middle managers are given substantial decision-making authority. At Southwest, flight teams are assigned a great deal of decision-making authority, but at American Airlines the scope for decision making at the team level is more tightly circumscribed. A closely related coordination problem is how information flows through the organization. Some organizations have relatively open access to critical business information within the firm, and others have information systems that channel specific information to specific subsets of employees. Because decision makers need access to information, the allocation of decision rights and the design of information flows must be consistent.

## The Incentive Problem

Because an organization is made up of many individuals and groups, it would be surprising to find that they all have objectives identical to those of the firm's owners. The objective of the stockholders is profit-maximization, but most employees have other concerns as well and may be willing to pursue their objectives at the expense of the firm's. For example, the design team at an advertising firm might care more about winning a Clio design award than about producing an advertisement that sells more of the client's product. Similarly, an individual manager may be more interested in the impact of his actions on his career opportunities than in the profitability of his unit or firm. Or a divisional manager, with an eye on the CEO's job, may believe that enhancing her own division's performance, even at the expense of another's, is a route to success. Regardless of the source of goal differences, an appropriate organization design must take them into account and moderate their impact on firm performance.[4]

These problems arise at the level both of the individual (i.e., the person willing to sacrifice the good of the unit to enhance his own career) and the subunit (i.e., a sub-

---

[4] The incentive problem is in a class of problems economists refer to as principal-agent problems. In these, there is some principal (the firm's stockholders, for example) who works through some agent (the managers of the firm, for example). When the objectives of the principal and the agent are inconsistent, the principal has the problem of designing the contract with the agent in a way that aligns the agent's incentives with those of the principal. The literature on incentive problems is large, and exploring it fully is beyond the scope of this book. See Baron and Kreps, *Strategic Human Resources: Frameworks for General Managers* (New York: John Wiley, 1999) and Lazear, *Personnel Economics for Managers* (New York; John Wiley, 1997) for more comprehensive discussions.

unit pursuing its own goals without regard to the profits of the firm). In the latter case, the problem arises because the members of subunits have objectives in common with each other that are inconsistent with promoting the overall performance of the firm. Since our primary concern in this chapter is to think about how the firm should organize its activities, we will focus mostly on the incentives of a subunit rather than on those of an individual. The nature of the problem and the available solutions, however, is the same whether we are thinking about an individual or a team of individuals with objectives in common.

In some respects, it is puzzling that an incentive problem exists even when we recognize that employees have concerns that are more complex than simple profit-maximization. After all, any subunit operates within a hierarchical structure that ultimately reports to a board of directors charged with representing shareholders' interests. So why aren't subunits simply told what to do?

Part of the problem, of course, is that the managers to whom the subunit reports often do not know precisely what they want the group to do. Some of the information on which the unit's decisions are properly based originates in the unit itself, for example. The sales group has more immediate and comprehensive information about the intensity of competition and the state of demand than do its superiors and should use this information in setting prices. If it observes that demand is falling or competition is becoming more intense, it should reduce prices to maximize firm profits. But if the unit is evaluated based on the number of sales made, it has an incentive to drop price regardless of the state of the market. Senior managers might then observe lower prices and an increase in sales along with a report from the sales division that prices were lowered in response to actions by competitors. This is a problem of *hidden information:* superiors simply do not have all the information possessed by those who make the decisions.

Superiors often find it difficult to observe exactly what actions the unit has taken. Although it is fairly easy to observe prices and sales, many actions are much more difficult to discern. Consider, for example, the kind of effort required for innovation. Because the innovative process is fraught with uncertainty, false starts, and unexpected outcomes, an outsider cannot know precisely how hard the unit is working at the task. Does failure after a month of effort mean that the unit wasn't working hard, or is failure simply part of the innovation process? Sometimes careful monitoring can give a reasonably good idea about what actions have been taken and whether those actions were appropriate. Often, however, even sophisticated, pervasive, and costly monitoring mechanisms produce information that is incomplete and even misleading. Collecting accurate information is made more difficult if the unit has an incentive to disguise what it is doing. When superiors cannot observe exactly what a unit is doing, there is a problem of *hidden action.*

The *incentive problem,* then, is to elicit the right amount and type of effort in the presence of hidden information and hidden action. The *coordination problem* is to achieve an efficient deployment of assets. These two problems can be described by the following metaphor. Solving the coordination problem is like building an efficient transportation infrastructure within the firm. Managers, for example, want to build a system of streets that allows employees to move information and other resources around in a way that makes them as productive as possible. Some streets should be simple two-lane roads, and others should be high-speed, limited-access highways. Some parts of the infrastructure should be nodes that are connected directly to many other parts; others need only minimal connection, and so forth. If the coordination problem is building the best road system for the tasks the firm must accomplish, the incentive problem is getting employees to use the roads. Employees, unless the incentive problem is solved, will use those parts of the infrastructure that get them where they want to be rather than where the firm wants them to be. This metaphor also implies, correctly, that these problems are interrelated; it is easier to get employees to use a road that is itself easy to travel. In the next section, we discuss the tools available to managers who must build the roads and direct the traffic.

## 4.5  MEETING THE CHALLENGE

The firm can manipulate many components of organization design to address the coordination and incentive problems. For example, when we think of how a firm is organized, we often think first of how it is divided into subunits. This is an important component of organization, but it is only one. How those subunits relate to one another is also important, as are the firm's formal and informal mechanisms for decision making. The organization's norms and the mechanisms for sustaining or changing them are also likely to be important, as are its compensation schemes, career ladders, and so forth. To bring order to the plethora of design elements, we have organized them into three categories as illustrated in Figure 4-3: architecture, routines, and culture (ARC).

Briefly, we define these components of organization as follows:

- **Architecture.** This includes how the firm is divided into subunits, the reporting relationships among them, the formal and informal mechanisms that link them, the hierarchical structure that governs them, and the recruiting and compensation policies applied to the people filling the positions within the organizational structure.

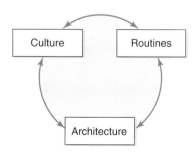

FIGURE 4-3   Elements of Organizational Design

- **Routines.** Most of the activities and decisions a firm engages in each day are similar to the ones it had to deal with the day before. The enormous amount of repetition allows a firm to develop formal and informal procedures, processes, and habits for doing the things it does. These "generally accepted methods for doing things" are the firm's routines. Many routines are neither fully codified nor even rationally determined by anyone, but evolve over time until, after much repetition, those participating in them take them for granted.
- **Culture.** "Culture" refers to the commonly held values and beliefs of individuals within the organization and, accordingly, the evaluative criteria used to make both large and small decisions.

To organize our discussion of how managers might use the levers of architecture, routines, and culture to attack the incentive and coordination problems, we first discuss each component separately. Then, in the following chapter, we turn to the problem of putting all the elements together.

## Architecture: Structure

The most easily observed parts of the firm's architecture are displayed in its organization chart. The organization chart depicts the architectural *structure* that divides individuals into groups and organizes them into a governing hierarchy through reporting relationships. The architecture also includes the compensation and information systems a firm uses to evaluate individuals and groups. These latter parts of architecture are treated separately because they are used primarily to address the incentive problem. The compensation and monitoring system is one way the firm induces its employees to drive on its roads, to return to our infrastructure metaphor. The part we call structure is used primarily for addressing the coordination problem. This is about how the firm builds its road system.

Constructing an organizational structure, then, is about dividing people into subunits and defining the linkages among these groups. Some of the linkages consist of reporting relationships and channels through which superiors exercise control and allocate assets. Other linkages are horizontal, allowing subunits to function more efficiently by sharing information and resources. We begin by discussing the problem of creating subunits, and then we turn to the problem of linking them.

Because communication and resource sharing are more easily accomplished *within* subunits than *across* them, the delineation of subunits profoundly affects resource and information flows within the firm. The extent to which people have ready access to the information and resources essential to performing their jobs depends on how they are grouped. For example, many large, primarily domestic firms have responded to the challenge of globalization by creating a subunit to develop global markets for existing products. This unit researches market opportunities abroad, sets up marketing and distribution in other countries, and encourages other subunits to be more responsive to international markets. The rationale for creating a separate unit is often to make it easier for senior managers to direct resources to developing international markets. One unintentional consequence, however, is to isolate the international concerns from the mainstream business of the firm. What the international group learns about other markets, for example, is not readily communicated to the domestically focused units that are much more likely to respond to messages from their own marketing people.

This example is just one of the many specific embodiments of the long-standing debate in the organization literature about the optimal approach to delineating subunits. In particular, scholars and managers have struggled over whether "functional" or "divisional" structures are a better way to solve the coordination problem. In a functional organization, depicted in Figure 4-4, individuals are grouped according to the tasks they perform. Thus, for example, all human resources people are grouped together, as are all salespeople, all research and development people, and so on.

By contrast, in a divisional organization, the primary subunits are formed based on some business logic rather than on a functional logic. For example, divisions might be based on geography, customers, or technology. Figure 4-5 illustrates a divisional organization based on geography. As in the figure, each division may have functional subdivisions. However, the grouping by division is the dominant feature of the organization structure, and divisional lines divide functional specialists from one another.

The functional organization helps firms realize the benefits of specialization by facilitating information sharing and learning among technical specialists. Over time, the specialists become increasingly expert at performing their particular function. For example, grouping all the engineers together provides more opportunity for cross-fertilization of engineering knowledge than there would be in a divisional structure that separated engineers in each division from one another. Two manufacturing divisions, each of which makes a distinct product line, may have a common process problem involving molded plastics, for example. If one group solves the problem, the organization might benefit from having a mechanism for sharing that solution with the other division. If the engineers are grouped together, this diffusion happens easily. If the engineers are separated by product line, it will be more difficult.

A functional delineation of subgroups also promotes individual investment in learning within that functional specialty. In the typical functional design, a well-

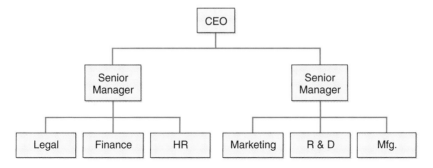

**FIGURE 4-4**    A Functional Architecture

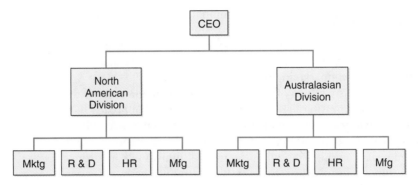

**FIGURE 4-5**    A Divisional Architecture

developed hierarchy within each function encourages the development and retention of the functional specialists. When the engineers are grouped together, for example, there is usually a clear engineering hierarchy, and the positions in it are well-defined stepping stones along a career path. Since the route to advancement within the function is clear, employees are motivated to specialize and invest in the human capital necessary to advance within the hierarchy. In a divisional structure, by contrast, the route to advancing one's career is typically less clear and may not be best approached by investing in function-specific skills.[5]

Despite these advantages of a functional organization, the divisional form has become increasingly common primarily because it is better at facilitating coordination *across* functions. If they are in the same subunit, those responsible for design and manufacturing are likely to learn more quickly about changes in customer tastes from the sales force than they would in a functional organization. In functional organizations, sales and marketing personnel may find themselves making unrealistic commitments to customers because they are unaware of the constraints in the design and production process. The divisional form is superior to the functional form at facilitating the coordination of different functions because it is designed precisely to accomplish this.

The value of the divisional approach increases as the firm increases in scale and scope. As the business historian Alfred Chandler has shown, the multidivisional form arose early in the twentieth century in the United States because the functional form was not well suited to the size and scope of industrial enterprises such as General Electric and DuPont. According to Chandler, improvements in the transportation and communication infrastructure and increasingly efficient capital markets made it possible and desirable for firms to grow into large and diverse commercial enterprises. As the enterprises grew in size and complexity, however, a general loss of accountability

---

[5] One can move to positions with responsibility for a more important region, a more profitable product, or a more prestigious customer. However, even if divisions can be ranked by prominence within the firm, there is still much less clarity about how career paths unfold through those divisions.

and a breakdown in communication occurred. Segmenting the activities of the firm according to divisions rather than functions, Chandler claims, enhanced accountability and communication.[6]

Regardless of how an organization resolves the functional versus divisional debate, some resources and information must cross group boundaries. One of the roles played by the senior managers overseeing multiple subunits is to function as an overarching governance structure that can communicate information and share resources among groups. Communication with and among senior managers is one way to coordinate the actions of the subunits. This process, however, requires that information collected by the subunits be passed up through the hierarchy, evaluated by senior managers, and addressed by commands and resources passed down through the hierarchy. How effectively this process accomplishes coordination is affected by how "flat" or "tall" the hierarchy is, that is, how many layers the organization structure has. Smaller, more focused firms tend to have flatter hierarchies. As the firm grows, it adds employees, and to keep the number of employees supervised by one person from growing too large, it tends to add layers to its hierarchy. At one time, General Electric had as many as nine layers of management! In flat organization structures, a request for cooperation need only "go up" the hierarchy a few steps before it reaches someone who can authorize the necessary interaction among groups.

However flat the structure, information is inevitably lost as it moves across formal boundaries. The CEO of IBM once purportedly complained that every time reports moved up another step in the hierarchy, 20 percent of the bad news was filtered out. By the time information reached the CEO, it was all good news. Passing information along consumes resources, causes delays, and degrades the information by introducing noise and distortion. This cost of passing along information is the rationale for allocating decision-making rights to those with the most immediate access to the relevant information. If the marketing group for a product is given broad discretion to set prices, it can respond quickly and appropriately to the information it gets from its customers.

The problem of pushing decision making down the hierarchy is that those closest to customers, for example, may not have vital pieces of information that others who are further removed possess. In particular, they may not know how their decisions will affect other subunits. Hewlett-Packard, for example, has separate subunits for desktop printers and the replaceable ink cartridges for them. Those in the printer group may fail to take into account that the prices they charge for printers affect demand for replacement cartridges and vice versa. Recognizing this problem, the managers to whom both groups report might want either to make these decisions themselves or to create other formal linking mechanisms that will allow the decisions to be coordinated.

The assignment of decision rights, then, and the flow of information must be closely linked. One basic principle of organization design is to assign authority to

---

[6] Alfred Chandler, *Scale and Scope* (Cambridge, MA: Harvard University Press, 1990).

those who have information. If information is largely decentralized within the organization, a strong argument can be made for decentralizing decision making as well. The countervailing force is the need for closely coordinated action that argues for centralized decision making accompanied by linkages that are effective at transmitting information up through the hierarchy. Typically, it is possible to decentralize decisions that require little coordination and to centralize authority for those decisions that require more coordination.

An alternative approach to resorting to hierarchy for achieving coordination is to rely on horizontal linkages. Horizontal linking mechanisms facilitate information and resource flows without affecting the organization of the subunits. Thus, an appropriate linking mechanism may allow for some cooperation across units without sacrificing the gains from specialization and decentralization. For example, a firm can use a functional structure to facilitate technical excellence within each function and still achieve some cross-functional sharing of information or knowledge.

## Examples of Horizontal Linkages

Horizontal linkages can be created in many ways, as can be illustrated with some examples. Those at the top of this list are generally less costly in the sense that they require less formally allocated time and resources. Those at the bottom of the list, however, are more formal and robust in that they can create effective linkages even when the boundaries of the subunits are difficult to cross. In formal organizations where lines of control and communication are rigidly followed, accomplishing effective coordination through horizontal linkages that cut across the hierarchy is difficult. In these circumstances, a more formal horizontal linkage may be necessary.

- **Personal networks.** Personal networks can be effective conduits for resources and information. They do not have to be established by management, but instead may arise through the actions of individual employees to meet particular needs. This characteristic is particularly valuable in a volatile environment where management may have limited insight into which linkages would be useful. However, relying on personal networks has some drawbacks. First, in a large, complex organization, individuals may not be aware of all the potential sources of information or resources. Second, these networks have no formal authority; no individual can force another to cooperate. Third, although personal networks can often be valuable for bilateral coordination, they are less effective in addressing more widespread problems that concern many groups.

- **Liaisons.** The liaison role—a formally designated linkage between units— may be useful when managers can identify a need for an intergroup linkage that personal networks are unlikely to support. FCB-Publicis (a recently dissolved alliance of two advertising agencies), for example, used liaisons to link operations in different countries when serving a global client. When it had an account with a multinational firm in the United States and another account with that same firm in France and Spain, it would rely on a liaison to coordinate the country-specific operations.

- **Task forces or teams.** A task force is a group formed for a limited time to address a particular issue, frequently one that concerns multiple units. For example, suppose that a multinational organization, divided into country-specific units, has had trouble extending its markets from its commercial base into the growing public sectors. Senior management might form a task force devoted to this topic that would assimilate and disseminate information across units. Unlike a liaison role, a task force generally has some formal authority to implement its conclusions, or it reports directly to someone who does have that authority. Teams are similar to task forces in scope but tend to have a more open-ended duration. So a firm may use a team to address issues that are of ongoing concern to several organizational units. For example, management in a multidivisional organization might create a cross-divisional manufacturing team to track and disseminate information on best practice in manufacturing processes. Like task forces, teams generally are removed from day-to-day workflow.

- **"Integrators."** Integrators also have some formal authority but are usually more closely intertwined with day-to-day operations than either task forces or teams. For example, Novo-Nordisk, a Danish pharmaceutical and chemical firm, relies on a 14-person team of "facilitators" to transfer best practice among and evaluate the performance of, approximately 300 units within the company. Over a three-year period, facilitators meet with each unit, help set performance goals, and provide information about practices observed in other units that the unit they are meeting with might find useful. A facilitator must have a wide range of contacts within the firm, share the perspectives of the groups with whom he works, and be able to exercise influence on the basis of technical expertise. So, for instance, at Novo-Nordisk, the facilitators are recruited from a broad cross-section of both staff and line functions. With each unit they evaluate, their experience and knowledge grow, further enhancing their ability to play the integrating role.

Interdependence among subunits is a key factor in selecting among the options for linking them. As an example of largely independent subunits, consider an oil firm that is also diversified into products unrelated to petroleum. It is unlikely that the activities in the petroleum divisions will affect the outcomes of activities undertaken by employees in the other divisions.[7] At the other extreme, divisions engaged in designing a system may be very interdependent. In engine design, for example, a change in the size, cost, energy requirements, physical location, or durability of one component can have significant implications for the design (and designers) of other components. As a consequence, there is a lot of interdependence among those who design different parts of the car. To allow the organization to respond effectively to

---

[7] Whenever units are part of the same firm, they have *some* interdependence. A bad year for one unit, for example, may affect the resources the firm makes available to another. When the price of oil plummeted in 1986, oil companies reduced their investment in nonoil businesses in response to the cash-flow constraint created by poor performance in the oil divisions (see Owen Lamont "Cash Flow and Investment: Evidence from Internal Capital Markets," *The Journal of Finance* 52, No. 1, (February 1997), pp. 83–109).

this kind of technological interdependence, an automobile firm's organization design will have a subunit structure and linking mechanisms that facilitate complex and frequent interconnections. We use the term "tightly coupled" to refer to organization designs with those characteristics. A more "loosely coupled" design is appropriate when the units really are largely independent or when the interface between them is standardized. Indeed, some interfaces are so standardized that assemblers can buy components off the shelf; the component designers are so loosely coupled that they are not even part of the same firm!

So far, we have limited our discussion of the organization's structure to solving the coordination problem, but architectural structure can also respond to the incentive problem. For example, the extent to which hidden action and hidden information exist within the unit depends on how the unit is defined. The incentive problem for a unit that is distinct from other units and has its own profit and loss reporting is more easily solved than it is when a unit's performance is difficult to evaluate. We therefore discuss the incentive problem in greater detail and the role that compensation and rewards can play in ameliorating it. We then return to how structure can support compensation and rewards in dealing with that problem.

## Architecture: Compensation and Rewards

One of the primary ways our understanding of organizations has advanced in recent years is in the area of defining and solving the incentive problem. We have learned that hidden action and hidden information make it impossible to observe precisely what a unit has done and what it knew when it did it. As a result, if a firm wants its employees to behave in a way that is best for the firm, it cannot simply tell them what to do and then check to see that they did it.

Fortunately, a firm can sometimes *induce* the behavior it desires by creating the proper incentives. Financial incentives tied to the performance of the unit are often a powerful instrument for inducing profit-maximizing behavior. For example, consider a setting in which the members of the unit are highly motivated by financial rewards and in which the firm can easily measure what a unit contributes to the firm's profit. In this situation, the firm can align the actions of the unit fairly closely with the firm's goals by tying the compensation of the unit's managers to the unit's profit contribution. This approach to inducing people to take the actions the firm wants them to take is now commonly used. Firms with separate divisions frequently give each division its own profit and loss accountability and tie the compensation of division managers to divisional performance.

Although tying pay to profitability will, in principle, solve the incentive problem, certain problems limit how effective such plans are in practice. For example, these types of compensation schemes can lead to substantial variation in compensation over time. The same hard work might produce more profit when the macroeconomic climate is good than when it is bad. If employees are risk averse, they are either unwilling to bear this risk or must at least be compensated for doing so.

Moreover, it is often difficult to ascertain the profit impact of a unit's activities. For example, a product design unit does not generate profits on its own. One possible solution to this problem is to tie the compensation of the unit's manager to the profit of the whole firm rather than to that of the unit. However, that tends to result in weak incentives for most employees. For example, consider a large firm like Asea Brown Boveri (ABB), a European firm that designs and manufactures large-scale power generation equipment and has over 200,000 employees in over 140 countries. A manager of a design group for a single system knows that her unit might be able to contribute some amount to firm productivity. But she also knows that whatever contribution the subunit makes will be swamped by the combined contribution of the other units and—possibly—by changes in the market context. So realizing any return on the unit's hard work is uncertain. Indeed, the subunit's payment might not be affected by how hard it works. Furthermore, even if its contribution does lead to an overall profit increase, the employees in the unit will share the reward with the 200,000 other employees in the company. At best, the unit will get only a small share of any profit increment it can generate.

This argument is relevant for all employees in the organization unless they are members of the firm's top management. The most senior members of the firm recognize that their impact on firm performance can be large enough to survive the combined actions of other employees and the environment. Furthermore, since there are only a few top managers, they can expect to get a larger share of the profit increment for which they are responsible. This is why one sees large option grants and other forms of contingent compensation offered to CEOs and other members of the top management team and less incentive pay for those further down in the hierarchy.

Because tying compensation to *overall* firm profits doesn't provide much incentive to act as the firm would like (at least for most of its workers) and the profit contribution of the subunit can be difficult to measure, firms typically tie compensation to some combination of imperfect indicators of unit performance. For example, firms have used the results of customer satisfaction surveys, the owner's assessment of how hard everyone seems to be working when she stops by the firm for a surprise visit, the number of patents awarded, meeting time-to-market schedules, and so forth. In deciding which indicators might be best, the senior managers must use their knowledge of the organization, including the nature of the tasks performed by a subunit, the information available, and the cost of monitoring.

In selecting indicators, managers can follow four rules of thumb. First, as one would expect, indicators that are highly correlated with the direct profit impact of the unit's work are more useful than indicators that are only weakly correlated with it. Thus the profitability of ABB in the country served by a design unit is a better indicator than the worldwide performance of ABB because the group has more effect on ABB's profitability in that country than on ABB's overall profitability. Note that it is profit impact that one wants to be correlated with the indicator; managers want to avoid indicators that can be manipulated without affecting the firm's profit. A medical laboratory, for example, once set up an incentive scheme that made technician pay sensitive to the variance in lab test turnaround times. The idea was to be able to give customers a reliable estimate of how long it would take to get lab test results. The effect was that the technicians dramatically reduced the variance in duration by holding up results that otherwise would have been available much earlier than others. Average turnaround time increased!

Second, it is useful to have indicators that allow one to "net out" the effects of factors beyond the control of the unit. For example, if the country goes into an economic decline, the firm does not want to punish the design unit for the sales decline. More generally, many elements contribute to a unit's performance that have little to do with the unit's actions and for which, therefore, the unit should not be rewarded or punished. Benchmarking the unit's performance against other units or firms that face many of the same challenges is one way to address this problem. Relative performance is frequently used, for example, in evaluating the performance of senior managers. The board of directors should ask how well the firm has done relative to its competitors. Using the performance of other firms has the advantage of responding to the hidden information problem. If a unit's performance is evaluated based on its own reports of the economic conditions it faced, the unit has an incentive to exaggerate its difficulties.

Third, since no one indicator tells you exactly what you want to know, there is a benefit to including several indicators in the incentive scheme. We have already suggested, for example, that managers should consider both the profit generated by the unit and factors that might affect that profit but are beyond the control of the unit. This means that the indicators should include some measure(s) of profit and some measure(s) of factors external to the unit that might affect its profits. More generally, including multiple dimensions minimizes the effect of errors in any one indicator. For example, a manager's assessment of a design unit's contribution might be one of the best indicators of performance available. But, like all indicators, it will be imperfect. More specifically, it will be "noisy" and it might be "biased." "Bias" means that the assessment is systematically wrong. The manager may simply like the head of the unit and therefore give it higher marks than it deserves, for example. "Noise" means the assessment is imprecise, but it is as likely to be too favorable as it is to be too harsh. Even if the alternative indicators available are less good (i.e., have more noise or bias), including additional indicators improves the combined information. The idea is similar to the benefits of forming a stock market portfolio in preference to investing in a single, even high-quality, stock. A portfolio can eliminate idiosyncratic risk, creating a return that is a good indicator of the health of the economy.

There is, of course, a limit to the number of indicators one wants to use. One reason for this is that information collection is costly, an issue we return to below. Another is that as the number of indicators used rises, the people in the unit may find it increasingly difficult to anticipate how the overall score is affected by what they do. When there are many indicators, no single one seems to count much toward the performance evaluation. If employees have little incentive to attend to any particular criterion, the incentive effects of the entire package will be negligible. This concern casts doubt on the efficacy of the increasingly popular "balanced scorecard" approach in which employees are rated according to a large array of indicators.

Finally, managers should consider the cost of monitoring. Some indicators may allow an accurate assessment of the unit's performance but be extremely costly to administer. The so-called 360 degree evaluation schemes—in which an individual employee is evaluated by superiors, peers, subordinates, and often key external constituencies as well—can provide refined information on individual performance but are extremely time-consuming. Constructing more accurate measures makes it easier to reward the "right" behavior and therefore will induce employees to take the actions the firm desires. But the cost of collecting the information might offset the gain. Information collected through an extremely detailed cost accounting procedure might be useful in providing incentives, for example, but the cost of collecting the data and doing the required analysis may be greater than the increase in revenues created by getting more of the desired behavior.

The problem of finding indicators that are informative is particularly severe for effort that involves cooperation among subunits. We alluded to this problem earlier when we commented that the design group typically does not have profit and loss responsibility because the value of its output is hard to disentangle from the value provided by manufacturing and distribution. Suppose the product is wildly successful. Who should get credit for the profits it generates? The basic problem is that there are generally few good indicators of the value each subunit contributes to the overall outcome even when that can be easily valued. One way firms try to solve this problem is by establishing transfer prices that are benchmarked to market prices. Often, however, there are no market prices because what is exchanged has no market counterpart. It is hard to know what the value of a particular design might be. Furthermore, much cooperative effort involves the exchange of information. This is difficult both to value and to track.

The firm's problem is complicated because the mechanisms put in place to get the subunit to be productive on its own may give it an incentive to avoid cooperation. Investment banks, for example, are notorious for building high-powered incentives for individual traders. More than half a trader's income, for example, is often in the form of a bonus for individual performance. Since a person can work no more than 24 hours a day, someone whose pay is so strongly tied to his own performance faces a huge incentive to avoid spending any time helping other workers. The opportunity cost of diverting time to cooperation is just too high. If the pay-for-performance scheme also involves a relative performance component so that top performers within the firm are disproportionately rewarded, a trader may even have an incentive to devote some time to impairing the performance of his co-workers.

Earlier, we mentioned that architectural structure can also affect the incentive problem. One way it can do so is by affecting the importance of cooperation across units. Consider, for example, a firm's decision about whether to market its products under a single brand or under multiple brands. Some firms, like 3M, Sony, IBM, Nike, or Xerox, build the brand name at the level of the firm, prominently attaching the name of the firm to many of its products. Other firms, like Procter & Gamble, PepsiCo, or Johnson & Johnson, build brands around individual products, segments, or divisions. Finally, others adopt a mixed approach to branding. In Europe, Daimler-Benz uses the Mercedes brand for both cars and trucks. In the United States, Daimler-Benz adopts a multibrand strategy, producing passenger cars under the Mercedes name and commercial trucks under the Freightliner and Sterling brands.

Although marketing concerns usually drive this branding decision, it has less obvious, but important, organizational implications. If a brand cuts across two separate organizational units, the identities and performances of the two units are inter-

twined. The decision of one unit to offer an inferior product has negative consequences for the other unit. Conversely, if one unit can improve its product, its actions
create positive effects for the other. The upside of linking identities is that each unit
now has a self-interested reason to assist the other; a failure to provide assistance can
directly harm the unit's own performance by damaging the common brand. However, this linking also has a clear downside. Because the overall perception of the
brand is a result of the aggregate effort of both subunits, neither realizes the full benefits or bears the full cost of its actions. As a result, even when the managers of each
subunit are rewarded based on the performance of their own unit, neither manager
has the right incentives to devote resources to supporting the common brand name.
Contrast this situation with a firm in which each subunit has its own brand. Each
manager has the right incentives to support her brand because the brand has no value
for other units, and she is rewarded based on her subunit's performance. Although a
common brand induces more cooperation, it also dilutes the incentives for individual
performance.

Achieving high levels of cooperation will not be equally important for all organizations. One reason an investment bank has high-powered incentives for individual
performance is that its profit is affected more by the aggregate of individual performance than it is by the level of cooperation among its units. Many other firms depend
much more on cooperation among subunits. A firm for which innovation is critical,
for example, tends to stress cooperation more. This is in part because rewarding individual performance is harder for this kind of firm. It is harder to tie firm performance
to a specific unit's R&D performance, and the returns to any unit's initiative are so
variable that tying compensation to them would lead to large variance in compensation over time. Equally important, however, the success of the R&D units often
depends on cooperation with other units within the firm.

The difficulty of inducing cooperative behavior with strong financial incentives or
carefully drawn organizational boundaries underscores the importance of other elements of organization design in solving the incentive problem. The focus here is on
compensation schemes and boundaries because they are powerful tools and can be
manipulated much more easily than many other elements of organization design.
They clearly are not a panacea for the incentive problem, however, and managers
should recognize that other elements can also be brought to bear on the problem.
Recognizing the limits of architecture, we now turn to the contributions of routines
and culture.

## Routines

Much of the day-to-day activity and decision making within a firm are accomplished
through the exercise of routines. As a simple example, consider a firm's routines for
repairing its products. A customer's call about a problem is routed to the repair
department. Often, someone responsible for "triage" will determine the precise
nature of the problem and route the call to a qualified repair person. If the expert
cannot resolve the problem over the phone, the customer will be told how to return
the product. When the product is returned, it is routed to the appropriate repair

personnel. After making the repair, these people route the paperwork to the warranty department and the repaired product to shipping. Each of the people involved in this process understands the circumstances that require them to act, the tasks for which they are responsible, and how to hand off specific tasks for which they do not have responsibility.

The key to routines is that they embody established *interfaces* among the parties that must interact in the performance of a process. The interfaces consist of common expectations about what will flow across them and a protocol for accomplishing the transfer. The shipping department knows that it will receive parts and the paperwork that tells it where the part should be shipped. On an assembly line, each worker knows what subassembly should be arriving at her workstation and how it will arrive. Having finished her work, she knows how the subassembly should pass to the next set of actors.

There are large coordination gains to this kind of routinization. Each employee can become expert at some subprocess. The shipping department, for example, gets good at packaging and handling the interactions with various common carriers because this is all that it does. Routines, therefore, support the realization of gains from specialization. Perhaps more importantly, because interfaces are standardized, there are huge informational efficiencies. As tasks proceed from one unit to another, only minimal amounts of information need be communicated between units. Each unit need know only what is essential for it to play its part, including how to interpret the information it receives and transmit the information necessary for the next step to the next unit.

Importantly, routines do not just apply to linear processes of the kind illustrated by the repair example. Firms also have routines for decision making, for example. In some organizations, group decisions are generally made by consensus. Strong opposition from even one person within a group can prevent the group from pursuing a particular plan. Other organizations make decisions by majority rule. Still others have some implicit weighting scheme based on rank, seniority, or expertise. Most organizations do not reevaluate these decision rules every time a decision is made. Rather, the organization has a decision routine that it applies each time a decision must be made.

Since many routines cross group boundaries, they facilitate coordination among groups by simplifying the interface. A routine way for employees in one division to access the resources in another division enables the firm to coordinate in ways that would be difficult if the firm had to make a new resource-sharing decision each time. Routines, once taken for granted, may obviate the need for structural linking mechanisms or intervention by managers. Moreover, in contrast to linking processes that function well for infrequent coordination, routines are excellent devices for repeated coordination because they develop from and rely on repetition.

Routines also ameliorate the incentive problem. First, they create opportunities to get better indicators of performance. Standardized interfaces make standardized indicators possible. In our repair example, the triage person can easily record referrals to repair people in a database. Similarly, shipping can record when the repaired part is received for shipment, and the warranty department can record when the warranty information is received. Routines also ameliorate incentive problems by "automating" activities for which it is otherwise difficult to provide incentives. By standardizing the interfaces among units, routines facilitate cooperation.

## Culture

The commonly held values and beliefs of an organization both constrain and enable the actions firms can take. Employees regard a decision they perceive to be consistent with common values and beliefs as substantively appropriate and worthy of support. Similarly, they view a decision-making process as procedurally just if they believe it conforms to the sanctioned criteria, even when they dislike the outcome. The converse, of course, is also true. Members of the organization will resist any course of action that appears to violate the culture of the firm.

Culture, then, provides the opportunity for inducing cooperation that otherwise would be difficult to achieve. Subunits are generally reluctant to give up resources, especially when they have difficulty understanding how those resources might be applied elsewhere. A culture that promotes communication and resource sharing can economize on the hierarchy and structural linking mechanisms necessary to accomplish resource and information sharing. Cooperation is particularly likely if there is a well-developed "norm of reciprocity": the belief that one is obligated to help those who have helped oneself.

Many companies consciously combine financial incentives and culture to elicit a balance of individual performance and cooperation. Hewlett-Packard (HP), for example, creates strong financial incentives at the divisional level by assigning profit and loss responsibility to divisions and, with few exceptions, does not allow one division to subsidize another. If a division cannot generate a profit on its own, it effectively dies. Given these strong division-level incentives, one would expect to see limited cooperation across divisions. The strong financial incentives for individual divisions, however, are balanced by a corporate culture that fosters interdivisional cooperation. Because this culture is important, HP has made it as explicit as possible, describing it as "The HP Way." HP's statement of its corporate objectives begins: "The achievements of an organization are the result of the combined efforts of each individual in the organization working toward common objectives. These objectives should be realistic, should be clearly understood by everyone in the organization and should reflect the organization's basic character and personality."[8]

Common beliefs about the firm and its external context also can help employees focus on those tasks that are important for the competitive advantage of the firm. Southwest Airlines' strategy requires its employees to pay attention to customers. If employees believe that this is necessary for the firm to succeed, they are more likely to regard dancing in the aisles as reasonable behavior. Furthermore, one of the reasons employees at Southwest trust senior managers to make the right decisions is that employees and managers have a common view of the world. Another is that Southwest has created an implicit contract with its employees that it will treat them fairly, con-

[8] You can find this statement and a description of "The HP Way" on their Web site www.hp.com/abouthp/hpway.html, accessed March 2000.

sider their perspective, and be responsive to their views of how the organization should change.

Culture can also play a vital role in resolving the foundation of the incentive problem. Recall that our discussion of incentives is premised on the notion that the firm and subordinate unit (or individuals) have different goals. However, suppose that this were not true; suppose that the firm and subunit have the same objectives. Then, management need not worry about offering incentives to the unit to pursue the firm's goals because the unit *wants* to pursue those goals. One view of culture is that it affects what people want to do *in the absence of pecuniary* rewards. Suppose, for example, that the competitive advantage of an organization hinges on innovation and product quality. If the employees derive considerable satisfaction from developing and being associated with high-quality products, then the firm has less need to offer financial incentives for this behavior. A manager who wants to induce a particular behavior that is difficult or costly to include in a pay-for-performance scheme may find that a strong culture can be a more effective means of evoking that particular behavior than pecuniary incentives.

## 4.6 ARC ANALYSIS

In this chapter, we have introduced some of the key concepts of organization design and developed a framework for approaching the complex problem of building a high-performance organization. We summarize that framework in Figure 4-6 under the label *ARC Analysis.* As illustrated in the figure, any effective design must address two general problems: *coordinating* the deployment of the firm's assets and aligning the *incentives* of its employees and units with those of the firm. The managers charged with designing the organization have three organizational levers to tackle these problems: *architecture, routines,* and *culture* (ARC). As indicated by the arrows connecting them in the figure, these levers interact, and an effective design depends on the three elements of ARC working in concert. We also noted that the coordination and incen-

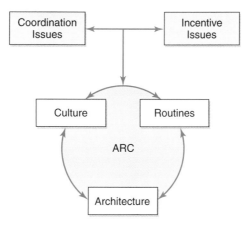

**FIGURE 4-6**   ARC Analysis: Building an Effective Organization

tive problems are intertwined. The way the coordination problem is solved, for example, affects the incentive problems the design must resolve. The bidirectional arrow between these problems in the figure is meant to represent this interdependence.

This framework suggests that managers must have a deep understanding of the elements of the firm's ARC, how those elements fit together, and how they address the firm's incentive and coordination problem. This is easy advice to give, but, as we have seen throughout the chapter, it is difficult to follow. Because organization design has many elements with intricate relationships among them, it poses formidable problems. The complexity that makes organization design difficult, however, also means that getting it right can create a competitive advantage that is difficult for others to match.

One way to approach this problem is to have a systematic approach to collecting information on the design challenge facing the firm and the elements of its architecture, culture, and routines. In Figure 4-7 we have listed some of the questions that managers who want to collect and evaluate this kind of information might usefully pose (and answer!). In Part A, we present some of the questions that are helpful for thinking through what kind of design problems the firm faces. This is the "green field" part of the problem. The idea here is to step back from the existing organization and ask what the firm needs to do (its coordination problem) and how its employees and units will be motivated to do it (the incentive problem). It is "green field" because it ignores the existing organization of the firm. It does not ask what problems the current organization addresses or fails to address, but what problems would be addressed if management could build an entirely new organization. As we shall see in the next chapter, defining these questions and arriving at answers are intimately tied to the firm's strategy. It is the strategy that determines the central design issues for the firm.

Part B of the figure brings us back to the current organization of the firm. The questions illustrated here are those that enable the managers to conduct a detailed analysis of the firm's current ARC. The answers to the questions posed in this stage should produce a rich description of the firm's structure, compensation and reward systems, routines, and culture. Once this description is complete, the manager is in a good position to identify any inconsistencies among the elements that make the organization less effective than it could be. Now the manager also has the information to ask whether the organization as it is currently designed is responsive to the key coordination and incentive problems it needs to solve. Laying out the details of the organization is a necessary step to understanding what parts of its design are appropriate and what parts should be reconsidered.

## 4.7  SUMMARY

A firm's competitive advantage often has its basis in the firm's organization. An effective organization design must address the specific coordination and incentive problems the firm faces and must do so in a way that supports the firm's strategy. The components of organization design that a firm can manipulate to address its coordination and incentive problems are its architecture, routines, and culture (ARC). The

## Part A: Defining the Problem

**Coordination Problem**
- How does critical information reach the firm?
- How should information flow through the firm?
- Who should make which decisions?
- What activities should be grouped together?
- What cross-unit linkages should be created?
- What activities should be routinized?
- What norms and decision rules should be supported?
- What beliefs about the firm and its environment are important?

**Incentive Problem**
- What activities are most critical to the performance of the firm?
- What performance dimensions can be measured and monitored?
- Where will incentive pay be most effective?
- What kind of culture will support productive behavior?
- What hiring and performance review routines are appropriate?

## Part B: Assessing the Firm's Response

| Architecture | | Routines | Culture |
|---|---|---|---|
| Structure | Compensation and Rewards | | |
| • Is the structure divisional or functional?<br>• How is it divided into subunits?<br>• What formal linking mechanisms exist?<br>  • Personal networks?<br>  • Liaisons?<br>  • Task forces?<br>  • Integrators?<br>• How interdependent are subunits?<br>• How frequently are they interdependent?<br>• What structures exist for resource allocation?<br>• What structures exist for sharing information?<br>• How tall/flat is the hierarchy?<br>• Where and how are decision rights allocated? | • How high is compensation relative to other firms in the industry?<br>• How important are nonfinancial elements of compensation?<br>• How important is incentive compensation?<br>• How closely is compensation tied to performance of the unit?<br>• How is performance measured?<br>• Does compensation depend on impact on other units? If so, how is that measured?<br>• How important and prevalent is promotion from within? | • What routines exist for resource allocation?<br>• What routines exist for sharing information among subunits?<br>• What routines exist for coordinating across boundaries between subunits?<br>• What routines exist for coordinating activity within subunits?<br>• What routines exist that give senior management visibility into what is happening at lower levels?<br>• What interfaces exist that facilitate the use of routines?<br>• How are the interfaces defined? maintained? What is the process for ensuring routines survive over time and are disseminated across the organization? | • How strong is the culture?<br>• What are its key characteristics?<br>• What norms support the culture?<br>• What "stories" are key to the maintenance of the culture?<br>• Does the culture support cooperation across units?<br>• Does the culture reduce the need for financial incentives to induce cooperation?<br>• Do the firms' recruitment policies reinforce the culture? |

**FIGURE 4-7** ARC Analysis Questions

framework developed here is helpful for creating an internally consistent ARC that effectively addresses the incentive and coordination problems the firm faces.

The framework developed in this chapter only brings us part way, however, to answering the basic question with which we began this chapter: How does the internal context of the firm determine its competitive advantage? Put differently, how does the manager know what the key incentive and coordination problems are for her firm? We asserted that these are determined by the firm's strategy, but we have not directly addressed how this connection works. In the next chapter we turn to thinking through the linkage between strategy and organization design.

# 5

# ORGANIZATION AND COMPETITIVE ADVANTAGE

## 5.1 INTRODUCTION

A manager is concerned with organization because it affects the success of the firm's strategy. We have argued that a strategy should contain a set of objectives, a statement of scope, a clearly stated competitive advantage, and logic that explains how the internal context of the firm will enable it to achieve its objectives given its external context. In Chapter 4 we developed tools that allow us to think systematically about organization design. In this chapter we focus on the logic that connects that organization design with competitive advantage. The central question here is: "Is the firm organized to support the competitive advantage it needs to achieve its objectives?" To answer this question, the firm's managers must first understand the specific organization design problems implied by its strategy. Once the firm's managers have identified what specific coordination and incentive issues are implicit in the strategy they are pursuing, they can build an appropriate architecture, routines, and culture (ARC).

Alignment between strategy and organization is critical to meeting the firm's strategic objectives. A high-service retailer like Harrod's should be organized differently from one that focuses on low costs such as Kmart. The organization of a firm like the game company, Sega, whose strategy hinges on rapid time-to-market, should be different from that of a steel company whose product development cycle is considerably slower and whose customers care more about reliability and price than innovation. Because organization and strategy are interdependent, we need, and in the next section will develop, a conceptual framework for exploring the relationship between strategy and organization.

Although this framework helps ensure that the organization "fits" the strategy, we also need to recognize that the relationship between a firm's organization and its competitive advantage changes over time. As the firm seeks to deepen its current advantage or build new competitive advantage, it has to change the way it deploys its resources. The firm must create an organization that supports the changes it needs to make. In section 5.3 we discuss two different approaches to organization design that enable a firm to meet this challenge. One design is particularly suitable for a firm intent on creating the continual and incremental change necessary to maintain its existing competitive advantage. Firms with this design and intent are called "exploiters" because they are focused on successfully exploiting the competitive advantage they already have.

The second design type is better suited to a firm that is attempting to create a new competitive advantage either because the firm wants to change its strategic scope or because it needs to exploit new technologies. Firms that are predominantly in the business of continually creating new capabilities, for example, fall in this category. Firms organized to generate a stream of advantageous capabilities or positions are called "explorer" firms.[1]

Almost no firms are pure explorers or exploiters. Most firms need to be proficient at both exploration and exploitation to be successful over the long haul. Although successful firms typically have elements of both exploration and exploitation, the organization design requirements of each are sufficiently distinct that it is difficult for the same firm to be equally good at both exploring and exploiting. Indeed, most managers can readily identify whether their firm is better equipped to explore or exploit. It is then a short step to evaluating whether the explorer-exploiter mix the firm is pursuing fits its external environment and its strategy. It is sometimes easy to see, for example, that a firm's historical strength in exploiting its current market segment is preventing it from seeing and therefore, seizing, new strategic opportunities. Or a firm's continual preoccupation with catching the next wave of technology may blind it to the opportunities for more profitably exploiting its current technology. The language of "explorers" and "exploiters" therefore provides useful shorthand for evaluating the firm's approach to maintaining or changing its competitive advantage—shorthand that we will return to in later chapters. However, we emphasize that it is shorthand, and though useful as a conceptual device, most firms resemble neither extreme, but rather must both explore and exploit to be successful. In the last section we discuss the problem of combining exploration and exploitation.

## 5.2  ALIGNING STRATEGY AND ORGANIZATION

In Chapter 4, we developed the concept of ARC analysis. This framework can be used to articulate the firm's key coordination and incentive problems and to assess whether its ARC effectively addresses those challenges. However, a firm can have a consistent and elegant solution to a set of coordination and incentive problems and still have a woefully inadequate design from a strategic perspective. The design must not only "work," it must do the work that is necessary to achieve the firm's strategic goals. In particular, as suggested by Figure 5-1, it must fit with the competitive advantage at the center of the firm's strategy. When there is a good fit between the

---

[1] The terms, "explorer" and "exploiter" were coined by Jim March in "Exploration and Exploitation in Organizational Learning," *Organization Science*, 2, No. 1 (February 1991), 71–87.

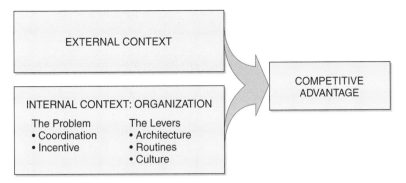

**FIGURE 5-1**    The Link between Internal Context and Competitive Advantage

firm's design and its competitive advantage, we say that the organization is "strategically aligned" with the strategy. Strategic alignment is a key strategy concept and our main focus in this section of the chapter.

As an example of strategic alignment, a firm with a competitive advantage of being the low-cost provider in its industry should have an ARC designed to achieve low costs. This type of firm might want to provide incentives that reward implementing cost-reducing process innovations and make the efficient flow of appropriate cost accounting information to key decision makers an important part of its coordination plan. It may also want to institute performance pay for its salespeople that rewards them for sales volumes, so that the firm can take advantage of production savings associated with large-scale manufacturing. If the firm is producing a commodity product like concrete, it may not be interested in customer feedback and need not be concerned about creating mechanisms for sales and manufacturing to exchange information with each other. By contrast, a firm with a competitive advantage based on time-to-market will want to provide incentives for timely design and to create an organization structure that features communication among marketing, design, and manufacturing groups. For this type of firm, information about cost control may be much less important than information about customer needs and about designs that are appropriate for rapid production.

Because organization design is complex, it is useful to have a framework for thinking through how strategic alignment might be accomplished. The framework we use, illustrated in Figure 5-2, combines the ARC Analysis introduced in Chapter 4 with the overall approach to understanding the determinants of firm performance discussed in Chapters 1–3.

As illustrated in Figure 5-2, we begin our analysis with a strategy that has a well-defined competitive advantage and then explore its organizational implications. This ordering should seem backwards, and indeed it completely reverses the logic in Figure 5-1. Up to now, we have largely taken the internal and external context of the firm as given and asked what performance-improving strategy a firm might develop to mitigate the problems and exploit the opportunities in that context. Here, we reverse this direction to ask a different question: If the manager has a strategy in mind that is

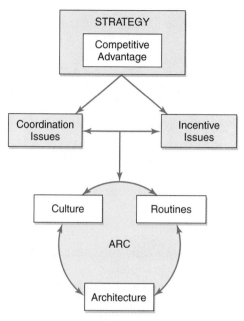

**FIGURE 5-2**   Strategic Alignment

appropriate for the firm's external context, what organization design will best enable the firm to carry out that strategy effectively?[2]

Given a clearly defined strategy, a manager must decide what coordination and incentive problems are most important if the firm is to achieve the competitive advantage its strategy requires. In what areas must the firm excel, and what behavior is most important if the firm is to meet its strategic objectives? In Figure 4-7, we presented a list of questions that the firm might ask about its coordination and incentive problems. An example on the coordination side is *"How does critical information reach the firm?"* Answering a question like this requires some way to assess what information is critical. Returning to our prior examples, a firm with a competitive advantage based on low cost might think information about productivity is most important, whereas a firm with a competitive advantage of time-to-market might think information about customer needs and competitor capabilities is most important. Similarly on the incentive side, how the manager responds to the question *"What kind of culture will support productive behavior?"* depends on knowing what behavior will best support the firm's competitive advantage. If sustaining volumes high enough to reap economies of scale is critical to the

---

[2] We should emphasize that we do not think strategies typically precede organization designs. Indeed, the more usual situation is that a firm exists and its managers are evaluating and refining—or even dramatically changing—its strategy. They may then turn to changing the organizational design, but it is only with new ventures that managers have the luxury of starting with a strategy and then building an organization. The diagram in Figure 5-2 is intended only to represent an analytic framework that allows a manager to explore how well the organization and strategy are aligned. We start with the firm's strategy because undertaking this exploration requires that the manager have a clear idea of what the strategy is.

firm's competitive advantage, having a culture that values salespeople who exceed quota is better than having a culture that values building close customer relationships.

The ARC of the firm is the manager's solution to the coordination and incentive problems implied by the firm's strategy. Because the optimal design depends on the strategy, there is no single "best" design. Managers can't simply impose some organizational template that will function well regardless of the competitive advantage the firm wants to pursue: They must go through a process like the one illustrated in Figure 5-2. Although the lack of a "one-size-fits-all" design requires that managers create a customized organization, starting with the imperatives of competitive advantage can also simplify the organizational design problem. Organizations are so complex that even the most diligent and creative manager will be unable to address all the design problems in her firm. Fortunately, it is not necessary to do that. What the manager must address effectively are those design problems that are most important for successfully supporting the firm's competitive advantage. This makes it essential to get certain aspects of organization right while making others less important.

## Applying ARC Analysis to Assess Strategic Alignment: Southwest Airlines Revisited

To show how organization is linked to competitive advantage and what is implied by getting the key aspects of design "right," we begin by returning to the Southwest Airlines example of Chapter 4. A streamlined version of Southwest's strategy statement might read something like this: "Our strategy is to provide air service unsurpassed in customer value in selected point-to-point, short-haul markets with substantial business traffic. We deliver customer value by providing reliable, low price, customer-driven service." The competitive advantage in this statement is providing business travelers with reliable, friendly service combined with a low-cost structure that allows Southwest to offer low prices. With this strategy in mind, we can revisit the ARC analysis framework to diagnose Southwest's design.

The first step is to identify the key coordination and incentive problems implied by Southwest's strategy: combining operational efficiency with outstanding customer service. Operational efficiency means using fewer resources than its competitors to deliver the same product. Outstanding customer service means meeting the needs of its target customers better than its competitors. In the top panel of Figure 5-3, we have identified some of the specific coordination problems that might be important for Southwest. More generally, the coordination issues for this competitive advantage are to design an organization that collects and uses information on customer needs effectively while implementing mechanisms to deliver efficient service and to monitor cost and service performance. The incentive problem is to build an organization that recognizes and rewards behavior that balances cost minimization and customer service. These are also illustrated in Figure 5-3.

With the key coordination and incentive problems identified, we can review Southwest's ARC to see how Southwest addresses these problems. In the lower panel of Figure 5-3, we've summarized some of the important characteristics of Southwest's organization. At Southwest, the cross-functional team responsible for a particular

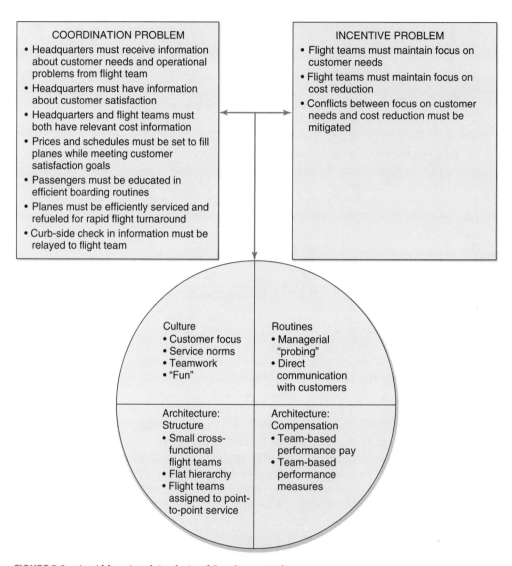

**FIGURE 5-3**   An Abbreviated Analysis of Southwest Airlines

route has most of the information necessary to make decisions that affect it. As a result, team members are well positioned to see and resolve problems that might delay flights. They control how quickly flights are turned around at the airport and how efficiently passengers are boarded and seated.

They also are the people who know most about the customers on that route and can make small changes to accommodate idiosyncratic problems that their frequent flyers might have. For example, a pilot has the discretion to return to the gate if a passenger has boarded the wrong plane. A culture that makes heroes of teams who provide exemplary service by any means necessary supports the efforts of these teams. When the teams encounter problems that they cannot solve, Southwest's flat hierarchy and the accessibility of its managers give them a way to ask for systemwide changes in policies or resource allocation that will enable them to perform better.

The teams also bear the cost of their decisions. The pilot who takes the plane back to the gate knows exactly what her action will mean for the flight's on-time arrival and what she and the rest of the team will have to do to make up for lost time. Any baggage handler who sees a bag going on the wrong plane can weigh the consequences of delaying the loading process by retrieving it. He also knows that his team members will support his decision because they, in turn, will count on his support when they need it.

These advantages of decentralization come at a cost to Southwest, however. Because teams make most decisions without needing to consult managers, less information about what is happening at the interface with the customer is automatically transmitted up the hierarchy. Yet it is vitally important that headquarters obtain this information if it is to disseminate best practice throughout the company and become aware of pervasive problems that need more centralized attention. Southwest attempts to improve information flows to headquarters in at least two ways. First, managers do a lot of "managing by walking around." By constantly probing throughout the firm, they can piece together a picture of what is happening lower down in the company.

Second, Southwest leverages its strong relationships with its customers to encourage direct communication with the company. Southwest responds carefully to customer letters (both of praise and complaint). For example, Southwest learned from customers' letters that a new policy allowing customers to get boarding cards when they checked in at the ticket desk rather than the gate annoyed its regular customers. Regular customers were used to being able to predict their seat assignments based on their time of arrival at the gate and could no longer do so. Southwest changed the policy. Headquarters also uses the examples of outstanding service it learns of through letters to reinforce that behavior throughout the firm by disseminating success stories to all employees.

Handling the coordination problem in this largely decentralized way also makes it fairly easy to resolve the incentive problem. Because many of the factors that determine customer satisfaction and operational efficiency are largely under the control of the local teams, it is easy to measure and provide incentives for that performance. Because team performance is easy to measure, Southwest can tie compensation to it. And because the teams are relatively small, each team member can expect to get a reasonable share of the reward. Finally, because the team members understand the contributions each member makes, it is difficult for any single member to violate the group norm. Shirking by individuals therefore is probably not a problem. While some of those incentives are financial, an advantage of the strong Southwest culture is that recognition by customers and other employees of outstanding performance is itself a reward.

In Chapter 4, we emphasized that sound organizational design requires organizational consistency. By this we mean that the firm must ensure that the entire design hangs together, with each element complementing the others and with no contradictions among them. For example, an organization designed to maximize the opportunities to learn from salespeople who are in direct contact with customers should probably have a fairly flat structure, so that few filtering layers get in the way of feedback from the salespeople to senior managers. It should complement the architecture with a culture of trust and commitment in which salespeople feel that it is important to share their ideas and in which they will not be punished for doing that. One would also expect to see routines in place that facilitate information flows, such as forums for regular contact between senior management and salespeople as well as routines for considering and acting on the feedback received.

A review of our ARC analysis for Southwest indicates that its organization design has this feature. The design combines a decentralized decision-making process with a production system in which almost all the information relevant to those decisions is readily and easily accessed by the teams. The incentive scheme that is based on team performance fits nicely with the decentralized decision making. Rewarding the teams based on the performance of the team as a unit encourages their members to support each other to maximize their own well-being. The flat hierarchy makes it easier for managers to get information by walking around and, in the process, to reinforce the culture of customer focus.

Consistent as Southwest's approach might be, it would simply not work for many of its competitors. Competitors that operate hub-and-spoke airlines cannot grant that much autonomy to the teams on specific routes. These firms also rely on product quality for competitive advantage, but their appeal is different. United Airlines, for example, delivers customer value by providing a large network of flights that allows passengers to reach many destinations without changing airlines. The value of this network is enhanced by frequent flyer programs that reward high mileage customers with free flights to many locations. Operational efficiency is achieved not by simplified, no frills service but by consolidating maintenance service at hubs and using the hub-and-spoke system to increase the number of passengers on each flight. Instead of offering a single, low fare, United offers a complex web of discounts that contributes to full flights and imposes higher costs on those travelers who are more willing to pay high prices. Implementing this kind of competitive advantage requires centralized decision making.

This is apparent in the problem of just getting planes in and out of airports on time. Airlines whose competitive advantage depends on an efficient hub-and-spoke system face the daunting task of coordinating disparate flights, all of which must arrive from and leave a hub within a short window of time. They achieve this coordination through a centralized process in which a small number of decision makers respond to exceptions with the aid of computer optimization programs. In this setting, the crews of particular flights are cogs in a much larger machine whose behavior is largely circumscribed by official policies and routines. No pilot will be called a hero for delaying a flight to accommodate a passenger who got on the wrong plane because the cost of that decision reverberates throughout the system. The hub-and-spoke operation creates a process-based interdependence among the units, which means that the coordination problem cannot be solved through decentralization. As a result, the incentive problem is also more complex.

## Other Examples: Sony, Apple Computer, and Silicon Graphics

The linkages between competitive advantage and organization are not, of course, unique to airlines. In Chapter 3, for example, we mentioned that Sony has a competitive advantage based on its capability of designing consumer electronics that are small and easy to make. A firm like this is an interesting contrast to one like Apple Computer whose strategy has depended on being quick to market with cutting-edge technology. A company like Apple may be willing to accept higher manufacturing cost if that buys it performance, a tradeoff that Sony would not make. These differences in focus are particularly interesting because Apple and Sony have collaborated on projects (such as some of Apple's Powerbook laptop computers), and differences in the way they are organized have led to conflicts within these cooperative ventures.[3]

Sony's miniaturization capability hinges on a set of well-defined and well-understood engineering processes that go beyond the design and development of any particular project. Sony engineers understand that once a component (e.g., a battery) has been allocated a particular space within the product (e.g., a camcorder), that space allocation is no longer negotiable. When Apple entered into a joint venture with Sony and tried to incorporate this decision-rule into the design process for its own laptop computer, Apple's managers found that it did not fit with Apple's culture, which tolerated almost any last-minute change if it led to a more "insanely great" product. Let's assume, for the sake of argument, that the ARC of each of these firms is organizationally consistent and aligned with its distinctive competitive advantage. The problems these firms had in working together successfully underscore the importance of organizational design for performance. It was difficult for Sony to allow for the kind of design changes Apple wanted to make and still perform in a manner consistent with its competitive advantage. Similarly, Apple engineers were unable to get some of the design features they felt made Apple products so appealing to its customers when they were forced to adhere to the design-process guidelines Sony imposed.

Similarly, a company whose competitive advantage depends, at least in part, on rapid time-to-market must adapt its routines to that strategy. Silicon Graphics, for example, has attempted to compete by being the first to market with state-of-the-art technology in high-end computer workstations. Pursuing this form of competitive advantage creates a tension for the design engineers. Being state-of-the-art requires being flexible about technology because the firm needs to incorporate the most current developments in every product. On the other hand, being first to market requires efficient manufacturing. Unfortunately, efficient manufacturing is often at odds with being flexible enough to incorporate the latest technology. Consequently, Silicon Graphics was forced to create routines and linkages between design and manufacturing to coordinate activity, so that designs did not need to be "frozen" until late in the design process, but once "frozen" could be quickly manufactured.

---

[3] See Saloner, Garth, and Hank Chesbrough, "Apple Computer in the Portable Computer Market (A) and (B)," Stanford Business School, S-SM-1 and S-SM-2, April 1992.

## 5.3  BUILDING AND CREATING COMPETITIVE ADVANTAGE

The framework summarized in Figure 5-2 works well when the firm's competitive advantage is clearly defined and the firm has or can readily acquire the resources necessary to pursue it. But achieving competitive advantage is not a static goal. Even if the firm's strategy doesn't change, the behavior of its competitors usually forces it to refine and deepen its competitive advantage. A low-cost firm today will not be low cost tomorrow unless it can continually improve its production and distribution processes to stay one step ahead of competitors. Wal-Mart's computerized supply chain management system was a huge competitive advantage when it pioneered this kind of system. These systems, however, are now more widely used, and Wal-Mart has had to improve its system and its other supply chain management processes to retain a cost advantage.

As a firm's environment changes or as it becomes aware of new opportunities, it may also want to create new forms of competitive advantage. Sometimes the change is forced on the firm by evolution within its industry or by changes elsewhere in the economy. Sometimes the change is created within the firm as it discovers a way to serve customers it had not reached before, or new channels for distributing its goods, or new technologies that allow it to fundamentally change its product offerings. We want to focus on the organizational implications of such changes in competitive advantage. Our shift in focus is illustrated in Figure 5-4, where we reproduce Figure 5-2 with the addition of arrows flowing from ARC back to competitive advantage.

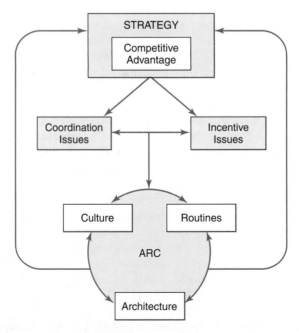

**FIGURE 5-4**    Strategic Alignment Implications

As the examples suggest, competitive advantage is dynamic in two senses. First, firms must continually develop and deepen current advantage if they are to meet the challenge of competition. Second, over time the firm may want to alter its strategy to pursue some other form of competitive advantage. As we stated in the introduction, we refer to the first kind of activity as "exploiting" a competitive advantage and the second as "exploring" new competitive advantages. Although every firm must engage in both of these activities, the extent to which a firm emphasizes one or the other varies. There are firms whose approach more closely resembles that of "exploiters," and others who are more like "explorers." Often the environment dictates which mode will be more successful. In a mature, stable industry, for example, exploitation may be more important for superior performance. In an industry buffeted by substantive technological or competitive change, more exploration might be optimal.

These two types of activities have very different organizational requirements. The ARC that supports exploitation is distinct from the ARC that supports exploration. Since the typical firm must both explore and exploit, doing both poses a big managerial challenge. Managers must find a way to incorporate two different sets of organizational demands within the same firm. To make this challenge concrete, we begin by treating the two extreme forms: pure explorers (that concentrate on developing new sources of competitive advantage) and pure exploiters (that concentrate on reinforcing current advantage). After examining the constellations of organizational design elements that are best suited to each of these types, we return to the issue of trying to pursue both in a single organization.

## Explorers and Exploiters

Exploiters and explorers follow different business models. Since the exploiter model is predicated on continually improving the firm's products and how they are delivered, that approach can be described as "doing better what we already do." Exploiters have a well-defined domain in which they operate, and they focus on occupying that domain more successfully. They perform well to the extent that they can stay ahead of competitors. This is a standard approach to achieving the kind of sustainable competitive advantage discussed in Chapter 3. Firms that compete on the basis of low cost in competitive, mature industries are usually exploiter firms. Since the industry is mature, so is the technology of production in the industry, and the firms that cannot produce at the lowest possible costs cannot survive. A good exploiter is a firm that sticks to its knitting and knits well.

Explorer firms, in contrast, hope to prosper by finding completely novel ways of doing things, rather than doing the same things a little better. They worry about the needs of new customer segments, emerging market opportunities, and how to leverage the firm's resources in completely new ways. Rather than doing better in a given domain, these firms strive to change domains. If, for example, we compare two firms that manufacture television screens, an exploiter is likely to concentrate on improving resolution, performance, and cost of conventional TV monitors while an explorer would devote its resources to investigating flat panel displays in current and potential markets. To perform well, explorers must achieve substantial first-mover advantage. They prosper by seeing opportunities first and rapidly deploying the resources necessary to seize them. These firms are adept at developing new forms of competitive advantage and then moving on before imitators can chip away at their position.

A useful analogy that we will use repeatedly in this section is to think of the firm as a mountain climber whose goal is to climb as high as it can. Broadly speaking, the firm has a couple of options. One is to devote all its energy to climbing as high as it can up the mountain it is on now. This would involve climbing as efficiently as possible and, to the extent that the firm spends time planning and scouting, to direct that effort toward finding the best possible route up the mountain it is on. Another approach is to spend some energy and resources climbing the current mountain, but to focus on scouting other mountains in case there are higher and/or more easily climbed mountains. Clearly, the former is an exploiter and the latter an explorer.

Explorers and exploiters should, and do, have different learning behaviors. Exploiters focus on understanding more about an established terrain. They tend to display lots of incremental innovation in products and processes. The questions that guide the organization's learning originate from what it already does well and would like to do better. So, for example, a manufacturing facility might look for ways to shave a few pennies off its unit production costs, and a software development operation might focus on refining routines for documenting changes in requirements. Resources are devoted to understanding all the possible routes up the mountain and ways of covering each mountain face with less effort. These activities tend to keep the firm within the domain of the technologies, products, and customers with which it is familiar. They typically focus on serving their existing customers' needs well and on beating their current competitors.

The continual improvement methods used by Japanese automobile manufacturers in the 1980s (collectively termed the *kaizen* method) are an example of learning well suited to exploiter firms. Firms learn in the *kaizen* method by developing processes and structures that leverage the insights of the workers directly involved in the manufacturing process. Quality circles whose members are production workers are used to discover ways to improve manufacturing reliability. This kind of activity is focused on doing somewhat better what the firm is already doing. A quality circle would not be expected, for example, to propose an entirely different product or a completely novel production methodology. Rather, its focus is on improving its existing processes and products. By pointing out that an automobile headlight is sometimes damaged when the grille is put in, for example, the workers might try to see if it is possible to reverse the order of headlight and grille assembly. In this way the *kaizen* model emphasizes the power of hundreds of small incremental improvements to add up to a dramatic quality improvement or cost reduction.

Explorer firms pursue different learning paths and objectives. They go after innovations that are likely to take them outside the domains they currently occupy. They spend resources on understanding the needs of clients for whom their current products have no appeal. They encourage engineers to experiment freely with new product ideas or new ways to produce. The old Bell Labs that AT&T operated when it had a regulated monopoly on U.S. telephone service is an example of the kind of R&D facility one would expect to see at an explorer firm. Researchers there were given broad license to explore whatever avenue they thought would lead to interesting technology even when it would not be immediately useful in telephony, the company's core product line. Semiconductors were invented there in the late 1940s but were not widely used in AT&T products until the 1970s. The 3M Corporation has also been cited as a model for this kind of learning. 3M's domain has been defined broadly, and it has a history of funding product research and development for which the final application is uncertain.

One way to understand the different learning modes is to think through one of the classic models of organization learning: variation, selection, and retention (VSR). In the VSR model, successful innovations start with lots of variation. In our mountain-climbing analogy, the best way to climb higher is to collect information on many possible paths to the top of the mountain. The more paths that are explored, the more likely it is that the best path to the top will be among them. Selection occurs when the organization applies some criteria for selecting among the possible paths. In our analogy, the selection criterion is based on getting to the top while expending as few resources as are necessary to make the climb. Once the path is selected, retention occurs when the organization establishes mechanisms for ensuring that everyone stays on the selected path and moves along it expeditiously.

For example, the VSR framework can be used to help us understand how British Petroleum (BP) approached the problem of learning to drill for oil in a radically different environment than it had previously. In the 1970s, the firm had substantial experience in land-based petroleum extraction. It had gotten very good at locating and extracting oil within this familiar domain. But it now faced the problem of drilling for oil beneath the rough, cold waters of the North Sea. Dry-land extraction techniques were not well suited to this new problem. To develop new tools and techniques, the company engaged in a series of experiments designed to test a wide variety of approaches. That is, the company deliberately fostered *variation*. As the results of the experiments came in, BP had to find a way to *select* among the various approaches. Some tools or techniques clearly failed, but others were at least moderately successful and the company needed to develop routines for choosing among them. These routines required applying performance measures *and* deciding who got to make the final decisions. How much weight should be given to the engineers who ran the experiments? How much to engineers more familiar with the company's needs in other areas?

BP's solution was to allow its business unit managers to make independent judgments about which approach(es) to adopt. Although this approach allowed the firm to tailor the extraction process to the local drilling environments, it opened up the possibility that some of the knowledge it had created would be "lost." Organizational learning *(retention)* occurs when the knowledge is incorporated into the accepted ways of doing things; knowledge must be codified and disseminated through the firm if it is to contribute to the firm's capabilities. To retain innovations in an organization with decentralized decision making, BP relies on a sophisticated information technology system and a culture that support the development of personal networks among its employees.

An important difference between explorers and exploiters can be seen at the variation stage. Exploiters investigate paths on the current mountain, while explorers collect information on several mountains. If these two types search out exactly the same number of paths, the exploiter will have a better chance of finding the best way up one mountain. The explorer is less likely to find the best path up any one mountain but may find a better mountain to climb. Because the explorer looks at more mountains, the paths it investigates will have more variation. Given infinite resources applied to the problem, the explorer will do at least as well as the exploiter and will probably find a better path, that is, a path that reaches a higher altitude at less cost.[4] With limited resources, the odds that the explorer will find a better path depend on how good the exploiter's mountain is relative to all the other mountains the explorer might discover.

If the explorer organization has an advantage in the variation stage, the exploiter is better positioned for selection and retention. It will be much easier for the exploiter to figure out which of the various paths before it is the best path because it knows more about the topology of its mountain than the explorer has about the topology of the several mountains it is exploring. The exploiter faces less uncertainty. It also will find it easier to move its organization along the selected path because the organization itself is on familiar terrain. The climbers probably already have much of the equipment and training they will need. The explorer may have to invest substantial amounts in training and equipment to climb a mountain it has never encountered before.

These two business models and the forms of learning typically associated with them are supported best by different architectures, routines, and cultures. Many specific elements of ARC tend to be different in exploiters and explorers, but most of these differences are examples of just three main dimensions in which exploiters and explorers differ: the degree of interdependence among the organization's activities; the extent to which the process of change is centrally controlled; and the share of resources the firm devotes to activities outside its core domain. We discuss each of these dimensions in turn below and then describe what they mean for the ARC of exploiters and explorers.

## Interdependence and Tight-Coupling

One important way in which organization designs differ is in the degree of interdependence they create among the various subunits of the firm. In Chapter 4 we introduced the terms "tightly coupled" and "loosely coupled" to describe the degree of interdependence among the subunits of an organization.

---

[4] It might be helpful to think about this process in a different way as drawing balls from urns. Each ball has a number on it, and the objective is to get a high number. The balls are divided randomly among many urns. The exploiter draws from one urn, and the explorer draws from many. Unless the exploiter's urn happens to contain the ball with the highest number, the explorer will eventually get a higher draw than the highest possible draw from the exploiters urn. The explorer's draws have more variance and are therefore more likely to result in very high (and very low) numbers.

The amount of interdependence among a firm's units is often a logical consequence of the strategy the firm is following. For example, compare the order completion process at a company like Dell that makes personal computers to order and sells directly to final customers with a company that manufactures a standardized line of computers and sells them to final customers through independent retailers. At Dell, because there are many possible configurations of computers and each is produced to order, all the elements of the process are highly interdependent. The parts must be available as soon as the order is received. Someone must be available to do the testing as soon as the computer is assembled. If an error is found, assembly must be quickly rescheduled to correct the defect. Shipping services must be immediately available when the machine is ready to go. This high degree of interdependence calls for a tightly coupled organization design: The customer order process, production scheduling, testing, and shipping departments all need to be tightly coupled if customers are to be served expeditiously. In contrast, a computer assembler producing a narrower line in much larger batches can rely on inventories to buffer any difference between order flow and operations. So, for example, production can be scheduled largely independently of product shipping because this type of computer assembler ships from finished goods inventories. It can effectively use a loosely coupled design.

Note that in this example the amount of interdependence among the firms' units is not the result of their product's characteristics because the basic technology of the product is the same for both types of computer assemblers. Instead, it is the result of how the companies have chosen to pursue competitive advantage. Dell's strategy is to sell direct, offering knowledgeable buyers lots of options without long delivery lags. Firms selling into retail channels typically sell to less technologically sophisticated buyers who have neither the knowledge nor the inclination to purchase a customized machine direct from the manufacturer. The difference in the approach to selling computers is reflected in a difference in organizational design, and tight coupling in particular. This is, indeed, another example of alignment between organization design and strategy.

As suggested in Chapter 4, many elements of ARC can contribute to more or less independence among a firm's units and hence to how tightly coupled they are. An organization structure based on functional units will usually display tighter coupling than one based on divisional units. A firm that invests resources in creating and maintaining linking mechanisms will display tighter coupling. Organizations with central routines that require tightly integrated processing—such as those that Dell has for handling customer orders—will exhibit tighter coupling, as will those whose cultures foster cooperation and good communication.

There are both advantages and disadvantages to tightly coupled designs. A tightly coupled organization is more at risk from the poor performance of a single subunit. A production process that uses just-in-time production with only minimal work-in-progress inventory, for example, can perform only as well as its least efficient unit. If one production unit falls behind temporarily, the others have no stocks of work-in-progress to fall back on and no final inventory to shield customers from the disruption. Similarly, when each unit has its own sales force, it is less affected by poor customer relations when another subunit treats a customer badly that both units share. On the other hand, the reputation for extraordinary customer service created by one subunit is equally unlikely to enhance the position of the other. Loosely coupled organizations are likely to have more redundancy than tightly coupled ones. Having multiple sales forces is a clear example of this. A tightly coupled organization is better suited to using a common resource because it has mechanisms to coordinate the sharing of resources. Similarly, it is also more likely to make use of best practice across geographies or other subunits.

The main point here is that both the tight- and loose-coupling forms can be part of consistent organizations and the degree of interdependence is a design variable for the managers of the firm. How tightly coupled the firm should be depends on its strategy and, in particular, on how it pursues competitive advantage.

Although exploiter firms can have strategies that make loose coupling of some or all of its organizational units optimal, they are usually more effective when they have a tightly coupled organization. One reason for this is that exploiter firms typically depend on efficiency for at least part of their competitive advantage and therefore want to avoid the redundancy often associated with loosely coupled organizations. Strong interdependence also allows the firm to exploit any economies of scale and replicate best practice effectively. The kind of learning pursued by an exploiter firm that is intent on deepening its competitive advantage is also well suited to a high degree of interdependence. Small, incremental changes are less likely to require substantial adjustments in other, interdependent parts of the firm. For these reasons, exploiter firms often view effective organization design as something that leads to a well-oiled machine that runs like clockwork. They deploy every possible resource to reach the well-understood objectives of the firm, each unit carrying out its own piece of the master plan. When changes are made, they are either "local" and do not affect other units, or companywide but with effects that are simple and predictable. When the adaptations required of several, interdependent units can be easily described, they also can be readily communicated through the formal and informal linking mechanisms that are in place to achieve interdependence.

Explorer firms, on the other hand, are likely to see advantages in at least some loose coupling. The extensive change necessary to create new competitive advantage is often better facilitated by a loosely coupled design. Loose coupling is beneficial because the outcome of any particular exploration is uncertain. When a unit is tightly coupled to others, it cannot explore on its own; it requires the cooperation of other units. The more that others in the organization must be induced to participate in the project, the less likely the project is to succeed. Other units may either have a different perception of the merits of the undertaking or may even stand to lose (albeit less than the organization gains) from its success. The broader the participation, the more likely that some conflict of interest will foster an internal political struggle within the organization. This can increase both the cost to the organization of pursuing the opportunity and the probability that the project will fail from a lack of wholehearted participation.

Explorers also tend to be loosely coupled so that parts of the organization can experiment without having to be concerned with how their experimentation will affect other highly interdependent parts of the firm. In tightly coupled firms, by contrast, not only must the exploratory venture obtain the cooperation of other groups within the firm, but its failure can negatively affect all of them. Even if it is eventually successful, the venture may interfere with the efficient operation of many other parts of the firm while it is being pursued. To return to the mountain-climbing metaphor, when all the climbers are roped together, no individual climber can undertake independent exploratory action without endangering the well-being of all the other climbers. It might be better to untie the exploration team from the rest of the expedition.

## Organizational Slack

Organizations also vary in how much discretion they allow subunits. In some organizations, optimal performance requires that each unit fully commit its resources to reaching operational objectives. Indeed, we commonly think of "efficient" organizations as those that fully commit their resources to specified activities and seek productivity gains by wringing out waste. In this way of thinking, an efficient design is one in which resources are directed to specific, well-articulated objectives. These objectives may be established centrally or through some development process undertaken jointly by central and unit managers. However the objectives are established, all managers share them and understand that the firm's resources are to be devoted to them.

Although this is one efficient design, the resources of the firm can also be fully and efficiently utilized without common understanding of the precise way they are to be used. That is, the firm may choose to allow the unit managers complete discretion over how to deploy at least some of those resources. When resources are allocated in this way, the firm's goal is to give employees the time and resources to experiment, learn, research, think, and reflect. The rationale for this kind of investment is that it will eventually benefit the firm, though perhaps not in a way that directly affects its current performance. When funds are explicitly allocated in this way, the firms are choosing to operate with some organizational "slack." The term "slack" here does not connote waste; rather, it represents an investment in innovation and change that cannot be immediately tied to the unit's current performance.

An example of slack is a practice at 3M called "bootlegging" in which researchers are granted 15% of their work time to pursue projects of their own choosing. They are allowed this time to undertake research activities that cannot be rationalized in terms of 3M's current competitive advantage. Indeed, any useful output from these projects is likely to be outside the firm's current domain. 3M researchers have produced some of the company's important innovations (the Post-It note may be the most famous example) during their bootlegging time. Other examples of organizational slack include paying a salesperson to develop relationships with customers who have no need for the firm's existing products; providing sabbaticals to employees to pursue their own intellectual development; or sending employees to an executive education program to acquire general management skills.

Any of these "slack" activities might lead to new insights into profitable opportunities the firm might pursue, but the outcome is highly uncertain. More importantly, they are unlikely to produce the kind of incremental learning necessary for successful exploitation. For firms intent on exploiting current competitive advantage, organizational slack is unproductive. Their focus is concentrated on what they already do; experimentation that might take them far afield is not only not useful, it also wastes resources that could be put to better use within the firm's current focus. Consequently, these firms do not need organizational slack. Explorers, on the other hand, embrace organizational slack. Because non-routine or non-incremental innovations and learning often arise out of slack elements of an organization, explorers devote a relative abundance of assets to giving individuals and units the freedom to experiment and search for new ways of doing things. If the mountain climbers don't get the time to get off the current mountain, they will never discover other mountains!

Slack activities are nearly always only loosely coupled with the other activities in the organization. What a researcher does on her "own" time is, by intent, not closely connected with other activities she or others in the organization pursue as part of their contribution to the firm's current competitive advantage. While slack implies some loose coupling, the reverse claim does not hold: loose coupling does not imply organizational slack. Two units can be independent of each other, and yet each of their resources can be fully committed to specific operational objectives.

## Central Direction

Organizations also vary in the extent to which their activities intended to produce change are centrally directed and coordinated. Exploiter firms are more likely to exercise centralized control of change because the cost of centralized decision making is lower for them than it is for explorer firms and the benefits are higher. The benefit of coordination is that the firm's resources can be systematically applied to move in the direction determined by central managers. A mountain-climbing team with a well-defined route will be more efficient when each member of the team knows her role and has the kinds and amount of resources she needs to fulfill it. The cost of centralization is the risk that the entire organization may be headed in the wrong direction, but this risk is relatively low for exploiter firms. They have been climbing this mountain for some time and can make well-informed choices about what kind of investments are likely to be productive.

The benefits to central coordination of change are especially high for exploiters when their operations are also tightly coupled. If changes in one part of the organization require changes in another, activities have to be coordinated. One can easily imagine a situation, for example, in which several changes made simultaneously could dramatically improve firm performance, but any of these changes made unilaterally would actually impair it. When a different unit must undertake each change, it is unlikely that all the changes will be made simultaneously or in the right sequence without some coordination. Centralized direction of resources is a particularly effective way to accomplish this.

Note that centralized control of change-oriented activities does not mean that exploiter firms maintain tight central control of all activities. Quite the contrary. Within the current domain, most of the activities pursued by exploiter firms require careful implementation of a stable strategy. As a result, these firms can delegate many routine matters. This delegation promotes efficient operation within the firm's domain and allows the senior managers to devote their attention to ensuring that any incremental changes are made in appropriate directions and are implemented in a coordinated fashion.

Central direction of change-oriented activities is much more problematic in explorer firms. For these firms, the direction of change is less certain, and benefits can accrue from allowing units to pursue independent paths. While central direction of resources does not *necessarily* imply that all units operate within the current domain, central direction is often the enemy of exploration in practice. Managers responsible for central direction inevitably have opinions about which directions might be more fruitfully pursued, and those beliefs are likely to affect which exploratory projects the firm approves. Consequently, when resources are centrally directed, the range of exploratory activities is likely to be narrower. When resource allocation for change activities is decentralized, there is less risk that the entire organization will pursue the same, necessarily risky, path.

The experience of McDonald's fast-food chain illustrates the effect of centralized direction of change. Change in the form of new product introductions and marketing innovations is essential for McDonald's to build and maintain competitive advantage. For various reasons, the McDonald's chain of fast-food outlets includes locations that are owned and operated by McDonald's employees and locations that are owned and managed by independent franchisees. Innovations introduced at the company-owned outlets are initiated and directed by the senior managers at McDonald's. At outlets owned by franchisees, the independent managers can (within the limits of their franchise agreement) experiment on their own. As our discussion of the strengths and weaknesses of centralized direction suggests, the franchised locations as a group are more innovative than the company-owned locations. Each franchisee tries things the central development group would not attempt and, since there are many independent franchisees, the range of innovations they produce is much larger than that initiated by the corporate office.

## The ARC of Explorers and Exploiters

As we have argued, and as illustrated in Table 5.1, exploiters tend to rely on incremental learning and therefore typically devote more resources to the selection and retention stages of learning and less to generating variance compared to explorers. They typically have less organizational slack, are more tightly coupled, and have more centralized direction than do explorers. These differences have profound implications for the overall ARC that will be most effective for each of these two types of firms. Perhaps the most obvious difference is in the architectural structure of the organization. Because exploiters are more tightly coupled and centralized, they typically have stronger linking mechanisms and a more hierarchical decision making process.

Explorers and exploiters are also likely to have different cultures. An exploiter organization is tightly focused and task-oriented. It has low tolerance for tardiness because the high degree of interdependence means that each task dovetails with oth-

**TABLE 5-1**   Explorer and Exploiter Profiles

| Characteristic | Exploiters | Explorers |
| --- | --- | --- |
| Interdependence among units | Tightly coupled | Loosely coupled |
| Discretionary resources | No organizational slack | Substantial organizational slack |
| Direction of change-activities | Centralized | Decentralized |
| Learning mode | Incremental within the defined domain | Outside the defined domain |
| Environmental fit | Well suited to stable environments | Well suited to rapidly changing environments |

ers. Hitting targets is culturally ingrained, and the firm's stories emphasize extraordinary feats of execution (the team that pulled out all the stops to get the product to the customer on time, for example). In contrast, employees at explorer organizations feel—and are—less tightly programmed. Risk-taking is encouraged, and failure is tolerated. Stories focus on the deviant behavior or extraordinary creativity that led to huge, unanticipated success. These types of firms make heroes of the employee who figured out a use (Post-its) for an apparently inadequate adhesive; or the employee who, contrary to protocol, licked his finger, discovered that the white powder on which he was working was sweet, and figured out that he had a new artificial sweetener (NutraSweet)—literally—on his hands.

Explorers and exploiters also differ in their hiring practices. Explorers need employees with a high tolerance for ambiguity and who value the process of searching for new ideas or technologies in their own right. In Silicon Valley, for example, engineers often distinguish companies and their projects in terms of a "coolness" factor. A "cool" project involves novel, cutting-edge technology, and its commercial success is often far from certain. Engineers drawn to cool projects are often less interested in the more meticulous, detailed development work that is necessary once a cool project is successfully transformed into a commercial product. Similarly, among the Web development firms clustered "South of Market" in San Francisco, the organizational cultures of the start-ups favor speed, creativity, novelty, and flair and are often (deliberately) located in old brick warehouses with exposed wooden beams rather than in more staid physical surroundings.

Exploiters have more pervasive monitoring systems and well-defined accountability because interdependencies heighten the consequences of failures-to-perform. Incentives are closely tied to specified tasks. Exploiters have numerous routines, finely honed from years of continual improvement, that ensure that all the interdependent entities are properly coordinated. In contrast, in explorer firms, incentives recognize and reward innovation. Time allocations are much less closely monitored. The firm's routines focus less on managing interdependencies among known tasks and more on identifying and developing the innovations that flow from projects. If an explorer is to harvest the fruits of its exploration, it must have routines and structures that inform management about the innovations that are produced. Their ARC must include a process both for assessing how the innovations might interact with the developments elsewhere in the firm, or might point to an entirely new direction, and for evaluating their market potential.

As should be clear by now, the distinct explorer and exploiter business models lead to firms with different competencies. Neither approach is always better. Here again the mountain-climbing analogy is useful. The exploiter will get higher up the current mountain than will the explorer because an exploiter devotes all its energy to climbing that mountain. Consequently, if the mountain being climbed is the best mountain, the exploiter will do better than the explorer. However, if a perfect mountain is just half a mile away, the exploiter will never find it, whereas the explorer may find it and then will quickly climb higher. The exploiter will outperform the explorer within a given realm of existing activity, but the explorer will do better if changing domains proves to be fruitful.

Managers who are introduced to the explorer–exploiter distinction can readily tell which label better describes their firm (or at least their part of the firm). That is the strength of the explorer–exploiter concept. By understanding the firm's explorer and exploiter competencies and organizational underpinnings, the manager is better able to predict how the firm will perform at maintaining and changing its competitive advantage over time. He will recognize the competencies the firm's organization gives to its pursuit of competitive advantage. He will also understand the limitations those competencies create for the realm of activities in which the firm is weak.

For example, managers in exploiter firms often lament that it is always the firm's competitors that first seize new opportunities that (with hindsight) their own firm ought to have captured. They will even sometimes complain that they had the same idea themselves but couldn't get the attention of, or resources from, more senior mangers to develop it. It is little consolation to them to know that the firm missed the opportunity not because it is badly managed, but because *it is well managed to operate within its current domain.* By focusing well on its current domain, a well-managed exploiter inevitably misses opportunities. Conversely, managers in explorer organizations will lament that other firms reap the benefits of their innovations while they watch their original dominant market share dwindle. Again the fact that this fate is part of the firm's destiny (and strength) as an explorer does not necessarily ease their pain.

Knowing why the firm is behaving as it is may not make the firm's deficiencies easier to swallow, but it is an important first step in diagnosis and change. A manager who knows, for example, that the firm's success at exploitation makes it weak in exploration is more likely to think about when exploitation alone is likely to fail the firm than a manager who is unaware of the problem. He may be more attuned to changes in the environment that portend a weakened competitive position because competitors have opened new domains than a manager who has no idea that new domains are possible. He also may devote resources to some exploration, while maintaining the focus on the firm's current domain. To do this effectively, he will need to find some way to combine exploration and exploitation within the same firm. In the next section, we turn to the problems he is likely to encounter in this effort.

## 5.4  COMBINING EXPLORATION AND EXPLOITATION

If both exploration and exploitation have advantages, it is natural to think about doing both. Why can't a firm have the best of both worlds and be the consummate explorer and the most efficient exploiter? The reason is that it is hard to be good at both; the optimal organizational designs consistent with each approach are so different. One is loosely coupled, the other tightly coupled. One embraces organizational slack, the other deploys all its resources to explicit ends. As already discussed, the organizational implications go beyond these differences to include many other elements of ARC. The very organizational design elements that make firms good at exploiting are likely to inhibit exploring, and vice versa. Consequently, no firm can be a world-class exploiter and explorer at the same time.

However, pure explorer and pure exploiter firms are unlikely to survive over the long haul. Firms may, for example, be successful at exploiting a current competitive advantage within a stable environment for many years. Inevitably, however, the environment will change to make that competitive advantage no longer advantageous. Other firms catch up, or the landscape changes. Anticipating this eventuality, and perhaps wanting to be in the forefront of any change that promises new opportunities, most exploiter firms devote some resources to exploratory activities. Similarly, a pure explorer is unlikely to be successful. Once an explorer discovers something new, it generally will want to become pretty good at it. It is nice to come up with the Post-It note, but once you have it, you want to make the most of it—to exploit it, in fact. If the firm is not good at exploiting its innovation, imitators will eventually overtake it.

There are only two ways to survive, even in the medium term, as a pure explorer. One way is if the innovations the firm creates are protected by some barrier to imitation of the kind discussed in Chapter 3 that prevent more efficient exploiters from taking over the market. If the firm continues to explore, however, most of the new opportunities it uncovers will probably not enjoy these kinds of barriers. Generally, sustainable competitive advantage requires some investment by the firm, the kind of investment in which exploiter firms are proficient. The other path along which a pure explorer might find some success is to enjoy its first-mover advantage for as long as it can and then move on to the next venture. For example, 3M recently divested a division that manufactured floppy disks, blank VHS tapes, and similar products because this division performed poorly under 3M's management. As these markets became commodity markets with many competitors, 3M's first-mover advantage deteriorated, and the burden of inefficient operations became unsupportable. It is therefore not coincidental that pure explorer firms are rare. Those who have explored successfully but have failed at exploiting the fruits of their exploration have long since disappeared. Either they have failed, or, as with many biotechnology firms, they have been acquired by successful established firms with the capabilities necessary for exploitation.

Since it is difficult for a firm to survive as either a pure explorer or a pure exploiter, the issue, then, is how a firm can combine elements of both. For a variety of reasons, this is perhaps even more difficult than excelling at either pure form. However, while challenging, it is the job of senior management to develop and nurture an ARC that enables the firm to chart a course between the extremes. Generally, this requires navigating gray areas in which both exploration and exploitation are prized.

To accomplish this, a firm must build a culture that fits both exploration and exploitation. It is difficult, however, for the same firm to make heroes of both renegade explorers and consummate exploiters. To the employees who are devoted to exploitation, the explorers look like reckless adventurers who depend on luck and live off the hard work of the exploiters in the firm. The exploiters also know that if these adventurers succeed, they might endanger the careers of the exploiters. The explorers, on the other hand, have little sympathy for the processes on which exploiters depend. They tend to view exploiters as unduly bound to old ways of seeing the world and blind to the opportunities that lie all around. Although it might be clear what culture to prescribe for explorers or exploiters, it is more difficult for a culture to support a hybrid organization because its norms and values must tolerate more ambiguity. Managing a hybrid organization requires a culture that allows diversity.

The architecture of the firm also must support both exploratory and exploitative activity. Within most firms, there are many units that are basically exploiters in their approach. Though focused on exploitation, occasionally these units will nonetheless spawn new opportunities that could open up new domains for the firm. Often it is middle managers who must recognize and bring forward the new opportunities that arise out of the work of their units. The advantage of giving this responsibility to these managers is that they are the managers most familiar with what their units have produced; other managers may have no way to recognize the new development. The problem is that the same managers who are charged with exploitation are also responsible for nurturing exploration. If they are to do both, the rewards for these activities must be carefully balanced. If the rewards to exploration are too high, achieving consistently superior exploitation will be difficult because managers will focus on exploration. On the other hand, if all of the focus is on performing well at exploitation, managers will have no incentive to champion good ideas that might take the firm into new domains.

Although making managers responsible for both exploitation and exploration is the most common approach, some firms separate responsibility for these functions. They have people in some units focused on exploitation, while others, usually in senior management, focus on exploration. A related approach is to concentrate the responsibility for exploration within one functional unit. In many firms, the business development function has responsibility for overseeing and nurturing the firm's exploration. The advantage of separating exploratory and exploitative behavior is that some units can focus on exploiting within the firm's current domain without being distracted by exploration, while others are responsible for scouting out new possible domains without having to sustain the firm's current competitive advantage.

Even when responsibility is separated in this way, neither senior management nor the business development group conducts much of the actual exploration themselves. Instead, their responsibility is to scan the firm for promising new developments and assess the opportunities they represent. Scanning the firm is productive because even units that are pure exploiters in their intent will learn serendipitously outside their current domain. This especially occurs in technology-driven organizations in which R&D directed at one problem often unexpectedly yields fruitful results for another. However, in pure exploiter organizations, such opportunities will tend to be lost because everyone is so focused on exploitation that they pay little attention to learning that might take them outside the current domain. An active and perceptive business development group or group of senior managers can try to capture and mold those opportunities.

Some firms have gone even further and have attempted to divide their exploration and exploitation activities between different divisions. One firm renowned for following the divisional solution to the problem is the Xerox Corporation with its Palo Alto Research Center (PARC). Although Xerox was highly focused on the photocopier market, Xerox PARC was given resources to indulge in a wide variety of research activities not explicitly related to photocopiers. Moreover, the researchers were also given the freedom to pursue research of their own interests without any master plan of where the research would take the company. This investment in organizational slack was extraordinarily productive. Many of the innovations that characterized the PC revolution originated at Xerox PARC, including the mouse and the graphical user interface that inspired the Apple Macintosh and, indirectly, Microsoft's Windows-based operating system. Xerox PARC also produced the ethernet, one of the key initial systems from which the current Internet developed. It seems unlikely that Xerox Parc would have achieved this rich array of innovation if its engineers had been asked to focus on the demands of Xerox's competitive advantage in photocopying.

At first blush, it seems that Xerox was able to be both a good exploiter in photocopying and a good explorer in other domains. However, it is not enough for a firm that is good at exploitation in its current domain simply to explore in others. It must also be able to reap the benefits of that exploration. Although Xerox PARC produced many incredibly valuable innovations, Xerox Corporation rarely captured the value of these innovations. Instead, it let firms like Apple exploit the innovations. Xerox's inability to capture value from these innovations was not a result of poor management. Rather, it arose precisely because Xerox was so well managed and well designed to exploit the domain of copiers. The research outputs at Xerox PARC were not useful for Xerox's current competitive advantage, and Xerox had no structures or processes in place to capture value from activities that were far afield from its current domain. Indeed, only because Xerox was extremely successful in the copier business did it have the luxury of supporting unrelated exploratory activity that produced little benefit for the firm.

The point here is twofold. First, firms need both to exploit and explore if they are to perform well over the long run. Second, it is not enough for a firm that is good at exploiting its current advantage also to be good at discovering potentially profitable new domains. The firm must also find a way to exploit these opportunities by integrating them into the firm's strategy. Xerox had a well-defined strategy in copiers, but it had no way to alter or extend its strategy to exploit the opportunities Xerox PARC developed. In the language of the variation-selection-retention model introduced earlier, Xerox PARC was superb at generating variation, but Xerox had no mechanisms to select among the many promising developments and no way to exploit (retain) them. The challenge managers face is both to explore and to exploit within the same firm *and* to make the strategic changes necessary to reap the benefits from exploration.

## 5.5  COSTS OF ORGANIZATIONAL CHANGE

Before moving on we want to note that undertaking organizational change that might help deepen or change a firm's competitive advantage has costs as well as benefits. The costs can be of two types. First, the uncertainty employees are exposed to when the organization is changed tends to lead to lower productivity and increased turnover during the transition. No matter how well designed the process of change might be, it takes time for people to understand and come to terms with how new incentives will be implemented, how new routines will be specified, and how new values will be enacted. Second, the overall organization will probably go through a period in which the design is worse than it was before the change was undertaken. It is difficult—if not impossible—to alter several elements of an organization at once if only because some aspects of the organization are easier to change than others. To return to the transportation metaphor, the new road system may be much better than the old, but while the roads are torn up to build the new system, traffic conditions deteriorate. All organization change takes time, and periods of transition when things do not work well are inevitable. Some changes take longer than others. Architectural elements typically can be changed more quickly than routines and culture. This also means that the disruption to operations is more intense when the firm needs to change several elements because the firm must then endure a period when some of the new design is in place, but the other elements have not yet adjusted.

Although we have argued that a firm must be organized to accommodate both continual exploitation and exploration, we do not mean that a company should be continuously changing its organization design. While organization change is sometimes necessary, it also has both coordination and incentive effects that should not be underestimated. At least in the short term, change will tend to disrupt coordination. Because change requires that individuals figure out new ways to address old tasks and solve new ones, coordination will be more difficult in moving to a new design. Moreover, if change within an organization continues over an extended period, it is likely to weaken incentives by eroding employees' beliefs that behaviors and outcomes valued today will be valued tomorrow. If an employee cannot be confident about what behavior or activities will be rewarded in the future, she is likely to avoid expending effort that has only a long-term payoff. If a company frequently changes its structure, for example, employees become less willing to take the time and energy to form good working relationships because they know that the relationships will probably not last long.

The challenge is not to change the organization design continually , but to create a design that will accommodate change in the firm's activities. Sometimes, however, the strategic change the firm needs to make is so substantive that a major change in organizational design is required and justified. The issue of strategic change is a major subject of Chapters 11 and 15. There are also some unique organizational issues that confront global organizations, and we examine those in Chapter 13.

## 5.6  SUMMARY

In this chapter we argued that the firm's organization must not only be internally consistent it must also be aligned with its strategy. We also emphasized that the firm's competitive advantage is likely to change over time and that how the firm learns and, therefore, its capacity to seek new competitive advantage is governed by its approach to exploitation and exploration.

We have also seen that for a firm to engage in effective strategic change, it is not enough to explore new possible forms of competitive advantage. It must also capture new competitive advantages in coherent and logical strategies and put an organization and resources in place that can capitalize on the opportunities that the exploration uncovers. As Jim March noted in introducing the explorer and exploiter terminology, "maintaining an appropriate balance between exploration and exploitation is a primary factor in … survival and prosperity."[5] We emphasized that the costs of organizational change must be factored in when attempting to change the balance.

We turn our attention now from the firm's internal context to its external context. Just as we have introduced a framework for analyzing the firm's internal context, we introduce a framework for understanding its external context. The next few chapters, then, will introduce the tools managers need to assess the challenges and opportunities in their firms' external context.

---

[5] James March, *ibid*, 71.

# 6

# EXTERNAL CONTEXT: INDUSTRY ANALYSIS

## 6.1 INTRODUCTION

In the preceding chapters, we argued that a firm's performance is determined by the interaction of its context, both internal and external, and by the actions its managers pursue. In this chapter we begin the task of understanding how the firm's external context, particularly its market environment, affects its performance. Our goal in this analysis is to provide the tools a general manager of a firm in any industry needs to answer two related questions. The first is: *What characteristics of my market context are important determinants of my firm's profitability?* Suppose, for example, that a division manager notes that the sales of her products are declining. To understand why this has occurred, she must think about competitors' behavior (have they dropped their prices? have they improved their products?), industry demand (has demand declined for all firms in the industry?), the effects of firm entry (are new entrants absorbing a larger share of demand?), and so forth. Answering questions like these allows her to identify the external factors contributing to the change in performance.

But the manager also needs to answer a second question: *Given my market context and my firm's assets, what strategic actions can I take to improve my firm's performance?* Analyzing the external context is also crucial for answering this question. Selecting the most effective action depends on understanding the nature of the problem. Just as a doctor must tailor treatment to the cause of his patient's symptoms, a manager's response to a problem will be more effective when she understands what is causing it. To continue the sales example, a decline in sales is only a symptom—like a high fever—that many distinct problems can cause. A response that is effective when the decline is caused by price-cutting by rival firms may be less effective when a general decline in demand for the product is causing sales to decline. In the former case, share is lost to rivals, and the manager wants to find a way to make his products relatively more attractive to potential customers. In the latter, the manager wants to find a way to increase demand for the industry's products.

Our discussion concentrates on the market environment and ignores the public sector's effect on firm performance. Though not usually the focus of strategic management, governments can have important effects on how firms perform. One basic role governments play is to set the rules that govern competition and contracts. Antitrust laws, for example, restrict how competing firms can lawfully cooperate, and contract law constrains firms from making profits by reneging on contracts. But the effect of public sector policies goes beyond the impact of antitrust and contract law. Environmental regulation, licensing requirements, safety standards, government purchasing requirements, and taxes and subsidies, for example, can all have substantial effects on industry profitability. Addressing the many roles the public sector can play in shaping a firm's strategic options and decisions is beyond the scope of this book.[1] However, because many of the strategic decisions discussed here may raise antitrust issues, these laws are briefly summarized when they are relevant to our discussion.

We begin by providing some examples of the effect of industry characteristics on firm performance in the next section. In the third section, we introduce the concept of industry analysis and provide a brief history of how economists and strategic management scholars have approached it. In the fourth section, we present the industry analysis framework we use. The elements introduced there will be treated in greater detail in the next four chapters of the book. Before embarking on this more detailed explanation, however, in the last section we comment on how industries are defined and why industry definition matters.

## 6.2  THE EFFECTS OF INDUSTRY CHARACTERISTICS ON FIRM PERFORMANCE

All firms are affected by global, national, and regional economic conditions. Business cycles, exchange rate shifts, interest rates, and so forth can affect profitability. Although these effects can be important, we are more interested in the effects of the firm's specific context. Like all firms, Saatchi and Saatchi's advertising revenue, for example, is affected by the overall level of consumer demand. But its profitability is also affected by factors specific to the advertising industry. The growth in alternative channels for advertising content, for instance, might induce new firms to enter the advertising industry changing the firm's competitive environment. It is this kind of effect that interests us in this chapter.

The performance effects of industry characteristics are often most obvious when a fundamental change in the industry takes place. For example:

- The OPEC-led price increases for crude oil in the 1970s had a dramatic impact on the profitability of firms in the plastics industry in which petroleum derivatives are an important input. In this industry, the common technology of production makes all the firms vulnerable to the effects of an increased price of petroleum.

---

[1] See, for example, David P. Baron, *Business and Its Environment*, Third Edition (New York: Prentice Hall, 2000) for a book that focuses on these issues.

- The introduction of Advanced Photo System (APS) cameras and film in the mid-1990s reduced the demand for 35mm film processing. Since APS photo processing requires more sophisticated technology than 35mm film, photo processors either adopt new technology or suffer a decline in market share. Moreover, digital cameras can eliminate photo processing altogether, and if widely adopted will threaten the viability of many photo processors.

- The entry of foreign competitors into the U.S. passenger car market reduced the profitability of U.S. automakers in the 1970s and 1980s. The profits of U.S. firms were affected both by the general increase in competition created by the influx of foreign firms and by a shift in demand that favored the smaller cars produced by the new entrants.

- Changes in the computer industry over the last three decades and the resulting changes in how businesses use computers have changed the nature of competition in the information technology (IT) services business. As system integration and data management have become more central concerns to users, firms wanting to provide IT outsourcing have had to change their service offerings and, in the process, have encountered new competitors. New firms have become industry leaders as the old leaders struggled to adapt.

- The emergence of stock trading on the Internet and online brokerage firms like e-Trade threaten conventional brokerage houses and have forced them to adapt. Those, like Schwab, that have adapted most quickly have gained market share from their rivals.

Managers who see the profound effect of industry change on the profits of incumbent firms understand that the firm's external context is important. Less well understood are the magnitude and durability of industry effects. Figure 6-1 shows that these differences can be dramatic and persistent. The figure presents the ratio of market value to asset value for selected U.S. industries from 1980–1990. The numerator is the firms' market value (number of shares multiplied by stock price), and the denominator is the replacement costs of the firm's capital assets.[2] For an individual firm, this ratio is a measure of how well the firm is performing. A ratio above 1, for example, implies that the firm is adding value to the assets it controls. Throughout the 1980s the firms in the pharmaceutical industry, on average, outperformed firms in the steel, toiletries, and vehicles and parts industries. At the beginning of the 1980s, the ratio for pharmaceuticals was more than six times higher than the ratio for the steel industry. By the end of the decade, the difference was enormous. Over the same period, toiletries manufacturers also did much better than the steel and vehicle industries.

Because differences in industry performance can be large and long-lasting, managers need to understand what determines them. Industry analysis is a framework for anticipating systematic differences in average firm performance. It can, for example, identify the characteristics of the steel and pharmaceutical industries that led to the starkly different performance profiles illustrated in Figure 6-1.

---

[2] This ratio is known as average Tobin's q in the finance and economics literatures.

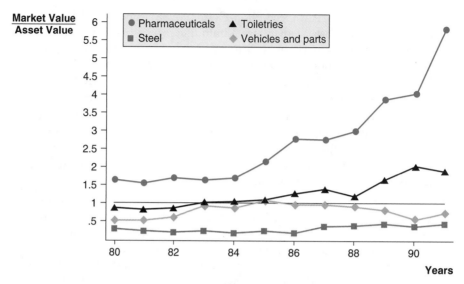

**FIGURE 6-1**    Ratio of Market to Asset Value for Selected Industries
*Source:* Authors' calculations from data made available by Professor Browyn Hall.

Average firm profitability varies across industries, as does performance among firms in the same industry. This variation occurs in part because firms in the same industry make different strategic decisions. For example, consider the U.S. steel industry. Figure 6-2 displays the steel industry ratio from Figure 6-1 and the ratios for selected U.S. steel firms. During this period the mature U.S. steel industry suffered from an aging capital stock: the U.S. firms were competing with European and Asian firms that were rebuilt after World War II and took advantage of technological changes in steel production. Bethlehem Steel and Armco are representative of these older U.S. firms. In the 1960s, a new form of steel manufacturing emerged (the so-called mini-mills) that used recycled steel and operated at a much smaller scale than the traditional steel firms. Sharp performance differences between the mini-mills and the older firms rapidly became apparent. Among the leading firms in this new group is Nucor. As Figure 6-2 shows, the ratios for Bethlehem and Armco are both consistently well below 1. Nucor, on the other hand, has a ratio consistently above 1 and is performing markedly better than the older firms.

Both the industry characteristics *and* the firm's response to those characteristics matter. How much of a firm's performance is accounted for by the firm's industry and how much is accounted for by the choices that the firm makes vary from case to case. Studies that have attempted to separate these two effects typically find that the industry accounts for about 20 percent of the variance in firm performance.[3] These studies

[3] Richard Schmalensee, "Do Markets Differ Much?," *American Economic Review* (June 1985); Anita M. McGahan and Michael E. Porter, "How Much Does Industry Matter, Really?," *Strategic Management Journal*, forthcoming (1997); and Richard P. Rumelt, "How Much Does Industry Matter?," *Strategic Management Journal*, 18 (1997), 15–30. (1991), 167–185.

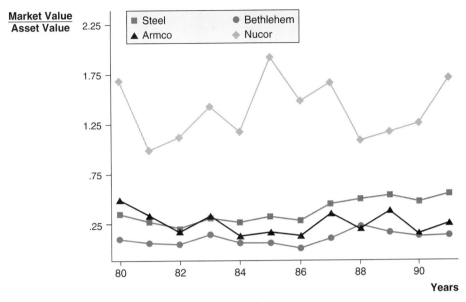

**FIGURE 6-2**   Ratio of Market Value to Asset Value for Steel and Selected Steel Manufacturers
*Source:* Authors' calculations from data made available by Professor Bronwyn Hall.

provide systematic evidence that is consistent with the examples we have seen: industry characteristics can substantially affect firm performance.[4]

Although the magnitude of industry effects is of interest, an industry analysis would be useful even if the effects were small. Think about the questions with which we started: "What characteristics of the industry are important?" and "how can a manager enhance performance given those characteristics?" An answer to the first question identifies industry characteristics that affect incumbent firms and, therefore, contribute to average profitability. The actions managers take (along with some luck, perhaps) are responsible for the variation across firms. Those firms that do better than the others in the industry are those whose managers carry out a strategy that mitigates the challenges and exploits the opportunities that industry characteristics pose. Setting luck aside, they succeed because these managers understand the industry.

## 6.3   ORGANIZING INDUSTRY ANALYSIS

Economists and students of strategic management have devoted considerable time and effort to identifying the industry characteristics that are important for firm per-

---

[4] This assertion leads immediately to the question of how these differences can persist. If everyone knows that firms in the pharmaceutical business are doing better than firms in the steel industry, why don't firms abandon the steel industry and move into pharmaceuticals? The answer has to do with barriers to entering an industry and the costs of exiting, topics we will discuss shortly.

formance and to understanding how they work. These characteristics include the number of firms in the industry, the level and pattern of promotional expenditures, the rate and nature of technological competition, the relative sizes of firms, consumer preferences for the product and for related products, the rate of demand growth, the extent of product differentiation, the pricing behavior of the leading firms, the minimum efficient scale of production, buyer switching costs, demand-side economies of scale, and the specificity of plant and equipment to the industry. The list could go on and on.

Faced with a bewildering array of potentially important characteristics, scholars have developed conceptual frameworks to organize the analysis and to provide a systematic way of covering all the bases. One of the earliest such frameworks is the Structure-Conduct-Performance (SCP) paradigm illustrated in Figure 6-3.[5] The underlying premise of the SCP paradigm is that the structure of the industry and the conduct (behavior) of its incumbent firms interact to create performance. Because the SCP framework was designed to understand how governments might intervene to increase social welfare, its performance measure is social performance, not profitability. That is, this framework is concerned with how well the industry performs in creating value for society, its impact on employment, its contribution to economic growth, and so forth. The box describing the potential impact of Public Policy is, therefore, an integral part of this framework. Aside from this difference in focus, the basic ideas of the SCP have been influential in shaping how strategic management scholars analyze industries.

In the SCP framework, the immediate determinant of industry performance is the behavior of firms (including pricing, product strategy, and so on). Firm behavior, in turn, is driven primarily by the market structure in which the firms compete. The basic idea is that a firm operating in an industry with many other competitors will be driven to have an efficient cost structure and to price close to cost to survive the competitive pressure. As the number of firms in the industry declines and competitive pressures abate, the firm can behave in ways that increase its profits (at the expense of social welfare) through, for example, charging higher prices. Industry structure, in turn, depends on underlying supply and demand conditions. The "dashed" arrows in the figure are also important. In particular, firms may be able to engage in activities that influence market structure and even the underlying supply and demand conditions that the industry faces.

The SCP framework, modified to place firm performance as the centerpiece, has been the basis of many of the frameworks proposed for industry analysis in strategic management. The most famous of these is the framework Michael Porter developed in the early 1980s.[6] Porter's framework, popularly known as the Five Forces, has been

---

[5] This formulation can be traced to the work of Mason in the 1930s and Bain in the 1950s. See Edward S. Mason, "Price and Production Policies of Large-Scale Enterprise," *American Economic Review* 29 (March 1939), 61–74; and Joe S. Bain, *Barriers to New Competition* (Cambridge, MA: Harvard University Press, 1956).

[6] Michael E. Porter, *Competitive Strategy* (New York: Free Press, 1980).

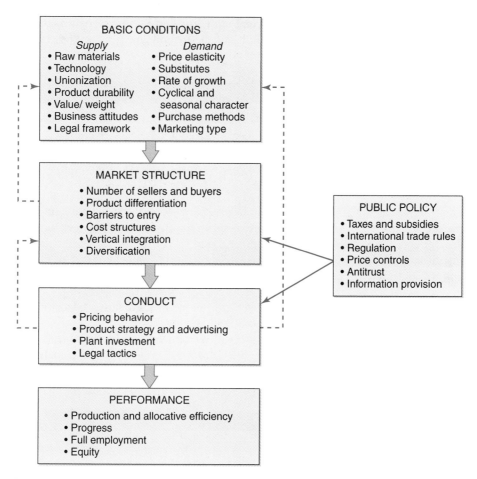

**FIGURE 6-3**   The Structure-Conduct-Performance Paradigm

*Source:* Industrial Market Structure and Economic Performance, Third Edition (Palo Alto: Houghton-Mifflin, 1990).

used and extended by many economists and strategic management scholars. The framework used here owes much both to the original SCP paradigm and to Porter's reformulation of it.

For any framework, the starting point for industry analysis is a well-defined industry. In our examples, we have casually referred to the automotive industry, the steel industry, or the pharmaceutical industry as if these industries had clearly recognized boundaries. In fact, the boundaries of an industry can be difficult to define. We will return to this topic later. For now, let us take as given that the industry is well defined. In particular, we will assume that we know what products or services are inside the industry and which are outside it.

Given a well-defined industry, Porter's initial insight was to recognize that the characteristics important to the profitability of the incumbent firms can be classified in these categories:

- the intensity of competition among the incumbent firms
- the ability of suppliers of inputs or buyers of industry products to restrain industry profits
- the behavior of firms producing closely related goods and services not included in the industry
- the potential for entry into the industry by firms currently not among the incumbents

In his original formulation, Porter summarized these forces in a diagram similar to Figure 6-4. There, we represent the intensity of competition as "competitors," the roles of buyers and suppliers as "buyer power" and "supplier power," the behavior of firms producing closely related products as "substitutes," and the effect of entry as "potential entrants." In keeping with the advances in economics and organization theory since 1980, we will use a modified version of the Porter framework. For example, our treatment of substitutes will be somewhat different. Nonetheless, our formulation is closely related to the one Porter proposed two decades ago.

In the next section of this chapter, we will introduce the analytic framework we will be using. First, however, we want to reemphasize the objective of the analysis. In

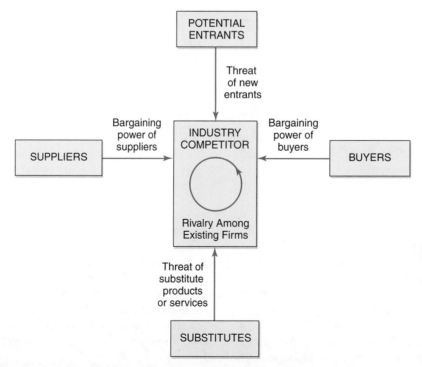

**FIGURE 6-4**  Porter's "Five Forces" Industry Analysis Framework

particular, it is important to understand that an industry analysis is not designed simply to uncover the financial profitability of the incumbent firms. Strategic management scholars frequently use questions like "how attractive is this industry?" and "how profitable is the average firm?" to mean "let's conduct an industry analysis." As a result, students may think that the obvious response is to calculate profitability for the incumbents and take an average. But, for our purposes, this information, even if available, would be woefully incomplete. We really want to know *why* the firms are, on average, so profitable (or unprofitable). We want to develop the information necessary to evaluate and formulate firm strategy. In keeping with our earlier definition of strategy, this means we want the information that enables us to choose a product scope and a source of competitive advantage that is consistent with the market environment. If all you know about a firm is its financial profitability, you know almost nothing about its current strategy and haven't a clue about how it might redeploy its assets to increase its profitability.

Because we want to identify important industry characteristics, an industry analysis examines the factors that affect all the firms in the industry or in major segments of it. Changes in the price of gasoline, government environmental regulation, and the increased competition of compressed design cycles, for example, affect all firms in the automobile industry. We can think of this as an analysis of the conditions facing the "average" or "typical" firm. As we will note, a firm that does unusually well in a given industry probably does so because something about it enables it to mitigate the problems or to exploit the opportunities all firms in the industry face. This is what we mean by competitive advantage.

Traditionally, we conduct the analysis from the perspective of incumbent firms—that is, firms active in the industry at the time of the analysis. This point is most clearly relevant for our discussion of entry barriers. All else being equal, incumbent firms are better off if outside firms have difficulty entering the industry. We will therefore say that the industry is more attractive when entry barriers are higher. However, the analysis could also be done from the perspective of a potential entrant.

Finally, an industry analysis focuses on the *long-run* performance of the industry. Short-run movements in profitability can occur because of transitory movements in input prices or cyclical changes in demand, for example. Although managers have to accommodate these changes, we want to uncover the fundamental, structural conditions that affect performance.

## 6.4    A FRAMEWORK FOR INDUSTRY ANALYSIS

Every industry is part of a value chain. As illustrated in Figure 6-5, upstream are the firms and other suppliers that contribute the inputs that industry incumbents use. Suppliers include firms selling components, materials, services or other inputs, workers supplying labor, and debtholders supplying capital.[7] Downstream from the incumbent firms are buyers: the firms or final consumers who buy from the firms in the

---

[7] Since we assume that the firm's objective is to maximize stockholder wealth, we think of stockholders as the firm's owners rather than as input suppliers.

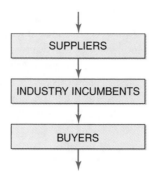

**FIGURE 6-5**    An Illustrative Value Chain

industry. We call the entire chain from raw materials to final consumers a "value chain" because each link in the chain adds some value to its inputs.[8]

All the participants in the chain contribute to the final value it creates, and each participant would like to maximize the share of that value that it captures as profit. A full analysis of the value chain would determine how all the value created by the chain is divided among its participants. But because we generally are interested in thinking about the situation facing some particular industry within the chain, we focus on identifying the factors that determine how successfully the incumbent firms in that industry capture the value generated by the value chain to which it belongs.

The logic of industry analysis, then, is as follows: The value chain in which the industry's firms participate creates some value. The participants in the chain will somehow divide that value among themselves. An industry analysis identifies the factors that determine how much value is created and how it is divided. The objective is to enable firms to think systematically about how they might increase the total value created and maximize the share of it they capture as profit. As we argued in Chapter 3, it is not enough simply to exhort firms to engage in "value-adding" activities: Because value creation is not enough to ensure that value is captured, the second step—analyzing value capture—is essential.

Consider an example. The personal computer industry value chain creates tremendous value. Component producers (makers of disk drives, memory chips, monitors, and microprocessors, for example), firms that put the components together, and the distribution channels for the final product each create some of this value. Although it is difficult to determine precisely how much each industry in this chain contributes to the total value, it seems unlikely that the share Intel and Microsoft capture is equal to the value these firms create. Rather, Intel has used its dominance of the microprocessor market to capture a large share of the total value the chain creates, regardless of where that value is created. Similarly, Microsoft has leveraged its domi-

---

[8] The term "value chain" sometimes denotes the set of activities performed within a single firm. While the idea that the activities firms perform add value is common to both uses, we reserve this term for the collection of firms and industries that participates in the production of a good or service.

nance of the operating system to dominate related software markets and to extract value generated elsewhere in the chain. Computer assemblers have been less successful in capturing value because they compete intensely with each other. Industry analysis is intended to understand how industry characteristics shape these variations in value capture.

## Value Creation: Potential Industry Earnings (PIE)

The greatest value the incumbents as a group could hope to capture is the entire value added by the chain: the value to the final buyers of the goods or services produced less the value of the resources that are used to produce them. We call this value Potential Industry Earnings or PIE. If we consider a simple example in which the chain has only three layers (final buyers, incumbent firms, and single layer of suppliers), we could represent PIE in Figure 6-6.

In the figure the total value of the product to the final buyers is the entire area under the industry demand curve.[9] The demand curve represents the buyers' willingness to pay for the incumbent firms' products. For the first unit they buy, buyers are willing to pay an amount equal to the height of the demand curve at its intercept with the y-axis (point A). For additional units, willingness to pay declines. The line labeled "opportunity cost of resources" represents the industry cost curve. The opportunity cost is the minimum payment that must be made to acquire the resources necessary to produce any given amount of the product. It is called opportunity cost because it is the

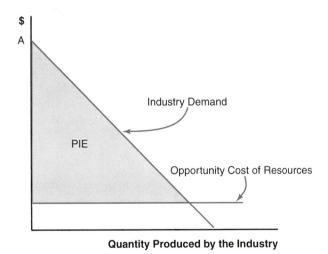

**FIGURE 6-6**  Potential Industry Earnings in a Simple Value Chain

---

[9] This is the demand curve for the industry as a whole, not for a single firm. Similarly, the cost curve is the curve for the industry. In the figure, opportunity cost per unit of output does not change with the level of output, but that is not always the case.

value of those resources if deployed in their next best alternative to being deployed here.[10] Potential industry earnings, then, is the total value created minus the opportunity cost of the resources required to produce that value, or the area defined by the industry demand and opportunity cost curves.

Even in this simple chain, the modifier "potential" in PIE is important: An industry can rarely capture all this value. Usually, suppliers will capture some PIE: the payment made to them will often be greater than the opportunity cost of resources. Similarly, buyers who pay a price less than the maximum they are willing to pay will also typically capture some. Competition among the incumbent firm will also dissipate some, and some will be lost to new entrants on the threat of entry.

Conceptually, then, two kinds of factors can affect the attractiveness of an industry. The first includes those that affect the value created by its value chain. All else being equal, participating in a chain that creates more value is preferable. Given the current state of technology, for example, the PIE for the electric car industry is probably small; indeed, the opportunity cost of producing, distributing, and maintaining electric cars may be higher than the value consumers place on the cars. Because PIE is, at best, small, no for-profit firm would choose to participate in the value chain without regulatory coercion. The second class of factors includes those that determine how the value created in the chain is divided. Given potential industry earnings, an industry is more attractive the greater the share of the created value it can capture.

This analysis is applicable to more complicated value chains in which there are many layers and a given industry buys inputs from multiple upstream industries and/or sells to many downstream industries. Think, for example, of the bulk chemical industry that supplies inputs for hundreds of downstream industries. These industries are all, in principle, in the value chain for the bulk chemical industry, but the entire value this chain generates comes close to the value of GDP. It is ridiculous to think that the bulk chemical industry could capture a large share of this value. Nonetheless, the same kind of factors that are important in simpler chains affects the profitability of the bulk chemical manufacturers. The practical difficulty in analyzing complex chains is just one of tractability; it is hard to examine each segment of these chains in detail. Practitioners of industry analysis usually resolve this problem by focusing on the segments closest to the industry of interest.

## Determinants of PIE

A glance at the PIE diagram in Figure 6-6 informs us that the size of PIE in this simple example is determined by the factors that shape industry demand and the opportunity cost of resources. Anything that changes industry demand or the industry's opportunity cost of resources will affect the size of PIE. Figure 6-7 summarizes some of the primary forces that make PIE larger.

---

[10] Opportunity cost may be easier to understand from the perspective of an individual firm. For example, a firm seeking to hire a software engineer will offer a compensation package that is at least equal to the compensation the engineer could earn at another firm. This is the opportunity cost of the engineer.

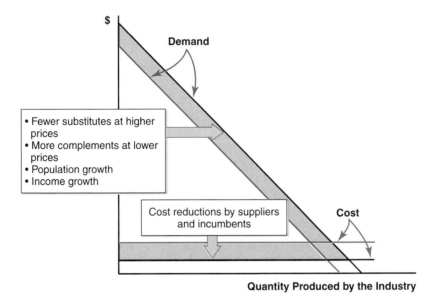

**FIGURE 6-7**    Forces that Increase Potential Industry Earnings (PIE)

The state of technology and the market forces acting upstream determine the opportunity cost of resources. A technological advance that changes how inputs are produced can, for example, shift the opportunity cost curve. Or fluctuations in the amount of some input available to the market can shift the curve: a war in oil-producing regions, for example, will probably increase the opportunity cost of petroleum products. Because the opportunity cost for the industry also includes the costs incurred by the industry's activities, any cost reductions by industry incumbents will also shift the opportunity cost curve.

Although these changes in opportunity cost affect the size of PIE, strategic management has focused more on demand-side effects. Traditional industry analysis, for example, highlights the role of substitutes in affecting industry demand. Substitutes are products or services produced by firms in other industries that buyers can use in lieu of those produced by the incumbent firms. For the coal industry, petroleum products are a substitute. For AT&T and the other long-distance carriers, e-mail is a substitute. For metal can producers, plastic and glass containers are substitutes. For manufacturers of electric shavers, razors are a substitute. Buyers' willingness to pay for coal, long-distance telephone service, metal cans, and shavers depends on how "close" they feel these substitutes are and on the prices of these substitutes.

Some substitutes are "closer" to the industry's products than others. Closeness is determined by buyers' perceptions; technological attributes contribute to these perceptions but are not necessarily dispositive. Glass, for example, is a closer substitute for metal for beer containers than is plastic in part because the technological attributes of glass are more suitable to bottling beer. But the final arbiter of closeness is buyer behavior, and many buying patterns seem to defy standard measures of technological closeness. Indeed, an important reason that glass is still used to bottle beer in the United States is the affinity some beer drinkers have for the "long-neck" bottles in which most beer used to be bottled.

The combination of perceived quality and price drives buyer behavior. *Existing* substitutes change the size of PIE when their prices change. Holding constant the price of metal cans, a decline in the price of glass bottles reduces the demand for metal cans. In the PIE diagram in Figure 6-7, this decline would be represented by an inward shift in the demand curve for the metal can industry.[11] Changes in the price of a close substitute will affect the demand for the industry's products more profoundly than changes in the price of more distant substitute will. Indeed, by "close" we mean that a small change in price will lead a substantial share of buyers to switch products. The introduction of *new* substitutes also affects PIE. The demand for record players, for example, declined when compact discs were introduced, and innovations in laser eye surgery will diminish the demand for eyeglasses. Again, this would be represented by an inward shift of the industry demand curve causing a reduction in PIE for the record player and eyeglasses industries, respectively.

Although traditional analyses focused on substitutes, *complements* can also affect PIE. Complements are goods or services not produced by the incumbent firms but used in conjunction with their products. Examples of complements are 35mm cameras, film, and camera lenses, as are automotive tires and engines and computer hardware and software. In contrast to the effect of substitutes, a drop in the relative price of a complement or the introduction of a new complement will *increase* demand for the industry's product. The versatility of a 35mm camera is enhanced when a variety of lenses can be used with it. As a result, the introduction of new lenses shifts film demand outward, increasing PIE.

Population growth, changes in income, and shifts in consumer tastes also affect industry demand. As consumer income rises, demand for most products increases, and the mix of products purchased usually changes. Luxury products, for example, receive a disproportionate share of the increase in demand when income rises. Holding constant the income distribution, population growth also increases demand and, with changing demographics, can also change its composition. Shifts in consumer tastes change primarily the composition of demand. Advertising, for example, seeks to induce consumers to shift expenditures to the advertised product by influencing their preferences.

Finally, it is important to note that while we can identify factors that affect PIE, determining the precise size of PIE is not easy. Frequently, managers who are analyz-

---

[11] Industry demand curves show the relationship between the price of a product and the amount of it that will be purchased. They assume that the prices of products outside the industry are held constant. If those prices change, the industry demand curve shifts. Even when the prices of outside goods and services are held constant, however, they affect industry demand. The slope of the demand curve tells us that buyers reduce the quantity purchased when the price of the product increases, all other prices held constant. This happens in two ways. First, buyers simply "do without" the product. Second, buyers switch to substitute products. When the price of beer rises, consumers drink less liquid ("do without") and switch some of their beer consumption to other beverages. Products with closer substitutes have more elastic demand: The revenue change they realize for a given change in price is larger.

ing their industry or another industry they are thinking about entering will look at industry revenues or historical profitability. Neither of these is an accurate guide to the size of PIE because they reflect both PIE *and* the share of PIE that the incumbent firms can retain. If, for example, suppliers can extract a large share of PIE, observed industry profitability will substantially underestimate PIE. Measuring PIE would require estimating opportunity cost and industry demand. In our simple, three-layer supply chain, this might be possible. In more complex value chains, it would be a daunting task.

Fortunately, we don't need to estimate PIE in general. Rather, we want to do two things. First, identify those factors that might affect it (substitutes, complements, population growth, etc.), so that we have some sense of whether the industry is likely to become more or less attractive as a result of changes in PIE. Second, we want to have some idea of how attractive an industry might be if incumbent firms could capture a substantial share of PIE. This is the rationale for looking at data on historical profitability. Past performance is a useful guide to how attractive the industry might be if everything stays the same. Managers therefore typically base forecasts on "doing as well as before." But if a firm can develop a strategy that increases the share of the PIE it captures, it can do better than before. Whether it can do so depends in part on the forces that constrain the share of profits the incumbent firms can retain.

### An Example of Value Creation: Lobster PIE

As an example of the factors that affect PIE, consider the lobster fishing industry in northeast North America.[12] The lobster harvesting industry is composed of hundreds of small boat owners who are licensed by the U.S. or Canadian governments to fish for lobster in the territorial waters of those countries. This industry is part of a value chain for lobsters that starts with lobsters foraging on the cold bottom of the Atlantic Ocean and ends with a consumer savoring a freshly cooked lobster. The supply chain for lobsters is composed of the lobster harvesters at one end, consumers at the other, and wholesale and retail operations in between. The value of PIE in this chain, and therefore the PIE for the lobster industry, is the difference between the value to consumers of lobsters and the resource costs of getting a lobster to them. We begin by considering the value to consumers before turning to costs.

Lobsters have many potential uses, and there is a multitude of consumers with different tastes and demographic characteristics. Consumers for whom lobster is a delicacy, eaten at home on special occasions or served in fine restaurants, make up the highest portions of the demand curve. These consumers have the highest willingness to pay. It is easy to imagine that wealthy individuals with a particular fondness for lobster might be willing to pay $100 a pound or more for it. For such consumers, the relevant substitutes are likely to be other delicacies such as caviar, crab, quail, fine cuts of beef, and so on. Somewhat lower down the demand curve are consumers who would

---

[12] This example draws on the Harvard Business School case "Prelude Corporation," 373-052, for much of the institutional detail on the lobster fishing industry. However, our purpose here is to provide an illustrative example, and we have not remained true to the facts in that case in all instances.

consider many other meals—salmon, steak, linguine—to be adequate substitutes for lobster and whose willingness to pay is correspondingly lower. Even lower down the demand curve are those who use lobster only as input to a dish for which a white fish, such as cod, is an adequate substitute, or adding it to soups or salads where lobster is typically less highly valued than when it is the centerpiece of the meal. There have even been cases in history, considerably further down the demand curve, where eating lobster was considered a hardship. In colonial America, contracts of indentured servants sometimes included provisions that limited the number of times per week that they would have to eat lobster! The number of consumers of each kind determines the demand curve for lobster.

Since relatively few consumers would pay hundreds of dollars a pound for lobster, and many would substitute lobster for fish if their prices were the same, the demand curve for lobster could have a shape like the one shown in Figure 6-8.[13] The steep portion of the curve captures those consumers for whom there no good substitutes for lobster. They have a high willingness to pay and are also probably not very sensitive to price: A small change in the price of lobster will have almost no effect on the quantity of lobster they purchase. The flatter segment reflects consumers who are more willing to consume substitutes and thus are more sensitive to price. A small change in the price of lobster substantially affects how much lobster these consumers will purchase.

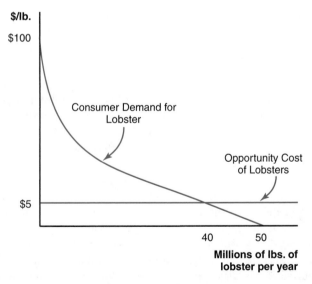

**FIGURE 6-8**   Potential Industry Earnings (PIE) for the Lobster Industry

---

[13] The demand curve depicted here has been sketched for illustrative purposes and has not been estimated from data on consumer demand. While economists have developed sophisticated methods for estimating demand, our purpose here is simply to give some flavor of how a demand curve can represent consumer tastes and income.

Managers in the lobster industry need to be aware of the characteristics of demand for their product, but they also need to understand factors that might affect that demand over time. One factor is the health of the economy, which affects consumers' discretionary income and hence their willingness to pay for luxury items. Especially, perhaps, for consumers not at the top of the demand curve, a decline in disposable income might curtail expenditures on lobster dinners. A second factor is consumer concerns about cholesterol that might favor lobster over some substitutes like red meat. A third factor might be concerns about ocean pollution that would tend to reduce demand for lobsters because they are ocean-bottom feeders.

Figure 6-8 also illustrates the opportunity cost of resources ($5 a pound). Several different segments of the value chain bear the cost of getting a lobster from the ocean floor to the final customer's plate. This value chain is illustrated in Figure 6-9 where the opportunity costs are broken down into the costs incurred at each stage of the chain.

The first stage consists of the industry that is our focus: lobster fishing. A typical lobster fishing operation is run by two people who take out the fishing boat, lay and raise the lobster traps, sell the catch to wholesalers at the next stage of the supply chain, and maintain their boats and equipment. The relevant opportunity cost of the labor involved is the income the harvesters could receive if they spent their lobster-fishing time in their next best alternative. Also included in the opportunity costs of the resources at this layer of the supply chain is the cost of the equipment (boat, traps, etc.). Spreading the equipment and labor costs over the number of pounds of lobster harvested, we have estimated those costs at about $2 a pound. The main factors that affect these costs are changes in the opportunity costs of time for the workers (which in turn depends mainly on the general health of the local economy) and the cost of equipment (boats, lobster pots, and tackle). Advances in the "technology" for harvesting lobsters, such as aquaculture, might significantly affect the opportunity costs of resources expended on harvesting.

The next stage of the value chain (also estimated to cost around $2 a pound) is the cost of getting the lobster from the dock to the retailer. This includes the costs of pur-

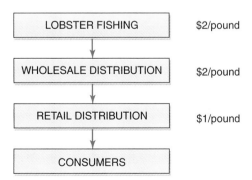

**FIGURE 6-9**   Incremental Opportunity Cost in the Lobster Industry Value Chain

chasing lobster from the harvesters at the dock (excluding the price paid to the lobster harvesters), transporting lobster to storage tanks, storage, making a sale to the retail segment, transporting lobster from storage to retailers, and administering a wholesale operation. The final stage is retailing. The costs here depend on the form of retailer (whether restaurant or supermarket, for example). While the analysis might be different for each of these segments, to simplify we assume that the costs here are about $1/pound. The sum of these costs is the $5 per pound shown in Figure 6-8.

Given the demand and cost figures shown in Figure 6-8, potential earnings in the lobster fishing industry are roughly $1 billion a year![14] More important than the precise figure is understanding the main features that determine it. In more complex industries, indeed, it is difficult to collect the cost data that would support even a back-of-the-envelope calculation of PIE. But we can still think through the determinants of PIE. On the demand side, this includes understanding the different groups of consumers who constitute demand, the substitutes that determine each group's willingness to pay, and the factors that shift demand over time. On the cost side, this requires understanding the structure of the supply chain, the cost structure of each segment, and the factors that could change these costs. Having a mental picture of the determinants of PIE is the starting point for managers' analyses of their industry.

## Capturing Value: Dividing PIE

Participating in a chain that creates substantial value is necessary for dramatic industry profitability, but it is hardly sufficient. It is little comfort to the stockholders of the average personal computer assembly firm to note that the value the entire desktop computer industry creates is enormous. Their segment of the value chain retains little of that value. The value the overall chain generates, however, is important to stockholders at Intel because Intel captures a large share of it. Understanding why PIE is divided the way it is represents an important step toward understanding how share can be defended and attacked.

Porter identified four forces that determine how PIE is allocated within the value chain: competition, entry, buyer power, and supplier power. To complete our overview of the framework, we briefly discuss each of these categories. They are treated more completely in succeeding chapters and are summarized here in Figure 6-10.

### Competition

To isolate the effects of competition, let us assume that no other layer in the chain is capturing PIE (no buyer or supplier power) and entry is impossible. Even under these unusually favorable conditions, the share of PIE incumbents capture may be small if

---

[14] You can perform a rough calculation by breaking PIE into segments for "high" willingness to pay consumers and others, which breaks PIE roughly into an "upper" triangle and a "lower" triangle. If, for example, extrapolating the lower segment of the demand curve back to the y-axis intersects that axis at about $45, the area of that lower triangle is roughly ($45/pound – $5/pound) * (40m. pounds) ÷ 2 = $800 million. A similar calculation for the "upper" triangle yields additional PIE of around $200 million.

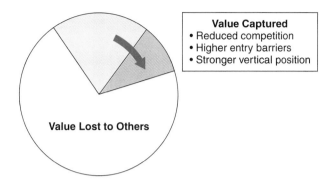

**Value Captured**
- Reduced competition
- Higher entry barriers
- Stronger vertical position

**Value Lost to Others**

**FIGURE 6-10**   Forces Increasing the Share of PIE Retained by Incumbents

competition among them is sufficiently intense. By contrast, if competition is muted, the incumbents may capture a large share of PIE. We can illustrate the dramatic effects of variation in competitive intensity by thinking about the two polar cases: monopoly (where competition is absent) and perfect competition (where competition is intense). In the case of monopoly, the single incumbent firm will earn a high return on investment because no PIE is lost through competitive pricing, advertising, or product development. In the case of perfect competition, the firms will earn returns only sufficient to clear the investment hurdle as they compete away PIE by aggressive pricing and product development aimed at stealing share from competitors. Although most industries are between these two extremes, competitive intensity always affects how much PIE incumbent firms can retain.

The primary rule of thumb used to assess competitive intensity is based on the distribution of market shares. An industry in which no firm has a large market share is typically more competitive than one in which one firm or a few firms have a large share. In the language often used by economists: An industry in which market share is "concentrated" in the hands of a few firms is likely to be less competitive than one in which market share is dispersed among many small firms. This relationship between market share concentration and competitive intensity has led analysts to develop various ways to measure concentration. One common measure is a concentration ratio. A three-firm concentration ration (CR3), for example, is the percentage of industry sales accounted for by the three largest firms in the industry. Another measure is the Hirschman-Herfindahl Index (HHI), which sums the squared market shares of each firm in the industry.[15]

Product differentiation and the behavior of competitors also affect competitive intensity. The more differentiated the firms' products are from each other, the less

[15] An industry with three firms with shares of 10%, 60%, and 30% would have an HHI $=\left[\frac{1}{10}\right]^2 + \left[\frac{6}{10}\right]^2 + \left[\frac{3}{10}\right]^2 = 0.67832$. Typically, the HHI is multiplied by 10,000 when it is reported, so the HHI for this industry would be 6,782. An industry with a single firm would have an HHI of 10,000. An industry with 100 equal-sized firms would have an HHI of 100.

competitive the firms will be. Price competition in commodity products like metals tends to be more intense than price competition in differentiated consumers goods like shampoo or snack foods. Firm behavior can also affect competitive intensity in some industries. Many commodity markets have or have had international cartels that attempt to control production and set prices (copper, crude oil, aluminum, and diamonds, for example). Typically, these cartels can initially increase prices by reducing supply but cannot enforce high prices over the long run. Both the emergence and the decline of cooperation dramatically affect commodity prices, even though the number and size distribution of firms have not changed.

## Entry and Incumbency Advantage

If firms in an industry are earning high returns, other firms will want to enter the industry. This behavior parallels our discussion of sustainable advantage in Chapter 3: Success breeds imitation. If nothing impedes the entry of new competitors, entry will eventually lead to increased competition in the industry. As we suggested in our discussion of competition, this will reduce profitability for the industry as a whole. For incumbents, entry tends to lead to lower prices (and/or increased nonprice competition) *and* smaller market shares than incumbents enjoyed preentry. When entry barriers are low, competitive intensity will eventually increase. Indeed, one of the things sustaining a perfectly competitive industry structure is the low-entry barrier, just as high-entry barriers sustain monopoly.

An entry barrier is anything that puts a new entrant at a significant competitive disadvantage relative to an established firm. Note that low profitability is not in itself an entry barrier. If industry profitability is low, firms may not *want* to enter but might be *able* to compete on an equal footing if they did enter. An entry barrier is something that prevents entry by creating a competitive disadvantage for new entrants: It makes firms unable to enter successfully. To emphasize this important point, it is helpful to think of entry barriers as an advantage of incumbency rather than as anything that keeps firms from entering the industry. Entry barriers can take many forms, but the most common types include:

- **Barriers from production or distribution technology.** Sometimes the technology of production or distribution confers some advantage on large firms. Small-scale automobile production, for example, is not economically feasible. The size of an efficient automotive firm limits the number of firms that can compete successfully in the automobile industry.

- **Barriers from brand name or reputation.** Incumbent firms may have a well-established brand name built up by years of promotion. To compete successfully, a new entrant will have to make a similar investment or do something else that gives buyers a reason to switch. An incumbent firm also might have established a reputation for "fair dealing." Again, a new entrant will need to expend the resources to offset this reputational advantage.

- **Legal barriers.** Sometimes barriers established by governments protect incumbent firms against entry. Trade barriers, for example, protect domestic firms against foreign competitors, and patents protect patent holders against imitation.

Because entry is bad for incumbent firms, they have an incentive to *create* entry barriers if none exists. They might, for example, expend resources to lobby for trade barriers that would disadvantage foreign firms. Or they might invest in excessive brand development (i.e., an investment in brands greater than the level that would maximize profits if entry were impossible) to discourage entry. These investments to create entry barriers are another way the absence of "natural" entry barriers dissipates PIE.

### An Example of the Effects of Competition and Entry

The preceding discussion argued that average profitability declines as the number of firms in the industry increases and as the products in the industry become more alike. Substantial evidence indicates that this is a general pattern. One particularly clear example comes from the pharmaceutical industry. New drugs are usually patented, allowing the firm holding the patent to behave as a monopolist for the life of the patent. When the patent expires, other firms enter with generic versions of the drug. If the number of competitors matters, prices should fall as more firms enter the industry. Figure 6-11 displays some of the results from a study of how prices behave when this happens.[16]

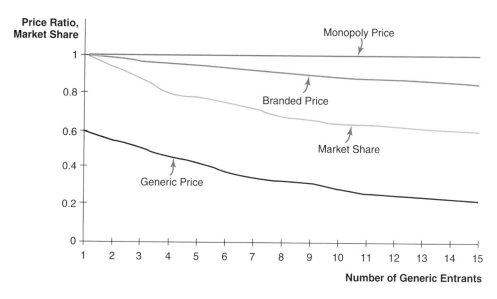

**FIGURE 6-11**   Entry and Price in the Pharmaceutical Industry

---

[16] Caves, Hurwicz, and Whinston, "Patent Expiration, Entry and Competition in the U.S. Pharmaceutical Industry," *Brookings Papers on Microeconomic Activity.* 1991. The authors of this text constructed Figure 6-11 based on data reported in the article.

The line labeled Monopoly Price represents the price the branded firm would charge in the absence of competition from producers of generic drugs. All prices represented in this figure have been divided by the monopoly price. So the normalized monopoly price is always 1, and all other prices are percentages of the monopoly price. The Branded Price curve shows the decline in the branded drug price from the monopoly price as more generic firms enter the market. The Generic Price curve shows the decline in generic price as more generic firms enter the market. The line labeled Market Share is the market share of the branded product.

This graph shows several interesting things.

- Note that the branded product can charge a price premium. The branded product retains a relatively large market share, even though generic prices are always substantially below the branded price. In this example, the brand's reputation was not a high enough barrier to prevent entry, but it continues to give the original firm a competitive advantage.

- Both branded and generic prices fall as more firms enter the market. This confirms our argument that competition intensifies when more firms are in the market.

- While all prices decline as the number of firms increases, entry affects branded prices less than generic prices. Increasing the number of generic entrants from 1 to 20 cuts the generic price in half but reduces the branded price by less than 15%. This is consistent with our claim that differentiation blunts competition. The generic drugs are much more similar to each other than they are to the pioneer branded drug. (Remember we are talking about *perceived*, not technical, equivalence.)

- The market share of the branded product declines by slightly over 30%. This pattern might have been different if the branded firm had fought back by lowering its price more. Then, of course, the branded price would fall more, but its market share would be higher.

What the graph does not show, but the study documents, is that promotional expenditures on a branded drug typically increased just before the drug's patent expired. This is consistent with an attempt by the incumbent firm to increase brand equity to disadvantage entrants.

## Vertical Power: Buyer or Supplier Power

Conceptually, buyer and supplier power are similar; it is just that they affect the industry from different directions. We can therefore think of them as manifestations of the general problem of "vertical power," that is, the ability of a participant (or group of participants acting together) elsewhere in the chain to capture some PIE. A supplier might accomplish this by raising the input price the industry incumbents must pay, and a buyer might accomplish this by depressing the output price the industry incumbents can charge.[17] Because buyer power is the converse of supplier power, we focus here on understanding supplier power.

---

[17]Buyers or suppliers could also exert power by providing lower quality or service for the same price.

This part of industry analysis is particularly sensitive to how expansively we define PIE. If we define PIE over the entire value chain, "suppliers" means any participant upstream from the incumbent firm in the value chain. In principle, the effect on the incumbent firms can be the same whether firms immediately above the industry or firms farther upstream exercise supplier power. If any supplier along the chain can raise its price above its opportunity cost of resources, that high price will reverberate through the chain, and our incumbents will face higher input prices. In practice, a price increase that happens at a greater remove from the industry may be harder for the incumbent firms to perceive and/or resist. For expository purposes, we will proceed as if the potential source of supplier power were the segment immediately above the industry in which we are interested.

The first thing to think about in evaluating the ability of suppliers to capture PIE is how competitive the suppliers are. If the supplying industry is intensely competitive, no firm in it can exert supplier power. Another way to think about this is to ask how easily an incumbent firm could buy the input from another supplier were its current supplier to raise its price. A long-distance telephone service has to buy access to the local phone companies' systems. The long-distance carrier may have its own interstate phone lines, but it relies on the local phone companies serving the origination and termination phones to complete every call it carries. In the United States, the local phone companies have long had a virtual monopoly of their service areas. Because the long-distance carrier has no alternative way to buy access, an unregulated local phone company would be able to charge a very high price for access. Its control over this input to long-distance service gives it bargaining power in determining the price of the input. If the local phone markets were perfectly competitive, the long-distance firms could easily change suppliers. Conversely, most commodity products, such as copper, steel, wire, and so on, are fairly homogeneous, so that firms buying them as inputs can easily switch suppliers. Since those commodities are also available from many firms, suppliers have virtually no power.

Note that what matters is the relative bargaining strength of *individual* industry incumbents and *individual* suppliers. When, for example, crude oil producers act as a group, they are a powerful supplier group relative to individual U.S. gasoline refiners. But if they do not coordinate their actions, no individual producer has much bargaining power over any refiner. If an individual producer attempts to raise its price, a refiner will simply buy from someone else. If there were a single airline, it would have greater bargaining power than the only two commercial aircraft manufacturers in the world: Airbus and Boeing. There are many airlines, however, few of which are large enough to have any bargaining power. This gives the advantage in bargaining power to Airbus and Boeing.

Imagine how a manager feels about negotiations with the firm's suppliers and buyers. At one extreme, the manager is "shaking in his boots" as he contemplates those negotiations. At the other, he is quite relaxed. The manager's feelings are a good indication of how much power the firm's buyers or suppliers have. A manager contemplating negotiating a copper contract can be pretty relaxed since he can play many suppliers against one another and be rather indifferent about which one he chooses. On the other hand, a manager negotiating an order for new aircraft is probably apprehensive because he has only two potential suppliers. The airline manager may also prefer to buy from a single supplier because his firm's maintenance costs are lower if it can carry a common parts inventory for all its planes, and its labor costs are lower if its mechanics can specialize in servicing fewer plane types. As a result, the people negotiating the contract on both sides of the table know that the airline will pay a premium to avoid switching.

### Dividing the Lobster PIE

To illustrate the forces affecting an industry's ability to capture value, we return to the lobster fishing example. How much of the $1 billion a year of PIE that the lobster fishing and distribution firms in North America create does the lobster fishing industry there capture? To answer this question, we briefly examine supplier power, entry, competition, and buyer power in the lobster fishing industry:

- **Supplier power.** The primary supplier is the ocean, which despite its awesome natural power, exerts no economic power over the industry! The owners of the fishing operation or their relatives typically provide labor, so the bargaining power of labor is usually not a factor. Additional labor, if needed, is acquired in a competitive market for part-time workers, so that supplier power is low there too. Other inputs, such as boats, lobster pots, and so on, are also competitively supplied. Supplier power is virtually nonexistent in this market. Lobster harvesters, then, are getting their inputs at roughly their opportunity cost, so they lose no PIE to suppliers.

- **Entry.** The fact that there are already over 4000 fishing enterprises in the industry speaks volumes about the ease of entry. Anyone who can buy or finance a small boat and some lobster pots and who understands the "technology" of lobster fishing can enter the industry. Moreover, lobster fishing has no economies of scale, so that a large incumbent firm has no cost advantage over a small entrant. The only significant barrier to entry in this industry is a nonmarket barrier; harvesters must buy a license. While this may prevent a vacationer from entering the industry during his weekend at the shore, it has clearly not kept out thousands of small operators. We conclude that the barriers to entry are low. On the one hand, low-entry barriers mean that incumbents have not incurred large costs attempting to erect barriers. On the other, it has meant that many firms are in the industry, thereby increasing competition.

- **Competition.** The thousands of competing fishing enterprises catching an undifferentiated product make lobster fishing a competitive industry. Buyers regard lobsters of a given size and condition as commodities, that is, holding the size and condition of the lobsters constant, a lobster caught by Bob will sell for the same price as one caught by John. In a market in which thousands of sellers compete to sell a commodity product, price will be driven down to the opportunity costs of the resources employed to produce the product. Competition is extremely intense, and the price that harvesters get for their lobster will equal, on average, the opportunity costs of harvesting the lobster, or $2 a pound.

- **Buyer power.** Given how competitive the industry is, the question of buyer power is moot. An assessment of buyer power often implies a balancing of opposing bargaining strengths. Here, however, at least one side of this "tug of war can exert no power." Harvesters simply bring their catch to shore and sell it at the going market price. For completeness, however, it is worth assessing how much power the buyers could exert if they had to do so. If the lobster harvesters tried to bargain with their buyers, they would find the buyers to be formidable. Unlike the fragmented lobster fishing industry, wholesale distribution is concentrated. There are a number of reasons for this—the need to supply retailers with a broad range of products, economies of scale in storage and distribution, and the ability to control entry into the fish markets—which we need not go into in any depth here. The point is that with only two major distributors and some smaller ones to sell to, lobster harvesters have few options. Moreover, lobsters must be sold alive. Therefore, since the wholesalers have large storage facilities and most harvesters do not, the wholesalers can make low "take-it-or-leave-it" offers that the harvesters virtually have to accept. If the lobster harvesters bargained over price, it would be they who were shaking in their boots, not the wholesalers!

The overall picture is not a happy one for the lobster harvesters. Despite their significant role in creating around a billion dollars a year in value, they capture none of it. They receive merely the opportunity costs that they put into the venture, including a normal profit on the money they invest.

To see who does capture the value in this supply chain, look at Figure 6-12. As shown there, the average price of a lobster to a consumer is estimated to be $6 a pound. That means that the total revenues earned by all the participants in the supply

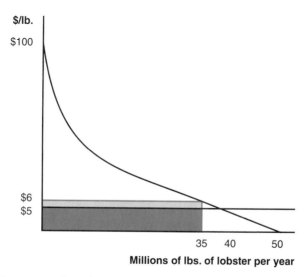

**FIGURE 6-12**    Revenues and Profit in the Lobster Industry

chain are about $210 million. (The total amount sold is 35 million pounds a year.) As an aside, note from these numbers and from the figure that revenues are only loosely related to PIE. A total of $70 million of revenue goes to the lobster harvesters and covers the $70 million in costs they incur. At a price of $6 a pound, only $1 per pound, or a total of $35 million (the light blue area in the figure), represents value captured as profit. Consumers who pay less for their lobster dinners than they would be willing to pay capture most of PIE. To determine which segment of the value chain captures the $35 million, we would also need to examine the ability of retailers to capture value. Given that retailing is a fairly competitive business as well, however, we can conclude that wholesalers capture most of the $35 million.

The primary conclusion to draw from this example is to distinguish between value creation and value capture. Lobster fishing contributes to a chain that creates substantial value. However, the structural characteristics of the harvesting industry—most importantly, the ease of entry and the consequently intense competition—prevent industry participants from capturing the value they help create.

## 6.5  INDUSTRY DEFINITION

Industry analysis is a tool used by general managers of a specific line-of-business who must understand the threats and opportunities in their market environment. Although there are some economywide factors (e.g., business cycles, interest rates, and so forth) that affect performance, we are most concerned with the factors in the firm's immediate environment. It is these industry characteristics that define the distinctive strategic challenge faced by the firm and that industry analysis is designed to address. To apply the industry analysis framework, however, we must first define the industry. To assess the threat of buyer or supplier power, we must know who the important buyers and suppliers are; to assess the state of competition, we must know who the competitors are; to gauge entry barriers, we must know the boundaries of the industry.

Managers conducting an industry analysis usually start with a firm (or firms) in which they are interested. The industry definition problem, then, is to determine in what industry (industries) the firm participates. Consider Pacific Bell, a telecommunication firm with a product line that includes the following products and services:

- On-premise[18] telephone system switching equipment and service
- Long-distance access
- Telephone system software including voice mail, automatic call distributors, and call monitoring

These products and services have different suppliers: long-distance access might be purchased from the long-distance carriers, and switching hardware might be purchased from one of the major switch manufacturers, for example. Asking whether suppliers have power over industry incumbents could have different answers for these two products. Furthermore, Pacific Bell's products face different competitors. In re-selling

---

[18] "On-premise" means that the switching hardware is physically located in the buyer's firm.

long-distance service, it competes with the primary long-distance carriers and other re-sellers. In on-premise switching equipment, it might compete primarily with other regional Bell operating companies and with independent suppliers of switching hardware. The characteristics of competition within these two sets of competitors might be different.

Thus, although the point of departure for defining an industry is usually the products of some firm, defining an industry based on those products is problematic for two reasons. First, the firm's products may span more than one industry. Are long-distance re-selling and on-premise switching equipment in the same industry? Or think of a more extreme example: In what single industry could we classify General Electric's products? Second, the industry usually includes products the firm does not produce. Even though in the early 2000s, most supermarkets do not offer online shopping with home delivery, that does not mean that competitors like Weban and Peapod that do should be excluded from an analysis of their industry.

## Industry Definition Based on "Close" Substitutes

If the firm's products are not an adequate guide to defining the bounds of the industry, what else could we use? The basic idea is to include products that are close substitutes in the industry and to place outside the industry products that are not close substitutes. In making this decision, remember that whether a product is a close substitute for another depends not on the technical characteristics of these products but on how their potential buyers perceive them. To a chemist the water coming out of the tap and the water sold in plastic bottles in the supermarket may be technically similar, but if consumers will pay a large premium for bottled water, the products are not close substitutes. Conversely, if consumers perceive little difference between news delivered on the Internet and in newspapers, those news sources are good substitutes despite the differences in the technology that deliver them.

The exhortation to include only close substitutes would be more useful if it were straightforward to decide whether a given product is close enough to include. In applying antitrust law, government agencies face a similar industry definition problem, and the approach taken by the U.S. Department of Justice (USDOJ) to this problem is instructive. The USDOJ determines what potential substitutes should be included in the industry using the following exercise. Start with a narrowly defined product (e.g., on-premise call switching hardware) and then ask: If a single firm sold this product, could that firm raise the price 5 to 10 percent? If there are close substitutes for this product, the answer will be "no." Now expand the definition slightly to include the most obvious substitutes (e.g., off-premise call-switching hardware) and ask the question again. Go on in this fashion until the answer is "yes." The smallest group of products for which the answer is "yes" constitutes an industry.

Note two things. First, the phrase "could raise price" means that the price increase would be profitable because a substantial share of buyers would be retained despite the increase. Second, it is not enough simply to ask whether some buyers are currently purchasing substitutes for the product in question. Even a monopolist will find it to be in its interests to raise its price to the point where some buyers are buying an alternative product. The question is whether many consumers will switch to the substitute given a small price increase. A monopoly firm will retain enough customers to make the high price profitable.

Even with an algorithm like this, however, there will be some uncertainty about where to draw the line. In a court of law, this uncertainty can lead to lengthy (and expensive) arguments about exactly what products should be inside or outside the industry. The parties to an antitrust dispute will tend to define the industry in quite different ways. When the U.S. government accused IBM of monopolizing the computer market, for example, the government proposed a narrow definition of the market. The government defined the market to be "general purpose electronic computer systems," by which it meant to exclude computers such as minicomputers, supercomputers, scientific computers, as well as computers used primarily for typesetting, communications processing, and so on. The government's definition would lead to the conclusion that IBM had a dominant market share in its industry. IBM's attorneys favored an industry definition that included a wide range of products. By arguing for a definition that included many products IBM did not produce, they hoped to induce the Court to conclude that IBM had only a modest market share. How an industry is defined can have a dramatic impact on antitrust decisions, and many arcane legal and economic arguments are usually made by the attorneys and expert witnesses on each side of the case.

Fortunately, we don't have to meet legal standards to conduct an industry analysis. For our purposes, we can admit that the precise boundaries are arbitrary. We are more willing to do so because we have a built-in safety net. Remember that an industry definition separates firms into "incumbents" and "substitutes." Suppose we mistakenly draw the line too tightly and count some firms as outside the industry who really should be inside. We might then conclude that competition among incumbents is less intense than it really is (because we have overlooked some competitors), but we will also conclude that PIE is smaller than it really is (because the industry as we've defined it has some close substitutes). The overall effect on our assessment of industry attractiveness might therefore be negligible.

## Industry Definitions for Systems of Complementary Products

An additional complication arises when the products involved are systems of complementary components. Some of the telephone system software is hardware-specific, and some is not. Should that affect our definition of the industry? This is a difficult question, and reasonable people disagree (even outside the law courts). Think of an automobile. It includes a body, an engine, and tires. From the consumer's point of view, the automobile (including the tires and engine it comes with) is a single product and should be included in a single industry. There is also a tire industry. When a consumer replaces the tires on her car, she thinks about which tire company's product she wants to buy. There is, however, no separate engine industry from the consumer's point of view: For all practical purposes, only a Ford engine can be used in a Ford automobile. The reason is that the interface between the engine and the rest of the car is so complex that switching engines is technically difficult.

The standard approach to this type of problem is to view the complementary products as being in separate industries when they are sold separately and in competition with other products. Ford engines, for example, are sold only for Ford cars. An owner of a Ford car who has to replace the engine does not consider whether to buy a competing engine supplied by another manufacturer. Or consider again IBM's mainframe products. A mainframe system requires the hardware containing the CPU, an operating system to run the hardware, and a host of peripheral equipment. Many firms attempted to enter the market for IBM-compatible peripherals because the interfaces were so well defined that buyers could switch, say, an IBM disk drive for one made by a competitor. The interface between the operating system and the hardware, however, was so complex that only a few firms (Amdahl Corporation being the main one) attempted to produce a fully IBM-compatible computer.

## 6.6 SUMMARY

In this chapter we have begun the exploration of how the firm's external context affects its performance. We demonstrated that a variety of industry characteristics affect performance and have examined several frameworks for organizing and analyzing those characteristics. Our main focus was on potential industry earnings, or PIE. We examined the determinants of PIE and the factors that determine who captures the value created by the industry value chain, including competition, entry and incumbency advantages, and vertical (buyer or supplier) power. We concluded with a discussion of industry definition.

Having provided a broad overview of industry analysis in this chapter, in subsequent chapters we will delve more deeply into its constituent parts. Chapters 7 and 8 are devoted to competitor analysis. In particular, Chapter 7 discusses the spectrum of competitive intensity and competition among differentiated products, whereas Chapter 8 examines competition in industries with few firms. Chapter 9 is devoted to entry barriers, both those that occur naturally as well as those that the incumbent firms themselves erect. Chapter 10 returns to the concept of the value chain to discuss buyer and supplier power and how firms can form relationships with buyers and suppliers to increase the value the chain creates.

# 7

# THE SPECTRUM OF COMPETITION AND NICHE MARKETS

## 7.1 INTRODUCTION

In the preceding chapter, we introduced the idea that competitive intensity within the industry affects the performance of the industry's firms; the share of PIE incumbent firms capture will decline as competition becomes more intense. Although all managers feel the pressure of competition and must act to limit its effects on profits, the intensity of the pressure varies enormously across industries. For example, the manager of a plastics company offering products protected by patents faces little competition and has the luxury of being able to maximize product performance without losing much sleep over competitors' behavior. In contrast, the manager of a line of laptop computers knows that falling behind technologically, pricing too high, or advertising in the wrong places or at the wrong times can cost him market share and profits as rivals take advantage of his missteps. This chapter and the next develop the tools that help managers understand why competition in their industry happens as it does and to develop an effective competitive strategy.

Because competitive intensity varies dramatically from one industry to another, we begin by identifying a *spectrum* of competitive landscapes. Within this spectrum, each landscape poses different strategic challenges. At one extreme are monopolistic industries in which managers can make strategic decisions without worrying about the competitive response of other incumbent firms. Competition is so mild at this end of the spectrum that the monopolist can hope to retain a large share of PIE. At the other, the structure of the industry imposes competition so intense that it sharply constrains a manager's options. In these industries, the incumbents will retain little PIE. In between are the competitive landscapes in which managerial decision making most affects competitive intensity and therefore the share of PIE that incumbent firms retain. These are the landscapes with which we will be most concerned.

In particular, this chapter focuses on niche markets in which product differentiation enables managers to reduce competitive intensity. Understanding these markets requires thinking carefully about how product differentiation works, what types of differentiation are possible, and how the manager of a firm producing differentiated products should think about competition. In Chapter 8, we turn to industries in which rivalry among large players largely determines competitive intensity. A manager whose firm is competing in this type of industry needs to understand and manage the strategic interaction among these large firms.

Although we will not focus on the extremes of perfect competition or monopoly, knowing how competition works in these structures can help us understand more complicated settings. We will therefore describe these extreme cases briefly in the next Section where we lay out the spectrum of competition in more detail. For those who want a more detailed treatment of monopoly and perfect competition, we also discuss these structures in the appendix to this chapter.

We then turn to understanding the nature of the managerial challenge and opportunity posed by competing in niche markets. To provide a sense of the richness of the strategic opportunities that product differentiation introduces, we discuss examples of niche market strategies in the retail clothing industry. Then we identify the underlying sources of product differentiation and characterize the broad types of differentiation firms encounter. Next we discuss how product differentiation enables firms to occupy niches and explore how this affects pricing behavior. (A more analytical discussion of these issues is contained in the appendix.) Finally we briefly discuss choosing product position.

## 7.2   THE SPECTRUM OF COMPETITION

The variety and richness of competitive context are illustrated in Figure 7-1, where we classify industry structures along a spectrum of competition. At the lower end of the spectrum, where competition is least intense, is the monopoly structure: industries that have a single firm. This is the most favorable position for a firm to be in the spectrum of competitive intensity. Unless a monopolist faces powerful buyers or suppliers or new competitors enter its market, it will capture a large share of PIE. AT&T, for example, had a near monopoly on local and long-distance phone service in the United States before 1984 and was highly profitable despite the pricing constraints government regulators imposed. Before its patent on an artificial sweetener expired, NutraSweet sold its sweetener for an average price of $70 per pound. When its patent expired and competing firms entered the market, the price rapidly dropped to about $20 per pound.

In an industry with a single incumbent firm, no profit is dissipated by competition. By definition, the prices chosen by competitors do not constrain the monopolist's choices. The manager of a monopoly needs to consider only the demand for its prod-

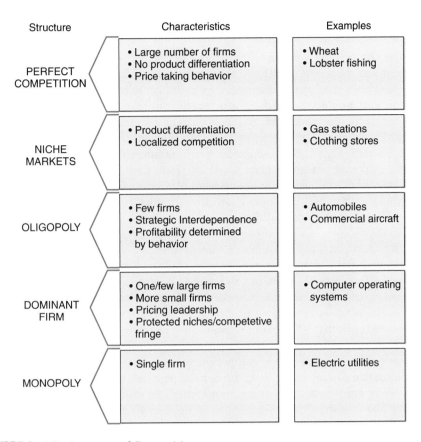

**FIGURE 7-1**   The Spectrum of Competition

uct and his firm's cost structure.[1] Because its potential customers either have to buy its product or "do without," the monopolist can achieve attractive margins. In every other industry structure, the choices competing firms make also affect a firm's profits. When a firm has competitors, its customers have more attractive alternatives than simply "doing without" because they can turn to the products offered by competing

---

[1] Put more carefully, the monopolist need not worry about the prices chosen by any firm within its industry (because there are none). Firms outside the industry have a muted effect on the monopolist's product. Because the price of imperfect substitutes affects the monopolist's demand curve, decisions by the firms producing these substitutes have some effect on demand for the monopolist's products. But, as discussed in Chapter 6, if the industry has been defined so that all the close substitutes are inside it, these effects will be small. Suppose, for example, only one firm produced paper suitable for standard copying machines and computer output printers. There are substitutes for this product—electronic copies, for example—but our paper monopolist would have substantial discretion in its pricing decisions. If, however, several firms produced paper suitable for these tasks, the pricing decisions of these competitors would have a huge effect on our paper producer.

firms. The demand for a firm's products will therefore depend on the prices and characteristics of competitors' products.

Perfect competition is at the other extreme of competitive intensity: Competition sharply reduces the share of PIE incumbents can capture. A perfectly competitive industry has many small firms. Furthermore, each firm sells the same product that all other firms in the industry sell; there is no product differentiation. Commodity markets for agricultural products are examples of industries located near this end of the spectrum. A manager of a firm in an industry like this cannot control the price his firm can charge for its output. Because products are undifferentiated, buyers will change suppliers to take advantage of even small differences in price, so the firm cannot charge a price above the price competing firms offer. In these markets, a manager can try to achieve a cost advantage over competitors but has no scope for strategic decisions about price or product quality.

In a perfectly competitive industry, firms compete fiercely, and price-cost margins are driven to zero. As a result, the firms earn only a "normal" profit. To stay in business in the long run, a firm must earn at least a "normal" profit; that is, it must earn enough revenue to cover its payments to input suppliers plus an amount that makes its owners willing to keep their capital invested in the firm. Normal profit is included in the firm's cost. What we refer to as "profit" is, more precisely, *economic* profit: in excess of the normal profit that a firm would earn in a perfectly competitive industry.[2]

One step removed from perfect competition are so-called niche industries. These industries are similar to perfectly competitive ones in that they contain many small firms. Unlike firms in perfectly competitive industries, however, firms in niche industries can differentiate their products. Sometimes the differentiation is geographic. There are many supermarket firms, for example, and all are small relative to world demand. But supermarkets serve local customers and may have a large share of the sales in their geographic segment. In this sense, these firms resemble "local" monopolists. In other niche markets, the segmentation is based on product attributes rather than geography. There are national retailers who compete directly with each other in terms of territory served; they are located in the same shopping areas. But these firms differentiate their products based on quality, service, and the demographic group they target. In general, firms can differentiate their products because demand is segmented: Potential buyers purchase locally or have different product preferences. In either case, product differentiation reduces competitive intensity relative to perfect competition.

A step removed from the monopoly end of the spectrum is the "dominant firm" structure in which a single firm has a large share of the market and faces only much smaller competitors who share the rest of the market. For many years, IBM's share of

---

[2] If a firm in a competitive industry can produce at a lower cost than its competitors, its cost advantage will earn it an economic profit. However, this situation cannot long endure in a perfectly competitive market because firms that are not efficient will be forced out of the industry. In the short run, inefficient producers may be able to survive if more efficient firms have capacity constraints. In the long run, however, the low-cost firms will add capacity, and competition among them will drive the market price to their marginal cost. The higher-cost firms, if they cannot achieve a competitive cost position, will then be driven out of the industry.

the world market for mainframe computers was above 60 percent, and, while several other small players were in the market, IBM faced no major competitor. In the United States, EDS dominated the information technology outsourcing business in the 1970s and early 1980s. Microsoft currently has a dominant position in computer operating systems. Cisco Systems has a commanding share of the network infrastructure market, and Intel is the market share leader in personal computer microprocessors. In these markets, the large firm usually acts as the industry leader. It makes decisions about its prices, for example, which become the standard for the pricing decisions of its small competitors.

In the middle of the spectrum is the "oligopoly" structure where the industry incumbents are a few, large firms. The U.S. automobile industry before the 1970s, the U.S. market for long-distance telephone services in the 1980s, the market for Unix workstations in the 1990s, and online book sellers and Internet portals in the year 2000 are examples of oligopolies. In these industries, several competitors, each with a large market share, face one another. The actions of each of these large players affect the industry as a whole. Where the firms are manufacturing companies, an increase in output by one firm will drive down industry price, for example. This is the industry structure in which rivalry, that is, conscious strategic interplay among specific firms, is important. In these markets, a firm must consider both the direct effect of its actions on its performance and the indirect effects that will occur because its rivals will respond to those actions. When Boeing is thinking about when to introduce its next generation of commercial aircraft, it must take into account demand for the product and the cost of developing it. It must also think about what its only competitor, Airbus, will do. If Boeing delays introducing the product to reduce the cost of development, for example, it may cede substantial market share to Airbus.[3]

## Structure and Behavior

Across this entire spectrum, two types of conditions affect competitive intensity: market structure and firm behavior. By *market structure* we mean the number and relative sizes of the firms in the industry and the structure of industry demand. Because buyers think of corn as an undifferentiated product and there are many small corn producers, the market for corn is competitive. By *behavior*, we mean choices incumbent firms make that affect how competitive the industry will be *given* its structure. If Boeing and Airbus were to design their products to appeal to different market segments, the market for commercial aircraft would be less competitive than it is when these firms compete for the same customers.

Whether structure or behavior matters more in determining competitive intensity depends on where the industry is in the spectrum. Market structure is overwhelmingly important at the two extremes: Competitive intensity is inevitably high when many small firms produce an undifferentiated product and is inevitably mild

---

[3] Often, industry structure is a "combination" of the dominant firm and oligopoly forms. There is an oligopoly of major players as well as small firms. The combined actions of the large firms determine the character of competition in the industry, and the small firms follow the large firms' lead.

when there is a single incumbent. In-between these extremes, however, firm behavior has a greater impact, and managers must think about how their actions will affect their competitive environment.

In niche markets, firms' decisions about the demand segment(s) in which they will compete can have substantial competitive effects. In the dominant firm structure, the behavior of the dominant firm is an important determinant of competitive intensity: This firm can, for example, set a high price and allow the other firms to live comfortably under its price umbrella, or it can price aggressively to drive up its market share. In an oligopolistic industry, the situation is more complex. The actions of these firms affect the competitive intensity of the industry. A manager setting strategy at one such firm must not only take into account the direct effect of her actions, but also consider how her rival firms' responses will affect competition.

Behavior is so important in oligopoly structures that this market structure is the "wild card" in the spectrum of competition. We can be confident that profit will be quite modest at the competitive end of the spectrum and quite high at the monopoly end. Firms in industries with a single dominant firm also tend to perform well. Although performance across niche markets varies, the firms in these markets tend to perform better than perfectly competitive firms and substantially less well than monopoly firms. But in oligopoly, anything can happen. In some oligopolies, firms approach monopoly profit rates; in others, performance is closer to perfectly competitive levels. For this reason, in Figure 7-1 we have emphasized that behavior determines profitability in oligopolies. This characteristic of oligopolies also is at odds with our notion of a spectrum of competition. Oligopoly is correctly placed in the middle in terms of industry structure. In terms of profitability, however, its position is uncertain.

As we have seen, the lack of product differentiation is one of the industry characteristics that make competition so intense in perfectly competitive industries. Managers who can differentiate their product offerings from those of their competitors have an opportunity to reduce the profit-destroying effects of competition. To understand how this works, we devote the rest of this chapter to exploring niche markets. We focus on niche markets because they are the simplest setting in which to discuss product differentiation. Differentiation also affects competitive intensity in oligopolistic and dominant firm industries, but its effects are more difficult to assess because other dimensions of firm behavior also impact competition in these environments. In niche markets, only product differentiation separates the firms from the rigors of perfect competition.

## 7.3  NICHE MARKETS AND PRODUCT DIFFERENTIATION

If all markets with more than one incumbent firm were perfectly competitive, strategic management would be a thin field of study, and general managers could ignore strategic thinking. When a manager works with a good or service for which many competing firms produce good substitutes, his search for sustainable competitive advantage is unlikely to be rewarding. Indeed, it will require all the firms' resources simply to maintain parity with its rivals. As the Red Queen explains in Lewis Carroll's

*Through The Looking Glass,* "[I]t takes all the running you can do to keep in the same place." In this situation, the competitive forces in its markets severely curtail the firm's strategic flexibility.

Fortunately for the field of strategic management and the contribution of strategic thinking to firm performance, most managers have responsibility for products or services for which no other firm produces really good substitutes. Once a firm's offerings are seen to be at least somewhat different from those of its rivals, the manager has more control over the firm's destiny. He has an array of tools (product selection, pricing, promotion and so on) that potentially provide leverage against competitors. By offering a distinctive product that appeals to a particular market segment, the manager can create a competitive advantage there that firms with different products cannot match. This is the reason we have distinguished the niche market structure from perfectly competitive markets in the spectrum of competition.

Although the manager in a niche market has more freedom to operate than she would if other firms in her industry produced identical products, her products are not so strongly differentiated that she can behave like an unconstrained monopolist. There are imperfect substitutes for her product to which her buyers can turn. Furthermore, there usually are some competitors who are well positioned to enter her niche if it is sufficiently attractive. Both of these factors restrain profitability. Indeed, as we shall see, a manager in these "niche" markets faces decisions that have the flavor of both competitive and monopoly markets. Some of her buyers are strongly committed to her product and will not switch to competing products to take advantage of small differences in price. Others are more willing to switch to competitors' products, and the manager will lose these customers if her price is above her competitors' prices.

## Building, Defending, and Exploiting a Market Niche: Benetton and The Gap

Clothing production and retailing tend to be competitive businesses, largely because entry barriers are not high enough to protect incumbent firms from would-be entrants. As a result, many firms compete in the retail portion of the clothing value chain, and the potential profits implicit in the lack of buyer and supplier power and in the strong demand for clothing are lost. Average, long-term performance for these firms is only slightly better than those typical of perfectly competitive markets.

Within this gloomy overall picture, however, some firms perform well. Two of these firms are Benetton and The Gap. Each of them first had tremendous success in its home country (Italy and the United States, respectively) and expanded internationally to become one of the strongest clothing brands in the world. As with most firms, these two companies' successes cannot be attributed to any one element of their business strategies. Nonetheless, how each of these firms has managed to differentiate its products has been a critically important component of its strategies.

The Gap and Benetton have each succeeded in creating and supporting distinct product positioning and branding strategies. Each has located its products in a niche in which it has become a leading brand. The Gap has targeted children, teens, and young adults for its line of stylish, well-made casual clothing. While Benetton also does well with teens and young adults, its somewhat more sophisticated clothing line also attracts an older clientele and provides a less casual wardrobe. The Gap has built its product lines around a core of khakis and jeans; the Benetton core is colorful knitwear. The different focus of the firms' product lines has enabled them to avoid head-to-head competition with each other. The very strong brand images they developed have also distinguished their products from other competitors' products. Both The Gap and Benetton have achieved this through product styling and product promotion. For both The Gap and Benetton, a successful branding campaign has created a loyal customer base that is difficult for another clothing retailer to capture with lower prices. This has reduced price competition with other firms.

The Gap and Benetton extended this basic advantage as they became global firms. Both firms have developed brands with global appeal within their target segments. The look promoted by The Gap is familiar to international audiences from U.S. television shows and movies, reinforcing an "American" image for its product. Conversely, Benetton's Italian origins and more sophisticated look create a "Continental" image for its products outside Europe. As a result, each firm has captured share in many geographic markets. These shares are big enough to support many specialized company outlets. This extensive retail presence in turn helps build the brand image, strengthening the brands' appeals to the local target markets.

Building a global presence has also allowed The Gap and Benetton to reduce unit costs by exploiting economies of scale as they export their successful formulas. Economies of scale are associated with the creation and promotion of a global brand both because the fixed costs of creating advertising and in-store promotions can be spread over many stores and because the international ubiquity of advertising, stores, and clothing strengthens the international brand. International distribution also enables the firms to exploit economies of scale in manufacturing because they can spread the costs of designing and producing the targeted (and hence narrow) range of products over substantial volumes. The combination of diminished price pressure from a strong brand and efficient manufacturing and distribution systems from operating at a global scale generate attractive margins.

Many of the ingredients of the market success of these firms are no longer secret. The business press has published a spate of stories analyzing their strategies. Even so, these firms occupy positions that imitators cannot easily attack. Each has a first-mover advantage in its niche. An imitator might benefit from the development of the niche by these pioneering firms: to the extent that the firms have created a well-defined customer base, a follower firm might be able to build a brand name more quickly. However, any imitator has to deal with the entrenched firm. Neither Benetton nor The Gap would be likely to remain passive if faced with increased competition in its niche. Indeed, although these firms are small relative to the entire retail clothing market, each is large relative to its own niche. As a result, any potential entrant must think about how to build a brand while protecting itself against the retaliatory strategies that a well-financed and experienced incumbent with a loyal customer base can pursue. And the only reward to a newcomer, even if it were successful, would be to share the niche with the incumbent. This is a much less attractive prospect than creating and dominating a new niche.

In summary, at the heart of both The Gap and Benetton's success is a clear and distinctive product positioning and branding strategy. Because loyal consumers of these firms' products do not perceive the offerings of rival firms to be good substitutes, The Gap and Benetton are protected from the rigors of perfect competition. By creating and defending a strong brand position, they can stake out niches in which they are not subject to head-to-head competition with one another or with other equally strong rivals. The attractiveness of their offerings to the customers in their market niches gives them a limited degree of market power, that is, the ability to sustain margins that would be impossible under perfect competition. Although The Gap and Benetton surely do not have the market power a monopolist enjoys, they nonetheless benefit from a respite from competition within their niches that a monopolist enjoys more broadly. The result is that the financial performance of these firms has surpassed the average for their industry. For example, in early 2000 the five-year average gross margins for Benetton and The Gap were 37.8 and 37.9 percent versus an industry average of around 35 percent over the same period, and net profit margins were 7.9 and 8.5 percent, respectively, versus an industry average of around 5.3 percent.[4]

## 7.4  CONSUMER PREFERENCES AND PRODUCT DIFFERENTIATION

The underlying phenomenon enabling firms like Benetton or The Gap to create and dominate a niche is variation in buyers' tastes. If all potential buyers had the same taste, product differentiation could not exist: Given any constellation of prices and products, every consumer would make the same choice. Anticipating this outcome, no firm would diverge from the only price-product bundle consumers would buy. Because there is a range of consumer tastes, however, The Gap and Benetton can target a subset of consumers. Their success at identifying a subset and catering to its preferences suggests that these firms understand how consumer tastes differ and how product and pricing decisions will affect profits *given* those differences. Next, we develop a framework that illuminates the generic ways in which consumers compare products. Then, we explore what this process implies for managers who must make strategic decisions for the firm.

### Preferences and Products

First, it is important to understand that what consumers care about (other than price) is product characteristics. We can think of consumer preferences, therefore, as preferences about the main *characteristics* that existing (or potential) products possess. When consumer preferences are displayed graphically, the result is sometimes called a "characteristics" or "perceptual" map. These maps are commonly used in marketing where, typically, products are arrayed in two- (or higher) dimensional space according to their primary characteristics. Note, however, that these maps are defined not by the product characteristics themselves but by consumer preferences over them. The dif-

---

[4] Yahoo Market Guide (http://yahoo.marketguide.com), March 29, 2000.

ference is important for two reasons. First, because we can map consumer preferences about the characteristics of existing products, we can also map consumer preferences over products that do not yet exist. Second, and more fundamentally, the structure of the map depends on consumer preferences. If consumers don't care about a particular characteristic, it cannot be mapped. And the rankings implicit in the map depend only on consumer preferences. If, for example, consumers think that mauve refrigerators are better than white ones or that slow computers are better than fast ones, the mapping should reflect these rankings.

Perhaps the easiest preference map to understand is one in which geographic location alone determines consumer preferences. All else equal, for example, motorists prefer to buy gasoline at a station located close to them to buying gasoline at a more distant station.[5] Consumers typically purchase gasoline at stations convenient to their standard travel routes; they buy gasoline on the way to work or shopping. Consequently, only a few stations routinely compete for each consumer's business. For each consumer, one could construct a map showing her most preferred point of purchase and other locations at which she sometimes purchases (less preferred points of purchase) or would never purchase (points of purchase providing no value to her).

While literally mapping potential buyers in geographic space provides a vivid image, it is often more useful to think of *figuratively* mapping preferences over other product attributes. A simple example of this (one that we will refer to repeatedly) is breakfast cereals. Imagine that consumers care only about how crunchy the cereal is. We can therefore envisage consumer preferences as being located along a line representing the continuum from the extreme of "turns-immediately-to-mush-in-the-presence-of-milk" to the other extreme of "maintains-the-texture-of-wood-chips-even-after-two-hours-of-emersion." In Figure 7-2 we have parsimoniously labeled the directions "soggy" and "crunchy." In this figure, each consumer's preferences place him on some point along the line. Peter, who likes a less crunchy cereal than Paul, is located to Paul's left.[6]

Of course, most mappings, including that for cereals, are more complicated than the one in Figure 7-2. For example, in evaluating automobiles, consumers care about size, styling, power, seating configuration, fuel efficiency, driving ease, amenities, and

**FIGURE 7-2** Consumer Preference for Cereal "Crunchiness"

[5] The "all else equal" matters here. Consumers also care about prices, other services the station offers, and so forth. All preference maps make some assumption about price levels and the levels of other, unmapped characteristics.

[6] "Crunchiness" is only one of many attributes that affect consumer preferences for cereals. However, it is a relevant one as empirical work by Aviv Nevo ("Measuring Market Power in the Ready-To-Eat Cereal Industry," *Econometrica*, forthcoming) illustrates.

so on. Although some of these attributes, like horsepower, are easily quantifiable, others—such as styling—are more difficult to measure than "crunchiness." Even for characteristics that have no "scientific" or "engineering" measure, those who study consumer behavior find that some scale that captures consumer preferences can be constructed. The combination of styling and amenities, for example, might be captured in a scale that runs from "elegant" to "functional." Furthermore, including all the characteristics consumers care about implies that the product characteristics space will be multidimensional. Multiple dimensions make the mapping problem more complex but do not change the basic principles involved. We can still imagine a map that locates consumer preferences.

In discussing these maps, we have implicitly assumed that each consumer occupies a unique position. This is clearly not true in general. Think about cars again for a moment; households with enough income to support more than one vehicle often choose two distinct product types. A family might, for example, want one fuel-efficient, compact car for adult commuting and another large vehicle for transporting children and their equipment. This family would have two "most" preferred points in the map. This possibility doesn't change our basic arguments, and setting it aside allows us to think of consumer locations and preference locations as being the same.

Once we have mapped consumer tastes, we can then easily locate a particular product on the map. The characteristics of each product determine its location. Figure 7-3 illustrates how three brands of cereal might be located by how crunchy consumers think they are.[7] How consumers view them determines the relative position of products. For example, among U.S. beers, if we say Budweiser is similar to Miller and distinct from Samuel Adams, we mean that consumers who prefer Budweiser to Samuel Adams will also probably prefer Miller to Samuel Adams. When we array these products in a perceptual map, the consumers who most prefer Budweiser will be relatively far away from consumers who most prefer Samuel Adams and relatively close to consumers who most prefer Miller. To use another beverage example, most Coke lovers do not consider Dr. Pepper to be "close" to Coke, but many do think of Pepsi as reasonably "close." In perceptual maps, this means that Coke and Pepsi will be closer together than will Dr. Pepper and Pepsi or Coke.[8]

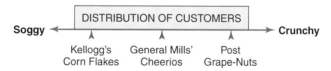

**FIGURE 7-3**  Location of Cereal Brands

---

[7] How crunchy a cereal is depends on how long it has been in milk. The array in Figure 7-3 is probably most accurate after only about 30 seconds in milk. After 5 minutes or more most cereals are pretty soggy!

[8] Another simplification we impose is that all consumers would describe the space in the same way. Consumers could disagree about the location of a product. Some might think that Budweiser and Miller beers are dissimilar, for example, while others cannot tell them apart.

Because there are typically fewer products than consumer locations, some consumers are more fortunate than others. Any consumer who most prefers the amount of crunchiness that General Mills' Cheerios cereal has, for example, has an ideal crunchiness point that is in the same location as Cheerios. He doesn't sacrifice any amount of crunchy satisfaction from not having a product that exactly matches his taste. He and others at this location obviously prefer Cheerios to any of the other existing brands and to any other possible brand with a different crunchiness. As one moves to the left of Cheerios, consumers value Cheerios less and Kellogg's Corn Flakes more. Customers close to Cheerios location probably still prefer it to its less crunchy competitor, but its advantage will be lower. The farther away a consumer is located from a given product, the more crunchiness satisfaction he must sacrifice to consume it.

Figure 7-4 illustrates a more complex map which the Saturn division of General Motors used in the early 1990s.[9] The figure classifies cars on two axes: Family/Functional to Personal/Sporty and Prestige/Luxury to Economy/Practical. These categories illustrate the difference between technical and taste dimensions. From an engineering standpoint, "Family/Functional" is not particularly meaningful. Presumably it implies something about passenger and cargo space and perhaps something about styling, but the positions on this axis have no precise technical analog. In contrast, the consumers surveyed to construct this map find these categories more useful than the many engineering specifications that might be listed for these vehicles.

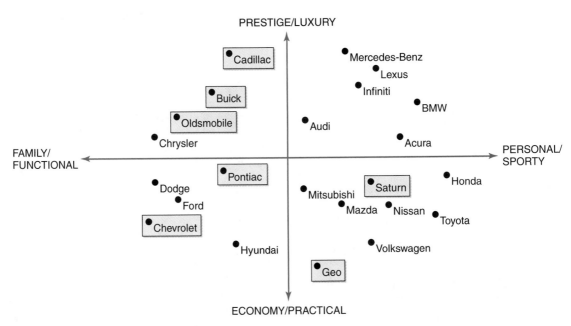

**FIGURE 7-4**    Mapping the U.S. Automotive Market

[9] This figure is based on a product map that appears in "Saturn: A Different Kind of Car Company," a Harvard Business School Case (No. 9-795-010) by Greg Keller and Anita McGahan.

This map also illustrates the problem of defining the appropriate level of analysis. As it is drawn, each entry includes multiple car models. Ford, for example, produced many models in this period, giving it a much broader presence than is indicated in this map, which places all Ford products at a single point. GM has six divisions (as well as its joint venture with Toyota which produces the Geo) represented on this map, each of which is denoted by shading in the figure. This gives the impression that GM products are more diverse than, say, Ford's or Toyota's. This might be appropriate: GM does have more products than any other firm on the map. But it also makes the other manufacturers look more focused than they are and may, if not analyzed carefully, imply that GM is more insulated from competition in some of its product lines than it really is.

## Horizontal and Vertical Product Differentiation

As the cereal example illustrates, the dispersion of consumer preferences creates the possibility that products will be differentiated in the minds of consumers. There are two distinct types of differentiation: vertical and horizontal. Briefly, products are said to be horizontally differentiated when buyers *disagree* about which product is better. Some people prefer frozen yogurt to ice cream, and others prefer ice cream to frozen yogurt. As a result, if both products are offered at the same price, some consumers will buy ice cream, and others will buy frozen yogurt. The differentiation between these products, like that in the cereal example, is horizontal. Products are *vertically* differentiated when consumers *agree* about how to rank them. Nearly everyone would agree that a Ritz Carlton is a more luxurious place to stay than a Travelodge. As a consequence, if a night at the Ritz were offered at the same price as a night at a Travelodge, few would stay at the Travelodge.[10] The differentiation between them is vertical. The cost–quality framework presented in Chapter 3 is based on vertical differentiation.

Many consumer products such as soft drinks, beer, and shampoos are horizontally differentiated goods. People disagree, for example, about which beer tastes best and will, when prices are equal, purchase different beers. When prices differ, they will also affect the choices consumers make. If Samuel Adams were more expensive than Miller, for example, some of those who prefer Samuel Adams when it cost the same as Miller would choose to buy Miller. Producer goods can also be horizontally differentiated. An engineer at an airplane manufacturer would probably choose a different type of steel for her products than a construction engineer would choose for his. These buyers use steel for different purposes and therefore value characteristics like weight and strength differently.

When products are vertically differentiated, they can be ordered by perceived quality. Some clothing retailers, for example, offer designer clothes, high service, and an attractive ambiance. These "premium stores" are different from the mass merchants that sell medium or low-quality products in a self-service, spartan setting. Products are vertically differentiated when people agree on how the products are

---

[10] There will always be *some* disagreement about product rankings, and many products will have both vertical and horizontal dimensions to their differentiation. Often, however, we can think of the primary mode of differentiation as horizontal or vertical.

ranked. Suppose designer and mass merchandise clothes were offered for sale at the same price and in the same settings. If all consumers agree about the relative ranking of these products, only designer goods will be sold.

When prices are not the same, consumers choosing among vertically differentiated products make different purchasing decisions because they have different incomes or use the product in different ways or vary in some other way that leads them to make different price–quality tradeoffs. A wealthy consumer may buy an expensive Rado or Rolex watch because he places more value on quality relative to price than does a less wealthy consumer. A homeowner may purchase a less durable and less expensive stove than a professional chef because the homeowner uses the stove under less demanding conditions than the chef and therefore makes a different price–durability tradeoff. A more affluent customer may pay a premium for banking service because she has more complex financial service needs than a less affluent investor or she is more willing to pay for time-saving service. These different choices do not mean that the buyers disagree about which watch is better made or which stove performs better or which bank provides better service.

In discussing vertical differentiation, we have casually described products as having "lower" or "higher" quality. This is quality as *perceived* by potential buyers, not a description of the product's physical characteristics. Mercedes may make "better" cars than Chevrolet based solely on technical criteria, but that is not directly relevant. In fact, whether we are talking about horizontally or vertically differentiated goods, only differences as *perceived by the consumer* matter because these are the perceptions that guide purchasing decisions. A common mistake made by technology-driven companies is to assume that customers prefer products with better technical characteristics. But this need not be the case, even when prices are equal. Conversely, consumers can have strong preferences among products that seem to be technically similar. One of the authors knows a 10-year-old customer who, on being told by a waiter that he was unsure whether his soda fountain served "Classic Coke" or "New Coke," ordered milk rather than risk getting her less preferred cola!

## 7.5  DIFFERENTIATION AND COMPETITION

A key factor intensifying competition at the perfect competition end of the spectrum is that the products each firm produces are undifferentiated from its competitors' products. As a result, buyers decide which firm to patronize based only on price. If there are many paperclip retailers, and one paperclip is just like another, consumers will select the lowest priced paperclips. When firms produce differentiated products, however, buyers make their choices based on product characteristics as well as price.

Although we have argued that this difference in how consumers make choices means that differentiation will soften price competition, we have been vague about *how* this happens. In this section, we look more closely at this claim. Here we take product locations as given. That is, we are not concerned with where firms should locate their products in the map. Instead, we discuss how a given product location affects competition. We turn to the location choice problem in the next section.

## Niches and Neighbors

To see how differentiation affects competition, we return to the cereal example. We saw that consumers who are farther away from Cheerios value it less than do consumers close to it. Extending this argument, consumers whose most preferred point on the crunchiness continuum is very far away from Cheerios' location probably wouldn't buy it at any price, no matter how low. They just don't like it. It is then easy to see that price competition among cereals is much reduced if the competing brands are "far enough" away from each other. If, to return to Figure 7-2, Post Grape-Nuts is far enough to the right of Cheerios and Corn Flakes is far enough to the left, then these three products will not compete with each other. The only customers who like Cheerios would not like Grape-Nuts or Corn Flakes. There will be no overlap between the consumers who are attracted to Cheerios and those who are attracted to the other two products. In this case Cheerios would have a virtual monopoly *in its market segment.*[11]

More likely, however, the demand segments to which the products appeal overlap, and these firms compete for the consumers located in the area(s) of overlap. Some consumers probably like both Cheerios and Grape-Nuts enough to buy either of them if its price is low enough. Cheerios and Grape-Nuts will compete for these consumers. However, to the extent that consumers care about crunchiness, Grape-Nuts and Corn Flakes are less likely to compete for many customers. Any customer who is buying Grape-Nuts might, if its price increased, switch to Cheerios but is less likely to switch to Corn Flakes.

This leads us to a straightforward conclusion: *Each product competes more intensely with products that are closer to it.* For our hotel example from Chapter 3, this implies that the Ritz Carlton would compete more intensely with the Sheraton than with the Travelodge. If the Travelodge were to increase its advertising, the Ritz might lose a few customers to it, but an advertising campaign of the same magnitude by the Sheraton would have a much larger effect on the Ritz Carlton's market share. Because the competitive impacts of other firms' actions are unequal, a manager who is attempting to assess the effects of a change in prices or an entry by a new firm, for example, has to think about the location at which the change occurs.

For a more fully developed example, consider the personal computer (PC) industry in the United States. A careful analysis of demand data for the 1980s[12] reveals four distinct market segments defined by whether the PC is identified with a well-known producer (a branded product) and whether the product is on the tech-

---

[11] In this situation, it might seem rather odd to include Cheerios and its two closest competitors in the same market. Per our discussion in Chapter 6, these two cereals are very imperfect substitutes for Cheerios. If this were an accurate picture of consumer preferences over crunchiness and crunchiness were the only attribute consumers cared about, we should think of Cheerios as a monopolist in its own industry.

[12] The information presented here comes from Bresnahan, Stern, and Trajentenberg. "Market Segmentation, Transitory Market Power, and Ranks from Innovation: Personal Computers in the late 1980's," *RAND Journal of Economics*, 1997, S17–S44. This study classified a product as branded if produced by IBM, Compaq, Hewlett-Packard, or AT&T. The technological frontier was defined by the microprocessor used in the PCs.

**TABLE 7-1**    Segmentation in the Personal Computer Industry

| | Origins of Increased Demand | | | | |
| Home Segment | Frontier, Branded | Not Frontier, Branded | Frontier, Not Branded | Not Frontier, Not Branded | New Demand |
|---|---|---|---|---|---|
| Frontier, Branded | **63%** | 16% | 4% | 0% | 16% |
| Not Frontier, Branded | 3% | **66%** | 0% | 0% | 31% |
| Frontier, Not Branded | 12% | 1% | **54%** | 3% | 30% |
| Not Frontier, Not Branded | 0% | 1% | 3% | **64%** | 31% |

nological frontier. Researchers have examined how a new entrant into a specific segment would affect the demand facing the incumbent firms. The entrant gains market share by growing the market for PCs as a whole and by stealing share from incumbent firms. Table 7-1 shows how share gains for a hypothetical entrant would be distributed. For example, as the third row of numbers shows, if an entrant to the unbranded, frontier segment were to sell 100 PCs, 30 of them would go to buyers who would otherwise not have purchased a PC, and 54 would go to buyers who would otherwise have purchased another unbranded, frontier product. Only 16 of them would go to buyers who otherwise would have purchased a computer in another demand segment.

No matter which segment we consider, most of the sales the entrant achieves come from competing products in the same segment (called the home segment in the table). Across all segments, 54 to 66 percent of a new product's sales comes from other products in its segment, and only 5 to 20 percent comes from products in other segments. This is exactly the pattern we would expect: products compete most intensely with those in their segment. We saw a similar pattern in the effects of entry on generic and branded drug prices in Chapter 6. Entry by another generic drug affects demand for other generics more than demand for the branded product.

The terminology of "niches" arises because differentiated products compete most intensively with those closest to them. As the example from the PC market illustrates, variation in consumer preferences creates the possibility that demand niches will emerge in which there are "pockets" of consumers whose preferences are similar to each other and dissimilar to those held by consumers in other "pockets." Consumers shopping for a high-end, luxury car may compare Infiniti, BMW, and Mercedes automobiles. Consumers searching for basic, reliable transportation may compare Toyota, Ford, Honda, and Chrysler products. These are two distinct product niches. The presence of pockets of preference means that firms can locate their products in a niche where the products appeal strongly to a specific subset of buyers and are insulated from competition by products in other niches. The Gap and Benetton each have a niche of this sort.

When demand can be characterized by distinct segments, the firms whose products are in the same niche are said to be in the same *strategic group*. This terminology is used because a firm's strategy is much more strongly conditioned by the actions of other firms within its niche than by firms in other niches.[13] High-performance luxury cars might be such a niche, and Mercedes, BMW, and Infiniti would be members of a strategic group.

Niches are often small relative to the demand for the overall product. The automobile market is large, but the high-end segment that Jaguar and Porsche serve, for example, is much smaller. In effect, differentiation reduces the size of the market relevant to each firm. In perfect competition, each firm competes directly with every other firm in the industry, and each firm is small relative to the entire market. In niche markets, each firm is small relative to the entire market, but the entire market is not the relevant market for any individual firm. Rather, it is the size of the market segment that the individual firm serves and the number of other competitors that serve that segment that determine competitive intensity. This is what we mean, in Figure 7-1, where we describe competition as "localized" in niche markets.

## Differentiation Softens Competition

Since each product competes more intensely with products closer to it, competition within the industry will be less intense when the products of competing firms are more differentiated from each other.[14] Differentiation reduces competition through two effects. First, holding prices constant, increasing the differentiation among products leads to an increase in the number of potential buyers who prefer a specific product. Second, increasing the differentiation among products leads to higher prices. We discuss each of these effects below.

*The first effect of increased differentiation is to increase each firm's sales.* To understand why, consider the effect of a decline in differentiation when prices are unchanged. As products crowd together more closely, each product has fewer customers who prefer it to all other products. Suppose, for example, the three cereal brands hold their prices fixed and Post makes Grape-Nuts less crunchy while Kellogg's makes Corn Flakes crunchier. Some of the customers who preferred Cheerios to its competitors before but were to its left will now prefer Corn Flakes. And some who were to its right will now prefer Grape-Nuts. More generally, when a firm's products are more differentiated from its competitors' products, each firm's sales volume will increase, holding all prices constant.

---

[13] Strategic groups are also found in other market structures and are sometimes based on competitive advantage rather than the positioning of their products. For example, oligopoly markets are sometimes composed of groups of firms adopting different strategies, some of whose competitive advantage is based on low costs and others who differentiate based on quality.

[14] In the context of our cereal saga, "more differentiated" means that the brands are farther away from each other in the crunchiness map. Moving away from the spatial metaphor for differentiation, an industry in which the firm's products are less good substitutes for each other will be less competitive than an industry in which they are better substitutes for each other.

The market for 35mm single-lens reflex cameras over the past 30 years vividly illustrates this phenomenon. In the early 1970s, Nikon dominated the "high end" of this market; its only competitor in this segment had a very small market share. The range of perceived quality below those premium brands was crowded, with Pentax, Minolta, Canon, Yashica, Nikon (with its Nikormat brand), and several others all competing fiercely. Over the past decade, some of these "midrange" camera manufacturers, most notably Canon and Minolta, have made a successful run at the high end, wresting share from Nikon. Nikon has responded to the intensified competition at the high end by attacking the "midrange" more aggressively with a line of cameras sporting the Nikon (rather than Nikormat) brand. The overall result is that Nikon has lost market share to Canon in the high-quality segment, and Canon has suffered from the more aggressive behavior of Nikon in the medium-quality segment.

Even if all the camera manufacturers had held their prices constant, Nikon's loss in market share in the premium segment would have reduced its profits in that segment. In fact, however, diminished differentiation was also accompanied by a reduction in market prices. This is a common effect: *Prices are higher when products are more differentiated.* The following argument explains why this happens. When products are undifferentiated, *all* buyers will switch to the low-price firm to benefit from even a small difference in price. But when the products are differentiated, the same price difference will lead to less switching. For example, if General Mills drops the price of Cheerios slightly, its sales will increase as it steals share from Kellogg's and Post. However, it will not get all the other firms' customers. Some of them will stay with the competing brands because they prefer them to Cheerios, even though its price is now slightly lower than it was. As a result, the gain from a price reduction is smaller when products are differentiated. With less incentive to cut prices, price competition will be less intense than it is when products are undifferentiated.

A good example of this phenomenon comes from the pricing of personal computers in the late 1980s. There were essentially two "flavors" of personal computers: Apple and the computers using the DOS (or Windows) operating system and Intel microprocessors. Many firms competed in the latter segment, but IBM's brand name was preeminent among them in the early days. Indeed, these computers were referred to as IBM-compatibles during this period. The higher perceived quality endowed by IBM's brand name enabled IBM to charge a significant price premium over its rivals. Over time, consumers realized that the manufacturers of DOS/Windows machines were mainly assemblers of others' components, a perception reinforced by Microsoft's branding of its Windows product and Intel's "Intel Inside" campaign. As a result, computers became less differentiated by the computer maker's brand name, and price competition among PC assemblers increased dramatically resulting in lower overall prices.

Another good example comes from e-commerce. In the traditional "bricks and mortar" world, brands that are sold through different outlets are differentiated both by attributes of the brand and by geography. However on the Internet the geographic element of differentiation is eliminated. Consequently firms competing on the Internet experience greater price competition pressure than in the offline world. While it is still possible to differentiate by quality of service, ease-of-use of the site, time-to-delivery, and so on, consumers who care only about price can easily search out the firm offering the lowest price (by using a comparison-shopping service like *mysimon.com*, for example).

Globalization has also demonstrated the profit-destroying effects of a decline in differentiation in many industries. As geographic differentiation breaks down, industries become more competitive. Domestic financial services firms, for example, have often been protected from competition by regulatory barriers that the home country imposed to prevent entry by foreign competitors. These barriers are gradually being relaxed, and the domestic financial firms are now facing international competitors. Each new firm enters a local market to increase its expected profits. However, as time passes and more firms enter, the entry of each new firm reduces the profits of those already in the market. If entry is costless, it will continue until all competitors earn a normal return. The initial incumbents who had been protected from competition may be driven out of the market altogether because the international firms entering the market typically have a lower cost structure, a broader range of products, and greater financial resources. In the U.S. banking sector, a similar story is unfolding on a state-by-state basis as state regulations are being relaxed on the number of branches banks can have and on interstate banking. As a result, the banking industry is moving from a situation in which a few small banks serve each geographic region to one in which a few, large banks face each other in many regional markets.

Note that we have assumed that a different firm owns each of the brands in the market. If one firm owned all the cereals, pricing would be different from what it was in the case we examined. In particular, a firm views stealing market share differently when the brand from which it is stealing share is one of its own! A firm that takes this effect into account will price less aggressively when it owns the neighboring brands, and overall prices will be higher.

In the early days of the U.S. ready-made breakfast cereal market, for example, there were few initial competitors, and their products were very different. As a result, price competition among them was not intense. Over time, however, hundreds of brands have been introduced, filling the product space and creating close competitors for each existing brand. Had each of these new brands been introduced by a new firm, this industry would have become much more competitive. Instead, the incumbent firms introduced most of the new brands. With just three firms owning a large fraction of all brands, competition has remained muted. This point has also been demonstrated in the automobile industry where, in the United States in the 1950s, many competing brands were owned by the "Big 3": General Motors, Ford, and Chrysler. This concentration of brand ownership reduced competition in the industry. In particular, each of the Big 3 priced a particular model less aggressively when it also owned the neighboring models.[15]

Our discussion about how prices are determined in markets with product differentiation illustrates an important conclusion of the chapter. The behavior of firms in

---

[15] See Timothy Bresnahan, "Competition and Collusion in the American Automobile Oligopoly: The 1955 Price War," *Journal of Industrial Economics* 34, No. 4 (1987).

niche markets contains elements of both perfectly competitive and monopoly markets. Typically, when products are differentiated, the firms will charge a price higher than the competitive price but lower than the price a monopolist would charge. The price is higher than the competitive price because each firm has customers who have a strong preference for its product relative to its competitors' products. These consumers will not switch to competing brands for a small difference in price. The price will be lower than the monopoly price because each firm also wants to sell to customers who find competitors' products attractive but will switch to benefit from small price differences.

## Price Competition and Market Share

The cereal example is one in which the products are horizontally differentiated, but the conclusion that increased differentiation tends to reduce price competition is also true for vertically differentiated products. As our camera example suggests, when products are vertically differentiated, each product competes more intensively with products closer to it, and differentiation reduces competitive intensity. Nonetheless, some important differences exist in how price affects market share and profitability in the two cases. To understand the differences, let's think about two competing products: widgets and gidgets. This odd product example has been chosen not because it is a favorite in economics texts, which it is, but because no one knows what gidgets or widgets are. We are therefore free to suppose anything we like about how they might be related to each other. Buyers could compare these products in any of three ways: They could see them as undifferentiated, vertically differentiated, or horizontally differentiated.

Now suppose I make widgets, and you make gidgets. I know you are charging a price of $1.00 and believe you will continue to do so. I want to know what happens to demand for my widgets at the various prices I might charge. To find out, I turn to the demand analysis in Table 7-2. The market shares in the table illustrate the effect of the interaction of price and market share for each type of differentiation. The first column of the table lists the possibilities for my price, varying it from $0.25 to $1.75. The remaining columns show what happens to my market share at each of these prices when your price is $1.00.

If consumers think of our products as very close substitutes for each other, I get the entire market when my price is lower than your price, and I make no sales when my price is higher than yours. When our prices are equal, we split the market. In the undifferentiated case, customers choose only on the basis of price because nothing else distinguishes the products. A small price advantage (disadvantage) leads to a large gain (loss) in share.

If consumers see our products as horizontally differentiated, I get some share of the market at all prices.[16] My share declines if I charge a higher price, but I still get some share when my price is above $1.00, and I don't get the entire market when my

---

[16] Given your price, there will be some high price at which I make no sales. In this illustration, the price at which my share drops to zero is higher than $1.75.

**TABLE 7-2**   Illustration of Product Demand, Price, and Product Differentiation (Competitor's Price = 1.00)

| "My" Price | My Market Share with No Differentiation | My Market Share with Vertical Differentiation | | My Market Share with Horizontal Differentiation |
| --- | --- | --- | --- | --- |
| | | If I Am High Quality | If I Am Low Quality | |
| 0.25 | 1.0 | 1.00 | 0.80 | 0.99 |
| 0.50 | 1.0 | 1.00 | 0.60 | 0.90 |
| 0.75 | 1.0 | 1.00 | 0.20 | 0.70 |
| 0.99 | 1.0 | 1.00 | 0.05 | 0.58 |
| 1.00 | 0.5 | 1.00 | 0.00 | 0.50 |
| 1.01 | 0.0 | 0.95 | 0.00 | 0.42 |
| 1.25 | 0.0 | 0.80 | 0.00 | 0.30 |
| 1.50 | 0.0 | 0.40 | 0.00 | 0.10 |
| 1.75 | 0.0 | 0.20 | 0.00 | 0.01 |

price is below $1.00. In this case, buyers' tastes differ, and each buyer has some preferred product, that is, the one he would always buy if the prices were equal. When prices are unequal, some buyers switch to the lower-priced product, but others stick with the higher-priced brand. The latter are consumers who prefer the higher-priced brand even if they have to pay a premium for it.

Buyers are also willing to pay a premium for the product they prefer when products are vertically differentiated. But in this case all consumers prefer the same product. As a result, market shares respond differently to price differentials than they would if the products were horizontally differentiated. Suppose consumers view my product as the higher quality good. Then, when my price is equal to or below yours, I get the entire market. No consumer will buy your product at an equal or higher price when they think my product has higher quality. My share declines only when my price is above yours. The converse is true if I have the low-quality product.

These examples illustrate that it is important for managers to understand how products are differentiated when making pricing decisions. The type of differentiation also influences how changes in the base of potential consumers affect product demand. For example, a decline in buyers' income usually depresses demand for all products. If the product is horizontally differentiated, all products may be affected equally. For vertically differentiated products, however, an income decline tends to increase the demand share of lower quality products. Thus, for example, demand for automobiles in developing countries is more concentrated in the lower half of the automobile quality distribution than is demand in the United States. And a decline in the U.S. stock market tends to depress demand for "high-quality" goods disproportionately because it disproportionately affects the income of those consumers who earn enough to be more willing to pay a high price for quality.

## 7.6 PRODUCT POSITIONING

Although we have analyzed what happens when firms' products are more or less differentiated, we have not directly addressed the question of choosing a position in product space. We now want to discuss this problem.

Up to now, it has been assumed that consumers are evenly distributed across the map. To discuss product positioning, however, we must first recognize that potential buyers typically populate some sections of product space more densely than others. Returning to the 35mm camera example introduced earlier, we find that many more cameras of medium quality are sold than cameras of the highest quality. More people seem to prefer cola-type soft drinks to citrus-flavored soft drinks than vice versa. When demand is uneven, most managers' first impulse is to locate their product where demand is greater. They are following the familiar marketing advice: "Locate close to your customers."

This kind of behavior is especially prevalent in political contexts. In the U.S. presidential primary elections (through which the two major parties select candidates for the presidency), competitors in each party often attempt to appeal to the core of their voter base. For example, Democratic candidates stake out positions close to the heart of the core of the Democratic Party. Consequently, in the primaries Democratic candidates appear significantly less conservative than their Republican counterparts. Once the primaries are over, however, the victor in each party has a large incentive to become more "centrist" in order to woo voters in the middle of the political spectrum regardless of their party affiliation (while trying to ensure that core party voters do not become so disenchanted that they decide not to vote!).

For firms, however, locating close to customers may mean sacrificing some of the advantages of differentiation. If the managers of Cheerios noticed, for example, that there were fewer customers near its location than near Grape-Nuts', they might be tempted to make Cheerios crunchier. In making this decision, however, they would also need to consider how this action would affect the market price. The move might increase Cheerios' potential market[17] (despite the fact that its overlap with Grape-Nuts would increase), but it would also lead to more price competition and lower prices. The sad reality is that locating close to your customers often also means locating close to your competitors. As a result, staying in a smaller niche can be more profitable than entering a larger niche with more competitors. This effect of competition on price is one that political candidates do not need to take into account; consequently, locating close to a competitor is less disadvantageous for them than it is for firms.

Choosing a location, then, means balancing two conflicting dictums: *Locate close to your customers* and *locate away from your competitors*. Many successful firms have played a niche strategy even at the cost of not serving the major market segments. Wal-Mart's strategy of locating its stores in small towns where it faced no competition from other

---

[17] Above we claimed that a decline in differentiation would lead to a reduction in sales, and now we appear to be claiming the opposite. The difference is that before we were assuming that potential consumers were evenly distributed along the line, that is, that there are as many consumers close to Cheerios as there are to Grape-Nuts. Here, we are thinking about what happens when there are more consumers close to Grape-Nuts.

large-scale retailers is a clear example. Most of the retail demand was in urban areas, but so was most of the competition. That Wal-Mart eventually entered urban markets also demonstrates the limits of playing a niche strategy. If Wal-Mart were to match the growth in later years that it had achieved early on, it could not afford to stay out of the center of the demand distribution.

Perceptual maps are sometimes useful for assessing the attractiveness of various positions. Figure 7-4, for example, illustrates the weakness of the U.S. automobile man-ufacturers that General Motors wanted to exploit when it created the Saturn division. All the U.S. manufactures are clustered to the left in the diagram because the "Fam-ily/Functional" category includes larger cars. This clustering of U.S. competitors in the large car segment dates back to the 1950s and 1960s when gasoline prices were low and there was no credible competition from foreign producers. The U.S. manufacturers located their products close to their customers, judging that this segment of the demand distribution was so large that moving farther away from each other was unprofitable. As late as the 1980s, the only strong U.S. entrant in the "Personal/Sporty" segment was the Geo, a joint venture of General Motors and Toyota.

This clustering, though advantageous for the U.S. manufacturers prior to the 1970s, became a liability in the 1970s and 1980s. Over these two decades, the price of gasoline increased and disposable incomes rose. The higher price of gasoline made fuel-efficient, smaller cars more attractive. Higher incomes increased the number of families owning more than one car. Together these two effects increased the demand for the Personal/Sporty category. Not only were the existing products of U.S. manu-facturers poorly positioned to respond to these changes in demand, but they now faced Japanese and European manufacturers whose products were ideally positioned for this segment. With the Geo nameplate making little headway in this segment in the 1980s, General Motors decided to launch a major push into the small car segment dominated by foreign firms with the new Saturn division.

As this example suggests, first-mover advantages can significantly affect profitability in niche markets. It is no accident that foreign entrants into the U.S. market entered the niche the U.S. producers had left open. It would have been difficult for the foreign firms to compete in that portion of the demand distribution that entrenched U.S. firms already populated. These incumbents had a clear first-mover advantage in these seg-ments, but they had no such advantage in the segments they had not entered. In the automotive industry, the niches are fairly distinct. Ford's brand equity, for example, made it a formidable competitor in its segment but did not prevent other firms from competing successfully in other segments. Once U.S. manufacturers decided to contest the Personal/Sporty segments, they were second movers. Firms like Honda and Toyota now had the first-mover advantage, and U.S. manufacturers had to play catch-up. In the strategy literature, the impediments to changing position from one strategic group to another are called *mobility barriers*.[18] A firm protected by mobility barriers may have positional competitive advantage based on its incumbency in its market niche.

---

[18] There is nothing logical about this terminology, but "entry barriers" usually denotes the impediments to coming into an industry rather than to moving from one strategic group to another within the same industry.

A primary reason for mobility barriers is the time and resources necessary to establish a position in consumers' minds. The Gap brand name, for example, has been built over many years of sustained promotional expenditures, and any new entrant will have to commit similar resources to create an equally powerful brand within The Gap's market segment. Furthermore, a firm already well established in another segment may find it difficult to compete in a new segment without jeopardizing its existing brand name. For this reason the Coca-Cola Company was extremely reluctant to use the "Coke" brand on any but its flagship product. Similarly, when The Gap wanted to expand into additional segments, it used different brand names: Old Navy for its lower quality retail stores and Banana Republic for its more sophisticated, young adult retail outlets. A well-developed brand name, then, gives the firm an advantage in its niche but may not be a good tool for overcoming the mobility barriers that protect the firms in another niche.

## 7.7  SUMMARY

We have introduced the idea that competitive intensity can vary across industries or across time within the same industry. The primary determinants of competitive intensity are market structure and firm behavior. The market structures that define perfect competition and monopoly necessarily imply that incumbents in competitive markets will face fierce competition while monopolists will face very little. In-between the extremes, product differentiation and firm behavior affect competitive intensity.

Products can be differentiated horizontally or vertically. Vertically differentiated products differ in perceived quality. Horizontally differentiated products differ in attributes over which consumers have differing preferences. We have illustrated the effect of product differentiation by showing how each product competes more intensely with products that are closer to it. More importantly, we have examined why increased differentiation both increases each firm's market size and softens competition. We also demonstrated that managers should take into account whether products are horizontally or vertically differentiated in making pricing decisions. Finally, we examined the factors that managers must consider in deciding how to position their products.

Having analyzed how product differentiation can reduce competitive intensity even when many firms are in the market, in the next chapter we discuss how firm behavior affects competitive intensity in markets where share is concentrated in the hands of a few firms.

## APPENDIX: MONOPOLY, COMPETITION, AND NICHE MARKETS

In this appendix, we summarize some basic economics of monopoly, perfect competition, and niche markets. The treatment is more formal than the one in the body of the text and is intended for those who would like additional insight into how competition works in these markets. Our discussion is necessarily condensed, and those who would like to read more should consult one of the many excellent microeconomics texts.

To simplify the graphical presentation, we make some assumptions about the shape of demand and supply curves, but our conclusions do not depend on these shapes. We also will assume that the industry is embedded in a simple value chain in which it sells to final consumers and buys from a single layer of supplying firms. To set aside the possibility that other segments in the chain may capture value, we will also assume there is no buyer or supplier power. Under these assumptions, PIE is the area defined by the industry demand and cost curves as drawn in Figure 7-A1.

## Monopoly

If protected by high barriers to entry, a monopoly firm will capture a large share of PIE by sustaining a high price–cost margin. To see how the manager of a monopoly firm might think about setting a price, let's return to the lobster industry that we discussed in Chapter 6 and consider the situation facing the manager of a (hypothetical) monopoly retailer of lobsters. As a monopolist, he faces the industry demand curve as shown in Figure 7A-1. Suppose the firm were charging a high price ($\bar{P}$, for example) that is far above the firm's unit cost and at which it makes few sales. The manager is unhappy with the low sales volume and is thinking about increasing the quantity of lobster the firm sells by lowering its price. To decide whether this is a good idea, he must think through the profit implications of a price reduction.

Reducing price would have two opposing effects on the firm's revenue. It would increase the number of lobsters sold because some consumers unwilling to pay $\bar{P}$ would now be willing to buy. This is the effect the manager likes, and the revenue from these *new* sales has a positive effect on the firm's revenue. But the lowered price will reduce the revenue earned from sales *that would have been made at the initial, higher*

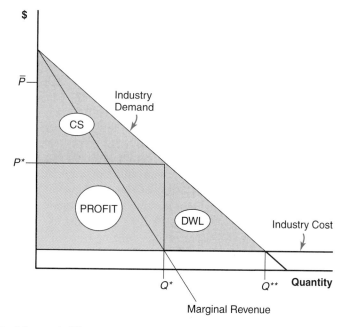

**FIGURE 7A-1**    Monopoly Firm

*price.* This has a negative effect on the firm's revenue. The combination of these two effects is the revenue effect of a small change in price or "marginal revenue." Since we started this discussion with a price at which few lobsters were sold, marginal revenue from the price reduction would probably be positive.

Note also that the loss in revenue on the "old" customers as the price declines implies that marginal revenue will be less than price as illustrated in Figure 7A-1. To see why this must be true, think about what happens when the firm is selling $Q^*$ lobsters and reduces the price just enough to sell one more lobster. The new price is the revenue on the additional sale. The marginal revenue from that sale is the new price *minus* the reduction in revenue from dropping the price on all $Q^*-1$ units that would have sold at the old, higher price. Marginal revenue only equals price on the first unit sold. For that unit, there are no "old" customers who would have paid a higher price.

Just as the monopoly firm's demand curve is the demand curve for the industry, its cost curve is the industry supply curve. On the cost side, the increase in sales induced by the price reduction will also increase total cost. The retailer will have to buy additional lobsters and may need to make other changes that will increase the total cost of business to accommodate the increase in sales. The change in cost associated with the output change is "marginal cost."

The price reduction our lobster monopolist contemplates, then, will increase profits as long as the increase in revenue is greater than the increase in cost. When marginal revenue is higher than marginal cost, the increase in revenue from dropping the price will be larger than the increase in total cost. On the other hand, if marginal revenue were lower than marginal cost, the manager could increase profits by raising the price because the cost savings would outweigh the loss in revenue. The optimal price for the monopolist is the one at which marginal revenue and marginal cost are equal. In the diagram, this occurs at the quantity $Q,^*$ which implies a monopoly price of $P^*$. The optimal price will be above marginal cost because price is higher than marginal revenue. The margin between price and unit cost is, of course, the reason for monopoly profit.

The optimal price for the monopolist to charge depends, then, on both its costs and on industry demand. If the price of inputs were to fall, for example, the manager of a monopoly would maximize the firm's profit by reducing its price. In this sense, monopolists "pass along" (some share of) cost changes. Our monopoly retailer would reduce the retail price of lobster to consumers if the wholesale price of lobster were to decline. Analogously, an increase in cost or demand leads to an increase in the profit-maximizing price. If the price of a complement falls, for example, demand for the monopolist's product will increase, and the profit-maximizing price will be higher. Vacationers in the northeastern United States purchase a large share of lobsters sold at retail. If the cost of such a vacation were to decline, the demand for lobsters would probably increase, and the monopolist's profit-maximizing price of lobsters would also rise.

A monopolist can capture a large share of PIE in the form of profit. But if, as we have supposed, the monopolist charges the same price to all its customers, it will not capture all of PIE. For example, a wealthy lobster lover may be willing to pay $100 a pound for lobster. If a hypothetical monopoly retailer of lobsters charged that much, however, it would sell few lobsters. By our logic above, the monopolist would increase its profit by lowering its price and selling to many more people. A lobster retailer might find the profit-maximizing price to be, say, $10 a pound. But that means that those consumers willing to pay more than this capture some of PIE. In particular, our high-income, lobster-infatuated buyer would get $90 per pound in value for which he did not pay. As a result, some of the value goes to consumers in the form of "consumer surplus" (denoted CS in Figure 7-A1). The "consumer" part of this label arises from the fact that the usual examples are from industries in which buyers are the final consumers. It might be more useful to think of this as "buyer surplus." The "surplus" part of the label means "getting more than you paid for."[19]

Another piece of PIE that the monopolist does not capture is what economists call "deadweight loss." Deadweight loss (DWL in the figure) is the part of PIE that no one captures because it is not created. Some buyers are willing to pay *more* than the cost of producing the product but less than the current price. These people would pay more for a lobster than the opportunity cost of getting it to their plates in a restaurant but are not willing to cover the hefty markup our hypothetical monopolist charges. In particular, $(Q^{**}-Q^*)$ additional units could be sold for a price that would more than cover opportunity cost. The monopolist sacrifices the opportunity to supply these customers because it would have to reduce its price to do so, and the lost profits on existing customers would more than offset the addition to profits the monopolist would achieve by selling to customers it does not currently serve.

If the monopolist were to expand its output beyond $Q^*$, it would reduce DWL, increase CS, and reduce profit. Reducing DWL will increase the sum of profit and CS, but the manager of the firm doesn't care about the sum. He cares only about the company's profit, and that is maximized by charging a price that leads to some deadweight loss. In contrast, in the United States, government agencies responsible for enforcing antitrust laws want to maximize total surplus, that is, the sum of CS and profit. Put differently, they want to minimize deadweight loss. Because DWL arises only when a firm has some market power (i.e., can charge a price above marginal cost), antitrust authorities are concerned about curbing market power.

The situation changes when the monopolist can charge different prices for the units of output it sells—or "price discriminate" in economics terminology. If it could perfectly price discriminate, it would charge a different price for each unit sold: the highest price any buyer would be willing to pay for that unit. The first unit would be sold for a price equal to the maximum any consumer is willing to pay, the second for only slightly less, and so forth until the last unit was sold at a price just equal to marginal cost. In that event, the monopolist could capture all of PIE! In practice, of course, a firm cannot price discriminate perfectly. Managers frequently find a way to price discriminate less perfectly, however, as will be discussed in the Appendix to Chapter 10. For now, we simply note that a monopolist will capture a large share of PIE if it cannot price discriminate and an even larger share if it can.

---

[19] Economists sometimes use "producer surplus" instead of "profit." This usage is directly analogous to consumer surplus. Profit is whatever the firm gets in revenue that it doesn't pay for in cost.

The world has few true monopolies (and lobster retailing is certainly not one of them). Most monopolies exist because regulatory barriers protect them. Many countries reserve some segments of the electrical power industry for a monopoly firm, for example. One reason true monopoly markets in unregulated industries are rare is that monopoly profits attract entry and therefore tend to be short-lived. Polaroid's patents, for example, gave it a profitable monopoly in instant photography for several years until Kodak entered the market. Nonetheless, since even some more competitive markets have elements of monopoly behavior, you should keep the monopolistic benchmark in mind.

## Perfect Competition

A perfectly competitive industry has many small firms, each of which sells an undifferentiated product. Each firm is so small relative to the overall size of the industry that no single firm can affect the price it gets for its product. One wheat farmer going out of business has no effect on the market price of wheat. Contrast this to what would happen to the market price if a monopolist were to reduce its output substantially. Because firms in a perfectly competitive industry cannot affect the market price, they are said to be "price takers." They can sell all they produce at the market price, and they can sell nothing at a price greater than the market price.

Figure 7-A2 depicts the situation facing the manager of a perfectly competitive firm. Because the industry contains more than one firm, the firm's demand curve is not the same as the industry demand curve, and its cost curve is not the industry supply

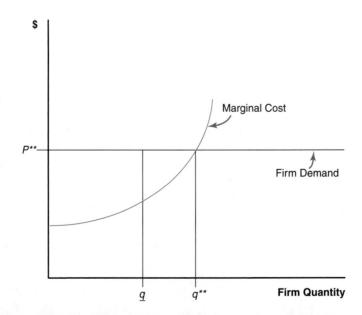

**FIGURE 7A-2**  Competitive Firm

curve. The demand and cost drawn in Figure 7-A2, then, are for the firm, not for the industry. A perfectly competitive firm faces a horizontal demand curve at a level determined by the market price. This is the diagrammatic representation of the fact that the firm's output choices have no effect on market price; it can sell any amount it produces at the market price.

In a perfectly competitive industry, firms choose to produce the output at which their marginal cost is just equal to the market price. Let's return to lobster retailing, but now imagine that this industry is perfectly competitive. Under monopoly, our manager thought about what price to charge. A seller in a perfectly competitive market, however, cannot choose price. Our lobster seller can now only decide what quantity of lobsters to sell *given* the market price. Suppose our manager were producing at some output like $q$ where its marginal cost is below the market price. If he produces an additional unit, the cost of doing so will be less than the price for which he can sell it. He will continue to increase the firm's output until his marginal cost is equal to the market price, as it is at $q^*$. Any output larger than $q^*$ would cost more than the amount for which it can be sold.

The tradeoff facing a competitive firm considering a change in its output is similar in logic to that facing the monopoly firm but importantly different in one detail. Both types of firms think through the gains and losses from, say, increasing output.[20] In doing so, both consider the change in revenue and in cost. Assuming they start from a point where marginal revenue is above marginal cost, both will increase output until marginal revenue equals marginal cost. For the competitive firm, however, marginal revenue is equal to the market price: No matter what amount it produces, it can sell it at exactly the market price. For the monopolist, changing its output changes the market price; it can only get buyers to make additional purchases from it by reducing its price.

Figure 7-A2 illustrates the situation facing an individual firm in a perfectly competitive industry. To compare competitive industry performance to a monopolistic industry, we can aggregate the competitive firms to the industry level. Unlike the demand curve facing the individual competitive firms, the industry demand curve is downward sloping; when industry output increases as all (or many) firms expand their output, the price must fall to induce buyers to purchase the larger output. The industry cost curve is the aggregate of the individual firm's marginal cost curves. Now suppose that we hold industry demand and opportunity cost constant and we change only the competitive structure of the industry. How would prices and profits compare between the perfectly competitive and monopolistic structures?

To answer this question, we return to Figure 7-A1 which illustrates the monopoly outcome. The monopolist prices at $P^*$, leading to the profits, consumer surplus, and deadweight loss, are illustrated in the figure. If a competitive industry had the same

---

[20] In describing the monopoly problem, we talked about the monopolist choosing price. We could have just as easily, however, framed the problem as choosing what quantity to sell: For every quantity, the demand curve determines the price. The difference between monopoly and competition is not whether the firm chooses price or quantity, but that a monopolist can increase the price it gets by reducing its output and a competitive firm cannot.

supply curve and industry demand, it would produce $Q^{**}$. Since the supply curve is the sum of its marginal cost curves, $Q^{**}$ is the quantity at which price and marginal cost are equal. The market price ($P^{**}$) will be lower, and consumer surplus will equal the sum of the areas denoted Profit, CS, and DWL. The firms earn no (economic) profit, and there is no DWL. Instead, buyers get all of PIE. They do so not because they are powerful, but because the incumbent firms compete fiercely, driving the price to the marginal cost of the resources they must use to produce the products. In short, a competitive structure is better for buyers because consumer surplus is higher, and a monopoly structure is better for the industry because profits are higher. It is the absence of deadweight loss (or, equivalently, the maximization of consumer surplus plus firm profit) in the competitive structure that appeals to those who enforce U.S. antitrust laws.

## Niche Markets

In this chapter, we argued that differentiation affects competitive intensity. Here we develop that argument more completely. To do so, we will return to the cereal example but add some detail and tools. Because the logic here is more complicated than in the monopoly or perfectly competitive cases, we will simplify our discussion by assuming that producing and selling product has no cost. With a marginal cost of zero, the firms maximize profit by maximizing revenue.

We assume that we can represent consumer tastes by locating consumers along a line as in Figure 7-2, but initially suppose that Cheerios is the only brand in the cereal market. We also want to assume that consumers are evenly distributed; that is, the same number of consumers are at every location along this line. This is called a uniform distribution. Consumers' tastes are not usually distributed this way. The marketing group at a fast-food chain, for example, expends considerable resources to assess whether more consumers prefer small, crunchy french fries or larger, less crunchy

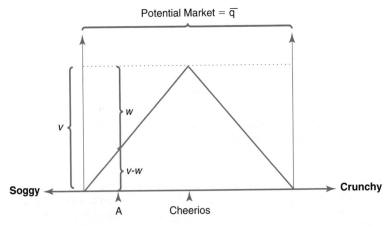

**FIGURE 7A-3**   The Market for Cheerios When It Faces No Nearby Competitors

ones. In our cereal example, we suspect that most consumers would prefer a moderately crunchy cereal to either of the extremes. If so, we might expect the consumer distribution to have the familiar bell shape of the normal distribution. For simplicity, however, we will assume that consumers are evenly distributed.

We suppose further that all consumers value their "ideal" product, that is, a product that has their most desired degree of crunchiness, at $v. Consumers whose ideal crunchiness is precisely the amount they believe Cheerios to have, then, would be willing to pay up to $v for Cheerios. Consumers whose ideal is either a little more or a little less crunchy than Cheerios value it somewhat less. For simplicity, we will assume that value declines linearly as the distance from the ideal increases in drawing Figure 7-A3. For example, the consumer whose ideal is located at A would also be willing to pay $v for her ideal cereal, but she is only willing to pay $(v-w) for Cheerios because of the distance that she must "travel" (in terms of compromise from her ideal) to consume it. The loss to her, relative to having a cereal that precisely matches her tastes, is $w.[21]

Eventually, once we have moved far enough away from where Cheerios is located, consumers' ideal cereals are so far away from the characteristics of Cheerios that the consumers do not place a positive value on Cheerios. That is, for some consumers $v–$w<0. This allows us to be more specific about the notion of *potential* market: The total number of consumers whose net value for a box of Cheerios is positive ($v–$w>0) is the brand's potential market size and is denoted $\bar{q}$ in Figure 7-A3. If Cheerios were to be priced at zero, it would sell to all consumers in its potential market.

Other cereal brands will have no effect on Cheerios if they are located far enough away. In the top panel of Figure 7-A4, for example, the potential markets of Cheerios, Grape-Nuts, and Corn Flakes—the two brands closest to Cheerios in product characteristics—do not overlap. That is, no consumer values both Cheerios and Grape-Nuts or both Cheerios and Corn Flakes. Because there is no overlap, the presence of these other brands does not affect the potential market for Cheerios; its potential market size is still $\bar{q}$ Product differentiation is strong enough to nullify any competition among the three crunchies. And since the brands closest to Cheerios offer no competition to it, no brand farther away will either. General Mills has an effective monopoly over the consumers who value Cheerios. In this situation, General Mills will choose a price that maximizes its profits following the same logic we described above for the monopoly case.

The bottom panel of Figure 7-A4 depicts the more typical situation in which Cheerios faces some competition because the closest brands are much closer to it. In this situation, Cheerios' potential market overlaps its neighbors' potential markets. Consumers at each of the solid vertical lines in the lower panel value the product of the neighbor as highly as they do Cheerios. Outside those solid lines, even those consumers within Cheerios' potential market prefer the products of another firm to Cheerios. If all three firms set their prices equal to zero, the consumers inside the solid

---

[21] Note that $w, the amount by which the value of Cheerios declines, depends on the location of the customer. A consumer located at the edge of Cheerios' potential market, for example, would have $w = $v. Any customer outside this potential market would have $w > $v.

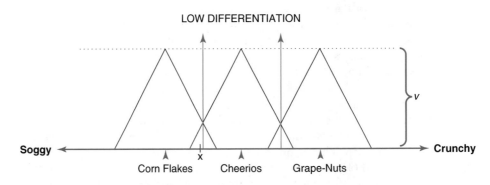

**FIGURE 7A-4**   Effects of Differentiation on Sales

lines would choose Cheerios, and those outside those lines would choose to buy from one of its neighbors.

To understand this point more clearly, think about a specific consumer located at point $X$ in both panels in Figure 7-A4. Consumer $X$ places some value on Cheerios; that is, for this consumer $\$v - \$w > 0$ for Cheerios. In the top panel, there is no other cereal she would buy. At a price of zero, she will buy Cheerios. Once Cheerios has closer neighbors, however, her choice will change. In the bottom panel, Cheerios and Consumer $X$ are in the same locations as before, but the two other brands have moved in. As shown in the bottom panel, Consumer $X$ now places a positive value on Corn Flakes as well. Indeed, when all firms charge a price of $\$0$, she gets more value from that product than from Cheerios. Her preferences have not changed, but as neighbors have crowded in toward Cheerios, one has located closer to her most preferred point than Cheerios is.

Of course, even in the lower panel, Cheerios has a *potential* market of $\bar{q}$, and it can achieve that potential if, for example, its neighbors were to charge very high prices.

The point is that in contrast to the top panel, the number of consumers who will buy from Cheerios when the three brands charge equal prices has been reduced. This leads us to one of the conclusions in the body of the chapter: When a firm's products are more differentiated from its competitors' products, each firm's sales volume will increase. Furthermore, in the top panel of Figure 7-A4, the number of consumers in Cheerios' potential market who buy its product is entirely in its own hands; Cheerios simply sets the price that maximizes its profits without regard to any other cereal brand. In the bottom panel, however, the number who buy Cheerios at any price it chooses also depends on the prices its neighbors choose.

Cheerios' *actual* market share, then, depends on the location of competing firms *and* on the prices General Mills and its rivals charge. To see more precisely what effect prices have, it is easier to return to Cheerios when it faces no close competitors and therefore needs to consider only the effect of its own price. A price of $0 defines Cheerios' potential market for its cereal. For any price greater than $0, not all of those in the potential market will buy its product. As Figure 7-A5 shows, if General Mills sets a price equal of $p$ for Cheerios, the value any consumer would gain from buying the product would be less by the amount $p$ compared to Figure 7-A3 where $p$ was implicitly set equal to zero. Our consumer A from Figure 7-A3 is now just willing to purchase Cheerios (i.e., for her $v - w - p = 0$). Those to her left who are in Cheerios' potential market are no longer willing to buy.

To select the price that will maximize its profits, the firm would balance the higher revenue that comes from a higher price against the reduction in the number of consumers who would buy the product at a higher price. In Figure 7-A5, the light blue shaded rectangle gives Cheerios' revenues. At higher prices the vertical part of the rectangle is higher, but the horizontal segment shrinks because fewer consumers purchase Cheerios. Because Cheerios has a monopoly, consumers who decide that the price is too high simply don't buy cereal. As in our earlier discussion of monopoly

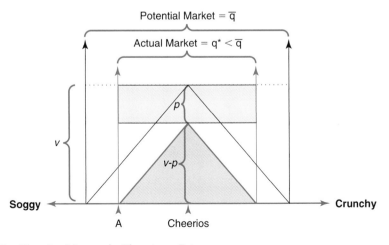

**FIGURE 7A-5**   Cheerios Monopoly Charging a Price = $p$

pricing, General Mills, would balance marginal revenue from a change in price of Cheerios with marginal cost.

When Cheerios has competitors, Figure 7-A6 illustrates what happens when General Mills charges $p$, but its rivals charge a price equal to zero. Here, because General Mills is charging more than its neighbors, some consumers who would have preferred Cheerios at equal prices now choose to buy Corn Flakes or Grape-Nuts. To select the price that maximizes its profits, General Mills will go through the now familiar logic of taking into account the two revenue effects of any price change. If it lowers its price below $p$, for example, it will earn less revenue than before on the sales it makes to those who would have purchased from it at $p$. That is, it will sacrifice some revenue it could have made by "milking" its current customers by charging them higher prices. Second, it will pick up additional sales as some of the people buying from its neighbors when it priced at $p$ switch to Cheerios at the lower price. By lowering its price, Cheerios can steal some market share from its neighbors. The combined revenue effect is the marginal revenue resulting from the price change. General Mills would then choose the price for Cheerios that equates marginal revenue and its marginal cost.[22]

Its neighbors are not likely to hold their prices constant as General Mills changes its price. Rather, they too will explore the effects of various prices and face a calculation similar to the one we just went through for General Mills with Cheerios. The outcome of this reasoning will be a set of prices at which each of the firms is doing as well as possible given the prices its competitors are charging. Each firm sets a price to balance the gain from stealing market share from its neighbors by charging lower prices against the benefits of "milking" its current customers through higher prices.

Note that the farther we move from the case of homogeneous products, that is, as products are increasingly differentiated, the more price competition declines. This occurs because the tradeoff between "milk the existing customers" versus "steal

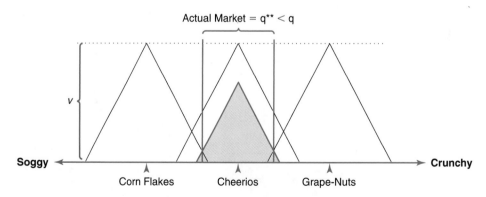

**FIGURE 7A-6**   Cheerios Charges Price = $p$ When Its Competitors Charge Price = 0

---

[22] This logic will be familiar from the discussion of the monopoly pricing. Here, however, the increase in revenue comes out of competitor's hides.

market share" changes as neighbors move away from the firm. To see this clearly, go back to the lower panel of Figure 7-A4. If all firms charge a price of zero, the vertical lines define the consumers buying from Cheerios. Call this the "high-differentiation" scenario. Now imagine that its neighbors are even closer to its location. This decline in differentiation would move in the vertical lines, reducing Cheerios' actual market. Call this the "low-differentiation" scenario. Now, think about what would happen if General Mills were to drop its price for Cheerios just enough to steal one customer from each of its competitors. Its revenue gain from stealing market share would be the same in both scenarios: the new price times two. In both scenarios, General Mills suffers some revenue loss on the customers who would have bought it at the old price. But this loss is greater in the high-differentiation scenario because there Cheerios had more customers to begin with. Firms therefore have a greater incentive to cut price when there is less product differentiation. This increased incentive to cut price makes price competition more intense and leads to lower equilibrium prices.

# CHAPTER

# 8

# COMPETITION IN CONCENTRATED MARKETS

## 8.1 INTRODUCTION

Most well-known firms are major players in their industries. The pharmaceutical, automobile, semiconductor, airline, telecommunication, investment banking, bulk chemical, and petroleum industries are but a handful of the industries whose incumbent firms include important, identifiable players. These firms are large enough to affect industry pricing and, more generally, to determine the competitive characteristics of their industries. When Ford changes its prices for automobiles, its decision affects the demand for the cars of every automobile firm selling in Ford's major markets, and all firms will respond. When Northern Telecom introduces a new generation of phone switching equipment in the United States, all firms selling switching equipment in the United States must either respond or lose business. In contrast, The Gap, despite its prominence in one segment of the retail clothing industry (see Chapter 7), has a small share of all clothing sales, and thousands of clothing retailers are largely unaffected by the decisions it makes.

Industries containing firms with substantial market share are called *concentrated industries* because market share is concentrated in the hands of a few firms. In the spectrum of competition defined in Chapter 6, these industries occupy the space between niche and monopoly markets. Although the terminology distinguishes among these industries according to how market share is distributed in them, what is important from a managerial perspective is how the major players in these industries can affect industry outcomes. A manager at a leading firm in a concentrated industry knows that her decisions about price or product characteristics will affect all the other players in the industry. If one leading firm competes aggressively, competition will intensify for all firms in the industry. As a result, a manager of a major firm in a concentrated industry must recognize that its competitors will respond to any strategic choice she makes, just as she will have to respond to the decisions they make because those decisions will affect her firm's performance.

Within the broad category of concentrated industries, two general structural patterns prevail. In one, a few firms hold a large share of industry sales, but no firm, by itself, dominates the industry. An industry in which five firms each have a 20 percent market share would be a clear example, as would the industries cited in the opening paragraph of this chapter. These industries are called oligopolies. Less common are dominant firm industries in which a large firm competes with many, much smaller firms. Sometimes, the dominant firm serves most of the market, and a raft of niche firms compete for small segments of the rest of the market. Kodak, for example, had been the dominant seller of photographic film in the United States until the 1990s. The regional Bell telephone companies in the United States have been the dominant firms providing local telephone service in their respective service areas, while wireless operators often compete in niches within the same service area.

These two market structures, oligopoly and dominant firm, can be much less competitive than perfectly competitive markets. If high entry barriers protect the industries, and powerful buyers or suppliers are unable to capture any PIE, the firms in these industries may be extremely profitable. Even under these favorable circumstances, however, competitive forces among the incumbent firms can dissipate a large share of potential industry earnings. Indeed, the same industry can evolve from a situation in which the leading firms are extremely profitable to one in which competition among firms drives profits to perfectly competitive levels. In the U.S. automobile industry, for example, the fortunes of the largest firms changed significantly during the twentieth century. This rich set of competitive possibilities makes oligopolies and dominant firm industries fruitful settings for applying strategic thinking. In this chapter, we present a way for managers to think about competition in concentrated markets that will help them assess how their actions will affect firm performance.

We begin by discussing oligopoly. To simplify the discussion and to distinguish between the oligopoly and dominant firm structures, we will discuss oligopolies as if they always involved only large firms. Then we discuss dominant firm industries as if they were invariably composed of one dominant player and small fringe firms. In fact, many industries have a few large players and some much smaller firms. In these industries, the leading firms face both the competitive problems of an oligopoly because they are competing with other major players and the problems of a dominant firm structure because the smaller competitors, in aggregate but not individually, constrain the profitability of the leading firms.

## 8.2  OLIGOPOLY: THE ELEMENTS OF STRATEGIC INTERACTION

In Chapter 6, we emphasized two distinguishing features of oligopoly: (1) These industries contain a few, large firms, and (2) the behavior of these firms determines how profitable the incumbent firms in the industry will be. These features are related. Because the firms are large ("large" here means having a large market share), their actions affect market outcomes. Think about an industry that only has two firms (a "duopoly"), each of which has half the market. If one of the firms in the market increases its output by 10 percent and the other firm holds its output constant, industry output will increase by 5 percent, and prices will have to fall to induce buyers to purchase the expanded supply. This will cause the profits at the firm that did not increase its output to fall. The actions of one firm in an oligopoly affect market outcomes—price and market shares in this case—and they also affect the profits of its competitors.

Since the actions of each firm affect the performance of other firms, each can expect its own actions to spark a reaction by its rivals. The reaction of competing firms can profoundly affect the profitability of the initial action. A firm may, for example, decide to compete primarily on the basis of low costs. If its competitors decide to compete on the basis of other attributes, such as service quality or time-to-market, the industry incumbents may avoid intense price competition because they are not competing "head-to-head" on any dimension. But if all rival firms pursue a low-cost strategy, the intense competition among them may depress profitability for all of them. Or a firm anticipating a demand increase may announce a large addition to its capacity. If its rivals respond by aggressively adding capacity, the entire industry may experience excess capacity even if demand increases as expected. If, however, its rivals respond to this announcement by curtailing their own capacity expansion plans, the industry may not experience excess capacity. In this case, the first mover will have a large increase in market share, but prices will not be depressed by competition among firms holding excess capacity. It is these kinds of strategic interaction among firms that make behavior in oligopolies so interesting to strategic management scholars and challenging to managers.

Outcomes differ in oligopolies because the details of strategic interaction are important. Industries differ, for example, in how quickly firms can add or retire capacity, and this affects competitive intensity. Some products are inherently difficult to differentiate, and the firms producing them have to compete primarily through price. Whether incumbent firms have high exit barriers can affect competitive intensity in the long run. Oligopolies in which firms expect to compete with each other for a long time may be less competitive than industries with a more limited time horizon.

Simply knowing that details matter is not very helpful, however. Instead, a manager of an oligopolistic firm needs to think systematically about strategic interaction in her particular industry. Figure 8-1 summarizes the framework we use to analyze strategic interactions. Each of the elements listed there represents a class of characteristics that can have important effects on the outcome of strategic interactions. We will describe each of them briefly here and then proceed to a series of examples designed to illustrate how and why these elements are important.

- **Players.** The players in an industry are the firms whose actions affect each other. Often a manager knows who his important rivals are. Boeing knows it has to think about Airbus, for example. Sometimes, however, rivals are less obvious as when a software firm suddenly faces a competing product from a firm that had not previously been an active competitor.[1]

---

[1] Furthermore, some players may not be rival firms at all. It is possible that a supplier, for example, may take actions that disadvantage some subset of the firms in the purchasing industry. In this chapter, we will largely ignore the possibility that there are important actors outside the industry but will return to this topic in Chapter 10.

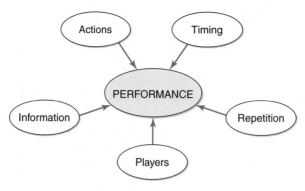

**FIGURE 8-1** Elements of Strategic Interaction

- **Actions.** The choices available to incumbent firms can affect competition. Can competitors expand output, or are they constrained by capacity? Can they differentiate their products, or do they produce a commodity? Can they make their product compatible or incompatible with those of their rivals, or is compatibility unimportant?

- **Timing.** Timing can matter. Sometimes firms can move preemptively and gain a first-mover advantage, for example. In other situations, a firm may want to wait until its competitor has moved first.

- **Information.** Which firms know what and when they know it can affect performance. If a firm has information before its competitors do, it may be able to exploit that knowledge. Other times, a manager at one firm may want to convey information to managers at competing firms to influence the decisions they make.

- **Repetition.** Sometimes firms know that they will be competing for only a short time, but oligopolistic firms often have a long competitive history and anticipate a long competitive future with each other. The fact that they interact repeatedly introduces the possibility of building and exploiting reputation or of behaving more cooperatively than would otherwise be possible.

Below, we provide some simple examples that show how these characteristics can affect industry outcomes. We rely on simple examples because real-life situations are so complex that they require an in-depth analysis to determine what is driving the outcome. We will also suggest some more textured examples as we go along. First, however, we want to emphasize four important characteristics of oligopolistic interaction.

First, to formulate strategy for a firm in an oligopoly a manager must anticipate how rival firms will respond. Devising a new strategy that would be a brilliant success if your rivals continued to do exactly what they are doing now is not enough. If your firm makes important strategic moves, your rivals will respond to them. A general manager at Boeing who has to decide whether to introduce a new line of commercial aircraft must ask, "How will Airbus respond? Can it introduce a competing product? How long will it take Airbus to do so? How will that affect my profit stream from this product?" It is like a chess game in which a player cannot win unless he can understand what his competitor can and will do.

Second, a manager should recognize that all firms will act in their own best interests. This means that when assessing how a rival firm will respond, a manager should adopt its perspective and ask, "If I had the internal context of Firm Y, what response would be optimal?" Airbus's response to Boeing's product introduction might be different from the response Boeing would make if Airbus were the first to introduce the same product. Do not assume that your rival sees the world the way you do. Each firm has a unique internal context that shapes its responses. A manager who controls assets that are different from yours or who operates within an organizational design that is different from yours will probably make choices you would not have made. What is profit-maximizing for you may not be profit-maximizing for your competitors. You have to put yourself in your rival's shoes to anticipate how he will respond.

Third, a manager must recognize that managers at rival firms are thinking the same way about her firm. They expect her to pursue a strategy that will maximize her profits given her context. She may want them to believe that she will take a particular course of action, but they will only believe that if they think that the action is profit-maximizing for her firm. For example, to convince competitors that her firm is committed to maintaining market share, a manager may announce that she will match any price cut a rival makes even if it bankrupts her firm. If her rivals believe this, they will have good reason to avoid price cuts that she will match at any cost. But if they believe that she has an alternative course of action that will be more profitable for her firm, they will not take this threat seriously. They know that, when faced with tremendous losses, she will withdraw from the market segment that is most costly for her to serve. Competitors will disregard any claim that a firm will pursue a course of action that is not in its own best interest.

Finally, no firm can make choices for the other firms. One sometimes hears references to firms "disciplining" rivals or "imposing order on the market," but either action is usually impossible. For example, it only takes one firm to start a price war, and the other firms cannot force it to raise its prices. The only effective way to influence the behavior of rivals is to act in a way makes it profitable for them to do what you want them to do.

For those who would like to see a somewhat more formal analysis of the material in this chapter, we discuss the underlying principles of strategic interaction in more detail in the appendix to this book. However, the discussion in the appendix is not necessary to understand the basic issues of oligopolistic interaction we present here.

### Differences in Actions

Industries differ in the kinds of actions managers can take. To see how these differences might be important, consider the security trading industry versus the petroleum refining industry. On the U.S. Nasdaq and the London International Stock Exchange, registered "market makers" compete for order flow for stocks traded. A market maker for Cisco, for example, will post prices at which it is willing to buy and sell Cisco stock. The market maker posting the lowest selling price for the stock attracts all potential buyers who have no reason to buy at any price above the lowest one available. Analogously, the market maker posting the highest buying price will attract potential sellers. If there were only one market maker, he could maintain a large spread between the buy and sell prices. To prevent this from happening, the governing body of the Nasdaq requires that there be at least two market makers for each listed stock. When there are two or more market makers, price competition turns out to be quite intense. Because the market makers cannot differentiate their product (one share of Cisco stock is just like another) and cannot affect industry output (at any given time, all of Cisco's shares are potentially for sale), they are forced to behave like perfectly competitive firms. Only if they can somehow alter the nature of competition will they earn an attractive return.[2]

In contrast, refiners producing and selling heating oil have refining schedules that are very difficult to change in the short run. It is very costly to change substantially the volume of heating oil produced by any given refinery. In essence, the refiners choose how much heating oil they will produce and bring that amount to market. The market price is determined by the demand for heating oil when the product comes to market and the total amount of heating oil that has been produced for sale. A refiner setting its production schedule for the coming month can decide to expand his output, but he cannot capture the entire market. Other refiners will continue to bring the product to market, and the combined volume will determine the market price. Markets for heating oil refining tend to be less competitive than securities markets.

What makes one of these markets more competitive than the other? A key difference is the actions through which the firms compete. A market maker chooses a *price* at which it will sell a stock, and that price determines how much it will sell. If it posts the low price, it will capture all the demand for that stock. A refiner chooses a *capacity*, and it cannot sell more than it is able to produce. If it were to set a price that generated a demand greater than its capacity, it could not increase its market share. Competition among firms that choose prices turns out to be more intense than competition among firms that choose capacities. Let's look at some simple stylized examples that allow us to investigate why this happens.

In each case we simplify by assuming that there are only two firms in the industry. Further, to postpone issues that arise when the firms compete with each other repeatedly, we make the absurd assumption that our firms compete only on one particular day. The "industries" we use for illustrative purposes are fishing and apple selling. As you will see, verisimilitude is not our intent. Rather, we want to show that the details of the competitive environment can have a huge effect on competitive intensity.

- **Fishing.** In this industry each of the two competing firms owns one boat. Each firm chooses how many pounds of fish to catch, and each incurs the same cost no matter how many it catches. The boats leave from the same dock in the morning, spend all day at sea working separate fishing grounds, return at

---

[2] The potential gain from avoiding the intense competition imposed by the structure of these markets was made clear in a recent investigation of trading practices on the Nasdaq in which the firms acting as market makers were found to have colluded to maintain more lucrative margins than would otherwise have prevailed.

the same time to the same dock, and sell their entire catch to wholesalers on the dock. Table 8-1 shows demand for fish at their dock. If the boats bring in a combined catch of 30 pounds, the market price to "sell" it all will be $0 per pound and industry revenue will be $0. If together they offer only five pounds of fish, the price will be $25 per pound and industry revenue will be $125. Even though catching more fish does not affect cost, bringing more fish to market reduces the margin per pound of fish by driving down the market price.

- **Apple selling.** In this industry, two farmers each own an apple orchard. Their efforts during the growing season have been very productive, for their trees are now laden with apples. The farmers have nothing to do now but sit at their respective stalls selling apples. The orchards are situated near a train station. The farmers post their prices on a board at the station, and travelers can shop at the stall of their choice. Demand is exactly the same as that for fish in the preceding example (simply replace "fish" with "apples"). Apples not sold on the one day our industry "exists" are worthless.

Although these two industries have similar characteristics, competitive intensity will be quite different in each. Note that we have implied that marginal cost, the cost of catching one more pound of fish or selling one more pound of apples, is zero for both industries. Since firms in these industries have the same marginal costs and the industries have the same demand, we can measure competitive intensity by price. If the industries were perfectly competitive, the price in each would be $0 (i.e., equal to marginal cost), and the quantity sold in each would be 30 pounds. In Table 8-1, we

**TABLE 8-1**    The Demand for Fish and Industry Revenue

| Price per Pound ($) | Pounds Sold | Industry Revenue ($) | Price per Pound ($) | Pounds Sold | Industry Revenue ($) |
|---|---|---|---|---|---|
| 0 | 30 | 0 | 16 | 14 | 224 |
| 1 | 29 | 29 | 17 | 13 | 221 |
| 2 | 28 | 56 | 18 | 12 | 216 |
| 3 | 27 | 81 | 19 | 11 | 209 |
| 4 | 26 | 104 | 20 | 10 | 200 |
| 5 | 25 | 125 | 21 | 9 | 189 |
| 6 | 24 | 146 | 22 | 8 | 176 |
| 7 | 23 | 161 | 23 | 7 | 161 |
| 8 | 22 | 176 | 24 | 6 | 146 |
| 9 | 21 | 189 | 25 | 5 | 125 |
| 10 | 20 | 200 | 26 | 4 | 104 |
| 11 | 19 | 209 | 27 | 3 | 81 |
| 12 | 18 | 216 | 28 | 2 | 56 |
| 13 | 17 | 221 | 29 | 1 | 29 |
| 14 | 16 | 224 | 30 | 0 | 0 |
| 15 | 15 | 225 | | | |

have also calculated the revenue (price times quantity) that a monopoly firm would realize if it were to choose the price listed in the price column. Since production is free in these examples, the price that maximizes revenue is also the price that maximizes profit. The data in Table 8-1 indicate that a monopoly firm would choose a price of $15 and sell 15 pounds, making a profit of $225.

To compare the duopoly outcome to the polar cases of monopoly and perfect competition, we need to figure out what the duopoly outcome will be. Let's first consider the apple industry. Here, each farmer only has to decide the price at which he is willing to sell his apples. What price should we expect the farmers to charge? Suppose they each thought of charging $15 a pound. If they both charged $15, each would sell 7.5 pounds and each would earn profits of $112.50.[3] Together, the firms earn the monopoly profit with these choices. In assessing this outcome, however, one of the farmers ought to reason that if he cut his price to $14 when his rival is charging $15, he would attract all of the buyers and sell 16 pounds of apples for revenue of $224. When products are undifferentiated, all buyers will want to purchase from the firm with the lowest price. Total industry revenue will be lower (by a dollar), but the low-price farmer expects to do better by undercutting his rival's price and getting all the sales than he would by holding to the monopoly price and getting only half the sales. But anticipating this incentive to undercut his price, the other farmer ought to charge $13, and so on. The only prices at which neither farmer would have an incentive to cut price further is $0. The market price will be $0, and 30 pounds of apples will be sold![4]

This outcome, in which price is equal to marginal cost even though the industry only has two firms, strikes many observers as unreasonable. One might believe, for example, that the farmers would understand that their greed would lead to exceptionally low performance and that they would therefore avoid cutting prices. We will return to the question of whether the farmers could avoid intense competition later. First, however, we want to think about the competitive outcome in the similar-looking fishing industry to identify exactly what makes competition so intense in the orchards.

In the fishing example, the firms face a somewhat different decision. Here prices will be determined by how many pounds of fish are caught, and each firm decides not what price to charge but how much fish to bring to market. To see what difference this makes, let's start again with each firm getting half of the monopoly profit. To do that, each would catch 7.5 pounds of fish. In the orchard example, one farmer realized he could do better by undercutting the monopoly price. Here, one firm will consider deviating from the monopoly outcome by catching and selling one more pound of fish. If one of the firms decides to catch 8.5 rather than 7.5 pounds, the total catch rises to 16 pounds and the price falls to $14. Industry profit falls to $224, but the profit of the firm producing the larger output rises from $112.5 to $119.

---

[3] One needs not assume that the sales are divided evenly when the firms have the same price, and any other assumption would not affect our argument. An equal division seems natural when the products are undifferentiated as they are here.

[4] To be precise, the market price would be the smallest increment in price possible. That is, if prices can be quoted in pennies, the market price would be $0.01. If both firms charge that price, neither has an incentive to unilaterally lower its price to capture market share.

As in the example of the apple orchards, then, each fishing firm has an incentive to deviate from the outcome that maximizes the combined profits of the two firms. It is willing to do so because each firm cares only about its own profit. In both cases, as one firm "undercuts" the other by shaving the price on apples or increasing the quantity of fish it brings to market, its gain is smaller than the losses this action imposes on the other firm. When, for example, one boat decides to catch 8.5 rather than 7.5 pounds, the gain in its profit is $6.50, and the rival firm loses $7.50 in profit. Clearly, if the same firm owned both boats, it would take into account the impact of the increased catch by one boat on total firm revenues and would not expand the catch above a total of 15 pounds of fish.[5] Competition dissipates PIE because competing firms maximize only their individual profits and do so at the expense of their rivals.

The fishing industry, like the apple industry, cannot sustain monopoly levels of output and price. But will the market price here be as dismally low as it is for the apple growers? To answer this question, suppose that each fishing firm plans to catch 15 pounds of fish, so that total output will be 30 pounds. The market price would be $0 as in the orchard example, and each boat would then earn a profit of $0. But now if one boat unilaterally decides to cut back and catch only 14 pounds of fish, the price for all the fish caught would rise to $1 and that boat's profit would increase to $14! Since each firm can do better by unilaterally changing its output, each firm will catch less than 15 pounds of fish. The fishing firms are going to do better than the perfectly competitive equilibrium.

Although we have yet to describe what the market price will be, the fact that it is higher than what the apple growers get implies that the nature of competition in these two examples is fundamentally different. This seems surprising given how similar these markets are. In both markets, the products are undifferentiated; the firms have marginal costs of zero; the products they bring to market cannot be stored; and industry demand is the same. The only difference between them is that the farmers have no capacity constraint when they sell their apples; each has enough apples to supply total industry demand. As a result, when one firm has a lower price than the other, it captures the entire market. The fishing firms, however, are essentially choosing capacity by choosing what quantities to bring to market. Once the boat arrives at the dock, it will offer its entire catch for sale, but the total catch limits the total amount sold. If one firm expands its output, it thereby reduces the market price but does not capture the entire market. The rival firm still sells its output.

When one of the farmers unilaterally drops his price, two things happen: The two firms together sell more apples, and the firm that cuts its price gets all of the market. The incentive to cut price, then, is large. When a fisher unilaterally increases output, the price falls, and the two firms together sell more fish. But the firm that expands its output doesn't capture the entire market because its rival still sells the output it was selling before. The incentive to "cut price" by expanding output is therefore smaller. Competition is more intense in the orchards because each firm can steal its rival's

---

[5] Of course, this firm would also recognize that it doesn't need two boats since one can catch 15 fish as easily as 2.

entire share. Competition is less intense at the docks because the rival firm continues to sell whatever output it brings to the market.

We have so far not "solved" the fishing example; what will the market price be at the dock? To answer this question, consider the data in Table 8-2, which show each firm's profits as a function of the pounds of fish it catches and the pounds its rival catches. The first number in each cell of the table is the profit of Boat 1, and the second is the profit of Boat 2. If, for example, Boat 1 catches 3 pounds and Boat 2 catches 2 pounds (the shaded cell), Boat 1's profit is $75 and Boat 2's is $50. You can use this table to figure out what each firm should do, given what the other firm does. To think about this from Boat 1's perspective, suppose that Boat 2 was planning to catch no fish. The best Boat 1 can do in this case—that is, the response that maximizes its profit—is to catch 15 pounds and earn a profit of $225, as we can see by looking across the first row. This result should not be surprising: If Boat 2 were catching no fish, Boat 1 could maximize its profits by catching the pounds of fish a monopolist would catch. The important point here is that Boat 1 could use this table to figure out how many pounds of fish to catch for each catch Boat 2 might offer for sale.

Of course, Boat 1 doesn't know what Boat 2 will do. We can nonetheless think about what a reasonable outcome might be. Indeed, the logic we used earlier will help us out here as well. We argued, for example, that the monopoly outcome would not be an equilibrium because each firm would reason that it could do better by catching more fish. Similarly, the competitive outcome is not an equilibrium because each firm can increase its profits by reducing its catch. So, what we want in an equilibrium is a set of catches from which neither firm has an incentive to deviate unilaterally. Put more informally, we think an equilibrium should be some outcome in which each firm is happy with its choice once it sees what its rival has done. Both firms may prefer a different outcome, but given what its rival has done, each recognizes that it has made the best possible choice.

We can use Table 8-2 to locate the outcome for which this is true. We already know that if Boat 2 catches 0 pounds, Boat 1 should catch 15 pounds. Similarly, if Boat 2 were to catch 1 pound, the data in the table show that Boat 1 should catch either 14 or 15 pounds, earning $210 in either case. In fact (as we show in the book's appendix), this "tie" is an artifact of restricting the entries in the table to whole pounds of fish. Boat 1 would really like to catch 14.5 pounds if Boat 2 caught 2 pounds. If we work through the rest of the table for Boat 1 in the same way, we will find how many pounds of fish Boat 1 would like to catch for each possible catch of Boat 2. In Table 8-2 we have circled the corresponding profit figures for those outcomes where there is not a tie. We can do the same thing for Boat 2 (looking down the columns of Table 8-2 this time), and find the best choice Boat 2 can make given what Boat 1 has done. These profit numbers are circled and on a grey background (again for the cases where there is no "tie"). In one cell, both numbers are circled: a case where each boat catches 10 pounds of fish and makes a profit of $100. This is the only outcome in which neither firm will regret its decision given the catch its competitor has brought to market. Because neither boat would want to change the size of its catch given the size of its competitor's catch, this outcome is an equilibrium. The equilibrium outcome of this competition, then, has both firms earning $100. The fishing firm duopolists don't do

**TABLE 8-2**   How Many Fish to Catch: Firm Profits for Each Level of Outputs

*Pounds of Fish Caught by Boat 1*

|  |  | 0 | 1 | 2 | 3 | 4 | 5 | 6 | 7 | 8 | 9 | 10 | 11 | 12 | 13 | 14 | 15 |
|---|---|---|---|---|---|---|---|---|---|---|---|---|---|---|---|---|---|
| | 0 | 0 | 29 | 56 | 81 | 104 | 125 | 144 | 161 | 176 | 189 | 200 | 209 | 216 | 221 | 224 | (225) |
| | | 0 | 0 | 0 | 0 | 0 | 0 | 0 | 0 | 0 | 0 | 0 | 0 | 0 | 0 | 0 | 0 |
| | 1 | 0 | 28 | 54 | 78 | 100 | 120 | 138 | 154 | 168 | 180 | 190 | 198 | 204 | 208 | 210 | 210 |
| | | 29 | 28 | 27 | 26 | 25 | 24 | 23 | 22 | 22 | 21 | 20 | 19 | 18 | 17 | 16 | 15 |
| | 2 | 0 | 27 | 52 | 75 | 96 | 115 | 132 | 147 | 160 | 171 | 180 | 187 | 192 | 195 | (196) | 195 |
| | | 56 | 54 | 52 | 50 | 48 | 46 | 44 | 42 | 40 | 38 | 36 | 34 | 32 | 30 | 28 | 26 |
| | 3 | 0 | 26 | 50 | 72 | 92 | 110 | 126 | 140 | 142 | 162 | 170 | 176 | 180 | 182 | 182 | 180 |
| | | 81 | 78 | 75 | 72 | 69 | 66 | 63 | 60 | 57 | 54 | 51 | 48 | 45 | 42 | 39 | 36 |
| | 4 | 0 | 25 | 48 | 69 | 88 | 105 | 120 | 133 | 144 | 153 | 160 | 165 | 168 | (169) | 168 | 165 |
| | | 104 | 100 | 96 | 92 | 88 | 84 | 80 | 76 | 72 | 68 | 64 | 60 | 56 | 52 | 48 | 44 |
| | 5 | 0 | 24 | 46 | 66 | 84 | 100 | 114 | 126 | 136 | 144 | 150 | 154 | 156 | 156 | 154 | 150 |
| | | 125 | 120 | 115 | 110 | 105 | 100 | 95 | 90 | 85 | 80 | 75 | 70 | 65 | 60 | 55 | 50 |
| *Pounds of Fish Caught by Boat 2* | 6 | 0 | 23 | 44 | 63 | 80 | 95 | 108 | 119 | 128 | 135 | 140 | 143 | (144) | 143 | 140 | 135 |
| | | 144 | 138 | 132 | 126 | 120 | 114 | 108 | 102 | 96 | 90 | 84 | 78 | 72 | 66 | 60 | 54 |
| | 7 | 0 | 22 | 42 | 60 | 76 | 90 | 102 | 112 | 120 | 126 | 130 | 132 | 132 | 130 | 126 | 120 |
| | | 161 | 154 | 147 | 140 | 133 | 126 | 119 | 112 | 105 | 98 | 91 | 84 | 77 | 70 | 63 | 56 |
| | 8 | 0 | 21 | 40 | 57 | 72 | 85 | 96 | 105 | 112 | 117 | 120 | (121) | 120 | 117 | 112 | 105 |
| | | 176 | 168 | 160 | 152 | 144 | 136 | 128 | 120 | 112 | 104 | 96 | 88 | 80 | 72 | (64) | 56 |
| | 9 | 0 | 20 | 38 | 54 | 68 | 80 | 90 | 98 | 104 | 108 | 110 | 110 | 108 | 104 | 98 | 90 |
| | | 189 | 180 | 171 | 162 | 153 | 144 | 135 | 126 | 117 | 108 | 99 | 90 | (81) | 72 | 63 | 54 |
| | 10 | 0 | 19 | 36 | 51 | 64 | 75 | 84 | 91 | 96 | 99 | (100) | 99 | 96 | 91 | 84 | 75 |
| | | 200 | 190 | 180 | 170 | 160 | 150 | 140 | 130 | 120 | 110 | (100) | 90 | 80 | 70 | 60 | 50 |
| | 11 | 0 | 18 | 34 | 48 | 60 | 70 | 78 | 84 | 88 | 90 | 90 | 88 | 84 | 78 | 70 | 60 |
| | | 209 | 198 | 187 | 176 | 165 | 154 | 143 | 132 | (131) | 110 | 99 | 88 | 77 | 66 | 55 | 44 |
| | 12 | 0 | 17 | 32 | 45 | 56 | 65 | 72 | 77 | 80 | (81) | 80 | 77 | 72 | 65 | 56 | 45 |
| | | 216 | 204 | 192 | 180 | 168 | 156 | (144) | 132 | 120 | 108 | 96 | 84 | 72 | 60 | 48 | 36 |
| | 13 | 0 | 16 | 30 | 42 | 52 | 60 | 66 | 70 | 72 | 72 | 70 | 66 | 60 | 52 | 42 | 30 |
| | | 221 | 208 | 195 | 182 | (169) | 156 | 143 | 130 | 117 | 104 | 91 | 78 | 65 | 52 | 39 | 26 |
| | 14 | 0 | 15 | 28 | 39 | 48 | 55 | 60 | 63 | (64) | 63 | 60 | 55 | 48 | 39 | 28 | 15 |
| | | 224 | 210 | (196) | 182 | 168 | 154 | 140 | 126 | 112 | 98 | 84 | 70 | 56 | 42 | 28 | 14 |
| | 15 | 0 | 14 | 26 | 36 | 44 | 50 | 54 | 56 | 56 | 54 | 50 | 44 | 36 | 26 | 14 | 0 |
| | | (225) | 210 | 195 | 180 | 165 | 150 | 135 | 120 | 105 | 90 | 75 | 60 | 45 | 30 | 15 | 0 |

as well together as a monopoly firm would have done, but they are better off than their apple-selling counterparts.

A first reading of the fishing and apple-growing examples might not have suggested such different outcomes. The details of how firms compete are important, not just in this simple example, but in assessing competition in oligopolies in general. This means that to assess the intensity of competition an analyst must understand the details of how competition works. For a manager, the intensity of competition in her industry may be all too apparent. But to make the best choices for her firm, she has to understand what forces affect competitive intensity in her market.

The detail that matters in these two examples is whether firms are choosing what price to charge or what quantity to sell.[6] In terms of the elements of Table 8-2, there is a difference in what actions the firms can take. The apple growers can only compete by choosing price because they have enough capacity to supply the entire market and nothing else to do with their apples. The fishing firms, on the other hand, are choosing capacity and then selling all they produce. This detail matters because a key determinant of the intensity of competition is the strength of a firm's incentive to "steal share" from its rivals. A manager contemplating a competitive action must weigh the benefit of stealing share against the costs of trying to steal it. When an apple farmer is considering a price cut of $1, the gain from a small change is huge because he captures the whole market, and the loss is small because the price to current customers is reduced only slightly. In the case of capacities, however, the gain from increasing capacity is small. Increasing capacity does not allow the firm to "steal" share the way cutting price does. To sell another pound of fish, the firm must add one pound to the total catch, thereby depressing the overall market price by $1 and selling only one more pound of fish. The fishers gain much less than the apple farmer who reduces price by $1 and gains the entire market. And the cost in lost revenue on current sales is the same.

If the farmers could reduce their capacity at the train station, they would be better off. In the long run, they need to plant fewer apple trees, differentiate their products, or find other markets to absorb the capacity. In the short run, they can do little to reduce competition. In contrast, the boats can restrict how much they bring to market. As a result, they achieve a better outcome than the apple growers. The fishing firms would like to do even better than they are doing but will not be able to do better by choosing optimal capacity because they are already doing that.

It is tempting to dismiss these examples as an intellectual exercise with no applicability to the decisions managers face in real industries. As the securities markets and petroleum refining examples described earlier illustrate, however, there is more to this analysis than apples and fish. Furthermore, the general principle that the actions firms can take affect competitive intensity applies to much more than just whether they are

---

[6] Note that even a fishing boat may post a price at which it will sell its fish, just as petroleum refiners post a price at which they will sell heating oil. But these firms are actually choosing quantities in the sense that they are setting the price that will let them sell all that they have produced. Quantities are determining the price. The apple farmers are setting prices because they have each already produced enough to fill industry demand. Prices are determining quantities.

choosing prices or quantities. For example, competitive intensity tends to be fairly low when firms compete through advertising and promotion instead of through prices. There are two reasons for this. First, although a strong advertising campaign may increase share somewhat at the margin, markets in which advertising is important generally have some degree of product differentiation. Consequently, even a successful advertising campaign is likely to persuade only a relatively small number of people to switch from one seller to another. Second, although advertising will likely lead customers to value one firm's products over another's, it will also enhance customers' perceived valuation of the entire product category. An advertisement for Coca-Cola may cause some customers to switch from Pepsi to Coke, but it also increases overall demand for soda.

Although competition through advertising tends to be softer than competition through prices of undifferentiated products, competition through product characteristics can be more or less intense. We have talked at length about how product differentiation usually leads to softer competition. However, in markets where technological change is rapid and consumers strongly prefer state-of-the-art products, nonprice competition can be intense. In such a setting, a firm that is first to market with the latest technology tends to "win" that round of the technology battle, gaining a large share of industry sales at an attractive margin. As a result, in these markets firms make large investments in research and development in order to be the winner, dissipating much of the industry PIE in product development competition.

## Timing

In the preceding examples, we assumed that the firms made their decisions at the same time. When one firm can move first, it complicates the problem. Suppose a manager knows she can move first. She also knows that her competitor will respond to whatever she does and that this response will affect her profits. Any manager who knows that her rivals' actions will affect her bottom line wants to anticipate them. To do this, she looks at the problem from her competitor's perspective and figures out what its profit-maximizing response would be. Her profit calculations will take her action *and* her rival's response into account. She has a first-mover advantage if she can do better by moving first.

The fishing example is useful for considering how a firm that moves first might gain a competitive advantage. Assume that Boat 1 gets to move first. Maybe it sneaks out in the dark of night and comes back with its catch before the other ship has even left the dock. More realistically, a firm may be the first to exploit a new opportunity. In any case, we need to ask if and why moving first is advantageous.

Boat 1 knows what Boat 2 will choose to do for every catch Boat 1 brings to the dock. Table 8-2 tells Boat 1 that if it catches 0 pounds, Boat 2 will catch 15. If Boat 1 catches 3 pounds, Boat 2 will catch 13, and so forth. So Boat 1 needs to choose the catch that will maximize its profits given what it knows Boat 2's response will be. Looking at the data, we see that Boat 1 should choose to catch 15 pounds. Boat 2 will respond by catching 7 pounds, and their profits will be $120 and $56, respectively. Because Boat 2 knows that at least 15 pounds will be on the market (those brought in by Boat 1), it will catch less fish than it did when the firms made their choices simultaneously. In this case, having a first-mover advantage increases Boat 1's profit from $100 to $120 and reduces Boat 2's profits from $100 to $56.

Does Boat 1 really need to bring the fish at the dock to get a first-mover advantage? Can't it just tell Boat 2 that it plans to catch 15 pounds? Won't Boat 2 then respond by only catching 7 pounds? This brings us back to the question of credibility. Before Boat 1 has made an irrevocable choice, Boat 2 has no reason to believe its threat to catch 15 pounds. Boat 2 can just as easily respond by announcing that it plans to catch 15 pounds, hoping that Boat 1 will respond by catching only 7. To be credible, Boat 1 needs to be able to *commit* to catching 15 pounds. When it moves first, it has the power to commit. When the boats move simultaneously, it does not.

The issue of being a "credible first mover" often arises when firms think about adding capacity. They frequently announce capacity increases well ahead of time, hoping that their rivals will take the planned capacity (which does not yet exist) into account when making their capacity decisions. If they do, the first firm to announce will have a first-mover advantage. Capacity plans, however, are not usually irrevocable, and firms often announce they are scaling back expansion plans because the market environment suggests that expansion will be less rewarding than they initially thought it would be. Because a mere announcement is not a credible commitment, rivals may respond that they, too, will install additional capacity. In this case, we are back to the initial problem facing the fishing firms: Each is choosing capacity, and the choice is simultaneous. Simply announcing a proposed capacity increase, then, will not usually get a first-mover advantage. If, however, the first mover has a big enough lead on its rivals, so that they know that it will have capacity on-line before they can even obtain the financing they need to begin expansion, the first mover might have a credible advantage.

Although we commonly speak of a first-mover "advantage," it is not always advantageous to move first. Let's return to our orchard example and ask what happens if one of the farmers posts his price at the station first and is unable to change the price once it is posted. If he posts a price above $0, the second farmer will simply undercut his price and take the entire market. The only price he can post that will not be undercut is $0. Moving first confers no advantage and has no effect on the market outcome.

Notice also that moving preemptively by making a credible commitment also has a down side. A commitment is credible because it ties the firm's hands. We have focused on the strategic value of commitment, but commitment works only because the firm gives up some flexibility. Flexibility is valuable in many situations. A firm that can add capacity quickly can wait for demand uncertainty to be resolved before building capacity. Waiting for information improves the probability that the firm's decisions will make the appropriate investment. Waiting may also have the value of not revealing strategy; if the firm can gain an advantage from catching rivals by surprise, premature public commitment will sacrifice it. In short, waiting gives the firm the value of retaining "real options." Like financial options, real options have value, and a strategic commitment sacrifices that value. In a richer, more realistic setting, the firm must weigh the value of commitment (in our examples, the advantage of moving first) against the value of waiting. In the appendix to this text, we provide a framework for valuing real options.

## Players

One of the most important characteristics affecting competitive intensity is how many players there are. Often oligopolies become more competitive as the number of incumbent firms increases (holding constant industry demand). This is primarily because each firm's incentive to steal market share is greater when more firms are in the industry. To see why, consider what happens if our fishing industry example had, say, 20 firms. Could they sustain an equilibrium in which the price is as high as it is with only two firms? They could not; the price would be lower. To see why, suppose the 20 firms were catching one pound each. This would make industry output and price the same as when each of two firms caught 10 pounds, which seemed like a reasonable equilibrium for the duopoly case. If our 20 boats caught one pound each, the market price would be $10, and each firm would earn a profit of $10. A boat that catches one more pound, however, increases the total pounds caught to 21, thus driving the price down to $9 but increasing its profit to $18. Because its profits increase when it catches another pound of fish when the others are still catching one pound each, each boat has an incentive to catch more fish. As a result, more fish will be caught, and the market price will be lower in a 20-firm industry than in a duopoly.

The incentive to produce more output when there are more firms comes from the difference in the total sales of each firm. When there are two firms, each is selling 10 of the 20 pounds. If one firm catches one more pound, it will drive the market price down by $1. This price drop costs it $10 on the fish it would have sold at the higher price. Since the firm gets only $9 for the additional pound, it will choose not to expand its output. But any firm in the 20-firm case is selling only 1 pound at the initial price and therefore loses only $1 when the price falls. It therefore is willing to expand its output to pursue the $9 it gets for the additional pound. The basic logic here is much more general than the stylized fishing example might suggest. As the number of firms in an industry increases (holding the size of the market constant), there are more firms with smaller market shares. As a result, a reduction in price costs them less in lost revenue from existing customers (of whom they have fewer) compared to the potential increase in revenue they hope to gain from new customers.[7]

This logic does not always work, however. That more firms means more intense competition is only a rule of thumb and not a law of nature. Indeed, in our apple-growing industry, adding more firms does not affect competitive intensity because competition is already intense with just two firms. This is why the governing body of Nasdaq permits a stock to be traded that has only two market makers for it; they believe that competition between the two dealers will drive down profit margins to the

---

[7] Competition can also become more intense as the number of firms grows because the firms find it harder to establish and maintain tacit cooperation. Below, we explore the conditions under which oligopolists can avoid the competition that prevents them from being as profitable (collectively) as a monopolist. As part of that discussion, we will see why having more firms in the industry makes cooperation more difficult.

competitive level. In industries in which having fewer competitors improves the performance of the incumbents, managers might want to limit the number of new entrants, encourage consolidation among existing competitors, or make it easy for competitors to exit from the industry. In industries where competition is intense even with few incumbents, these strategies will be less effective.

## Information

Many types of information can affect competitive intensity. One type is what the firms know or believe about each other. Suppose you know that a rival firm is on the verge of bankruptcy. You should then anticipate that the firm might be desperate for cash flow and will price aggressively to build short-run revenue. Knowing this detail, you would be foolish to behave as if the low prices would remain in effect for a long time. Your rival will either go out of business, allowing you to raise prices, or will recover and want to raise prices itself. Or, to provide another example, a low-cost firm will generally be willing to produce more than its higher-cost rivals because it has attractive margins even at lower prices. If its competitors know that its costs are lower than theirs, they will rationally reduce their output to maintain higher prices. This will happen only if they have information about their competitor's costs. Otherwise they might interpret the low price as just an attempt to steal market share by sacrificing margin and will respond with their own price cuts.

A second type of information that can shape competition is information about actions other firms have taken. A firm that moves first gets a competitive advantage from doing so only if its rival learns that it has moved. Attempting to preempt the rival's capacity expansion by expanding first has no effect if the rival does not know about the expansion. Finally, information about market conditions is important. For example, let's return to the fishing boats but assume that demand for fish could be either high or low when the boats come in with their catch. If both boats know that demand will be high, they will catch more fish. However, if only one boat knows demand will be high and believes that the other boat will decide to catch only enough to satisfy average demand, it might want to catch even more. So not only does the state of market demand matter, but the information that each firm has about demand, about the other's information about demand, and so on, all affects competitive intensity.

Because information affects behavior, firms sometimes try to influence a rival's actions by providing information. For example, if you and I are locked in a battle in which only one of us can win, and if I can convince you that I will never give up, you will choose to abandon the fight immediately because fighting is costly, and if I never give up, you can never win. You have a similar incentive to make me believe that you will never give up. Indeed, we would both like to communicate our determination to fight forever even if we really plan to capitulate tomorrow.

In this kind of setting, a firm wants to think about how it can credibly communicate information to a rival. In this example, we both want to communicate something that is not true but that we would each like the other to believe. In other cases, a firm wants to communicate something that is true but may be difficult for the rival to observe and believe. This is called "signaling." Signaling is necessary only if the rival would not normally see the true information. If the firm can reveal the information directly, it may want to do so. For example, if I want to convey that I have a lower cost production process, I can invite your engineers into my plant and show them exactly why my costs are lower than yours. Of course, that would also teach your engineers how to lower your costs. So, I may prefer to find some way to signal that my costs are low without revealing exactly why they are low. My problem is how to communicate information in a credible way.

The effectiveness of signaling depends on a number of factors. First, the rival firms must see the signal and interpret it properly. Rival firms often misunderstand communications. They observe a drop in *list* price, for example, but do not know how that will translate into *transaction* prices. Are transaction prices supposed to fall by the same amount? the same percentage? Is it an across-the-board reduction, or is it a reduction only to selected customers?

Assuming that the firms can solve the communication problem, they still have to solve the credibility problem. Suppose the firm wants to convey the following to its rivals: "I have lower production costs than the rest of you. My profit-maximizing price is therefore lower than yours. So the low price you observe is not a temporary grab for market share. It is the price I will charge in equilibrium. You have no reason to respond by cutting your price to punish me. You should accept that I will be the low-price firm and make your decisions accordingly." Remember that in this example the signaling firm really has low costs and is trying to convey information that its rivals want to have. The problem is that a firm that is not low cost would like to convey the same message.

To be more concrete, think about our apple industry but give up the notion that apples can be brought to market at no cost. If both farmers have a marginal cost of selling apples of, say, $1.00, the equilibrium price will be $1.00. If one farmer has a marginal cost of $1.00 and the other a marginal cost of $2.00, the lower cost farmer will cut price until it is just below his rival's marginal cost. The low-cost farmer will earn a profit, and the high-cost farmer will either have to go home or sell each of his apples at a loss. If the higher-cost firm is convinced that its rival really is low cost and can therefore afford to charge this low price forever, it would be better off leaving the market now. If it thinks that its rival is bluffing, however, it has a reason to match the price cut and wait for its rival to raise the price back to a remunerative level. In this case, the appropriate response for the competing firm is something like, "Prices are too low in this market, but I will not be undersold, and I remain committed to the market."

To summarize, the low-cost firm has information about its cost that its rival cannot observe. Both firms would be better off if the information could be credibly communicated. The low-cost firm would be better off because its rival would withdraw, and it could then behave as a monopolist. The rival would be better off because it would incur losses as long as it remained in the market; it is better off withdrawing sooner rather than later. Unfortunately, a firm that does not have low costs has an incentive to claim that it does have low costs in order to bluff its rival into withdrawing. As a result, the simple claim that "I have low costs" is insufficient. Even charging a low price may not be sufficient.

A firm that wants to convey a low-cost position, then, has to do something more. It has to send a message that a high-cost firm would not imitate. It could announce a deep price cut and offer to take orders over the next six months at that price. If the rival knows that a firm without low costs could not afford to make that kind of commitment to buyers, it will believe that the communicating firm is indeed low cost and will act accordingly. This is ultimately what makes a signal credible: The communicating firm would find it impossible or too costly to send the signal if the signal were not true. In our simple story, posting a price for apples that is less than $2.00 would work as a credible signal because we've assumed that the two farmers post a price only once. A firm that has a marginal cost of $2.00 or greater would be unwilling to sell all its output for less than $2.00. In more complex settings, because the firm can raise its price when its rival withdraws, the firm finds it harder to make a credible signal.

We have used the term "signaling" in the same way it is used in the economics literature—that is, to mean communicating something credibly when there is an incentive to mislead. In popular usage, "signaling" often means nothing more than "talking." If I simply announce that the cost at my new plant is 50 percent lower than with my old technology, my rivals may well be suspicious of my claim. I have said something, but they know I would like them to believe that my costs are low even if they are not. "Signaling" low cost requires that I do something to make my claim credible. The signal will be credible only if it is one that is too costly for an impostor to send.

Communication that is not costly is called "cheap talk." Cheap talk will be credible only when the communicator has no incentive to lie. When two cars meet at an intersection, one driver may indicate that he is turning left. This communication is cheap talk, but it is credible because the talker has no incentive to mislead the other driver. Indeed, the talker has every incentive to communicate precisely what he will in fact be doing. In this case, the cars have a coordination problem, not a conflict of interest. In industries, coordination problems can arise when all the firms benefit from pursuing the same course of action. All the firms producing computer peripherals, for example, benefit from a standardized interface with the computer. These firms may not care exactly what the interface is as long as it is standardized. In this case, an announcement by IBM (or some other large computer firm) that it will build interfaces to some specific standard may be cheap talk, but it might also be credible and followed by other firms. If a firm has an incentive to mislead its rival, however, cheap talk will not be credible.

## Repetition

Faced with the devastating effects competition can have on profitability, managers frequently bemoan the "insanity" that drives firms to undercut each other continually. In the drive to increase its profits, each competitor acts to maximize its profits at the expense of its competitors' profits. Because all firms engage in this activity, profitability at all of them declines. Each firm knows that all of them would all be better off if they could all agree to be less competitive. Why can't they just say "no" to competition?

One reason is that certain types of interfirm agreements violate antitrust laws. Laws governing agreements that might reduce competition vary across countries, but most governments impose some limits on them. The United States prohibits agreements to set prices, for example. We will summarize the relevant law in Section 8.4.

Another, more fundamental reason that firms cannot cooperate is that each firm has a very strong incentive to deviate or "cheat" to increase its profits.[8] Suppose, for example, that our apple farmers are thinking about whether to cooperate, in which case they could each charge $15, sell 15 pounds, and earn a profit of $112.50. They know that if they compete, the price (and their profits) will be $0. Cooperation seems to be the more attractive alternative. But now, think about what happens if one of them, say Farmer 2, cooperates by charging $15. Farmer 1 must decide whether to price at $15 or cheat by selling his apples for $14. This situation is illustrated in Table 8-3 where the first (second) number in each cell is the profits of Farmer 1 (2). When Farmer 2 is cooperating, Farmer 1 can also cooperate and earn $112.50, or cheat and earn $224 (a rightward move in the top row of the table). Facing this temptation, Farmer 1 will cheat. Of course, if Farmer 2 believes that Farmer 1 will cooperate, Farmer 2 faces an identical temptation, and he, too, will cheat. Furthermore, if either believes that the other will cheat, the best he can do is to cheat too. The result is that they both cheat. If the undercutting stopped at $14, the cheating would make them both somewhat worse off because they would each earn $112 instead of $112.50. The undercutting, of course, doesn't stop at $14 because the situation simply repeats itself at that price. If Farmer 2 is charging $14, Farmer 1 has an incentive to cut his price to $13, and so forth. Indeed, the farmers end up back at the equilibrium price of $0![9] This happens even though each firm would be better off if both were to cooperate.

It is particularly important to understand why firms find it hard to cooperate: No firm can reduce the incentive for another to cheat by not cheating itself. Often

**TABLE 8-3**    The Incentive to Cheat by Lowering Price

| | | Price Charged by Farmer 1 | |
|---|---|---|---|
| | | Cooperate (Price is $15) | Cheat (Price is $14) |
| *Price Charged by Farmer 2* | Cooperate (Price is $15) | 112.50, 112.50 | 224, 0 |
| | Cheat (Price is $14) | 0, 224 | 112, 112 |

---

[8] We use the terms "cooperating" and "cheating" because the firms have agreed to undertake an action—charge the monopoly price, for example. Abiding by the agreement is "cooperating," and violating it is "cheating."

[9] The situation in Table 8-3 is a version of the classic Prisoners' Dilemma discussed more fully in the Appendix to this book.

[10] Note that Farmer 2 has created a first-mover *dis*advantage by committing to a high price.

people think that firms should reason as follows: "If I maintain a high price, my rival will recognize that it won't be hurt by also charging a high price. So if I can convince it that I will price at the monopoly price, it will want to cooperate." This reasoning is fallacious. Suppose Farmer 2 does something that prevents him from charging a price less than $15. It is not obvious what that might be without violating the law, but let us set that problem aside for the moment. Recognizing this commitment, Farmer 1 now knows he can price at $14 and make $224.[10] If Farmer 1 is fulfilling his fiduciary responsibility to his stockholders, he has to make the profit-maximizing decision and set a price of $14. Even though his competitor is charging a high price, Farmer 1 would be hurt by cooperating because he would forgo $111.50 of profit. Indeed, the closer Farmer 2's price is to the monopoly price, the more Farmer 1 has to lose by cooperating. Recognizing this, Farmer 2 would be unwilling to make the commitment.

The problem that firms face in this example is that the value of cheating is greater than the value of cooperating. To sustain cooperation, they must somehow reengineer the world to make the value of cooperation greater than the value of cheating. One way to do so would be to sign a contract with a large penalty for breach. Most countries, including the United States, forbid price fixing contracts. To cooperate, then, the firms have to come to some agreement that is *self-enforcing*. The profits a firm will earn when it cooperates must outweigh the gains it will get from cheating, even though the firm cannot enter into an agreement that the courts will enforce. The example we have worked through suggests that cooperating cannot be more profitable than cheating when firms compete against each other only once. Without some enforceable contract, cooperation is impossible without repeated interaction, and oligopoly firms will therefore have lower margins than a monopoly firm would have.

Outside the simple examples of fish and apples, however, firms do repeatedly interact with each other, which opens up additional opportunities for sustaining cooperation. Suppose Farmers 1 and 2 meet in this market every autumn. Farmer 2 can now post a price of $15 and say to Farmer 1: "If you match my price this year, I will set a price of $15 next year as well. But if you charge a price less than $15 this year, I will charge a price of $0 next year and every year thereafter." Farmer 1 now calculates: "If I post a price at $14 this year, I will make $224. But next year and every year thereafter, I will make only $0. If I charge a price of $15 this year and every other year, I will make $112.50 every year." Even with future profits discounted substantially, cooperating becomes the more profitable path.

Although repeated interaction might make cooperation possible, it does not guarantee that it will occur. To soften competition through cooperation, firms must solve a number of related problems. First, they must "agree" about what constitutes cooperative behavior. "Agree" is in quotes here because an explicit agreement is unlawful; the cooperation must be tacit. If Farmer 2 did what we suggested in the preceding paragraph, he would have violated U.S. law. Firms must somehow come to a common understanding of what price to charge without directly communicating with each other.

In our simple example, the farmers might easily agree about what the "correct" price is, but in the more complicated settings real oligopolists face, such agreement may be difficult. Reaching agreement is more complicated when products are differentiated because the firms may then need to agree about several different prices. It is also more difficult when firms have different production costs. A firm with a lower marginal cost than its rival will also want to have a lower cooperative price. Furthermore, although we have focused on price competition, firms also compete in other dimensions. They advertise and invest in new product development, for example. To reduce competition effectively, the firms may need to agree not only on price, but also on the appropriate levels for many kinds of competitive expenditures. Disagreements about what the firms would like to see happen in the market are difficult enough to resolve when firms can communicate directly; they can be impossible to resolve when communication must be indirect.

Even if the firms can come to a common understanding, they must be able to monitor compliance and punish deviations quickly. In the apple example, we assumed that each farmer could easily tell how much his rival was charging. In practice, firms often cannot ascertain what other firms charge. Even when firms do list their prices, many transactions may involve a discounted price. One way to tell whether your rival has secretly cut prices is to infer it from a drop in demand for your product. When demand is constant, this works pretty well, but when demand changes, it is difficult to distinguish between the effects of a decline in industry demand and a secret price cut by a rival. If competitors cannot detect a price cut, they cannot respond by refusing to cooperate in the future, and cheating becomes more profitable. Similarly, if a firm cannot respond quickly to cheating by its rival, the gains to cheating are larger.

Reaching and enforcing an agreement without communication that would violate antitrust laws, then, are difficult. Moreover, any unexpected change can disrupt cooperation. The introduction of a new product, the entry of a new competitor, or a change in demand or cost might require "renegotiating" the entire agreement. The more unexpected changes there are, the more unlikely it is that cooperation can be sustained.

Cooperation is also less likely when there are more firms in the industry. More firms make it more difficult to reach agreement about what constitutes cooperation. More firms also make cheating relatively more attractive. Suppose, for example, that there were five apple sellers instead of two. Now, if all sellers cooperate, each gets one-fifth of monopoly profits each period instead of one-half. The gain to cooperation has declined. The gain to cheating, however, has remained the same. If a single firm drops its price to $14, it makes $224 no matter how many other firms are in the industry. As the number of firms increases, it becomes more difficult for the gain from cooperating to outweigh the gain from cheating.

Cooperation is also less likely when the future becomes less important. For example, suppose two firms are cooperating, and one is suddenly facing bankruptcy because of losses in an unrelated line of business. Both firms now recognize that they may not be competitors in the future, so the anticipated gain from cooperating declines, but the potential gain from cheating (which is earned immediately) does not.

The point here is that avoiding competition through more cooperative behavior is difficult at best. The problems the OPEC cartel faces are instructive. The OPEC countries can and do negotiate openly and enter into explicit agreements to cut back production in order to maintain the targeted price for crude oil. They decide who can sell how much, and they have established procedures for monitoring compliance. The member countries also know that they will be competing against each other for a long time. Their product is fairly homogeneous, and there are many ways to estimate world demand. Even under these unusually favorable conditions, however, member countries have repeatedly violated the various agreements because it was in their best interest to do so.

Nonetheless, firms that have been competing with one another over a long period, particularly when the product has remained fairly stable, may be able to mitigate some of the effects of competition. These firms know both the market and each other well. As a result, they can respond to subtle cues from each other that allow them to avoid fierce competition.

Consider the following example from the steel industry in the United States. In the mid-1960s, price competition was becoming increasingly intense despite the efforts of a leading player, U.S. Steel, to maintain price stability. List prices declined, and some of U.S. Steel's competitors were also routinely offering secret price discounts off list prices. In late 1968, watching its market share slipping, U.S. Steel abandoned its policy of not discounting its list prices and joined those who had been offering secret price cuts. Bethlehem Steel—another major firm—discovered that U.S. Steel had offered one of Bethlehem's important customers a secret discount. Bethlehem responded by announcing a drop in its *list* price of hot-rolled steel sheets from $113.50 a ton to $88.50, a 22 percent price cut! Bethlehem also announced that "prices should go up, not down" but that Bethlehem "must be competitive." Three weeks later, U.S. Steel raised its list price to $125. Nine days later, Bethlehem raised its price to $117. U.S. Steel matched it. A few months later, Bethlehem raised its list price to $129, and U.S. Steel again matched it. These price changes tell a fairly obvious story. Bethlehem Steel says, "We're tired of these secret price cuts, and we're not going to take it any more" ($89). U.S. Steel responds, "You're right, we're sorry, what price do you like" ($125)? Bethlehem Steel says "$117." U.S. Steel says, "OK." Bethlehem Steel says, "Well if we can agree on $117, how about $129?" Again U.S. Steel says, "OK."

Leading prices up in this manner is easier when the industry has a focal firm to act as an informal leader. Often the leader is one of the largest firms in the industry. To the extent that the other firms follow the lead of the focal firm, the industry may be less competitive than its numbers alone would suggest. Some have argued, for example, that General Motors has been the leader for U.S. automobile firms:

> General Motors is clearly the price leader in the industry. It initiates general rounds of price increases; it can by refusing to follow prevent either of its two U.S. rivals from leading price alterations; and, finally its price changes establish the de facto price ceilings for Ford and Chrysler.[11]

---

[11] Walter Adams and Gerald Brock, "The Automobile Industry" in *The Structure of American Industry*, 7th ed. Walter Adams (New York: Macmillan, 1986).

If the leader firm sets a relatively high price and the others follow, competition can be reduced. However, the leader cannot *make* the other firms follow. If Ford and Chrysler believe it is no longer in their interest to follow General Motors, they will not do so. If one of the major players in steel had declined to follow U.S. Steel's price increase, prices would have remained low.

Price leadership behavior has been observed in markets as different as cigarettes, plywood, and airlines. Consider, for example, a conversation played out in the pages of *The New York Times* in March 1983. Following the deregulation of the industry in the late 1970s, the United States airline industry entered an unstable period that included frequent price wars. Then, on March 15, 1983, the *Times* carried an article headlined "American to Base Fares on Mileage" and reported American Airlines' announcement that it would use a simple, distanced-based formula to determine prices.[12] American's senior vice president for marketing was quoted as saying that the new fare structure would reduce "fare confusion" and make ticket prices "more equitable." In the same article, a TWA official stated, "At first glance it is a good move. … It's very businesslike." United Airlines commented that it "wanted to see if the new fares would increase revenue yields in its markets."

The next day, the *Times* reported that a spokesman for United Airlines had announced that it would adopt American's fare plan. The following day, an article headlined "Most Big Airlines Back American's Fare Plan" announced that TWA and Continental said they would apply the new fare structure to their entire route systems. TWA said, "[T]he proposal … represents an excellent attempt to rationalize a pricing system that has gotten totally out of hand." Eastern and Western also announced support of the basic concept of the plan, even though they had not yet adopted it. Delta reportedly said that the plan was a good one and it would decide that day whether to go along with it. By the end of the week, the reporter covering the story reported that most airlines were rallying behind the proposal.

The stock market apparently agreed that the widely adopted plan would be good for profits. Table 8–4 reports an estimate of the above-market returns earned by the major airlines' stockholders earned over the three days in which this conversation took place in the newspapers.[13]

As the table shows, an investment in a portfolio of the airlines made before the first announcement would have returned a 6 percent profit in three days. The total stock market valuation of these companies increased by close to half a billion dollars over this time span. American Airlines fared particularly well with a 12 percent return and a $109 million increase in stock market valuation. Perhaps American's advantage in choosing the structure of the new price schedule was partly responsible for its unusually good return.

These steel and airline stories demonstrate that firms can compete less aggressively when they recognize their interdependence; when they are sufficiently familiar

---

[12] "American to Base Fares on Mileage," *The New York Times*, March 15, 1983.

[13] The analysis in this table was performed by Julio Rotemberg and Garth Saloner and was reported in an earlier draft of a paper that was published as "Collusive Price Leadership," *Journal of Industrial Economics* 34 (September 1990), 93–111.

**TABLE 8-4**   Stock Market Response to "Simplified Pricing"

| Airline | Return (%) | Increase in Value ($m) |
|---|---|---|
| American Airlines | 12 | 109.2 |
| Delta Air Lines | 4 | 83.0 |
| Eastern Air Lines | 4 | 8.2 |
| Northwest Air Lines | 6 | 60.5 |
| Ozark Holdings | 5 | 8.9 |
| PSA | 6 | 6.9 |
| Pan American | 5 | 4.9 |
| Piedmont Aviation | 2 | 6.7 |
| Republic Airlines | 16 | 30.8 |
| Texas Air | 4 | 4.6 |
| TWA | 9 | 44.6 |
| United Air Lines | 9 | 91.6 |
| US Air | 4 | 29.6 |
| Western Airlines | 4 | 3.8 |
| Equally weighted portfolio | 6 | |
| Total | | 493.5 |

with their competitive environment and each other to reach an informal agreement without direct communication; and when they expect to compete with each other in the future. These conditions are not trivial, however. The forces of competition can sometimes be repressed but are not eliminated.

Firms have subverted several temporary "truces" in the airline industry, for example, because they have found, for one reason or another, that the benefits of cooperating were not sufficiently high. Sometimes, airlines near bankruptcy have precipitated a price war. Other firms have used their United States traffic primarily to feed their international flights and therefore had more to gain from cutting prices on U.S. routes. When firms have different returns to cooperation, the low-return firms constrain the ability of the high-return firms to realize those gains. To be effective, the "agreement" must appeal to all the firms in the industry (or at least to all the major players).

## Summary

Competitive intensity in an oligopoly depends on certain subtleties in the setting in which competition takes place. We have emphasized the main determinants of competitive intensity: players, actions, information, timing, and repetition. Although many useful generalizations about competition in oligopolies can be drawn, a lot depends on the details of the situation. Moreover, the various elements of the setting interact. So, although a duopoly generally experiences less competitive intensity than an oligopoly with several firms, even a duopoly may struggle if the informational conditions aren't right or if interactions are so infrequent that repetition is not an important factor. Conversely, an oligopoly with six or seven firms may be quite profitable, provided the players know one another well, have had a long history of cooperation, have good information about one another, and are in a setting where it is difficult to steal significant market share in the short run by "upsetting the apple cart." A manager in an oligopolistic industry, therefore, must understand what characteristics of the environment determine the level of competitive intensity. Failure to understand the details can lead to costly mistakes as rivals react in unexpected ways.

## 8.3  DOMINANT FIRMS

Unlike oligopoly markets, which have at least two major players, the classic dominant firm structure has a single large firm and a number of much smaller firms. When the firms' offerings are differentiated, the dominant firm produces the leading products targeted to a broad spectrum of buyers. In contrast, each of the small firms plays a niche strategy in which it targets a small subset of buyers. For many years, EDS had a commanding share of the outsourced information technology business. The industry had many other, much smaller firms, that often specialized in responding to industry or business-specific information technology needs and, therefore, competed for only a narrow segment of the overall outsourcing market.

The dominant firm functions as the industry leader. It sets a price for its product, for example, knowing the smaller firms will take that price as the industry standard, benchmarking their prices to it. In this type of market, the behavior of the large firm determines competitive intensity. If it has a substantial competitive advantage over its smaller competitors, it can act much like a monopolist. By not pricing aggressively, for example, it will cede some share to the smaller firms, but it will have a large gain from "milking" its customer base. This is the scenario we had in mind in Chapter 6 when we placed a dominant firm next to the monopoly structure in the spectrum of competition. If it has no real competitive advantage, a dominant firm may feel it must protect its share against encroachment by firms that are smaller but not otherwise at a substantial disadvantage. It may then need to behave more aggressively, and the industry will be more competitive.

For the dominant firm structure to persist, the dominant firm must have some advantage over its much smaller competitors. Put differently, why don't the small firms undercut the price of the dominant firm slightly and take its share? The incentive to do so is enormous given the share they would gain. The answer is that something usually differentiates the product of the dominant firm from those of the small firms. For more than 20 years, for example, Coca-Cola dominated the U.S. market for soft drinks; no competitor had a significant market share. Supporting Coke's dominance was the fact that it was the first firm to build a national brand name in soft drinks and have a national distribution network. Any challenger would have to build these resources and deal with Coke's response to its challenge. Pepsi eventually mounted a sustained attack on Coke's position and became a strong rival. But it took a long time and a well-developed, well-executed attack strategy to do so. Simply charging a lower price was not enough.

IBM in mainframe computers is another example. In Europe, a number of firms had much smaller shares of the mainframe market (e.g., Siemens, Nixdorf, Olivetti). For the most part, these firms were domestic and had particularly strong positions with their national governments, which supported domestic firms. In contrast, IBM had a strong multinational position and was favored by firms that had multinational operations and that valued the IBM reputation for service and quality. The structure in which IBM was the dominant firm in a market with several niche players persisted for many years.

These examples emphasize how difficult it can be for small firms to attack a dominant firm successfully. The likelihood of an attack by a fringe firm is also reduced by what the attacking firm is giving up. As long as the dominant firm is setting a price "umbrella" that allows the fringe firm to make more profit than it would if there were no dominant firm, the incentive to attack is diminished. If the dominant firm is setting a high price, the smaller firms may be more profitable than they would be if competition among the many small firms set the market price. Being the dominant firm is better than being a firm that lives in the shadow of the elephant. But living in the shadow of an elephant is better than living in the glare of unprotected competition.

If the small firms are reluctant to attack, why doesn't the dominant firm attack them? One answer goes back to our discussion of the gains and losses from lowering price. A dominant firm that drops its price to attack a small firm gives up revenue on its large customer base to gain a small market share. This may not be worthwhile. This reasoning is much less compelling if the dominant firm can selectively lower price. Suppose the contact lens industry has a dominant firm and another firm that provides specialty lenses only for people with light-sensitive eyes. If the dominant firm can lower price only to the specialty market without losing revenue on its other customers, it may do it. In this example, the small firm is much more vulnerable to competition from the dominant firm.

Niche firms are also sometimes protected by the mobility barriers we discussed in Chapter 7. The technology allowing a small contact lens firm to produce specialty lenses may be proprietary, for example. In other examples, a close relationship with a few buyers protects the niche firms. A niche firm may have customized its product for them, sell them other complementary products, or be a national champion, for example.

Some markets that we would classify under the dominant firm heading have a structure more like that of the metal can industry in the 1980s: a few large firms and many small firms. In this situation, the dominant group is an oligopoly, and the discussion of how they might compete with each other described in the oligopoly section applies. In particular, if the large firms can mute the competition among themselves, they can establish a price umbrella for the small firms that is like the one a single dominant firm creates. However, they may end up competing fiercely. If so, there will be no price umbrella, and the small firms may be casualties in the competition. When, for example, Coke and Pepsi were fighting over the U.S. market in the 1970s and 1980s, profits at the smaller firms (e.g., Seven-Up) suffered. It is nice to stand in the shelter of the elephants' shadow when they are at peace, but if the elephants start fighting, the small firms can get trampled.

## 8.4  ANTITRUST

Concentrated markets raise two types of antitrust issues. First, firms that are large relative to the size of the markets they serve can affect industry outcomes. They can, for example, undertake activities that will force other, less well-positioned, firms out of the market. However, size alone, even dominating size, does not violate U.S. laws. In a U.S. Steel case, the court made this point clear: "the law does not make mere size an offense or the existence of unexerted power an offense. It … requires overt acts." But what kinds of acts? Section 2 of the Sherman Act declares that any acts that represent "monopolization or attempts to monopolize" an industry are unlawful. One act that falls under this description is "price predation." A firm that charges a price below a reasonable measure of cost with the intent to drive out a competing firm is said to have engaged in predatory pricing. A firm that denies access to some facility that is necessary for the survival of competing firms (a so-called *essential facility*) can also be charged under this statute. For example, if an airline owns a widely used computerized reservation system, it cannot lawfully refuse to list the flights of competing airlines on the system. Many acts that might violate this statute arise in the context of attempts to block entry, and we will return to this topic in Chapter 9.

The second antitrust issue is collusion. If "competing" firms can agree not to compete, they will be much more profitable. They also will violate the laws against collusion. In the remainder of this section, we summarize some of the laws relevant to collusion to indicate the kinds of actions managers in these firms should take when formulating competitive strategies.

### Collusion and Antitrust

In the United States, Section 1 of the Sherman Act that prohibits "contracts, combinations, and conspiracies in restraint of trade" covers price fixing and collusion more generally. By *price fixing*, we mean agreements that have the effect of fixing prices. For example, an agreement between the fishing boats that each would catch 7.5 pounds of fish would "fix" the market price at monopoly levels. Similarly, agreements to divide markets geographically or in some other way that means firms do not compete for sales can effectively fix price.

Under Section 1, an agreement whose sole purpose is to fix prices is per se illegal. That is, the courts do not ask whether the behavior is "reasonable" or in the public interest. If the agreement fixes prices, it is unlawful no matter what else it might do. One could argue, for example, that when there is excess capacity, uncontrolled competition might make it impossible for two firms to cover their average costs. Without cooperation, one of the firms might be forced out of the industry, leaving a monopolist to charge a much higher price. In some early antitrust cases, firms argued that they had fixed prices only to avoid such ruinous competition in the face of excess capacity and that the prices they had set were fair. Such arguments seldom persuade the courts.

Although the law clearly makes an agreement to fix prices unlawful, what constitutes an agreement is often less clear. In some famous cases, the government obtained evidence that representatives of the firms involved communicated directly and fixed prices explicitly. In a recent case involving makers of bulk chemicals, company representatives met in hotels and discussed how to set production quotas and monitor production, and how they would set up a trade group to disguise the conspiracy. Unfortunately for them, one of the participants was cooperating with a law enforcement agency and tape recorded the conversations.[14]

In the absence of this kind of direct communication, the courts can have difficulty determining whether a "contract, combination or conspiracy" has occurred. Suppose, for example, that the firms have made public announcements about prices and the state of the industry. Is this unlawful? How different are the situations in the steel and airline industries discussed above from one in which the firms get together and secretly reach an agreement about price? In the steel example, if one can imagine the conversation that is taking place, is this different from having the conversation actually take place? And if, as in the airline example, the conversation is taking place in the newspaper, is that different from the conversation taking place in secret?

In the early years of antitrust enforcement, the U.S. courts adopted the perspective that there was little difference. In a series of cases, the courts developed the "conscious parallelism doctrine." As this name suggests, the courts drew a parallel between explicit price fixing and situations in which firms, though not meeting to fix prices, were consciously acting cooperatively. The American Tobacco case offers a clear exposition of this doctrine. After the Tobacco Trust was dissolved into several independent firms in 1911, the firms struggled to reach a pricing equilibrium for over a decade. In the early 1920s, the three major firms, Reynolds, American Tobacco, and Liggett and Myers, developed a pattern of price leadership in which one of the firms (usually Reynolds) would lead a price change and the others would exactly match that price, usually within a day. Between 1923 and 1941, the "standard brands" these firms offered had eight price changes, six of which Reynolds led.

The court concluded that this pricing pattern was neither coincidental nor competitive in its intent. The court also maintained that there was "a unity of purpose for a common design and understanding, or meeting of minds in an unlawful arrangement" and that "the conclusion that a conspiracy is established is justified." One problem with interpreting evidence of this kind as an indication of collusion is that similar pricing patterns can also be a normal, noncollusive outcome. Even if firms are behaving competitively, prices must occasionally adjust to changes in market conditions, and if the change affects all the firms, their prices will move in parallel. Perhaps because of the difficulty of distinguishing this kind of normal, competitive behavior from "consciously parallel" collusive activity, since the mid-1950s the courts have ruled that mere parallel action in an oligopoly, without additional evidence of unlawful behavior, is not in and of itself illegal.

Antitrust laws outside the United States can be different. A complete review of these laws is beyond our scope, but we want to emphasize that no common under-

---

[14] "The Tale of the Secret Tapes," Kurt Eichenwald. *The New York Times*, November 16, 1997, Section 3, p. 1.

standing exists about precisely what acts are lawful or the conditions under which certain acts become unlawful or even the rationale for having antitrust laws.[15] In the United States, the overarching rationale for antitrust laws is the belief that competition leads to socially desirable outcomes. The law, then, is designed to promote competition. In most of the rest of the world, the belief that competition is a social good is less firmly held. Outside the United States, courts can be more sympathetic to arguments that some observed deviation from competitive outcomes has desirable social effects.

Within Europe, each country has laws that govern domestic price fixing, and Article 85 of the Treaty of Rome governs collusion within the European Economic Community. Like Section 1 of the Sherman Act, it forbids interfirm agreements that are intended to limit competition. The kinds of arrangements Article 85 prohibits are similar to those the Sherman Act outlaws. Nonetheless, different kinds of behavior are likely to be found to be in violation of the law. For example, an agreement to set price is unlawful under Article 85 unless it qualifies for an exemption. U.S. law does not allow for exemptions. On the other hand, U.S. law treats technology development agreements as presumptively lawful unless they can be shown to have anticompetitive effects, whereas the European law treats these agreements the same way it treats agreements on price.

Japan's law on interfirm agreements has been moving closer to the European and U.S. position but still allows for cartels and other agreements to cooperate that are "in the public interest." Japan has no general prohibition against cartels; indeed, the government itself orchestrates some of them. Since the 1970s, different agencies within the government have disagreed about what practices violate the existing law. For example, the Ministry of International Trade and Industry has argued that collusion that promotes the competitive position of Japanese firms abroad is "in the public interest." At the same time, the Japan Fair Trade Commission has argued for a more rigorous adherence to existing laws against collusion.

## 8.5  SUMMARY

In this chapter we have examined competition in concentrated markets. We have discussed both industries with a small number of large firms, oligopolies, and markets where there is a large dominant firm. When an industry includes large firms, competitive intensity will be determined by the details of how those firms compete. The actions the firms can take, the information they have, the number and characteristics of the large players, the timing of moves, and the time horizon over which firms compete can all affect competitive intensity. We illustrated the importance of the institutional details of an industry for its competitive dynamics through two detailed examples in which most of the characteristics of the markets were the same but the

---

[15] The information on antitrust outside the United States is based on F. M. Scherer and D. Ross, *Industrial Market Structure and Economic Performance*, 3rd ed. (Boston: Houghton Mifflin, 1990), and a Stanford University teaching note by D. Lane and F. Scott Morton, "Antitrust Laws in Countries Other Than the United States."

competitive outcome differed greatly because of seemingly minor changes in the way the firms competed.

In concentrated industries, a manager's understanding of precisely how competition works in the industry is most critical. A manager must not only understand how the actions his firm takes will affect the industry, but must also anticipate the reactions of rival firms. Because collusion is most likely to arise in concentrated industries, we also included a brief review of relevant antitrust laws.

Typically, an industry will remain concentrated and the established firms will enjoy incumbency advantages only if entry by other firms is difficult. We therefore turn next to entry barriers.

# *9*

# ENTRY AND THE ADVANTAGE OF INCUMBENCY

## 9.1 INTRODUCTION

When incumbent firms are performing well, other firms want to join the party. For example, the profits of incumbent pharmaceutical firms have enticed entry by a horde of small biotechnology firms, and the profits of successful software companies have encouraged thousands of software ventures. Sometimes even the expectation of strong performance can promote entry; the number of on-line retailing firms has exploded, even though many incumbents have never earned a profit.

Incumbents dislike entry for two reasons. First, successful entry implies that the incumbents' *share* of industry profits must decline. Some incumbents may lose more share from entry than others, but, as a group, their share must decline. Second, entry frequently leads to *greater competitive intensity* within an industry because competition usually increases as the number of firms in an industry increases.[1] As the industry becomes more competitive, the combined profit the incumbent firms earn declines. Entry, then, can depress aggregate profits by making the industry more competitive and can reduce the share of industry profits the original firms retain. On the other hand, as we argued in Chapter 6 (and illustrate in Figure 9-1), if barriers to entry exist, the incumbent firms might retain a substantial share of potential industry earnings over the long run. A study of entry barriers is therefore an essential part of industry analysis.

---

[1] Aggregate industry profits could increase as new firms enter because they bring new products or production processes to the industry. Aggregate industry profits could also increase in the early stages of an industry as new firms enter because subsequent entry "legitimizes" the offerings in the market. For example, when IBM entered the personal computer market, it legitimized the PC as a viable market, leading software companies to write enough programs for the PC to enable consumers to derive greater value from the product. Except in unusual circumstances, however, entry means that the industry incumbents become less profitable.

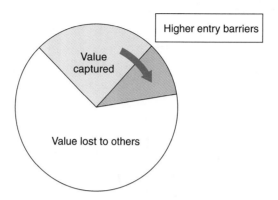

**FIGURE 9-1**    Entry Barriers Increase the Share of PIE Retained by Incumbents

Entry barriers are conditions that make the industry less attractive to a potential entrant than it is to the incumbent firms. Because this asymmetry in competitive positioning is fundamental to entry barriers, we will often refer to entry barriers as "incumbency advantages." This terminology emphasizes that an entry barrier gives a competitive advantage to an incumbent firm *because it is an incumbent*.[2] Often, the advantage arises from an early mover advantage that the incumbents share. They might, for example, have lower cost or greater consumer appeal simply because they have been in the industry for some time. If there are no incumbency advantages, incumbents cannot capture a significant share of PIE over the long run.

As the language suggests, incumbency advantages are similar in effect to the competitive advantages we discussed in Chapter 3 and elsewhere. Indeed, in the rare case when the incumbent is a monopoly firm, any of the competitive advantages we have already discussed could be considered an incumbency advantage. In the more usual case when the industry has several competitors, however, entry barriers are an advantage the incumbent firms share. One firm might have a patent that gives it a competitive advantage over any other firm, but the advantage from a patent is no greater over potential entrants than it is over incumbent competitors. Furthermore, the fact that the advantaged firm already faces successful competitors suggests that entrants might be able to compete profitably. The patent, then, is not an incumbency advantage. In contrast, when firm reputation is important, firms that are already competing successfully in the industry have an advantage over a new entrant that has no established reputation. Reputation is an incumbency advantage because it makes each successful incumbent better positioned than a new entrant.

---

[2] Note that low pre-entry profits are not a barrier to entry. If all the firms in an industry are losing money, for example, a firm that can exactly match the cost and consumer appeal of the incumbents might decide that entry is not attractive. But the potential entrant is not disadvantaged relative to the incumbents; it could enter and earn the same miserable returns the incumbent firms earn. Only if its entry made industry conditions worse would the potential entrant face an incumbency advantage.

In this chapter, we examine some common entry barriers, provide examples of entry barrier effects, and, finally, discuss how firms might strategically create entry barriers.

## 9.2.  TYPES OF INCUMBENCY ADVANTAGE

In this section, we describe some of the most common entry barriers, accepting the barriers as conditions that simply exist. We will, for example, talk about the barriers from economies of scale in production technology as if the technology were a given. Once we understand how these barriers work, we will later discuss how incumbent firms might choose to *create* entry barriers.

### Scale Advantages

One of the most frequently cited entry barriers in the literature is *economies of scale*. By this we mean that average costs decline as the firm produces more output (at least over some range). Economies of scale can arise at the level of an individual machine. The most efficient way to make paper, for example, is to run high-capacity machines with as little downtime as possible. A cost-efficient machine for producing business and writing paper can produce over 1500 tons of paper a day. Smaller machines can be used, but they entail higher costs per ton of paper. Scale economies can also arise at the level of the plant that operates most efficiently when several machines, each of which has its own efficient scale, operate together. The cost of paper making is reduced when the pulp used as an input is produced in the same plant to avoid the cost of drying the pulp for transport to a distant paper-making plant. The combined scale effects of pulp and paper making determine the most efficient scale for the plant. Scale economies can also arise at the level of the firm. A central R&D unit, for example, might produce a breakthrough in the process of breaking down wood fibers that will reduce the cost of production at all the firms' paper-making plants. The greater the volume of output at the firm, the more units the cost reduction will affect and the more units over which the fixed cost of R&D can be spread. Or the cost of selling premium papers might be lower when the same sales staff sells products produced at different plants.

Whatever the source, scale economies imply that the unit cost of output declines in the scale of operation. To understand how scale economies might be a barrier to entry, think about a simple example in which spreading a fixed cost over larger and larger volumes of output reduces average cost. As the term suggests, a fixed cost is one that does not vary with the amount the firm produces or sells. The cost of an advertising campaign to launch a new product is a good example of a fixed cost. Although the firm might choose a larger or smaller advertising campaign depending on how much it hopes to sell, the actual advertising costs (the costs spent on developing the ads and buying media space) do not themselves depend on how much of the product the firm subsequently sells. Similarly, an Internet site like Amazon.com has some fixed costs (such as the cost of developing its site) and some variable costs (such as the costs of fulfilling each order).

To see why scale advantages can be a barrier to entry, suppose that a commodity industry has a single firm that incurs some fixed cost during each period it produces output and has a constant variable cost it must pay for each unit of output it produces. Figure 9-2 illustrates this situation. Here the firm has a constant variable cost of $c$ per unit of output and a fixed cost of $A$ per period that gives rise to a total average cost that declines with output per period. If the firm produces $q$ units of output in a period, for example, the sum of the two shaded areas (i.e., $q \times c + A$) represents its total costs. Of these, the lightly shaded area is the total variable cost ($q$ times $c$), and the darkly shaded area is the fixed costs.[3]

Figure 9-3 adds the industry demand curve for the product to the information in Figure 9-2. In Figure 9-3, the monopolist makes a profit because its revenue ($p \times q$) is greater than the sum of its costs. The sum of the two most darkly shaded areas gives its *gross* profit (revenue minus total variable cost). Since this exceeds the fixed costs, the firm makes a net profit equal to the most darkly shaded area. If $p$ is the price that maximizes gross profit, the firm can do no better than charge a price equal to $p$ because net profit is always just gross profit minus $A$. We can now say something about what it means to have "large" fixed costs. If fixed cost is greater than the largest gross revenue a monopolist can earn, it is too large for even a monopoly firm to be profitable. We don't see industries with fixed costs this large, of course, because no firm would produce under this circumstance. The point is that "large" means large relative to the gross profit the firms (or a monopolist in this case) can earn.

When the monopoly incumbent is earning an above-normal profit, other firms will consider entry. Suppose some firm can produce the product with the *same* variable

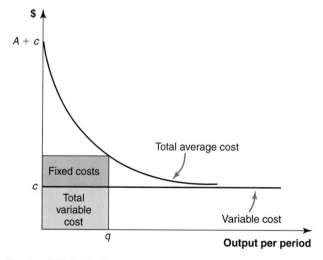

**FIGURE 9-2**   Fixed and Variable Costs

---

[3] Fixed costs are always equal to $A$, no matter what output the firm produces. In Figure 9-2, the vertical height of the "fixed cost" block is $A/q$, or average fixed cost. Multiplying average fixed cost by output gets us back to $A$, the area of the fixed cost block.

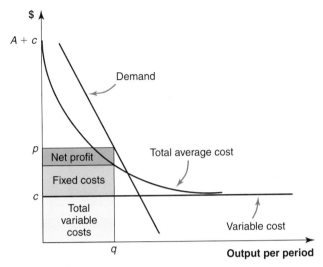

**FIGURE 9-3**    Covering Fixed Costs

and fixed cost as the incumbent; that is, the incumbent does not have a more efficient production process. If that firm enters the industry, the two competitors will charge identical prices for the undifferentiated product; otherwise the higher-priced firm will make no sales. Suppose that they divide the market equally.[4] Even if the price remained at the monopoly level, each firm would now earn half the gross profit the former monopolist earned. Each would still earn a positive gross margin on each unit it sells because the monopoly price is above variable cost, but each firm's gross profit may now be less than the fixed cost each must bear. Figure 9-4 illustrates this situation where each firm's total cost when it produces $q/2$ units is less than its revenue, as can easily be seen from the fact that its average total cost is greater than the price[5] In this example, the monopoly firm was profitable, but entry of a second firm would make both firms unprofitable.

The situation for the entrant is even grimmer than we have painted it so far because the price will probably not remain at the monopoly level. Competition for market share will drive the price below the monopoly level. So each firm will earn *less than half* the gross profit the monopolist earned. The potential entrant should anticipate the gross profit it will earn given that it shares the market with the incumbent *and* that the post-entry price will be lower than the pre-entry price. If the potential entrant anticipates that its gross profit will not cover its fixed cost, it will not enter.[6] The logic would be exactly the same if the market had several incumbent

---

[4] Our point does not depend on how the market is divided; assuming an equal division just makes the arithmetic simple.

[5] Here revenue is given by price times $q/2$ and is less than total cost (which is the sum of the shaded areas).

[6] It might still choose to enter if it believes the incumbent will exit the industry, and it will become the monopolist. We examine this unusual case later

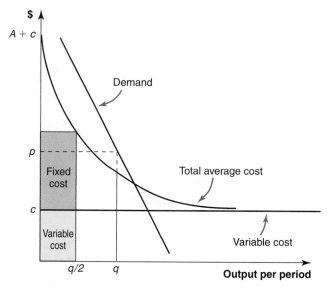

**FIGURE 9-4**   Covering Fixed Costs with Two Firms

firms, all of whom were earning above-normal profit. The potential entrant must think about what share of sales it can expect to get and the price at which it will make those sales. The upshot is that economies of scale can block entry even when the potential entrant is as efficient as the incumbents and when incumbents are earning above-normal returns.

Holding market demand constant, we find that fixed costs are more likely to be a barrier to entry when they are large relative to expected gross profit. If, for example, fixed costs were less than 1 percent of the monopolist's gross profit, they would probably not deter entry. If, however, they were 90 percent of the monopolist's gross profit, entry would probably be unprofitable. The conclusion, then, that high fixed costs can be a barrier to entry is correct, but only if "high" means high relative to the gross profit the incumbent firms earn. So, for example, although the typical fixed cost of bringing a new drug to the U.S. market exceeds $200 million, this has not stopped a flood of biotech firms from entering the pharmaceutical industry because the expected profit flow from their investment is much greater than $200 million.

In the foregoing, we assumed that there was only one way to produce this product, that is, that production necessarily entailed a fixed cost of $A$ and a unit cost of $c$. This is unrealistic. Indeed, potential entrants choose the scale at which they will operate and the technology they use, thus determining their fixed cost and unit cost. A firm might choose to operate a large-scale plant that produces at a low unit cost of output or a smaller plant that produces at a higher unit cost. For example, a brewery can use extremely large vats and fully automated bottling lines or smaller vats and bottling technology that requires more human intervention. What economists call *minimum efficient scale (MES)* affects the optimum choice. MES is the minimum amount of output per period a plant must have to minimize long-run, total average cost. This concept appears in industry analyses in the form of statements like "the cost of an MES plant is $20 million." This means that a firm that wants to minimize its long-run (total) average cost must invest $20 million and incur a fixed cost that is equal to the cost of capital necessary to support that investment. MES is a long-run concept because it involves choosing the size of the plant as well as the level of output, given the plant.[7]

Suppose MES is large relative to industry demand. Figure 9-5 illustrates this situation. Here, a U-shaped long-run average cost curve represents the production technology of the single incumbent. Each output level on this curve represents a different-sized plant operated as efficiently as possible. MES occurs at $q^*$. At outputs less than $q^*$, the firm experiences economies of scale; that is, it could achieve lower total average costs by building a larger plant. At larger outputs, the firm first faces constant returns to scale (small increases in scale do not affect average cost) and, ultimately, *decreasing* returns to scale. In the example, the industry demand curve intersects the firm's long-run total average cost curve at $q^*$, and the incumbent charges a price of $p$, earning an attractive profit.

Now let's consider the entrant's problem. If it builds a large plant to be cost competitive with the incumbent, it will have to capture a large share of industry sales to earn a reasonable return on its investment. If, for example, it were to match the size of the incumbent's plant and the incumbent maintained its pre-entry output level, industry output would have to rise to $2q$. Because prices must fall to sell the increased output, this would lead to much lower profits for both firms. In equilibrium, each firm might find it optimal to produce somewhat less than $q$, but it seems clear that large-scale entry will trigger a fierce battle for market share. Profits might fall so low that

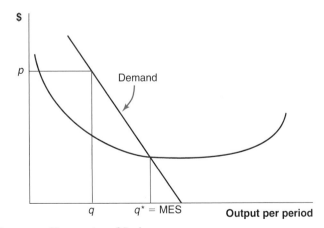

**FIGURE 9-5**   Long-run Economies of Scale

---

[7] The fixed cost example in Figure 9-2 might now be reinterpreted as follows: The fixed cost of $A$ is the cost of capital necessary to support the cost of an MES plant. That is, the monopolist has a fixed cost of $A$ because that is the cost associated with the most efficient scale plant. Given that it has this plant, it must choose how much output to produce each period.

neither firm earns even a normal return on its investment. Alternatively, the entrant could come in with a much smaller plant that places it at a cost disadvantage. This makes it less well positioned to survive post-entry price competition, but it also might reduce post-entry competition. The incumbent might prefer to let the entrant have a small share to avoid the sharp decline in price necessary to dislodge it. The fact that MES is large relative to industry demand, then, leaves the entrant with two choices. It can enter at a large scale and face a price war or at a small scale and have, at best, a limited presence in the market. In either case, scale economies might persuade the firm that entry is unattractive.

MES is important only if it is large relative to demand. If MES occurs at 1 percent of industry demand, it will not constitute a barrier to entry unless many firms are already in the industry. Even if MES occurs at a large scale, however, it will only be a barrier to entry if the cost disadvantage from being below MES is also large. If, for example, MES is two-thirds of industry output, but the cost penalty is only 2 percent for producing at one-fiftieth MES, small-scale entry against an incumbent monopolist might be profitable. In this case, the incumbent would have to drop its price almost to its cost to drive out a small-scale entrant and might well prefer to keep its price near the monopoly level and cede share.

Note that we have overlooked the possibility that the entrant could replace an incumbent firm. Suppose the incumbent firms are earning an above-normal profit, but entry would lead to all the firms earning a return that makes the investment unattractive. We have described this case as one in which barriers to entry are high, and we have assumed the entrant would decide to stay out. However, a potential entrant could look at the profits the incumbents are earning and decide to enter, drive an incumbent from the industry, and take its position as a profitable firm.

Although this can happen, two kinds of factors often protect the incumbents. First, the profit stream has to be worth the cost of the fight. One sometimes sees fights among several firms competing for a market that cannot possibly support them all. These fights consume a substantial share of the potential profit. Indeed, each firm has an incentive to continue to fight if the cost of fighting for one more period is less than the expected profits from fighting (i.e., the profit from being the winner times the probability that your opponent will quit). Anticipating that the fight will be too costly, the firm might stay out. Second, the incumbent may have sunk costs that make its cost of exit high. We will have more to say about this second point.

## Incumbency Advantage from Cumulative Investment

An incumbency advantage can also arise when the firms in the industry make investments that must be spread over time and that, cumulatively, reduce current cost. Unlike the scale advantages we discussed earlier, these cost advantages grow over time. Scale advantages occur within a production period. Scale effects imply that the cost of paper will be lower when produced on a machine with a capacity that reaches MES. But whether the machine was run at full capacity in prior periods does not affect the cost of running the machine at full capacity this period. In contrast, the effects of cumulative investment imply that costs this period are lower when the firm has produced more output in prior periods.

The best known example of these kinds of investment is learning economies. However, as we suggest in the next section, investments made in the past can lower current costs in other ways. We first discuss learning economies and then suggest other ways that past investment might reduce current costs.

**Learning Economies**

Learning economies are cost savings that come with experience and are a good example of an advantage that comes from incumbency.[8] Because the incumbents have more experience producing and selling their products than do potential entrants, learning economies can put entrants at a cost disadvantage. The concept of learning economies was first analyzed in the context of economies in production that firms realize as they produce more output, but learning economies can also occur in distribution, R&D, marketing, or other activities.

These effects can occur through learning by individuals. People spend less and less time on repetitive tasks the more they do them, for example, and similar effects occur in production processes as individuals become more efficient at their particular tasks. Learning also occurs at the level of the firm as it develops routines for coordination that make the organization as a whole more efficient. The learning-based cost reductions in production processes, for example, come not only from the cumulative effect of the learning of individuals involved in the process, but also from organizational learning about how to improve the way teams work, how to configure the production process, and so forth.

Early evidence on the strength of the learning curve came from studies on the number of hours it took to build warships during the Second World War. As individual workers became expert in their specialized tasks and as manufacturers learned how to organize production better, the number of hours required to build a ship fell dramatically. Since the 1970s, these effects have become more widely appreciated because they can have a particularly dramatic effect in high-technology industries. The popular understanding of these effects has also been promoted because some consulting firms proclaimed "learning curves" to be a primary source of competitive advantage.

Figure 9-6 illustrates the effect of learning economies on cost. We have graphed the decline in the unit cost of production as the number of units produced increases. If this were, for example, the cost of producing one bit of computer memory, the cost savings might come from learning about the production process for a particular memory chip that leads to higher yield rates and from learning how to pack more bits onto a single chip. In Figure 9-6, the decline in cost tapers off eventually. For many products this is a reasonable assumption. The learning benefits from producing more of a particular 16-bit memory chip, for example, will eventually be exhausted. But, as this example also suggests, when the product changes, learning effects can again become

---

[8] Learning economies are also called "learning curves," "learning-by-doing," or "experience economies."

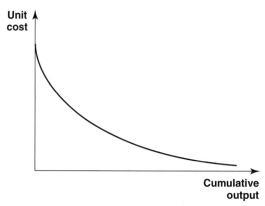

**FIGURE 9-6**   An Example of Learning Economies

important. The introduction of 32-bit chips led to an immediate decline in the cost per bit relative to the 16-bit technology and began another learning process for cost reductions in the 32-bit product.

Figure 9-6 also implies that unit costs are constantly decreasing in cumulative output and that individuals and organizations never "forget" what they have learned. In fact, there is some evidence that firms can "forget." A recent study of Lockheed's production of airframes for large aircraft, for example, found that when production was disrupted, it was less efficient when it re-started than it had been when it stopped. In this example, changes in demand compounded by shortages in component supplies disrupted production. During these disruptions, Lockheed laid off personnel, and the consequent loss of tacit knowledge may have contributed to the loss of efficiency when production ramped up again.[9] In any case, Lockheed probably would have been more efficient—even at its low points—than a new entrant with no learning.

With learning economies, a new entrant has to catch up with the incumbent who has a cost advantage through cumulative output. How great an incumbency advantage this creates depends on two things: how much output an entrant has to produce to match the cost structure of an incumbent and how large the cost reduction is. If learning economies are exhausted after producing one month of output, for example, they cannot be a substantial entry barrier. Similarly, if the total cost reduction is only 2 percent, the incumbent will not have much of a cost advantage.

As a result, learning economies are most important when the curve is moderately sloped rather than either initially steep or shallow. Consider three examples of learning curves in Figure 9-7, and think of the efficacy of learning-based entry barriers when the incumbent firms are located to the right of point $Q_A$. For both the shallow curve *(A)* and the steep curve *(B)*, the incumbent's aggregate cost advantage is not great, although for different reasons in the two cases. For the shallow curve *(A)*, the

[9] C. Lanier Benkard, "Learning and Forgetting: The Dynamics of Aircraft Production," *National Bureau of Economic Research*, Working Paper No. 7127, 1999.

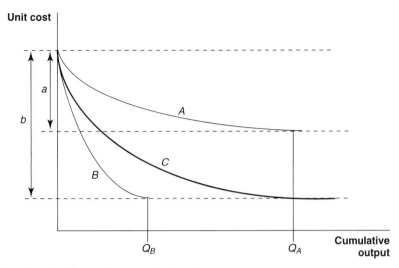

**FIGURE 9-7**    Learning Economies as a Barrier to Entry

entrant's cost disadvantage is never large (at most it is *a*). For the steep curve *(B)*, the cost of being behind initially is large (as large as *b*), but it doesn't take much output for the entrant to catch up ($Q_B$ is small), and once it has caught up, the entrant is at parity with the incumbent. The curve with the moderate slope *(C)* represents the greatest barrier to entry because the incumbent's cost advantage is greater for every unit of the entrant's output (before $Q_A$) than in either of the other two cases.

**Innovation Advantage**

A related phenomenon can occur in competition in innovation. If the learning that produces one innovation increases the probability that the R&D team responsible for it will also produce the next innovation, R&D has incumbency advantages. This can happen because the innovation process has "stages." For example, a series of problems might have to be solved sequentially to achieve a breakthrough. If a research team can keep the knowledge it gains from solving one stage early from its competitors, it has an advantage over them. More commonly, a firm develops a stock of knowledge that enables those within the firm to innovate more quickly because they are already engaged with the current technology. In the digital animation industry, for example, early innovators develop a library of software tools that they can use to increase the speed of later innovation. In either case, the payoff from R&D has a cumulative nature that implies an incumbency advantage.

The cumulative advantage of R&D lies behind some public sector investments. Concern that domestic firms will fall permanently behind foreign competitors in some technology has motivated several well-known, government-supported R&D efforts. Japan, for example, has sponsored several cross-firm research efforts in semiconductor and other computer-related technologies. Even without government support, a firm sometimes pursues product development when the investment will keep them in the race to produce other state-of-the-art products even when the product it sells is not currently profitable. Firms can make these kinds of investments because they are active in the industry. Nonparticipants will fall farther and farther behind.

## Promotional Advantage

As we suggested in a prior section, advertising that affects demand through repetition over time might be a source of a cost-based incumbency advantage. Marketing scholars argue that advertisements have a cumulative effect; brands are built over time, and a firm cannot replicate the effects of five years of advertising by spending the same total amount in one year because the effect takes time as well as dollars. Coca-Cola and Pepsi-Cola have the benefits of decades of cumulative brand advertising. Because incumbents have had the opportunity to build a brand throughout their tenure in the industry, they have an advantage: Their current marketing cost (adjusted for its effectiveness) will be lower than the entrant's.

## Incumbency Advantage from Consumer Loyalty

Our discussion of advertising touched on a common source of incumbency advantage. We argued that cumulative advertising reduces the current cost of influencing buyers and therefore constitutes an advantage to an incumbent who has already done a lot of advertising. The incumbent has built a brand name over time that gives its product offerings a reputation with buyers that a new entrant cannot match without a comparable investment over a comparable time horizon. Here, we turn to how these effects might be reinforced when customers have difficulty distinguishing between product characteristics and find it costly to switch to a different supplier.

The advantage that an incumbent firm has over potential entrants because of its established brand will be especially strong if the product is an *experience good*. An experience good is one the buyer has to experience to learn how valuable it is. This is usually because the product's value is consumer-specific or because consumers cannot easily learn how the brand performs through word-of-mouth or publications like *Consumer Reports*. For example, consider a headache medicine. Since people respond differently to each medication, the best guide to how a brand works for you is your own experience.

In an experience good market with well-established incumbents, many of the potential buyers in the market will have already tried existing products. Typically, potential buyers will start with one brand and, if they are happy with it, will not try other brands. Only buyers who are not happy with the first brand they try (and attribute their dissatisfaction to the brand rather than to the product class) will try another brand. This gives incumbent firms a large first-mover advantage. A new entrant into the market will find it difficult to entice customers who are happy with an existing brand. This is so *even if the entrant's product is identical* to the incumbent's.

These buyers are happy with their current choice and believe that they may not like the new product as much once they use it. They therefore have little incentive to expend money and time trying the new product. Customers who have decided to consume none of the existing brands after trying one or two might also be difficult to attract. If they attribute their dissatisfaction to the product type rather than to the specific brands they have tried, they may be more reluctant to try the new brand than they were to experiment initially. The entrant's best chance might lie with those who are buying one of the current brands but are not particularly happy with it. These buyers like the product class and might be willing to take a chance that the new brand is preferable. Overall, however, because the entrant cannot demonstrate its product's quality to those who do not try it, the existing brands have a strong first-mover advantage. The advantage that incumbent drugs have over later entrants that we illustrated in Chapter 6 is a classic example of this effect.

### Incumbency Advantage from Switching Costs and Demand-Side Increasing Returns

Incumbents can also be advantaged when it is costly for buyers to switch to the entrant's product. Switching costs might exist because complementary products are compatible only with the buyer's current product. A classic example is razors and razorblades: If blades fit only one brand of razor, consumers tend to buy blades for the razor they already own. Switching costs block entry into the blade markets. Auto parts suppliers also have "locked- in" customers for many car parts. Sparkplugs are standardized, but many other engine parts are customized to the car model. Once you own the car, you have a high cost of switching to other auto parts suppliers. In both of these cases, a system of components locks the buyer in once she has chosen the initial product. We will say more about competition and customer lock-in in Chapter 12. For now, note that a new entrant will have difficulty attracting customers in a market where most are already committed to a competing system.

There are several main sources of switching costs:

- **Durable productive assets.** The firm must often incur significant costs if it wants to change suppliers for durable productive assets. For example, many firms are locked into the proprietary computer operating systems of vendor companies. With massive applications written on those operating systems, the cost of switching to other vendors is often significant.

- **Training.** A firm's employee base is trained to work with its current trading partners and/or their equipment. At the simplest level, a firm that has trained its workers to operate a particular manufacturer's equipment must incur retraining costs if it changes that equipment. In other cases, the firm's employees will have been trained to use the systems that the firm needs to work effectively with its suppliers or buyers. For example, Wal-Mart's suppliers must learn to use Wal-Mart's information systems.

- **Complementary assets.** Consumers are also locked in when the firm whose product they have purchased also sells complementary products. An example is the purchase of service contracts for telephone equipment. More generally, this occurs for many products with so-called aftermarkets: The original product is sold with all the components, and new components, replacements, and follow-on service are purchased later on. Examples include razor blades, printer cartridges, and software upgrades. Not all aftermarket products involve switching costs. For example, auto tires are typically not specific to a make of car.

- **Transactions costs.** These are the costs incurred in finding, qualifying, and developing relationships with new suppliers. These costs are lower when the input is homogeneous, so that the buyers don't need to evaluate product differences. They also are lower when an organized market for finding sellers exists. Commodity markets like those for bulk chemicals often have both characteristics. Transaction costs are reduced even more when electronic markets, such as Chemdex, are created that bring buyers and sellers together in an efficient way.

- **Loyalty programs.** Frequent flyer programs are a classic example of how firms attempt to make it costly for customers to switch to competitors. These programs introduced in the early 1980s gave airline customers "free miles" for every mile they flew on a paid ticket. Once customers had collected a specified number of miles, they could trade them in for a "free" ticket. Since these "free miles" could be redeemed only at the airline where they were earned, these programs gave consumers an incentive to fly only one airline to accumulate point totals more quickly.

Another source of incumbency advantage comes from "network effects" or "demand-side increasing returns." These terms describe products whose value to an individual buyer increases when many other people also consume the same brand. Telephone networks are a classic example: Your phone's value to you increases with the number of people you can reach via the telephone network to which it is connected. Computer software also has this characteristic: A given word processing package is more valuable when you can exchange documents produced in its format with many other people. These effects make buyers want to stay with the dominant product. If there were only one telephone network and no entrant could connect a competing system to it, no entry would occur. This is why regulators who want to induce entry require that an incumbent telephone firm allow entrants to route calls over its network. We will say more about competition and entry in these markets in Chapter 12.

### Incumbency Advantage from Sunk Costs

High costs of *exiting* the industry can also create an entry barrier for potential new entrants. To see how this seemingly paradoxical situation can arise, consider the following story. There are two towns located on the coast of France. Suppose that freight could be transported between the two towns by railroad or ship and that the fixed and marginal costs of transportation are the same for the two modes. But the fixed costs of shipping by sea are all from the cost of the ships, and the fixed cost of shipping by rail is spread over the cost of the track and the train. Suppose fixed costs are high enough relative to the profits that can be earned in this industry that only one mode of transport will exist in equilibrium. If, through some miscalculation, both firms entered the market, both would lose money and, eventually, one would leave. Which firm would leave?

The answer is that the sunk costs of the track give an advantage to the railroad! A sunk cost is an investment in some asset that has no equally valuable use elsewhere. For the railroad, the cost of building the track—because it cannot be used elsewhere once built—is entirely a sunk cost. Once the track is built, the owners of the railroad will accept a below-normal return on it because they have no choice; the owners of the ship will sail away to a market where the ship will earn at least a normal return. Note that the sunk cost here is not literally a cost of exit. The railroad has already committed to investing in the track and will pay for it whether it stays in the industry or exits. Indeed, the railroad managers disregard the cost in making their decisions because it is unavoidable. If the entire cost of operating the railroad were a sunk cost, the managers would choose to operate the railroad even if the profit per period were almost zero.

The lesson here is that an incumbent who has no place to go is a formidable competitor. If the railroad is in the market first, the ship will not enter. If the ship is in the market first, however, the railroad might enter because it can commit to staying and fighting. This counterintuitive result arises from the strategic interaction between the firms. Normally, we would favor the ship in this situation because its ability to leave the market if it so desires gives it an *option value*. In a strategic situation, however, option value may be less than the value of being able to *commit*. We discuss option value and the value of commitment in more detail in the Appendix at the end of the book.

## Firm Scope

The literature on entry barriers frequently mentions a "full line" of products and economies of scope as a source of incumbency advantage. Economies of scope are cost savings a firm achieves from having multiple products. They exist whenever the cost associated with producing and selling two products together is lower than the sum of the cost of producing and selling the two products separately. For example, the cost to the BIC Company of producing both disposable lighters and disposable pens might be lower than the total cost would be if two separate firms produced lighters and pens. Economies of scope might come from sharing plant or equipment, obtaining volume discounts on common materials, or applying the expertise developed in producing pens to lighters. Moreover, if demand for pens and lighters is not perfectly correlated, capacity utilization will be greater as production moves to pens when demand for lighters is low, and vice versa. Scope economies might also come from establishing a brand name and in distribution and sales. Because BIC began as a pen company, and many of the same channels that sell disposable pens also sell disposable lighters, the marginal cost of selling and distributing lighters under the BIC name is considerably less than the cost would be to establish a new brand name, sales force, and distribution.

Similarly, it is less costly for eBay to add new categories of products to its auction site than it is for a new company to begin to offer those products from scratch. Although eBay began by offering collectibles, it quickly added other used products like cameras. More recently, it has added products that are best sold regionally in its local markets section of its site, as well as a section for higher priced collectibles.

There are similar advantages to offering a full line of products, but here the cost savings are on the buyers' side. It is costly for buyers to procure inputs from many vendors. The costs associated with evaluating and monitoring vendors, managing inbound logistics, billing, and so forth represent transaction costs that often increase with the number of vendors. As a result, firms often prefer to purchase from suppliers that can provide a broad product line. Because this reduces transactions costs for the buyer, the total cost of accomplishing the sale are lower, and the seller and buyer can share the savings. For example, multinational firms often prefer "one-stop" shopping for all their voice and data communication needs. They want a single point of contact for resolving telecommunication problems anywhere in the world, and they prefer consolidated billing for their worldwide telecommunication expenses. Offering this kind of one-stop shopping is a tremendous logistical challenge for telecommunication firms. To be able to do it, a telecommunication firm must have a presence in many countries and across a broad variety of communication media. The savings to customers, however, can be substantial, and solving the logistical problem can give a telecom firm a large competitive advantage over a firm that has only a regional presence.

Although both economies of scope and full-line advantages might be important sources of cost advantage, they do not necessarily constitute a barrier to entry. If having multiple products is simply a matter of investing more, an entrant can replicate the incumbent's product line. These multiproduct economies can, however, contribute to creating an entry barrier if they are coupled with some other barrier. The following example might be helpful on this point. Suppose there are common costs in small and large car production that imply economies of scope when they are produced by the same firm. If there are no barriers to entry in either segment, the presence of economies of scope will not create them. But if the firms in the large car segment are so entrenched that it is not possible to enter against them in that segment (perhaps because their brand positions are too well established or because they enjoy economies of scale in production), they might be able to leverage scope economies to create an entry barrier in the small car segment, too. This is because a firm contemplating entry into *the small car segment only* would now face competitors with lower production costs in that segment because their competitors are also entrenched in the other segment.

## 9.3  ENTRY BARRIERS AT WORK

We have emphasized that successful entry has two negative effects on incumbent firms. It reduces the share of profit they can retain, and it can lead to an increase in competition that reduces aggregate profit. Although these effects are bad news for incumbent firms, they can also prevent entry from occurring. In this section we show that entry barriers work exactly as the theory suggests.

To set the stage, suppose that an isolated rural town is *just* large enough (i.e., has just enough demand) to support one new car dealership. Because the car dealership has no nearby competition, it will charge a price that is above its marginal cost. Even though it is charging high prices, however, it is earning only a "normal" profit; that is what we mean by the town being just large enough to support one dealer. Demand is just sufficient to allow the dealership to cover its fixed and marginal cost. Suppose the market grows by 50 percent. The original dealer might now be making a handsome profit as the only local firm, but no other dealer will want to enter because demand would not support two firms. Now suppose the town grows to *twice* its original size. While only one firm is in the market, it will earn much more than a normal profit, but demand is sufficient for two firms to earn a normal profit at the current price. Will a second dealership open? Probably not. If a second dealership enters, the increase in competition will depress car prices, and both firms will earn less than the original firm was earning in the original market.

Timothy Bresnahan and Peter Reiss examined this situation in a variety of industries in small, isolated towns in the United States. Table 9-1 shows what they found. The variable $S_M$ represents their estimate of the size of the town at which the first firm enters. So, for example, a town of 664 people is just large enough to support one new car dealer. If the second car dealer to contemplate entering the town did not expect its entry to lead to increased competition, it would be willing to enter a town that is precisely twice that size; that is, we would expect to see two car dealers in a town with 1328 people. If the second dealer, however, expected a competitive response from the incumbent, it would only enter a town with a much larger population than 1328. The variable $S_D$ represents the average size at which a second firm enters. As Table 9-1 shows, for a car dealer, that number is 1538, 16 percent higher than 1328.

The ratio $S_D/S_M$ is a way to summarize the data. If entry were not expected to depress prices, this ratio would be 2. If entrants anticipated a competitive response from the incumbent, it would be greater than 2. As Table 9-1 shows, typically the ratio is around 3. This implies that a second firm will enter only when the market conditions are considerably more favorable than those under which the first firm would enter, presumably because it expects a competitive response from the incumbent. These data also imply that the first mover may gain significant incumbency advantages because there is a range of market size where incumbency is profitable and yet entry does not occur.

**TABLE 9-1**   Entry Thresholds in Small Towns

*Entry Thresholds for "Professional" Industries*

| Variable | Physicians | Dentists | Veterinarians | Drug-stores | Opticians | Auto Dealers |
|---|---|---|---|---|---|---|
| $S_M$ | 730 | 722 | 1000 | 583 | 1886 | 664 |
| $S_D$ | 2463 | 2304 | 4256 | 1778 | 5481 | 1538 |
| $S_D/S_M$ | 3.378 | 3.195 | 4.255 | 3.040 | 2.907 | 2.315 |

*Entry Thresholds for "Retail" Industries*

| Variable | Barbers | Cooling Contractors | Electricians | Heating Contractors | Plumbers | Movie Theaters | Tire Dealers |
|---|---|---|---|---|---|---|---|
| $S_M$ | 941.9 | 6858 | 1057 | 3014 | 1559 | 1985 | 618 |
| $S_D$ | 2534.9 | 15313 | 3292 | 5315 | 3311 | 6000 | 1690 |
| $S_D/S_M$ | 2.692 | 2.201 | 3.112 | 1.763 | 2.125 | 3.022 | 2.731 |

*Source:* Timothy B. Bresnahan and Peter Reiss, "Do Entry Conditions Vary across Markets?" In Martin Baily and Clifford Winston, eds., *Brookings Papers on Economic Activity: Special Issue on Macroeconomics, No. 3* 1987, (Washington: The Brooking Institution) 833–871 (at 859).

## 9.4   STRATEGICALLY CREATING INCUMBENCY ADVANTAGE

Some barriers to entry arise as byproducts of the competitive behavior of incumbent firms. For example, suppose the incumbent firms in an industry ignored the possibility of entry and focused only on competition with each other. To compete for market share, they might invest in building brand. This could also create customer loyalty that would create a barrier to entry. If firms do not specifically take entry barriers into account when they invest in branding, the brand is only incidentally an entry barrier. However, firms could realize that brand can be an incumbency advantage and take that benefit into account when they make investment decisions. When a firm changes its behavior specifically to create a barrier to entry, it is *strategically* investing in incumbency advantage. In the branding example, this would mean that an incumbent firm is spending more on branding than it would if it were not trying to use branding to make entry more difficult. In this section, we suggest how incumbent firms might strategically invest in creating entry barriers.

### Packing the Product Space

In markets where consumers have different tastes, firms might introduce multiple products to increase their share of sales. Auto manufacturers offer more than one kind of car; brewers offer several brands of beer; cereal manufacturers sell many cereals; and snack food makers typically sell many different snacks. Although some of this behavior is standard competition for market share, the incumbent firms might also be attempting to leave no opening in the product space uncovered for potential entrants. That is, they may introduce more products than they would if they were not concerned about the possibility of entry. In effect, they are sacrificing some short-term profit by engaging in "excessive" product development. They do this to prevent an even greater loss of profit that might occur if a new entrant offered the incremental products.

Both of the reasons why entry lowers incumbents' profits that we discussed before apply here, too. First, the incumbent must share the market with the entrant. That is, the entrant now gets some of the sales the incumbent would have made. Second, the incumbent and the entrant compete on prices. If the incumbent introduces the new product, its initial product will lose market share, but the incumbent will avoid increased price competition. The incumbent will not engage in price competition against itself!

Although packing the product space is just one kind of investment the incumbent might make to block entry, we will use it to illustrate how an incumbent firm should think about strategically investing in entry barriers. In Figure 9-8 we have drawn a tree that illustrates how the incumbent's decisions affect the entrant's choices. There, the incumbent firm *(I)* makes the first move. It decides whether to introduce the number of products that maximizes its profit, taking only current competitors into account (denoted as "few products"), or enough products to deter entry as well ("many products"). Given the decision the incumbent has made, the entrant *(E)* must then decide whether to enter with its product ("enter") or not ("stay out").

Four combinations of moves are possible: *I* can choose few, and *E* can respond with enter (leading to Outcome 1) or stay out (leading to Outcome 2); or *I* can choose many, and *E* can respond with enter (leading to Outcome 3) or stay out (leading to Outcome 4).

The matrix in Figure 9-9 displays some hypothetical profits that each of these four scenarios would produce. Each cell in this matrix represents one of the four out-

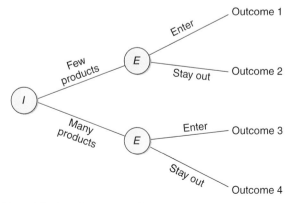

**FIGURE 9-8**  The Entry Blocking Investment Decision

INCUMBENT

|  | Few Products | Many Products |
|---|---|---|
| **Enter** | Outcome 1<br>($50, $40) | Outcome 2<br>($45, −$10) |
| **Stay Out** | Outcome 3<br>($80, $0) | Outcome 4<br>($70, $0) |

ENTRANT

**FIGURE 9-9**   Payoffs in the Entry Blocking Decision

comes from Figure 9-8. In each cell, the first number in parentheses is the incumbent's profit, and the second is the entrant's profit. If, for example, the incumbent chooses "many" and the entrant responds with "enter," we are in the cell for Outcome 3 where the incumbent earns $60 and the entrant *loses* $10. Comparing the entrant's profits in the cells for Outcomes 3 and 4, we can tell that if the incumbent chooses to pack the product space, the entrant would prefer to stay out and earn $0 rather than enter and lose $10. Outcome 3, then, won't occur. Analogously, if the incumbent chooses "few," the entrant will choose "enter" because it prefers a profit of $40 to a profit of $0. Outcome 2, then, won't occur either.

Since only Outcomes 1 and 4 might actually happen, the incumbent is effectively choosing between them when deciding whether to introduce products. If the incumbent packs the product space, the entrant will stay out, and the incumbent will earn $60. If the incumbent ignores the entry threat and responds only to current competition, it will suffer entry and earn $50. In this circumstance, the incumbent will choose to pack the product space, thereby blocking entry. This is the equilibrium outcome to the "competition" between the incumbent and the potential entrant.

The numbers in Figure 9-9 are arbitrary, chosen to get the outcome in which the incumbent blocks entry to be the equilibrium. Different numbers could lead to a different outcome. Nonetheless, this example illustrates three general characteristics about strategic entry-blocking behavior:

- Investing to block entry is costly. The incumbent would be better off if producing few products would block entry.
- The entrant can always choose to stay out, earning whatever profit it can gain by deploying its resources in the next best alternative. We've represented the next best alternative as resulting in a profit of $0, but this need not be the case. The better the entrant's alternatives, the more easily the incumbent can block entry.
- It is important that the incumbent make its investment decision before entry occurs. If the entrant can move first, it will choose to enter because the incumbent will respond by choosing to produce few products. Moving first has advantages.

This last point emphasizes that incumbent firms should be proactive in thinking about entry. Incumbency lets them erect entry barriers, but they can waste this opportunity if they wait to act until entry has occurred.[10]

## Blocking Entry through Contract or Vertical Integration

Time Warner's acquisition of Turner Broadcasting raised some concern with the federal government because the combined entity gained control over the most popular cable channels, channels every cable system operator has to offer. The concern was that the firm could threaten to withhold these popular channels from any cable firm that agreed to carry a competing channel. This practice is called vertical foreclosure. The "foreclosure" language means that Time Warner could shut out (foreclose) competitors from access to cable system operators. The foreclosure would be vertical because it would be accomplished by threatening (allegedly) to withhold a vital input (essential cable channels) from downstream firms (cable system operators). The acquisition was allowed only after Time Warner agreed to restrictions the government believed would prevent foreclosure.

## Signaling to Prevent Entry

Fear of an aggressive response by the incumbents can make entry unattractive. If entry triggers a substantial price decline, it may prove to be unprofitable for the entrant, even though entry would have been profitable had prices remained at the pre-entry level. However, this logic works only if the entrant can anticipate that the price will fall if it enters. If it believes that the incumbents cannot profitably reduce their current prices, the potential entrant is less likely to think that its entry will trigger a sharp price decline. If, for example, competition already has pushed prices to the incumbent firms' marginal cost, an entrant can reasonably anticipate that its entry will not affect prices.

In industries where entry is most attractive, however, incumbents are pricing above marginal cost, and potential entrants have to assess how much their entry will reduce the market price. Suppose, for example, a firm is contemplating entering a market that has a single incumbent firm. Suppose the incumbent's production cost is lower than the potential entrant's would be because the incumbent has a lower-cost production process that is a trade secret. If the entrant were to come in, the incumbent's profit-maximizing response would be to undercut the new firm's prices, driving it out of the industry. Of course, even though the entrant ultimately exits, the incumbent is better off if entry had not occurred in the first place because it will have sacrificed profit to win the battle.[11] Fortunately for the incumbent, the entrant can anticipate its defeat and will not enter, thereby saving itself the costs of entry.

---

[10] The last point also raises (again) the issue of credibility; the incumbent must somehow commit to producing many products. Otherwise, the entrant can come in and make it unprofitable for the incumbent to continue to produce many products.

[11] The incumbent also will have to explain to buyers why its prices fell when the competitor was present and then rose again when the competitive threat ended. No customer likes to be reminded just how much profit suppliers are making at its expense.

This logic, however, only works if the potential entrant *believes* that the incumbent has a cost advantage. An entry barrier (a cost advantage by incumbent firms in this example) prevents entry only if the entrant understands the barrier. In our product-packing story, we assumed the entrant could observe the number of products the incumbent firms offer. But, as in our current example, the entrant may have no way to observe how great the incumbent's advantage is. The incumbent wants to make sure the potential entrant understands that it will be at a crippling cost disadvantage should it choose to enter. Since the entrant also wants to know this, both firms will be better off if the incumbent can communicate how low its costs are.

At first glance, this problem might seem easy to solve. The incumbent simply announces its cost structure, and the entrant takes advantage of the information by refraining from entering. The problem is that *any* incumbent—even one with no cost advantage—would benefit from convincing potential entrants that its costs are low. More generally, every incumbent firm benefits from having a reputation for meeting entry with aggressive price competition. Our hypothetical incumbent really is a low-cost firm but must convey this to the entrant who knows that every incumbent tries to act like a low-cost firm. If the incumbent simply says it is low cost, the entrant will ignore the claim. If the incumbent reveals its trade secrets, it will give up its competitive advantage.

The incumbent could solve this problem by setting its pre-entry price low enough so that only a low-cost firm could make money at that price. Observing that a higher-cost incumbent would lose money at that price, the potential entrant would logically infer that the incumbent's costs are low and that entry is not worthwhile. This particular tactic is called *limit pricing* because its intent is to limit entry. We can generalize this example to any competitive advantage that is hard for entrants to evaluate. It is also an example of *signaling* (discussed in Chapter 8 and in more detail in the Appendix to the book) because the incumbent is using a low price to signal to potential entrants that its costs are low.

An incumbent might also prevent entry if it can convince potential entrants that its management will fight even when fighting is not a profit-maximizing move. That is, having a reputation for "irrational" competitive responses can sometimes be valuable! A firm could establish a reputation for responding aggressively no matter what by fighting in a series of battles for market share. But note that the firm has to fight these battles even though they are not profit-maximizing for it. The only way to gain a reputation for being crazy is to act crazy. If one is to believe the business press, CEOs can embody a reputation for irrational aggression. In media markets, Rupert Murdoch (CEO of News Corporation) appears to have built a reputation for waging relentless and costly battles for market share.

## Entry Barriers and Antitrust

Attempts to build entry barriers, if successful, increase market concentration and diminish competition. It is not surprising, therefore, that the kinds of actions described earlier are often subject to antitrust scrutiny. In the United States, Section 2 of the Sherman Act prohibits "monopolization or attempts to monopolize." For example, aggressive pricing to drive an entrant out of the industry can lead to a charge of "predatory pricing." In principle, the courts have viewed investments made to create entry barriers as predatory, even though no actual firm has been preyed upon because no entry has occurred. When Alcoa had a near monopoly on U.S. aluminum refining, for example, it paid the primary suppliers of low-cost energy to withhold energy from any new firm that wanted to compete with Alcoa. The courts found that this practice violated antitrust law. Cases have also been brought (for example, against Kellogg's in the cereal industry) for "packing the product space" (i.e., for producing many different varieties in a product class). Moreover, the antitrust authorities can use Section 7 of the Clayton Act, which regulates mergers, to prevent vertical mergers that lead to foreclosure.

Although we cannot discuss the antitrust environment in depth here, three general remarks are in order. The first is that the stated purpose of antitrust laws is to protect competition, and not competitors. That is, the antitrust authorities and the courts ask whether competition has been reduced (and thus buyers have been harmed), and not merely whether a competitor has been harmed. So, for example, if an entrant is kept out of the industry because it is inefficient and not because the incumbent is abusing its market power, the entrant will not receive a sympathetic hearing.

Second, action taken by incumbent firms with market power will be viewed differently from the same action taken by firms in a more competitive industry. Since consumers are hurt when incumbents with market power abuse that power, and since competitive firms don't have any market power to abuse, competitive firms that pack the product space will not be charged with anticompetitive behavior.

Finally, a firm that is charged with eliminating competition so that it can then use its power to raise prices is not likely to be found in violation of the antitrust laws unless it is also protected by other entry barriers. So, for example, an effective defense against a charge of predatory pricing is for the alleged predator to show that entry would occur if it were to attempt to raise prices. In a recent case against American Airlines, competitors claimed that American was pricing below cost to drive them from the industry. They failed to convince the court largely because they could not make the case that American would be able to raise prices eventually without inducing new entry.

## 9.5  SUMMARY

Often incumbent firms have profitable positions in an industry, even though there are equally capable potential entrants. They have these incumbency advantages because barriers to entry exist. In this chapter, we have examined the main kinds of entry barriers that arise in practice. Some of these barriers to entry might arise naturally without firms having to focus on the problem of new entrants. These include scale advantages, advantages from cumulative investment (such as learning economies and innovation advantages), advantages from having a product that customers know from experience is high quality, and advantages from switching costs and demand-side increasing returns.

Other barriers to entry require the firm to focus on entry. These include packing the product space or developing a reputation for aggressively fighting new entrants. If no "natural" barriers to entry exist, then incumbents will try to construct or erect these barriers. The ability of incumbents to do this is subject to the appropriate antitrust regulations, which we briefly discussed.

Barriers to entry are an important determinant of industry attractiveness for incumbents because without them, incumbents always risk losing a share of Potential Industry Earnings (PIE) to new entrants. We examined each of these barriers and provided evidence from a variety of markets in small towns. This evidence indicates that in many of those markets incumbency is profitable and yet entry doesn't occur, suggesting significant incumbency advantages. We move now from this discussion of how much PIE is lost to new entrants to a discussion of how PIE is divided among the participants in the value chain.

# 10

# CREATING AND CAPTURING VALUE IN THE VALUE CHAIN

## 10.1 INTRODUCTION

In prior chapters, we have discussed how a firm's external environment affects its performance. By thinking about competition among incumbent firms and the advantages they might have over potential entrants, we have come to see how industry structure, firm behavior, demand conditions, and cost structure can affect the profitability of incumbent firms. In this chapter, we extend our analysis to the value chain in which the industry is embedded. To do this, we must return to a discussion of the value the chain creates and how its segments divide that value.

In the next section we provide a broad overview of the problems of value creation and value capture within the context of the segments of the industry value chain. We show how value creation and capture are related and provide an example. Having provided a broad overview, in the following section we explore the relationships among value capture, value creation, and buyer and supplier power in more detail. Then we examine which of the firms in the value chain are able to capture value and how they do so. We do this by studying different kinds of market structures in the various layers of the value chain. In the final section, we turn from the adversarial considerations inherent in value capture to more cooperative issues of developing relationships with other firms in the value chain with the objective of creating value.

## 10.2 VALUE CREATION AND VALUE CAPTURE

In keeping with our framework for industry analysis, we are interested in how the characteristics of segments in the value chain and the links among them affect the division of value (PIE). Consider an industry that manufactures consumer goods that a separate retail industry distributes, for example. We want to identify what deter-

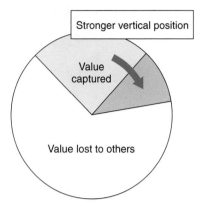

**FIGURE 10-1** A Stronger Vertical Position Increases the Share of PIE Incumbents Retain

mines the value that the manufacturing segment, the retailing segment, and the final consumers in this chain each capture. How value is captured is at the heart of industry analysis because it affects the share the industry incumbents are able to retain. As illustrated in Figure 10-1, the value extraction problem faced by the incumbents is to maximize the share they are able to capture by reducing the share captured by other segments in the chain.

Broadening our perspective to include other segments of the chain also enables us to think about value creation. Industry analysis largely ignores the question of how much value is created. We have taken the size of PIE as given and instead have focused on how competition and entry determine the share of PIE the industry incumbents can retain. By including the entire chain in our discussion, we can think about the factors that affect how much value is created. In particular, in subsequent sections we will consider how relationships between firms in different segments of a chain can create value. Figure 10-2 illustrates the value creation problem faced by the firms in the chain.

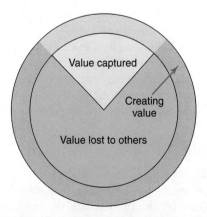

**FIGURE 10-2** Creating Value Increases the Size of the PIE and the Size of the Firm's Slice

Although it is convenient to think about value capture and value creation separately, these are related activities. Indeed, a firm can sometimes use the same tactics to pursue them both. As we will see, for example, if a firm has market power in its segment, the value its chain creates and the share it captures are typically higher when all the other industries in the chain are fragmented. In this case, value creation and value capture can be furthered by encouraging competition in the other segments. Often, however, pursuing capture has an adverse effect on value creation. A monopoly firm, for example, increases the share of the value it captures by raising its price above its cost. But, as we have seen in Chapter 7, this reduces the total value generated by the chain.

Because firms pursue both value capture and value creation, companies within a chain can both compete and cooperate with each other. Value capture tends to be adversarial; holding total value constant, we see that one segment's gain is another segment's loss. Value creation, however, is often cooperative. By holding shares constant, profits in both segments can be increased if the firms in a chain cooperate to expand the total value the chain creates. As a result, the relationships among firms in different segments of a chain can be both adversarial and cooperative. A relationship may be adversarial when firms are negotiating the terms of trade between themselves, but cooperative when they work together to increase the value they jointly create.

Wal-Mart's relationship with its suppliers highlights this dual quality and illustrates how relationships in the value chain can affect firm performance. On the value capture side, Wal-Mart is renowned in the mass-market segment of the retail industry for the tough negotiating stance it takes with its trading partners. Because its strategy is premised on being the lowest priced firm in its market segment, minimizing its costs is important to Wal-Mart's success. Because Wal-Mart buys in large quantities, its suppliers want to retain it as a customer. This gives it leverage in setting the terms of trade. Wal-Mart has also introduced its own store brands to increase its bargaining power with its suppliers. Everything about how Wal-Mart negotiates with its suppliers is designed to gain it the best possible terms. Wal-Mart conducts the negotiations in decidedly unluxurious surroundings at its corporate offices in a small town in Arkansas. Its negotiators are famously hard-nosed. Product representatives responsible for the Wal-Mart account report that "negotiation" is an inappropriate term for the inflexible demands Wal-Mart makes.

Yet, Wal-Mart is also well known for the innovative ways it partners with its suppliers to improve efficiency and increase value. It pioneered the idea that value could be created by giving suppliers access to its own sales and inventory data and allowing them to make stock replenishment decisions. Many suppliers dream of being able to decide how much of their product retailers will carry, and many retailers who balk at giving their suppliers so much power have resisted vendor replenishment. In contrast, Wal-Mart has reasoned that tightening the link between supplier and retailer enhances the overall value of the relationship by reducing logistics costs. Suppliers can time delivery and production to minimize their cost of serving Wal-Mart. Since a supplier also "owns" the product until the final customer buys it, the supplier has an incentive to minimize the inventory Wal-Mart holds. Essentially, Wal-Mart has sold the logistics problem to its major suppliers by giving them the authority to manage that problem as efficiently as possible. This has increased the value that Wal-Mart and its suppliers can capture.

Having provided an overview and example of value creation and capture, we proceed to a more precise discussion of the value chain and the relationships among value creation, capture, and buyer and supplier power.

## 10.3 THE VALUE CHAIN AND BUYER OR SUPPLY POWER

Traditionally, a value chain is said to have suppliers "upstream" and buyers "downstream." An industry's suppliers might include workers, financiers, and producers of intermediate goods it uses as inputs. If a firm sells directly to final consumers, there are no downstream firms. From Wal-Mart's perspective, Procter and Gamble and other product manufacturers are upstream and only consumers are downstream. Often, however, segments of buying firms are downstream. Figure 10-3 illustrates this structure of the value chain. We will focus on this structure because we can best understand the effects of buyer and supplier power when our incumbent buys from and sells to other firms.

For most value chains, a simple model like that shown in Figure 10-3 is a compelling representation of the flow of goods and services. This perspective is particularly appropriate for considering pricing (a subject that will command a lot of our attention) because the party charging a price is logically upstream to the one paying it. However, in some industries participants have a more complicated relationship. For example, in the live entertainment industry, it sometimes makes sense to think of the production company as the supplier to the owner of the theatre and, in other cases, to think of the theatre as an input to the production of the live performance. The difference in perspective depends largely on whether the entrepreneur is the theatre or the production company. In a repertory theater, the theater directors determine what plays will be offered and hire the actors and other personnel for each play. It therefore makes sense to think of the buyer as the theatre and of the personnel as suppliers. When Broadway shows are syndicated, however, a production company often hires a

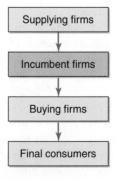

**FIGURE 10-3**   A Value Chain

theater and the play's personnel. In this case, it might make more sense to think of the theater as a supplier.

Fortunately, even when one might argue about which segment is the supplier and which is the buyer, the way these labels are assigned doesn't affect how much value is generated or how it is distributed among the segments. Furthermore, we usually don't need to think about the issues in relationships among buyers and suppliers separately because they are opposite sides of the same coin. In any given relationship, what matters for value capture, for example, is the relative ability of the firms to affect the transaction price. Factors that increase relative supplier power will reduce relative buyer power.

When we talk about "value" we mean the value of the product to its final consumers minus the opportunity cost of the resources required to produce it. This restates the definition of Potential Industry Earnings (PIE) from Chapter 6, and we will use the terms "PIE" and "value created" interchangeably. The value created is distributed among the participating segments in the chain. Although no segment can capture more than the total value the chain creates, any other relationship between value created and value captured is possible. In particular, although every segment in the chain typically adds something to PIE, a segment that adds more value does not always capture more value. Indeed, the participants in some sector can capture either more or less value than the segment creates.

To see why this is so, think of the following (obviously counterfactual) example. A county that contains the only coal deposits in England has a single landowner and many potential coal miners. Assume further that coal mining is the only possible economic activity for which the land can be used, that the workers cannot seek other employment, and that all workers are equally good coal miners. The total value this coal value chain creates is the value of coal to its final consumers minus the opportunity cost of the land, the workers, and the downstream segments of the chain. Because this is the only coal produced in England, the value to final consumers is large. Since neither the land nor the miners have any alternative uses, the opportunity cost of these resources is low. As a result, this chain creates substantial value; PIE is large.

It is impossible to decide exactly how much of this value is created by the land and how much by the coal miners. However, we can predict that the landowner will capture much more of the value than the workers. Any worker can easily be replaced by another; so the coal mine operator will pay only the workers' opportunity cost. As a result, the workers will capture *none* of the created value. In contrast, the landowner, will earn a return well above the land's opportunity cost. Indeed, he might capture a substantial share of the total value in the form of monopoly profits.

To drive the point home, suppose instead that the county had many landowners each of whom owned a small fraction of the coal-bearing land. Suppose, moreover, that a workers' union controlled who was allowed to work as a coal miner and collectively bargained for their wages. The workers would capture most of the value, and the landowners would capture little. In each case, the value each segment creates is unaltered, but the value each segment captures differs significantly.

"Supplier power" is the ability to capture PIE by demanding a payment in excess of opportunity cost. In the first version of the preceding example, the landowner is the monopoly supplier of an input and thus has considerable power to affect its price. The workers, in contrast, have no supplier power. "Buyer power" is the ability to capture value by demanding to pay less than the price one is willing to pay. If the landowner formed his own monopoly coal-mining firm, he would have buyer power in the labor market because he would be the only employer.

Note that neither buyer nor supplier power arises simply because the input in question has no good substitutes. One industry, for example, may supply an indispensable input to another, but that does not mean that the firms in the supplying industry have supplier power. If one firm in the supplying industry attempts to raise the price of the input, the purchasing firms might turn to a rival supplier. If they can do that easily, no supplying firm will have power. The key characteristic of buyer or supplier power is the ability to affect the terms at which the parties exchange goods. A powerful supplying firm can demand a price greater than the minimum price at which it is willing to supply the input. A powerful buying firm can demand a price lower than the price it is willing to pay for the input.

Although exercising buyer or supplier power is a common way for firms to capture value, it is not the only way. Consider firms producing a commodity product, for example. If there is some cost asymmetry among these firms, the lower cost firms will be more profitable than the higher cost firms. Competition implies that the market price will be equal to the marginal cost of production. When there are cost differences among firms, the higher marginal cost will determine price, allowing the lower-cost firms to earn a super-normal profit.[1] In our discussion of value capture, we focus on buyer and supplier power because these are the issues tied to the characteristics of the value chain. We will set aside cost differences by assuming that all firms in a segment have the same costs.

## 10.4   CAPTURING VALUE

The examples in the previous section illustrate an essential point: *Competition limits buyer or supplier power.* Firms in a perfectly competitive industry have no buyer or supplier power. An individual coal miner cannot negotiate for a wage above his opportunity cost when there are many workers who are perfect substitutes for him. To return to an example from Chapter 6, a single lobster company among thousands of small firms fishing for lobster in the Atlantic cannot negotiate a price for its catch because its product is a commodity. It simply brings its catch to the dock and sells lobsters at the market price. In both cases, the suppliers are participants in a perfectly competitive market. For the coal miners, it is the labor market; for the lobster fishers, it is the market for lobsters at the dock.

These two markets are competitive because they have many small suppliers of products that are good substitutes for each other. But competition can prevent the

---

[1] In the long run, cost differences are unlikely to persist in commodity markets. Eventually, the lower-cost firms will expand production, or other low-cost firms will enter, driving the higher-cost firms from the market.

exercise of buyer or supplier power no matter why the industry is competitive. For example, an industry that has only two firms might be competitive if the incumbents fight for market share. If this competition leads them to price at cost, they cannot capture value by exerting supplier power.

In short, any buyer who is purchasing from firms in an intensely competitive industry need not be concerned about falling victim to supplier power. That is, a firm must have market power to have supplier power.[2] Analogously, any supplier selling to firms in an intensely competitive industry need not be concerned about falling victim to buyer power. That is, a firm can only exert buyer power when it can affect the price at which it purchases inputs. And finally, any firm *participating* in an intensely competitive industry can exert little supplier or buyer power in its interactions with other segments.

Because competition within each segment of the chain affects buyer and supplier power, the nature of competition in all segments of the value chain affects value capture. To understand how this works, let's discuss several examples. First, we will look at who captures value when none of the participants in the chain has any buyer or supplier power. Then we will discuss what happens when firms in only one segment can affect transaction prices. Finally, we will think about a chain in which firms in two (or more) segments can affect transaction prices.

In the following discussion, we will assume that each layer of the value chain contains only one industry. Although most firms in a given industry actually purchase from firms in many other industries (think, for example, about how many industries must supply General Motors), this complication does not change the nature of the analysis. When there are multiple supplying industries, the analysis we describe must be performed for each of them. Similarly, firms, particularly those producing far upstream in the value chain, often also sell to many industries. Again, a firm must decide whether any of its buyers can affect pricing. In this case, however, there may be spillovers from one buying industry to another. Suppose our industry sells the same product to many downstream industries and the purchasing firms can easily re-sell that product. Then, any firm will have to charge only one price for its output. If, instead, the supplying firm were to charge a high price to a firm with no buyer power and a lower price to another firm that does have buyer power, the firm buying at a low price would simply re-sell the product to the firm that had been quoted a higher price. Unless the supplying firm can prevent re-sale, selling to one industry in which the purchasing firms have buying power can depress the price the firm can charge to all industries.

## Value Capture without Buyer or Supplier Power

Suppose each segment (except the final consumers) in some value chain is a competitive industry. This chain creates value as firms transform inputs into more valuable

---

[2] Indeed, "supplier power" is another term for "market power in output markets." "Buyer power" is another term for "market power in input markets." We use the terms "supplier power" and "buyer power" because they are traditional in the strategy literature.

outputs. But a perfectly competitive firm charges a price equal to its marginal opportunity cost and therefore cannot capture the value it creates. Who gets the value? In this case, the final consumers capture it all, even though *consumers have no market power and therefore no buyer power.*

To understand the intuition for this outcome, let's use a numerical example. In this example, the value chain looks like the one in Figure 10-3: three layers of firms and a group of final consumers. Each firm in this chain has a marginal cost equal to $1: It costs each of them $1 per unit to transform its inputs to outputs. Thus each unit delivered to consumers has used $3 worth of resource. (The inputs the initial upstream firms use are free.)

Table 10-1 summarizes the amount of value this chain creates and its distribution among the participants. The second column of the table shows that the first unit the chain produces is worth $10 to the consumer. Since it cost $3 to provide, the value created by manufacturing and selling this unit is $7. The next unit is worth $9 to consumers and adds another $6 of value. If eight units are produced, the consumers value the eighth unit at $3, exactly the cost of providing it. If additional units were provided, they would cost more to provide than they are worth to consumers, and the firms would be unable to cover their costs. At most, then, this value chain will produce eight units of product. By doing so, it would create a total value of $28.

Each firm in the most upstream segment of the chain (segment 1) incurs a marginal cost of $1 and will therefore charge a price of $1. Each firm in segment 2 buys its input from segment 1 at a cost of $1 and incurs an additional cost of $1 per unit to transform it. It therefore charges a price of $2 for its product. Similarly, the third segment will charge a price of $3. This is the price consumers face, and they will therefore purchase eight units. The equilibrium outcome is a price of $3 and a quantity of

**TABLE 10-1**    Value Creation and Capture in a Chain with No Buyer or Supplier Power[a]

| Units Produced and Sold | Buyer Value for Marginal Unit ($) | Marginal Value Created ($) | Total Value Created ($) | Segment 1 ($) | Segment 2 ($) | Segment 3 ($) | Consumers ($) |
|---|---|---|---|---|---|---|---|
| | *Value Created* | | | *Total Value Captured* | | | |
| 1 | 10 | 7 | 7 | 0 | 0 | 0 | 7 |
| 2 | 9 | 6 | 13 | 0 | 0 | 0 | 13 |
| 3 | 8 | 5 | 18 | 0 | 0 | 0 | 18 |
| 4 | 7 | 4 | 22 | 0 | 0 | 0 | 22 |
| 5 | 6 | 3 | 25 | 0 | 0 | 0 | 25 |
| 6 | 5 | 2 | 27 | 0 | 0 | 0 | 27 |
| 7 | 4 | 1 | 28 | 0 | 0 | 0 | 28 |
| **8** | **3** | **0** | **28** | **0** | **0** | **0** | **28** |

[a] Firms in each segment price at marginal cost. The firms charge $1 in segment 1, $2 in segment 2, and $3 in segment 3. With a price of $3, consumers will buy eight-units. Consumers value eight units at $52 and pay $24 for them. Consumers therefore capture $28. (The bold print denotes the equilibrium outcome.)

8. In aggregate, consumers value the product at $52 and pay only $24 for it, capturing all the value ($28) the chain creates.

All the value goes to the final consumers because the firms in the other segments compete vigorously. At any point in this value chain, the buyers benefit from the competition that occurs in the levels upstream from them. A firm in segment 2, for example, gets inputs at their opportunity costs because the firms in segment 1 are competing intensely with each other, and the outcome of the competition determines the price to the firms in segment 2. In turn, competition in its segment drives the firm in segment 2 to sell its product at a price no greater than its opportunity cost. The final buyers, however, compete with no one. Consumers, therefore, buy the product at its market price but consume its full value. They therefore get all the value the chain creates.

If the entire value chain for lobsters were intensely competitive, we could all eat lobster with the additional satisfaction of knowing that we were capturing all the value in that chain. The value chain for writing paper has a structure somewhat like this. Timber growing, paper machinery manufacture, paper manufacturing and distribution, and retailing are all pretty competitive industries, with the result that consumers capture most of the value created.

## Value Capture by a Single Powerful Supplier (or Buyer)

Suppose a firm in one segment in the chain has buyer or supplier power. Because it has significant market power, this firm can set its output price. No other firm in the chain has this luxury. We can see the effect of this by slightly altering our numerical example. As before, we will assume that segments 1 and 3 are perfectly competitive industries. Segment 2, however, is now a monopoly industry. Since all the segment 1 firms have a single customer, our monopolist will have substantial buyer power. Similarly, it will have substantial supplier power over the firms in segment 3 because it is their only supplier. When OPEC succeeds in operating as a cartel, the oil industry resembles this structure. OPEC's suppliers, such as firms that drill for oil or operate oil wells, are in competitive industries, and the downstream buyers (oil refiners, distributors, and retailers) are fairly competitive as well.

Table 10-2 summarizes the results. The change in structure does not affect consumer valuation of the product or the cost of producing, so the first three columns of Table 10-2 are identical to their counterparts in Table 10-1. The competitive firms in segment 1 behave exactly as they did before, charging a price equal to $1. They are selling to a powerful buyer, but this makes no difference to them. Competition among them drives their price to marginal cost, and the powerful buyer can do no additional damage. Even a powerful buyer cannot force a firm to supply at a price below its opportunity cost. To go back to our coal mining example, the coal mining operators can hire a worker at his opportunity cost even if there are many competing coal mines. In contrast, Wal-Mart, needs buyer power to offset the supplier power that some of the large producers of the branded products it sells have.

The segment 2 monopolist has a marginal cost of $2 and will charge as much as it can for any given level of output. It knows that the third segment in the chain will have

**TABLE 10-2**   Value Creation and Capture with a Single Monopolist[a]

| Units Produced and Sold | Buyer Value for Marginal Unit ($) | Total Value Created ($) | Prices for Output | | | Total Value Captured | | | |
|---|---|---|---|---|---|---|---|---|---|
| | | | Segment 1 ($) | Segment 2 (monopoly) ($) | Segment 3 ($) | Segment 1 ($) | Segment 2 ($) | Segment 3 ($) | Consumers ($) |
| 1 | 10 | 7 | 1 | 9 | 10 | 0 | 7 | 0 | 0 |
| 2 | 9 | 13 | 1 | 8 | 9 | 0 | 12 | 0 | 1 |
| 3 | 8 | 18 | 1 | 7 | 8 | 0 | 15 | 0 | 3 |
| **4** | **7** | **22** | **1** | **6** | **7** | **0** | **16** | **0** | **6** |
| 5 | 6 | 25 | 1 | 5 | 6 | 0 | 14 | 0 | 11 |
| 6 | 5 | 27 | 1 | 4 | 5 | 0 | 12 | 0 | 15 |
| 7 | 4 | 28 | 1 | 3 | 4 | 0 | 7 | 0 | 21 |
| 8 | 3 | 28 | 1 | 2 | 3 | 0 | 0 | 0 | 28 |

[a] Each firm in the competitive segments charges a price that just covers its marginal cost. For each quantity produced, the monopolist charges the marginal consumer valuation. The most profitable output (highest value captured) for the monopolist is four units sold at $7. Of the $22 of value created with this output, the monopolist captures $16, and consumers capture $6.

to add $1 to the price of its input to cover its cost. The monopolist can then charge a price that is equal to the consumers' marginal valuation minus one dollar. If it were to produce only one unit, it would sell it for $9, the consumer would get it for $10, and the monopolist would make a per unit profit of $7. To sell two units, the monopolist would have to drop its price to $8, so that the final price would be $9 and its per unit profit $6. The Prices for Output columns of Table 10-2 report the prices the monopolist would charge for each level of output.

The Total Value Captured columns of the table report the profits for all the firms in the chain and the value consumers capture. The price that maximizes profits for the monopolist in segment 2 is $6. At this price, four units are sold, PIE is $22, and the monopolist makes $4 on each, for a profit of $16. Its supplier power has allowed it to capture a large share of the value the chain has created. The two competitive segments still cannot capture value. They are not made worse off because a monopolist is in the chain. Consumers, however, are worse off because both their *share* of the value created and the *total value* created have declined. The monopoly firm has captured value by reducing output from the competitive level (compare these results with those in Table 10-1). As a result, some consumers who are willing to pay more than the cost of providing the good cannot buy it.

Consumers can still capture some value even without the benefits of a competitive supply chain. This happens because we have assumed that the monopolist has to charge a single price for its output. If it offers one unit, it can sell it for $10. To get consumers to buy two units, the price for both units must drop to $9. If, however, the company can price discriminate in some way among consumers who place different value on the product, it will increase the share of total value it captures. If the company could charge a different price for each unit, it would capture all of PIE by charging $10 for the first unit, $9 for the second, $8 for the third, and so forth.

Sometimes firms cannot price discriminate at all, and they can seldom discriminate finely enough to prevent buyers from capturing some of the value created. Frequently, however, firms can construct some form of price discrimination that increases their share of value they capture. We discuss how firms might do this in the appendix to this chapter.

This simple example implies that a firm with a monopoly in one segment of a chain in which all other segments are competitive cannot improve its profits by obtaining a monopoly in another segment as well. In some more complicated settings, this may not be true. We will see an example of how a firm with a monopoly in one segment might increase its profits by also monopolizing another segment in Chapter 12. But the general point is worth emphasizing. A firm with a dominant position in one segment of a value chain should not assume that it will be better off if it also dominates another segment. Instead, it should assess whether extending its dominance will increase the value it can capture.

Strategic management scholars frequently claim that a large supplier is powerful. The word "large" here has two different meanings. First, it can mean that the purchasing firm buys only a small share of the supplier's output. For example, a paperclip manufacturer buys only a small fraction of its steel supplier's output. If this disparity in size denotes a disparity in power, the large supplier is powerful. In the example of Table 10-2, the monopoly firm in segment 2 is much larger (in this sense) than the many, competitive firms in segment 3. But the power relationship comes from a difference in market power, not a difference in size. In the paperclip example, the paperclip firm may buy only a small share of some steel supplier's output, but the supplying firm might have no power because the steel industry is competitive.

Second, "large" can mean that the supplying firm provides an input that represents a large share of the purchasing firm's cost. Although a supplier with supplier power will charge a higher price for the same input than a supplier who does not have supplier power (and therefore will have a larger share of cost), cost share is irrelevant to market power. To return to the steel industry example, even though steel represents a significant share of the cost of an automobile, if the steel industry is competitive, steel firms have no supplier power.

## Value Capture When Buyers and Suppliers Are Powerful

In the previous example, firms had some ability to affect transaction prices in only one segment. As a consequence, the market outcome was the standard monopoly result we would get even without considering the other firms in the value chain.[3] More commonly, firms in several segments in a value chain have at least some buyer or supplier power. As a result, more than one segment of firms shares the value captured. When

---

[3] More precisely, a vertically integrated monopolist with marginal cost equal to $3 who sells directly to consumers with the demand in this example would maximize profits by selling its product for $7. The competitive firms add some cost, but this cost is unavoidable and even a vertically integrated monopolist would incur it.

more than one segment of the chain has firms with some power, two kinds of effects come into play: double marginalization and bargaining over transaction price.

## Double Marginalization

"Double marginalization" is a formidable name for a simple idea. We can illustrate it by making a slight change in our last example. As before, suppose segment 1 is competitive and segment 2 is a monopoly, but segment 3 is now a niche market. Think of a monopoly manufacturing firm (in segment 2) selling its product to consumers through many local retailers (in segment 3). With this change, firms in segment 3 now have some supplier power but no buyer power. Individual retailers have no buyer power because we assume that the manufacturer could easily replace each retailer with another firm willing to serve the same niche. Firms that operate fast-food franchises, for example, might easily replace one local outlet with another. But each niche firm has some supplier power because it has some customers for whom purchasing from another distributor is not a good substitute. Some customers prefer a particular retailer because of its location, for example. These customers are unwilling to switch to another retailer for a small difference in price.

Another example occurs in the market for medium format cameras.[4] In this market, at least at the high end, Hasselblad is the manufacturer of choice and wields considerable market power. Hasselblad's suppliers are parts suppliers who are in competition with one another.[5] Its buyers are regional distributors who have little power since Hasselblad has a choice of potential distributors in each region from which to choose. However, since each geography typically has only one distributor, distributors have some supplier power over the retailers in their region.

Because the first segment remains competitive, the firms in it will be driven to price at marginal cost as before. Our monopolist's buyer power is still unimportant, and its supplier power still enables it to capture some value. Now, however, its buyers also have some supplier power which affects the share the monopolist can extract. When segment 3 was competitive, the monopolist could anticipate that each firm in it would add a markup of $1, the cost each firm incurs to bring the good to consumers. Now, however, each firm in segment 3 will add a markup greater than $1; its supplier power will allow it to add a positive price–cost margin on top of the margin our monopolist creates. These two margins are the source of the name "*double* maginalization."

In this case, two industries are now capturing some of the value. As a result, the *share* the monopolist captures has declined. This is a general rule. When buyer or supplier power exists in more than one segment, each segment will capture some of the value in the chain. The decline in share also implies that imperfect competition in another segment will adversely affect the absolute amount of value the monopolist

---

[4] Medium format is defined by negative sizes of $6 \times 7$, $6 \times 6$ or $4.5 \times 6$ centimeters.

[5] The lenses are provided by Carl Zeiss. However, Hasselblad and Zeiss cooperate in all aspects of the production and marketing of the system, and it is more appropriate for these purposes to think of them as together comprising one layer of the value chain.

captures. When all other segments are competitive, our single monopolist captures exactly the profits a vertically integrated monopolist would earn (assuming that a firm could integrate all three segments without changing the costs incurred in the value chain). Since the firms in any chain cannot extract more than this, the monopolist's profits have declined because it is sharing the value created.[6]

Double marginalization means that firms with supplier or buyer power will be better off when the other firms in the value chain are in perfectly competitive industries. We already knew that firms prefer to have market power in their own industries to mitigate the effects of competition on value capture. We now know that firms also prefer their buyers to have no supplier power. If a firm can increase its own supplier power or reduce supplier power elsewhere in the chain, it can increase its profits.

## Bargaining between Powerful Buyers and Suppliers

In the prior example, our segment 2 monopolist could dictate its price, even though some supplier power existed downstream because the retailers in that example had no buyer power. When a powerful supplier faces a powerful buyer, the situation is different. Both the supplier and the buyer can influence the terms at which they transact. To see how this affects value capture, we can use an example in which there is a single buyer.

In this example, the buyer is a pharmaceutical firm with a monopoly position in the market for insulin. The supplier is a small biotechnology firm with a proprietary new form of insulin[7] but no production or distribution capacity. As a result, the biotech firm must sell insulin to the pharmaceutical firm, which then distributes it to consumers. If the new insulin becomes available to consumers, it will completely replace the old product. The pharmaceutical firm expects net revenues from the new drug (revenues minus its production and distribution expenses) to be $100 million. The net revenue it earns on its existing insulin product is $40 million. To make matters simple, suppose it has cost the biotech firm nothing to develop the new drug.[8] As

---

[6] As in other sections of this chapter, the results change when we allow the firms to use a pricing scheme that is more sophisticated than a single per unit price. If, for example, our segment 2 monopolist could charge the retailers some lump-sum payment (an advertising charge or franchise fee, perhaps), the double marginalization problem could be solved. The monopolist would charge a price equal to its marginal cost and a fixed fee equal to monopoly profits. Further, if segment 2 were an oligopoly market, double marginalization could make the firms more profitable. These effects, however, depend on the firms being able to charge downstream firms a lump-sum payment that is large enough to extract all the value the chain creates. In our view, most firms cannot do this and are better off when no supplier power exists elsewhere in the chain.

[7] This example is loosely based on the situation facing Genentech (the biotechnology firm) and Eli Lilly in 1987. Genentech had discovered a way to make synthetic insulin, and Eli Lilly had over 80 percent of the U.S. insulin market for an older, less pure insulin product. (Insulin is used to treat diabetes.)

[8] Without this unrealistic assumption, the outcome of the bargaining depends on whether the development investment has already been made when the bargaining takes place.

noted in prior examples, consumers should capture some of the value this new drug creates even when the pharmaceutical firm has a monopoly. To focus on bargaining between the firms, however, let's assume that consumers capture no value. Then, the total value this new product creates (assuming the firms can reach an agreement that lets it come to market) is $60m (the increase in net revenue).

The biotech firm wants to charge the pharmaceutical firm a high price, and the pharmaceutical firm wants to pay a low price. They will bargain over the price the pharmaceutical firm pays. Table 10-3 shows the possible prices and the resulting value each firm captures.

As shown in the table, $60m is the maximum amount the pharmaceutical firm will be willing to pay. It could continue to sell its old product on which it earns net revenues of $40m. Continuing to sell the old product is, in the language of bargaining, its outside option. The value of that option is $40m. The most it would be willing to pay for the new product, then, is the $60m increase in net revenues associated with it. The biotech firm has no alternative: it would be willing to accept any price above $0. If it could get a price of $60m for its drug, the biotech firm would capture the entire value created. At a price of $0, the pharmaceutical firm would capture all the value created.

Although we can be fairly confident that the final price in this situation will be no higher than $60m and no lower than $0, we still don't know what the price will be. The firms could split the gains from proceeding with the new drug evenly by setting the price at $30m. (Each then gains $30m.) Indeed, experiments in which players bargain over a fixed sum confirm that a 50-50 split is common. But it is obviously not the only outcome, and each firm would like to capture a greater share. Whether a firm can capture a larger share depends on its bargaining position.

A firm's bargaining position arises from the details of the bargaining situation. Because we have posited that each firm is a monopoly, they might have equal bargaining power. If, however, one of the firms faced competition, the other might be in a

**TABLE 10-3**   Value Allocation When Each Firm Has a Monopoly Position[a]

| Value Created by New Drug ($m) | Price ($m) | Incremental Pharmaceutical Firm Profits ($m) | Biotech Firm Profits ($m) |
|---|---|---|---|
| 60 | 0 | 60 | 0 |
| 60 | 10 | 50 | 10 |
| 60 | 20 | 40 | 20 |
| 60 | 30 | 30 | 30 |
| 60 | 40 | 20 | 40 |
| 60 | 50 | 10 | 50 |
| 60 | 60 | 0 | 60 |

[a] The second column shows the price the pharmaceutical firm pays. Given those prices, the third column shows the *incremental* profit the pharmaceutical firm would earn (the net revenue on the new drug minus the net revenue on the old minus the price it pays for the new drug). The fourth column reports the profits the biotech firm makes.

better bargaining position. To see how this might work, suppose the biotech firm could threaten to vertically integrate into manufacturing and distribution and retain sole ownership of the new drug. Because it would probably be less efficient than the established firm, let us assume that its cost of distribution and manufacturing would be $20m higher, so its net revenue from these activities would be only $80m (versus the $100m the pharmaceutical firm would generate with this product). The vertical integration option increases the biotech firm's bargaining power by increasing the value of its outside option. The minimum price it will accept if it can threaten to vertically integrate is $80m.

But this doesn't seem to make sense. The pharmaceutical firm was only willing to pay up to $60m before. Why will it pay $80m now? Because without the threat of vertical integration, the pharmaceutical firm had a monopoly on the insulin market. Because it can vertically integrate, however, the biotech firm can wrest the market away from the incumbent and capture $80m of value. All that the pharmaceutical firm brings to the bargaining table is its distribution advantage, which is worth $20m. Since it depends on the biotech firm to utilize even that advantage, the pharmaceutical firm will get somewhere between $0 and $20m (depending on the outcome of the bargaining), and the biotechnology firm will get the rest.

A better alternative to vertical integration for the biotechnology firm might be to offer the drug to another pharmaceutical firm that is not currently in the insulin market. A firm with existing distribution and manufacturing capacity will probably be more efficient than the vertically integrated biotech firm. If the other pharmaceutical firm is as efficient as the current insulin monopolist, it, too, can earn net revenues of $100m for the new drug. With both pharmaceutical firms willing to pay up to $100m, the competition between them will allow the biotech firm to capture both the entire incremental value to the pharmaceutical firm the new drug creates *and* all the profits from the old drug as well.[9]

This example illustrates the general outcome when each side of the transaction can affect price: The firms will bargain over the transaction price, and each will probably capture some of the value. The buying power of firms in adjacent segments reduces the value a supplying monopolist in one segment of the value chain captures. Aside from this basic point, this example also illustrates three other common characteristics of bargaining between two firms.

First, both parties want the transaction to go forward. Although the biotech firm could vertically integrate, there are prices for the drug at which both firms would be better off than they are under the vertical integration option. More generally, there are gains from trade when some buyer values the product more than the seller does. If the buyer and seller cannot come to terms, they lose this value. Second, the final price cannot be one that makes either firm worse off than it would be if the transaction did not go through. This is why the firm's alternatives set the price range: The buyer will

---

[9] Note that this is an example of a firm capturing more value than it creates. Here it is clear that the biotech firm adds—at best—$60m in value. If it vertically integrates, its inefficiency at production and distribution actually reduces the value it adds to $40m. But it captures all the value it creates and all the value the other firm was creating.

pay no more than the increase in value that owning the product will allow it to realize, and the supplier will not accept less than its incremental cost of supply.

Finally, the negotiated price reflects the relative bargaining power of the two firms. The firm with greater bargaining power will get the larger share. We have focused on outside option value as a primary determinant of bargaining power, but other factors can also come into play. The start-up biotech firm, for example, might be much more cash constrained than the pharmaceutical firms. This means that its cost of delay will be higher; if the deal isn't struck soon, the biotech firm will be out of business. The pharmaceutical firm would prefer to earn profits earlier rather than later but can more easily bear the cost of delay. As a result, it might get the drug for a lower price by agreeing to a quick settlement or by front-loading the payment.

Negotiating skill can also affect bargaining power. For example, since outside options generally leave some range for negotiation, a firm might increase its share by establishing some price as a "natural" division. A 50-50 split, for example, seems to be a natural outcome when firms have equal bargaining power. However, a firm could get a larger share by somehow making some other division a natural outcome. For example, suppose the biotech firm has expended $10m on drug development. It might argue that (even though those expenses don't affect the economics of the deal going forward) those expenses should be reimbursed. The pharmaceutical firm might agree simply to consummate the deal.

Whatever the precise outcome, a supplying firm with supplier power would prefer that its buyers have no power. As with double marginalization, power elsewhere in the chain reduces the value that the powerful incumbent firms can capture. In the next section, we suggest how a firm might reduce the power of firms in other segments.

## Reducing Power in Other Segments

Because competition among buyers or suppliers is the most potent weapon against supplier or buyer power, any strategy that encourages increased competition in other segments can be profit enhancing. We have touched on the possibility that vertical integration could mitigate the power of other segments. In principle, the *threat* of vertical integration should suffice. In practice, this threat may or may not be credible. General Motors can credibly threaten to bring component manufacturing in-house because it already has a substantial presence in component manufacturing. Pepsi can threaten to forward integrate into bottling operations to counteract buyer power because it has demonstrated its ability and willingness to operate bottling operations. However, Dell Computer cannot credibly threaten to backward integrate into microprocessor design and manufacture because the required capability is too far from its area of expertise.

To make the threat of competition credible, a company can pursue a strategy of "tapered" integration; it builds some capacity in another segment but not enough to serve its entire demand for inputs or to handle its entire output. Tapered integration gives the firm a credible claim that it has an alternative to trading with its powerful buyer or supplier and requires fewer resources than full integration. If, however, bringing the activity in-house involves important scale or learning economies, the firm may find the in-house operation much less efficient than the outside alternative. More generally, an outside firm that is dedicated to the activity might be a more efficient producer than the firm's in-house operation. Managers at GM, for example, often prefer to source from outside the company even when an in-house supplier exists because they believe the outside producer is more efficient.

Because in-house production is often at a competitive disadvantage to supply by another segment, encouraging independent competitors is usually a better alternative. In general, a firm can influence the number of its suppliers or buyers. In many industries, for example, a company must work with a potential supplier to ensure that the supplier's output meets the specifications necessary to serve as input into the firm's production process (a process known as qualification). Qualifying multiple suppliers, or ensuring that potential suppliers could easily be qualified, reduces supplier power. Toyota, for example, generally maintains strong relationships with two suppliers for almost any part it purchases. Even if a firm has a favorite supplier, maintaining a second source of supply lessens that supplier's ability to threaten the firm and enables it to capture more PIE. In some settings, holding an auction for inputs not only invites firms to prove that they are qualified, but it may also induce competition more effectively than negotiating with the suppliers separately.

The firm also might benefit by maintaining flexibility about the inputs it uses in its production process if the supplier of one of those inputs has significant market power. For example, building a product that can use different component brands might be more costly, but it could increase the firm's profit if it induced competition among the branded component makers. Alternatively, a buyer can influence the number of suppliers by opting for generic or standardized requirements. For example, GM standardized parts in its car design partly because it allowed GM to go to more suppliers for those parts.

So far, we have assumed that buyers and sellers are adversaries. That is, the buyer's gain is the seller's loss, and vice versa. Sometimes, however, a buyer and seller can create more value if they cooperate rather than compete. As we shall see, cooperative relationships typically trade off value capture for value creation.

## 10.5  CREATING VALUE

The value a chain creates depends on the investments made by the firms in the chain. Firms can invest in cost reduction or product development activities to increase the value they create.[10] As we argue later in this section, the relationships formed between firms in different segments can affect these investments, and therefore the value created. Creating additional value through crafting relationships with buyers or suppliers might add more to firm profitability than clever value extraction strategies can.

Firms can create tremendous value by working closely with their buyers and suppliers. Japanese manufacturers across a variety of industries—such as automobiles and

---

[10] Firms outside the chain that produce complementary or substitute products can also change the PIE the value chain creates by changing their products or the cost of producing them. To focus on the activities within the chain, we are implicitly holding the value of complements and substitutes constant.

electronic devices—generally develop strong cooperative relationships with their suppliers. Although we noted earlier that Toyota maintains two suppliers for any part that it purchases from the outside, it also fosters strong cooperative relationships with its suppliers, which often include sharing information on costs and manufacturing routines to improve the quality and efficiency of the manufacturing process.

A cooperative working relationship to maximize value creation is not always easy. Firms entering cooperative agreements do not simply give up on value capture, which often creates a conflict with their upstream or downstream partners. Instead, creating and maintaining these relationships generally require each firm to protect its own interests while simultaneously creating value for its partner.

The managerial challenge here is similar to the organizational design challenge within the firm. Senior managers have to design an organization that solves the coordination and incentive problems using the tools of architecture, routines, and culture (ARC). Managers responsible for crafting and maintaining relationships with other firms face the same two problems, albeit in different form. They have to design a relationship that coordinates resource acquisition and deployment across firm boundaries. A relationship with a buyer, for example, may require that the two firms coordinate inventory and delivery processes. They must also confront the incentive problem. Since both firms want to capture value, their managers have divergent interests. The relationship must somehow provide the right incentives for the two firms to solve the coordination problem.

Although the basic concepts of organization design are similar whether the relationship is between units of the same firm or between units in different firms, new issues arise because two firms are involved. In particular, the form of the relationship is a more prominent concern. Within a firm, workers are usually employees, and the firm usually controls physical assets. When a relationship involves two firms, their managers need to decide how and to what extent assets at one firm will be controlled by managers at another. Can the managers at your partner firm decide how much of your capacity to devote to a particular product? Can they decide what quality product you will produce? Should all decisions be made by consensus? Or should some decisions be made by consensus and others by managers at one firm or the other? Or should an independent joint venture make all decisions?

As suggested by these questions and demonstrated by the proliferation of strategic alliances among firms in recent years, interfirm relationships can take many forms. Vertical integration is at one extreme. The $8 billion acquisition of Turner Broadcast Systems by Time Warner, for example, created a vertically integrated unit that had a substantial presence in both cable television broadcasting and the production of television programming. Market transactions are at the other extreme.

Simple market transactions are sales that take place without any other contract between the firms. Most daily purchases of consumer products are simple market transactions, as are many transactions between firms.

In between these extremes are various "relational contracts." Relational contracts differ in duration, scope, and complexity. For example, natural gas companies sign long-term supply contracts with their buyers that commit the firms to transacting and limit the transaction prices. Joint ventures usually involve the creation of a third entity by two (or more) firms and are therefore complex contracts with a substantial scope and relatively long duration. An example is GM and Toyota's New United Motor Manufacturing Inc. (NUMMI) relationship to produce a small car for the U.S. market using resources from both firms. A supply contract may be much simpler and more limited in scope, and could be of any duration. The organization design problem is to construct a relationship that best addresses the coordination and incentive problems that firms must resolve to maximize the value their relationship enables them to create and capture.

A manager thinking about setting up any relational contract should first work out why it will add value. Why will transacting within a relational contract make the firm better off than it would be with a simple market transaction? Simple market transactions are our benchmark because most transactions are organized this way. We also use this as a benchmark because casual commentary in the business press (as well as some of the strategic management literature) suggests that vertical integration or relational contracts have some "natural" advantage. These commentators often underestimate the costs of the relationship and forget that it is costly to hire workers and direct the allocation of other resources efficiently. Getting incentives right inside a firm is difficult; monitoring can be as difficult (if not more difficult) inside the firm than it is across firm boundaries. When a unit is on its own in the market, its profitability and revenues become signals of its performance and quality. In contrast, when a unit is situated within a large, complex organization, where units share costs and where all levels in the organization do not necessarily report costs and revenue, getting clear indicators of a unit's performance and quality is much harder.

We also use market transactions as the benchmark because many managers have a bias toward exerting control. Managers who have a problem with input supply or channel relationships frequently feel frustrated because they cannot "make" these parts of the value chain work "properly." The manager's instinct is to exert control when things aren't working to her satisfaction, and she may feel, for example, that vertical integration is a good solution. Unfortunately, it is usually not the best solution. The same manager who at 10:00 A.M. proclaims that her division would be more profitable if she had an in-house sales force that she could direct, instead of independent distributors whom she must persuade, will at 11:00 A.M. declare that she cannot make her (vertically integrated) R&D lab understand that deadlines matter. Vertical integration—or any relationship between firms in the value chain—does not solve all the existing problems and usually creates new ones. Managers who are thinking about forming a vertical relationship should understand specifically how the relationship will create value.

## Opportunities for Creating Value: The Coordination Problem

Firms form relational contacts because they believe that the relationship can resolve some coordination problem. A manufacturing firm with a competitive advantage based on innovation might, for example, be able to create value by establishing an ongoing relationship with an outside law firm for managing intellectual property rights. Although the manufacturing firm could hire in-house counsel, it is usually less costly to hire specialized expertise on an as-needed basis. An outside firm can spread its investment in specialized expertise over many clients. Outside counsel also has a disadvantage, however: The manufacturing firm may be concerned that its proprietary knowledge could be leaked by the law firm or that its interests might conflict with those of the law firm's other clients. To allay these concerns and still reap the cost benefits of outside counsel, the manufacturer might choose to set up a long-term contract with its outside counsel that specifies the obligations of both parties.

More generally, vertical relationships can add value by reducing transaction costs. Transactions between firms often involve more than agreeing to buy a well-specified product at a particular price. Firms must assess the characteristics and prices of alternative inputs; sellers must seek out buyers; and both firms must make arrangements for a delivery schedule and for handling delays or disagreements about the quality or characteristics of the product. All these activities consume resources. Furthermore, most transactions are repeated; a company buys inputs repeatedly, and the aggregate cost of even simple transactions can be large. Establishing relationships with buyers or suppliers can sometimes reduce these costs by, for example, enabling information to be exchanged more easily. As the firms work with each other over time and anticipate an on-going relationship, they invest in learning about the other firm. Simply knowing whom to call at the other firm can facilitate the transactions. As the parties learn more about the systems and personnel at the other firm, they can further reduce these costs.

As the preceding examples suggest, relationships can create value by encouraging the companies to make investments that are valuable only if the relationship continues. The time a procurement staff spends getting to know the marketing people at another firm is useful only if the firms continue to interact. To design an appropriate patenting strategy, a law firm may have to invest in understanding the particular applications for its client's intellectual property. Investments of this type are called *relationship-specific investments* because they create assets that are more valuable within an on-going relationship than they are outside it. Put differently, the value of the assets when used within the relationship is higher than their value would be in their next best use.

Despite the forbidding name, relationship-specific investments are not exotic. They take many forms and characterize at least some of the transactions at most firms. For example, coal-burning power plants can reduce the cost of supplying electricity by locating close to a coal mine because transporting coal is much more costly than transporting electricity. Component manufacturers and original equipment manufacturers (OEMs) create a better product if the component manufacturer makes capital investments in machinery that is customized to that OEM. Business consulting firms make investments in learning about industries and specific firms that are valuable only if the client renews the consulting contract.

These types of investments have two key characteristics. First, they create value. Both parties to the relationship want to make the investment. Second, the value they create is specific to the relationship. Customized components cannot be sold to other firms. Locating a generating plant next to one coal mine makes it more costly for the plant to use coal from another mine. The combined effect of these two characteristics implies that a simple market transaction will not work in these cases. Without some contractual protection, the firms will not make the investment and will not create the value.

A numerical example may make these points clearly. Suppose there are two manufacturers of water meters. Water meters are enclosed in a bronze case produced with specialized casting equipment. Waterworks Company has an in-house foundry that has a variable cost of $7 per case and sells 1 million meters a year. Marmot, Inc. is paying $8 per meter case, which includes a per unit charge to cover the cost of transportation from a distant foundry. Marmot also sells 1 million meters a year. If a new, specialized foundry were constructed near Marmot, the foundry's variable cost of producing water meter cases would be $5. To simplify the discussion, assume that the foundry lasts only one year and that the total fixed cost of establishing and running a foundry to produce 1 million water meter cases is $2.2m. If the foundry were located next to Marmot, it would cost $1 per unit to ship the completed cases to Waterworks' location.

An enterprising business student, writing a term paper on the industry, recognizes that building this foundry would create value. She incorporates immediately and becomes Maincases, Inc. She builds the foundry and offers to sell water meter cases to Marmot for $7.99, a price that would give her a profit of $790,000. Marmot responds that it would be overjoyed to purchase her entire output at a unit price of $6.01. At this point, the firms negotiate over the final price. The cases are worth $8 to Marmot and $6 to Maincases, which is the maximum amount Waterworks would be willing to pay for them. The negotiating will be over who gets the $2 of value on the table. If Marmot and Maincases have equal bargaining power, they may split the difference evenly, and the resulting price will be $7. At this price, Maincases will have lost $200,000.

If Maincases' founder is smart and forward-looking, she will refuse to build the foundry without some prior agreement on price. Marmot's only options then would be to continue to pay $8, build a foundry itself, or try to solve the problem by entering into a one-year contract with Maincases. Since Marmot was willing to pay $8 per meter before without building its own foundry, we can assume that it does not have the resources to build or operate a foundry. Its best option is to contract with Maincases. When the contract is negotiated before the foundry is built, the entrepreneur can refuse to accept any price below $7.20.

The foundry in this example is a valuable and relationship-specific investment. It potentially creates a value of $2m that the two firms can share, but to realize the potential, the transaction must be carried out. If they can negotiate a contract specifying how the value will be shared before the investment is made, the firms will settle on a division that makes them both better off. Otherwise, the investment won't be made. Any firm foolish enough to make an investment of this type without a contract is unlikely to realize a reasonable return on its investment. The colorful name used to describe the possibility of expropriating relationship-specific investments is the "hold-up problem." Although things look fine *ex ante* (before the foundry is built), *ex post* the other firm "holds up" the investing firm. When both firms are making a relationship-specific investment, identifying who is the bandit and who is the victim can be difficult, but the result is the same. Fearing that their investment will be expropriated, neither party will make a relationship-specific investment without a contract.

In many value-creating relationships between firms, one or both parties must make relationship-specific investments. Wal-Mart's suppliers have to invest in the information technology necessary to use Wal-Mart's information systems. Toyota and GM had to invest in relationship-specific resources for the NUMMI venture. Although some long-term contracts only save on future negotiation and search costs, the contracts that involve relationship-specific investments can create the greatest value.

## Contracting to Create Value: The Incentive Problem

The hold-up problem exists because the incentives of the two firms are not aligned. Both want the investment to be made because it creates value. However, once one firm makes the investment, the other has an incentive to capture as much of the value created as possible. As with other incentive problems, an appropriate contract can resolve the hold-up problem. In the simple water meter example, writing a contract that solves the problem is fairly easy. More commonly, it can be difficult.

The example of the bargaining between the biotechnology and pharmaceutical firms over the value a new drug creates is another example of a relationship-specific investment. The biotech firm developing the insulin drug knew that it would face a single potential buyer. Recognizing that a pharmaceutical firm could expropriate its product development investment if it did not negotiate a deal *ex ante*, the biotech firm might have considered signing a contract *before* making the investment. However, a contract that protected both firms would be difficult to write. The firms could not have known in advance whether discovering the drug would cost $5m or $20m, for example. To deal with the uncertainty, the pharmaceutical firm could offer a "cost plus" contract that guaranteed the biotech firm's costs would be covered and granted it a share of the profits. But then the biotech firm would have an incentive to use this money to fund research on other drugs that it could offer to other firms. Because monitoring research is difficult, the biotech firm could easily apply the funds to other uses.

The firms would also have to reach some agreement about who owns the ancillary intellectual property. In the real case on which this example is based, both firms knew that they would have to solve a series of problems to develop this drug. Solving each would be a technical breakthrough that produced potentially valuable technology. If the pharmaceutical firm funds the research and development process, should it own all the intellectual property or only the property directly necessary to produce the drug? How should these technologies be valued? Appraising the value of a known drug with a well-established market is relatively easy. Evaluating technical advances in the process of drug discovery that might be applied to many other drugs is more difficult. In fact, the firms did not sort out these issues even in the contract they signed after the drug was created. It took years of litigation to decide which firm owned various pieces of intellectual property.

The point here is that, except in simple cases, the formal contracts that govern a relationship will be incomplete. The formal contract will explicitly cover contingencies that are easily anticipated, but unanticipated events often occur. This becomes more likely as the duration, scope, or complexity of the relationship increases. A similar problem occurs inside firms. Although there are formal agreements about compensation, title, and the general job description for each employee, for example, these formal, explicit contracts cannot completely specify what a worker's responsibilities are in every contingency. Instead, much of the employer-employee relationship is governed by an informal, implicit contract that requires the employee to respond to any reasonable request the employer makes and requires the employer to protect the employee against risks that cannot be reasonably avoided. What is reasonable is defined by a commonly understood set of routines and norms within the firm. The implicit contract supported by the norms and routines enables the firm to change its activities without rewriting thousands of explicit contracts. The firm's owners and its employees can share the value this flexibility creates.

The same kind of implicit contracts can develop between firms, but they may be more difficult to develop and maintain. Although employees may choose to pursue their own self-interest at the expense of the firm's owners, this incentive is stronger for two firms. Each firm's management has an obligation to its owner to extract as much value as possible. Furthermore, the routines and norms that support relationships within the firm may not extend to relationships outside the firm. Indeed, sometimes firms with very different cultures want to form a long-term relationship that involves relationship-specific investments.

One way firms avoid the hold-up problem when explicit contracts are incomplete is to focus on the long-term gain from the relationship. In Chapter 8, we introduced the idea that competing firms might refrain from "cheating" on a tacit agreement to cooperate if they recognize that on-going cooperation can yield greater gain than the immediate gain they can earn by cheating. In a similar way, firms in a long-term relationship could make relationship-specific investments with the understanding that the gain from continuing the relationship would be greater than the gain from exploiting the opportunity for hold-up. Some scholars of interfirm agreements believe that agreements are sustained by an atmosphere of trust that encourages each firm to refrain from incessantly weighing the tangible perceived benefits and costs. Each knows that the future will correct today's imbalance. Trust also reduces transaction costs by reducing risk. When a firm knows that its partner will behave fairly, it need not create costly contractual terms for insurance. For example, "take-or-pay" contracts prevent the buyer from refusing to buy the product once the supplying firm has made a relationship-specific investment for producing it. The purchaser agrees to buy an agreed-upon amount at a specified price ("take") or pay a large penalty ("pay"). As a result, when demand is less robust than expected, the purchasing firm sometimes buys output that is less valuable than its cost of production. If both firms knew that neither would hold the other up, this problem would not arise and the cost of take-or-pay would not be incurred.

It is one thing to say that "an atmosphere of trust" can be beneficial; it is another to create and maintain that atmosphere. A firm's culture and routines might support implicit contracts. But what supports this kind of relationship between firms? That support could come from the firms' larger social context or a firm could build a trustworthy reputation.

In arguing for the effects of a broader social context, some have claimed that the cultural differences between Japan and the West explain why long-term relationships between firms are more common in Japan. Sociologists have noted that a key characteristic of the relationships between Japanese firms is a commitment to resolve problems by instituting a dialogue rather than by ending the relationship and starting another. The buyer tries to work with the seller in order to address deficiencies in the seller's performance, for example, rather than simply switching to another seller. Each party also gives more weight to its obligation to its partner than it does to any advantage it might gain from violating the trust between them. Because these relationships were first observed among Japanese firms, some scholars believed that this type of relationship was part of Japanese culture. They argued that relationships that depend on goodwill and reciprocity were inconsistent with the individualistic values of Western culture.

The adoption of these kinds of relationships in the United States and Europe in recent years, however, has challenged this conclusion. When Japanese automobile firms set up factories in the United States, they formed successful long-term relationships with U.S. suppliers. Furthermore, American automobile firms like Ford and Chrysler quickly and successfully followed the Japanese example in managing supplier relationships. This does not mean that cultural values do not affect a firm's comfort level with these types of relationships. But it does suggest that national characteristics do not in themselves determine the success or failure of a long-term relationship.

Other analysts have focused on firm-specific reputations. Within any particular society, the extent to which firms enter cooperative relationships varies. Even within a given industry, some incumbent firms are more likely than others to be involved in long-term buyer–supplier relationships. A firm known for "doing the right thing" can develop a reputation for cooperative behavior. Other firms expect this firm to behave cooperatively because they believe that its managers have a set of values that makes them more trustworthy than managers at other firms. The potential partners of the firm with a reputation for fair dealing recognize that it is in the firm's best long-term interest to continue to behave cooperatively. A firm that takes advantage of a partner may gain some temporary advantage, but if the violation becomes public it can damage the firm's other relationships. The firm may then find that its other partners are reluctant to trust it. Similarly, potential partners' beliefs about how that firm will behave will hamper its attempts to enter into new relationships. Conversely, a firm with a reputation for treating its partners well can contract with others more easily.

Because trust is central to these relationships and because trust takes time to develop, long-term relationships usually evolve. One study of relationships in the high-technology sector proposes that implicit contracts have three phases.[11] Phase I establishes the preconditions for initiating the relationship. Firms select potential

---

[11] Andrea Larson, "Network Dyads in Entrepreneurial Settings: A Study of the Governance of Exchange Relationships," *Administrative Science Quarterly* 37 (1992), 76–104.

partners based on the reputations of managers and/or of firms. The more that each party knows about the other and about how the other has performed in previous long-term relationships, the more confident they are that they can predict the other party's future performance. Accordingly, positive personal relationships and reputations enhance cooperation in the earliest stage of a relationship.

In Phase II, the parties to the relationship enter a trial period during which rules and procedures are established, clear expectations are formed, and some initial level of trust and feeling of reciprocity is established. Typically, one firm assumes the role of initiator during Phase II, taking responsibility for moving the relationship forward. In Phase III, there is a key transition in terms of the level of integration and control. Operational integration may take place; that is, the relationship can become an integral part of each firm's operations rather than being a stand-alone entity separate from its main activities. There also may be strategic integration. Both firms manage the relationship as a central asset in their strategic objectives. In the earlier phases, operational and strategic integration involves too much risk for each firm.

The importance of implicit contracts in relationships should not obscure the role of explicit contracts. Explicit contracts establish a framework for the relationship and ensure that both parties agree to certain terms in the beginning. Explicit contracts are necessarily incomplete and imperfect, but they provide essential protection. You can trust your partner more easily when a contract curtails its temptation to betray that trust. Explicit contracts limit the exposure of both parties.

Explicit contracts are also important because the firms' interests may change over time. When the relationship starts, for example, each may anticipate that the future flow of benefits will reward them for not taking temporary advantage of their partners. But changes in demand or technology, or even within the firms themselves, can affect that balance. Both explicit and implicit contracts are useful for finding ways to alter or end the relationship. Changing the explicit contract lets both parties rethink their positions and evaluate what the changes mean.

## 10.6  SUMMARY

The way firms manage buyer–supplier relationships and the competitive structure of the segments within the value chain determine which firms capture the value that the chain creates. Lack of competition in one's own segment of the value chain and intense competition elsewhere facilitate value capture. From the buyers' perspective, supplier power is unlikely to reduce the share buyers capture when suppliers are competitive. Thus increasing the competition among suppliers will reduce supplier power. When suppliers have power, the buyer will be better off if it also has a strong bargaining position.

Although value capture is adversarial, value creation is often enhanced if the firms in adjacent layers can establish long-term cooperative relationships. The essence of such long-term relationships is the partners' belief that the investments they make today will be rewarded in the future through continued interactions. Value capture is about enhancing the firm's own buyer and supplier power at its buyers' and suppliers' expense. Value creation is often about deliberately creating a powerful buyer and supplier by creating more value through exchanges within the relationship than outside it. Focusing exclusively on value capture and preventing opportunism by trading partners in the short run can prevent firms from enjoying even greater gains from cooperation in the long run.

We have now completed our examination of the major determinants of value creation and capture. In Chapter 6 and in this chapter, we discussed how the value chain creates value. In Chapters 7 and 8 we described the factors that determine whether that value is dissipated by competition among incumbent firms. In Chapter 9 we analyzed whether value can be captured by new entrants. Finally, in this chapter we focused on whether participants in other layers of the value chain can capture value. The structure of the value chain, of course, changes with time. In the next chapter we focus on change in the firm's external environment and the management challenges that change raises.

## APPENDIX: PRICE DISCRIMINATION

In this chapter, we have focused on the effects of buyer or supplier power. We have also noted, however, that offering every buyer the same price limits a powerful supplier's ability to capture value. Similarly, a powerful buyer cannot extract all the value from its suppliers when it must pay them all the same price. When buyers (for example) have different valuations for the product but face the same price, high-value buyers get a great deal. If the price is $10, a buyer who is willing to pay no more than $10 is left with no value, but a buyer willing to pay $100 is left with $90 of value. The seller could extract more value if it could charge one buyer $10 and the other $100.

To do this, the seller needs to know who is who. Knowing that customers differ in their willingness to pay for your product isn't very helpful unless there's some way to find out who is willing to pay a high price and who will purchase only at a lower price. The seller also needs to be able to charge different prices. The sophisticated pricing schemes airlines employ that result in customers on the same plane paying more than 20 different fares require a large investment in information technology and technical personnel. Finally, the firm must be able to prevent re-sale of its product. If the product can be re-sold, the customer charged the lower price will simply re-sell it to the customer who was quoted a higher price. When a firm can surmount these difficulties, it can price discriminate.

To explore how firms can price discriminate, we focus on discriminating among buyers, but the arguments apply equally well to discriminating among suppliers. If suppliers differ in their willingness to supply the product, buyers who can price discriminate will gain. Suppose, for example, that some supplier has a lower cost but can't supply enough of an input to meet the buyer's entire demand. Then the buyer would like to purchase as much as possible at a low price from the low-cost firm and offer the higher price necessary to complete its purchases only to the high-cost firm. We also focus on the case where a powerful supplier faces buyers who have no power. A total absence of buyer power is not necessary for price discrimination, but making this assumption lets us concentrate on the price discrimination problem while setting the bargaining problem aside.

Ideally, a firm likes to be able to charge each buyer an individual price exactly equal to its willingness to pay for the product.[12] Charging each buyer its willingness to pay is called *perfect price discrimination* and it requires acquiring and processing lots of information about individual buyers. The informational requirements are so high that one seldom sees this type of price discrimination. How can a firm know that I am willing to pay $2 more for a given dishwasher than my next door neighbor? A few examples come close, however. Colleges collect substantial information on the ability of students (and their families) to pay college expenses. A student who receives financial aid is offered a discounted price that is customized precisely to his ability to pay. Auto dealers don't achieve perfect price discrimination, but they work hard to strike a customized deal with every buyer. As they negotiate, two factors limit their ability to extract value. First, they have less direct information than colleges on willingness to pay; they have to infer this information from the bargaining process or what they can readily observe about the customer. Second, cars—unlike college education—can be re-sold. Auto-buying services that negotiate for buyers combine both of these features. Because the seller doesn't know who the final buyer is, it is at an informational disadvantage. Second, the buying service effectively buys at a low- (or moderate-) value buyer's price and re-sells to any customer whose value is equal to or above that.

Although perfect price discrimination is rare, a firm can adjust its product and pricing offerings to achieve some price discrimination in many ways. One approach is to find an observable characteristic that is at least a rough proxy for buyers' valuations and to offer different prices or products based on that characteristic. Examples include discounts for seniors, students, children and other groups. These pricing schemes are profitable if willingness to pay is related to the observable characteristic—for example, if the student's typical willingness to pay is lower than that of the general population. One of the more clever forms of this kind of price discrimination is a sign written only in Chinese in a Chinatown restaurant announcing that no tips are necessary. This results in a lower overall price for Chinese-speaking customers who may have a lower willingness to pay because they know more about the restaurant's alternatives. This form of price discrimination is less effective than perfect price discrimination because willingness to pay within each category varies. Some students, for example, have a higher willingness to pay than buyers in the general population.

Another more common approach to price discriminating is to find a rough proxy for willingness to pay and to construct a set of products and prices that get consumers to sort themselves according to their willingness to pay. Consider the simple example in Table 10.A1. As the table illustrates, the quality-conscious buyer has a higher will-

---

[12] More precisely, a price that just equals the buyer's willingness to pay for the product from that firm. If the supplier is a monopoly, the willingness to pay for the product in general and from that firm is the same. More commonly, powerful suppliers have competitors, which limits the price levels the firm can charge. Competition does not, however, prevent firms from price discriminating, and the examples we discuss in this appendix are about industries with multiple firms. A monopoly firm that can charge each customer what it is willing to pay will leave no value to buyers. A firm with competitors will leave some value because competition drives down prices, but it can still price discriminate to avoid leaving more value with those buyers who have higher valuations.

**TABLE 10-A1**    Separating Consumers by Their Preferences for Quality

|  | High-Quality Product ($) | Standard-Quality Product ($) |
|---|---|---|
| Quality-conscious buyer's valuation | 10 | 6 |
| Price-conscious buyer's valuation | 6 | 5 |
| Firm's cost per unit | 4 | 3 |

ingness to pay for both the high- and standard-quality products than the price-conscious buyer. If each buyer only wants one product, the firm's apparent choice is to sell either the high-quality item for $10 or the standard-quality item for $5. Its profits from these options are $6 and $4, respectively. Obviously, it would choose to sell the high-quality product. (Note that these choices are better than charging $6 and selling two units of the high-quality product, or charging $6 and selling one unit of the standard-quality product.)

But the firm can do better. To understand how, see what happens if the firm produces both products and sells the high-quality one for $8.99 and the standard-quality item for $5. At these prices the quality-conscious buyer will buy the high-quality offering because it gives her $1.01 of value compared to only $1.00 from the standard-quality product. In contrast, the price-conscious buyer is willing to buy the standard-quality item but not the high-quality one. The firm therefore sells one unit of the high-quality item and one of the standard-quality one, for a profit of $6.99.

Even if the firm cannot tell quality-conscious from price-conscious buyers, by adjusting its quality and price offerings appropriately, *it can induce the buyers to self-select to the offering that makes them happiest.* In the process, the firm does better than it would by charging a single price. Note, however, that in this example the firm cannot do as well as it could in a world of perfect price discrimination. The reason is that to induce the quality-conscious buyer to choose the high-quality offering, the firm must ensure that she is no worse off buying it than she would be if she purchased the standard-quality one. One way to do this is to raise the price of the standard-quality product. But the firm also wants to sell to the price-conscious buyer, and that limits to no more than $5 the price it can charge for the standard-quality offering. At that price, the quality-conscious buyer would capture some value from buying it ($1 worth). So, the quality-conscious buyer must also get at least $1 of surplus when she buys the high-quality product. Its price then cannot be higher than $8.99.

There are many other examples of this type of price discrimination, involving different mechanisms to induce buyers to self-select according to their willingness to pay. Discount coupons are one common mechanism. Consumers with the highest willingness to pay are often those who also value their time most highly and are less willing to take the time to clip coupons. Consequently, a firm that offers coupons induces price-sensitive buyers to clip coupons (and receive a lower net price), while less price-sensitive buyers pay the full price.

Another classic example can occur when a seller offers both a primary good and complementary products. In the days when computer programs were written on punch cards, for example, IBM required its mainframe computer customers to purchase punch cards from IBM. By charging high prices for these cards, IBM could charge significantly higher total prices to customers who used many cards and therefore presumably had a higher valuation for their computers. Such pricing tactics are common when a product is sold with a consumable that meters usage—for example, toner fluid in copier machines or cartridges in printers. These are examples of *tying*, since one product (in these cases the consumables) is tied to the purchase of another.

In other circumstances, a firm has an incentive to offer its products both separately and in a *bundle* in which they are sold together. This practice is common in software markets, for example. To see how this works, consider the simple example in Table 10-A2 where we assume the firm's cost is $0.

If the firm sells Products A and B separately, it maximizes profits by charging $200 for each, which enables it to sell two of each for a total of $800. The firm can do even better if it can bundle, however, by charging $300 for each product and $400 for a bundle consisting of both A and B. Consumer 1 will buy B, consumer 2 will buy A, and consumer 3 will buy the bundle. Total revenues are now $1000. The firm has exploited the fact that some users highly value only one product and others (like Consumer 3) moderately value both. By offering a selection of bundles and prices, the buyers self-select according to their willingness to pay.

The passage of time provides another avenue for price discrimination. This happens, for example, when buyers' impatience is correlated with their willingness to pay. Wealthy buyers often are willing to pay more and are less inclined to wait. The firm can then price discriminate by charging higher prices today and lower prices in the future. Even if wealthy buyers know that prices will fall later, they may nonetheless buy today at the higher prices. Those who are more patient and also have a lower willingness to pay will wait for the prices to decrease. Stores "sales" are an example. Buyers who are price sensitive and patient wait for the sales, but impatient, price-insensitive buyers indulge their desire for instant gratification by buying immediately.

Airline discounts for advance purchase tickets and Saturday night stayovers are a related technique. Since more travelers who make plans late are business travelers with a higher willingness to pay than vacationers, airlines can (and do) charge more for booking a ticket with little advance notice. Similarly, cheaper flights for trips that involve a Saturday night stayover serve to distinguish (albeit imperfectly) between business travelers who want to be home on the weekend and vacation travelers who want to be away on the weekend.

**TABLE 10-A2**   The Effect of Bundling

|  | Value of Product A ($) | Value of Product B ($) |
|---|---|---|
| Consumer 1 | 0 | 300 |
| Consumer 2 | 300 | 0 |
| Consumer 3 | 200 | 200 |

To implement them, all these types of price discrimination require the firm to prevent re-sale. Preventing re-sale can be easy if the item is customized to the individual buyer. More generally, re-sale is impossible when a service is being provided rather than a product—a college education, say, rather than a car. In other cases, preventing re-sale is much more difficult, although firms have shown great creativity in preventing it. One way to prevent it is to alter the product characteristics according to the targeted market segment. In one case, a certain kind of cement could be used both in industrial applications and in dental bonding. Because the firm making the cement could charge much higher prices in the dental market, it attempted to prevent the re-sale of the industrial cement to dentists by adding a small amount of arsenic, rendering the cement unusable in dental work (with unfortunate legal ramifications as it turned out)!

In extreme cases, firms may use vertical integration to prevent re-sale. For example, an aluminum manufacturer might want to charge lower prices to some buyers than to others. Typically, for example, manufacturers of metal cans and cookware are less willing to pay than are aircraft manufacturers. However, if aluminum companies charge lower prices to the firms that make cans and cookware, those firms can re-sell the aluminum to the aircraft manufacturers. One way to achieve at least partial price discrimination is for the aluminum manufacturers to forward integrate into cans and cookware where buyers have a low willingness to pay. By charging themselves a low internal transfer price and others a high market price, they can achieve the benefits of price discrimination. Because they then own the downstream unit, they can prevent re-sale. This is the favored explanation for Alcoa's pattern of vertical integration into cookware, electric cable, and automobile parts but not aircraft when it was a monopoly supplier of aluminum in the early twentieth century.

The principles of price discrimination do not just apply to firms that discriminate among buyers. A good example of discrimination among suppliers is the behavior of paper mills that purchase lumber. Often, a paper mill has some market power because it is one of only a few buyers of trees in a region, and cut trees are costly to transport. Most sellers, on the other hand, own relatively small lots and have few good alternative uses for their timber. Thus, for example, if there are two mills 100 miles apart, the landowners located near one of the mills will prefer to sell their trees to that mill even if the mill's price is lower than that of its distant competitor. Because the mills arrange contracts with each seller individually, the (net of transportation cost) price for lots close to one mill or the other is higher than the price for identical trees from lots midway between the two mills.

Antitrust restrictions can limit a firm's ability to use price discrimination. In the United States, for example, the Robinson-Patman Act prohibits price discrimination that a firm uses to harm its rivals and create or maintain market power, or that harms competition among the seller's customers. Although firms are occasionally prosecuted for price discrimination in the United States, the government no longer enforces these laws with much enthusiasm. One reason for this change is that at the time the law was passed, the government believed that price discrimination was always bad for consumers. Economists now recognize that this is not necessarily true. Think of the financial aid example cited earlier. Are buyers of a college education harmed because colleges use a sliding scale for financial aid? Or think of senior discounts. If discounts allow senior citizens to buy a product they otherwise could not afford to purchase, is this bad for consumers? Typically, price discrimination leads to prices both above and below the price that the firm would charge if it could only charge a single price. As a result, price discrimination makes for winners and losers. Because price discrimination may be good or bad for consumers overall and is difficult to prove (firms can always find some explanation other than price discrimination for differences in their prices), today it is seldom litigated in the United States.

# 11

# STRATEGIC MANAGEMENT IN A CHANGING ENVIRONMENT

## 11.1 INTRODUCTION

Change may be the greatest strategic challenge general managers face. If the firm's environment never changed, managers could set strategy once and then devote their time to implementing it. When the firm's external context changes significantly, however, managers must recognize the change, understand how it will affect the firm's strategy, and adjust the strategy and internal context accordingly. The challenge is all the more daunting because change is usually accompanied by some uncertainty. A given change can portend a new, long-run trend, or it may be merely a transitory deviation. It is difficult to assess which of several possible outcomes might be the new status quo and which are promises or threats that will never fully materialize.

Much of this book has not explicitly addressed change or presented our basic frameworks in a dynamic context. Fortunately, this does not mean that these frameworks are not useful in a dynamic world. It is precisely because the paths of industries and firms take unexpected turns that the manager must maintain a mental map of the relationship among the firm's environments (both internal and external), actions, and performance. Figure 11-1 reproduces a figure first introduced in Chapter 1, which illustrates the relationships among internal context, external context, action, firm performance, and change. Changes in the firm's context frequently mean that the actions that will maximize its profit may also change. The firm's strategy may now no longer be aligned with its external and internal contexts. The firm must understand exactly what has changed in these relationships to know how it should adapt. When the nature of the change is uncertain, the firm has to know what might occur and how it should respond to the most likely outcomes.

Change often originates outside the firm. A new technology that a competitor introduces, for example, can transform competition in an industry. Or a government's

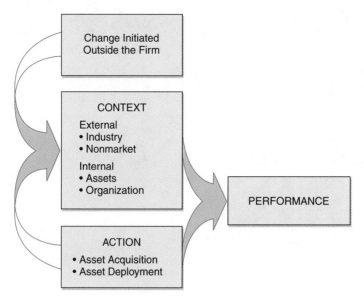

**FIGURE 11-1**   Dynamics of Business Strategy

new trade policy can open up new markets. Change can also originate within the firm. It may be your own firm whose technology changes its industry. In any case, the change will affect the firm's external context, which, in turn, will have implications for its strategy and how it organizes its assets. This chapter provides tools for dealing with changes in the firm's environment and formulating strategy in periods of change.

We begin by using the example of the automobile industry to discuss external change. Next, we use industry analysis to categorize how external change can affect firm performance. We then turn to the dynamics of industry evolution and changes in the organization of the value chain. Finally, we explore the challenges managers face in formulating strategy in periods of change.

## 11.2   THE EVOLUTION OF THE U.S. AUTOMOBILE INDUSTRY[1]

The automobile industry emerged in the 1890s when entrepreneurs experimented with gasoline engines, steam engines, and electric motors as sources of propulsion. The first automobile manufacturers were a far cry from today's massive companies. Entry into the new industry was easy, and many small firms were founded. A new firm would design a vehicle, promote it, and take orders. To fill orders, these firms contracted for components with machine shops, engine suppliers, and other manufacturers of components from wheels to bodies. The automobile manufacturers functioned largely as designers, assemblers, and marketers. By 1910, over 30 automobile companies were supplying fewer than 200,000 cars per year.

---

[1] The material in this section is based on information in "Automobiles," Chapter 3 in Walter Adams and James Brock, eds., *The Structure of American Industry*, 9th ed. (New York: Prentice Hall, 1995), 65–92.

Automobile production soon accelerated: Total industry sales were 462,000 in 1913, 896,000 in 1915, and 1,746,000 in 1917, reaching 3,735,000 by 1925. The driving force behind the initial market expansion was the strategy followed by the Ford Motor Company. Ford believed that demand for automobiles was so elastic that reducing their price would lead to a large increase in demand. To support a price cut, Ford undertook a cost reduction plan that combined standardization of parts and products, specialization of labor by task, and mass production. This was a classic low cost strategy. By driving costs down, Ford could lower prices, expand the market, and generate the volume necessary to reap economies of scale in production. By 1921, Ford's Model T had captured half the market.

The next engine of demand creation was General Motors' (GM) differentiation strategy. In contrast to Ford, GM sought to increase the market and its share by producing a wide range of models that it updated each year. GM believed that the market for automobiles was large enough to support many models at efficient scales of production and that product proliferation would further stimulate demand within several niche markets. To build its product line, GM acquired many independent firms and reorganized itself as a multidivision firm with distinct automobile families. GM believed that producing many models within a common firm would allow it to reap economies of scope across models and economies of scale for specific processes. This strategy led to GM's dominance of the market.

The successful strategies that Ford and GM—and later Chrysler—pursued led to continuing consolidation within the industry. The "Big Three" had 68 percent of U.S. auto production in 1923 and 98 percent around 1970. As the Big Three firms emerged as the industry's clear winners, their sales grew dramatically. Other countries experienced a similar pattern of consolidation in their automobile industries over a similar time frame.

Although the large U.S. firms benefited from the growth of the market, the size of the market also attracted entry by foreign firms. These entrants first established a significant presence by serving the small-car segment that the U.S. firms had largely ignored. Leveraging their position in small cars, foreign producers reduced the Big Three's share to about 75 percent by the late 1970s. This shift was the result both of a change in fuel prices that made small cars more attractive and technological advances in product design and manufacture that enabled Japanese and European firms to produce high quality cars. By the end of the 1970s, the U.S. firms were producing cars that were technologically inferior and out of sync with consumer demand. These once dominant firms were reduced to appealing for government subsidies and trade barriers to protect them from foreign competition. In the 1980s, the U.S. firms changed their asset base and their architecture, routines, and culture (ARC) to build the basis for a new competitive advantage. By the late 1990s, the Big Three were approaching technological parity with their foreign competitors and had leveraged their experience in producing large cars and trucks into the new minivan and Sport Utility Vehicle segments. These accomplishments revived their fortunes.

Throughout the industry's history, the leading firms have repeatedly transformed their relationship with the value chain. Initially, the industry was disintegrated; that is, the automobile companies neither produced most of their products' components themselves nor had long-term contracts with suppliers. Over time, however, automobile firms have increased the span of activities they perform in-house. For example, by the mid-1970s, GM produced about two-thirds of its components internally and Ford a little less than half.[2] In addition, firms that specialized in automotive components produced many of the outsourced components in close working relationships with the Big Three firms. The contracts governing these relationships gave the automobile firms substantial control over their suppliers' activities. Recently, the automotive firms have reduced in-house production, sometimes spinning off units that produced components for the firm. They also have developed more cooperative relationships with independent suppliers.

The evolution of the automobile industry is a good example of how changes in firms' environments can affect their performance. The rise of multinational automobile companies able to compete in the U.S. market has profoundly affected the profitability of the U.S. companies. The industry also illustrates the systematic dynamics of industry emergence, growth, and maturity that often characterize industry life cycles. The substantial changes these firms have made to the organization of their industry's value chain also is characteristic of the dynamics found in other industries. Finally—and most importantly from our perspective—the way these firms responded to the threats and opportunities in their environment shows the importance of formulating a strategic response to change. Ford and GM first dominated their industry because they formulated and implemented innovative strategies. Later, faced with a competitive challenge by new, international competitors, the domestic firms had to change their strategies to prosper in a new environment.

## 11.3 CHANGE AND COMPETITIVE ADVANTAGE

A sustainable competitive advantage is central to a successful strategy, and changes in the firm's environment can affect its competitive advantage. Firms that once had a substantial incumbency advantage may face new, strong competitors. Shifts in technology may destroy dominant firms' once impregnable positional advantage. As these changes occur, each firm must adapt its strategy to exploit the new opportunity or fend off the new threat. Small independent drug stores, for example, tailored their services to a local community of customers. Their primary competitive advantages were location and customer relationships. When large, efficient chain stores entered these local markets, the focus of competition shifted over time to cost and breadth of product line. The incumbent firms were not well positioned to compete on this basis. Unable to compete in the new environment, most of these local retailers were driven out of business.

In Chapter 6 we presented a framework for assessing the firm's external context, and we can return to it here. As Figure 11-2 suggests, the framework was based on understanding how value is created and how that value is allocated. We referred to the

---

[2] Kirk Monteverde and David Teece, "Supplier Switching Costs and Vertical Integration in the Automobile Industry," *The Bell Journal of Economics* (Spring 1982), 206–213.

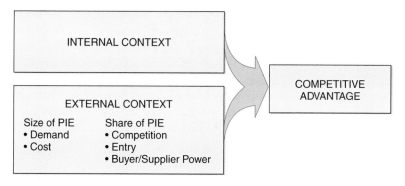

**FIGURE 11-2**    Change and Competitive Advantage

value the chain creates as Potential Industry Earnings, or PIE. The share of PIE that the incumbent firms as a group can capture depends on how intense competition among them is, how high the barriers to entry are, and how much value buyers or suppliers can capture. Because change can affect any of these factors, the framework is a useful way to think about the effects of change.

Any change affecting PIE can also affect the performance of incumbent firms. Recall that the difference between the final buyers' valuation of the goods and services that the value chain provides and the opportunity cost at which it can provide them determines an industry's PIE. Changes to PIE can come from either the demand or cost side and from a variety of sources. A common demand-side change is the emergence of new substitutes or complements from new technology. The development of automobiles, for example, reduced the demand for bicycles. A change in consumer tastes can also affect demand. A new concern with health and processed food created the bottled water industry. Long-term changes in income can also affect demand, shifting it toward luxury products, for example. On the cost side, changes in the prices of raw inputs can profoundly affect PIE. Increases in the price of refined petroleum products, for example, affected the competitive advantage of firms producing plastic containers and of oil-burning electric power plants. Technology shocks also affect costs. "Cracking" technologies transformed oil refining and made petroleum a much more cost-effective energy source. Computer-aided design has allowed firms to perform the same design tasks at a lower cost than before and to manage complex design processes that would have been impossible with the old technologies.

Even if PIE is unchanged, changes in competition, in the advantage of incumbency, and in the bargaining power of buyers or suppliers can dramatically affect the fortunes of the incumbent firms. For example:

- **Competition.** Many external forces affect the competitive intensity of an industry. The public sector, particularly deregulation, privatization, and trade policy, has been one of the most important sources of these forces in the last 25 years. For example, most features of the U.S. airline industry, including pricing, were subject to regulatory oversight until 1978. Under regulation, airlines competed more on quality (service, meals, comfort, etc.) than on price. After deregulation, however, price competition heated up. The recent privatization of electric power generation in the United Kingdom was intended to produce more competition and the efficiencies that are associated with competition. Changes in the behavior of rival firms can also affect competitive intensity. For example, in an industry where implicit collusion is maintained through relationships among top executives at the largest firms, a leadership change can destabilize the cooperative atmosphere.

- **Threat of entry.** Any change that reduces incumbents' advantages over potential entrants can affect the performance of incumbent firms. The introduction of "mini mill" technology in the steel industry, for example, enabled firms to enter at a much smaller scale than was previously required for efficiency. More generally, entrants often use new technologies to overcome the incumbents' advantage. New technologies allow entrants to differentiate their products from those of the incumbents or to provide them at a lower cost. The Internet provided a way for new entrants to compete with established brokerage firms. Deregulation can also eliminate entry barriers, as when, for example, the government lifts prohibitions that prevent telecommunication companies from entering each other's markets.

- **Buyer and supplier power.** When a firm in one layer of the value chain achieves a dominant position, it diminishes the ability of the firms in other layers to capture value. Such changes can be evolutionary and thus anticipated. But they can also be sudden and unexpected, as when Intel rocketed to a dominant position in the microprocessor market for personal computers. More recently, electronic commerce has caused dramatic changes in the positions of firms in the value chain. For example, the ability of consumers to buy directly from on-line toy distributors is a shock with which conventional bricks-and-mortar toy stores must contend.

This is by no means an exhaustive list of the changes a firm might encounter. Our purpose is simply to illustrate that any specific change can affect industry profitability. A change in manufacturing or distribution technology, for example, can affect both cost and entry barriers. The development of a new product might affect both demand and buyer power. A manager who perceives a change needs to think through the effects it will have. If it affects entry barriers, for example, he should think carefully about which of his customers are most likely to switch to new suppliers and should strengthen his firm's relationship with them before entry occurs. If it significantly reduces costs, competition might become more cost-based (at least in the short run). The firm would quickly need to prepare for this possibility.

In short, external change means that a general manager has to rethink her mental map of the relationships among the firm's external context, strategic assets, and competitive advantage. Keeping track of *all* the changes that are occurring is often impossible. Some of the relevant changes can occur in other industries, and their effects may not be immediately apparent. Even within an industry, change is continual, and managers often cannot distinguish long-term shifts from short-term fluctuations. Long-term changes may require reformulating the firm's strategy, but short-term fluctuations usually do not. It can even be difficult to determine the important long-term changes from those that will scarcely affect the firm's performance.

It is here that having a clear mental map of the industry and a strategy based on that map can help. To develop the strategy, managers must identify the key external features on which the strategy depends and must keep tracking them. A change in one of these features can render the entire strategy and the internal context supporting it inappropriate. For example, the rise in managed care and changes in government reimbursement policies in the U.S. health care industry have placed tremendous pressures on teaching hospitals that once depended on fee-for-service payment systems, minimal monitoring of hospital charges, and subsidies in government reimbursement to generate revenue to support their teaching mission. When the insurance industry moved to per capita payments and rigorous cost control, these hospitals had to redesign their organizations and try to compete on the basis of cost. The pressure was intensified when the government reduced Medicare payments to hospitals. By contrast, these same hospitals had adjusted easily to major technological changes in the delivery of health care because these changes did not threaten their competitive position. Indeed, these hospitals were usually among the first to adopt new technology because their capabilities and organization were designed to identify and accommodate changes in medical science. They were not, however, designed to be responsive to their buyers. As a result, the managers at these hospitals were slow to recognize the importance of changes in the insurance industry and public policies and were not well positioned to respond once they did recognize the changes. If they had developed a strategy to identify the key environmental characteristics on which their prosperity depended they might have been able to react more quickly.

## 11.4  INDUSTRY LIFE CYCLE

Some factors that have affected the automobile industry over the years have been unpredictable, short-term fluctuations. For example, short-term movements in exchange rates, interest rates, and consumer spending over the business cycle affect the sales of domestic models. But the kind of systematic, long-term changes in demand growth and industry structure that characterize many industries have also shaped the automobile industry. One of these patterns is the reorganization of the value chain, a topic we will return to later in this chapter. The other is the pattern called the industry life cycle. As Figure 11-3 illustrates, this view of industry evolution describes four stages of sales: emergence, growth, maturity, and decline.

Although the predominant feature of each stage in the cycle is a different rate of demand growth (or decline), many other characteristics of the firms and industry structure also change over the cycle. As the industry moves through this cycle, the number and size distribution of firms in the industry, the mode of competition among firms, barriers to entry, and the role of suppliers and buyers tend to change. In this section, we discuss some of the more important features of the life cycle and its implications for managers who formulate business strategy.

Although managers who want to both anticipate and respond to change must understand the long-term dynamics of the life cycle, there are two important caveats about the life cycle concept. First, the neat structure of industry change illustrated by Figure 11-3 is often at odds with the actual development of an industry. Industries that appear to be maturing, for example, can revert to being growth industries when technologies change or new segments open up. Or rapid technological change can turn what looks like an industry in the early stages of strong demand growth into a declining industry. Or industries that appear to be moving into the growth stage can stall, entering a limbo in which firms stay alive but never thrive. No industry has to follow the stages in Figure 11-3. Rather, a manager should use this profile to think about what problems industry evolution presents to her firm. Second, the *rate* at which the industry goes through this life cycle varies from industry to industry. Some scholars refer to industries as having different "clock speeds."[3] For example, rapidly changing industries are said to operate on "Internet time." The speed of change increases the managerial challenge, and the firm must adapt its approach accordingly. As we shall see in more detail in Chapter 15, rapid change means that the firm's strategy-setting process must be much faster and more flexible.

## Emergence

Uncertainty and ferment are the hallmarks of an industry's emergence stage. For example, the early years of the automobile industry were years of experimentation in which entrepreneurs tried different technological approaches and strategies: Firms promoting gasoline engine technology for cars competed not only with one another but also with those trying to develop electric or steam-powered models. Indeed, the competition among different approaches is what distinguishes competition in the emergence stage of an industry. Typically, one approach triumphs in the market, and success at this stage depends on choosing the right approach. Many firms fail because

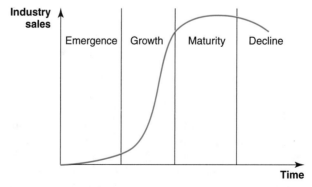

**FIGURE 11-3**  The Industry Life Cycle

---

[3] See Charles H. Fine, *Clock Speed* (New York: Perseus Books, 1998).

they pursue the wrong approach. The best electronic car firm was an early casualty in the battle of automobile technologies.

To participate in the early stage of an industry, a firm must bring together a number of skills and strategic assets. One common ingredient of a successful new venture is inventing a new technology, product, or approach. Invention, however, is only one part of the task early-stage firms face. The greater challenge is to understand the opportunity the innovation creates and to bring together the resources to seize it. It is difficult to shape a new venture in an emerging industry because competing alternative approaches make the environment extremely uncertain. If outsiders are to commit the resources that most new ventures need, they must be persuaded that the approach chosen by the firm is likely to succeed.

Because shepherding a new venture requires traveling through unmapped territory, the entrepreneur needs courage and an ability to focus on the venture's chosen direction in the face of conflicting environmental signals. Joseph Schumpeter summarized these qualities and the role of the entrepreneur in this setting as follows:

> To act with confidence beyond the range of familiar beacons and to overcome resistance requires aptitudes that are present in only a small fraction of the population and define the entrepreneurial type as well as the entrepreneurial function. This function does not essentially consist in either inventing anything or otherwise creating the conditions which the enterprise exploits. It consists of getting things done.[4]

The intense competition characteristic of this stage makes the entrepreneur's task more challenging. The path to success is uncertain, but each participant recognizes that if he succeeds he can establish an enduring first-mover advantage. Moving quickly can affect both which approach wins market acceptance and which firm will be best positioned. Furthermore, because there is no accepted technological paradigm and no firm has yet established a strong competitive position, entry barriers are typically low. As a result, many firms enter the competition, and the ensuing contest resembles a gold rush, with many prospectors attempting to stake out claims.

Competition for positional advantage on the Internet is an excellent example of early-stage competition. It is no surprise that analysts' discussions of Internet ventures focus on the search for workable "business models." A viable business model is a strategy that has a reasonable probability of succeeding if well executed. In the early stage, various business models compete. Some firms attract Web surfers, for example, by offering them free service along with paid advertising, following the familiar radio and television model. Others charge users directly for service. Still others use the Internet to sell goods traditionally sold through other channels or seek revenue by charging other sites for referrals. In each case, the firms struggle to attract enough customers to generate revenue to support their cost structure. To complicate matters, the success of any of these approaches depends critically on what others do because there is competition for Web traffic. No wonder the stock prices of these companies are so volatile. Investors asked to back these nascent ventures do not know what will succeed and

---

[4] Joseph Schumpeter, *Capitalism, Socialism, and Democracy*, (New York: Harper & Row, 1942), 132.

what will fail. When there is tremendous uncertainty, small bits of information strongly affect peoples' expectations. As a result, the stock prices of new Internet ventures experience large, sudden changes.

Entrepreneurs and investors face four main sources of uncertainty in emerging markets: technological, market, organizational, and strategic.

- **Technological uncertainty.** Fundamental technological change can create new industries. The application of solid-state physics to electronic switching and amplifying created the semiconductor industry. The information technology industry emerged from technological changes in computing. Because new technologies often give birth to new industries, early participants must place bets on which technologies will prevail. One part of this wager is purely technological: What technologies will work? In the discovery phases of innovation, the viability of a new technology is never obvious. Before the transistor was discovered, no one knew whether solid-state devices could amplify current. When the Department of Defense asked IBM and other research laboratories to develop a computing machine, no one was sure that it would lead to anything more useful than a mechanical adding machine. No one knows when or if a vaccine (let alone a cure) for the AIDS virus will be developed. The problem becomes more complex when there are competing technological designs. Then the question becomes not only whether anything will work, but also which design will work better than the others.

- **Market uncertainty.** When a product is different from those currently on the market, it is difficult to anticipate how much demand it will command. How much demand will there be for 500 cable television channels? How much will people pay for an electric car? IBM initially estimated that fewer than 20 computers would satisfy world demand. Similarly, EMI dramatically underestimated the demand for its CT scan technology. More often, however, firms overestimate eventual demand. Engineers become enamored of their new technology and became convinced that the world will embrace it. Uncertainty about how much the new technology will cost makes it even more complicated to estimate market acceptance. How much will companies need to charge for the new product? How quickly will costs (and prices) decline enough to attract a lot of buyers? Firms resolve demand uncertainty only when they overcome technological uncertainty and bring products to market.

- **Organizational uncertainty.** In the emerging stage, the relative capabilities of the participating firms and the optimal organization design are both uncertain. The technology may be feasible, but can *my* firm develop it? Will my firm develop it before another firm can? What organizational structure will be most successful? For new enterprises, organizational design is typically intertwined with financing issues. The start-up firm must decide how to accommodate the demands of key resource holders. For an established firm embarking on a new venture, organizational issues typically revolve around how the new venture should fit into the existing organization. Should an existing division manage the venture? Should the firm create an autonomous or semiautonomous new entity to purse the new opportunity?

- **Strategic uncertainty.** Selecting the best business model requires placing strategic bets. What strategic logic will succeed in this market? Should the firm specialize and achieve economies of scale as Ford did, or should it pursue product differentiation and economies of scope as GM did? Is being first to market the most important source of competitive advantage, or can a superior but late product capture the market?

The combined uncertainty in these markets means that new ventures compete with one another, not just to develop the new technology and compete in the marketplace, but also to acquire the resources to succeed. A fledgling enterprise needs to attract people, capital, customers, and alliance partners. All these are in scarce supply, and their owners have to decide which competing organization and strategic alternative to back. Even established firms can feel resource-acquisition pressures. Although existing firms have internal human and physical assets that they can deploy to back new ventures, these internal ventures must vie for customers and alliance partners outside the firm and must also compete for resources with other (perhaps more proven) alternatives within it. The competition for resources helps explain why the market tends to grow relatively slowly in this phase; none of the resource holders is confident enough to place large bets on any one alternative. Only the promise of extraordinary profits for the winning venture can induce investors to participate at this point.

Because outcomes are uncertain, the entrepreneur must develop a strategy that accommodates uncertainty. Her strategy will depend on her view of what the industry will look like. The firm must place bets on technologies and market demand. The manager must find a balance between driving the firm in one direction to take advantage of coordinated activity and hedging its bets if her beliefs about the future are wrong. Vision and the manager's ability to get resource-holders to believe in that vision are particularly important in this period. Uncertainty undermines the willingness of employees and outsiders to make the investments that the firm needs to succeed. A manager who can persuade employees and outsiders that his vision of the future is correct (or at least highly probable) will get investments at less cost than a manager who either has no compelling vision or cannot sell the one he has.

Over time, the uncertainty about which approach will be more successful in the market is resolved, and the industry enters a "shake-out" period. Ventures that have backed the wrong technology or embraced badly flawed strategies wither as financial capital providers are unwilling to make additional investment and key human capital providers decide to place their bets elsewhere. Established firms shut down their new venture. Start-up firms go out of business altogether.

The mortality rates for independent start-ups in the later phases of emergence are a striking example of the well-documented fact that younger firms are more likely to fail than older ones. Organizational sociologists call this phenomenon the "liability of newness." In emerging industries, new firms take tremendous risks, and many will fail. Some make reasonable bets and formulate sound strategies but still bet on the wrong scenario. Others are too inexperienced and make mistakes or cannot acquire the resources they need to succeed. Others simply choose the wrong strategy. For many reasons, they are winnowed out. The survivors manage to avoid the problems that doomed their less fortunate rivals. *Ex post*, it is clear that the survivors placed winning bets and followed better strategies. As a result, these older firms will have a lower mortality rate in the future than did the entire cohort of new firms.[5]

This process by which the winning approach emerges resembles the variation-selection-retention evolutionary processes described in Chapter 5. There the concern was with evolutionary change within the firm (and organizational learning, in particular); here the focus is on industry evolution. Nonetheless, the underlying process is similar. Here, the many approaches to technological, market, organizational, and strategic options that firms adopt are the "variation" in evolutionary processes. The environmental fitness of the many different varieties is uncertain. The winnowing out of these varieties as the market separates the more fit from the less fit is a process of "selection." Market forces select the variations that will succeed in the particular demand and supply environment. For example, it becomes apparent that consumers prefer a product and/or a product proves to be less costly to produce. The selection may not be purely "technological" in the sense that the best design wins. Rather, the design for which demand is greatest will win.

"Retention" occurs when the winning approaches emerge and the surviving firms imitate the more successful features of their rivals' approaches. In addition, new entrants that now understand what makes for success in the industry and believe they are well positioned to compete on that basis will imitate the successful incumbents. The success of particular organizational and strategic approaches gives rise to what organizational ecologists call a process of legitimation. Entrants can obtain the resources they need to enter by pointing to other firms that already have succeeded. At the same time, mavericks find it harder to obtain the resources they need to compete because a successful paradigm has been established. Accordingly, the "winning" approaches are "retained" and perpetuated. There is much less variety among the survivors than among the original contenders.

Selection produces a strategic and a technological paradigm. As the emergent phase ends, the characteristics of the new market become apparent. How firms will compete becomes clear, and uncertainty diminishes. The emergence of a "dominant design" often resolves technological uncertainty. A dominant design is the technological approach that becomes the accepted industry solution. Sometimes this is embodied in formal industry standards, but more often an informal consensus develops. So, for example, the gasoline engine became the standard for the automobile industry. Firms that backed the losing design usually cannot switch to the dominant design, and so they often go under.

---

[5] See Glenn R. Carroll and Michael T. Hannan, *The Demography of Corporations and Industries* (Princeton, NJ: Princeton University Press, 1999).

## Growth

As the emergent stage ends, a consensus forms about both the technology and the kinds of organizational structures and strategies that will succeed. The locus of competition begins to shift from vision and acquiring resources to production and distribution. Innovation remains important, but the focus of research and development shifts from product to process innovation and/or from fundamental to incremental innovation. The winners in the growth stage are the firms that produce the most attractive products within the class of products that won out during the emergent phase. As competition shifts to efficient execution, costs and prices fall. Lower prices and product refinements expand the market, and scale and learning economies emerge. The consolidation that began in the emergent stage with the shake-out of losing firms continues. The firms that have the most effective strategies and the best implementation gobble up or drive out less effective competitors in a push to spread best practices and exploit firm-level economies of scale. The growth rate of successful firms soars.

Competition among the successful firms is muted by the growth of industry demand. Because the market is growing rapidly, a firm does not need to steal customers from competitors in order to grow. It can achieve very high performance by solidifying its position in the market. There is little need for it to attack competitors who appeal to other segments or even to fight fiercely for each customer with firms offering very similar products. Incumbent firms benefit from demand growth because it allows increased sales without the reduced margins generated by intense competition.

The growth fueling the profits of incumbents attracts new entrants but enables incumbents and newcomers to coexist. Although the established incumbents are more durable on average, many new entrants also thrive. One way new entrants succeed even when the industry is populated with large, successful firms is that the incumbents leave unfilled niches for the entrants to occupy. Each established firm develops a well-defined strategic scope, and its growth comes primarily from the growth of that segment of the market. Its profitability derives from reaping economies of scale and learning how to attract and serve customers within its chosen strategic scope. As the market grows, however, so do pockets of demand where the buyers have slightly different needs from those the incumbents serve well. Incumbents have advantages over entrants when new customers have the same preferences as existing customers. But entrants may be better positioned to serve customers with different needs. For example, new buyers may need a different channel or require a different set of complementary products or services. A new firm that does not have commitments to existing channels or a well-established product line might adopt these new business models more readily.

Although firm concentration often increases during the growth stage, entry and exit continue throughout the industry life cycle. In a study of many industries in all phases of the life cycle, researchers found that among the large participants in an industry in a given year, 39 percent were not industry participants five years earlier and 40 percent will no longer be industry participants five years later.[6]

---

[6] Dunne, Roberts, and Samuelson, "Patterns of Firm Entry and Exit in U.S. Manufacturing Industries," *Rand Journal of Economics*, Vol. 19, Winter 1988, 495–515.

In the growth phase, the general manager's focus shifts from exploration and competition among technological and market paradigms to solidifying and exploiting an established competitive advantage. In this phase, the role of strategy is more consistent with the view expressed in Chapter 2: Strategy helps managers make decisions based on their understanding of the firm's external environment and internal assets. In the growth stage, the domain of the firm is well defined and the characteristics of competition have become apparent, so the strategy is oriented toward the current, rather than the anticipated, environment. However, because rapid growth in demand is the hallmark of this stage, the strategy must include some blueprint to help the firm increase both the market and its share of it. To do this, the strategy must deal with the potential threat from new entrants as well as the current competition from incumbents.

## Maturity and Decline

The mature phase of the industry life cycle exhibits greater stability than either the emergence or growth stages. Continued consolidation, through mergers and acquisitions among the major firms, often accompanies the transition from growth to maturity. When the industry reaches maturity, the entrenched market leaders have well-established positions and fairly stable market shares. Innovation tends to be incremental, refining and improving what is already there. Firms focus on maintaining their competitive advantage within their established domains. This is the classic role of an "exploiter" organization discussed in Chapter 5.

The U.S. beer industry shows a typical pattern of consolidation. Table 11-1 illustrates the dramatic increase in the market shares of the leading firms from 1947 to 1992. The largest 5 and largest 10 firms accounted for only 19 percent and 28 percent of the market, respectively, in 1947, but by 1992 their shares had risen to 88 percent

**TABLE 11-1**  Company and Plant Concentration, 1947–1992

| Year | Independent Companies[a] | Separate Plants[a] |
| --- | --- | --- |
| 1947 | 404 | 465 |
| 1954 | 262 | 310 |
| 1958 | 211 | 252 |
| 1963 | 150 | 211 |
| 1967 | 124 | 153 |
| 1974 | 57 | 107 |
| 1978 | 44 | 96 |
| 1983 | 35 | 73 |
| 1986 | 33 | 67 |
| 1989 | 29 | 61 |
| 1992 | 29 | 58 |

[a] Excludes microbreweries of less than 10,000-barrel capacity.
*Source:* Kenneth K. Elzinga, "Beer," Chapter 5 in *The Structure of American Industry*, 9th ed. Walter Adams and James Brock, eds. (New York: Prentice Hall, 1995), 119–152, at 130.

and 93 percent! Excluding microbreweries (firms with capacities under 10,000 barrels a year), the number of companies plunged from 404 to 29, even though demand was growing (slowly) for most of this period. The number of plants with capacities in excess of 10,000 barrels per year also fell from 465 to 58, and the typical plant grew larger. Table 11-2 illustrates this growth in plant size.

Plants became large in order to exploit economies of scale in production. Fewer production locations, however, imply that beer has to be transported over greater distances. The declining cost of transportation and the development of refrigeration in this period made that possible. Although economies of scale in production and improved transportation technology explain larger plants, they do not account for the concentration of sales in the hands of a few large firms. If a separate firm owned each of the 58 plants, the largest 10 would have a share well below 93 percent. Instead, the largest firms own many large plants, and a combination of brand reputation, economies in distribution, and economies in national brand promotion appears to be driving concentration in this industry.

The trend toward concentration of market share among fewer firms with larger plants, large distribution networks, and well-established brand names masks another important trend in this industry: the rise of the microbreweries. Although the number of firms with capacities in excess of 10,000 barrels a year continued to decline, the *total* number of firms, including microbreweries, started to grow again in the mid-1980s and surged to more than 800 by 2000. The rise of the microbreweries is typical of the growth in the number of firms that often occurs in an industry after a period of steady consolidation: entry rises.

The increase in the number of firms in the beer industry is both less and more important than it appears. It is less important because microbreweries, though numerous, have only a tiny share of overall output. It is more important because it illustrates that new entrants often accomplish major innovation in mature industries. As we shall explore in greater detail later in this section, although established firms excel within the current modes of competition, they are often set in their ways and blinded to new opportunities and ways of doing things.

**TABLE 11-2**  Surviving Breweries by Capacity, 1959–1992

| Listed Capacity Barrels (000's) | 1959 | 1963 | 1967 | 1971 | 1975 | 1979 | 1983 | 1986 | 1989 | 1992 |
|---|---|---|---|---|---|---|---|---|---|---|
| 10–100 | 68 | 54 | 36 | 21 | 10 | 10 | 15 | 13 | 8 | 8 |
| 101–500 | 91 | 72 | 44 | 33 | 19 | 13 | 12 | 8 | 7 | 7 |
| 501–1000 | 30 | 33 | 35 | 32 | 13 | 8 | 2 | 3 | 3 | 3 |
| 1001–2000 | 18 | 17 | 18 | 21 | 13 | 11 | 13 | 10 | 5 | 5 |
| 2001–4000 | 8 | 10 | 10 | 12 | 12 | 13 | 9 | 10 | 6 | 5 |
| 4001+ | 2 | 3 | 4 | 7 | 15 | 20 | 23 | 23 | 20 | 22 |

*Source:* Kenneth K. Elzinga, "Beer," Chapter 5 in *The Structure of American Industry*, 9th ed., Walter Adams and James Brock, eds. (New York: Prentice Hall, 1995), 119–152, at 124.

In the mature phase, the failure rate is much higher among new entrants than among older, established firms. This is another example of the "liability of newness." The liability, however, is not youth itself. It arises because an older firm is more insulated from competition than a newer firm because the older firm is larger and has a more established market position. Age itself does not necessarily improve a firm's probability of survival. Carroll and Hannan report that in 21 industries, older firms were more likely to survive than younger ones in only 12 of them, once size was taken into account.[7] In this instance, older is not necessarily wiser.

Eventually, industry demand declines. Some local markets decline because the number of buyers falls, and others because buyers' tastes change. The demand for baby food, for example, grew explosively with the baby boom after World War II and then declined when these children moved on to solid food. However, most industries decline because new technologies lead to substitute products or services that consumers prefer. The buggy and buggy whip industries fell victim to the automobile, vinyl records to compact disks, and so on. Whatever the cause, firms can face a rapidly dwindling demand for their products and services.

There are two common, but often misguided, responses to finding oneself in an industry in which demand is declining. One is to exit immediately in the belief that declining industries must be unprofitable. This is not true. Decline can be profitable for incumbent firms. Makers of vacuum tubes, a product that semiconductor technologies completely replaced, earned a good return in the waning days of the industry. Had these firms been driven by sales growth, they might have abandoned this industry, sacrificing high margins for growth.

The other common mistake is to stay in as long as possible, fighting fiercely to maintain sales volume. With demand declining, PIE will also necessarily decline. If the firms in the industry don't accept a decline in sales volume, and instead intensify their competition, the *share* of PIE they retain will also fall. Staying in is profitable when the major players recognize that decline in sales volume is inevitable and therefore refrain from frantic competition to maintain volumes. This is more likely when all the firms recognize that the decline is permanent. If firms mistakenly think that the decline is just a temporary downturn, they may fight for market share. Their impulse is to take what they consider temporary losses, so that they can be in a better position when demand recovers. Once they recognize that demand will not recover, they have irrevocably lost an opportunity to be profitable.

If the incumbent firms have low exit costs, competition for the shrinking PIE also tends to be milder. As demand declines, some firms have to exit if the remaining firms are to be profitable. Exit costs dissuade firms from taking capacity out of the industry even when (without these costs) it would be profitable for them to do so. Exit costs can take several forms. Firms may have assets that have no (or much lower) value outside the current industry. Specialized plants or equipment, for example, may have little value outside its current use. Investment in assets that have no other (valuable) use is called "sunk" costs, and sunk costs create exit costs.

[7] Ibid.

Sometimes connections with another industry create exit costs. Water meter companies in the United States, for example, relied on a particular kind of hard rubber as an input. Because other industries had little demand for this product, no independent U.S. manufacturers stayed in the hard rubber business. The water meter companies, however, were willing to subsidize a hard rubber manufacturer to maintain the source of supply. The commitment of top managers to the line of business can also create an exit cost. The Polaroid Corporation, for example, maintained a large commitment to instant photography long after its decline became evident partly because Polaroid's founder was reluctant to accept the demise of the technology.

Once growth rates slow and the industry enters the mature or declining phases, a firm's ability to maintain its competitive advantage determines its ability to survive and prosper. The cushioning effects of growth that might allow a less efficient firm to do reasonably well or mask a weakness in the quality of the firm's product line are gone. Any competitive deficiencies will take a severe toll. The manager's task is to deepen competitive advantage and manipulate the competitive environment to avoid intense competition. A firm must always be ready for a full-scale competitive battle but should try not to trigger intense competition. Uncertainty is relatively low, and successful firms are consummate exploiters.

## 11.5  THE EVOLUTION OF INDUSTRY ORGANIZATION

As the industry moves through its life cycle, so, often, does the organization of its value chain. Recall that auto "manufacturers" began largely as assemblers of standardized components that other firms produced. The automobile firms neither owned the component producers nor required that most components be customized. Later on, the automakers produced many components in-house or required another firm to produce them under long-term contract to their custom specifications. In contrast, vertically integrated firms initially designed and produced new desktop printers for personal computers. The few outsourced components were produced to the specifications of the printer manufacturer.

### Horizontal vs. Vertical Organization

At any point in time, the production and assembly of components can be organized in two general ways. In one, independent firms produce standardized components, which an assembler (who may also produce some components) then combines. This is a "horizontally" organized industry. In the other, a single firm orchestrates the overall design, manufacture, and assembly. Although some components may be subcontracted, a single firm controls the architecture of the product and the specification of component characteristics. This is a "vertically" organized industry.

Andy Grove, CEO of Intel, first used "vertical" and "horizontal" to describe the change in the organization of the computer industry's value chain as the industry moved from dominance by mainframe computers to dominance by desktop computers.[8] Figure 11-4 illustrates the mainframe era: Large vertically integrated firms like IBM were responsible for almost everything that went into producing and using the computer, from the design and production of hardware components to providing service on the customers' premises. In contrast, Figure 11-5 illustrates the personal computer era: At least in its early years, the PC industry had a horizontal organization. Here each layer consists of firms competing to produce a different component used in the overall system. So, for example, the firms competing in the industry segment that produces microprocessors were not the same firms competing as computer assemblers or software suppliers.

Each of these ways of organizing the value chain has its strengths. The main advantage of the vertical form is that the components can be designed to work optimally together as a system. IBM not only supplied all the hardware and software for its mainframes; it also ensured that they comprised a working computer system. Mainframe users did not need to spend resources figuring out how to make the peripherals work with the computer or the software applications work with the operating system. When independent firms produce and assemble the components, making them work together may be more difficult, and a less-than-seamless fit may affect the performance of the final product. Moreover, when a single firm controls the architecture of the system, it can ensure that the components interface efficiently. In contrast, when a component must be designed to work with many other components in the adjacent

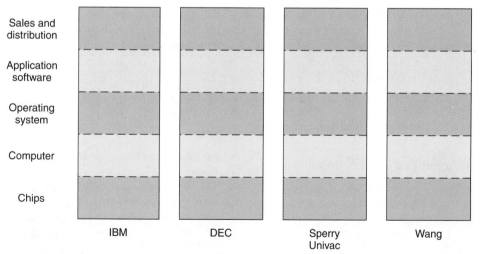

**FIGURE 11-4**  The "Old" Computer Industry

[8] See Andrew S. Grove, *Only the Paranoid Survive* (New York: Doubleday, 1996), as well as interviews in *Fortune* ("How Intel Makes Spending Pay Off," February 22, 1993, 56–61) and *The Wall Street Journal* ("Intel Plans to Consolidate Industry Lead with Salvo of Price Cuts," January 18, 1993, pp. B3 and B5).

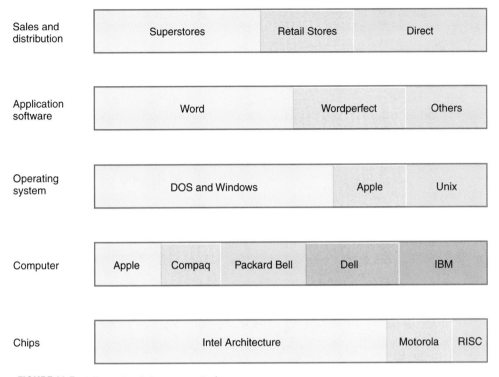

**FIGURE 11-5**  The "New" Computer Industry

"layers," a standardized interface must be developed and maintained, which can add costs to both layers.

In a horizontal organization, each segment of an industry can specialize in just one component and thus achieve the benefits of specialization. The small arms industry in the 1860s is a vivid example of how specialized a horizontally organized industry can be:

> The master gun-maker—the entrepreneur—seldom possessed a factory or workshop... Usually he owned merely a warehouse in the gun quarter, and his function was to acquire semi-finished parts and to give these out to specialized craftsmen, who undertook the assembly and finishing of the gun. He purchased materials from the barrel-makers, lock-makers, sight-stampers, trigger-makers, ramrod-forgers, gun-furniture makers, and, if he were engaged in the military branch, from bayonet-forgers. All of these were independent manufacturers executing the orders of several master gun-makers... Once the parts had been purchased from the "material-makers," as they were called, the next task was to hand them out to a long succession of "setters-up" each of whom performed a special operation in connection with the assembly and finishing of the gun. To name only a few, there were those who prepared the front sight and lump end of the barrel; the jiggers, who attended to the breach end; the stockers, who let in the barrel and lock and shaped the stock; the barrel-strippers, who prepared the gun for rifling and proof; the hardeners, polishers,

borers, and riflers, engravers, browners, and finally the lock-freers, who adjusted the working parts.[9]

A horizontal organization like this can increase the total value the chain creates. Independent specialists are often better at producing each part than a firm that produces multiple components would be. A firm that devotes all its energy to making gun barrels is likely to master the materials and manufacturing technology to produce this specific product efficiently. Although a firm could be organized with specialized divisions for each component, specialization and competition combine to make a horizontal structure perform well. If our barrel maker does not produce the desired product at the lowest possible cost, assemblers will buy barrels from competing barrel makers. Competition among specialized producers of a standardized product ensures that only the best products survive in the market. An integrated firm cannot easily replicate this effect. Even if it has independent divisions for each component, it cannot reproduce the effect of competition in-house. As a result, a series of horizontally organized specialists can perform better overall than a vertical system where each producer is likely to be a mediocre generalist, hobbled by at least one inferior internal component-producer.

The horizontally organized structure might also produce more value because of its superior ability to provide differentiated components from which assemblers can construct customized systems. When competing firms populate each layer, they typically vary in their capabilities and therefore in the kind of products they produce. This allows assemblers to select among components to build a differentiated system. Dell Computer attracts customers, for example, by presenting a menu of system options to its buyers from which they can "assemble" a customized computer tailored to their preferences. Dell can "mix and match" hardware and software from multiple vendors to provide this service. The specialized vendors can still realize economies of scale by selling to many assemblers. If Dell had to produce all its components in-house or under long-term contract, it would lose some of its flexibility and probably could not offer its buyers the same broad product menu.

Overall, then, there is a tradeoff between benefits to coordination and benefits to specialization and competition. When the benefits from coordination are higher, industries tend more toward the vertical system. When specialization benefits are higher, industries tend toward the horizontal system. At any point in time, most industries are between these two extremes. Typically, the assemblers control part of the component manufacture because the coordination gains are particularly high there. These same firms, however, may also purchase (or produce) many standardized components for which the gains from specialization are large. The auto manufacturers have never controlled tire production, for example, because the gain from specialization and competition is high in tires and the gain from coordination of this standardized product is low. But the automotive firms exert much greater control

---

[9] This account is from G. C. Allen, *The Industrial Development of Birmingham and the Black Country: 1860–1927* (London, 1929), quoted in George Stigler, "The Division of Labor Is Limited by the Extent of the Market," Chapter 12 in *The Organization of Industry* (Chicago: University of Chicago Press, 1968), 140.

over the production of engine controls where the gain to coordination is much higher.

Even when a horizontal structure would be more efficient, a kind of "chicken-and-egg" problem early in an industry life cycle could lead to a vertically organized industry. If the components for systems that the emerging industry produces have no other use, a firm in that industry may have to produce most components because no other market for the components exists. No firm was already making anything that could be used for electronic data storage before the computer was invented; no firm was making anything like ink jet printer heads before ink jet printers were developed. The first printer and computer firms had no place to go to find the components they needed. Not surprisingly, therefore, the early computer and printer industries were vertically organized. In other cases, some components for the new products are available elsewhere. The early automobile producers could turn to carriage makers to produce automobile bodies, for example. The manufacturers adapted many of the components, such as steering mechanisms and brakes, from horse-and-buggy era components.

Firms may also adopt a vertical organization initially because standardizing the interfaces among components takes time. When the dominant design of the system is not yet established, it is difficult to know exactly what the components will be, let alone have well-defined interfaces among them. As the industry evolves and certain designs become dominant, specialists can also emerge who focus on just one component of the dominant design.

The bicycle industry has gone through a vertical-to-horizontal cycle not once but twice.[10] In its early years—the mid-1800s—small, fully integrated firms in England, Germany, France, and the United States produced bicycles. By the late 1800s, demand had increased to a million bicycles a year. During this time, the industry settled on a single dominant design and shifted from vertical to horizontal organization as specialists emerged to produce each of the now standardized components. By around 1900 when demand peaked, there were over 300 bicycle producers, almost all of them assemblers of standardized components that specialists produced.

The arrival of the automobile sent this growth industry into decline. By 1905, industry demand for bicycles had fallen by three-quarters, and only 12 manufacturers survived. As the Depression of the 1930s further reduced demand, Schwinn decided to try stimulating demand by pursuing a unique, high-quality strategy. A better bicycle, however, required nonstandard parts. To obtain them, Schwinn had to move back toward "hand-in-glove" production with its suppliers in which a set of partnerships produced parts to order. Schwinn even brought the production of some previously outsourced parts back in-house. As Schwinn bicycles gained market share and dominated the industry, many competitors followed suit, and the pendulum swung back toward vertical organization.

In the 1990s, the mountain bike posed a new threat to industry incumbents. Demand for mountain bikes soared, but the leading manufacturers missed this trend

---

[10] This description of the bicycle industry is drawn from Fine, *Clock Speed*, ibid.

and their slow response opened the way for new entrants. Initially, enthusiasts built their own mountain bikes, often adding their own components to a sturdy frame from a much earlier generation bicycle. Initially, the structure of the mountain bike segment was largely horizontal. As the mountain bike segment grew, Shimano became the dominant component supplier. Most mountain bikes soon used Shimano brakes or gears. When the traditional manufacturers belatedly embraced the trend toward mountain bikes, they, too, relied on Shimano components. Shimano extended its dominance by bundling more and more of its components into subassemblies. Thus, for a while, the industry began to move back toward vertical organization. However, the vertical structure had been turned on its head, with the "component supplier" now the lynchpin of the value chain and the "manufacturer" a low value-added assembler and distributor.

As this example illustrates, the vertical organization of an industry tends to change as the industry evolves, but the pattern may be difficult to predict. Nonetheless, we can draw some general conclusions. First, early in the life of an industry, essential specialist component industries may not yet exist, so the pioneering firms have to undertake a broader range of activities than they would otherwise choose to do. So, even a firm that believes its capabilities relate to just one particular component of an overall system may have to produce (or develop relationships with other firms that produce for it) other components of the system. The bicycle industry provides two examples of this: at the outset of the industry, and later, when Schwinn set out to produce high-quality bicycles. Second, once the overall architecture of the system is established, new firms will be attracted to the production of particular components in which they believe that their own distinctive competencies give them a competitive advantage. Finally, periods of discontinuity in the industry's evolution tend to shake up its overall vertical organization. The advent of the mountain bike and the rise of Shimano provide an apt example.

## Organizational Implications of Industry Structure

The organization of an industry has implications for the organization of the firm, but the connection is less simple than one might think. If the industry is vertically organized, an incumbent firm may have to be vertically organized itself. If there are no independent suppliers for standardized components, the firm may have to control the production of components itself. Note, however, that this does not imply that the firm should be vertically integrated in the traditional sense. It need not *own* the component production capacity. It will, however, need to develop close working relationships with component suppliers and may need to create those suppliers. Because these suppliers typically won't be able to sell components to other firms, the contract with them will probably need to be long term and offer some protection for the investment they must make. The supplier who makes the investment to produce a part that only one firm will buy has to be concerned that its investment will be expropriated. As we noted in Chapter 10, the problem that assemblers of a coordinated system of customized components must overcome is asset specificity. Sometimes the best way to overcome the contracting problem is to produce the component in-house.

The connection between industry structure and firm organization is less tight in horizontally organized industries. When a firm competes in an industry that has well-developed horizontal layers, it has more choices about how to shape its relationships with its buyers and suppliers. For example, it can compete in a single layer, purchasing the best components available from supplying firms and selling a standardized product to buyers. This alternative allows the firm to achieve the benefits of specialization, but it must forgo the opportunity to improve its product by coordinating activities across layers.

Another alternative is to participate in multiple layers to achieve gains in coordination. It can contract with specialists within each horizontal layer, so that it can tightly coordinate their activities. The clothing industry, for example, has many specialized firms all along the value chain. Some clothing firms, however, are vertically organized. Benetton controls most elements of its value chain while actually performing few of these activities itself. For example, although Benetton is involved in styling (to ensure a "Benetton look") and dyeing (one of its core capabilities), and is responsible for global advertising and logistics (using a huge, fully automated distribution center in Italy), third parties under contract to Benetton perform many critical elements in the chain. Benetton does not conduct most design, manufacturing, and sales operations in-house. Although Schwinn's control of the vertical layers was less complete, it could procure many of the components it needed to produce high-quality bicycles from outside suppliers.

A firm that controls and coordinates the vertical supply chain within a horizontally organized industry while performing few of its activities itself is called a "vertical architect." Vertical organization allows the firm to gain the full benefits of coordination but prevents it from reaping the benefits of specialization and competition in the segments. The vertical architect, on the other hand, can select the most suitable vendors at each horizontal stage rather than have to purchase from an in-house division that may not be the best supplier. It can therefore avoid becoming a mediocre generalist whose products are hurt by weak components. Vertical architects have the freedom to scan—often globally—for the most efficient providers in each link of the value chain. What they do in-house is to carefully select, nurture, and manage a few core capabilities on which their distinctive competitive advantage depends. This is why Benetton has continued to perform the dyeing function that provides the vibrant colors that are its hallmark while it leaves other activities in which it has no competitive advantage to selected outside providers.

The vertical architect is well positioned to combine standardized and customized components. It can buy the best components at the best price from independent, competing specialists that produce standardized products. To secure the components that depend on coordination for their value, it can create a contractual relationship with specific vendors or produce the components in-house. In doing so, it may face the same asset specificity problems endemic to the vertically organized industry, but it can be much more selective about when to take on these problems. In short, it can incur the costs of control only when the benefits justify those costs.

On-going improvements in information technology may make the vertical architect approach more common than it has been. By lowering the costs of transacting, information technology makes it easier for the vertical architect to coordinate its suppliers. The dramatic increase in interfirm transactions through the Internet testifies to the ability of information technology to facilitate transactions across firms. Although this probably means that the vertical architect model will be more prevalent, the advances in information technology have also improved coordination *within* the firm. Global firms can coordinate specialized divisions more efficiently now than they could before. With improvements in both in-house and interfirm coordination, we cannot be certain that the vertical architect model will dominate industry organization.

## 11.6  MANAGING STRATEGIC CHANGE

Changes in information technology, the globalization of firms and supply chains, and the increasingly rapid pace of technological change in many industries mean that the external context of many firms is changing rapidly. Firms must adapt by finding new sources of competitive advantage and new ways to organize their assets. To handle these transitions, managers must understand the firm's current position and define where they want the firm to go even while its environment is changing. This means making fundamental decisions about the direction of the firm while its new environment is still unclear. Once managers know what changes they want to make, they must communicate the need for change to others in the firm and establish the process that will lead the firm to its new position. In this section, we review some of the challenges managers face in managing change.

It is difficult to effect strategic change within an established firm. Often managers at established firms are slow to recognize change around them and are reluctant or unable to change. The challenges for a general manager are to understand that change is necessary, decide what kind of change should be made, reformulate the firm's strategy, and reorganize its strategic assets—all the while getting the buy-in from others within the firm that is necessary to implement the envisioned change. Any manager who has attempted to change a firm knows how difficult all this can be. Managers who have experienced dramatic external change also know that they cannot avoid the challenge of managing change. No firm can remain an industry leader over the long run without changing its strategy and organization.

### Overcoming the Barriers to Strategic Change

When the firm's external context changes profoundly, the capabilities and market positions that led it to be successful in the old order need not carry over to the next. Schumpeter refers to the process by which generations of innovations rise, decline, and are replaced as "creative destruction"—creative because of the innovations that fuel the new phase and destruction because new capabilities destroy the old ones that had supported prior successes. This process is also called punctuated equilibria because periods of ferment, innovation, and change interrupt (punctuate) periods of order and stability (equilibria).

For an existing firm with a well-defined strategy in its current domain, these disruptions create a major challenge. Indeed, many leaders have failed to make the transition to the new order:

- Although Swiss firms dominated the watch industry, Japanese firms were the first to exploit quartz technology.
- The transition from electronic products based on vacuum tubes to electronics based on semiconductors resulted in complete turnover of market leadership in the electronics component industry.
- Although IBM was the dominant firm in the era of mainframe computers, the fledgling Apple Computer was the first to achieve major success in the market for personal computers.
- The rotary kiln transformed the process for making portland cement in the 1890s, leading to a dramatic turnover in cement producers in a four-year period.
- With each new generation of disk drives—as the diameter shrank from 14 inches to 8 inches, to 5.25 inches, to 3.5 inches—the incumbent firms stumbled and relative newcomers became the industry leaders.

Despite the many examples of firms failing to compete effectively when major environmental shifts occurred, the failure of established firms is not inevitable. Indeed, many established firms have made successful transitions:

- Merck has remained a major player in the pharmaceutical industry despite substantive change in how new drugs are discovered and developed.
- DuPont has maintained its position in the chemical industry over a long period in which the underlying technologies have changed dramatically.
- U.S. automobile manufacturers have integrated electronics in both production processes and products while remaining major contenders for world leadership in automobiles.

Why do some leading firms manage strategic change successfully and others fail? It is tempting to conclude that each failure is the result of poor management. But these firms dominated the old order, and it is unlikely that poorly managed firms could achieve and maintain market leadership. Indeed, many of them are acknowledged to be well managed.

Generally, failure arises not from poor management but from a poor fit between the strategy and organization the firm had in place to perform well in the old environment and the strategy and organization that it needs to succeed in the new order. Returning to the language of explorers and exploiters that we introduced in Chapter 5, we can say that the incumbent firms were well managed to make products within, and innovate incrementally in, their existing domains, not to explore new domains. Some analysts claim that a steadfast focus on performing well in the existing market against the current competitors *causes* successful incumbent firms to miss market shifts. James March, for example, refers to a "competence trap": Firms that strive for competence within a given strategy sometimes are trapped in it and miss the opportunity for strategic change.[11]

The competence trap exists because firms that are successful doing predictable things under stable conditions develop routines and procedures that make them good at what they do. As the routines become increasingly well adapted to the current environment, they are less generalizable and less appropriate for tackling new problems. Furthermore, the routines tend to become less well articulated as they get built into how the firm operates and how it views itself and its environment. The firm becomes more successful at what it does but less and less able to do anything else.

These routines and procedures include:

- Promotion and hiring routines that select people who operate well in the existing, stable environment but who may be uncomfortable taking risks or entering new areas.

- Incentives that reward individuals and units for maximizing profits from the existing business rather than encouraging investment for the long term in new technologies.

- Capital budgeting systems that seek to minimize risk and focus only on the "types of projects that we know will make us money."

- Organizational structures that hinder the cross-functional and cross-organizational learning that can be fundamental to innovation.

- Personal commitment to the current strategy that arises from specialized investment in human capital or a culture that exalts persistence and loyalty.

Although these routines and procedures help the firm to do what it knows how to do—often turning out a high volume of a product line that it understands well to an established line of customers—they can inhibit recognizing or introducing major innovation.

If competence always implies inability to change, why do some firms perform well through cycles of change? Perhaps because not all major changes are alike. Indeed, scholars have identified factors that affect the likelihood that new winners will displace established leaders at times of major change.

One key factor is whether the required change is competence enhancing or competence destroying. The competence trap is unlikely to hinder incumbents when technological change is incremental and enhances existing capabilities. In those settings, the very routines that make those firms successful are likely to lead them to embrace the new technologies. However, when radical technological change destroys currently valued competences, incumbents are more likely to fall victim to the competence trap.[12] This suggests, for example, that the transition to digital photography will

[11] See James G. March, "Exploration and Exploitation in Organization Learning," *Organization Science* 2 (1991), 71–87.

[12] See Michael L. Tushman and Philip Anderson, "Technological Discontinuities and Organizational Environments," *Administrative Science Quarterly* 31 (1986), 439–465.

be a major challenge for Kodak because its competitive advantage has been in film technologies that digital photography will make obsolete. When innovations are competence destroying, existing firms in other industries that happen to have the necessary capabilities might be more likely to carry the new technology forward. Similarly, new firms that have no established competence are more likely to embrace a new capability.

Recent work has also emphasized the importance of how the structure of technology interacts with the organizational structure of the firm. Clark and Henderson[13] argue that firms tend to be organized around their products' "components" or "modules." An automobile company, for example, might have a unit that develops brake systems and another that develops fuel injection. Fuel injection technology can change dramatically without affecting the brake system. In the Henderson–Clark terminology, a change that affects only one organizational unit would be a "modular change." However, as electronic controls moved from the component level (e.g., from electronic fuel injection) to controlling almost all of the automobile's functions, the structure of the system of components changed. Now, the same central processing unit in the car can (potentially) control brakes and fuel injection. The component development process at the brake and fuel injection facilities now have to be coordinated in a new way.

Henderson and Clark characterize the change that requires adaptation in multiple components as "architectural" and argue that it is much harder for firms to accomplish than modular changes. They present some examples of technological changes that were apparently incremental but defeated established industry leaders because the changes required organizational units to coordinate their activities. Two types of problems occur when firms face the need for architectural change. The most obvious is the one we have described: To adapt, the firm must reorganize its communication and coordination patterns. The less obvious problem is that the firm may have difficulty recognizing that a change has occurred because the change is happening at the boundaries of the established units. Firms that have built linking mechanisms among their organizational units may be less likely to stumble when they need to make an architectural change. Firms that frequently need to make architectural changes have used the mechanisms we described in Chapter 4 to confront this kind of problem. Hewlett-Packard, for example, has developed a corporate capability to combine the capabilities of its existing businesses in new business units that can meet emerging market needs.

Another line of research suggests that part of the competence trap lies in the network of relationships with the firm's customers.[14] One of the firm's competences lies in its ability to track and meet the needs of *existing* customers. The firm therefore

[13] See Rebecca M. Henderson and Kim B. Clark, "Architectural Innovation: The Reconfiguration of Existing Systems and the Failure of Established Firms," *Administrative Science Quarterly* 35 (1990), 9–30.

[14] This account of the disk drive industry is drawn from Clayton M. Christensen, *The Innovator's Dilemma* (Cambridge, Mass.: Harvard Business School Press, 1997), and Joseph L. Bower and Clayton M. Christensen, "Disruptive Technologies: Catching the Wave," *Harvard Business Review* (January–February 1999), 43–53.

tends to assess the market potential of new technologies based on the needs of its current customers. To avoid competing with established, incumbent firms, new entrants are more likely to seek customers that existing firms do not serve well. Their entry strategy often depends on finding unmet customer needs and uncovering new market segments. After they enter to serve those segments with a new technology, they are well positioned to serve the incumbent's established customer base as the virtues of the new technology become apparent.

For example, Seagate Technology was the leader in the market for 5.25-inch computer disk drives and was one of the early developers of the 3.5-inch format. But Seagate's existing customers showed no interest in the 3.5-inch drive, insisting on higher capacities. As a result, Seagate concentrated on the 5.25-inch drive. Its competitors, meanwhile, focused on selling to companies where small disk size was an advantage (portables and small desktop computers). Seagate had never served this segment and had vastly underestimated its potential market size. Conner Peripherals (whose founders included former Seagate employees) and Quantum dominated the 3.5-inch market and became leading figures in the disk drive industry.

Clay Christensen and others who have studied this phenomenon argue that established firms can avoid this form of competence trap by embedding projects to develop the new technologies in groups whose customers have a clear need for the new technology. Often these are smaller units in the firm who find concentrating on an emerging demand segment attractive. By focusing on a new market rather than the firm's main market, these groups avoid the inertia that the demands of the current customer base impose.

A competence trap based on established relationships within the organization or with existing suppliers and customers is consistent with a larger body of research in organizational sociology which argues that *where* an innovation is introduced can affect whether the organization adopts it. It might matter, for example, whether a change at a multinational firm is introduced first in the firm's large home market or in a small, new market. To analyze this issue, scholars describe organizations as a network of relationships among individuals. These networks tie together the individuals and those parts of the organization with which they are affiliated. As a result, some units within the organization are more tightly bound to one another than are others. Those units that have many ties to many parts of the organization are called the *core* of the organization, and the more autonomous units within the organization are the *periphery*. The core might serve the firm's home market and the periphery other geographic markets, for example.

Introducing a change at the core causes two conflicting effects. First, if it embraces the change, the core has the connections to encourage the periphery to adopt the change as well. Put the other way around, the core might not adopt even a successful innovation occuring in the periphery. This is an example of the old maxim that you cannot create change within an organization unless the senior managers buy into it. The senior managers are part of the core of the organization. Second, the core is more likely to resist change than is the periphery. The individuals in the core have ties to the rest of the organization and to its existing customers and suppliers. The core is therefore more sensitive to any resistance to the innovation. The core also contains the individuals who typically have the greatest investment in the status quo. They have much to lose if the innovation fails or if it succeeds so well that the core itself is transformed.

GM's handling of the Saturn division demonstrates these effects. The Saturn project had the backing of GM's top corporate management. In that sense, the core selected and sponsored it. But powerful constituencies within GM, primarily senior managers at the established divisions, also opposed the Saturn venture. Within these divisions were other core groups with considerable influence. To prevent these managers (and other well-connected opponents) from sabotaging or blocking the initiative, GM's corporate office decided to create a separate division for Saturn and to locate it far from GM's geographic center. As a result, the new division could adopt innovative practices that the older, established divisions of the firm would probably never have contemplated. Locating the project in the periphery led to greater innovation, and corporate backing gave it the resources it needed. This compromise, however, has not helped GM to diffuse the successful innovations produced at Saturn into the core of its established divisions.

The core and periphery concept illustrates a general dilemma faced by established firms wanting to pursue an opportunity that requires a fundamental change in their activities. On the one hand, the best reason for making a fundamental change is that it will benefit the existing organization. Connecting the new venture with the established firm, then, is important. For example, Seagate's strategic assets in disk drives could have been re-deployed to the next generation of products. On the other hand, even when synergies between the new ventures and the established activities of the firm exist, the change will impose costs on the current organization. As a result, the new venture may be more likely to succeed if it is insulated from the political processes in, and the inertia of, the parent company.

Fortunately, firms can organize a new venture in many ways to resolve this dilemma. The options available to the parent company range from establishing the new venture as a completely independent spinoff to fully integrating it with the firm's existing operations. Robert Burgelman suggests a framework for choosing among these options.[15] Figure 11-6 illustrates his approach. The axes of the figure are the two dimensions that he thinks are the most important determinants of how the venture should be organized. One dimension is the "strategic importance" of the new venture to the firm. He argues that ventures more central to the firm's strategy should be more integrated with the existing firm. In the extreme, if the firm's strategy absolutely depends on the success of the new venture, it may make sense to tie the venture more closely to the parent company.

For example, think about ventures to develop electric automobiles. Both Hewlett-Packard (HP) and General Motors have ventures in this emerging market. Clearly, electric cars are more closely related to GM's central strategy than to HP's. Many aspects of GM's approach to electric cars (pricing, distribution, advertising, etc.) have implications for gasoline cars. Moreover, success in electric cars directly affects its

[15] Robert A. Burgelman, "Designs for Corporate Entrepreneurship in Established Firms," *California Management Review* (1984), 154–166.

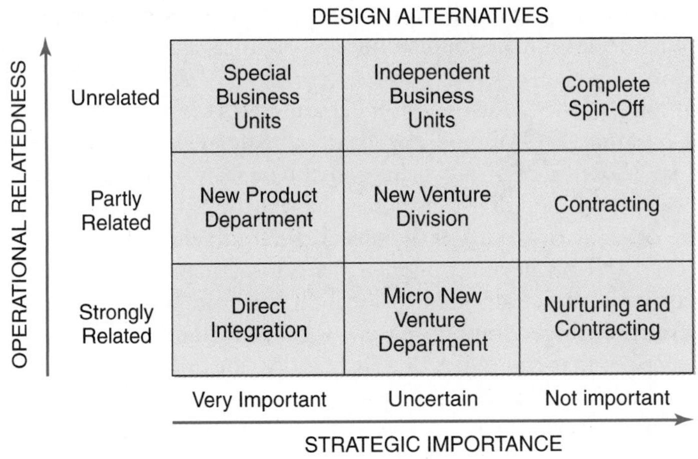

DESIGN ALTERNATIVES

| | | Very Important | Uncertain | Not important |
|---|---|---|---|---|
| OPERATIONAL RELATEDNESS | Unrelated | Special Business Units | Independent Business Units | Complete Spin-Off |
| | Partly Related | New Product Department | New Venture Division | Contracting |
| | Strongly Related | Direct Integration | Micro New Venture Department | Nurturing and Contracting |

STRATEGIC IMPORTANCE

**FIGURE 11-6**   Organization Designs for Corporate Entrepreneurship

strategic flexibility in gasoline cars because regulatory authorities set emissions allowances based on the performance of the firm's entire fleet of cars. HP's computer and printer businesses are largely unrelated to the technology, manufacture, or distribution of electric cars.

The electric car venture is also closely related to GM's primary business in an operational sense. For example, the electric car venture can exploit GM's know-how in body design, sourcing, and/or manufacture of many parts that electric cars share with gasoline cars, marketing know-how, and so on. Operational relatedness, the second dimension in the Burgelman framework, is much weaker for HP.

Putting the two dimensions together provides the set of prescriptions shown in Figure 11-6. Note that on the diagonal as both strategic and operational relatedness decline, the prescription changes from direct integration of the new venture division to complete spinoff. This seems reasonable: A new venture division may enable the parent company to leverage synergies with existing operations and to align the venture's activities with the firm's overall strategy, while insulating the new venture from the political and inertial forces in the company.

This framework is a useful starting point for deciding how to organize a new venture. However, many other variables need to be taken into account. The framework focuses on the structural features of the firms' architecture but neglects the other elements of the firm's ARC that might be critical to success in the new venture. For example, many successful new ventures in electronic commerce are start-ups with a distinctive culture. Their employees are young, work long hours, interact and dress casually (shoes, for example, are often discretionary), and so on. They are typically compensated with low base salaries but attractive stock options. Some of the desirable performance features that such organizations exhibit are great creativity and rapid speed to market. However, many established companies have difficulty accommodating such a "subculture" alongside a more traditional culture and yet cannot compete for the best talent without accommodating it. If the ARC that works for the new venture and the one that works for the established firm conflict, the parent firm may want to isolate the new venture even when it is operationally and strategically related to the existing firm.

## Managing Under Uncertainty: Scenario Analysis

However the venture is organized within the firm, the firm's managers will have to decide how much to invest, what technologies to pursue, what features the final product should have, what level of manufacturing capacity is appropriate, what initial market segments to target, and so forth. These decisions have to be made in an environment of tremendous uncertainty. To make them, the managers need some sense about what direction the industry will take. As discussed earlier, this is difficult to have in an emerging industry. It can also be hard in an established industry that is changing significantly. In the end, the manager's understanding of the industry and of the innovation is the basis for making educated guesses. There is no way to eliminate the uncertainty.

Tools are available, however, for approaching the decision problem systematically and, in particular, for discussing the decisions within the strategy formulation process.[16] Scenario planning is a tool that enables managers to see how their strategies are likely to perform and to conduct robustness tests and construct contingency plans. A scenario is an internally consistent, possible industry future—that is, a plausible picture of what the industry might look like in the future.

For example, a firm competing in the retail book industry might consider several scenarios, including the following two:

*Scenario 1:* Most book buyers can and do buy books on-line. On-line book sites capture the lion's share of retail book sales for books of all kinds. Two or three firms dominate on-line sales.

*Scenario 2:* Less than 20 percent of book buyers purchase books on-line. They restrict their on-line book purchases to a fairly narrow set of "popular books." There is only one dominant on-line book seller.

Clearly, many scenarios are possible. We have used just three variables to construct these examples: how many buyers purchase on-line, the range of books purchased on-line, and the structure of the on-line industry. We could construct many other scenarios by using other combinations of these variables or by considering other variables, for example, the adoption of on-line publishing.

Most managers can only handle three or four scenarios. The scenarios should serve the specific purposes of the firm developing them. That is, scenarios that are

---

[16] One approach to dealing with uncertainty is the decision tree. This involves mapping out all the possible things that can happen, assigning probabilities and payoffs to each possible path, and choosing the actions that yield the highest expected payoff. This approach is useful for structured decisions where a small number of variables are involved. However, it can become unwieldy in complex situations.

useful for one firm might not be useful for another firm in the same industry and vice versa. The goal in constructing the scenarios is to represent the future through a few plausible vignettes. Accordingly, the vignettes should be distinct, and the variables that are used to construct them should be those for which significant variation will affect the success of any strategy the firm pursues. If the scenarios are irrelevant to the strategic success of the firm, they will be useless in evaluating strategies.

Once developed, scenarios can serve several purposes. They can provide common language for the management team, and they can also provide a way to interpret and communicate about new events that affect the industry. For example, as events unfold, they make certain scenarios more likely and others less so. However, the main virtue of scenarios is in evaluating potential strategic options.

Managers can assess how each strategic option will fare in each scenario and thus how robust the strategy is for a range of possible industry developments. They can combine this information with their assessment of the likelihood of each scenario to evaluate the risks and rewards of each strategy. A strategy that maximizes the expected value of profits for a firm will rarely do well in all scenarios, however. A strategy that is focused and internally consistent will often involve placing a big bet on one, or a small subset, of the scenarios.

Firms that try to cover all possible scenarios may be spread too thin to do well in all circumstances. The point of testing a strategic option against all the scenarios is not to ensure that the strategy will do well in all circumstances, for few strategies will. Rather, the point is to be aware of the risks that the firm is taking and to identify the scenarios in which the strategy will do well. This is particularly important when innovation is a winner-take-all race. Pharmaceutical research, for example, where patents protect innovations, has a winner-take-all flavor. In circumstances where having a first-mover advantage matters, a competitive advantage in discovery is obviously important.

Similarly, when a dominant design is likely to arise, deciding to pursue a different approach often makes sense despite the risks of backing the wrong design. A firm that just "follows the crowd" can reduce its risk, and managers who follow the crowd are usually not blamed for doing what others do; they can always claim that they were following best practice. Even if the "crowd" is right, however, all the firms in it will share the market. It therefore can make sense for a firm to risk an approach that few others are pursuing because the payoff if it "wins" will be greater.

Finally, scenario analysis can be used for contingency planning. Even as the firm bets on certain scenarios, it can develop plans for what to do if a different, less favorable, scenario emerges.

## Strategic Change: An Example

Before leaving this chapter, we provide a detailed example that illustrates many of the main points in this section. The example is from the photocopying industry and the relationship between Xerox and Fuji Xerox.[17] Fuji Xerox is a joint venture between

---

[17] This account draws heavily on the HBS case "Xerox and Fuji Xerox" N9-391–156.

Xerox and Fuji Photo Film that was formed in 1962. It is considered one of the most long-lived and successful joint ventures in existence.

Before forming the joint venture with Fuji, Xerox had already formed one with the Rank Organization in Europe. That joint venture, Rank Xerox, was to manufacture and market photocopiers primarily for the Japanese market. Rank Xerox then formed the joint venture with Fuji, largely because Japanese government regulations required that foreign companies either license their product to a Japanese company or form a joint venture with one. Fuji Xerox would have manufacturing and marketing rights for Xerox products in Japan. Xerox owned 50 percent of Rank Xerox, which in turn owned 50 percent of Fuji Xerox.

Xerox wanted Fuji Xerox to be only a manufacturing and marketing vehicle for products that Xerox engineers would design at its headquarters in Rochester, New York. Within Xerox, there was a strong belief that the engineering knowledge in Rochester far exceeded the engineering knowledge in the rest of the company and that any attempts at new product development outside the United States would waste resources.

Management at Xerox and at Fuji Xerox had different views about the types of copiers that should be developed. Xerox emphasized large, expensive, high-margin machines at the upper end of the copier market. Consistent with this focus, it canceled a number of development projects in the 1960s and 1970s for copiers in the low- and medium-sized segments of the markets. These cancellations troubled Fuji because its primary competitors in this market, companies like Ricoh and Canon, were successfully offering smaller products for the Japanese market. Even though the quality of these small machines was considerably lower than that of the larger machines, the higher cost of office space in Japan meant that these low-end machines were popular there.

Therefore, contrary to Xerox's worldwide strategy of focusing on the higher end market, and its intention that Fuji Xerox focus its resources on manufacturing and marketing products designed in Rochester, Fuji Xerox started its own product development efforts. These efforts, begun in the early 1970s, focused on the small- and medium-sized copier segments. As these products were coming to fruition, the worldwide copier market was changing. In the 1970s, many of Xerox's key patents expired, and it suddenly faced many new competitors. Moreover, around the world, Xerox's high-end machines were losing ground to the increasingly competitive small- and medium-sized copiers.

In 1978, Fuji Xerox offered to sell the copiers that it had developed to Rank Xerox and Xerox to counter some of the international competition. Over the next year, Rank Xerox purchased 25,000 machines from Fuji Xerox, the largest purchase order that it had ever made. Xerox chose not to buy any. Over that year, Rank Xerox was able to defend its market share, and Xerox's market share declined. Eventually, Xerox started to call on Fuji Xerox for help not only in product design, but in improving its manufacturing routines as well. This collaboration resulted in small- and medium-sized products that enabled Xerox to win back the market share that it had lost.

The example of the Fuji Xerox venture is notable for a number of reasons. First, as in the example of Seagate and the disk drives, Xerox was perhaps unduly focused on current customers. Fuji Xerox, on the other hand, was exposed to a different set of customer needs. Second, it was probably easier for engineers within Fuji Xerox to pursue an alternative copier strategy because they were not in the core of the Xerox organization. They were therefore less vulnerable to the competence trap of those who were focused on the large copier market. Third, the core of Xerox was able to absorb the benefits of the innovation that occurred in the periphery once it woke up to the need to do so. Finally, this example illustrates an important point that we will return to in Chapter 15. Fundamental strategic change often comes about in unplanned ways, at least unplanned by the corporate center. Strategic evolution occurs as managers in the middle of the organization take strategic initiatives that are outside the scope their senior managers intended.

## SUMMARY

In this chapter we have provided frameworks for thinking strategically about external change. We have distinguished between a natural evolution that most industries undergo over their life cycle and occasional episodes where underlying forces of supply and demand shift. The management challenges and required strategic-thinking skills are different for each kind of change and for each stage of industry evolution.

In the emergent stage of the industry life cycle, entrepreneurship, both in the sense of discovering new opportunities and in Schumpeter's sense of doing what needs to be done to succeed, is at a premium. Within established companies, the equivalent skill is likely to be more prevalent within explorer-type organizations. As the industry paradigm begins to solidify after a shake-out in which dominant designs or forms emerge, the stage is set for the winners to grow. Here the focus shifts toward successful exploitation. This trend continues as the industry matures and the basis of competition shifts to a few key attributes, such as cost or differentiation. The organization of the value chain also tends to change over time. Sometimes it has a vertical structure, and sometimes it has a horizontal one. Moreover, although the relationship of the structure to the stage of industry evolution can be hard to predict, the industry often starts with a vertical structure that gives way to a horizontal structure over time.

Unfortunately, as successful companies go through the latter stages of the industry life cycle, their success at exploitation often causes them to become inwardly focused and rigid and to fall into "competence traps." Firms that are successful in the long run will be those that manage to maintain a balance between exploiting current success and finding and taking advantage of possible sources of future success. In Chapter 15 we discuss how a firm's strategy processes can help it to strike this balance. First, however, we examine some special issues involved in managing markets that exhibit demand-side increasing returns.

# 12

# STRATEGY IN MARKETS WITH DEMAND-SIDE INCREASING RETURNS

## 12.1 INTRODUCTION

In the late 1970s, several young companies offered a new product called a "microprocessor," a semiconductor device that would become the processing unit for desktop computers. Among the leading contenders in this emerging market were Intel and Zilog. By 1998, Intel had net revenues of $26 billion and net income of $6 billion. Only six public companies in the world had higher profits that year. Zilog, a privately held company, had 1998 revenues of $205 million and announced its first operating profit in two years. "Intel" is a household name, even though many of us don't understand what it sells. "Zilog" is a name that only firms purchasing electronic components recognize.

This tale of big winners and big losers is common in high-tech markets, particularly in the fields of computers and telecommunications. These are often "winner-takes-all" markets that a single firm eventually dominates, even though initially several well-positioned rivals heavily contested them. In Chapter 11, we noted that many industries experience a period of consolidation after the emergent phase of their life cycle. However, this pattern is much more pronounced in high-technology markets where an underlying product characteristic accentuates it: *The product's benefits to each user increase along with the number of other users.* As a result, consumers or firms choosing among alternative products want to choose the one that others are choosing. It is this phenomenon that propelled Intel's stellar performance and Zilog's stagnation. As more computer firms adopted Intel's microprocessor standard, the Intel family became increasingly attractive to all computer firms, and the Zilog family became relatively unattractive.

Buyer preferences in markets with this characteristic are different from those for more conventional products. For many products or services, a buyer is worse off if everyone else wants what she wants. For example, when she goes to a movie, she might prefer that others choose to attend at another time so that she can get a good seat in the theatre. For many other goods, users simply don't care how many others use it.[1] The products or services we are considering here, however, exhibit increasing returns to the size of the user population: The more people who use them, the *more* valuable they are.

This phenomenon has several labels: demand-side increasing returns, demand-side economies of scale, network externalities, network effects, or positive feedback economics. We prefer the term *demand-side increasing returns* (DSIR) because the phenomenon does not always involve a network. The following quotation from Bill Gates, CEO of Microsoft, who uses the label "network externalities," illustrates the strategic importance of DSIR:

> We look for opportunities with network externalities—where there are advantages to the vast majority of consumers to share a common standard. We look for businesses where we can garner large market shares, *not just 30%–35%.*[2]

Microsoft's strategy is to offer products that have DSIR and find ways to be the "big winner."

Because the DSIR phenomenon is central to the strategies of firms in many important industries, we devote this chapter to exploring how they affect the performance of competing firms. We begin by explaining the sources of DSIR. We then explore how they affect the nature of competition, and we discuss their implications for competition among systems of components. Next, we examine their impact on the adoption of a new technology. In the last section we discuss nonmarket standard-setting processes.

## 12.2 SOURCES OF DEMAND-SIDE INCREASING RETURNS (DSIR)

The benefits underlying DSIR are associated with compatibility and networks. Compatibility means that the products others use "work" with the product you use. A sparkplug is compatible with many engines; CDs can be played in most kinds of CD players. Networks facilitate transactions among users by connecting them to each other.

### Compatibility Benefits

The benefits of compatibility are familiar to anyone who uses a computer. Computer users want to share files and programs with others and to use the same applications and peripherals on different computers. They value *compatibility* among computers, applications, and peripherals. For example, someone who uses Microsoft Word can share documents more easily when everyone else also uses Microsoft Word. Compat-

---

[1] Of course, for all products, increasing demand (holding supply constant) tends to drive up prices. For simplicity, we ignore this pricing effect in this chapter and focus on cases where, implicitly, the positive effect of more users is stronger than the pricing effect.

[2] *Microsoft, 1995,* HBS Case 9-795-147, by Tarun Khanna and David Yoffie. Italics added.

ibility benefits imply that *standardization* has benefits. Each user of Word benefits from its status as the word processing standard.

The benefits of compatibility are by no means limited to the computer industry. Some other examples are:

- **Cameras and lenses.** For cameras with interchangeable lenses, the lens must be compatible with the lens mount on the camera body. Lens mounts are not standardized; a Nikon, Canon, or Minolta lens is usually not compatible with a camera that one of the other manufacturers makes. Independent lens manufacturers therefore have to make either different lenses for different cameras or lenses with interchangeable mountings.

- **VCRs and tapes.** The VCR will only play a tape of a particular format. VHS, beta, and 3/4″ are mutually incompatible formats. As anyone who rented videos when both VHS and beta had significant market shares can attest, the movie you wanted seemed only to be available in the format your home machine couldn't play! Through VHS's current dominance of this market, consumers can reap the benefits of standardization.

- **Typewriter keyboards.** Typewriter keyboards are an interesting example because the way we have "wired our brains" to find keys as we learned to type creates compatibility here. We have made ourselves compatible with the keyboard. In English-language countries, the standard keyboard is "QWERTY" (named after the first six letters on the left top row). Computer makers have offered other keyboard configurations but have not found many buyers for them.

- **Wrenches, nuts, and bolts.** Nuts and bolts must not only be of the same size, but must also have compatible threads. Wrenches must be of the same size as the nuts and the heads on the bolts. Although most countries have adopted standards to deal with this problem, these standards have not been harmonized across all countries.

- **Railway gauges**. Railroad cars and tracks must have compatible gauges. Because rail systems initially served only specific geographic regions, different regions adopted different gauges. This became a serious problem when these regional networks had to be integrated. In the United States, railways typically unloaded and reloaded freight at points where the gauge changed. Other countries developed rail carriages with adjustable wheel gauges. In the late 1800s, the U.S. rail system was finally harmonized by stopping train traffic, while thousands of workers adjusted the track gauges to a standard width. Switzerland still has a few local train routes where the gauge changes.

- **Language.** Europeans have long borne the cost of the lack of a common language, and firms that operate in multiple countries also increasingly have to bear these costs.

Compatibility benefits are so ubiquitous that these examples only scratch the surface. Autos and auto parts, bicycles and bicycle parts, electric current and outlets, and printers and ink cartridge are a few of the many other markets in which compatibility issues arise.

Although standardization is beneficial, users are not always happy about the standard that wins the market. Some people who use Microsoft Word and benefit from its widespread use by others would prefer that a different product dominated the market. Many believe that the QWERTY keyboard has a less efficient layout than other keyboards. We will discuss standards and product quality later in the chapter.

## Network Benefits

Perhaps the clearest examples of network benefits come from physical networks, such as a telephone system. The owner of the only telephone in the world would have only an interesting knickknack, as the Dilbert cartoon in Figure 12-1 illustrates for the videophone. The value of a telephone depends on being able to communicate with other people who also own telephones, and its value increases enormously as the network of telephone users grows.

It is easy to see the benefit from network size in telephones. Using Figure 12-2 as an illustration, imagine that A is the sole owner of the telephone. Like Dilbert in the videophone example, A has no one he can communicate with using his equipment. When B also buys a phone, calls can be made in two directions: from A to B and B to A. Adding the second user creates *two* directions in which messages can be sent. Adding a third user, C creates *four* additional directions in which messages can be sent (from A to C, from C to A, from B to C, and from C to B). Adding D creates *six* additional message routes, and so on. The point is that the number of directions in which messages can be sent increases at an increasing rate as the system adds users. B added 2, C added 4, and D added 6.[3] Because the value of the network to any user increases

**FIGURE 12-1**   Dilbert Is an Early Videophone Adopter (Dilbert © UFS. Reprinted by permission.)

[3] In general, the number of directions in which calls can be sent is equal to $N*(N-1)$, where $N$ is the number of "nodes" in the network. This means that the number of directions in which a message can be sent increases by roughly the square of the number of nodes. This is sometimes called the *rule of squares*, also known as Metcalfe's law. Networks are often more complex than this simple telephone example suggests, however. In particular, the value of the network can depend on who is in it and how it is structured. For example, an e-commerce network that large retailers use might be more valuable to vendors than one small retailers use, even if an equal number of retailers participate in each network. Because the value of the network can depend on its composition, a simple rule of squares to measure its benefits need not apply.

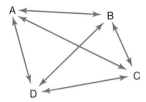

**FIGURE 12-2**   The Network Effect

with the number of directions in which messages can be sent, the value of a telephone also increases at an increasing rate.

In telephone systems and similarly constructed networks, each user is connected directly with every other user. In other networks, users interact via a central nexus. These "star" networks are illustrated in Figure 12-3. A clearinghouse is a star network. Banks increasingly rely on central clearinghouses to facilitate interbank transfers of funds. Similarly, physicians rely on information clearinghouses that the National Institutes of Health (NIH) maintains to track new developments in medical research. In both cases, the value of the clearinghouse to its users increases in the size of the network. As the number of banks using the system increases, a larger share of any single bank's transactions can go through the clearinghouse. As more publications cooperate with the NIH clearinghouse, it will include more relevant research. This means that physicians have access to more information and journals will reach more researchers.

The World Wide Web is a technology with even more rapidly increasing DSIR than the simple networks we have described. Each new Web site (or the addition of information to an existing site) increases the value of the Web to every existing user. Thus the value of the Web increases with the amount of content on it. It also increases

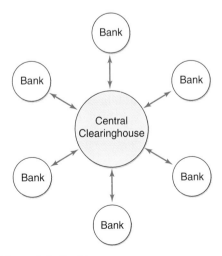

**FIGURE 12-3**   A "Star" Network in Banking

with the number of people who use it. Since each user can access each Web site, as the user base grows, so does the value of the content that is available. Thus, the overall social value of the Web increases both with the amount of content on it and the number of people who surf it.

So far, we have talked about how networks can connect people at different, but fixed, locations. Networks also have value because people change locations. For example, consider a network of automated teller machines (ATMs). One benefit of ATM networks is that the consumer has access to banking services at many locations. The more locations in which a person can find a compatible ATM, the larger the value of the ATM network to that person. Because people value network size, banks with larger networks can charge higher fees and/or attract more depositors. The large ATM network created by the 1999 merger of Bank of America and Nationsbank, for example, is used in advertisements to attract potential customers.

As the clearinghouse example suggests, network benefits can also occur even when no physical network connects the members. A club of baseball card traders enjoys network benefits. The more members it has, the greater the variety of cards they can trade, and so the more valuable the club is to its members. Similarly, the value potential sellers place on an auction increases with the number of buyers who participate in it. Those who study regional economics claim that network effects also impact the value of industrial clusters. As the number of similar firms located in a region increases, so does the benefit each firm earns from the proximity of others. In this example, network participants might be firms that exchange information on technology. The more firms that contribute to the common pool of technological know-how, the more valuable it is to belong to the network.

These examples suggest that there are also costs associated with network size. As networks grow, any constraint on the resources needed to sustain them can cause congestion. Lack of bandwidth causes congestion on the Web, slowing access time and delaying transactions. The increase in the cost of land in Silicon Valley as congestion increases raises the costs of taking advantage of the network benefits of locating there. These examples show that the rate at which the value of the network increases can eventually decline because of congestion costs (or even turn negative if the congestion costs outweigh the network benefits).

Although we have discussed compatibility and network effects separately, both can be present in the same technology. E-mail is an example. The network effects are particularly strong for e-mail because the same message can be sent to multiple recipients. But the value of some e-mail features requires compatibility between the sender's and receiver's software. Similarly, the value of the fax, like the telephone, depends on the number of others whom one can fax or receive faxes from. However, to enjoy the full extent of the DSIR, all users must use compatible transmission protocols.

Whether the underlying source of DSIR is compatibility or a network effect, it has dramatic implications for competition, as we will see next.

## 12.3  COMPETITION IN MARKETS WITH DEMAND-SIDE INCREASING RETURNS

Earlier, we claimed that DSIR contributes to the "big winner" phenomenon; in this section, we provide the logic to support this claim. As we will argue, DSIR can turn small advantages in market share into a large, enduring positional advantage. Once we have established the logic that ties DSIR to positional advantage, we will discuss how firms can use competitive strategies to gain and reinforce positional advantage rooted in DSIR.

### Installed Base and Tipping

If a product has DSIR, potential buyers care about how many people use it. Whether DSIR comes from compatibility, network benefits, or both, buyers want to purchase the same product that others purchase. A consumer deciding between VHS and beta VCRs in the 1980s would want to know how many others had already purchased each format and how many were likely to purchase each in the future. Similarly, if she were choosing between an Apple or Wintel (*win*dows operating system + in*tel* microprocessor), computer she would want to know how many of each type were already in use and what the market shares would be in the future. Because computers and VCRs are durable goods, she cares about both how many people use each type now and how many will be using them in the near future.

How many people already own a product will heavily influence her beliefs about how many people will use it in the future. The buyers who already use a product or technology are collectively called its *installed base* of users. If people can easily switch among products, installed base will be less important; the number of people using a brand of toothpaste today, for example, may not indicate how many will use that brand two years from now. However, many DSIR products have high switching costs that induce buyers to stay with their initial choice. As a result, a product with a large share of the installed base will retain most of those customers. Our new buyer, then, will assume that most of the installed base for a given product will contribute to the benefits she will get if she chooses to buy it. This gives the product with a larger installed base a competitive advantage. All else being equal, she would rather buy the product with the largest installed base. Furthermore, she knows that other new buyers will also prefer the product with the largest installed base. As a result, *all* the new buyers will choose the product with the largest installed base (again, assuming nothing else differentiates the products in the buyers' minds).

Because installed base looms large for potential buyers of products that have DSIR, markets for these products are inherently unstable: *they tend to "tip" toward a winner.* For example, consider the competition between VHS and beta in the market for videocassette recorders in the 1980s. In the early years, the market share advantage of VHS was not large. Suppose a consumer noticed that VHS had a 55 percent share. For many products, she would correctly interpret a 55–45 split as a stable configuration and assume that the two products would continue to enjoy a large market share.

But since VCRs have DSIR, the larger share would make VHS the more attractive choice. She and others would therefore choose VHS. As new users disproportionately adopted VHS, its lead grew, making it even more attractive to new buyers. As this cycle repeats, the product with a large installed base advantage becomes ever more dominant; the market "tips" toward a winner. Eventually, this cycle drove beta VCRs from the market.

As this example suggests, the strong firms or technologies that compete in markets with DSIR tend to become even stronger. This tendency is known as *positive feedback*. A large installed base yields current strength in the marketplace which results in stronger sales, which *feeds back* to increase the installed base. Figure 12-4 illustrates this positive feedback cycle. For the loser, of course, the feedback is negative. It loses some market share, so its installed base grows more slowly, the slow growth in market share leads to a greater loss, and so forth. The feedback loop for the loser, like beta, is a death spiral.

The assertion that DSIR products have high switching costs is crucial to the argument we have made. Installed base affects DSIR because people who are using the product today will continue to use it tomorrow because it is costly for them to switch. Because they use the product in the future, they contribute to the product's installed base which today's buyers expect to see in the future. If users could switch costlessly, today's installed base might have little effect on tomorrow's. Often, switching costs are high because many products with DSIR are durable and expensive. Computer or telephone systems are not replaced on a whim. Another reason is that users typically make significant investments in complementary products. With personal computers, for example, users purchase compatible software that may not be usable with a competing computer platform. These kinds of switching costs are even more significant for mainframe computers where customized software often is specific to the operating system. Indeed, some companies have established successful businesses by providing support

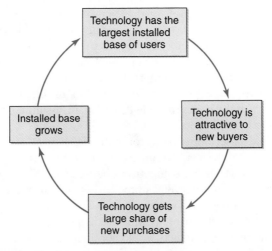

**FIGURE 12-4**  Positive Feedback

to firms' existing mainframe systems. For example, Computer Associates earned $3.5 billion in revenues in 1995–1996, making it the third largest software company, largely by being the leading supplier of systems management software that runs on IBM's mainframe and midrange operating systems.[4] Switching costs might also be high because the user has invested time in learning how to make the best use of the technology. Firms spend a lot of money training employees to use specific systems, and individuals have to learn the idiosyncrasies of particular software. Companies also develop large databases that are system specific, and converting them to other systems is often prohibitively costly.

Switching costs lock buyers into their current technology. Switching to an alternative product is costly, and a firm that wants to induce a consumer to switch must provide enough benefit to offset these costs. The extent of lock-in for a particular product changes over time. Sometimes it declines as the product ages. For example, the cost of switching to a new television technology (such as high-definition TV) tends to fall because the depreciated value of the existing stock of televisions consumers already own declines with time. Often, however, lock-in increases with time. For example lock-in to a computer platform becomes more effective over time as a firm continues to add to its existing databases, trains more employees to use the technology, or writes more applications.

Moreover, switching costs for products with DSIR can be high even if no individual switching costs are significant. That is, even when none of the potential switching costs we have described is large enough to create lock-in, the presence of DSIR can still create lock-in because no user wants to switch unless most other users also switch. An analogy might be helpful here. Suppose cowboys have to camp overnight in the desert. They need to keep their horses from wandering off but cannot find anything in this barren landscape to tie the horses to. They could hobble each horse (tie its front legs together), or they could tie the horses to each other. This second solution would be effective because horses are not good at coordinating an escape! In a similar way, DSIR ties users together. Unless users of a particular product with DSIR can coordinate a move to another product, they will be stuck with the one they have.

eBay is a striking example of how DSIR can create switching costs. It provides an Internet auction site where sellers and buyers can exchange items, such as baseball cards, photographic equipment, dolls, and so on. "Communities" of traders have developed who regard eBay as the premier electronic site on which to trade. They share information about items and about each another. Individuals have developed reputations for trustworthiness that make others who frequent the site willing to deal with them. eBay thrives precisely because its auction has attracted a large, loyal following. Although any individual participant can switch to a competing site, he would leave behind almost everyone with whom he wants to trade. Like the horses tied together, mutual interdependence ties eBay's users together, and they would have to make a coordinated effort to move to another auction site.

---

[4] See Carl Shapiro and Hal Varian, *Information Rules* (Boston: Harvard Business School Press, 1999) for details. That book is also an excellent reference for additional information on demand-side increasing returns and its implications for management.

The positive feedback loop in Figure 12-4, then, creates big winners and endows them with a positional advantage that is difficult for challengers to overcome. The winner may be a firm or a technology. The gasoline-powered engine was the winning technology in the early days of the automobile market. Because no firm owned this technology, however, many firms could compete by producing cars based on this winning standard. Sometimes, however, a firm has a proprietary claim on the technology and therefore owns the standard. Microsoft owns the standard for personal computer operating systems (Windows), a standard embraced by the vast majority of the installed base of personal computers in the United States. The power of this installed base suggests that Microsoft may control the personal computer standard for a long time. The decision of Judge Jackson in June 2000 to break Microsoft into two companies, an operating system company and an applications company, was predicated in part on the view that doing so might increase competition for the Windows operating system.

Even if no technology standard is involved, DSIR can create a winning firm because buyers prefer to make similar choices. eBay doesn't have a proprietary technology standard, but its large share of Internet auction users gives it a significant advantage over its competitors. eBay gained an initial advantage primarily by being a first mover in Internet auctions, but it could not prevent other firms from imitating its technology. DSIR, however, made eBay's first-mover advantage sustainable and propelled the market capitalization of this fledgling company to over $8 billion within months of its initial public offering. A similar phenomenon plays out in the market for telephone yellow page directories. It involves no proprietary know-how or technology, but each advertiser wants to appear in this book which most consumers consult to find products and services. Each consumer wants to consult the book with the most listings. As a result, each city usually has one dominant yellow page directory.

Even a *superior* new technology may be unable to displace a technology that has created large DSIR benefits. In appraising the new technology, new users will compare the value of its inherent superiority with the benefits of the larger installed base on the inferior, old technology. Unless the enhancements offered by the new technology can compensate new users for the loss of compatibility with the installed base, they will choose the old technology. Their decision means that the installed base on the old technology continues to grow, making it even more attractive to the buyers who follow them. It is therefore hard for the new technology to get off the ground, and it may fail to gain market acceptance, regardless of its superiority.

Despite the incumbent technology's enormous advantages, it cannot always fend off entry. For example, Super 8 movies replaced Standard 8, and compact disks replaced vinyl records. If the new technology is sufficiently better than the old one, some new users will adopt it and sacrifice the benefits of compatibility with the installed base. If many new adopters make this decision, they will build their own installed base on the new technology, blunting the costs of incompatibility with the installed base on the old technology. The mass adoption of the new technology strands the buyers who own the old technology. Their installed base stagnates and eventually declines, forcing them to incur the switching costs necessary to move to the new technology or live with reduced DSIR benefits.

Positive feedback and the consequent tendency for markets with DSIR to tip mean that a "niche" firm's position is much more precarious than in other markets. In earlier chapters, we noted that in many dominant firm markets, the niches under the dominant firm's umbrella can often be attractive market positions. Niche positions tend to be less attractive in markets with DSIR because in these markets a firm with a small installed base may not generate enough DSIR to remain viable. This dynamic exists in the market for desktop computer operating systems, for example, which is why Apple's current situation is precarious. Apple's share of current sales plunged in the mid-1990s from around 15 percent to about a third of that in just four years. Although many factors affected Apple's situation, its share of current sales declined largely because potential buyers believed that Apple was losing the operating system market to Microsoft.

## Competitive Strategies for Building DSIR

A firm with a large installed base can charge a price premium because of the DSIR benefits that its products offer. This price premium makes it attractive to be the market leader in DSIR markets. Bill Gates considers Microsoft's Windows and Office businesses to be two of the five most attractive businesses in the world. Because a large installed base creates a large and sustainable positional advantage, firms compete fiercely to build installed base. In markets with DSIR, competition often shifts from being primarily competition *within* markets to competition *for* markets. That is, firms devote most of their strategic energy to trying to become the big winner. Many of the competitive tactics in these markets are investments to ultimately achieve that position.

For example, although a firm that has an installed base lead *can* charge a premium for its product, it knows that a high price will affect its installed base in the future. By charging a high price today, the firm increases its current profits. However, its high price will dissuade some potential buyers from purchasing its product, thereby making its future installed base smaller than it would otherwise be. That in turn will make its product less valuable to consumers in the future. So *to build up its future installed base each firm has an incentive to charge less than it otherwise would.* An extreme form of this principle is "give-aways." Giving the product away is not normally regarded as a way to make money, but Microsoft with its Internet Explorer and Netscape with its Netscape Navigator used this tactic to build installed base. A less extreme version of the same principle is to charge a low introductory price to build market share, a tactic known as *penetration pricing.* Once a firm has an entrenched position as the winner, it can harvest its large installed base by raising its prices. A firm also has an incentive to persuade its installed base, many of whom purchased the product at introductory prices, to "upgrade" to more current—and expensive—versions of the product. It might do so by offering them an "upgrade" discount off the price offered to new buyers.

Although "give-aways" and penetration pricing are natural tactics for a new entrant attempting to make headway into a market, a large incumbent can also use these tactics to drive smaller competitors from its market. In Chapter 9 we saw that predatory pricing (pricing below cost) in conventional markets is often an unprofitable tactic. The problem with pricing low to drive out rivals or prevent entry is that the predatory firm eventually has to raise its price to make up for the losses that pricing below cost has created. However, when it raises its price, entry again becomes attractive. Without high barriers to entry, the firm cannot maintain high margins. However, driving competitors from markets with DSIR increases the size of the predatory firm's installed base. The low price and the belief that the competitor will leave the market attract potential buyers. The large installed base predation created may protect the predator against entry when it eventually raises its price.

Because a new, much more attractive technology can dislodge even a firm with large DSIR, the current winner has an incentive to invest in product enhancements to improve its product. However, the "cannibalism" effect blunts its incentive. It makes money on its current products, which its new products will make obsolete. In effect, it is eating its own profits by introducing new products. An entrant with no products to replace has a greater incentive to invest in new technology. The dominant firm, therefore, has an incentive to delay product innovation, but only if it can do so without losing the market. The dominant firm might delay investment *and* prevent successful entry by "pre-announcing" its new products. Suppose an entrant announces that it has a new, improved product that it will ship in three months. The incumbent can announce that it will have a new product available in, say, nine months, which will have all the features of the entrant's product. The customers who make up the installed base then compare the gain from waiting an additional six months *and* remaining with the large installed base with the gain from getting the product enhancements sooner but giving up the DSIR benefits associated with the incumbent's large installed base. By judiciously choosing to delay, the incumbent can reduce both the demand for the new entrant's product and its own investment in product development. Once potential entrants recognize that this will happen, entry may never occur, and the incumbent can reduce its product development expenditures even more.

Control Data Corporation (CDC) claimed that IBM used this tactic when it countered CDC's new product offering in the mainframe market by announcing an even better computer that would be available later. Although IBM denied it, CDC claimed that IBM determined the specifications for its pre-announced computer in a weekend retreat by marketing executives, without the benefit of input from engineering about what IBM could actually deliver. Similarly, software firms often complain about rivals' use of "vaporware": software that an incumbent firm promises will have all the attributes of the challenger's offering (and more), but that never appears or appears much later than promised.

Strategic incompatibility can also support the dominant firm's position. In the same case against IBM, for example, makers of peripherals charged that IBM changed the peripheral interfaces in its computers solely to make entrants' products incompatible with theirs.

Although it is difficult, firms with a small installed base can compete against incumbents in markets with DSIR. Niche firms, for example, aren't necessarily doomed. If there is enough product differentiation of the kind we described in Chapter 7, some consumers will be willing to purchase the product with the smaller installed base because their preference for the differentiation it offers outweighs the loss in DSIR. Apple's loyal following among those who prefer its desktop publishing and plug-and-play capabilities has helped it make significant sales even after its share of installed base fell. The lock-in of users unwilling to bear the switching costs of a change to the Wintel platform also protected Apple. In addition, Apple has found it easier to attract new users—those who have never before owned a computer and hence have no switching costs—than converts from other platforms. So, for example, Apple has targeted the youth market as one of the primary consumer segments for its new iMAC computers.

Firms with a dwindling or a small and stagnant installed base can also pursue compatibility with a larger installed base by providing *conversion technology* or an *adapter*. An adapter lets buyers who like the niche product enjoy the DSIR benefits from the larger installed base. In the mid-1970s when incompatibility among mainframe computers was rife, an estimated "one quarter of the total available computer power in the United States was being used to provide conversion systems between dissimilar, nonstandardized (or nonstandard) elements of computer systems."[5] Apple Computer used this tactic in response to its dwindling market share, when it offered computers that could run software written for the Wintel platform as well as its own.

## 12.4  SYSTEMS OF COMPONENTS

When the final product is a system of components that must work together, DSIR can affect competition between systems and among components. In this section, we address two common competitive issues. First, firms producing competing platforms must decide whether to make their systems compatible with their competitors' systems. Buyers usually prefer that systems be compatible, but the manufacturers may use incompatibilities to create or support competitive advantage. Second, a firm can sometimes increase its profits by leveraging its dominant position as the producer of one component into dominance of another component. We begin with system compatibility and then turn to leveraging market position.

### System Compatibility

Compatibility issues often arise when buyers combine components into a system, as in the case of cameras and lenses or stereo systems. The canonical case of compatibility in systems is that of computer hardware and software. A typical computer user cares about her ability to create documents (using word processing software and a printer), analyze data (using spreadsheet and/or financial analysis software), and surf the Internet (using a modem and a browser). The attractiveness of any manufacturer's component in this system depends on the availability and performance of compatible

---

[5] *Datamation*, October 15, 1985.

components. Components of a system are *complements;* the more there are and the higher their quality, the more attractive the system is.

The same firm sometimes produces all the components in a system, but most often it does not. When multiple firms produce system components, the demand facing each component manufacturer depends on a supply of complementary components created by other firms. Thus a firm attempting to introduce a component that will be part of a system of new components faces a "chicken-and-egg" problem. Think about a new operating system. If it is to win wide acceptance, many potential users and independent component suppliers must believe it will be widely adopted. Users want to adopt it only if other users will adopt it and if compatible software will be made available. Independent software vendors will invest in writing software for the new system only if they believe consumers will buy it. If software companies hesitate to commit resources to develop products for the new operating system, consumers will be reluctant to buy it. As consumer demand fails to develop, software companies become even more reluctant to support the new system.

Remember quadraphonic sound? It would not be surprising if you don't. It is an example of a technology that never managed to get off the ground and has virtually disappeared. Quadraphonic sound was a record playback system that used four channels instead of the two channels stereo uses. For it to catch on, many popular records would have had to have been produced in quadraphonic sound. But for that to have happened, record producers would have had to believe that many people were going to buy quadraphonic sound systems. This in turn would have required a lot of quadraphonic sound records to play on them. Battle over the standards for quadraphonic sound early in its development exacerbated this chicken-and-egg problem. The adoption process for quadraphonic sound stalled, and the technology is now virtually extinct.

Since complements are important to the success of systems with DSIR, a firm attempting to promote a technology wants to nurture the development of compatible complements. The strong alliance between Microsoft and Intel in the early years of the personal computer to promote the Wintel platform is a good example. So, too, is Apple's early "evangelists" program through which it nurtured independent software vendors producing Apple-compatible software. Alliances are particularly common in such settings because all the firms producing products for the system ensure that more complements are produced. Competition here is said to resemble competition among "ecosystems": Firms are members of an ecosystem that competes with other ecosystems, and having more members strengthens the competitive position of each group.

## Leveraging Market Position

A firm with a dominant market position in one component may be able to leverage that position into a dominant position in other components. For example, critics of Microsoft's business practices allege that it has used its dominant position in the PC operating system market to gain a strong position in the markets for applications, Internet browsers, application development tools, and related operating systems. A firm might leverage its strong position as a supplier of one component into a strong position as a supplier of another in a variety of ways. Suppose that a firm dominates the market for the operating system (OS) for a computer platform. It can use its control of the OS to gain control in another segment in several ways.[6]

- It can attack the applications market by giving its own application programs preferential access to specific OS features that enable applications to work better. Microsoft's competitors in word processing applications, for example, have long claimed that Microsoft uses undocumented features of its OS to make its own applications run faster or more smoothly. Others allege that Microsoft uses the Windows interface to its advantage. America Online (AOL), for example, complained that Microsoft disadvantaged AOL's product by including a desktop icon for Microsoft's MSN in the Windows 95 OS.

- It can dominate the market for the central processing unit (CPU) by withholding OS interface information from rival CPU manufacturers. For example, Amdahl alleged that IBM used control of its mainframe operating system to maintain its dominance over the CPU market. Since IBM controls the proprietary interface between its OS and the CPU, it could deny Amdahl access to IBM's OS and thus shut Amdahl out of the CPU market.

- It can attack other markets by bundling products with the operating system. For example, by integrating a memory manager into the operating system (and charging for it), the OS provider can own the market for those "add-ons." Once a computer assembler has paid for the memory manager built into the OS, it will not pay for another, competing memory manager. Similarly, a consumer who gets an application that comes bundled with the OS is unlikely to purchase a competing application at an additional cost.

Although these examples suggest that firms can leverage a dominant position, they do not prove that it would be profitable to do so. Just because a firm can leverage into an adjacent market doesn't mean that it should. A variant of the argument we made in Chapter 10 suggests that the firm can sometimes maximize profits by exploiting its monopoly in just one layer of the value chain. If a firm has monopolized one layer and all the other layers are competitive, the firm may be able to extract its monopoly profits for the whole chain simply by pricing appropriately in that layer. If

---

[6] The OS example addresses a common case in which a firm with dominance in one market leverages into a dominant position in an adjacent market. In some cases, however, a firm competing on an equal footing with others in one market can enter a new market, obtain dominance through DSIR there, and then leverage back into the original market. This occurred in airline computer reservation systems (CRSs). CRSs are subject to DSIR because the same system can be used to make bookings on many airlines, travel agents prefer not to have to use many different systems, and airlines do not want to support many different systems. By recognizing this feature of the reservation market, American Airlines and United Airlines secured dominant positions in the CRS market. They then leveraged this position back into the airlines market by giving themselves preferential treatment on the CRSs. For example, the first flights listed on American's Sabre system would be American flights. A series of court cases later regulated the "abuse" of the CRSs for competitive advantage.

competitive firms can supply the other components more efficiently, so much the better. The firm's dominance of one layer *and* the competitive conditions in the other layers mean that it can extract all the value the system creates. Leaving component production to the most efficient firms means the system will create more value.

In other circumstances, a firm dominating one component can increase the value it captures by gaining control of the market for another component. A firm with market power that bundles different products may be able to do better than a firm that only sells the products separately.[7] If bundling increases profitability, a firm that has market power in several components might be more profitable than a firm that has market power in only one.

A second motivation for leverage is that the firm might want to dominate another layer to protect its position in the market for the component it already dominates. Consider, for example, the situation illustrated in Figure 12-5. There, Domino is the dominant producer of Component 1. Many versions of Component 2 are compatible with Domino's Component 1, but few are compatible with its rivals' versions of Component 1. Because the dominant firm's product has more complements, more buyers want to purchase it. Indeed, it may have become dominant in Component 1 because of its success in persuading firms to produce to its standard.

Now suppose that a new technology becomes available (labeled Component 3 in Figure 12-6) that makes all versions of Component 2 compatible with all versions of Component 1. For argument's sake, suppose many competitive firms provide the new technology. The new layer expands consumer choice because consumers can now buy any version of Component 1 and Component 2; that is, they can "mix and match." But this is dangerous for Domino. Domino has lost the DSIR advantage that it obtained from having more compatible complements, and it is now likely to face much stronger competition from its rival producers of Component 1.

Observers have argued that the Internet provided just such a threat to Microsoft's dominance of its Windows OS. The combination of independently provided browsers and the Java programming language constitutes a layer that may enable applications to run on any operating system. By using its OS market position to leverage into the Internet market, however, Microsoft can secure a dominant position there, thus protecting its OS position. A firm with a dominant OS position has a similar incentive to

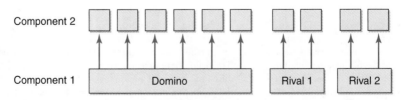

**FIGURE 12-5**   Domino Has a DSIR Advantage from Dominating Component 1

---

[7] See the appendix to Chapter 10 for details of this argument.

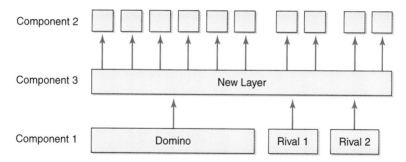

**FIGURE 12-6**    A New, Intermediate, Layer Emerges

dominate a market for applications development tools that make applications compatible with multiple operating systems.

## 12.5  TECHNOLOGY ADOPTION

We have described how the value a consumer gets from a product with DSIR depends on how many others adopt the same technology and the implications of DSIR for competition among products with different installed base shares. In this section, we discuss in more detail how DSIR affects whether the market adopts the technology in the first place. When DSIR are important, adopters are afraid that they will adopt the technology but that few others will. If this happens, adopters will be unable to enjoy the intended DSIR effects.

The behavior of penguins offers a useful natural analogy to this phenomenon. Nature documentaries often show penguins crowded together near the edge of an ice floe. They seem eager to enter the water and sometimes even appear ready to leap in, and yet they don't, even though they are hungry and want to go fishing. The problem is that although they are eager to get to the food in the water, they don't want to *be food in the water!* If only a few penguins jump in and a predator is lying in wait, they will probably be eaten. If all the penguins jump in at once, the risk that any particular penguin will end up as a meal is much lower. All the penguins are happy to go into the water if enough of them go in with them. Our adopters of new technology are the penguins: They are happy to adopt the technology as long as others do so too.

To see how the interdependencies among potential adopters play out, consider a simple example in which there is a single technology that might be adopted. Willingness to adopt depends on how many others are expected to adopt. This gives rise to an adoption curve of the kind illustrated in Figure 12-7. As the figure illustrates, some adopters are so enamored of the technology that they are willing to adopt even if no one else does. (This gives rise to a positive intercept on the *y*-axis.) Beyond that point, however, successive users are only willing to adopt if others also adopt. The upward slope of the curve illustrates that the more users are willing to adopt, the more other users are expected to adopt as well.

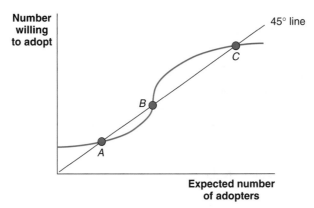

**FIGURE 12-7**   Illustrative Adoption Pattern

Figure 12-7 also includes a line at a 45° angle to the axes, which the curved line crosses three times. As we shall discuss later, there are good reasons to believe that consumer preferences for many technologies that exhibit DSIR resemble the data graphed in the figure. Although not all adoption profiles look like this (and we shall see what happens when they don't), we can use this figure to make some general points about the adoption process when DSIR are important.

How many potential users will adopt this technology? To answer this question, first think about the segment of the figure to the left of point *A*. Since that segment lies above the 45° line, for any number who are expected to adopt the technology, even more are willing to adopt it. So, for example, if 10,000 people were expected to adopt, a greater number, perhaps 12,000, would be willing to adopt. The result is a band-wagon effect ensuring that the process reaches at least *A*. Some people are willing to adopt even if no one else does; these are the hungriest penguins. Because these people adopt, some others are now willing to adopt. After those people adopt, still more adopt, and so on. This bandwagon leads to *A*.

Adoptions can get "stuck" at *A*, however, because the segment of the curve between *A* and *B* lies *below* the 45° line. In this segment, the number willing to adopt is always *less* than the number expected to adopt. The people in this segment are the less hungry penguins. They hesitate, but they do not want to be the last to adopt. For-tunately for the firm introducing the technology, this does not necessarily mean that the process will end at *A*. Note that if the process *somehow* got to *B*, all the users between *A* and *B* would be happy. Moreover, if users leap in and get the process to *B*, not only will they be happy, but the logic that got them to *A* would kick in again and take the process to point *C*.

The problem, then, is the potential adopters between *A* and *B*. Like the penguins, the users between *A* and *B* face a coordination problem. If they could *all* somehow agree to leap in, they would all do so happily. However, because they cannot get together and commit themselves to plunge in, they have to look to other means of coordination (or stay hungry). The firm introducing this technology would prefer to end up at *C* but may not be able to get more than *A* adopters. In the next section, we discuss how the firm might avoid stalling at *A*. First, however, we want to make some observations about the critical characteristics of the problem:

- **Expectations matter.** All potential adopters want to be doing what others are doing. So if everyone believes everyone will adopt, many people will in fact adopt and the outcome *C* will result. If people are pessimistic about the number of people who will adopt, the process will get stuck at *A*. What people *expect* to happen matters. In the language of game theory, there are multiple equilibria, and potential adopters' beliefs affect which equilibrium is achieved.

- **Bandwagons may emerge.** The potential adopters are watching one another like the penguins on the ice floe. If the adoption gains momentum, adopters will gain confidence that many others will adopt. As this realization dawns, the mass of potential adopters abandon their fears and jump on the bandwagon. This, of course, simply makes others even more confident, strengthening the bandwagon effect.

- **Early adopters jumpstart the process.** Some users are generally eager to try the new technology even if they are not optimistic that DSIR will kick in. Typically, then, the curve will start with a positive intercept on the vertical axis.

- **Intermediate adopters are difficult to attract.** Often, a segment of consumers in the "middle" of the demand distribution are unwilling to adopt unless they think others who value the technology even less than they do will also adopt. They represent the "critical mass" of adopters who must be persuaded to adopt if the bandwagon effect is to kick in. They create the steep section in Figure 12-7 around point *B*.

- **DSIR benefits don't increase forever.** DSIR probably have diminishing returns once the number of adopters becomes large enough. With 100 million telephone users, how valuable is the next person to get a phone? The flat section of the curve beyond point *C* in Figure 12-7 reflects these diminishing returns.

Not all products with DSIR experience the process we have just described. The adoption curve could look like the one shown in Figure 12-7 but be positioned differently. For example, if each user is more willing to adopt the technology (because it is more valuable to him) than Figure 12-7 suggests, the curve will shift up. If the curve shifts up enough, as Figure 12-8 illustrates, adoption will proceed immediately to *C* because even the intermediate adopters value the product enough to take the plunge without the assurance that a larger mass of penguins will go in with them. And, of course, if the technology is less valuable, the curve will shift down. If it shifts down enough, not even the most ardent consumer will buy the product. The phenomenon depicted in Figure 12-7, however, is real for many products. They acquire an initial, small number of users and then struggle to acquire a large installed base.

## 12.6  MANAGING THE ADOPTION PROCESS

Whether or not a firm faces competing technologies, it wants to build both actual and expected market share. If it fails to achieve enough market penetration, even a tech-

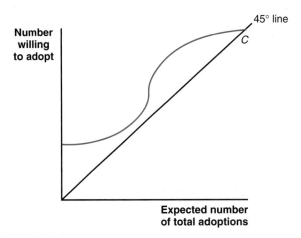

**FIGURE 12-8**   An Alternative Adoption Pattern

nology that a monopolist promotes will stall and probably disappear. If a technology has rivals to be the market standard, it may have to achieve a large market share to avoid a death spiral as DSIR increasingly favor its rival. In this section, we describe some factors that affect adoption processes and how firms have made these factors work in their favor.

## Marketing to Create Momentum

Because expectations tend to become self-fulfilling in the adoption of DSIR technologies, creating the belief that your technology will be the standard is critical to success. No firm has exhibited a better understanding of these dynamics than Microsoft did in launching Windows 95. There was a worldwide launch of the product on a particular day—August 24, 1995—with much advance fanfare (including the use of the Rolling Stones' "Start Me Up" as a theme song). Because of the single-day launch, Microsoft received enormous free advertising showing thousands of customers lining up to purchase the new OS (some of whom apparently didn't even own computers). The newscasts of these eager purchasers convinced many of the penguins to plunge into the icy waters themselves.

## Leveraging Reputation

The reputation of the firm promoting the technology matters. An offering by Microsoft is much more likely to gain wide adoption than an offering from an unknown company, even if the two products are of similar quality. If the sponsoring firm does not have an established reputation, it may decide to enter a strategic alliance with a firm that does. Leveraging IBM's reputation as a computer manufacturer helped create the dominance of the Wintel standard, for example.

## Committing to "Open" Standards

An "open standard" is one that all firms can use. The firms that developed the VHS technology, for example, allowed many VCR manufacturers to produce players embodying that technology. In contrast, Sony, restricted the number of manufacturers who could produce VCRs with the beta technology. Many believe that VHS triumphed over beta largely because it was an open standard. Although an open standard might propel adoption, the process of establishing a standard sometimes requires a lengthy standard-setting process that will slow down adoption as adopters wait for the standard to emerge. (We will have more to say about this matter in the next section.) Creating an open standard requires that any firm owning the technology relinquish its proprietary control. Open standards trade off the positional advantage of sole proprietorship for the positional advantage of a large installed base.

## Winning Over An Influential Buyer

The presence of an influential buyer can have a major impact, as the adoption of uniform product codes (UPCs) illustrates. The UPC is the identity of a product represented by the rectangle of vertical lines (barcode) that can be scanned at the checkout counter. This technology was available for years before it was adopted because of the chicken-and-egg problem discussed earlier. Package designers saw no merit in messing up their beautiful designs for a barcode for which no electronic scanners were in place. For their part, supermarkets saw no point in purchasing expensive scanning equipment when none of their manufacturers was putting a barcode on its products. This impasse was broken when a few large supermarket chains adopted scanning systems and required all their suppliers to use UPC codes. Once these large chains had committed, other supermarkets discovered that the UPC was showing up on the goods they were buying. They in turn adopted scanners and required that their remaining non-UPC suppliers get with the program. The UPC was soon all but universal.

## Advance Sign-Ups

One way to assuage the fears of the penguins in the middle is to show them that many others have already committed to adopting the technology. Many companies are willing to let it be known that they are committed to adopting at some unspecified future date. As the commitments grow, so does the confidence of potential adopters that the technology will take off.

## Winks at Pirates

In the early stages of the adoption profile for many desktop applications, software suppliers like Lotus had to decide how strongly to attack illegal copying of their products. When there are strong DSIR effects, a software manufacturer prefers that a student have an illegal copy of its software than not have its software at all. Consequently, in those early days manufacturers often turned a blind eye to illegal copying. As the market has consolidated, however, firms are enforcing intellectual property rights much more vigorously.

### Leasing

A firm can reduce the risk to its customers that its technology will not become widely adopted by leasing rather than selling it. By leasing its mainframes, IBM shifted the risk away from its buyers because buyers could always cancel the lease if the system did not catch on.

### Price Commitments

Firms will sometimes use long-term price contracts to assure buyers that they will not fall victim to price increases once they are locked into the technology. For example, to try to make its Java computer language ubiquitous, Sun Microsystems has granted long-term licenses to companies like IBM for only an initial fee.

## 12.7 STANDARDS-SETTING PROCESSES

Our discussion has focused on technology adoption governed only by markets. We have shown that DSIR benefits can help determine the winner in a battle for market share. Because these markets have a winner-take-all flavor, the battles often end with some product or architecture becoming the industry standard. This is sometimes called *de facto* standardization because it occurs through market processes. A fascinating aspect of situations in which DSIR are important, however, involves the many nonmarket institutions that work to establish standards through formal committees.

Most industry standards committees are voluntarily established by the firms in the industry. For example, the Secure Digital Music Initiative (SDMI) is a joint undertaking of firms with property rights to music. These firms have traditionally earned a return on their property by selling recordings to consumers. The emergence of the Internet as a channel for downloading digital copies of music (with or without the permission of the firm owning the copyright to it) both threatens these firms and opens a new opportunity for them to exploit. They formed the SDMI to develop a standard format for downloading and storing digital music that will prevent unauthorized copying and distribution. This effort is part of a huge voluntary standards community involving more than a hundred thousand people working on thousands of committees covering hundreds of industries around the world. In the United States, a central clearinghouse, the American National Standards Institute (ANSI), keeps track of standards. More than 220 trade associations and more than 1000 corporate members belong to ANSI. The International Organization for Standardization (ISO) oversees international standards. Both ANSI and ISO are nongovernmental, voluntary institutions.

These voluntary institutions exist because often the firms in an industry all benefit when a standard is set. Nuts and bolts manufacturers benefit from standard sizing, and electrical component manufacturers benefit from standardized interfaces for their products. Firms band together to create a standard because the market process for creating a *de facto* standard—even one that benefits everyone—can be difficult. Think again about the problem of adopting UPCs. UPCs reduce the transaction costs involved in ordering, inventorying, and selling retailers' products. But individual retailers would not invest in the necessary technology without the assurance of widespread adoption. One way to get that assurance—that is, to solve the coordination problem—is to get the firms to act collectively through a voluntary standards committee.

A standards committee seems to be an excellent mechanism for solving the coordination problem. Because these committees have to understand the technology involved in making a standards decision, these committees tend to have an "engineering bias." This suggests that they might have an incentive to pick the best technology and bring it to market. The committees also have rules about fairness and openness, so that all interested parties can participate and have their say. Finally, decisions usually require more than a simple majority vote, so the committees are unlikely to override the interests of a large minority. Voluntary standards committees are particularly effective when firms have a strong interest in having an industry standard established and when they do not have strong vested interest in *which* standard is adopted. When these two conditions are met, the standards committees are not highly politicized; engineering considerations dominate; and the consensus decision-making process leads to good results.

If the first condition is not met, firms will not have enough incentive to participate in the process. That is the *public goods* problem. Everyone wants to see a standard established, but no one wants to bear the costs of selecting one. In those situations, such as is the case with weights and measures, for example, governments usually establish the standards. The voluntary committee process can also fail if the firms care deeply about *which* standard is selected. For grocery scanners, for example, the competing standards involved technology from different firms. Even if it has to license its technology to get a standard adopted, the firm whose technology is adopted has a first-mover advantage. In these cases, standards committees are obviously less likely to be cooperative and to produce unbiased outcomes. Instead, the proceedings become highly politicized. Allied firms form opposing camps, with perhaps one firm agreeing to help an ally on one committee in return for the ally's assistance on another. In other cases, a firm that wants its proprietary technology to become a *de facto* market standard has an incentive to drag out the standards process in order to give it time to establish its own standard in the market. Once the market determines a *de facto* standard, the standards committee will come under heavy pressure to adopt it as the *de jure* standard as well.

The standards committee structure can also be valuable when a firm wants to commit to opening up its technology. A firm might want to commit for two reasons. First, based on its competitive advantage in that technology, it believes that it would win in head-to-head competition with other firms. In that case, the firm may prefer to give up its proprietary hold over the technology because it expects that its slice of the pie will be larger than its proprietary pie would be. Second, a firm may choose to give up its hold on its proprietary technology if, as discussed earlier, it is behind in the standards race with another firm and it believes that its technology will prevail only if it is open. Whatever the reason, it is difficult for a firm to commit credibly to making its technology open. Buyers understand that the firm has an incentive to renege on openness once the standard is widely adopted. Surrendering the technology to a standards committee that has open and fair procedures can demonstrate the firm's commitment.

## 12.8 SUMMARY

DSIR often arise either because of compatibility benefits or network benefits. Markets with DSIR differ from conventional markets in important ways. They tend to involve competition *for* the market as much as competition *in* the market. Installed base is important, and because these markets tend to "tip," the winner takes all, raising the stakes of competition. Consequently, firms often price aggressively, sometimes even giving the product away, in order to build momentum. Where products are sold in systems, firms sometimes have the ability and incentive to leverage dominance of one component into dominance of another, as the Microsoft antitrust case illustrates.

Users face a coordination problem when adopting new technology that has DSIR. Expectations are important, bandwagons emerge, early adopters jumpstart the process, and intermediate adopters ("penguins") are crucial but can be difficult to attract. Firms often manage the adoption process by marketing to create momentum, leveraging reputation, committing to open standards, targeting influential buyers, engaging in advance sign-ups, leasing rather than selling, and making long-lasting price commitments. Because coordination is important in markets with DSIR, industry standards committees play an especially important role.

Markets with DSIR also raise thorny antitrust issues. DSIR effects often determine important issues of industry structure early in the life of a technology when they create installed base. Because of its concern with monopolization, typically conventional antitrust enforcement only begins once a firm already has a significant market share and threatens to achieve dominance. In the kinds of technology markets discussed here, however, a firm may firmly establish dominance before it triggers antitrust scrutiny. The governmental antitrust machinery is battling to stay relevant in markets that move at much greater speed than they are used to.

In the following chapter, we examine strategic issues that arise from globalization.

# CHAPTER

# 13

# GLOBALIZATION AND STRATEGY

## 13.1 INTRODUCTION

One of the most striking and pervasive changes in business over the last few decades has been the internationalization of companies, industries, and economies. Increasingly, managers have to operate in diverse cultures, procure materials and components in international markets, and face the challenges that new, foreign competitors create. Firms have increased their international scope both to take advantage of the competitive advantages in new markets that they have already demonstrated in their existing ones and to gain new competitive advantages through globalization. Nike is a good example of a firm that has done both. Nike's founding strategy involved creating competitive advantage in the U.S. market by using low-cost, high-quality athletic shoe production in Japan. Because it outsourced production, Nike could focus on building its brand name and distribution in the United States. In later years, Nike was able to leverage its strong U.S. brand in international markets, creating one of the strongest global brands. When manufacturing costs increased in Japan, Nike moved to lower-cost producers in Korea, Taiwan, Indonesia, and Thailand. Thus Nike first sought competitive advantage in low-cost manufacture in Japan, later extended the competitive advantage of its strong U.S. brand into other countries, and then relocated production to maintain low-cost competitive advantage.

Decisions such as these by individual companies have created massive changes for entire industries that had been largely domestic. For example, non-U.S. firms have contributed to a massive restructuring of the U.S. film industry, which has resulted in huge media conglomerates with a presence in all the major geographic markets. Four of the leading firms in the U.S. industry (Twentieth Century Fox, Columbia, MGM/UA, and MCA) were acquired by non-U.S. firms.[1] The worldwide automobile industry has also been transformed as domestic firms have established production and

---

[1] B. R. Litman "Motion Picture Entertainment" in *The Structure of American Industry*, 8th ed., W. Adams and J. Brock, eds. (Englewood Cliffs, N. J.: Prentice Hall, 1995) p. 207.

sales in foreign markets. The world's largest automobile producers now include Japanese, U.S., and European firms, all of which have a substantial presence outside their home countries.

The growth of international trade suggests the magnitude of these changes. For example, in 1963 merchandise exports as a percentage of manufactured output in the United States, Britain, and Germany were 5.5, 17.8, and 21.2 percent, respectively. By 1993, those same percentages had risen to 18.9, 42.9, and 41.1 percent. The value of investments made in other countries has also increased dramatically. Between 1980 and 1996, for example, the value of cross-border transactions in bonds and equities increased by 50 times in the United States and Germany and by more than 100 times in France.

In this chapter, we review some of the forces contributing to this increase in globalization, identify the key challenges managers pursuing a multinational strategy must face, and discuss some alternative approaches to meeting those challenges. The fundamental tools we will rely on have been developed elsewhere in the book. Industry analysis, for example, requires the same tools in each external context. The answers may be different, but the questions are the same: How intense is competition? Are there barriers to entry? What about buyer and supplier power? The basic nature of the organization design also is independent of location. Again, the questions are the same, but the answers may be different in different external contexts.

Although we don't need to develop an entirely new set of tools, we should recognize that increasing a firm's international presence poses new challenges. The frameworks for analyzing the strategies of a purely domestic firm are still useful, but managers face a different mix of problems when their firms and industries become more global. To compete effectively, a firm must respond to globalization of its industry. Performance will deteriorate if the firm tries to pursue business as usual. Globalization requires a firm's managers to respond to more complex nonmarket and cultural issues, meet greater challenges in assessing and transferring best practice, and make more difficult resource allocation decisions.

We begin by exploring the implications of globalization for managers. We then examine how firms can gain strategically from globalization. We briefly explore some of the factors driving globalization of industries and economies before examining the challenges that globalization poses and how firms can be organized to meet those challenges.

## 13.2   IMPLICATIONS FOR MANAGERS

Although the scale and scope of changes in globalization are obvious, the implications for managers who develop firm strategy are less clear. Managers, for example, disagree about what it means for a firm to become more "global." One manager will assert that his firm is becoming more global by catering to variations in tastes across the world rather than by providing "one-size-fits-all" products or services. Another will counter that her firm is standardizing products across its various national operations to take advantage of scale economies. A third will claim that what is truly global about his firm is a set of common values across all its geographically dispersed units, while a fourth will point to the autonomy her firm gives to its regional units to accommodate local customs and norms. These are conflicting views about what it means to respond effectively to the challenge of participating in multiple national markets.

They may all be correct. There is no single definition of what it means to be a global firm. Instead, the most effective approach for a firm intent on becoming more global depends on the strategy it pursues. In earlier chapters, we argued that the firm's organization design must be aligned with its strategy. Similarly, a firm must align its approach to globalization with its strategy. A pharmaceutical firm like Ciba-Geigy, for example, sells products that are subject to extensive, country-specific regulation through distribution systems that are shaped by vastly different public sector health policies and channel infrastructures. As a result, it must allow for variations in distribution, product development, and nonmarket activities across countries. In contrast, a semiconductor manufacturer like Motorola typically sells a range of standardized products to large original equipment manufacturers (OEMs) and component distributors who themselves are multinational firms. Although pharmaceutical firms approach globalization by developing country-specific business strategies, semiconductor firms globalize by pursuing worldwide economies of scale in manufacture, product development, and distribution. The managers in these two types of firms quite reasonably have different views about what globalization means because they have very different strategies.

Just as managers have different views about globalization, so do strategic management scholars, and later in the chapter we present some of the leading views of how firms should respond to globalization. However, we want to emphasize one common thread in this literature: Managers must recognize that operating effectively in multiple countries requires them to accommodate variations in the firm's internal and external contexts. Returning to the now-familiar paradigm illustrated again in Figure 13-1, we find that a company that operates in several countries often faces several distinct external contexts. The managerial challenge that international operations pose, then, is to understand this diversity and exploit the opportunities it presents.

The firm's ability to meet this challenge effectively will depend on its internal context, particularly on how it is organized. As its operations become more dis-

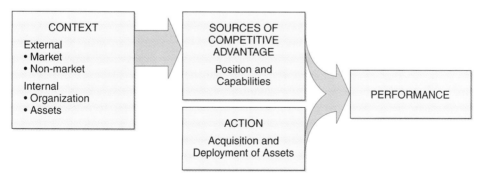

**FIGURE 13-1**   Sources of Competitive Advantage

persed, it is likely to face more complex coordination and incentive problems. Some of the increased complexity arises simply because its operations are larger and more dispersed. As a company gets larger and its operations become more spread out, coordination and incentive problems increase. But some of the increased complexity arises from the firm's operation in different external contexts. A firm that operates in countries with different national cultures, for example, may need to have country-specific architecture, routines, and cultures (ARCs) for its units. Even a simple decision to acquire a component from a foreign rather than a domestic supplier can profoundly affect the firm's ARC. Using a foreign supplier may require changing the contracts that govern the transaction, and it will certainly affect inventory controls and monitoring systems. We return to the question of how the firms should be organized to operate effectively in a global context later in this chapter.

## 13.3  STRATEGIC GAINS FROM GLOBALIZATION

Many firms expand internationally to take advantage, in new regions of the globe, of the competitive advantages they already possess in their current markets. Thus Benetton decided to expand outside its European base because it believed that the value of its brand would extend to other geographic markets. In a similar way, as Wal-Mart's market in the United States became saturated, it sought to apply its competitive cost advantage to distributing branded products to Latin America and Asia.

Indeed, some firms might have the same kind of competitive advantage in new markets that they have in existing markets but be even better positioned to exploit it. The increase in world gasoline prices in the 1970s precipitated the globalization of the automobile industry. Japanese automobile manufacturers who competed head to head in the Japanese market suddenly found that their fuel-efficient cars gave them a tremendous competitive advantage in the United States where no domestic producer offered a small, fuel-efficient car. Instead of fighting each other with similar products in Japan, they attacked the U.S. market share of competitors who were ill positioned to respond. Similarly, Crown Cork & Seal, one of several large metal can producers competing in the United States, expanded internationally by signing exclusive territory agreements with governments in emerging economies that had no domestic can-making firms. It thereby secured a first-mover advantage in those markets that it did not have in the United States.

Sometimes a firm might choose to expand its operations to *create* competitive advantage. This can occur, for example, when a firm's competitive advantage depends on its being able to operate in multiple national markets. The insulin industry provides an example. Before 1980, a dominant firm served each of the geographic regions into which the insulin market was divided. Worldwide, about half a dozen insulin manufacturers had near monopolies in their own regions. The application of recombinant DNA technology to insulin drugs, however, increased the R&D costs to produce insulin and required a larger investment in manufacturing capacity. The firms serving smaller markets found it difficult to cover these costs and had to ally with firms serving other regions. As a result, the insulin industry became more global, and the leading firms Novo-Nordisk and Eli Lilly became increasingly dominant because they participated in more markets.

This is an example of how minimum efficient scale can affect a firm's decision to enter new markets. The sales volume necessary to achieve low unit costs can exceed demand in the home country, driving firms to find new markets. Many of the best examples of scale economies as a driver for international expansion come from knowledge-based industries. Software, for example, has a marginal cost of almost zero. Once the product is developed, producing and distributing another copy of it is inexpensive. Development costs, however, can be substantial. As a result, the firm must have enough market to expect that its operating profits will cover the sunk cost of product development.

A firm might also seek competitive advantage from a global presence if it has international customers who prefer a single supplier. For example, multinational firms have sought to reduce transaction costs by insisting on a single advertising agency and a single telecommunication provider for their entire international network of businesses. To compete for the business of these multinational customers, advertising and telecommunications firms have needed to develop a multinational presence, either by forming strategic alliances or by expanding their own operations. A global presence gives these service firms a competitive advantage over local, domestic firms.

A firm might also create competitive advantage by locating its activities in countries that give it a cost advantage. Firms based in Europe and the United States have traditionally located some of their manufacturing and assembly operations offshore to take advantage of cheaper labor, for example. Recently, software firms and other information technology users have sought offshore programming services to reduce software development costs. As technologies become diffuse and economic development profiles change, so do low-cost locations. Japan, for example, has lost its labor cost advantage in electronics to less-developed economies. If rivals can obtain the same low costs by relocating their activities, relocating to cut costs ceases to be a competitive advantage. However, even if all firms can access low-cost production, any firm that does not find the lowest-cost location for its activities might find itself at a competitive *disadvantage*

Similarly, firms sometimes move parts of their business to foreign countries to take advantage of differences in public sector policies. Low corporate and personal tax rates generally encourage an inflow of capital. Ireland and Puerto Rico provide two compelling examples. Each offers corporate tax rates that are considerably lower than those in many other industrialized areas and has attracted considerable foreign direct investment as a result. Governments also sometimes offer subsidies for locating facilities within their countries or require firms to invest within their country before they are allowed to sell there.

A firm may also seek to enter a new country to facilitate learning. For example, Canon located an R&D facility in Silicon Valley rather than near its center in Japan because it wanted to learn from other firms with technological expertise in digital technology. Locating facilities in the geographic center of a technology might give a firm increased access to engineering or research talent. It might also facilitate the participation of the firm's engineers in the interfirm flow of ideas and teach them how to compete more effectively. For example, Philips located part of its optical storage unit and its multimedia division in Silicon Valley for these reasons. Historically, Philips had been competing in markets where technology moved more slowly and product cycles were longer than in the emerging digital technology in which it planned to compete in the future. By locating in Silicon Valley where suppliers supported high-speed development and where engineers were accustomed to shorter design cycles, Philips hoped to learn the design and manufacturing routines necessary to compete in industries with short product cycles.

Finally, a firm may locate some of its activities to affect a competitor's strategic decisions and actions. For example, a firm might enter the home market of a significant competitor to affect its rival's ability to compete aggressively outside that market. By building up capacity in its competitor's home market, the firm can credibly threaten to compete intensely there. Anxious to avoid intense competition in its home market where it is the dominant firm, the competitor may choose to move less aggressively in other markets in which the two firms compete.

Although any one of these reasons could motivate international expansion, they are not mutually exclusive, and firms often have several reasons to become more international. As firms increasingly operate in multiple countries, their actions affect the structure of their industries and the economies in which they operate. As firms become more global, so do industries and economies.

## 13.4  GLOBALIZATION OF INDUSTRIES AND ECONOMIES

Frequently, the same factors that push one firm in an industry to expand its geographic presence lead others in the industry to do the same. Taken together, the actions of these firms lead to a more global industry as the same firms become the primary players in national markets throughout the world. For example, the beer industry has slowly become more global since the 1960s, as firms like Heineken have begun to sell outside their traditional regional markets. Before then, competition was localized, and different firms were active in different regions of the world.

As companies attempt to leverage their competitive advantage in new markets or to create competitive advantage through multicountry operations, formerly national economies become part of a global economy. A general trend toward eliminating national restrictions on cross-border flows and the emergence of infrastructures that have facilitated expanded operations have promoted this move to more open economies in which goods and services move across national boundaries more freely.

Since the Second World War, numerous international agreements have lowered trade barriers. For example, in February 1997, after three years of negotiation, the World Trade Organization (WTO) brokered a telecommunications agreement among 69 governments. After January 1998, each signatory country's domestic telecommunications market would be open to foreign competition. Before this agreement, U.S. telecommunications carriers had been able to compete for business in markets representing only about 17 percent of the total population in the top 20 international markets. After the agreement, U.S. carriers had direct access to over 90 percent of the world telecom services market. Regional agreements, such as the North American Free Trade Agreement (NAFTA) and the European Union (EU), have also lowered barriers among participating nations. Similarly, constraints on the movement of human capital are also generally declining. Laborers in the EU are now allowed to move freely among EU countries, for example.

Regions are also becoming more closely linked economically because improvements in both international and national transportation infrastructures have reduced the costs of transporting goods. As transportation costs decline, firms can take better advantage of differences in labor costs, for example. Moving assembly offshore reduces cost only if the cost of transporting the components to the lower-wage location and of transporting the assembled product to its final market are sufficiently low. Equally important, the ability to manage a far-flung enterprise depends on the costs of moving information. The diffusion of telephony technologies and Internet-based systems has enhanced the ability of firms to coordinate a dispersed network of businesses. Finally, efforts to harmonize intellectual property laws, contract law, and other forms of the legal infrastructure have also facilitated international expansion.

Some have argued that the emergence of international media companies has created more homogeneous consumer tastes and thus facilitated the globalization of industries. They cite the widespread acceptance of Swatch watches and Nike shoes as examples of an emerging "global" taste for some products. In the 1950s and 1960s, European manufacturers of home appliances frequently had different models for the different European countries in which they sold their products. Since the 1970s, however, many of the country-based differences in tastes have disappeared, and many manufacturers are selling fewer models in more countries. Distinct market segments for appliances remain, but these segments are common across countries.

Although homogenization has occurred for some products, preferences for others remain localized. Even though firms sell automobiles in all regions of the world, different regions value different features of cars. National variations in such things as the cost of fuel, the width of roads, the amount of time people spend in cars, and per capita income mean that consumers in different regions of the world have different needs. This helps explain why no successful global car has emerged, despite leading manufacturers' efforts to promote "world cars."

The increasing internationalization of business creates strategic challenges for managers of international firms and for the purely domestic firms that must cope with new competitors. We now turn to a discussion of these challenges.

## 13.5  STRATEGIC CHALLENGES

In Chapter 4 and 5, we developed the idea of strategic alignment: The firm's internal context (its ARC: architecture, routines, and culture) must be appropriate for its strategy. This means that an international firm's organization design must accommodate the specific challenges that operating across national boundaries pose. These challenges can be grouped into three categories: local responsiveness, global efficiency, and learning in a global context.

## The Challenge of Local Responsiveness

Every country has social and economic features that distinguish it from its neighbors. Our concern is how these differences affect the firm's strategy and organization. Consider, for example, Canada and the United States. Both countries derive their legal context from English Common Law; most of their citizens share a common language; in both countries infrastructures are similar; and so forth. As a result, although each country has different laws governing employment relations, so that firms operating on both sides of the common border have to accommodate country-specific practices, firms can usually handle these differences through fairly minor organizational changes. Dealing with such differences is unlikely to have *strategic* effects. That is, a Canadian company with a strategy developed for its domestic market can probably bring the strategy and the key elements of its internal context that are aligned with it to its U.S. operation. Something about the competitive context in the United States could make entry unattractive. But the Canadian company is unlikely to encounter strong barriers to implementing its strategy that are based on national differences in the general social or economic context. Canada and the United States are similar enough for local responsiveness not to be a major challenge.

At the other extreme, firms from developed economies that are attempting to compete in emerging economies often have major local responsiveness problems. Differences in the legal environment and in the transportation, communication, and utility infrastructures can make it extremely hard for foreign firms to formulate an effective strategy. Consider the challenges that foreign brewers faced when they sought to enter the Chinese beer market in the 1990s. On the one hand, many aspects of the Chinese market made it attractive for foreign entrants in this period. Demand for beer was growing at approximately 10 percent per year and China was expected to be the largest beer market in the world early in the twenty-first century. Moreover, major domestic brewers tended to concentrate on one city or region, and no domestic brewer had more than 4 percent of the overall market share.

Foreign producers found, however, that they had to change their strategies and operational practices to compete in the Chinese market. The Chinese government generally required foreign brewers to have a local alliance partner, but appropriate partners were hard to find. The electrical power infrastructure was inadequate, and production processes had to be adapted to take into account frequent electricity brownouts. Obtaining sufficient clean water was also a problem. The transportation infrastructure was overloaded, expensive, and unreliable. It cost more to transport a container from southern China to Hong Kong than from Hong Kong to Europe or America. Temperature-controlled transport was unavailable, leading to spoilage. Moreover, no large-scale, efficient distributors existed. A typical state-owned brewery might rely on 2000 primary distributors, and most distributors had poor procedures for tracking inventory.

In this environment, companies like Kirin or Anheuser Busch could not pursue the same competitive advantage they had developed in their home countries. In its home country, each of these firms depends on economies of scale. It supports its brand position through national advertising. Its breweries operate efficiently at large scale and depend on a stable energy supply as well as large amounts of clean water. Each firm distributes its product through a well-developed network of moderate-to-large distributors who deliver the product in good condition and in time to meet demand. This strategy would be all but impossible to replicate in China. Indeed, despite a large influx of brewers from Europe, Asia, and the United States, most analysts believe that as of 1998 no foreign brewer had profitable operations in the Chinese market. Short-term overcapacity explains some of the dismal performance, but the difficulty of exploiting the competitive advantage these firms had in their home markets in this very different external context may make Chinese operations unprofitable for foreign brewers for some time.[2]

Foreign firms entering a new market may confront laws, regulations, and institutional procedures that are different from those faced before. Many countries require foreign firms to ally with a domestic partner and to use "local content."[3] Firms also must adapt to how buyers or governments will respond to establishing local production facilities or using local suppliers. For example, Boeing uses Asian suppliers for its commercial planes because it believes that its affiliation with them will enhance the receptivity of Asian airlines to a Boeing bid. In contrast, when Honda opened automobile production facilities in the United States, it found that the reputation for poor quality work in U.S. auto plants led potential buyers to ask whether "their" Honda had been produced in Japan.

Although the formal requirements are usually clear, the informal requirements that local customs and beliefs impose are often less obvious. Both formal laws and informal norms about employment practices tend to vary widely across countries, for example. When it first established operations in China, Anheuser Busch was unaware that employers were required to provide employees with lunch. When it provided lunch, the firm was startled to find that many more people were eating at the plant than were working there. Firms also sometimes find that officials must be bribed to furnish a license or permit. This poses problems when paying bribes violates the firm's own norms or the laws of its home country.

Adapting to local requirements is more difficult when they are not explicit. An outsider always has problems acquiring tacit knowledge, but it can be important to succeeding in a new environment. Consider Marks & Spencer's experience in Spain. The British firm's initial sales of women's clothing were lower than expected. Eventually, managers discovered that part of the problem was that they were not decorating their mannequins with jewelry. Spanish shoppers were much more accustomed than their British counterparts to seeing mannequins wearing jewelry. To Spaniards, the Marks & Spencer displays made the clothing look less attractive. Like so many cultural differences, this one was not one that people were particularly conscious of, so none of its local participants had alerted Marks & Spencer to the problem.

---

[2] For more information, see "Lion Nathan and the Chinese Beer Industry," Case SM-47, Graduate School of Business, Stanford University.

[3] "Local content" requires that some share of a firm's output or components be manufactured within the country in which the product is sold.

So far, we have considered the challenge of local responsiveness in terms of the problems encountered in extending a firm's current strategy to a different external environment. However, there is also an internal challenge. Even if the firm's existing strategy remains useful in the new external environment, the organizational underpinning that supported it in the home country may not work in the new environment. A firm's internal context is tied to its broader social context. For example, engineers in Silicon Valley often change employers. As a result, firms located there develop human resource policies that minimize the cost of high employee turnover. For firms used to operating in a social context of stable, lifetime employment, adapting these kinds of policies required a substantial change in their ARC.

One of the first systematic attempts to describe differences in national cultures was based on a survey of over 100,000 employees of a large U.S. multinational firm that operated in 40 different countries.[4] The researchers concluded that two dimensions described the primary distinguishing cultural characteristics: "individualist *vs.* collectivist" and "hierarchical *vs.* egalitarian" (which is also called *power distance*). The researchers developed scales to map countries along these two dimensions, and an illustrative mapping appears in Figure 13-2.

Individualist–collectivist measures the extent to which individuals can avoid strong obligations to their group and still remain consistent with established norms.

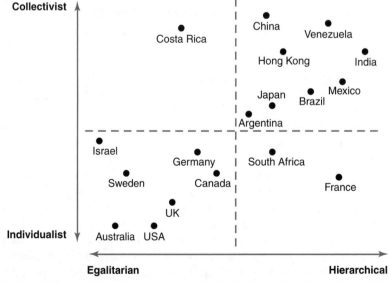

**FIGURE 13-2**  Distribution of Selected Countries on Individualism-Collectivism and Power Distance Scales [*Source:* Geert H. Hofstede, *Cultures and Organizations: Software of the Mind*, New York: McGraw-Hill, 1997.]

---

[4] Geert H. Hofstede, *Cultures and Organizations: Software of the Mind* (New York: McGraw-Hill, 1997).

In individualist cultures, it is acceptable for individuals to place their self-interest above the interest of others, and there is a strong belief that individuals should be evaluated on the basis of their own performance alone. Collectivist cultures strongly disapprove of an individual who tries to avoid obligations to his group, and individuals are evaluated according to the performance of the group. One example of how the individualist–collectivist distinction affects behavior is in the practice of nepotism. In an individualist culture, nepotism is generally regarded as unethical because these cultures distribute rewards based on an individual's merits rather than on the group to which he belongs. In contrast, in a collectivist culture, failure to favor a friend or relative is widely regarded as unethical. A firm with units in both types of cultures has to decide whether to allow nepotism in one location but not another or to push a countercultural policy on employees in one location.

Power distance refers to a society's willingness to accept an uneven distribution of power in institutions and organizations. In a high power-distance culture, superiors are shown deference by their subordinates, and the directives of superiors are rarely questioned. In a low power-distance culture, superiors are only able to secure the cooperation of subordinates through consultation and discussion. In a low power-distance culture, the firm's decision-making process is more likely to involve committees and liaison work to make the decision and to "sell it" to the rest of the organization once it has been made. In high power-distance cultures, decision making can be more easily concentrated in the hands of upper-level managers who then inform the other members of the firm of the outcome. Again, a firm that operates in both environments has to decide how to resolve the conflicting organizational demands.[5]

Although the figure illustrates two dimensions along which national cultures differ, firms from countries that seem to be similar in the figure can still face different organization constraints. In Figure 13-2, the United States and Germany, for example, are fairly close together. But when Daimler and Chrysler merged in 1998, the difference in the compensation structures for senior and upper-level middle managers in the two firms was a major concern. Compensation packages for U.S. senior managers are much higher on average than the packages European firms offer. Upper-level executives at Chrysler had compensation packages that were two or three times greater than their Daimler counterparts. Preserving these variations within the newly merged firm posed a problem of internal equity. Lowering the salaries of Chrysler employees would cause many of them to leave, and those employees with the highest market value would leave first. Even though it was expensive and posed problems in the context of European culture, DaimlerChrysler seems to have decided to increase the salaries of its German managers.

---

[5] Two features of the country mapping illustrated in Figure 13-2 are worth noting. First, a country's location on an axis reflects the position of the *average* respondent from that country. Within each country, there is considerable variance. Even if we focus on respondents from a country located in one corner of the diagram, we could still find many respondents holding views close to those held by individuals in the opposite corner of the diagram. Second, there is a positive relationship between collectivist and high power-distance beliefs. Countries that are collectivist tend also to be high power distance; conversely, those countries that are individualist tend to be low power distance.

We have provided several examples of how firms might need to adapt their strategies and internal contexts to operate internationally. Managers who have to make this kind of adaptation first must understand what kinds of changes are necessary. Second, they need to weigh how much variation in ARC the firm can accommodate. Finally, they should judge whether these changes will prevent them from leveraging their current advantage. Although a firm might theoretically pursue radically different strategies in different locations, doing so raises questions about whether common organization is the best way to implement these strategies.

## The Challenge of Global Efficiency

A firm is "globally efficient" when it produces and distributes goods at lowest cost. The issue here is how the firm should geographically configure its activities to make this happen. Where should it locate its operations? How many locations should it have? As suggested earlier, configuring a global supply chain requires addressing issues related to exploiting scale economies, accounting for transportation costs, leveraging variations in input costs, and managing a dispersed operation. To minimize costs, these various factors must be carefully balanced.

Intel, for example, was founded in Silicon Valley in the 1960s and initially had all its operations located there, even though it sold its products worldwide. As the semiconductor industry became more cost competitive, Intel began to move some labor-intensive, low-skill activities (packaging memory chips, for example) offshore. As the high-technology cluster in Silicon Valley developed, the cost of living and operating in the Valley increased. Intel responded by moving more of its activities out of the Valley, establishing centers for manufacturing in lower cost areas of the United States and in technology clusters abroad. Because these manufacturing activities involve state-of-the-art engineering, Intel sometimes has had to recruit engineers specifically to work in its new locations. For example, Intel has a program to subsidize the training and relocation costs of young engineers in the United States who will relocate to Intel's facilities in Ireland.

On the one hand, the opportunity to exploit economies of scale suggests that the firm might restrict the number of locations in which scale-sensitive activities take place. On the other hand, to take advantage of variation in factor costs, respond to nonmarket requirements for local production content, or reduce the risks associated with political instability, the firm might choose more locations than scale economies would dictate. For example, a firm might want to locate research and development in countries where the supply of technical labor is more favorable and production activities in other countries with low labor costs, even when this geographical separation imposes some inefficiency on the firm. Similarly, if the firm operates in countries where political and economic conditions are volatile, it may want to diversify its geographic portfolio to reduce the risk of losing access to vital capacity because of policy shifts or political upheaval. Finally, although a variety of financial structures allow firms to hedge against exchange rate risk, managers also need to be sensitive to these risks when making large investments. All these factors tend to push firms toward having multiple locations.

In deciding how many locations to have, firms often underestimate the logistical costs of managing a process that spans multiple locations. These costs are particularly high when the production process demands minimizing inventory of work in progress. Improvements in information technology have facilitated firms' ability to manage logistics efficiently, but the challenge is still daunting.

Perhaps even more frequently ignored are the costs of communication. This involves the cost of getting information from one place to another, but it also includes the costs the firm incurs because it is difficult for employees in one location to take into account the needs of employees located somewhere else. Just as employees in a single business in a multibusiness firm find it difficult to anticipate how their actions might affect other businesses, geographically separated units cannot readily anticipate these effects on each other. As we note below, this affects companywide learning. It also leads individual units to invest too much (from the company's perspective) in activities that adversely affect other units and not enough in activities that positively affect them.

The kinds of local adaptation required for diverse local contexts often exacerbate the problem. For example, we noted earlier that local norms may make nepotism efficient at one manufacturing site and not at another, and a firm may allow each unit to decide its own policy. However, this approach may lead employees in the individualist culture to refuse to accept employees reassigned from the collectivist unit because the former believe that the hiring practices of the latter result in less able workers on average. In this case, letting one unit engage in nepotism while disallowing it at another limits the firm's ability to reallocate its human resources effectively.

However many activity locations a firm might choose to have, it also has to choose *where* to locate them. Labor supply is often a deciding factor. Firms that rely on labor-intensive factory assembly will seek to locate plants in countries with low labor costs. Managers should recognize that wages alone do not determine cost. Because labor productivity also varies, managers also need to assess the cost of labor required to produce the product. Suppose a worker in Country A can be hired at $2.00 per hour and can produce 10 pots per hour, while a worker in Country B must be paid $3.00 per hour but can produce 20 pots per hour. Clearly, the labor cost per pot is lower in Country B ($0.15) than in Country A ($0.20) because the workers in B are also more productive. Figure 13-3 illustrates that a strong relationship exists between wages and productivity across continents. While an engineer in Hungary might receive a salary that is one-fourth or one-fifth that of an engineer in Britain, the British engineer is still competitive because Britain's infrastructure allows him to be three or four times as productive as his Hungarian counterpart.

## The Challenge of Learning

As companies struggle to formulate strategy and design organizations that are appropriate for multicountry operations, they often must also cope with rapid technological change. A firm must therefore be able to learn what is necessary to deepen its current competitive advantage and build new competencies to remain a strong competitor in a global industry.

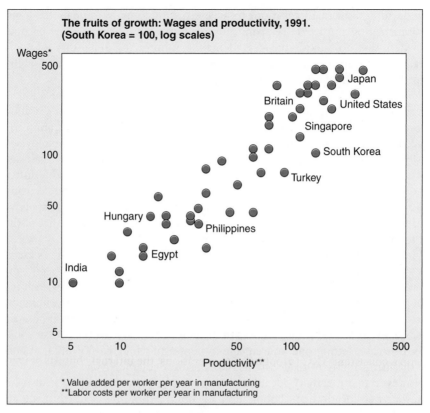

**FIGURE 13-3**   The Relationship between Wages and Productivity (*Source:* Dani Rodrik: Reprinted in *The Economist*, September 20, 1997, p. 38.)

A firm with a broad international presence might benefit from being exposed to a wide variety of problems and solutions. In each of its locations, it can collect information about local customers and suppliers, competitors, and technology. Moreover, it brings its own local human capital to bear on the information it collects. To the extent that customers, suppliers, technology, and human capital vary by country, an international firm is exposed to more variation in how problems are defined and solutions are formulated than a purely domestic firm would be. Ford engineers, for example, found that dust interfered with the quality of its assembly-line production in its Brazilian plants. To mitigate this problem, the engineers there developed dust-resistant techniques that other Ford plants worldwide quickly adopted. Although most of the plants outside Brazil did not have as severe problems from dust and therefore had not addressed this issue, they still benefited from the innovation produced in Brazil.

Another example comes from the drilling practices at British Petroleum (BP) in the Gulf of Mexico where BP faced a rapid increase in the price of deep water drilling rigs. One possible solution was to reduce costs by using the rigs more efficiently. Local drilling engineers had benchmarked their operations against others in the region and determined that they were already among the most efficient. However, when they compared their productivity to that of other BP units around the world, they discovered that they could improve performance by refining their processes for selecting drill bits and drill tool assembly. Within a year, BP had cut the drilling time per well in half in the Gulf.[6]

In both of these examples, a local unit solved a problem that was acute in its area. The resulting benefits were large enough to motivate the investment in learning necessary to find a solution. Moreover, both companies had mechanisms for recognizing the contribution these solutions made to their competitive advantage and for diffusing the innovation throughout the company. Ford's engineers in Brazil produced an innovation that was new to the company but would have had only a local impact had Ford not been able to replicate it in its other plants. BP's engineers in Mexico solved their local problem by accessing learning that other BP units had accomplished.

Recognizing the value of an innovation and transferring it to the rest of the firm are particularly challenging for a global firm. Because its international operations are so varied, the firm must distinguish between variants that can add value in other locations and those that are idiosyncratic to one location. Even when a firm has attempted to develop a consistent ARC throughout its operations, the internal contexts of its various units will inevitably be different. Moreover, *external* contexts are inherently different. As a result, the same variation that produces innovation in the first place makes it difficult to recognize which innovations have value for the firm as a whole. It is difficult to decide which experiments that were successful in one part of the firm will also be successful in others. Conversely, failure in one location does not mean the innovation might not have value elsewhere.

Given the scope of the selection problem, the company faces a dilemma in deciding how centralized its selection mechanism should be. The more centralized the selection process, the more difficult it is for decision makers to know what local innovations have occurred. On the other hand, the more decentralized the selection process, the less likely it is that management will understand how widely applicable the change may be. As we saw in Chapter 4, one way firms respond to this problem is to form linking mechanisms that encourage both horizontal and vertical communication. A horizontal mechanism might be a forum for engineers from different units to meet on a regular basis or standardizing procedures for benchmarking across units, for example. Horizontal mechanisms support a decentralized selection process. Vertical communication supports a centralized selection process. Reporting and monitoring

---

[6] *British Petroleum (B): Focus on Learning*, Case 16B, Graduate School of Business, Stanford University.

systems that give central decision makers the information they need to understand innovations that occur at the local level are an example.

Once it has decided to adopt an innovation in its other locations, a firm has to have a mechanism for implementing it. Firms with centralized decision making often impose adoption. But some firms have a central group—an *ad hoc* or continuing committee made up of technical staff, for example—that decides which innovations are valuable but has no direct authority to mandate adoption. It can make recommendations to another central body that does have that authority, or it may be asked to "sell" the idea to regional units. When selection is decentralized, so are most implementation decisions, and again responsibility may be divided between those who select and those who implement.

## 13.6  ORGANIZING TO MEET THE CHALLENGE

Considered independently, each of the challenges of local responsiveness, global efficiency, and learning poses a formidable organizational task. However, the problem is compounded because the design choices that enhance a firm's ability to address one of them often undercut its ability to deal with another. For example, the more a firm seeks to be locally responsive by customizing processes and products, the more difficult it will be for it to reap global economies of scale or to select and transfer innovations effectively. The more the firm pursues a strategy of global efficiency, the more difficult it is to maintain the variation that facilitates local responsiveness and learning. As these problems become more pressing, firms experiment with organization design, reworking their ARC as they find that clinging to the old, ineffective design costs more than reorganizing.

### Federated vs. Centralized

Historically, multinational firms have adopted two different types of architectures. One is a highly decentralized, country-based "federation" typified by European multinationals such as Nestle, Shell, Unilever, and Philips. As these firms developed in the postwar period, each country operation within them typically contained a full complement of functions from R&D to sales, made its own decisions about product features and pricing, and built up its own supplier relationships. The corporate head-office was little more than a holding company, rarely intervening and often facing opposition when it tried to reallocate resources from one local unit to another. A second type of multinational was the tightly coupled, centralized architecture, typified in the 1980s by Japanese firms, such as Matsushita or Toyota, where a large, powerful corporate office made worldwide decisions. Local units served as knowledge conduits, feeding market information back to the center, and as distribution points for the exported products that arrived from centralized production facilities.

Each of these architectures has strengths and weaknesses. The federated architecture is more locally responsive than the decentralized model but is less likely to achieve global efficiency. A country unit in this model will have the information and the decision-making authority to structure its operations to fit its national environment. But global efficiency is difficult to achieve because the top of the federated structure has neither the information nor the power to allocate resources. As a consequence, corporate headquarters finds it difficult to rationalize worldwide operations, achieve scale economies, and shift resources to where they would provide the greatest value.

The centralized model is more likely to achieve global efficiency and less likely to accommodate local adaptation. Those at corporate headquarters have better information and can allocate resources. However, they face the complex managerial task of optimizing resource allocation decisions across many countries and time zones. Although this model may lend itself to economies of scale in production, it can also produce serious managerial diseconomies because the corporate office makes most important decisions.

Moreover, neither of these approaches is well designed to foster learning. The federation model may encourage learning at the local level but has no mechanisms to compare different approaches to similar problems or to disseminate best practice across country groups. In terms of the variation–selection–retention model discussed in Chapter 5, a centralized architecture does not lend itself to variance, while the federated architecture does not lend itself to efficient selection or retention. Thus neither form fosters learning.

The federated structure is best suited to producing goods where local responsiveness is the key competitive advantage. If tastes are highly differentiated by country or business practices are subject to country-specific regulation, this kind of organization might work well. However, for commodity products where cost is the key competitive advantage, the more centralized architecture would probably work better. Unfortunately, neither approach is appropriate for rapidly changing industries, and, as a result, these old models are becoming less relevant.

In response to the obvious weaknesses of these models, multinational firms in the 1990s searched for a middle ground. Thus, for example, Procter & Gamble, which traditionally had conformed to the centralized model, has been decentralizing while its traditionally federated competitor, Unilever, has been attempting to link units by, for example, encouraging cross-national coordination in product development and introduction. A similar convergence is occurring in the automobile industry. General Motors, which historically had completely separated its international and U.S. divisions, is now building linkages between those units. Meanwhile, Toyota, an archetype of the centralized model, is allowing greater local variation.

It is too early to know where this experimentation will lead or which paths will prove most useful. However, international business scholars have suggested several models for firm organization. We briefly review some of the better-known models and the circumstances in which each might be most appropriate.

## Building the Middle Ground

Three main models attempt to address the challenges of globalization by pursuing a middle way between the centralized and federated structures. They are not the only ways a firm might organize, but they are examples of how the organizational challenges might be addressed.

## The Regional Organization

In his 1990 book, *The Borderless World*, Kenichi Ohmae[7] argues that the world economy has three primary and distinct regional markets—North America, Europe, and Asia. Especially for commodity goods, each region has a set of demand conditions that are relatively homogeneous within the region but differ among the three regions. A global firm thus needs to establish a complete supply chain within each region and create a corporate headquarters that is "geographically de-centered." A full supply chain within each region, Ohmae argues, allows the organization to be locally responsive and minimizes the costs trade barriers impose. A de-centered headquarters has no national home and facilitates regional responsiveness. Ohmae suggests that a litmus test for whether corporate is de-centered is if the CEO could come from any region.

This model is close to the decentralized, country-based organization characteristic of the multinational corporations that arose after World War II. However, Ohmae's model aggregates country operations by region and can thus obtain scale economies that the less aggregated model could not achieve. If a region has significant local variation, a firm organized this way will give up some local responsiveness in exchange for greater operating efficiency. If the units are standardized within regions, this organization sacrifices some of the learning advantage from variation that the federated approach produces, but it may be better at selection and adaptation.

## Locational Advantage

In *The Competitive Advantage of Nations* (1990), Michael Porter argues that competitive advantage in the global context is intimately bound to location.[8] He sees competitive advantage as a product of the firm's external environment and notes that there is typically a high level of geographic concentration among the leading firms within a global industry. As examples, consider Swiss watches, Dutch flowers, U.S. furniture, Italian clothing, or Japanese automobile manufacturers. Firms located in these areas of agglomeration, Porter argues, benefit from the presence of other leading firms and have a competitive advantage over firms located outside these geographic clusters.

Porter argues that four attributes of a location foster strong competition in a global context: (1) factor conditions, (2) demand conditions, (3) related and supporting industries, and (4) firm strategy, structure, and rivalry. Figure 13-4 reproduces his description of the regional factors that make industry clusters important to how businesses perform. If these industry-specific factors are indeed important, companies should center their businesses in the most advantageous locations. Note that the home base for a business unit need not be the same as the corporate headquarters, and the home base for one business in a multibusiness firms need not be the same as the home base for another. For example, when Sony entered the movie industry, it did not build

[7] Kenichi Ohmae, *The Borderless World: Power and Strategy in the Interlinked Economy* (New York: Harper-Business, 1999.).

[8] Michael E. Porter, *The Competitive Advantage of Nations* (New York: The Free Press, 1998).

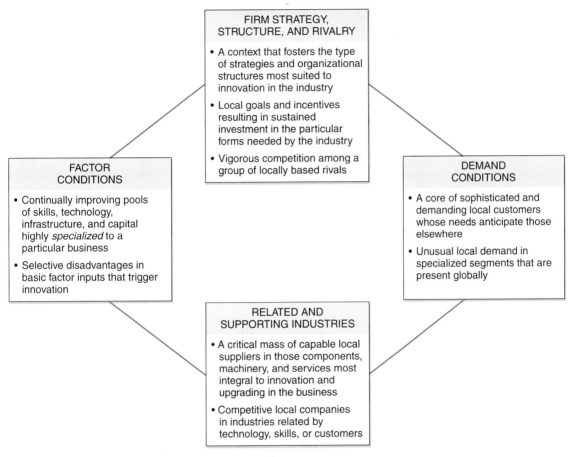

**FIGURE 13-4**   Selected Location-Based Determinants of Competitive Advantage: The "Diamond" (*Source:* Reprinted from Michael E. Porter and Rebecca E. Wayland, "Global Competition and the Localization of Competitive Advantage," *Advances in Strategic Management*, Vol. 11A, p. 84.)

a film studio in Japan. Instead, it acquired an established U.S. firm, Columbia Pictures. Although Sony centered its film production activity in California, it kept its R&D for its electronics business in Japan near its center of excellence.

Many of the local conditions Porter identifies as fostering a strong global competitor are industry characteristics that we described as making an industry *unattractive* in Chapter 6. Porter's underlying argument is Darwinian. Tough local conditions, he says, lead to fiercer, smarter competitors. In such an environment, a competitor must be strong or fail. Conversely, in an attractive local industry, a weak, inefficient competitor can often flourish until it encounters competition from international firms.

On a business unit basis, the locational advantage model is closer to the old centralized model than to the federation model and is probably better at generating global efficiency than at enabling local responsiveness. The older centralized model, however, paid scant attention to where the "center" should be located. It generally took the country of origin as the center. The locational advantage model considers how the center should obtain the capability it needs to be globally efficient.

The locational advantage model thinks of a multibusiness firm as a collection of business units; this is not a model of how the firm as a whole should be put together but of how to organize activities. Like the federation model, Porter's view of the firm is unclear about what contribution headquarters makes. In the federation model, corporate does little to facilitate local responsiveness but can require the local units to make some concessions to the center, thus detracting from their ability to be locally focused. Similarly, the locational advantage model has no clear mechanism through which the center can contribute to the performance of the individual units, each of which is situated in the area of its locational advantage.

## The Transnational Corporation

To identify the firm characteristics that best confront the challenges that globalization poses, Bartlett and Ghoshal developed a model of the transnational corporation.[9] A transnational corporation rejects the sharp, historical dichotomy between local responsiveness and global efficiency by analyzing firms at the activity level rather than at the level of the firm itself. Scale-sensitive activities would be centralized to reap economies of scale, for example, while other activities for which local responsiveness is more important would be decentralized. A firm may thus have production centralized in one location but globally disperse its marketing. Although the transnational corporation might well locate centralized activities in geographic areas that provide the most fertile ground for them, Bartlett and Ghoshal have little to say about where activities should be located.

The recent movement to "platform" production in the automobile industry illustrates how firms selectively choose which activities to centralize and which to decentralize. In "platform" production, designers and engineers try to identify those parts and features of a car about which its globally dispersed consumers have similar preferences. The designers and engineers then respond to local variation by adding unique country-specific features to this basic platform. The automobile firm can thereby realize global economies of scale in those features of the car that are common worldwide, while still responding to local demand for those features where variation is important to the firm's competitive advantage.

The transnational corporation tries to accomplish both local responsiveness and global efficiency by dispersing the firm's supply chain. When the company's supply chain is globally dispersed, the firm's performance hinges on its ability to coordinate activities across those dispersed segments. Thus, corporate headquarters must ensure coordination across units. Indeed, the ability to coordinate globally dispersed assets is perhaps the most essential capability of the transnational corporation.

---

[9] Christopher A. Bartlett and Sumantra Ghoshal, *Managing Across Borders: The Transnational Solution*, 2nd ed. (Boston: Harvard Business School Press, 1998.)

In both the transnational corporation and the locational advantage models, learning is highly centralized. A center of excellence is set up to become the repository of leading technical or strategic knowledge, and the ideas that emerge from this center are then sent out to peripheral units if and when those ideas are applicable. As we noted earlier, centralized learning models are weak in generating the variation necessary for innovation. If no learning that originates in one business unit can be applied in another, concentrating a business in one location might be a good model for selecting among the innovations that occur and ensuring that the firm implements valuable innovations. Similarly, if learning is activity-specific, the transnational corporation might be good at selection and retention. But if learning needs to be transferred across geographic units, these designs will face the same problem the decentralized models encounter.

## 13.7  SUMMARY

We have considered the drivers behind globalization at the firm, industry, and country level. We illustrated how some firms expand internationally to take advantage of the competitive advantages they already possess in their current markets and how they can create new competitive advantages by expanding their operations geographically. We then examined three challenges implicit in globalization: the challenge of local responsiveness, the challenge of global efficiency, and the challenge of learning. Finally, we explored the implications of these challenges for the way the firm is organized.

In addressing these issues, we have also answered a question we raised earlier: How are the strategic challenges global firms face different from the challenges that firms competing within the border of one nation face? We have seen at least four reasons why strategic management is different for multinational firms. First, variations in the public sector environment are a much more salient concern for global firms. Second, differences in social and market contexts are greater, and it is thus harder for global firms to develop a common organizational culture, share understanding of organizational activities, and identify what practices they can and should transfer across contexts. Third, the logistical complexity of managing the organization is greater. Although improvements in information technology and transportation have made it easier for firms to confront this complexity, global firms find it harder to match people to problems and ensure accountability. Fourth, because of these first three problems, individual managers are less likely to be aware of what they do not know. In a global firm, the challenge of collecting the information to make a sound decision is much greater.

In the following chapter we discuss the specific strategic challenges of the multi-business company.

# 14

# CORPORATE STRATEGY: MANAGING FOR VALUE IN A MULTIBUSINESS COMPANY

## 14.1 INTRODUCTION

In earlier chapters, we explored the challenge facing a general manager who formulates strategy for a business competing in a specific industry. Figure 14-1 illustrates the framework we have used and depicts business performance as the combined effect of context and action. The role of the strategist is to provide the business with a guide to choosing the actions that will enhance its performance given the firm's internal and external contexts. This manager, we have argued, must develop a deep understanding of the industry in which his firm competes. That understanding, along with a hardheaded assessment of the firm's assets and organization, is the basis for identifying and pursuing competitive advantage. This now-familiar description captures the scope of the strategic management problem faced by the general manager of a single business.

Sometimes, however, this business is part of a larger firm composed of multiple businesses. For example, Hewlett-Packard has an inkjet printer business, a laser printer business, and a computer business. Our treatment of strategic management thus far would be appropriate for the head of, say, the desktop printer group. But it does little to illuminate the strategic role of the corporate managers[1] to whom he reports or how being part of a larger organization affects his role. If strategy formulation and implementation occur at the business unit level, what strategic responsibilities do corporate managers have?

---

[1] We will use the terminology "corporate manager," or sometimes simply "corporate," to refer to those senior managers to whom managers of the firm's businesses report. Looking ahead to Figure 14-2, for example, the general manager of Business A would have the strategic role we have discussed throughout the text. The corporate manager would be senior to this manager and responsible for the overall performance of the firm.

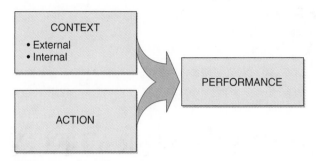

**FIGURE 14-1**   Business Unit Strategy

A key strategic difference between the roles of the business unit managers and the corporate managers is one of breadth. The manager of a business unit is responsible for the performance of that unit, whereas the corporate managers of the firm are responsible for the performance of the company as a whole. We have said much about how strategic thinking can contribute to the performance of the business unit as a stand-alone enterprise. The central question of corporate strategy is what additional contribution to performance can be made at the corporate level. How might embedding a business unit in a larger firm where corporate managers have the authority to review and influence the decisions made at the business level enhance performance?

That question is the focus of this chapter. We begin by embellishing the framework in Figure 14-1 to incorporate multiple business units. Then we discuss, in general terms, how diversification affects firm performance. Next we explore how a firm's competitive advantage in one business can contribute to its competitive advantage in another. Finally, we turn our attention to the ARC of the multibusiness firm and ask how organization design issues affect its ability to reap benefit from a multibusiness organization.

## 14.2   A FRAMEWORK FOR CORPORATE STRATEGY

To understand the difference between corporate and business strategy, think about the problem a new corporate manager faces. Most corporate managers come from within the firm, and a new vice president might have managed one of the businesses within her company. As the head of that business, she had mastered the art of understanding its external and internal contexts. She had crafted a strategy that allowed her managers to create and implement policies that gave the business a sustainable competitive advantage. Now her job has changed. Another manager now fills her old position, and he and several other business heads report to her. What is her role now?

One thing is clear: She should no longer be developing *business* strategy. Even if that were not the responsibility of others, she is not well positioned to fulfill this role.

Indeed, she may have only limited familiarity with the external and internal contexts for the businesses in the firm outside her old area. Even if she strives to become better acquainted with these businesses, the managers who run them on a day-to-day basis have better information on which to base decisions about strategic direction. She will largely rely on information they make available to her to assess their performance. If they are doing their jobs well, she cannot improve the performance of the individual units by altering their strategies. If she is to enhance firm performance, she must instead find ways to encourage them to make decisions that contribute to the firm's overall performance and that they would not make if they focused only on the performance of their unit.

Figure 14-2 illustrates her dilemma. There we show a company that is composed of two lines of business. Each business operates in an external economic and nonmarket environment. Some of the elements in these two external contexts overlap. General macroeconomic conditions, for example, affect both businesses, as do social conditions and the public sector. A war in the Middle East, a recession in Asia, or social upheaval in Russia is likely to affect the performance of each business. However, these contexts may also have important differences. If one business produces television programming, the emergence of new channels for electronically distributing

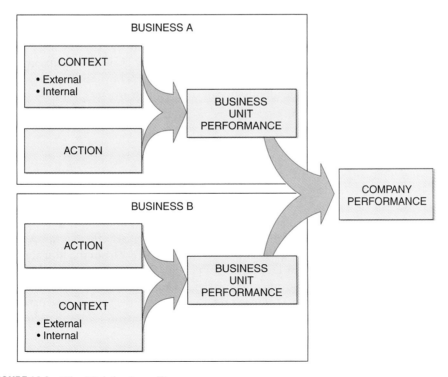

**FIGURE 14-2**  The Multibusiness Firm

entertainment content could affect it. If the other business makes heavy construction equipment, trade barriers for manufactured goods might affect it. It is unlikely, however, that the changes in trade barriers for manufactured goods will much affect the entertainment company or that the manufacturing firm need be concerned about how many channels consumers can use to receive entertainment. In short, if her company is really a "multibusiness" firm, its constituent businesses are competing in *different* external contexts.

This implies that the businesses might also rely on different internal contexts and pursue different strategies. The assets and organization that support an advantageous strategy in entertainment are likely to be different from those that maximize performance in manufacturing construction equipment. The entertainment business might have a strategy based on product differentiation and vertical integration into distribution, while the manufacturing business might pursue competitive advantage through operational efficiency and supply chain management. Thus, although multibusiness companies vary in how widely they are diversified, their constituent businesses are likely to have distinct internal and external contexts.

"Corporate" strategy and "business" strategy must therefore be distinct. Corporate strategy is not a "larger version" of business strategy. A diversified firm as a whole cannot develop the kind of strategy we described in Chapter 2. Rather, each business in the company should have a strategy with a set of goals, scope, clear competitive advantage, and a logic that is consistent with its distinctive external and internal context. In Figure 14-2, we have augmented the standard single business diagram by including a box labeled "company performance" based on the performance of the business units. Although it seems obvious that the goal of corporate managers is to improve the performance of the company as a whole, it is less obvious how they might do it. If each business is independently maximizing its performance, what is left for corporate to do?

## Managing Strategic Spillovers

We believe that corporate can add value by managing the "strategic spillovers" from one business unit to another. Spillovers occur because the actions one business unit takes in pursuit of its objectives can affect the performance of the company's other business units. When the managers of Walt Disney Corporation's studio division developed and promoted the animated film *The Lion King*, its efforts improved the performance in the theme park division because the characters from the film appeared at the parks. By contrast, when Disney's Miramax division produces films that some consider inconsistent with the uncontroversial, mainstream, family entertainment reputation of the theme parks, Miramax might negatively affect the theme park division. In Figure 14-3, we have illustrated these spillovers as arrows from the actions of each business unit to the performance of the other.

Spillovers like these mean that company performance might be more than just the summation of the various individual business unit outcomes. These spillovers are the reason that the performance of the whole company might be better than a simple

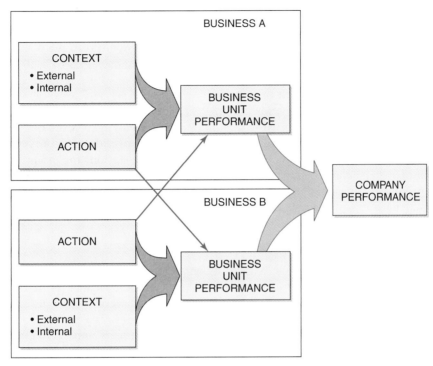

**FIGURE 14-3**   Business Unit Spillovers

portfolio of the business units as stand-alone enterprises. If putting the business units within a single firm increases the potential for positive spillovers, the combined performance of the units could be better than it would be if each unit operated as a separate firm.

We have called these interactions "strategic spillovers" to indicate that we are interested in inter-unit effects that can affect the outcome of a business unit's strategy. If the theme park division's strategy depends on a brand image that is synonymous with high-quality films, consistent with mainstream culture, Miramax's edgy, culturally challenging productions might impair the parks division's competitive advantage. The label "strategic spillover" also makes the point that these interactions can be negative or positive. A more common term in the strategy literature for "spillovers" is "synergies." This implies that the spillovers are always or predominantly positive. But when businesses are related in a way that makes positive spillovers possible, the spillovers can also be negative. Corporate managers need to manage spillovers to foster positive ones and limit the effects of negative ones.

When spillovers are important, the difference in the perspectives of corporate and business unit managers can affect company performance. Just as the position of the corporate manager makes it difficult for her to construct a good business strategy, it is difficult for the business manager to perceive and account for how his decisions will affect the performance of other business units. Both managers have important and different roles. A multibusiness firm has business unit managers to reap the benefits of strategic management at the business level. It has corporate managers to manage the strategic spillovers among these units.[2]

Corporate managers might manage spillovers by making decisions themselves. Corporate managers at Disney, for example, will intervene when they believe that business unit managers are poised to act in a way that seems against the best interests of the corporation. More often, however, corporate works through the business units. Rather than making every product development decision, for example, the corporate managers at Disney try to create a corporate culture and construct decision-making routines that lead its business unit managers to make decisions that will enhance the company's image as a source of mainstream, family entertainment.

## A Framework for Corporate Strategy

As the Disney example suggests, corporate managers can affect decision making by constructing the company's organizational design. Corporate managers design the overall architecture of the firm, contribute to the development of a corporate culture, and establish some of its important decision-making and business process routines. The firm's broad architecture will affect the interaction of its units through both structure and compensation. The structure of the organization affects what the unit can do on its own and what it must rely on other units to provide. The companywide compensation scheme affects the incentives that induce unit managers to take the objectives of the company as a whole into account. The corporate managers directly affect the routines for inter-unit functions (monitoring and control functions, for example). By diffusing best-practice and imposing standardization, corporate managers can also indirectly affect routines within the business units. To the extent that diverse businesses can have a common set of norms and beliefs, the corporate managers establish and maintain a company culture. One of the first things that Carly Fiorina focused on after assuming the CEO position at Hewlett-Packard was amending its famous corporate culture, for example.

Resource allocation is another major avenue through which corporate influences the activities of the business units. Corporate managers typically have a voice in the resources that are available to the business units. As a result, corporate managers can profoundly affect the internal contexts of the business units. Providing additional resources may allow the business to develop assets it otherwise could not deploy. Corporate managers also can target resources for specific activities within the business units, thereby affecting the mix of things the unit undertakes. And, of course, corporate managers can also reduce a unit's resources.

---

[2] A corporation also has a corporate office because it has legal responsibilities to fulfill. These, however, have little to do with adding value.

Whether corporate managers are working through resource allocation or organization design, their actions affect the units' internal contexts: the assets and organization of the business units. As the actions of the corporate managers alter these contexts, business unit managers respond by making small or large changes in their strategies. This affects the actions the units take and thus their performance as well. Ideally, the units will be creating more positive spillovers as a result, leading to an improvement in their combined performance.

Figure 14-4 pulls this discussion together into a framework for corporate strategy. In this framework, corporate managers promote the firm's overall performance by making resource allocation and organization design decisions that affect the internal contexts of the business units. This activity adds value to the company by managing the interactions among the constituent businesses.

Our new vice president can add value then by creating an organizational design and a resource allocation plan that lead the businesses to make decisions that promote the performance of the firm as a whole. We devote most of this chapter to fleshing out what this means. Before turning to this task, however, we want to emphasize that adding value in this way is not always possible. To do so, we briefly review the performance record of diversified firms.

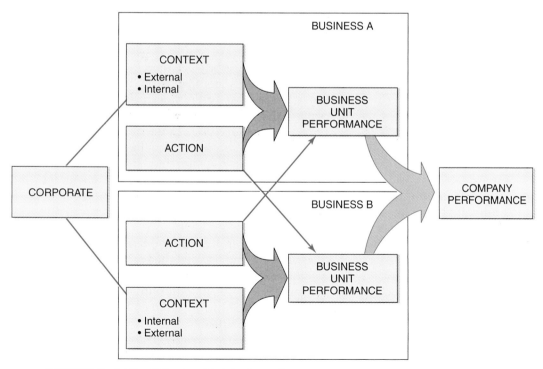

**FIGURE 14-4**   Adding Value in a Multibusiness Company

## 14.3  DOES CORPORATE ADD VALUE?

Although corporate *might* add value, there is no guarantee that it will. Although Disney is often cited as a firm that creates and captures value through the spillovers among its business units, other firms have destroyed value through diversification. Sometimes that value is unlocked in a leveraged buyout in which the firm is taken over and then split up into separate businesses. A classic example is the infamous buyout of RJR Nabisco by Kohlberg, Kravis, and Roberts (KKR) in 1988. KKR subsequently sold off the company's European business and its Del Monte foods division. In a similar vein, some acquisitions made by Disney have been questioned by analysts concerned about whether they will add value to the company. Does, for example, the ownership of the professional hockey team Disney acquired really add value to the firm? It is not surprising that some corporate combinations work better than others or that managers can make mistakes. But it is important to know whether a corporate strategy of diversification is *likely* to enhance firm performance. Does combining two (or more) different businesses within a single firm typically add value?

To answer this question, we must first be more precise about what we mean by "adding value." Consider a firm that produces both automotive glass and ball bearings and has a stock price of $100 per share. Suppose this firm were broken up into a ball-bearing firm and an automotive glass firm with the stock in each distributed to the stockholders of the original firm. For every share of the old, multibusiness company a stockholder owned, he would get one share in the new automotive glass company and one share in the new ball-bearing firm.

If the market value of one share of the new ball-bearing company plus one share of the automotive glass company is worth less than $100, breaking up the firm has destroyed value. Conversely, if the value of the stock prices of the businesses is greater when they are separate, as was the case after 3Com spun off the Palm Pilot in early 2000, breaking up the firm has added value. The stock prices value the expected profits of the businesses, and a decline implies that the stock market thinks that the two businesses were more valuable when they were in a single firm. Setting aside the details of this example, we see that adding value means that the long-run profits of the multibusiness firm are greater than the summed profits its businesses would earn if they were independent firms. The whole is greater than the sum of its parts.

Thinking about value added in this way shows why corporate managers of a diversified firm shoulder the burden of improving on what the businesses could do on their own. To return to our hypothetical firm, any investor could hold a portfolio that included stock from a company that produces only automotive glass and from a company that produces only ball bearings. Investors can build a portfolio to mimic any combination of businesses that a diversified firm might put together. To add value, then, diversified corporations must do something that investors cannot accomplish on their own.

## The Performance of Diversified Firms

How much value diversification creates or destroys, then, is the critical question for the firm's corporate managers.[3] They should consistently ask whether they currently add value to their businesses and if they can expect to do so in the future. Once the euphoria of achieving corporate managerial rank wears off, our new vice president might be sobered by a review of the managerial and economics literature on the performance of diversified firms.

The first thing she might note is the lack of consensus in the academic and business communities about whether diversification creates value. Some business leaders strongly advocate a "narrow" business focus. This "stick-to-your-knitting" view gained ground in the 1980s and 1990s. But others argue that diversification can create value. Given this division in the business community, it is not surprising that strategic management scholars are also not of a single mind about this issue.

The overall trend among management scholars, however, is to view diversification negatively. For example, Michael Porter concluded in 1987 that the "track record of corporate strategies has been dismal." He asserted that in the 33 companies he studied, "Only the lawyers, investment bankers and original sellers have prospered in most of the [diversification] acquisitions, not the shareholders."[4] Other research supports this dismal view of diversification. A recent study[5] of over 1400 large, publicly traded U.S. firms compared the performance of diversified firms to portfolios of undiversified firms. This study contrasts, for example, the performance of a firm with assets in forestry products and construction with the combined performance of an undiversified forest products firm and an undiversified construction firm. The basic question this study asks is whether the diversified firm outperformed a portfolio of undiversified firms put together to mimic the diversified firm's asset structure. If diversification adds value, the answer should be "yes."[6] Instead, the answer appears to be "no"; on average, diversification reduces value, and the diversification discount is fairly large. Although some large-sample studies do find value in diversification, the

---

[3] Whether corporate managers can meet this challenge is also important to the overall economy because so much economic activity occurs within diversified firms. Most large U.S. firms are at least somewhat diversified, for example. And in other economies, diversification is even more common. Those who study business structures in emerging economies note that even moderate-sized businesses tend to be diversified. If corporate managers cannot add value at these firms or—to take a darker view—if combining diverse businesses within a single firm actually destroys value, diversification can substantially hurt the economy.

[4] Michael E. Porter, "From Competitive Advantage to Corporate Strategy," *Harvard Business Review* (May–June 1987).

[5] Larry H.P. Lang and Rene M. Stulz, "Tobin's $q$, Corporate Diversification, and Firm Performance," *Journal of Political Economy*, 102, (1994), 1248–1280.

[6] It is possible that diversification adds value, but diversified firms are made up of poorly performing divisions that would do even worse as a stand-alone companies. If this is true, one would want to ask why diversification systematically collects weak divisions.

preponderance of the evidence suggests that diversified firms, on average, do not perform as well as focused firms in the United States.[7]

Although the evidence that diversification may destroy rather than add value is growing, it is less clear how this happens or why firms pursue diversification despite its negative effects on performance. One piece of the answer may be that the managers who should be thinking hard about how they might add value do not appear to be asking that question. Two prominent scholars of corporate strategy report the following:

> In 1990, we embarked on a field research project to assess the state of corporate strategy… In particular, we wanted to know if the individual parts of a firm were integrated into a coherent whole and how the competitiveness of a firm's individual units was affected by their presence in the larger corporation. The study involved on-site interviews with executives in over 40 firms. A harsh truth emerged from this research: In more than half of the companies we studied, corporate management could not effectively articulate how their firms added value to the businesses in their corporate portfolio."[8]

Another piece of the answer may be that large, diversified firms are a relatively recent phenomenon in the United States. The conglomerate form was not prevalent here before World War II. As a result, managers and scholars had little experience with its effects in the postwar years. The belief that diversification would add value reached its height in the United States in the 1960s with the formation of large conglomerates like Textron and ITT. In 1950, the 200 largest U.S. manufacturing firms (ranked by sales) had an average of 4.8 lines of business; by 1975, the leading 200 firms averaged 10.9 lines of business.[9] Fueled by a rising stock market and by the creation of new instruments for financing takeovers, managers sought to extend the reach of their firms through mergers and acquisitions. In all, 82 percent of the new businesses these 200 large firms entered after 1950 was accomplished through acquisitions.

There were two popular rationales for these expansions. First, in the 1950s and 1960s, the concept of "professional management" emerged. Business schools turned out waves of students who were more formally trained in management than ever before. There was a popular belief that these management skills could be applied to a wide variety of businesses. Second, in the late 1960s, the concepts of "portfolio planning" and "value-based strategy" within a conglomerate enterprise took hold. Firms like General Electric, aided by consulting firms, argued that corporate man-

---

[7] These data reflect the experience of U.S. firms. The value of diversification in other contexts, particularly in emerging economies where external capital markets are poorly developed, is probably different. We will return to this point below.

[8] David J. Collis and Cynthia A. Montgomery, *Corporate Strategy: Resources and Scope of the Firm* (Chicago, Ill: McGraw-Hill, 1997), p. 4.

[9] David J. Ravenscraft and F. M. Scherer, *Mergers, Sell-offs and Economic Efficiency*. (Washington: D.C.: The Brookings Institution, 1985).

agers could add value by judiciously allocating funds among their businesses to create a financially sound portfolio.

The optimistic view of conglomerates changed in the 1980s when the trend was toward corporate focus. As many conglomerates encountered performance problems, managers reduced the diversification of their companies. By the 1990s the dominant view in the academic world of corporate finance was that diversification was more likely to destroy than to add value. In the business world, the new mantra has been "focus" and building on core strengths. In strategic management, the most common view is that adding value through diversification is difficult. Many are now convinced that corporate can add value only if there are significant strategic spillovers of the type illustrated in Figure 14-4 among the businesses.

Some firms prosper as diversified enterprises. However, that the average diversified firm does not appear to add value should give pause to any manager who is considering diversification. He should ask why the particular diversification under consideration will be successful when so many are not. Managers should also ask whether their company's current level of diversification is warranted. Our new vice president can take some comfort from recognizing that her firm can be above average. To make it so, however, requires that she and her colleagues find a way to manage strategic spillovers within it.

## 14.4  STRATEGIC SPILLOVERS AND COMPETITIVE ADVANTAGE

Strategic spillovers are possible when assets within one business unit affect (actually or potentially) the performance of another. Since superior performance depends on competitive advantage, we are interested in spillovers that might affect the competitive advantage of other units. These assets might be a source of positional advantage. For example, a product innovation in one unit might confer a first-mover advantage on another unit that produces a complementary product. When Sun Microsystems' software division developed the Java language for developing applications on the Internet, its server division benefited greatly because its servers were well suited to running those applications. Or one unit could benefit from close customer and channel relationships that another unit developed. For example, Nike was able to distribute its hiking boots and walking shoes through many of the same channels that had been developed for its athletic shoes.

The assets affected by spillovers also might be the source of a capability-based advantage. For example, one business unit might acquire a system for inventory management that could be expanded to handle inventory in another business with little incremental cost. Or one business unit might develop a benchmarking process that another business unit could use. In both cases, the investments that the unit developing the asset made could enhance the other unit's performance. For example, Ford was able to apply its manufacturing capability to increase quality at Jaguar after its purchase of that company.

Corporate managers can help turn potential positive spillovers into actual and effective spillovers (or, conversely, prevent potential negative spillovers from degrading performance). They can do this by setting up a process to recognize and manage spillovers.

## Identifying and Managing Spillovers

Corporate managers must first *identify* spillovers. Most managers within a business unit do not know how their actions affect the performance of other units. These managers might be well informed about which investments will create value within their business but know nothing about the investment opportunities in other businesses. It is the managers responsible for overseeing a number of business units who can recognize that investments made in one unit might have a payoff in another unit. They might recognize these opportunities from personal contact with the units, by reviewing information the individual units provide, or because they have created communication channels that cross business unit boundaries. Corporate management might, for example, create a group with membership from several units that is charged with investigating opportunities for generating savings through supply chain management. A group like this might discover that the contracts used to manage supplier relationships in one unit can be applied in another. They can then alert corporate management to the need to provide the resources necessary to transfer supply chain management practices across units.

Corporate managers must also *provide the resources* necessary to exploit positive spillovers. To see why this is so important, think about the investment made in customer relationships by a single business unit. That unit's managers are concerned with the return (in increased sales or margins) that their unit might achieve by allocating additional resources to building customer relationships. They will choose an investment level that equates the marginal return (in their unit) on the investment with the marginal cost (to their unit) of the investment. Suppose, however, that their investment also benefits another unit at the firm that is serving the same customer. Because the investing unit does not take this positive spillover into account, it will invest too little from the perspective of the firm as a whole. In this example, the unit bears the full cost of the investment but gets only part of the return earned by the firm as a whole.[10]

This problem arises even when the asset generating the spillovers is crucial to the unit making the investment. Microsoft, for example, has used its positional advantage as the dominant supplier of operating systems for desktop computers to dominate the market for other desktop software. Sony's design-for-manufacturing capability has enabled it to compete successfully in a wide range of electronic product markets. In these examples, a competitive advantage in one business is used to build competitive advantage in another. In other cases, the asset is not particularly

---

[10] In economic language, the investment has an "externality"; some of the value is external to the division making the investment. This is similar to the problem of a firm making an investment in, for example, worker training. The firm considers the return it gets from its training investment, not the return that future employers might realize from its trainees. Some of the value the training creates is external to the firm.

valuable to the unit generating the spillover. Many "accidental" discoveries were of no particular use to the business in which the discovery was made but were (or could have been) exploited in another business inside the firm. Eli Lilly and other pharmaceutical firms, for example, devote resources to combing through their "libraries" of proprietary compounds to discover ways in which they could be applied to disease treatment. These compounds often are patented because the firms know they have some pharmacological effect. But because there was no known application for the effect within the group making the discovery, the compounds are shelved. As the researchers at the firm become aware of new applications, they can turn to the archives to find potentially useful compounds. In both cases, the unit making the investment will consider only its return and will therefore undervalue the asset.

As a result, corporate managers might want to *create a mechanism to increase the investment made in the asset.* They might increase the level of investment in customer relationships, for example, by devising a way for the investing unit to get "credit" for the value the investment created in other units. They might also encourage more investment by supplying additional funds to the investing unit and directing its managers to invest them in customer relations. They also might encourage the right level of investment by centralizing customer relations, creating a unit that manages customer relationships for both business units and is rewarded based on overall sales. Although the best mechanism for addressing the problem will be situation-specific, the general point is that business units will not make the correct level of investment unless corporate management takes an active role.

Corporate managers can also enable positive spillovers by *facilitating the cross-unit transfers of knowledge or information* necessary to accomplish the spillovers. Knowledge gained by one unit about a customer's needs creates no value for other units unless they are told about it. A supplier contracting processes must be adapted and extended to produce value in another unit. And the other units must be trained to implement a new benchmarking process if they are to benefit from it. These activities require that information flow across the boundaries of the business unit. Corporate managers can create the channels for these flows and provide the resources to ensure that units use the channels effectively.

## Sources of Spillovers

Positive spillovers can arise in many ways. One of the most common is through the reuse of knowledge or information. Proprietary knowledge or information can be a capability-based source of competitive advantage in more than one industry. Information has tremendous economies of scale; once captured, the firm can use it across its organization. Conveying the information requires expending resources, but the knowledge itself can be reused numerous times. The central role information plays in corporate strategy reflects this quality. In many firms, it shows up in the procedures corporate managers use to develop and disseminate best practice throughout the firm. For example, McKinsey and Co. expends great resources to ensure that learning developed in one part of the firm is made available to others through an extensive IT knowledge system. In other firms, it shows up as a central research and development lab, like HP Labs, where investment decisions can take into account the broad benefits that might accrue to the firm from research applicable to many of its businesses. In many firms, the information technology infrastructure is used to bring together data that can be used in many of its businesses. Applying a knowledge-based capability to multiple industries is a common rationale for how diversification might add value.

Scale economies might also be realized in other activities when corporate managers consolidate and coordinate functions across business units. There may be savings in the cost of accessing capital markets when firms centralize the finance operation or in human resource management when firms centralize the development of compensation schemes and recruiting processes. Unlike the scale economies in information, however, firms can eventually exhaust these economies of scale. Indeed, they often are exhausted within the confines of a single line of business.[11] Consolidation also can lead to inefficiency when firms sacrifice the gains from specialization to centralize an operation. Although a central human resource management function may perform routine tasks efficiently, it is unlikely to handle the diverse recruiting problems the firm's business units face as effectively. For example, a financial services business unit would probably not be well served by the recruiting and compensation practices that are well adapted for a manufacturing operation. Similarly, many companies are finding that they need groups with a "dot com" culture to develop their electronic commerce offerings.

Although size in a single business unit can exhaust scale economies, some diversification is central to realizing economies of scope. "Economies of scope" refers to the cost savings realized when two different products are produced within the same organization rather than at separate organizations. Economies of scope may arise because the products share a common input. The R&D lab described as a source of scale economies can also generate scope economies when the firm uses its output in different businesses. The lab, for example, may solve a problem in materials sciences that the firm can use to manufacture different products. Or a firm might leverage the positional advantage conferred by its reputation with its customers across multiple products.

This idea that the firm can use some of its assets in diverse applications is the most common rationale for diversification. Merck, for example, may have a capability in drug discovery that it can apply in numerous pharmaceutical markets. Or Procter and Gamble, might have a capability in developing consumer brands that it can use across many similar consumer products. Assets might also be more broadly defined capabilities. Some have argued that a major source of GE's corporate success across its widely diversified product portfolio is its ability to train managerial talent. However they are defined, exploiting these assets can justify diversification only if all the following conditions are met:

---

[11] Managers should also think about whether these gains could be achieved by outsourcing the function. Computerized transaction processing, for example, has large economies of scale that smaller firms can achieve by outsourcing data management to a firm like IBM or EDS.

- The assets cannot be sold on the open market. A glass patent might be useful in many industries, for example, but the firm owning it need not be active in all of them to extract value from the patent. It can, instead, license it to other firms that have the necessary complementary resources. In contrast, a positional advantage arising from a reputation for product quality might be less easily sold.

- The asset must be a source of sustainable competitive advantage in more than one industry. This goes back to our earlier discussion of what competitive advantage means. We argued that competitive advantage comes from position or capabilities (or some combination thereof) that are superior to the assets of one's competitors, valued by one's customers, and difficult to imitate. To form the rationale for diversification, an asset must confer this advantage in more than one industry.

- The firm must be able to acquire the other assets it needs to apply the one(s) it already owns. Many industries require the application of an entire bundle of valuable and difficult-to-acquire assets. Having only a piece of the puzzle might not be enough. EMI, for example, developed CT scanning technology but lacked the manufacturing and distribution assets necessary to exploit it effectively.

In practice, it is easier to determine whether these conditions are met when the asset itself is narrowly defined. A team with the programming expertise to write software applications efficiently has a capability that management can leverage across diverse software projects. The expertise is, at least in principle, measurable with a well-defined scope of application. More general assets could be more widely applied but are harder to identify and quantify. The early belief in diversification, for example, was based on the idea that "professional management" consisted of a set of capabilities that could be widely leveraged. As the performance of many conglomerates based on this belief deteriorated, analysts discovered that it was not easy to define good management or to assess how effective management in one industry could be leveraged into another.

Even for narrowly defined assets, potential spillovers are easier to describe than to realize. A manager contemplating a diversifying acquisition can be tempted to focus on the positive spillovers that might exist and ignore the costs that her firm must incur to realize them. Managers can also ignore the negative spillovers that will occur as the organization struggles to integrate the set of diverse business practices and cultures required to operate efficiently in diverse product markets. There may be some positive spillovers between financial services and automobile sales, for example, but these two businesses typically require different architectures, routines, and cultures. Melding them into a single firm is difficult. It can be so difficult that many diversified firms decide to allow substantial autonomy to their business units. For example, Dean Witter, a traditional full-service brokerage, continued to run the discount broker Lombard as a separate unit for several years after its acquisition. Although this avoids the problem of destroying value by imposing too much integration, it leads us back to our original question: If the business units operate best with little intervention by the cor-

| GOAL | APPROACH | TOOLS |
|------|----------|-------|
| Improve company performance by encouraging (discouraging) investment in positive (negative) spillovers. | • Identify potential spillovers<br>• Enable/impede spillovers through investment and information | • Resource allocation<br>• Organization design |

**FIGURE 14-5**   Managing Strategic Spillovers

porate parent, what value does corporate add? Indeed, after its merger with Morgan Stanley and facing significant competition from other brokerage firms that had an online capability, Morgan Stanley Dean Witter later integrated the Lombard operation into the corporate product line.

Diversified firms tend to be outperformed by undiversified firms in part because positive spillovers are difficult to identify and achieve and negative spillovers are difficult to identify and curtail. Without positive spillovers, the diversified firm's business units may perform no better than their undiversified rivals, and they must also bear the (often considerable) costs of the corporate structure. Moreover, even when the businesses benefit from exploiting a common asset, the potential for positive spillovers also makes negative spillovers more likely. If one unit at Procter and Gamble benefits from the channel relationships of another unit, it can also be hurt by the other unit's channel relationship. If one unit neglects or abuses its accounts, its bad reputation can extend to the other unit.

Figure 14-5 summarizes our discussion of managing spillovers. Corporate strategy seeks to improve the performance of the firm as a whole by managing the spillovers that enable the firm's performance to be greater than the sum of its parts. An important part of managing spillovers is to have a system that allows corporate managers to identify areas in which spillovers are occurring or could occur. Corporate managers can then help realize spillover benefits by encouraging investment in activities that generate positive spillovers and by enabling information to flow across unit boundaries. To accomplish these ends, corporate managers can use two levers: resource allocation and organization design.

## 14.5  LEVERS: RESOURCE ALLOCATION AND ORGANIZATION DESIGN

Suppose our new vice president is at a firm where the business units are wellmanaged. What concrete steps can she take to help these units perform better than they would on their own? The roles corporate headquarters play vary across firms, but most executives would agree that two of the most essential activities are resource allocation and organization design.

Resource allocation involves both financial and human capital. Capital allocation might include making decisions about acquisitions and divestitures that shape the scope of the businesses in which the firm will participate. It also includes developing a system for moving human and capital resources across existing business unit boundaries. Although those running businesses within the firm may be granted substantial autonomy to allocate resources within their business units, the flow of resources across business units or from center to business units is usually controlled by corporate.

Organization design issues that affect the company as a whole are also the responsibility of the corporate office. Coordinating activities across business units and establishing incentive systems to align the interests of business unit decision makers with those of the company's stockholders are problems that the corporate office must solve. Because business units at diversified firms compete in different industries with different strategies, they may need to have different organization designs. As a result, a business unit manager must have the autonomy to develop a design that is well suited to the business's external environment and strategy. But each unit must also fit within the overall architecture, routines, and culture of the company. Making one company out of many businesses and managing the organizational interfaces are the responsibilities of the corporate office.

Adding value through resource allocation and organization design are related problems. How resource allocation functions, for example, depends on how the firm defines its divisions, structures incentives, and develops a culture that encourages cooperation. Although we will point out areas of overlap between them as we go along, we begin by focusing primarily on resource allocation and then turn to organization design.

## Resource Allocation

Scholars and managers generally agree that resource allocation decisions are at the heart of managing a multibusiness firm. Whether the resource is people, capital, or information, corporate managers must decide how to distribute resources through the firm. They do this by acquiring and selling businesses and by allocating company resources among existing businesses.

### Allocating Financial Capital

One of the most dramatic ways corporate allocates capital is through acquisitions and divestitures. Although corporate can shape the firm's portfolio of businesses through this activity, this may not be the primary way it adds value to the firm. When it makes an acquisition, the firm pays a price that reflects the value of the acquired assets as a stand-alone enterprise. Suppose, for example, a car company acquires an independent information technology (IT) firm, as GM did in its acquisition of EDS. The car company will pay a price equal to expected future profits of the IT company as an independent firm. If this acquisition is to be profitable for the car company, its managers must make the IT firm more valuable inside the new firm than it was outside it. The acquisition *by itself* will not create value.[12]

Similarly, diversification does not automatically mean that more resources will be available to the business units. One common claim, for example, is that diversified firms can invest more because they have, on average, a lower cost of capital than undiversified firms. This argument has little theoretical or empirical support. Those who make it often argue that the returns from a diversified firm are less risky than the returns from an undiversified firm in the same way that returns on an investment portfolio can be less risky than the returns on a single asset. As a result, the argument goes, investors require a lower risk premium to provide funds to a diversified firm. However, investors can create diversified portfolios on their own. A bank, for example, can diversify its loan portfolio without lending to diversified firms. GE does not have a AAA bond rating because it is diversified but because it is a profitable firm with a low debt–equity ratio.

The cost-of-capital argument is about the total amount of investment available to the firm. A different argument for how corporate can add value is that, holding constant the total level of investment, corporate managers choose how to allocate those funds across their business units. If, for example, corporate managers have better information on the performance potential of their business units than an outside investor could have, internal capital markets might work better. They might have better information because a business unit can divulge proprietary information to corporate managers that would lose value if the information were known to outside investors. An exploration division of a mining company would be unwilling to reveal information about the potential value of a publicly owned tract to outsiders but would reveal it to corporate managers. Corporate also might gain inside information simply because it learns things about its businesses that is difficult to communicate to outsiders but is apparent to those in day-to-day contact with the business.

Although it seems plausible that corporate managers might have an information advantage over outside investors, several caveats should be applied before concluding that capital allocation within the firm can add value. First, because business units are "buried" within a larger, diversified firm, they are more difficult for the external capital market to evaluate than they would be if they operated as stand-alone firms. In this sense, diversification *creates* an information asymmetry between outside investors and corporate managers. That is, once the firm is diversified, corporate managers know more than outside investors. But claiming that this is an advantage of diversification is like claiming that aspirin is a benefit of influenza. A sick person might feel better with

---

[12] The argument for divestitures is similar. The diversified firm can only sell a business unit for a price that reflects its expected future profits outside the firm. Divestiture can therefore create value only if the unit is less valuable inside the firm than it is outside it. This was the rationale for the breakup of many large diversified firms in the 1980s; their managers discovered that the business units were more profitable outside the firm because the diversified firm was actually destroying value by owning the business units. Divestiture, of course, need not be a sign of failed management. Firms can acquire assets, make them more valuable, and then sell them at a higher price. "Turnarounds" of this type occur, but they probably represent a relatively small share of the diversification observed in the U.S. economy.

medication than without it, but that is no reason to get influenza. If corporate managers are adding value because they have better information to use when allocating capital than the market has, they must have information that the external capital markets would not have *if the business units were independent*. That is, they must know more about their business units than outside investors would know if the units were independent firms.

Second, diversification creates an information problem for corporate managers as well as for external capital markets. Independent businesses create informative signals about their performance. Stock prices, for example, are a good indicator of expected future cash flows for an independent firm. Corporate managers don't have any stock price to rely on. Indeed, in the 1980s, a tool called value-based corporate strategy was developed with which corporate managers could create something like a stock price for each business unit based on its projected cash flows. The theory was that they could then compare this internally constructed stock price with the average stock price of other firms in the same industry. This approach implied that the *external* market values assets correctly and that corporate managers had a responsibility to do *as well as* the market. Many leading diversified firms embraced this practice, which suggests that their managers had doubt about their supposed informational advantage.

We argued above that exploiting spillovers, or the potential to do so, was the best way to create value through diversification. With this in mind, internal capital markets may be effective because they take spillovers into account. Corporate managers may have no better information than outsiders about the independent performance potential of their business units, but they could have better information about how the investments in one business unit affect the returns that another unit earns. Furthermore, they can capture the benefits of the spillovers within the firm in a way independent firms cannot. If the firm's overall performance can be increased by taking spillovers into account in capital allocation decisions, internal capital markets can be a tool for adding value.

This brings us to the issue of whether capital allocation is a good tool for creating positive spillovers and discouraging negative ones. Note that simply increasing the investment in a business unit that is generating positive spillovers is not enough. Because a manager is primarily interested in the performance of his own unit, he will allocate any funds he receives to the uses that maximize his unit's performance. As a result, little of those additional funds may be spent on the activity that was creating the spillover. To encourage investment in the activity creating the spillover, corporate managers have to affect how the additional money is spent. To do this through the capital budget requires specifying and monitoring the expenditures that the business units make.

## Allocating Human Capital

Much of what we have said about capital allocation also applies to the movement of human resources across business unit boundaries. Here, of course, the benchmark is the external labor market: Can corporate managers direct the allocation of human resources more effectively than the external labor market? The arguments about spillovers apply to human as well as financial resources. Human capital should be allocated so that it is as productive as possible for the firm as a whole. However, the human problem is different from the financial one in important ways.

One of these ways is that people learn from experience. Allocating people to jobs does not mean just assigning the right type and amount of capital to a specific task. It is also about developing in people the skills to handle complex and demanding jobs. The potential to help workers invest in human capital provides another opportunity for corporate managers to create value. Corporate managers help establish the firm's hiring and promotion routines. They also can direct resources toward employee development. They might, for example, have well-developed routines for training, developing, and selecting their managers. They might offer formal training, rotate managers among positions, expose them to more senior managers, provide opportunities for managers to gain increasing levels of responsibility, and systematically review the progress of senior and middle managers.

Although corporate managers typically influence the broad direction of the firm's human resource management, nothing we have said so far suggests that diversification affects the impact of corporate on human resource management. Corporate fulfills this function at single business firms as well. But human resource management may be an area in which multibusiness firms are particularly well positioned to add value. A diversified firm can expose its managers to a wider variety of problems than a more focused firm can. Broad experience under diverse conditions is important for general managers because they must often make judgments with imperfect and incomplete information. As a result, they must depend on their own intuition when assessing how a particular strategy will work, given what they know or believe about the external environment and the business's internal context. The questions that matter most for firm performance usually have no obvious "right" answer, and hindsight seldom allows one to tell *ex post* what would have happened if the business had taken a different path. Managers can only develop a sense for the relationship between the strategic variables that are under the firm's control and the outcomes for the firm by fiddling with those variables and then seeing what happens.

There is no substitute for experience, and a diversified firm can provide richer experiences for executives than less diversified firms can. A multibusiness firm has multiple general manager positions, and a manager can head a business and still have corporate managers to turn to for mentoring and advice. Like management consultants, managers rotated through businesses have been exposed to a variety of strategies, contexts, and outcomes. They have seen the relationship in Figure 14-1 played out repeatedly. As a result, they can develop an intuition about what matters and how context and strategy interact. Unlike most management consultants, however, these managers have also implemented strategies and run businesses. General Electric is an example of a company famous for rotating its managers in this way.

Being able to provide this training within a single company has another advantage. Although individual managers can theoretically replicate this learning experience by moving among many different, less diversified firms over the course of their career, they will have difficulty conveying to their next employer the skills and learning they have acquired in their previous jobs. With every job change, a manager leaves some information about her abilities behind. This is much less a problem for a diversified firm that is rotating its managers through various divisions. Furthermore, as managers move from position to position within a firm, some things remain common. They don't have to learn new accounting systems, new personnel practices, and so on. The "corporate" functions remain the same. This allows the managers to focus on what is new about their new positions, that is, the strategic issues. Because less information is lost and learning is focused on strategic differences, a diversified company can run a more efficient manager development process than undiversified companies.

These factors may imply that a diversified firm could produce a corps of capable managers with the capability to think strategically. As a result, they may give the company an important corporate advantage: the ability to acquire new businesses and manage them well. This may be why many corporate managers at diversified firms call "the people part of the business" the most important thing they do. The "may" modifier we have used in this paragraph is important. We know of no systematic information supporting the claim that diversification can produce better trained managers. Anecdotal information and conversations with executives, however, are consistent with this claim.

The opportunity to participate in this process might also make a diversified firm attractive to managers who want to develop their human capital. People who recruit managerial candidates emphasize how hard it is to compete against firms that have a better career development system. These firms can offer a lower initial wage and still attract talent. There is a down side for the firm investing in training, of course. Once managers' competency and abilities are recognized outside the firm, other firms will try to recruit them. Even if experienced managers leave, however, the investment can still pay off the firm. Some managers will stay, and those who leave will have cost the firm less in wages than they would have in the absence of the career development process.

## Organization Design

The resource allocation process is embedded in the firm's architecture, routines, and culture. Its ARC will determine how effectively corporate can add value through resource allocation. Organization design can also contribute directly to the performance of the firm by, for example, creating routines for decision making or establishing a culture that promotes the firm's overall performance. In this section, we highlight aspects of organization design that are particularly important for multibusiness firms.

### Architecture and Firm Performance

The company's architecture affects the effectiveness of its resource allocation process and of the company as a whole. Indeed, whether there are spillovers across unit boundaries depends on how the firm defines the unit boundaries in the first place. In our discussion of corporate versus business strategy, we assumed that the businesses in which the company competes defined the business units within the diversified firm.

Thus a firm competing in the furniture and sports equipment industries would have an organizational unit for furniture and an organizational unit for sports equipment. Each of these units would have a general manager who was responsible for formulating a business strategy for his unit and who reported to corporate managers.

Although many multibusiness firms are organized in this way, most firms deviate from this profile to some extent. We have already suggested that some central functional structures (central R&D labs or accounting departments, for example) might be appropriate to realize economies of scale. Global firms may create country groups that cut across business units and are responsible for marketing all the firm's products in a specific region. All these organizational variations have spillover and, therefore, resource allocation implications. A central R&D lab that creates spillovers will absorb resource that otherwise would have gone to the business units, for example. The more the firm centralizes functions, the more it must reallocate resources.

Although, as we have pointed out, there may be good reasons to alter the basic equivalence between a business and a business unit, every business within a diversified firm needs a business strategy. The furniture business needs a strategy for competing in the furniture industry. Formulating, implementing, and evaluating this strategy are most easily accomplished when a general manager is responsible for that business. This is one reason for creating an organizational structure that directly reflects the businesses in which the company competes. Another reason is to evaluate and provide incentives for performance. It is hard to evaluate the contribution of a centralized accounting group or other cost center to the firm's performance. It is easier for the firm to evaluate its furniture business by comparing its performance to that of other furniture businesses.

The "strategic business unit" concept formally spells out the advantages of organizing the company along lines of business. GE developed this concept in the 1960s and 1970s, and it has rapidly spread among large U.S. firms. As the name suggests, the goal was to create business units that made strategic sense. To create these units, corporate can pose the following question: "Suppose we were to group this set of activities together. Could a general manger responsible for them develop a business strategy that is consistent with a well-defined external context?" In practice, this means grouping together activities that have a common external context. The strategy for a group, for example, must take into account buyer or supplier power. This is hard to do when the activities have different buyers or suppliers. Similarly, the strategy should be responsive to the competitive intensity and strength of rival firms. If there is no common set of rivals for the "business" as it is defined by corporate, it will be hard to develop a sensible business strategy.

The organization's structure is not the only design lever that corporate managers can use. Indeed, many of the organization design issues that we discussed in Chapter 4 are directly applicable to the design opportunities and challenges that corporate managers of a multibusiness firm face. Three issues, however, are especially prominent in multibusiness firms.

The first is one that has already appeared in our resource allocation discussion. Managing spillovers means inducing business unit managers to invest more in some activities and less in others than they would if they took only their stand-alone performance into account. Unless corporate managers can find a mechanism to reward a business manager for considering the effects of spillover, he has no reason to do so. Actually, he has reason *not* to make the kinds of investments the corporate managers might like. Managers usually care more about their own unit's performance than about that of other units. An incentive scheme that gives substantial weight to the performance of the manager's unit often reinforces this preference. Managers are also likely to have a strong emotional investment in how their unit performs and in the well-being of its employees. Investing in spillover-generating activity at the level that is good for the firm as a whole degrades the performance of a manager's unit. This is true even if his unit receives positive spillovers from other units. Although the positive spillovers it receives may make it perform better within the company than it would as an independent firm, it would do even better if it could receive those benefits *and* expend its resources to maximize only its own performance. Designing a compensation scheme to induce managers to take into account the performance of the firm as a whole is therefore particularly important at a diversified firm.

Second, corporate managers at these companies tend to be at least one step further removed from their firms' business activities than are the corporate managers at more focused firms. This makes communicating information to decision makers more of a problem within a multibusiness firm. Third, compared to the corporate managers at a single business company, corporate managers can make many more business-level decisions; a group vice president could "micro-manage" several businesses if she chose to do so. Furthermore, multibusiness companies have the problem of defining the authority granted to business unit managers when corporate managers can review and reverse their decisions. The organization design problem is to determine what decisions should be left to the business unit managers and which should be made by corporate managers. We discuss these two problems in the following sections.

### Routines for Information and Influence

Business units provide most of the information corporate managers need to make strategic decisions. Changes in the external contexts that the businesses face are difficult for corporate managers to observe directly. Experienced corporate managers often develop a "feel" for what matters in the external environment that makes them valuable as interpreters and decision makers. To be effective, however, they still need information that arises at the business level.

Corporate managers should therefore be concerned about how information flows from the business unit to the corporate office. The design of reporting routines, management information systems, and coordinating groups should take into account the kind of information corporate managers need to evaluate the decisions made by business unit managers. Companies have developed many design elements to bridge the information gap between businesses and the corporate office. For example, senior officers are encouraged to spend more time in the field and to talk with business unit personnel. Business unit managers are selected, in part, based on their ability to communicate with corporate managers. The company's routines for communication might include regular informal and formal meetings between corporate managers and business unit personnel.

But in the language of Chapter 4, building conduits for information solves only a "coordination" problem: It makes it relatively easy for business unit managers to transmit information to corporate managers. It does not solve the incentive problem. A business unit manager is not passive. He has his own agenda and cares about the level of resources allocated to his business unit. A unit manager's power within the firm and opportunities for advancement often depend on the success of his unit and the amount of resources he manages. Self-interest and concern about the employees in his unit also will lead him to try to get a larger share of company resources. The new vice president we introduced at the beginning of the chapter will be deluged with claims about the investment opportunities in the divisions she oversees and the consequences to the firm of diverting any resources away from any division.

Some of the information in these claims will be valuable to the new vice president because the units' managers know more than she does about the opportunities they face. Because the managers care primarily about their unit, however, they have an incentive to bias the information they give her. They also have an incentive to convey information that is *not* useful but might affect allocation decisions. They might, for example, develop relationships with those responsible for the decision or form coalitions with other managers to pursue common goals. Economists call these "influence" activities because their goal is to influence decisions. Since the time spent on these activities could be spent on other activities that have more value for the firm, they are costly and the costs associated with them are called influence costs. A manager could, for example, spend time either preparing an elaborate defense of his budget request or figuring out how to serve customers more effectively. The former activity might affect the resources he receives from the corporate office but might also contribute to wasting those resources in an ineffective business plan.

Not only do influence activities divert managerial resources from more valuable pursuits, but they can also have little net effect on the allocation of resources. Suppose no manager engaged in influence activities. Then each manager would know that any time he spent on these activities might substantially affect the resources his unit receives. If no other manager is submitting an annual resource plan that has much analytic support, he knows that it might be effective if he spent time making a strong case for more resources. Anticipating this, however, other managers will also spend resources building a persuasive case. When all his counterparts are spending resources to influence corporate managers' decisions, no business unit manager can afford to spend less time on influence activities. In the end, all this activity may cancel itself out and have no effect on how resources are allocated, but it will have consumed considerable resources. The resource allocation process becomes an arena of competition in which all the managers (and the company) would be better off if every manager cut back on influence activity.

Influence activities are one example of how internal politics can affect the resource allocation process. The distribution of power within the organization also affects this process. Some managers have more clout than others. Perhaps they are viewed as likely candidates for promotion. If you think that your colleague today will be your boss tomorrow, you may cede more resources to her than you otherwise might. Other managers have more political power within the organization because they are connected to a powerful constituency. Whatever the reason, it is naive to think that internal politics do not affect internal resource allocation.

Influence costs and other political considerations are not limited to multibusiness companies; they also operate in a firm that focuses on a single line of business. Typically, however, diversification creates another layer of management and, therefore, another place to affect decision making. Diversification across industries also tends to increase the diversity of views on what resource allocation is appropriate and therefore to increase the scope for conflict that power and influence can resolve. For these reasons, the internal capital markets in diversified firms may be less efficient than external capital markets. The external market may not be able to manage spillovers, but it is less subject to political manipulation than the internal market.

Firms can reduce the costs associated with influence activities in various ways. One of the most important may be reputation. Over time, corporate managers can identify those who habitually devote more time to influence activities and will begin not to trust the information those managers give them. A manager's reputation for influence activity may in fact make it more difficult for him to influence decisions. Another way to minimize influence activity is to restrict the kinds of information managers communicate to corporate managers or the channels through which they communicate it. The problem with this approach is that corporate managers need information and the cost of shutting down communication can outweigh any influence costs. Finally, firms can reduce influence costs by restricting the number or the impact of the decision corporate managers make.

## Routines and Norms for Intervention

Multibusiness companies vary in how much their corporate offices intervene in business unit decisions. Some conglomerates, like Johnson & Johnson, take the position that corporate should do very little in the way of allocating resources. Instead, as part of the firm's overall commitment to decentralization, the resources acquired and deployed by the individual businesses are largely controlled by those businesses. Corporate acts as a clearinghouse to assist the movement of people across business boundaries, but the impetus for reallocation comes from the businesses or the people, not from an overall corporate plan. Similarly, although corporate funds some relatively minor central services, J&J does not typically take financial capital away from one unit to give it to another.

At GE, in contrast, corporate takes a very active role in resource allocation. Corporate managers argue that moving capital from low-return to high-return businesses is an essential corporate function. The firm's managers also take an active role in developing managers by rotating them among business units. Whether the resources are capital or people, corporate managers allocate them to maximize the return to GE stockholders; the resources belong to GE, not to the divisions.

Each company must decide how interventionist to be. What works at one company with one business portfolio may not work at a different company with another portfolio. Whatever decision it makes, it must implement it consistently. A company cannot switch from hands-off to hands-on and back without harming its culture. The level of intervention also is tied to the firm's architecture and routines. A company should therefore develop "rules" that define how and when corporate managers will intervene.

In Chapter 4, we discussed how to design these rules. We argued, for example, that those with the best information should make decisions. For the multibusiness firm, this means that business units should be able to make decisions about their businesses unless those decisions have substantial spillovers for other parts of the firm. Granting business units autonomy leverages their specialized information and expertise. When coupled with an incentive scheme that rewards business unit performance, autonomy can maximize the profit of business units. But the business unit manager does not have the information to decide how his business decisions will affect other parts of the firm. When these effects are large, corporate managers must intervene.

The problem in applying these kinds of rules is to define those cases when corporate intervention will be beneficial. When are spillover effects large enough to warrant overriding the decisions of the business unit managers? This is often a hard call to make. Corporate management must weigh the incentive effects for the business unit managers against the potential benefits of intervention. If corporate frequently change the decisions of business unit managers, what incentive do they have to make reasonable decisions in the first place? How much time will they devote to influence activity as the corporate office becomes more interventionist? To what extent will they make decisions that are calculated to ward off intervention rather than to improve business unit performance?

Given how hard it is to weigh the costs and benefits of intervention, it might seem that corporate should use a case-by-case approach and intervene only when its analysis suggests that intervention would reap large benefits. This sounds sensible but can make intervention seem capricious. Every manager within the company knows that corporate managers have the authority to make decisions, but no one knows when they will exercise it. Every time business unit managers make a strategic decision they must think about whether it will trigger a corporate response. Will it lead to fewer resources for their division because corporate managers think it will negatively affect another division? How should managers change their decisions to minimize the likelihood of corporate intervention? In short, the *potential* for intervention can affect the behavior of business units.

Think, for example, of the problem facing the news division of ABC now that Disney Corporation owns its parent corporation. Before the acquisition, ABC News had aired a story that was sharply critical of Disney's environmental protection record. Would ABC have developed that story if Disney had owned it at the time? Would the reporters even have proposed such a story? More generally, the problem is that business unit managers within a larger corporation focus one eye on their competitive environment and another on the internal concerns of the corporation.

For this reason, companies try to develop a reputation for a consistent style of intervention. Johnson & Johnson's commitment to stay out of business unit decision making allows business units to act without having to guess how corporate will respond. To support its reputation and still allow corporate to intervene J&J has a well-established procedure for consultation and evaluation before corporate can exercise its authority. Indeed, a corporate manager at J&J must create buy-in from the business units for any decision.

At more interventionist companies, the corporate office may establish and adhere to a process for approving intervention. A well-documented capital budget process with multiple layers of review and consultation, for example, can provide all the firm's managers with a blueprint for how and when intervention might occur. It gives managers some warning about when resources might be reallocated to encourage or curtail spillovers, and it gives them the opportunity to argue for business-level plans that will allay corporate's concerns. This process tends to be cumbersome and may limit the corporation's ability to make major changes, but it encourages business unit managers to pursue profit-maximizing decisions rather than political actions.

Establishing bounds on intervention is difficult because the bounds are not completely credible. Corporate managers cannot really give up the power to intervene even when it is in their best interest to do so. This is a *commitment* problem. Corporate managers may want to promise that they will never exercise their authority in certain ways because business managers who believe this promise will act for the good of the firm in ways they otherwise would not. All the managers in the firm know, however, that the corporate managers will violate this promise if the company faces a problem. As a result, the promise is not credible, and managers always have some concern that corporate management will intervene.

Moreover, business unit managers frequently want corporate managers to intervene. Our new vice president will not only be deluged with glowing reports by managers of the investment opportunities in their businesses, she will also receive many requests by business unit managers to curb the behavior of other managers. Business unit managers naturally think that corporate should approve all their decisions but change other managers' decisions that negatively affect them. Corporate managers, then, feel pressure both from their own desire to act and from the business managers who want a larger share of resources or conflicts with other units resolved. If the business units don't feel that corporate is too conservative, corporate may not be doing a good job of managing its intervention.

## Corporate Direction

In addition to establishing a commitment to a consistent style of intervention, the company culture can have other advantages that warrant investment by corporate managers. Students of corporate leadership often emphasize that the CEO acts as a spokesperson for the corporation's values and vision. The CEO represents the firm both to the outside world and to the other employees at the firm itself. This role is evident in the prominence given to mission statements, in the repetition of the firm's values at every corporate function, and in the continual attempt to drive home a simple message about the direction of the corporation.

One famous example comes from the early part of Jack Welch's tenure as CEO of GE. By 1984, Welch had developed the formula that each of GE's businesses had to be "number one or number two" in its industry. If a GE business had no reasonable prospect of becoming so, GE would sell it or shut it down. For fifteen years, Welch and his corporate management team have relentlessly repeated this mantra. However, a moment's thought leads to the conclusion that this is not an optimal investment rule. Many businesses that are not number one or two are still profitable and attract investment. And some businesses may be number one or two in industries in which even the best firms make little profit. Moreover, it is not clear how one ranks businesses in an industry. Are they to be number one or two in sales, growth, profits, productivity, or innovation?

If this is not really an investment rule, why does it remain so important to GE's corporate managers? One explanation is that it is a shorthand way of referring to a culture of performance. Within GE it has created an acceptance for reducing investment in unproductive assets. Managers know that only performance, not tradition or personal attachment, will guide investments. This rule also emphasizes that performance will be judged by external standards; businesses must be compared to the competition, not to other GE businesses. Business units at large corporations often become inward looking, evaluating themselves relative to the rest of the firm. Over time, an inward-looking firm can find itself with a collection of mediocre assets. The motivational benefits of Welch's rule are also enormous. When personnel evaluation is coupled with resource allocation decisions, the tendency is to "play it safe" by setting goals for the unit that are relatively easy to achieve. If the company requires its business to become or stay number one or two in their industry, it is no longer a good career strategy for managers to set lower objectives just because they can easily meet them. The acceptable hurdles are now higher.

Although corporate managers need to influence the values and beliefs of members of the company, a multibusiness firm constrains their ability to do so. Just as it makes no sense to try to develop a common business strategy for a widely diversified firm, so it also makes no sense to try to develop a completely consistent culture. As with the other elements of organization design, each business unit must align its culture with its strategy. It is no more advantageous to try to mold a truly common culture than it is to have a companywide compensation policy. Instead, corporate managers need to focus on those aspects of culture that are consistent across its businesses.

Welch's concern was to make GE understand its competitive position in its various markets and recognize that resources must be allocated to areas of strength if GE was to survive. Welch also made productivity growth part of GE's cultural values. Again, this is a cultural attribute that can be applied across diverse industries and is consistent with the culture of best practice advocated at GE. At Merck, whose overall corporate performance depends on the innovations in its business units, corporate managers emphasize a culture of innovation. Its company heroes are those who make research breakthroughs, not those who improve output per worker.

## 14.6  SUMMARY

In this chapter we developed a framework for corporate strategy. We examined how the strategic role of corporate managers is different from that of the general manager of a business unit. We analyzed the performance of diversified firms and showed that although creating multibusiness firms was once widely viewed as an appropriate way to create value for the company's shareholders, the poor performance of diversified conglomerates in the last two decades has led to a dramatic shift of opinion. The most common presumption now is that diversification is unlikely to add value and perhaps is value destroying.

We described the dominant view that diversification adds value only when it creates or enhances synergy among the firm's businesses. We described how the firm can leverage the capabilities or positional advantage in one of its businesses to benefit another by identifying and exploiting spillovers. The potential for the firm to exploit spillovers is likely to be greatest when the businesses are closely related. We examined how to reap the possible benefits of diversification: Corporate managers need to create a resource allocation plan and organization design that support the synergy while minimizing the costs of diversification. Getting value from diversification is difficult both because real synergies are uncommon and because getting value from those that exist is a difficult managerial challenge.

We turn now to our final chapter in which we discuss the strategy process.

# 15

# THE STRATEGY PROCESS

## 15.1 INTRODUCTION

In this final chapter, we turn to the strategy process: how a firm's managers develop, implement, and change its strategy. Every firm has some set of routines for making the decisions central to its overall direction. Some have elaborate strategic planning processes in which managers throughout the firm contribute to an annual strategic planning document. Others rely on a small group of senior managers to make these decisions without any well-defined planning process. Still others adhere to no strict planning cycle, responding instead to the tempo of market changes. Indeed, there are almost as many "strategy processes" as there are firms!

There is good reason for this variation in process: Firms face different internal and external conditions, and their strategy processes reflect these differences. The less formal strategy processes that serve a small, focused firm well simply are inadequate for a firm with 500 senior managers spread over 50 countries and 10 lines of business. A firm competing in e-commerce cannot afford to wait for the next annual planning cycle to make strategy changes while its market changes dramatically every month. An organization in a stable external context with a successful strategy in place might devote fewer organizational resources to strategy process than a firm undergoing a fundamental strategic change.

Despite the wide variation in strategy processes, any successful process will include certain basic elements. Paramount among these is the formulation of a strategy with clear goals, scope, competitive advantage, and logic. Formulation of such a strategy is almost always affected by two different processes. The first is a set of activities that are intended to define the firm's strategy and are understood to be part of the strategy process. We refer to these as the *intentional* part of the strategy process. The second is a set of activities initiated by managers (who may not even be participants in the intentional process) that affect the firm's strategy but were not foreseen by the intentional process. We refer to these as the *autonomous* part of the strategy process.

We begin by laying out some principles that are fundamental to any effective process and discussing the intentional part of strategy process. We outline the basic strategy process steps and explain how the tools and frameworks developed in this book can be used in the process. We then discuss the *strategic plan* that is the center-piece of some formal strategy processes, describe the components of a typical strategic plan, and provide an example of a plan. Next we turn to the autonomous part of strategy process and the ways in which firms can integrate intentional and autonomous processes. Finally, we move from a focus on business strategy process to the corporate strategy process at a multibusiness firm.

## 15.2  SOME PRINCIPLES OF THE STRATEGY PROCESS

Before discussing the elements of strategy process, we will summarize the important characteristics of strategic management that we have emphasized throughout the book

- **Strategic thinking is more important than strategic planning.** Planning and the development of planning documents are no substitute for thinking. Many planning processes dwell too much on the "to do's" of tactical implementation and on resource allocation and too little on building a coherent mental model of the business. Furthermore, strategic thinking should not be a once-a-year formal exercise. It is an on-going frame of mind in which the general manager constantly tracks strategic assets and the external environment to ensure that the logic of the firm's strategy is aligned with the firm's internal and external contexts. Strategy is too important to do only once a year as an afterthought to budgeting and operational planning.

- **The essence of a strategy is a statement of objectives, scope, competitive advantage, and logic.** Every member of the management team should agree about these elements. Events will constantly challenge the definition of the vertical and horizontal scope of the firm, for example, and the basis of its competitive advantage will evolve. Consequently, the firm's strategy must also change over time. But the need for change in the future is no excuse for lack of clarity about the current strategy. The argument that "things are changing too fast to have a strategy" is often only an excuse for fuzzy thinking and laziness.

- **Strategy is an inherently creative process.** Despite our emphasis on conceptual frameworks that enable the strategist to think clearly about the firm's environment and its internal assets, strategic thinking is fundamentally creative. Once one understands the firm's current situation and has a view of the future, improving the firm's performance requires thinking up new opportunities for creating and capturing value by leveraging its strategic assets. Managers must then translate these new ideas into robust strategies and check their viability. But a major source of the value of strategic thinking arises when ideas are being generated. Too many strategy processes give idea generation short shrift.

- **Strategy is not just the responsibility or domain of the firm's most senior management.** Any manager who has to make choices whose outcomes depend on the firm's strategic assets and its environment can make better decisions by thinking strategically. Moreover, if strategy is to help coordinate the activities of disparate parts of the firm, all managers must understand the firm's strategy and their role in it.

- **The firm's organization and its strategy are intimately interrelated.** Over time, the firm's strategy becomes embedded in its culture and routines and aligned with its architecture. A firm pursuing a strategy in which low cost is important will have a culture that values frugality and incentives that reward it; a firm that is pursuing a strategy that involves providing premium service will hire people adept at maintaining customer relationships and have an architecture that supports those relationships; a firm whose strategy is predicated on constant innovation will have the structural attributes of an explorer. Because an organization is difficult to change and the firm's capabilities are deeply embedded in its organization, the firm may be foreclosed from certain kinds of strategic change, at least in the short and medium terms. Firms that attempt to imitate others' strategies without realizing the consequences for organizational change are unlikely to succeed.

- **No matter how much planning the firm does, the strategy will still evolve in unintended ways.** A great deal of external change is unpredictable. Environmental change will be surprisingly kind to some elements of the firm's strategy and unkind to others. If one segment of a firm's product line fails in the market, its strategic scope will have been changed through a process of market selection. Furthermore, the firm's own processes and actions can create new opportunities and consequences that will take the firm in unintended directions. Both Nutra-Sweet's artificial sweetener and 3-M's Post-it note were invented "by mistake," but both had large consequences for their firms. More commonly, autonomous experimentation by managers inside the firm will give rise to fruitful new avenues that may fundamentally change the firm's strategy.

- **Corporate strategy must add value to the business-level strategies.** Corporate strategy in a multibusiness firm must test the strategies of its various lines of business and ensure that the businesses provide more value as part of the whole than they would separately. That is, the *corporate* strategy process has two primary functions: (1) to provide frameworks that help the firm's businesses develop sound business-level strategy processes and guide corporate's evaluation of those strategies; and (2) to ensure that corporate adds value to the firm's businesses.

With these principles in mind, we can now discuss the strategy process at the business unit level.

## 15.3  BUSINESS STRATEGY PROCESS

Figure 15-1 illustrates the basic steps in strategy formulation and implementation for a business; these steps are the building blocks of strategy process. Whether the process is composed of explicit, formal routines or relies on informal and *ad hoc* activities, an effective process must somehow accomplish these steps. This basic process was first

**FIGURE 15-1**    Steps in Setting Business Strategy

introduced in Chapter 2. We return to it now with a more complete understanding of the analytic underpinnings of strategic management and can, therefore, go beyond our earlier treatment.

We have in mind here primarily the *intentional* strategy process. The flow of activities from strategy identification through implementation depicted in Figure 15-1 is most recognizable in the activities formally defined as the strategy process. Even here, however, these steps may not occur in a rigid sequence, and some steps may be much more important within the firm than others. The steps in Figure 15-1 should not be taken as a blueprint for defining the flow of the strategy process but as a description of a set of related activities that should be part of an effective strategy process.

## Strategy Identification

The first step in the strategy process is identifying the current strategy. This involves more than looking up the strategy that managers wrote down the last time strategy was formulated. A firm's strategic assets can change in unanticipated ways, and its managers can create unexpected change in its *de facto* strategy. It is important, then, to look carefully at what the firm actually *does* in each of its functional areas, target markets, and so on. By examining these policies and actions and the capabilities and position on which its performance depends, managers should be able to determine the firm's scope and competitive advantage, and infer the logic of its strategy. If the logic of its strategy cannot be inferred from what the firm is actually doing, its *de facto* strategy may not be logically consistent.

As part of articulating the firm's current strategy, its management needs to identify which assumptions about the firm's internal and external environment must hold if the strategy is to lead to strong performance. If the logic of the firm, for example, depends on high demand for state-of-the-art telecommunication services by small businesses, the firm should identify this assumption and adopt a system for assessing its validity. When managers believe that important changes might be occurring, it is especially useful to develop a set of variables that those responsible for formulating and evaluating strategy should track. They might, for example, want to watch the evolution of specific technologies they think will affect demand in their target segments or track the growth of demand for emerging technologies. Identifying key variables is useful for the strategy evaluation component of strategic planning, but having these variables in mind throughout the year can also help the firm respond to change between planning cycles.

## Strategy Evaluation

The next step is to evaluate the strategy by checking that the logic of the strategy is compelling. Doing so requires evaluating whether the firm's internal strategic assets and how they are organized are appropriate to the strategy that it is pursuing and whether the strategy exploits the opportunities and mitigates the threats in the firm's external environment. Although we could only allude to the strategy evaluation exercise in general terms in Chapter 2, in the intervening chapters we have developed a host of tools that managers can use to analyze whether the firm's strategy is aligned with both its strategic assets and its environment.

### Internal

We have seen that the firm's competitive advantage is based on its strategic assets. In particular, the logic of a successful strategy is predicated on the firm's positional advantage, its capabilities, or both. For the firm to succeed with its current strategy, its rivals must be unable to imitate its capabilities and the barriers to its positional advantage must remain intact. Another important element of internal consistency is the fit between the firm's strategy and its organization. Strategy and organization are, in many ways, two sides of the same coin. An ARC analysis provides a useful framework for identifying the elements of the firm's organization, both formal and informal. Once identified, the elements of organization can be evaluated for fit with the strategy.

Because the firm's internal and external environments are dynamic, a snapshot of its strategic assets and organization is not enough. The firm's ability to learn and adapt is as important as its current strategic assets. Managers must also align these *dynamic* elements of the firm's organization with its strategy. For example, a firm whose strategy is predicated on constant innovation must have an organizational capability consistent with that competitive advantage. The exploration–exploitation framework provides a useful shorthand for describing and diagnosing the firm's relative strength in developing new capabilities and positional advantages versus exploiting existing ones.

## External

Assessing the strategy's external consistency requires checking the strategy's alignment with the value chain in which the firm is situated and the industry in which it competes. The value that the firm can capture, and hence the overall performance its strategy will deliver, depends on the forces at work there. An industry analysis provides a systematic way of identifying those factors that matter. It begins by assessing which firms in the overall supply chain can capture the value in it and how the power of the upstream and downstream firms is changing. It also evaluates the nature and intensity of competition in the industry and how competition might be changing. Since the value that the firms in an industry can capture depends on the barriers to entry that protect them, the analysis must also assess the threat of entry and how to address it.

How the industry has changed, in both expected and unexpected ways, since the last strategic review is the most important factor in assessing whether to alter the strategy. Understanding where the industry is in its life cycle is useful, as is scanning for other changes in the external environment. It is important, for example, to determine whether demand-side increasing returns are developing in any part of the value chain because they provide particular opportunities for firms to capture value. Or the competitive structure of the industry may be changing as major competitors enter new geographic markets or introduce new products. The strategic review process should address any change that has implications for the logic of the current strategy.

If there is substantial uncertainty about the industry's future path, a scenario analysis can be useful. Scenario analysis helps managers capture the effects of uncertainty by constructing a manageable number of possible futures. Managers can then assess their current strategy's fit with each scenario. As new information arrives, they can focus on those scenarios that seem most likely and on those parts of their strategy that should be changed to be successful in them.

A particularly important part of industry analysis is tracking competitors' strategies and predicting their future moves. This requires assessing the value of the firm's strategic assets—its capabilities and position—*relative* to those of its competitors. The starting point to competitor analysis is to understand the spectrum of competition and where on that spectrum the industry is located. The next step is to understand the strengths, weaknesses, and changes in the strategies of the individual leading competitors. One useful tool for tracking competitors' strategies is an industry map. Since the two most common generic strategies are low-cost leadership and offering premium quality, mapping its position on the cost-quality frontier, for example, is often a particularly useful way of evaluating the firm's strategic position. It is important to see whether rivals have encroached on the firm's unique positioning and whether the firm and/or its rivals pushed out the frontier.

Figure 15-2 summarizes some of the concepts we have examined that are useful for assessing internal and external alignment of the firm's current strategy.

### Developing and Evaluating Strategic Options

The analysis of the firm's strategic assets and its environment might lead the firm to conclude that it does not need to fundamentally change its strategy. If, however, it identifies significant problems with the current strategy, the next step is to generate strategic options. Generating strategic options means developing fundamentally *different strategies*, each with a new scope or new competitive advantage and logic. A strategic option is not simply a list of interesting things the firm could do. Changes in the external environment or developments in its own positioning or capabilities usually generate many interesting actions the firm can take. However, many of these actions are just ways to implement the current strategy.

Take the example of Southwest Airlines described in Chapters 4 and 5. Southwest could do many things that would not imply a strategic change. It could, among other

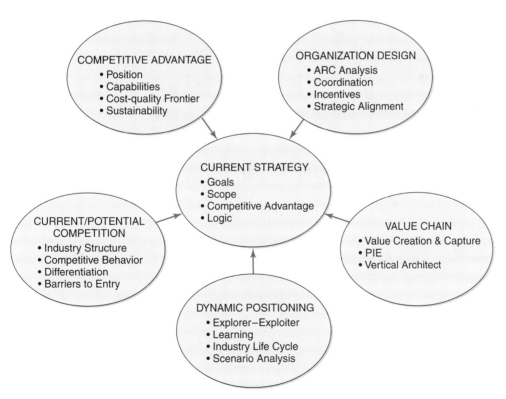

**FIGURE 15-2**   Inputs to Strategy Evaluation

things, change the number of flights within its current route coverage, change the seat configuration of its planes, and upgrade its flight reservation system. These are relatively minor adjustments within the existing strategy. However, other possible actions imply fundamental strategic change. Southwest might, for example, decide to expand into long-haul routes that take it outside its traditional base in the western and southwestern United States (a move it has recently made), to offer international flights, or to compete for upscale business travelers with business class service. Those would constitute significant changes in the logic of the existing strategy and would therefore require Southwest to reformulate its strategy.

Generating strategic options is both a creative and an analytic process. The drive toward an underlying logic requires an analytic process. Managers must be rigorous and remorseless in assessing the logic of the strategic options. However, the creative side is just as important. Creating strategic options potentially adds substantial value because it lets the firm imagine new ways to contribute and capture value. A strategic option embodies a vision of the firm's future role. Firms should not be too restrictive in generating options. Managers often err by quickly focusing on just a couple of options. Because much of the value a firm captures can be traced to the ingenuity of its strategic vision, managers need to brainstorm at this stage, generating many options before winnowing them down.

Once the firm has identified its strategic options, it needs procedures for evaluating and comparing them. Each strategic option must be subjected to the same tests of internal and external consistency applied to the current strategy. One difference in the evaluation process for the newly proposed strategies involves assessing internal consistency. Because a strategic option might require some assets the firm does not currently possess, it may not be consistent with the firm's current internal context. Indeed, key assets necessary to support a substantially different strategy are often missing. If the firm lacks the strategic assets necessary to implement an option, it must have the ability and a plan to acquire them.

## Selecting and Communicating the Strategy

Once one of the strategic options has been chosen, the final steps in setting strategy are communication and implementation. This can't be done until the strategy has been captured in some explicit strategy statement. How this is done in practice varies, but there is little point to developing a strategy if the people responsible for carrying it out don't know what it is! It is a mistake—and a common one—to assume that the strategy's logic will be as obvious to those who learn about it second-hand as it is to those who developed it. Managers involved in strategic planning sometimes present only the broad operational implications of a strategy to those who must carry it out rather than give them an overall view of the strategy itself. As a result, others in the organization have little sense of the strategic implications of the decisions they make. They do not know when an action violates the existing strategy, when to communicate information that is important to assessing the strategy, or how to best support the efforts of others within the organization. Failing to communicate the strategy consistently and clearly makes it unlikely that the strategy will contribute to firm performance.

## Strategy Process in a Rapidly Changing Environment

Firms that must contend with rapidly changing external environments face special strategic challenges. They simply cannot formulate strategy in as much detail as can firms in more stable environments. They also cannot formalize their strategy process as a routine annual planning process. They must have a process that allows them the flexibility to change their strategy much more frequently than that. As we noted in Chapter 11, they must operate on a faster "clock speed" than firms in more stable environments. To do this, they must have routines and structures to make strategic decisions more rapidly. For example, a firm's board of directors may have an executive committee that meets more frequently than the full board, can be called together on short notice, and can make decisions on behalf of the board. Firms can also cultivate a culture of flexibility in which they routinely reassign people among projects as strategic priorities are revised.

High technology start-ups often face a rapidly changing and uncertain external environment. Most start-ups set out knowing what business opportunity they intend to pursue and have a business plan that lays out the elements of a strategy and its implementation. The plan should include a well-thought-out logic in the form of a "business model" that explains how the firm will achieve its desired financial returns by pursuing its stated strategy. Despite this upfront planning, few start-ups end up with a business that bears more than a slight resemblance to what the business plan envisaged. The reason for this is that the initial plan included many assumptions and hypotheses, including what the firm's customers will want, what the firm can deliver, and what competition it will face. As the firm implements its plan, it collects information that validates or refutes these assumptions. This information requires it to refine and sometimes fundamentally change its implementation plans and perhaps even its strategy.

Netscape, for example, was founded in April 1994 with a strategy based on providing the best Internet browser.[1] It released its "Navigator" product in December 1994, which was met with huge demand. It dominated its rapidly growing market place and had an installed base of over 10 million users by the middle of 1995. In August 1995 the firm issued shares that gave it a market capitalization of $2.2 billion. Then, in December 1995, Microsoft announced it had developed a strategy to incorporate Internet technologies into all its products and, in particular, would incorporate its browser product into its desktop operating system. Within a week of this announcement, Netscape's stock price had dropped by 28 percent. Before the end of 1998, Microsoft's competitive advantage in leveraging its operating system had allowed it to overtake Netscape's lead in the browser market. As Netscape found

---

[1] This example draws on "The Browser Wars, 1994–1998" (Harvard Business School Case #9-798-094).

that it could not compete with Microsoft as a browser company, it re-positioned itself as an Internet portal and Web-site services company. In less than two years, the company had completely revised its strategic scope, its competitive advantage, and the logic of its strategy in response to the competitive realities of its external environment.

Since evolutionary processes are most powerful for firms in rapidly changing environments and for start-ups, well-thought-out strategy processes might seem least important in these environments. Moreover, since start-ups tend to be smaller than established firms, coordination among the start-up managerial team might seem to be easier, entailing less need for formal strategic processes. In fact, exactly the reverse tends to be the case. Precisely because such firms are forming and testing so many hypotheses about the logic of their strategies and because they update them so often, they need to be as clear as possible about what their working hypotheses are and what their strategic direction is at any point in time. Even though the start-up knows that it will frequently review its strategy and will end up at a far different place from where it started, it will benefit from the discipline of committing its strategy to paper (or computer slide presentation, so that it can be changed easily and often!). Articulating its strategy will help the firm develop a clear sense of the strategy's logic, identify the assumptions on which the strategy depends, and point everyone in the same strategic direction.

## 15.4  STRATEGIC PLANS

The strategy process illustrated in Figure 15-1 sometimes takes place as part of a formal, strategic planning process with a set of explicit planning steps that leads to a "strategic plan." Clearly, there is no "right" format for strategic planning or for a strategic plan. Many firms have no formal strategic plan, and other firms vary in how systematized the process is, how it is carried through, and what elements the strategic plan includes. Because the planning process must be tailored to the strategic needs of the business, there is little to be gained by reviewing these processes in detail. What we can do, however, is sketch the role of strategic planning in guiding the firm's behavior. We approach this task by focusing on the outcome: the firm's strategic plan.

Most strategic plans start from a general statement of mission and strategy that is then translated into specific objectives and action items, and finally into financial projections for the planning unit. A "typical" strategic plan for a line of business might include the following segments:

- A mission and/or vision statement
- A strategy statement including long-term goals
- An evaluation of the firm's assets, organization, and external environment
- A set of strategic benchmarks for assessing progress toward the long-term goals
- The major areas (or directions) in which progress must be made to achieve the long-term goals

- An outline of specific objectives within each major area or direction to be achieved within the planning period
- Action items, or tactics, to attain each objective
- A set of projected cash flows and measures of financial performance.

The first four segments are roughly consistent with what we have described as the strategy process in the previous section. The next four trace the implementation process that the strategy implies.

The mission and/or vision statement is a valuable part of the plan if it guides the development of the strategy statement as it might for a single business firm. In a large, multibusiness firm, however, the corporate mission and vision may be irrelevant to the particular business unit. If the business unit's mission or vision is much more specific than that of the corporation, the business unit may have its own statement of mission or vision.

The strategy statement, of course, includes a statement of goals, scope, competitive advantage, and logic. It typically includes an assessment of the firm's strategic assets and the external environment, together with an appraisal of the fit of the firm's strategy with the internal and external contexts. Often an industry analysis, scenario analysis, and statement of underlying assumptions are included here. The description of the firm's assets and organization highlights how they are aligned (or not yet aligned) with the firm's strategy. Benchmarks for measuring the firm's progress toward meeting its long-term goals are an essential element both for making future strategic planning efforts and for making "midcourse" corrections.

The plan lays out the implementation framework in successively finer steps. First, the firm identifies the main areas in which it needs to make progress over the planning period *and beyond* to achieve its long-term goals. Many firms call these "strategies", however, we call them "major directions" to preserve the distinctive meaning of "strategy" that we have used throughout the book. Second, the firm determines a set of specific objectives for each major direction. In contrast to the major directions, which extend beyond the current planning period, the objectives are specifically geared to the planning period. Finally, the firm establishes a specific set of action items, or tactics, that accomplish the objective. Action items should be specified in a way that makes it clear when the action has been completed. The firm should specify who is responsible for completing each action and how long each person or team should take to complete it.

This list includes two sets of benchmarks for gauging performance: strategic and financial. The strategic benchmarks might include market share, market share relative to specific competitors, product launch dates, a list of desired alliance partners, and dates by which the firm should establish these relationships. Especially when financial projections are uncertain, such benchmarks help indicate whether the strategy is on track.

A more concrete example of the implementation elements might be helpful. In Chapter 2, we constructed a strategy statement for Borders Books based on publicly available information. In Figure 15-3, we present some hypothetical directions, objectives, action items, and benchmarks that could be appropriate for that strategy. Note

*Major Directions.* Given its strategy statement, one might expect the major directions for Borders to include:*

- Establish store locations in every major metropolitan area in the United States and Canada.
- Increase revenue per square foot in existing stores.
- Ensure that in-store service levels are the best in the industry.
- Develop and maintain the best inventory management system in the industry.
- Increase net margins while maintaining or improving service levels.

Given Borders' strategy, these major directions represent the broad areas in which the company must make progress over the planning period and beyond in order to be successful. They should be consistent with the logic of the strategy, distilling the logic into broad areas of implementation. This also means that directions must be mutually reinforcing. For example, having outstanding in-store service and the best inventory management system in the industry both further the direction of increasing revenue per square foot in existing stores. And increasing net margins while maintaining or improving service levels provides the firm with the resources to improve its inventory management systems.

*Objectives:* Fleshing out the first major direction ("to provide stores in all major metropolitan areas in the United States and Canada"), the objectives for this major direction might read:

- Open 20 new stores by the end of the planning period.
- Review master plan for new store growth
- Do groundwork for opening of 22 new stores during the following planning period.
- Confront issues of public concern about the impact of book superstores on local communities.

*Action items:* The tactics drill down one level further, specifying the actions that must be taken to achieve the objective and assigning specific responsibility and completion times to them. An example that might fall under the third objective above (Do groundwork for opening of 22 new stores during the following planning period) might be: "Identify 40 possible sites by 6/22 (Todd, Susan, and Graham)".

*Financial and Strategic Benchmarks:* The strategic plan also includes a financial plan that translates the actions into expected financial performance. The main components of this are a set of (usually quarterly) income statements for the planning period and a cash-flow analysis. Obviously, the income statements should devolve from the strategy and therefore be consistent with the strategic plan. For example, revenue growth will be linked to the opening of new stores as well as the tactics aimed at increasing sales in existing stores. The gross and net margins that are targets in the strategic plan will also be reflected in the income statements, as will the expenditures on investments to improve the inventory management system and to maintain service levels (recruitment, training, etc.).

The strategic plan should also include some benchmarks for ensuring that strategic goals that are not well measured by the financial measures are being met. These might include benchmarks related to market share within the metropolitan areas that Borders currently operates as well as market share in the United States and Canada as a whole, some measures of the quality of the inventory management system (perhaps obtained from an independent "technology audit"), an appraisal of quality of service, customer satisfaction, and so on. Financial performance for the year might be on target, but if the firm is slipping in terms of staff satisfaction or the competitive advantage represented by its inventory management system, the firm could find itself in financial difficulty down the road.

*The material in this figure is hypothetical and prepared without any knowledge of Borders' actual strategic plan.

**FIGURE 15-3**    Examples of Major Directions, Objectives, Actions, and Benchmarks

that this example is entirely hypothetical; we have no information about Borders' strategic plan.

Although the typical plan contains most of the elements we have described, many planning processes focus too much on the budgeting and operational planning elements and too little on the strategy these elements should support. All too often, the imperatives of resource allocation and operations drive the planning process, transforming a process of strategic thinking into a lifeless ritual of documentation. Because these plans are often foils in political battles to allocate resources, the process becomes more about garnering resources than thinking about how to use resources most effectively. Conflict over strategic direction can result in broad compromises that "give everyone something." The political struggles and the focus on budget and operations often lead to a strategic plan that contains everything except a statement of strategy! Managers should focus on defining the firm's strategy and avoid getting bogged down in the plan's details. Their focus should be strategic thinking, not the traditional planning process, mired as it so often is in myriad implementation details. Those details are important. But it is the strategy that should drive them. Although the strategy statement is just one element of a strategic plan, it is almost certainly the most important one. If the strategy is unclear and the logic unsound, no amount of operational detail or investment will compensate for its weakness.

## 15.5 THE EVOLUTION OF STRATEGY

We have described the steps in strategy process and the elements of a strategic plan as if strategy processes were inevitably systematic and ordered. Anyone who has participated in strategy formulation and implementation, however, knows how poor a characterization this can be. They know that managers are not robots blindly executing a set of instructions. Managers will deviate from the plan if they encounter unforeseen contingencies that threaten the firm. They will take the initiative to reach for new opportunities. Even when managers don't deliberately deviate from the plan, the firm's routines can launch the firm down paths that take it far beyond the terrain mapped by the plan.

Most companies are replete with stories of successful ventures that were not envisaged in formal strategic plans and were even explicitly excluded from them. One example comes from Honda's entry into the U.S. motorcycle market.[2] Honda's senior management had prepared a detailed plan for entering the market with a strategy based on selling large motorcycles. Before the launch, however, its employees in the United States made an important and accidental discovery. They often traveled on mopeds to keep costs down and found that passing motorists and pedestrians asked them where they, too, could buy a motorized bike. The local Honda team responded to this market opportunity, and Honda "adopted" a small motorcycle strategy without any formal change of strategy by its senior managers in Japan. As local projects that deviate from the official strategy grow in size and success, they eventually are incorpo-

---

[2] See, for example, Richard T. Pascale, "Perspectives on Strategy: The Real Story Behind Honda's Success," *California Management Review* 26, No. 3 (1984), 47–72.

rated into the formal strategy, perhaps as part of the next planning cycle, and may become an acknowledged part of the firm's strategy. In such cases, strategy follows implementation rather than the other way around.

Two main forces—one external and the other internal—cause strategy to evolve in unforeseen ways. The *external* mechanism is market acceptance. Whatever the firm's plan might have been, it will—if it is to succeed—gravitate toward the products and services that its customers want. As products wither in the marketplace, the firm will shift attention and resources away from them. As customers embrace products, so will the strategy. It is always easier to find internal resources for products that meet the market test. These changes in the firm's offerings often require it to adapt its competitive advantage as well. For example, explosive growth in the market for electronic stock trading pushed Charles Schwab, the discount broker, to offer on-line trading to its customers to keep them with the firm. This early offering was so successful that Schwab devoted substantial resources to building a deep and state-of-the-art capability in Internet stock trading and managing customer relationships on-line. Although this capability involved the same basic activity Schwab has pursued before—buying and selling stocks for individual accounts and providing information to investors—it required radically different capabilities.

The firm's strategy also evolves *internally* through experimentation by managers. Often this occurs because line managers have enough autonomy to pursue ideas that look interesting *to them*, even though these ideas may be outside the firm's current strategy. Once one of these projects generates customer acceptance, resource allocation routines support it because the project meets rate of return goals for funding. That is, although budgets typically flow from the strategic plan, many resource allocation decisions made *within* the budget are governed by routines that give resources based on profitability, with only cursory reference to the articulated strategy. For example, Robert Burgelman suggests that Intel's routines for allocating capacity at its production facilities according to "margin per wafer" caused its strategy to drift toward producing microprocessors, even though its formal strategy was to focus on memory chips.[3]

Changes that are internally generated pose a challenge to the intentional strategic processes we have been discussing. At first blush, it seems difficult to reconcile the reality of informal resource allocation, for example, with creating value through intentional strategic processes. Some critics even suggest that these deviations mean that the intentional process has no point and can be counterproductive. They argue that substantive changes in the firm's strategy occur only through informal management processes. Senior managers may make pronouncements about strategic direction, but middle and line managers who respond more to their own information and the imperatives of their routines than they do to formal strategy statements develop the firm's *real* strategy. Some would also argue, since a firm's strategy can change only through informal processes, investing resources in formal, empty planning can impede change. At best, they would argue, intentional planning processes waste resources; at worst,

---

[3] Robert Burgelman, "Intraorganizational Ecology of Strategy Making and Organizational Adaptation: Theory and Field Research," *Organization Science* (1991), pp. 234–262.

they may impede the only viable sources of change, leaving the company unable to respond to a changing environment.

Others have argued, and we tend to agree, that firms can reconcile intentional processes with the changes created by the autonomous actions of managers that are inconsistent with the formal strategy. Even if the firm knows that it will "drift" from the course it has set, it still needs direction. Even if contingencies force a traveler to rethink the remainder of her journey, she is still better off having a plan than wandering aimlessly. Without a strategic plan, the firm's fortunes are left to the mercies of the completely uncoordinated activities of disparate groups within it. A strategy is crucial to coordinate purpose, especially in large complex organizations that have to delegate activities and authority. Without coordination of purpose, the firm may go nowhere.

## Autonomous and Intentional Strategic Changes

In practice, the strategy process usually involves both an intentional strategy process and an autonomous process. The intentional process may be based on formal strategic planning or less formal managerial interaction. What distinguishes intentional strategic process is that it consists of a set of decision-making and analytic routines that are *intended* to develop the firm's strategy. When managers make decisions that take the firm beyond its formal strategy, they engage in an "autonomous" strategy process; they are implementing a strategic change that is not directed by the strategy articulated through the intentional process.

All firms have both types of processes at work but vary in how important they are. At one extreme are firms that rely almost entirely on the independent or "autonomous" action of managers that fall outside any formal strategy. Firms at this extreme tend to have no formal strategic planning process, and its senior managers devote little time to intentional strategy process. At the other extreme are firms with strategy processes that are very formalized and in which management stringently resists any deviation from the formal strategy. Although most strategy processes are hybrids of intentional and autonomous processes, it is instructive to characterize the two extremes so that we can isolate the contributions each approach makes.

A firm's organizational design determines its approach to strategy process. In particular, the roles and responsibilities fulfilled by three groups of managers—*senior managers, middle managers,* and *line managers*—determine the relative importance of intentional and autonomous processes. How the organization defines the contribution these groups make to strategic process determines how rigid or flexible the firm's strategy is and how well it copes with anticipated and unanticipated changes.

In firms emphasizing intentional processes, senior managers typically formulate firm strategy. This does not mean that no other managerial layer participates in the process. Indeed, formal strategy processes typically gather input from all layers of management before determining strategy. However, the process is "top-down" in the sense that managers at the top of the organization use this information to formulate the strategy and then drive it down through the organization. Once senior managers set the strategy, middle managers work with line managers to develop an implementation plan and monitor progress toward its goals. Middle managers, then, are essentially a conduit for the authority of senior managers to line managers and for information from line managers to senior managers. Line managers implement the articulated strategy by carrying out the plan and provide information to middle managers. This extreme version leaves no role for autonomous action. Middle managers must approve any actions line managers contemplate that might be outside the scope of the strategy because line managers have no formal or informal authority to deviate from it. If middle managers determine that the proposal falls outside the articulated strategy, they will ask approval from senior managers before authorizing resource support for it. The structure of strategy making and implementation is bureaucratic, the compensation scheme is tied to implementation of the detailed plan, the culture emphasizes "following orders," and the routines are built around delivering on the plan.

Toward the completely autonomous process extreme, the line managers initiate the activities that, in aggregate, constitute firm strategy. They propose these initiatives to middle managers who evaluate them and, if they approve, provide the resources to implement them. Senior management articulates the firm's strategy based on the initiatives that the firm, in fact, is pursuing. Their role is to ensure that this process works well. They nurture a culture that supports this "initiative from the bottom" approach and ensure that other processes are consistent with it. In particular, they must ensure that the resource allocation routines are consistent with this strategy process. Line managers must understand that they will receive resources for worthwhile projects, and middle managers must be able to screen proposals that will contribute to firm performance. Middle managers are crucial here because they manage the resource allocation process that determines where the firm is going, and they train the line managers to think strategically. Senior managers mold strategy only by their impact on how the organization functions.

Although there are companies whose strategy processes resemble these extremes, most companies rely on a combination of intentional and autonomous processes. They have a formal, intentional process in which senior managers articulate strategy, line managers implement it, and middle managers are a conduit for information and resources between them. However, layered on this is a process in which a line manager can occasionally decide to pursue an action outside the formal plan. He will make a proposal to middle managers who can allocate resources even though the proposal falls outside the plan. If the venture is successful, senior managers will incorporate the proposal into the formally articulated strategy.

A hybrid process may look inefficient and cumbersome. Even though the firm has gone through an intentional strategy-setting exercise that culminates in a formal strategy and implementation plan, line managers take actions they know are outside that strategy's stated scope. Moreover, middle managers support them with the necessary resources. Finally, senior managers acknowledge that the strategy has indeed changed and alter the formal strategy accordingly! This sequence is especially strange because senior managers presumably can insist that the formal strategy be followed precisely and can set up incentives to ensure that it is. Senior managers do not exercise this authority because they believe that the combination of formalized strategy setting coupled with some degree of adaptation and autonomous change is the best way to ensure that strategy contributes to firm performance. To see why, consider the strengths and weaknesses of the processes at the extremes.

Organizations relying solely on intentional processes are tightly coordinated and can be tightly integrated because all their activities are planned. There is no working at cross-purposes or duplication of effort. Moreover, employees know where the firm is headed, and they recognize that they will be rewarded for any initiative that helps the organization move in that direction. As a result, they tend to be efficient at what they choose to pursue. Classic exploiter organizations tend to take this form. On the other hand, organizations that emphasize autonomous processes are more flexible and less likely to pass up good but unanticipated opportunities. Employees know that they will be rewarded for taking risks, even if those risks involve activities senior management did not anticipate. Classic explorer organizations tend to be organized in this way. We have already argued that firms need to be somewhere between the extremes of pure explorer and pure exploiter. Where they choose to be on the explorer–exploiter continuum should also determine where they should be on the strategy process continuum.

## 15.6 CORPORATE STRATEGY PROCESSES

A multibusiness corporation must have a strategy for each of its businesses and for the corporation as a whole. The strategy processes we have discussed so far are appropriate for a line of business whether it is part of a larger, multibusiness firm or a stand-alone enterprise. However, when the business is embedded in a larger firm, two distinct issues arise. The first is how the senior managers at the corporate level should participate in the process of developing line-of-business strategies. The second is how corporate managers can add value by developing a strategy for the company as a whole.

Both of these issues are affected by how strategically inter-related the firm's businesses are. As we discussed in Chapter 14, the strategies of the businesses within a multibusiness firm usually are inter-related. If the business units are so strategically independent that the corporation is just a holding company, corporate will probably not add value over what shareholders could achieve on their own by holding a portfolio of the separate companies. Nonetheless, to think about strategy process in a multibusiness firm, we begin with a situation where the businesses have no strategic interdependencies. Then we discuss the additional complications that arise when those interdependencies are present.

### Corporate Strategy Processes for Strategically Independent Businesses

In the absence of interdependencies, most multibusiness firms have a *corporate* strategic process that contains the steps illustrated in Figure 15-4. As the figure shows, each of the constituent businesses is responsible for developing its own strategy and implementation plan. For this purpose, the unit implements a strategy process of the kind we have described in Sections 15.3–15.5. If the businesses are independent, they can proceed with this process as if each were a separate business. Layered on the business unit strategy processes, however, is a *corporate* strategy process.

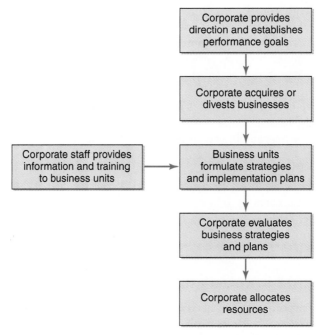

**FIGURE 15-4**  Corporate Strategy Process When Business Units Are Strategically Independent

The corporate managers are responsible for a process that sets goals for the overall company, selects the businesses in which the company will compete, supports the strategy processes of the various businesses, evaluates the business unit plans, and allocates the company's resources. These elements are illustrated as a process in Figure 15-4, beginning with corporate managers setting goals and culminating in the resource allocation. In reality, the processes are much more fluid. It is unlikely, for example, that the overall direction of the firm will be changed before each business strategy cycle or that acquisitions and divestitures will inevitably follow from corporate goal-setting. Instead, the diagram should be understood to illustrate the logic of the process. Business-level strategy, for example, should be responsive to the overall direction and goals of the firm and corporate decisions about which businesses to retain are often informed by the output of the business strategy process.

- **Setting corporate direction and goals.** Even when the business units are unrelated, corporate managers must articulate goals and direction for the firm as a whole. If the businesses that make up the firm are really in separate lines of business, corporate cannot develop a companywide strategy that has all the elements of a sound line-of-business level strategy. The firm as a whole cannot have a strategy with a well-defined set of goals, scope, competitive advantage, and logic. Corporate can and should, however, establish the direction and performance goals they expect the business units to pursue. Goals will likely be less specific than they are at the business unit level. For example, they might specify desired levels of corporate profitability and growth. The direction might specify the kinds of businesses, for example, industries and sectors, in which the firm will participate and how corporate intends to add value to its businesses.

- **Acquiring and divesting businesses.** Corporate headquarters decides which businesses to keep and which to exit. Often the information and analysis that flow from the strategic planning process itself guides these decisions. Unlike a mutual fund manager who chooses which stocks to hold based on their impact on the expected risk and return characteristics of her portfolio, a corporation decides whether value can be created by keeping the business within the corporation rather than by selling or closing it. Faced with the difficult question of which businesses to keep, corporate strategists have often resorted to simple frameworks of the kinds illustrated in Figures 15-5 and 15-6. Figure 15-5 is a resource allocation plan General Electric used (and McKinsey & Company developed), and Figure 15-6 is a framework promoted by the Boston Consulting Group. Both are intended to allow a parsimonious summary of how attractive any given business unit is to the corporate parent. Although each incorporates some important elements that affect business attractiveness, they may not be posing the right question for the corporate staff. Any investor would rather own a "star" than a "dog." The real issue for the managers of the corporation, however, is whether the value of the unit is greater if it is kept within the corporation than if it is divested. Ultimately, the answer to that question comes back to how the corporation proposes to add value to its businesses and whether it can add more value than another corporation could or than the business could achieve on its own.

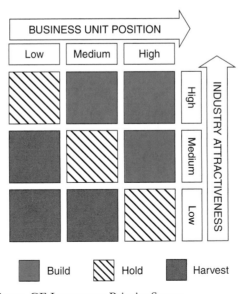

**FIGURE 15-5**   The McKinsey–GE Investment Priority Screen

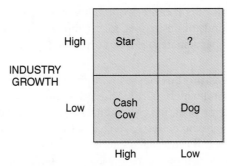

**FIGURE 15-6**    The BCG Typology for Assessing Investment Opportunities Facing a Diversified Firm

- **Providing staff support to the business units.** This support is generally of two kinds. The first consists of substantive information and analysis of the common external environment that the businesses face. It makes sense to centralize information gathering and analysis about macroeconomic trends, for example, and disseminate the results to each of the businesses. The second is to help structure the business-level strategy process. Since the corporate office oversees a number of business strategy processes, it is likely to know more about best-practice and can develop effective planning routines that can be adopted across businesses. This implies a training function. As managers are promoted into senior business unit roles, they need to be trained in strategic thinking. The business unit provides some of this training, but the corporate office is particularly well positioned to provide this training because of its on-going interaction with the planning processes at all the business units in the firm.

- **Evaluating business unit plans.** Ultimately, corporate headquarters must decide which businesses merit additional investment and which do not. Evaluating the business plans is therefore a critical corporate function. More importantly, however, the quality of the review they receive influences the quality of the business unit. A business-level management team that knows that its plans will receive thorough and intelligent scrutiny will do a better job developing the plan in the first place. This is a difficult role because corporate management typically knows less about the businesses than do the business unit managers. It is easier, however, if the corporation values strategic thinking above elaborate strategic planning in which strategy is disguised, buried, or absent. If the business-level *strategy* is crisp and clear, corporate management can evaluate and improve it.

- **Allocating resources.** The final step of the corporate strategy process is to allocate resources across business units based on evaluation of the business-level strategic plans.

### Corporate Strategy for Strategically Interdependent Businesses

In addition to the functions described above, corporate can use the information it gets through the strategic planning process to identify opportunities and threats that span business unit boundaries. Because corporate participates in the strategic planning process at the business unit level, it develops a broad knowledge of the strategic assets in its existing units and the units' external environments. As illustrated in Figure 15-7, it can therefore identify potential or actual effects one business unit has on another (called "spillovers" in the figure) and new opportunities that might lie at the boundaries of its existing units.

This activity involves a crucial business development function. By scanning the existing business units and their external environments, corporate can identify existing (or emerging) capabilities within the firm that have promise for meeting market needs outside the business units in which they currently reside. Corporate can then create new business units by pulling together resources from existing business. For example, corporate might combine the manufacturing know-how from one unit with the new technology developed in another and the customer relationships established by a third to create a new business.[4] When corporate managers recognize that they can create new business units from existing capabilities, they add a new dimension to the ways in

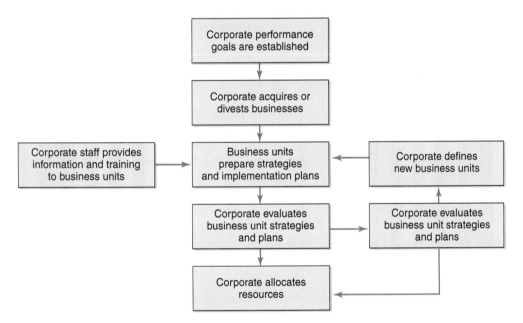

**FIGURE 15-7**    Expanded Corporate Strategy Process

---

[4] Shona L. Brown and Kathleen M. Eisenhardt ("Patching: Restitching Business Portfolios in Dynamic Markets," *Harvard Business Review*, May 1999) call this process "patching" to connote the idea of piecing together a new business opportunity from existing endeavors.

which they might add value. Without this function, corporate can change the business mix of the firm only by acquiring and divesting businesses.

Corporate also helps the business units respond to interdependencies by exploiting positive spillovers from one unit to another and avoiding negative spillovers. For example, it may be able to help a business unit use technology being developed in another business or establish structures and processes that coordinate the marketing efforts of several businesses that share customers. As described in Chapter 14, corporate commonly fulfills this role by encouraging the business units to make investment decisions that take spillovers to other business units into account.

## The Role of General Managers

Although we have focused on the role of corporate headquarters in the corporate strategy process, we should mention what being part of a multibusiness corporation implies for the heads of the business units. By "business unit head" we mean the general manager of a line of business. Functional managers within a firm often play important roles but are not central to the task of formulating and implementing business strategy. A Chief Information Officer or Human Resource Director, for example, might affect the performance of the firm's lines of business. But these positions do not have the strategic role assigned to the general manager of a line of business. Although we have devoted much of this book to describing the role such a general manager can play within a firm, we have largely ignored the possibility that the general manager's business unit is part of a larger firm.

When her line of business is embedded in a larger firm, the head of the business unit has to manage a complex set of relationships to chart a successful strategic course for her unit. To start with, she is the equivalent of the CEO for her business unit and as such has the prime responsibility for its strategic thinking and her unit's strategy process. However, she also has responsibility for presenting the unit's strategic plan to corporate and for obtaining the resources from it that the business needs. This is a difficult role because corporate often knows less about the details of the business unit than she does. She has to clearly articulate the opportunities and needs of the unit to those who decide how to allocate resources.

Precisely because there are usually interdependencies among the business units, a unit will often need resources that another unit controls. It might, for example, want to push its products through the channels that another unit manages. In that situation, the unit head has to persuade other business unit heads to cooperate. As we discussed in Chapter 14, although she may be able to get the support of corporate headquarters for this request, she cannot rely on them to intervene routinely on her unit's behalf. Instead, an effective unit manager must develop relationships with the managers at other units that allow them to share resources. Furthermore, the unit will sometimes find itself on a strategic collision course with another unit. In this situation, too, the unit head must resolve the conflict by negotiating with her counterparts in the other divisions.

Finally, the business unit head must communicate the needs of the firm as a whole to her subordinates. She will, of course, need their support to implement her unit's strategy. Although it is relatively easy to sell a strategy designed to improve the unit's performance, it is more difficult to persuade key players in the unit that they should share resources with other units or forego an opportunity for the good of the larger firm. The unit head must therefore manage "up, sideways, and down." The strategic role is an inherently political and difficult one requiring strategic thinking and organizational skill.

## 15.7  CONCLUDING REMARKS

The firm's strategy process is how its managers envision a possible future and guide the firm toward it. This "possible future" is a moving target: The firm and the environment change in both unexpected and anticipated ways. Consequently, "guiding the firm" does not mean just formulating a strategy for others to implement. The organization must be structured and its processes shaped so that it follows the right strategic path in a dynamic world. Planned and autonomous strategy processes must meld to yield the right outcome. Creating and managing an effective process present a difficult managerial challenge, but when a strategy process works well, it is one of the most fulfilling experiences in the professional life of a general manager.

A vision of what the firm can achieve must spring from the minds of the managers themselves. Preparing for the creative process of formulating a new strategy requires first and foremost developing and maintaining a mental model of the firm's strategic situation. We hope that the frameworks that we have developed in this book will help hone managers' abilities to think strategically and that the tools we have provided will help to structure that thinking. Mostly, however, we hope that these insights into organizations and strategy will help them structure their organizations and processes, so that strategic thinking becomes pervasive, effective, and rewarding.

# APPENDIX

# APPLYING GAME THEORY TO STRATEGIC MANAGEMENT

## A.1  INTRODUCTION

We have discussed many examples of situations in which a manager needs to think about how her competitors will respond to the actions she takes. We have also discussed many cases where she needs to think about how others *within* her firm (perhaps subordinates or managers of other business units) will behave. In both of these situations, there is "strategic interdependence" between her and the other actors: The outcome for all of the actors depends on their own actions and on those of others. Thus a firm's profitability depends not only on the prices of its own goods, but also on the prices of its competitors' products. A firm's success in innovating depends on whether its rivals are also innovating. Successful entry to an industry depends on the response of the incumbent and so on. Within the firm, the effectiveness of a business venture will depend on how its employees react to it; meeting their unit's performance goals often requires that business unit heads obtain the cooperation of other units; and managers at corporate headquarters must contemplate how business unit heads will respond if corporate management decides to intervene in the units' affairs.

Strategic interactions like these are analyzed with techniques and insights from game theory. Indeed, the insights obtained from application of those techniques have guided much of our discussion in the book. In the body of this text, we focus on the specific application of game theory rather than on its underlying principles. These principles, however, are applicable to a wider variety of circumstances than those we have mentioned in the text. Moreover, to fully grasp the discussion in the text, it is helpful to understand the underlying principles. In this appendix we discuss these principles. Because game theory and its application to strategic management are a vast subject, we can only survey the basic principles in a general way. The reader who wants more detail should consult one of the many fine texts that focus on those subjects.

## A.2  A FAMOUS EXAMPLE: THE PRISONERS' DILEMMA

We introduce the game-theory approach to analyzing strategic interactions with the famous "prisoners' dilemma" example. Although its concrete setting is far removed from managerial concerns, its underlying principle has many business applications. The example involves two prisoners arrested on suspicion of having committed a crime. The cunning district attorney separates them at the jail and then makes each of them the following offer: "Confess and I'll ask the judge to be lenient with you. How lenient, of course, depends on whether your accomplice also confesses, for your confession is worth less if he also confesses."

Suppose that Figure A-1 summarizes the jail time each prisoner expects to face. In this figure the number of years of jail time each can expect depends on the choices each of them makes. The first number in each cell represents "Prisoner 1's" expected jail time, and the second is "Prisoner 2's" jail time. If, for example, Prisoner 1 were to confess and Prisoner 2 did not, the numbers in the "northeast" cell of the table tell us that the prisoners would expect Prisoner 1 to serve no time and Prisoner 2 to serve 10 years. We can interpret the payoffs in the table roughly as follows. If neither confesses, the probability of conviction will be relatively low, so expected jail time (the length of the sentence if convicted times the probability of conviction) would be only one year for each. If both confess, by contrast, each can expect to get five years because either one confessing establishes his guilt, but each gets some credit for having cooperated with the Court. If one confesses and the other doesn't, the one who confesses gets a deal (no jail time), while the judge throws the book at the other (10 years) for his intransigence. Suppose that each prisoner only cares about minimizing his expected jail time. What choice should he make?

Before analyzing what each prisoner will do and what outcome we expect to occur, note that the setting we have described has a number of important features. First, there is more than one decision maker; each prisoner makes his own decision. Second, the setting makes it clear what information each has about the other's actions. As we shall see, it is crucial that the district attorney separates the actors, so that each

|  |  | Prisoner 2 | |
|---|---|---|---|
|  |  | Confess | Don't Confess |
| Prisoner 1 | Confess | 5, 5 | 0, 10 |
|  | Don't Confess | 10, 0 | 1, 1 |

**FIGURE A-1**  Expected Jail Time in the Prisoners' Dilemma

makes his decision independently. Third, the setting specifies what each decision maker can do. Each prisoner has a simple choice: "confess" or "don't confess." Finally, the outcome associated with each set of choices is specified; the actors know how choices will determine outcomes when they make their decisions.

These elements define a "game," and any setting for game-theoretic analysis is first parsed into these components. In game-theoretic terminology, the key defining elements of the game are the *players*, the *actions* each can take and when they can take them, what *information* each has at the time he acts, and the *payoffs* each receives given the actions that all the players take. Translating this setting and any other into these components has important consequences for understanding the outcome.

Returning to our example, we see that Prisoner 1 is better off confessing regardless of what decision Prisoner 2 makes. If Prisoner 2 does not confess, Prisoner 1 expects to get a year in prison if he also does not confess but no jail time if he confessess. If Prisoner 2 confesses, Prisoner 1 gets 10 years by not confessing but only 5 years if he also confesses. The situation is analogous for Prisoner 2. In the terminology of game theory, confessing is a *dominant strategy:* each player has a single "best" decision *no matter what the other does.* This logic leads us to conclude that the equilibrium outcome to this game is that each prisoner chooses to confess. Note, however, that although each confesses in order to minimize his expected jail time, the expected jail time for both will be lower if both choose "don't confess." When both players follow the logic we have laid out, they will confess and end up with 5 years in jail; if neither confesses, they will each expect to serve only one year! This is the prisoner's dilemma.

To many, this outcome is counterintuitive, and a chorus of protests often arises at this point in the analysis. One objection is that the prisoners should understand that, although there may be an individual gain to confessing, this will inevitably lead to the "bad" outcome where they both confess. If the prisoners could somehow cooperate with each other, they would probably agree not to confess because when neither confesses each gets minimal jail time. If each holds to the agreement, each will be better off. This is correct, of course, and is at the heart of what makes the dilemma interesting.

The setup has two important features that preclude agreement. The first is that the clever district attorney has separated the prisoners, so that they can't communicate and agree not to confess. You might argue that they shouldn't need to communicate because the "right" decision—that is, the one that makes them both better off—is obvious. They should realize that if they could communicate they would agree not to confess. But that brings us to the second problem: the agreement to refrain from confessing is not sustainable. Suppose that the district attorney allowed the prisoners to meet and bargain but then separated them again for their final decisions. Once separated, each would again have an incentive to "cheat" from the agreed-upon decision by confessing because each recognizes that confessing when his counterpart does not will lead to even less jail time. These features make the setting inherently *noncooperative.* This consideration is an important one because, for the most part, the game-theoretic tools and insights that we use in this book apply in noncooperative settings. We assume, for example, that firms cannot reach binding cooperative agreements on prices and that members of an organization cannot make a binding agreement to ignore their own self-interest.[1] It is precisely this noncooperative context that creates our prisoners' dilemma.

A different kind of objection to our analysis is that each prisoner might care about what happens to the other prisoner as well as to himself. Our prisoners may not be purely self-interested, and perhaps each should feel a little guilty about squealing on the other (especially since we have said nothing about whether they are guilty: the analysis applies whether or not they committed the crime!). This objection has more bite. We have assumed that each prisoner cares only about his jail time. If there is honor among thieves (or if they are innocent, honor among the imprisoned), the payoffs cannot be represented by the expected time in jail as in Figure A-1. Indeed, if the prisoners don't like jail time but also don't like to confess, the appropriate payoffs might lead each to have a dominant strategy of "not confess." In that case, neither confessing would be the equilibrium outcome. This objection highlights an important point: game-theoretic analysis only provides useful predictions for the game that is analyzed. If something important has been lost in translating the real-world setting to the model, the predictions are unlikely to be useful.

With this caveat in mind, let us return to our example and emphasize two things about the unhappy prediction in the prisoners' dilemma. First, as long as one buys the assumptions we have made along the way (the players are purely self-interested; they cannot reach a binding agreement; they care only about jail time, etc.), each prisoner's decision-rule is simple because it is optimal to confess *regardless of what the other does.* This is the dominant strategy feature we mentioned earlier. Second, again buying the assumptions of the model, neither prisoner has an incentive to change his decision. That is, when both confess, neither prisoner has any reason to regret his decision. Game-theoretic language describes this as having no incentive to "deviate unilaterally" from the equilibrium. We call an outcome from which no player has an incentive to deviate unilaterally a *Nash equilibrium.*[2]

To explore further the absence of incentive for unilateral deviation in Nash Equilibrium, suppose we allowed the prisoners to meet and discuss what they will do. We argued above that even if they could do this, they could not reach a "no confession" agreement that would affect their behavior. Regardless of whatever they said to each other in the meeting, each would still confess when the time came to make his actual decision. That is, both would have an incentive for unilateral deviation; the "no confession" outcome is not a Nash equilibrium. But suppose they met and agreed that

---

[1] By "binding" we mean an agreement that a third party enforces. In situations involving firms, this usually means that the firms cannot write a contract that the courts will enforce. Because it is unlawful in the United States for competing firms to agree on the prices they charge, for example, no court would enforce a price-fixing contract. Although most of the settings we have examined are noncooperative, a few are cooperative. For example, in some of the bargaining situations we discussed, we implicitly assumed that the parties *could* reach binding agreement.

[2] "Deviation" means to change the action. "Unilateral" means to change one's action assuming that the other's action is unchanged. "Nash" refers to John Nash who first developed this concept and was awarded the Nobel Prize in Economics in 1994. Note that the game doesn't actually allow the players to change their actions; they can't retract their confession. The point is that neither would *want* to do so even if he could.

each would confess (setting aside for now why they would bother to agree to such a bad outcome). Neither would have an incentive to deviate from this agreement. This means that Nash equilibria are *self-enforcing* in the sense that if the players agreed to behave in a manner consistent with a Nash equilibrium, neither would have an incentive to deviate unilaterally from that agreement.

Generally speaking (we shall discuss some refinements to this general conclusion later), game theory predicts that any equilibrium outcome of a game must be a Nash equilibrium. In the case of the prisoners' dilemma, this prediction seems obvious. Clearly, if each prisoner has a dominant strategy, neither will have an incentive to change his decision. However, in most interesting settings the players do not have dominant strategies. What is best for each to do depends on what the other will do and vice versa. In those settings, the Nash equilibrium concept has a lot more bite.

As a simple example, consider another famous example, the "battle of the sexes" game that has the payoffs illustrated in Figure A-2. In this example, a couple is considering whether to go to a movie or to dinner. The numbers in the table represent the value each gains from the outcome. The man prefers the movie to dinner and the woman prefers the reverse, but each prefers to go out together rather than on their own. What each wants to do depends on what the other does, and there is no dominant strategy. If she is going to dinner he prefers to go to dinner, but if she is going to the movie he prefers to go to the movie too.

Going to the movie is a Nash equilibrium. If the couple agreed over the breakfast table to go to the movie and to meet one another there, even if they don't communicate during the day and there is no binding agreement, we would expect them both to go to the movie. Going to the movie is a self-enforcing agreement from which neither has an incentive to deviate unilaterally. Of course, going to dinner is a Nash equilibrium too. (We could replace "movie" by "dinner" in this explanation, and the logic would still hold.) Thus game theory can help us narrow down our prediction here (the couple will go to dinner together or the movie together), but it cannot give a precise prediction.[3] Sometimes we can still predict the outcome because one of the multiple

|  |  | Her | |
|---|---|---|---|
|  |  | Movie | Dinner |
| Him | Movie | 2, 1 | 0, 0 |
|  | Dinner | 0, 0 | 1, 2 |

**FIGURE A-2**   Payoffs for the Battle of the Sexes

[3] This situation has more than one Nash equilibrium. With multiple equilibria it becomes difficult to predict the outcome. But this is not necessarily bad. The couple faces an interesting coordination problem, and we wouldn't believe an analysis that predicted with certainty that they would go to dinner! In addition to the equilibria discussed in the text there is also an equilibrium in which the players randomize between going to the movie and to dinner (a so-called *mixed strategy* equilibrium). Since we do not draw on mixed-strategy equilibria, we omit the details here.

equilibria is "focal." A focal outcome is one that the players expect to happen because they have seen it happen before or it is prominent in some other way.[4]

The important feature of this game for our purposes is not that there are multiple Nash equilibria but that neither player has a dominant strategy. This is true for most of the settings we examine. Fortunately, there is also often a unique Nash equilibrium so that the predictions from the game-theoretic analysis are still sharp. This is the case, for example, in the duopoly games we discussed in Chapter 8, which we analyze in more detail in the following section.

## A.3   NASH EQUILIBRIUM AND DUOPOLY

The logic that underlies the prisoners' dilemma applies in many competitive strategy situations. Consider, for example, the following simple competitive situation facing two firms. As in the prisoners' dilemma, each firm must make a single decision contemporaneously with the other, and the outcome will depend on both decisions. In this case suppose that they produce identical products and that each must consider how much to produce. Strategic interdependence comes from the fact that the price each will earn for the goods it produces depends on the total amount produced, and, in particular, the price declines with total production. (Demand curves slope downwards after all!) We label the firms 1 and 2 and suppose that the amount each chooses to produce is $q_1$ and $q_2$, respectively. For simplicity, we suppose that the market price for their product is given by the equation $P = 30 - Q$ where $Q$ is the total amount produced (and is therefore equal to $q_1 + q_2$).

Supposing for the moment that the firms have no variable costs, the profit that Firm 1 earns, which we write as $\Pi_1$, is equal to $Pq_1$, which can be rewritten as:

$$\Pi_1 = (30 - q_1 - q_2)q_1.$$

Written this way, the dependence of Firm 1's profit on the amount Firm 2 produces is clear: the more Firm 2 produces, the less profit Firm 1 can make.

Although we cannot predict how much Firm 1 will choose to produce without more analysis, this equation shows that we can easily calculate how much Firm 1 would produce if it knew how much Firm 2 were going to produce. Suppose, for example, that Firm 1 is certain that Firm 2 will produce a quantity of 20 units (so that $q_2 = 20$ in the above equation). In that case, Firm 1's profits are equal to $(10 - q_1)q_1$. It is relatively easy to calculate that Firm 1 should then produce 5 units.[5] So if Firm 1 believes that Firm 2 will produce 20 units, Firm 1 should produce 5 units. In the language of game theory, Firm 1's "best-response" to $q_2 = 20$ is $q_1 = 5$. Using this logic, we

---

[4] In experimental work, players can often select a focal equilibrium without direct communication between them. For example, if two Americans want to meet in Paris and set a date and time for the meeting but fail to specify a place, both might decide to go to the Eiffel Tower because that seems like an obvious place for tourists to meet each other.

[5] To see this, create a spreadsheet that calculates Firm 1's profits for each possible amount it could produce given that Firm 2 produces 20. Alternatively, using calculus set the derivative of Firm 1's profits with respect to $q_1$ equal to zero, giving the first-order condition $10 - 2q_1 = 0$.

can calculate Firm 1's best response to any amount Firm 2 might produce.[6] We have graphed the result as the solid line in Figure A-3.

Note that if Firm 2 produces 0, Firm 1's best response is to produce 15. Firm 1 would also choose to produce 15 if it were a monopoly. This makes sense because when Firm 2 produces nothing, Firm 1 should behave as a monopolist would. Note also that Firm 1's best response decreases the more it believes Firm 2 will produce. This also makes sense. The more Firm 2 produces, the lower the price will be for any given amount that Firm 1 produces, and so its profit-maximizing output will be lower too. For example, if Firm 2 produces 30 units, the price will be zero even if Firm 1 produces nothing, so producing 0 is Firm 1's best response.

Plotting Firm 1's best response tells us what it should do for each possible choice Firm 2 might make. We therefore know that any Nash equilibrium to this game must be a point on Firm 1's best-response curve. To see this, let's take some pair of outputs $q_1^*$ and $q_2^*$. Is the choice of $q_1^*$ by Firm 1 and $q_2^*$ by Firm 2 a Nash equilibrium if $q_1^*$ is not Firm 1's best response to $q_2^*$? No, because Firm 1 would have an incentive to deviate from this outcome. In particular, it would deviate to its best response to $q_2^*$.

We can perform the same analysis for Firm 2. Firm 2's best-response function is the dashed line in Figure A-3. (Since the firms' situation is symmetric, their best-response functions are too.) Since a Nash equilibrium must lie on both firms' best response functions, a unique equilibrium lies where the solid line intersects the dashed

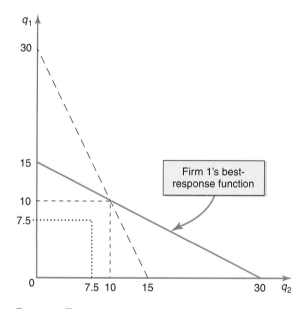

**FIGURE A-3**   Best-Response Functions

[6] Or again using calculus, the first-order condition for Firm 1 for any given amount of production by Firm 2 is $30 - q_2 - 2q_1 = 0$, so that Firm 1's best-response function is $q_1 = (30 - q_2)/2$. (Note, for example, that if $q_2 = 20$, this equation tells us that Firm 1's best response is 5.)

line. The predicted outputs are 10 for each firm. (To check that these outputs do constitute a Nash equilibrium, note that if Firm 2 produces 10, Firm 1 has no incentive to deviate from an output of 10, and vice versa.)

This analysis reproduces the game between the fishermen we described in Chapter 8. Indeed, the best-response diagram in Figure A-3 is consistent with the table of payoffs presented there. The best-response functions pick up the responses circled in Table 8-2. In the approach used here, the analysis is done for all outputs (and not just integers), so the best-response functions are easier to discern. This game in which firms simultaneously choose how much to produce is called the "Cournot" game in honor of the French economist Augustin Cournot who originated the game.

To say that the outcome where each firm produces 10 is a Nash equilibrium begs the question of how the firms arrive at that outcome. A significant difference between a setting like this where there is strategic interdependence and a setting where there is a single decision maker (a monopolist, for example) is that here what the firm should do depends on *what it thinks its rival will do*. Simply because an output of 10 is the Nash equilibrium is no guarantee that 10 is the amount the rival will produce. Nonetheless, there is reason to expect that the Nash equilibrium will be the result from a game with this kind of structure. There is considerable evidence that experienced players do indeed achieve the Nash outcome in experimental settings that have the structure of a Cournot game.[7]

However the firms arrive at the equilibrium, they produce more collectively than a monopolist would. We have already pointed out that a monopolist would produce 15, whereas the firms choosing outputs noncooperatively would produce a total of 20. Why don't they produce 7.5 each, thus earning a greater total profit and higher individual profits? For the same reasons as in the prisoners' dilemma game! Suppose, that the firms got together and decided to produce 7.5 each. Note from Figure A-3 that the point where each produces 7.5 is on neither firm's best-response function. If either thought the other were really going to produce 7.5, it would "cheat" and produce its best response to that (11.25). Thus, in the absence of a binding agreement, neither firm should expect the agreement to hold. The firms face a dilemma: each would like to restrain output below the Nash equilibrium level, but each knows that the other has an incentive to "cheat" and unilaterally raise output. Thus the duopolists cannot do as well as a monopolist can.

However, they do much better than they would if their industry were perfectly competitive. Recall from Chapter 6 that in a perfectly competitive industry with these characteristics, we expect price to equal marginal cost (which in this case is zero). These duopolists do better because it is costly for each firm to "steal" share from its rival. It can only increase its share by increasing its output. However, when it does so,

---

[7] This is not surprising. If a player observes that another player chooses not 10 but, say, 8, it would then choose 11 (its best response) the next time it plays. So too should other players. But then if it were the norm that players chose 11, an intelligent player would choose 9.5 (the best response to 11). And so on. Carrying this argument to its limit results in all players choosing an output of 10 (as they do in experiments). This nice convergence argument doesn't apply to all games but is a compelling argument for a Nash equilibrium here.

it also decreases the market price. With only two firms in the market, each has a large market share, so that this decrease in price causes a decline in revenue on the many units the firm was already supplying. Thus each firm's large market share makes it less willing to expand output.

We can solve the Cournot model for more than two firms. When the number of firms increases (holding everything else—including market demand—constant), the amount any individual firm produces declines and the aggregate amount the industry produces increases. As the number of firms becomes very large, the outcome approaches the competitive one. The reason is the converse of the logic in the preceding paragraph. With many firms in the industry, each firm's share is tiny. Consequently, when the firm expands its output slightly and thereby depresses the industry price, it does not lose much revenue from existing output. Since each firm behaves with less restraint than it would in duopoly, total output is larger.

The Cournot model teaches us that firms can show some mutual restraint when they do not have much to gain from deviating. To accentuate this point, contrast the Cournot setting with that of the apple sellers in Chapter 8. In that game two players face the same demand situation as in the fishing example, but each firm simultaneously announces a price. The firm with the lowest price supplies the entire market at that price; the firms divide the market equally if they have the same price. This game is also a well-known one, named for its originator Joseph Bertrand.

The unique Nash equilibrium in the Bertrand game is for both firms to charge a price of zero. To see why, note first that this is at least one equilibrium. If both firms charge zero, each earns zero. However, neither gains anything by raising or lowering price either. The firm unilaterally increasing its price continues to earn zero because it makes no sales. The firm unilaterally lowering its price captures the entire market but earns a loss on each apple it sells. Since neither has an incentive to deviate, both firms charging zero is a Nash equilibrium. Now note that no other pair of prices constitutes an equilibrium. If the firms are charging the same positive price, they share the market. But then either firm could double its output by slightly undercutting its rival's price, thereby (almost) doubling profits. Similarly, a situation where the firms charge different, positive prices cannot be an equilibrium either because the firm with the lower price could make a higher profit by raising its price slightly.[8]

These two games illustrate that a variety of factors influence how aggressively firms will compete. In particular, the extent of the prisoners' dilemma problem is affected by any factor that affects the value of unilaterally deviating from the "best" outcome for all firms. The market price in these games is lower than the monopoly price because each firm benefits from unilaterally undercutting that price. In the Bertrand game, that benefit is large because even a very small price advantage leads to a huge gain in market share. In the Cournot game, because firms "cheat" by increasing output, cheating lowers the market price, but the firm that cheats does not capture nearly as much of the market as it would for a comparable price drop in the Bertrand game. The benefit from deviating is small. In real market situations, firms often face

---

[8] Also, unless the firm with the lower price is already charging a price of 0, the firm with the higher price could make a profit by slightly undercutting the other's price.

multidimensional competition. They compete in price, product quality, innovation and so forth. In these situations many, often subtle, features of the markets and the firms' positions affect the severity of their "prisoners' dilemma".

One less subtle feature that affects how intensely firms compete in oligopolies is whether they interact repeatedly. An obvious complaint about the plight of the duopolists in the games we have looked at so far, especially the Bertrand variant, is that a firm might be less willing to cut prices today if it fears retaliation in the future. However, in the simple Bertrand and Cournot formulations we have examined here, there is no repetition and hence no fear of retaliation.

## A.4  THE EFFECT OF REPETITION

To see what difference repetition makes, suppose that time is divided into "periods" and that in each period two firms are engaged in the Bertrand game. Since the game is repeated, the firms' strategies can be much more complicated than in a one-period game because what they do can depend on the entire history of their interactions up to that point. This enables simple but powerful strategies of the following form: "I will charge the monopoly price (i.e., cooperate) as long as you do, but if you ever undercut me I will punish you by setting my price equal to marginal cost (i.e., revert to the one-period Bertrand strategy) in each subsequent period."

If one firm (call it "A") in a duopoly followed this strategy, one of the choices its rival (call it "R") would have would be always to cooperate. If it did so, it would earn one-half of the monopoly profits in every period. If we write monopoly profit as $\Pi$, each firm would then earn $\Pi/2$ every period because neither would ever "cheat." To convert this profit stream into net present value, suppose that \$1 next period is worth \$$\delta$ today (obviously $\delta$ is less than 1). Then, the net present value of that profit stream each would earn is $\Pi/2(1-\delta)$.[9]

In deciding whether to cooperate in this manner, Firm R has to compare that profit stream with what it would earn if it cheated. The best it can do if it cheats is to charge slightly less than the monopoly price and capture the entire market in the period in which it cheats. Its profits in that period are close to $\Pi$ (and we approximate it by $\Pi$). However, in all subsequent periods, it earns nothing if Firm A carries out its punishment threat. So Firm R must weigh the $\Pi$ it earns if it cheats against the $\Pi/2(1-\delta)$ it earns if it does not. It will therefore choose not to cheat as long as $\delta > 1/2$. We could make the same argument for Firm A; it would not cheat if Firm R were following the announced strategy and $\delta > 1/2$.

To summarize: as long as \$1 tomorrow is worth "enough" relative to \$1 today and both firms can credibly follow these strategies, neither firm will cheat, and they will share the monopoly profits forever. Repetition eliminates the prisoners' dilemma because cheating becomes less attractive owing to its adverse future consequences. We can now see (more precisely than in Chapter 8) how the firms' ability to sustain cooperation through the threat of "punishment" for cheating depends on a number of fac-

---

[9] The net present value of \$1 received each period is $\$1 + \$\delta + \$\delta^2 + \$\delta^3 + \ldots = \$1/(1-\delta)$.

tors. One is how important future profits are relative to current profits. In the simple example we have used, only $\delta$ affects the relative value of future profits; as $\delta$ gets closer to 1, future profits become more valuable and firms are less tempted to cheat. In richer examples, many other factors affect the value of future profits. If the firms anticipate that industry demand will decline in the future, for example, they will be more inclined to cheat.

A second important factor is how severe the punishment is expected to be. For example, suppose that a firm believed its rival would respond to cheating by charging a price of zero for only one period and then would resume cooperating. In that case, it would be worthwhile to cheat as long as $\Pi$ were greater than $\Pi/2 + \delta\Pi/2$, that is, $\delta < 1$, which is always the case. This is because the firm gets the full monopoly profits today if it cheats but gets half that amount today and another half next period if it cooperates. Because it would rather get the full monopoly profit today than the same amount spread over two periods, it has an incentive to cheat. Thus the firms must face the credible threat of a sufficiently prolonged price war to resist the temptation to cheat.

A third important factor is how many firms there are. Suppose, for example, there are three firms rather than two. With three firms, each earns $\Pi/3$ each period if it cooperates. However, if it cheats and cheating results in punishment forever, it earns $\Pi$ in the current period. The temptation to cheat is greater than in the two-firm case because the cheating firm gains more in the current period ($\Pi-\Pi/3$ rather than $\Pi-\Pi/2$) and gives up less in future periods (it loses $\Pi/3$ per period rather than $\Pi/2$). Carrying through the analysis from above, three firms can only cooperate if $\delta > {}^2/_3$. More generally, if there are $N$ firms, cooperation is sustainable only if $\delta > (N-1)/N$. The greater the number of firms, the more difficult it is to sustain cooperation.

We have skirted the issue of whether the threatened punishments are credible. Why should a firm believe that its rival will respond to cheating by reverting to the same behavior it follows in a one-period Bertrand game forever after? After all, once the next period arrives, what happened this period is "water under the bridge," and one might expect the firm to attempt to restore cooperation by charging the monopoly price. But if one's rival has decided that cheating is optimal once, why will it not cheat in the future? Why should it be trusted not to cheat again? Put differently, cheating may indicate that the rival has decided that playing cooperatively is not in its best interest. If the firm believes its rival will never cooperate, one plausible response is for the firm to resort to behaving each period as if it were in a one-period Bertrand game.

And if it anticipates this "punishment," the best the cheating firm can do is respond by also charging a price equal to marginal cost in the period after it cheats. That is, it is a Nash equilibrium for both firms to charge a price equal to marginal cost if either has cheated in a previous period. This suggests that we can use the concept of Nash equilibrium in games of repeated interaction. We must, however, refine the notion. If we call the remainder of the game from any point that is reached in a game, a "subgame" of the overall game, we can then think about whether the strategies the firms follow in any given subgame are a Nash equilibrium *for that subgame*. If they are not, we would not expect the firms to employ them because they would be better off following some other strategy at that point in the game. More formally, the equilibrium concept we will apply to games in which firms interact over time is that their strategies must be mutual best responses (i.e., be Nash equilibria) for every subgame of the game. A set of strategies that meets this criterion is called a *subgame perfect Nash equilibrium.*

The strategy of cooperating until one's rival cheats and then responding by charging marginal cost forever is a subgame perfect Nash equilibrium if $\delta$ is large enough. We have already argued that should your rival ever cheat it is a best response to mete out the punishment. Because punishment is credible, the best response when your rival is cooperating is to cooperate yourself. An equilibrium outcome (again, for large enough $\delta$) is that the firms will cooperate in each period.

All of this begs the question of how firms would develop strategies of this kind in practice. That is, why would they develop the expectation that cheating would be followed by punishment if punishment never happens because they never cheat? A simple (and decidedly non-game-theoretic) explanation is simply that a manager contemplating cutting price should anticipate that the managers at rival firms would be angered by cheating and lash out. A manager wanting to punish a rival might reasonably turn to marginal cost pricing. Retaliatory behavior, then, might soon lead to strategies of the kind described here. A different explanation is that a firm may not know what else to do. What is a manager to think when he observes a price cut by a rival? He might well think that until he sees his rival revert to more cooperative behavior that his rival will behave noncooperatively. If he expects the rival to be aggressive until he sees evidence to the contrary, he should behave aggressively himself. His rival might follow exactly the same logic, and cooperation would break down. Moreover, managers might develop these beliefs about what to expect once cheating has occurred by observing what happens in other industries. They may not need personal experience to develop the expectations that lead to the kinds of strategies we have described. However it happens, once these expectations are formed, they will lead to behavior of the kind we have described, resulting in the possibility that cooperation is sustained when firms interact repeatedly.

The idea of subgame perfection and the need for threats to be credible has relevance in a wide variety of settings. In many settings a firm would want to be able to credibly commit to some course of action. For example, a firm might want to commit to behaving very aggressively toward entrants to scare off potential entrants. Making this kind of commitment, however, reduces the firm's flexibility. Because the firm's external environment changes over time—often in ways that are difficult to predict— foregoing flexibility can also be costly. Thus, there is a tradeoff between the value of commitment and the value of flexibility.

## A.5   CREDIBILITY, COMMITMENT, AND FLEXIBILITY

As a firm implements its strategy in a changing environment, it faces many decisions about what resources to commit and when. In making these decisions, the firm must balance the benefits of flexibility with the benefits of commitment. There are often benefits to staging resource commitments. For example, if a firm believes it will eventually want to add 1000 units of capacity, it may want to add some amount immediately and then add the rest later if demand increases as it expects. By staging its capacity investment, the firm can give itself the option of making the second round of capacity investment only if future conditions make additional investment worthwhile. The option of adding capacity later is valuable. In some circumstances, however, it is also valuable to be able to commit to a future course of action. Your rival may be less aggressive in adding capacity, for example, if you are already committed to adding the full 1000 units. Next we discuss the value of flexibility, and then we turn to the value of commitment.

## The Value of Flexibility: Real Options

Options relating to the commitment of the firm's resources in the pursuit of its strategy are referred to as *real options*.[10] As an example, let us consider a more specific version of the capacity investment decision. Suppose, for example, that a firm has developed a new product and must decide whether to put the product into production, but it doesn't yet know what the demand for its product will be. To make matters more concrete, suppose the facility costs $100m to build and the operating profit generated by the product if demand is high will be $140m, while it will be only $50m if demand is low. If the firm believes that high and low demand are equally likely outcomes, it will choose not to produce the product because its expected profit is a negative $5m: the expected operating profit is $95m, less than the $100m cost of building the facility.

The firm could create a valuable real option by staging its investment in the facility, even if it is more expensive to build the facility that way. Suppose, for example, that the firm could provide the same capacity by building two smaller plants, each of which costs $60m. The total cost of building the two plants would now be $120m instead of $100m. However, if the firm can build the plants sequentially and can choose to build the second only if it discovers that demand is high, the project may now be worthwhile. By staging its production and giving itself the option of whether to go ahead with the second plant, the firm has created a valuable real option.

To see why, observe that if demand is low, the firm will elect not to build the second plant. In that case, its net loss is $10m (the operating profit of $50m less the cost of building one facility of $60m). However, if demand is high, it can go ahead and build the second facility. Its profit in that case is $20m (the operating profit of $140m less the construction cost of $120m). Since the firm now has an equal chance of making $20m and losing $10m (or an average of a positive $5m), it is profitable to go ahead with the project.

---

[10] The adjective "real" connotes that these options relate to the deployment of the firm's strategic assets as opposed to financial options which provide the owner the right to buy or sell an asset—usually a financial asset—at a predetermined price.

By investing in the more costly production facility that can be built in stages, the firm has bought itself the real option to ramp up to full capacity if demand is sufficiently high. That option is so valuable in this case that it represents the difference between a "go" and "no go" decision on whether to proceed with production. The expected value of going into production without the option was ($5m). The expected value with the real option is a positive $5m. Thus the total value of the real option in this example is $10m.

Real options are much more prevalent than financial options and come in many forms. For example, the real option in the above example is a *staging option*. Other common forms of real options are timing options (e.g., delaying a marketing campaign until more information about the desired target market becomes available), exit or abandonment options (e.g., the ability to easily exit an unsuccessful strategic relationship), and learning options (e.g., introducing and test marketing two variants of a product to learn about customer acceptance before rolling one out nationwide).[11]

Real options are valuable in an uncertain environment precisely because they enable the firm to expend resources when they are most likely to bear fruit. They derive their value from the *flexibility* they give the firm: the flexibility to add capacity when and where needed, to abandon unprofitable ventures, to delay committing resources until more information is available, and so on. Many managers underestimate the value of real options. Since firms can often attain a valuable option at low cost, for example, opportunities are sometimes squandered.

## Commitment and Credibility

Because flexibility is usually valuable, strategically creating the real options that provide flexibility often creates value. In some circumstances, however, it can be more valuable to *commit* and hence forego the benefits of flexibility. For example, some strategies succeed only if employees make investments in strategy-specific skills. A strategy might depend on close relationships with customers that are built only if employees expend the time and effort to create them. If the employees believe that the firm is likely to change its strategy to one in which these relationships are not valuable, they are unlikely to develop them in the first place. If the firm can credibly commit to its current strategy, it will be able to implement it more successfully.

Commitment is also valuable when it is important for a firm to put a stake in the ground in competition with a rival, as we discussed in Chapter 9. Suppose, for example, that an incumbent in an industry has two potential responses to entry: it can accommodate the entry, or it can fight it. Suppose further that the potential entrant would stay out if it were sure that the incumbent would fight. Then, if the incumbent can commit to fighting entry, it will deter it. In that case, commitment—by depriving the firm of the flexibility to accommodate—gives a strategic advantage.

But this is where the concept of subgame perfection applies with vigor. Under these circumstances, the firm wants to be able to threaten that it would meet entry by

[11] See Martha Amram and Nalin Kulatikala, "Disciplined Decisions," *Harvard Business Review*, January–February 1999, 95–104.

fighting. Yet a rational entrant should expect the firm to do what is in its best interests if entry actually occurs. If it is in the incumbant's interest to accommodate entry once it has occurred, the entrant should not put any weight on the threat of fighting. Instead it should enter, and the incumbent should accommodate the entry.

To formalize this discussion, we can apply subgame perfection to a simple example. Consider an incumbent monopolist is facing a potential entrant. If entry occurs, the two firms will compete as duopolists. Suppose that the entrant's choices at the outset are to "enter" or "stay out." If the potential entrant decides to enter, the incumbent firm has two choices: produce a moderate amount of output ("accommodate") or flood the market with output ("fight"). The accommodation choice might be thought of as behaving like a duopolist playing the Cournot game we described in Section A.2. The choice to fight would then mean producing a larger output, driving the market price below the level at which the entrant can earn a profit. If the entrant stays out, of course, the monopolist produces the output that maximizes its profit as the monopoly incumbent ("monopoly output"). Figure A-4 summarizes the payoffs associated with the four possible outcomes of this entry game. If, for example, the potential entrant stays out, it earns $0 and the incumbent earns $225.

Note that there are two Nash equilibria. In one, the potential entrant enters and the incumbent accommodates. In the other, the entrant stays out and the incumbent enjoys monopoly profits. This latter equilibrium arises because the entrant decides to stay out in anticipation of the incumbent's "fight" response to its entry. It appears that the incumbent has been able to deter entry by threatening to fight. However, this equilibrium is not subgame perfect. For if the entrant were to enter, the incumbent would rather accommodate than fight. But if the incumbent will accommodate, entry is profitable for the potential entrant and it should enter. The incumbent has nothing to back up its threat to fight. It is an idle threat, and the entrant should ignore it.

To see this point clearly, we write out the game in a different form in Figure A-5. This way of writing out the game (called the "extensive form") takes the sequence of actions into account. The first move belongs to the entrant who chooses between "enter" and "stay out." The incumbent then responds by choosing "fight" or "accommodate" if entry has occurred and by choosing "monopoly output" if it has not.

The entrant should think about the optimal actions for each player starting from the right-hand side and working backward in time. This ensures that each player is

|  |  | Potential Entrant | |
| --- | --- | --- | --- |
|  |  | Enter | Stay Out |
| Incumbent | Accommodate if entry, monopoly otherwise | 100, 80 | 225, 0 |
|  | Fight if entry, monopoly otherwise | 70, −50 | 225, 0 |

**FIGURE A-4**  Payoffs in the Entry Game

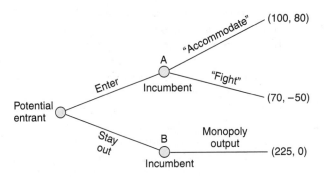

**FIGURE A-5**    The Extensive Form of the Entry Game

behaving optimally when any point in the game is reached. So, most importantly in this example, if node "A" is reached, the incumbent will choose "accommodate" rather than "fight" (and earn 100 rather than 70). Moving back in the tree, therefore, at the beginning the potential entrant knows it can ignore the "fight" part of the tree and can therefore choose between its uppermost and bottom branches (with respective payoffs of 80 and 0). It accordingly chooses to "enter."

It may be possible, however, for the incumbent to deter entry by *changing the game that is played after entry occurs*. Suppose, for example, that by taking a particular action (let us be silent for the moment on what such an action might be) the incumbent can change the game from the one we have been examining to the one in Figure A-6. The key difference is that the incumbent now prefers the "fight" branch of the tree (where it earns 120) over the "accommodate" branch (where it earns 100). Now if the potential entrant enters, the incumbent will behave aggressively. Thus the potential entrant is choosing between the middle and lowest branches of the tree. It will rationally choose to stay out.

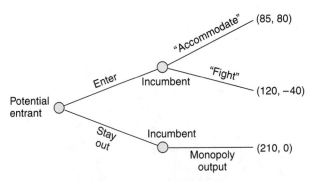

**FIGURE A-6**    The Extensive Form of the Modified Entry Game

The incumbent now enjoys monopoly profits because the threat to act aggressively has become credible. Importantly, in equilibrium the incumbent does not have to carry out the threat because the entrant rationally stays out. Since the incumbent does so much better when the entrant chooses to stay out, it would rationally be willing to spend a great deal to play the game in Figure A-6 rather than the game in Figure A-5.

What could the incumbent do to change the game in this way? It might make an investment that makes fighting a profit-maximizing response to entry. For example, *before* the entrant makes its entry decision, the incumbent can invest in a technology that lowers its marginal production cost. Since lower marginal cost implies that the incumbent's profit-maximizing output is larger, the investment will make the firm more aggressive. Two things are important here. First, the incumbent must do this before the entrant makes its entry decision; it must preempt entry or it will be back in the world of Figure A-5. Second, this investment would not be optimal if the firm were not anticipating that entry would occur. In Figure A-6, we have reduced the incumbent's payoffs for the top and bottom branches (relative to those in Figure A-5) to recognize that the incumbent must "give up" some profit to prevent entry. In the example, the investment has cost the firm $15 in profit but has allowed it to earn $210 rather than $100.

In these examples, the incumbent wants to commit to act aggressively to deter entry. In other cases, a firm may prefer to commit to act passively. For example, returning to the prisoners' dilemma nature of duopoly for a moment, if firms can take actions that make cheating *more costly to themselves*, they will reduce their own temptation to cheat and may make cooperative outcomes easier to obtain. For example, *a most-favored customer* contract under which a firm promises its existing customers that if it lowers its price to any customer they will also retroactively get the same low price can have this effect. By making this commitment, the firm essentially commits to punishing itself if it lowers prices. If that self-imposed punishment is large enough, the firm will have committed itself not to lower its prices!

These examples show that a firm can change the outcome of a game by making investments or by taking other actions that change the nature of the game that is being played. It does so by changing what it will be optimal for it to do when it faces decisions down the road. It essentially commits itself to certain courses of action, or at least it makes those actions more attractive than they would otherwise have been. Much like Odysseus who tied himself to the mast of his ship to be able to resist the song of the Sirens, the firm ties its own hands.

The advantage of commitment arises from its indirect effect on the firm's strategic *rival*. By convincing the rival that it will take a particular course of action, the firm changes the rival's behavior. The benefit of commitment is therefore indirect. The direct effect is to reduce the firm's own flexibility. Because of the value to real options described above, the firm must be fairly certain of the indirect strategic effect if it is to benefit from tying its own hands. In rapidly changing settings or when the nature and form of the strategic interactions that will occur are uncertain, flexibility is likely to be more valuable than commitment.

## A.6  STRATEGIC BEHAVIOR IN THE PRESENCE OF ASYMMETRIC INFORMATION

In the settings we have examined so far in this appendix, we have supposed that all the players know both all the relevant information about their opponents and what actions they have taken. These assumptions are obviously crucial since, for example, our potential entrant's entry decision in Figure A-6 depends on knowing the incumbent's payoffs to fighting and accommodating. Yet the potential entrant may have incomplete information about the incumbent's costs. Or, to take a different example, a firm may be unsure whether a rival "cheated" by expanding output or whether lower prices were the result of other market conditions.

In the following examples, we have highlighted two different ways in which the players can be imperfectly informed. In the examples, the players either don't know everything that there is to be known about their rivals or they aren't sure what actions the rivals have taken. As described in Chapter 4, these are the two most important categories of incomplete information:

- **Hidden information:** This category refers to situations where a player does not know an important characteristic of its rival. For example, it may not know its rival's cost structure, capacity, or inventory levels. Within the firm, managers may not know important attributes of the employees for whom they are setting incentive plans (e.g., their innate abilities).

- **Hidden action:** This category refers to situations where a player cannot tell precisely what action another player has taken: for example, the deal a rival firm made with its customers, or how hard the firm's own employees have worked or indeed precisely what they have done.

Sometimes hidden action and hidden information can work to a player's advantage. For example, an incumbent that has a high-cost structure may be happy that a potential entrant doesn't know that and instead believes that the incumbent has low costs. Or an employee who doesn't like to work hard may be happy that his manager cannot tell whether low output is the result of his own shirking or of adverse production conditions.

But hidden action and hidden information are usually disadvantageous to at least some of the players. First consider a problem of hidden information: Someone buying a used car would like to know whether the car has been well maintained or has any latent problems that will soon be revealed. The owner of the car typically has far better information about this than the buyer does. Hidden information frequently leads to problems of *adverse selection*. If buyers cannot somehow overcome their informational disadvantage, they will tend to treat all cars as "average." But then potential sellers of high-quality used cars have an incentive to hang on to them rather than put them up for sale.

To make this example more concrete, suppose that there are only two types of used cars: high quality and low quality. Suppose, too, that the high-quality cars are worth $10,000 and the low-quality $5,000 and that the sellers would rather keep their cars than sell them for less than their true value. Suppose that the stock of used cars is equally divided between high-quality and low-quality cars. If buyers know this but cannot observe car quality, they will pay no more than $7,500 for any car. However, at that price only the low-quality cars would be offered for sale. Knowing that, buyers would only be willing to pay $5,000 for any cars offered for sale. Thus the only Nash equilibrium in this simple example has only the low-quality cars being sold. The owner of a high-quality car cannot sell it for fair value because of adverse selection: the car is assumed to be of low quality in equilibrium.

Hidden action can similarly lead to problems. Suppose that an auto mechanic can work hard to repair a car or can do a mediocre job and that working hard is less desirable for the mechanic. Suppose further that the value of the repair for hard work is $500 but only $300 for mediocre work. Clearly, if the car owner cannot see how much effort the mechanic put into the job or discern that from observing the repair, the only equilibrium outcome is that the mechanic does the mediocre job and is paid $300. The problem is that since the mechanic has an incentive to shirk, his claims about the great job he did are not believable. This is an example of the *moral hazard* problem that arises from hidden action.

Because adverse selection and moral hazard lead to undesirable outcomes, participants in these markets often try to mitigate the presence of asymmetric information.

### Signaling

Consider the following simple example involving the labor market and education. Half of the workers in a particular market are highly productive, and half are less productive. Suppose that the value to employers of highly productive workers is $100,000 and that of less productive workers is $50,000 (over some relevant time frame). If the employers cannot tell the two types of workers apart, they will probably offer all workers $75,000. This is a good outcome for the less productive workers but not for the highly productive workers.

Now suppose that before seeking employment, the workers can get an education, which comes in discrete units (perhaps number of years of school), and that it is more costly for less productive workers to get an education (because it takes longer or is harder for the less productive workers). In particular, suppose that the costs per unit of education are, respectively, $30,000 and $10,000 for less productive and highly productive workers and that employers can see how much education workers have received but not how costly it was for them to obtain it.

One plausible, though not perhaps immediately intuitive, outcome is the following. Highly productive workers obtain two units of education, and less productive workers obtain none. Since workers with two units of education are then presumed to be highly productive (only highly productive workers get two units of education), they are paid $100,000. Workers with less education are assumed to be less productive and are paid $50,000. Why does this outcome represent a Nash equilibrium? Note first that the highly productive workers earn $80,000 net of their education expenses and the less productive workers earn $50,000. A highly productive worker who elects not to get two units of education is misinterpreted as being less productive and earns only $50,000. A less productive worker who attempts to masquerade as a highly productive worker by obtaining two units of education earns $100,000 but must pay $60,000 in education expenses and therefore nets $40,000. Therefore no one has an incentive to deviate, and the posited behavior forms a Nash equilibrium.

Note that the highly productive workers obtain education even though it does nothing to enhance their productivity! They *obtain an education because it signals their productivity*. Since it is more costly for less productive workers to get an education, the highly productive ones can credibly demonstrate that they are productive by engaging in an activity that sets them apart because it is too costly for the others to mimic. An employer can infer that an applicant who has obtained two units of education is a highly productive worker who is attempting to signal her high productivity. No less productive worker would find it to be in his interests to get that much education even if doing so would convince the employer that he was a highly productive worker.[12]

Signaling can occur in many competitive situations. For example, manufacturers of high-quality products will generally be willing to signal their higher quality by offering a longer warranty (which costs a manufacturer of low-quality products more to offer), or an incumbent firm facing potential entry might be willing to signal it has low costs by charging low prices (which would be more expensive for a high-cost firm to do).

## Screening

In the case of signaling, the parties about whom there is incomplete information act to make their characteristics known to the parties on the other side of the transaction. In screening, the uninformed party can structure a range of offers that induces the informed parties to reveal their information through the choices they make. A common example of screening mechanisms is the range of possible contracts auto insurers offer. An insurer knows that some drivers are more accident prone than others. Moreover, typically the driver knows more about his risk of accident than the insurer does. However, by appropriately structuring the kinds of insurance contracts it offers, the insurer may be able to induce the drivers to reveal some information about themselves. For example, the insurer might offer contracts that are

---

[12] In general, these situations have multiple Nash equilibria. For example, if employers draw no inference from the amount of education that workers obtain, no worker will find it worthwhile to obtain education. So no one would obtain education, and all workers would be "lumped together" and be paid $75,000, their average productivity. We call an equilibrium like that "pooling" because workers of all productivities are pooled together. In contrast, we call an equilibrium of the kind discussed in the text "separating" for obvious reasons. There are also generally multiple separating equilibria. For example, if employers insist that workers have three units of education before they are willing to conclude that workers are highly productive, the highly productive workers will still find it worthwhile to get three units rather than be labeled "less productive." However, such an equilibrium seems unintuitive because it will unreasonably label a worker who obtained two units of education as less productive, even though no less productive worker would ever be willing to obtain two units of education. Economists have proposed a variety of refinements of Nash equilibrium to rule out unintuitive equilibria.

inexpensive but have high co-payments in the event of an accident, and others that are more expensive and have lower co-payments in the event of an accident. If these contracts are structured appropriately, only low-risk drivers will choose the contract with a high co-payment (figuring that the probability they will have to pay the co-payment is relatively low). In this way, the drivers *self-select* according to their risk profiles.

### Reputation

Firms most often demonstrate their hidden attributes by developing a *reputation*. This can happen in many situations. For example, a firm that consistently acts aggressively toward new entrants can establish a reputation for toughness. A firm that consistently produces high-quality products may convince consumers that its future products will also be high quality. In these cases, past performance is a good indicator of future performance because a good reputation is a valuable asset that firms are reluctant to destroy. The mechanism is much like the one that sustains cooperation in repeated games, described above. A firm weighs the short-run benefit from *cheating* by, for example, offering a low-quality product against the long-term loss from no longer being able to charge a price premium.

## A.7  SUMMARY

The examples in this chapter show that managers face many different kinds of situations in which there are strategic interdependencies between them and other participants, either other firms or members of their own firms. In such situations, a manager must try to figure out how others will act and how they will react to the actions she takes. Especially when interactions unfold over time, questions of "what will they do if we do this" inevitably arise. Game theory provides some tools for guiding one's thinking in such situations, and in this appendix, we have tried to provide a broad overview of how game-theoretic thinking is inevitable and useful.

We began with the classic example of the prisoners' dilemma to illustrate why strategic interdependence matters and to introduce the main concepts and approach of game theory. We then applied that approach to the Cournot and Bertrand duopoly models which we had introduced in Chapter 8 in the guise of the fishing and apple-growing examples. Having a slightly more formal apparatus at our disposal here somewhat simplified and sharpened the analysis. We then illustrated how repetition can change matters, and, in particular, how it can facilitate cooperation in situations where cooperation would be impossible in a static setting. We then explored issues of commitment and flexibility, introducing the concept of real options and showing how in strategic settings lack of flexibility can sometimes actually be better. Finally, we introduced asymmetric information. We described the hidden information and hidden action problems and showed how signaling, screening, and reputation can ameliorate problems caused by asymmetric information.

In our experience participants rarely have enough information, and the situation can seldom be adequately simplified so that a formal game-theoretic model can provide a literal guide to action. Rather, in many situations game-theoretic frameworks provide logical reasoning and a structured lens to study phenomena, such as signaling, commitment, and reputation. In that sense, game theory is a good fit with the overall emphasis on strategic thinking in this book and supports our motivation for focusing on intuition, reasoning, and phenomena involving strategic interactions.

# CREDITS

Figure 6-3: F. M. Scherer and David Ross, *Industrial Market Structure and Economic Performance*, Third Edition. Copyright © 1990 by Houghton Mifflin Company. Adapted with permission.

Figure 6-4: Adapted with the permission of The Free Press, a Division of Simon & Schuster, Inc., from *Competitive Strategy: Techniques for Analyzing Industries and Competitors* by Michael E. Porter. Copyright © 1980, 1998 by The Free Press.

Figure 11-4 and Figure 11-5: From *Only the Paranoid Survive* by Andrew S. Grove, copyright © 1996 by Andrew S. Grove. Used by permission of Doubleday, a division of Random House, Inc.

Figure 11-6: Copyright © 1984, by The Regents of the University of California. Reprinted from the *California Management Review*, Vol. 26, No. 3. By permission of The Regents.

Figure 12-1: DILBERT © UFS. Reprinted by permission.

Figure 13-2: From *Cultures and Organizations: Software of the Mind*, First Edition, by Geert Hofstede, 1991. Copyright © Geert Hofstede. Used with permission.

# INDEX

## A

Abrahams, Jeffrey, 24$n$
Acquisitions, 368, 399
Actions, in oligopoly, 188, 189–197
Advance sign-ups, 325
Aguilar, Francis J., 9$n$, 30$n$
Airbus, 44, 141–142, 189
Alcoa, 237
Amazon.com, 37–38, 217
Amdahl Corporation, 147
American Airlines, 207, 208, 237, 319$n$
American National Standards Institute
(ANSI), 326
American Tobacco, 212
America Online (AOL), 40, 319
Anderson, Philip, 296$n$
Antitrust, 211–213
collusion in, 211–213
entry barriers and, 236–237
interfirm agreements and, 202–203,
213
price discrimination and, 268–269
price predation in, 211
Apple Computer, 11, 46, 101, 166, 295,
311, 315, 317, 318
Applied Materials, mission statement
of, 26$n$
ARC analysis, 75–90
architecture in, 75, 76–86, 89–90
competitive advantage and, 95–103,
111–113
coordination problem and, 87–90, 91
culture in, 76, 88–90
of multibusiness company, 371–377
organization design and, 75–90,
371–377
routines in, 76, 86–88, 89–90

strategic alignment and, 97–100
Architecture
compensation and rewards, 82–86
defined, 75
firm performance and, 371–373
structure, 76–82, 343–345
Armco, 122–123
Asea Brown Boveri (ABB), 12, 83
Asset analysis, 35–36
Asymmetric information, in games. *See*
Game theory
AT&T, 50–51, 105, 131, 150
Autonomous strategy process, 381,
395–397

## B

Bain, Joe S., 124$n$
Bandwagon effect, 322, 323
Bargaining power, 251–254
Barney, Jay B., 53, 53$n$
Baron, David P., 120$n$
Baron, James, 73$n$
Bartlett, Christopher A., 348$n$
Benchmarking
compensation and, 84
with market transactions, 257
of transfer prices, 85
Benetton, 155–157, 293, 332
Benkard, C. Lanier, 224$n$
Bennis, Warren, 27, 27$n$
Bertrand equilibrium. *See* Game theory
Bethlehem Steel, 122–123, 208
Bias, compensation and, 84
BIC Company, 56–57, 229–230
Blockbuster Entertainment Group,
mission statement of, 24

Boeing Corporation, 44, 52, 141–142, 153–154, 189, 337

Bootlegging, 109–110

Borders, Inc., 31–32, 34, 36, 37–38, 391–392

Boston Consulting Group, 399, 400

Bower, Joseph L., 297n

Branding, 44, 85–86

Bresnahan, Timothy, 163n, 167n, 231, 232

British Petroleum (BP), 105–106, 343

Brock, Gerald, 206n

Brock, James, 272n

Brown, Shona L., 401n

Bundling, and price discrimination, 267

Burgelman, Robert A., 15, 15n, 299, 394n

Business development function, 115

Business strategy, 2–10, 19–38
  corporate strategy versus, 351–352
  describing, 19–23
  dynamics of, 6–8
  goals of, 3–4
  mission statement and, 24–27
  nature of, 12–13
  strategy process and, 33–38, 383–390
  strategy statement, 28–32

Buyer power
  bargaining with powerful suppliers, 251–254
  change and, 276
  in Structure-Conduct-Performance (SCP) paradigm, 126–127
  value capture and, 247–254
  in value chain analysis, 143, 244
  vertical power, 140–142

Buyer preferences, 305–306


C

Canon, 166, 303, 333–334

Capability advantage, 49–55
  kinds of capabilities, 46–48

positional advantage versus, 41–43
  relationship to positional advantage, 51–55
  as sustainable competitive advantage, 49–50

Capacity, in oligopoly, 190–197

Carroll, Glenn R., 282n, 286

Causal ambiguity, 49

Caves, Richard, 139n

Centralized structure, 110–111, 344–345

Chandler, Alfred, 78–79

Change, strategic, 36–38, 271–304
  barriers to, 294–301
  and competitive advantage, 274–277
  costs of, 117
  in evolution of automobile industry, 272–274
  in evolution of industry organization, 287–294
  in evolution of strategy, 389–390, 393–397
  and industry life cycle, 277–287
  managing, 294–304

Characteristics maps, 157–161

Charles Schwab, 394

Cheap talk, 202

Christensen, Clayton M., 297n, 298

Chrysler, 207, 262, 273, 339

Ciba-Geigy, 331

Cisco Systems, 51, 153

Clark, Kim B., 297, 297n

Clayton Act, 237

Coca-Cola Company, 1, 12, 172, 209, 210, 226

Collectivism-individualism, 338–339

Collis, David J., 360n

Collusion, 211–213

Commitment problem, 377, 416. See also Game theory

Compaq Computer, 4–6, 7

Compatibility benefits
  for demand-side increasing returns, 306–308, 317–318
  system compatibility, 317–318

Compensation, 82–86
Competency trap, 296–298
Competition
    change and, 275–276
    in concentrated markets. *See*
        Dominant firm structure;
        Oligopoly
    and market share, 168–169
    in markets with demand-side
        increasing returns, 311–317
        competitive strategies for building
        DSIR, 315–317
        installed base and tipping, 311–315
    and product differentiation, 165–169
    product positioning and, 170–172
    spectrum of, 150–154. *See also*
        Spectrum of competition
    strategy of, 386–387
    in Structure-Conduct-Performance
        (SCP) paradigm, 126–127
    in value chain analysis, 136–138,
        139–140, 142
Competitive advantage, 39–63, 93–118
    ARC analysis and, 95–103, 111–113
    and business strategy, 21–22
    capability, 41–43, 46–48, 49–55, 66
    central direction and, 110–111
    change and, 274–277
    cost-quality frontier and, 59–62
    culture and, 89
    exploiters and, 94, 103–106, 108,
        109–116
    explorers and, 94, 103–106, 108–110,
        111–116
    interdependence and tight-coupling,
        106–109
    organizational slack and, 109–110
    organization design and, 65–67,
        93–118
    positional, 41–46, 50–55, 66
    and resource-based view of the firm,
        53–55
    strategic alignment for, 95–101
    strategic spillovers and, 361–366
    in strategy process, 382
    sustainable, 48–51
    value and, 39–40
Complements
    industry definitions of, 146–147
    nature of, 132
    price discrimination and, 266–267
    switching costs and, 228
Computer Associates, 313
Concentrated markets, 185–214
    antitrust and, 211–213, 236–237,
        268–269
    defined, 185
    *See also* Dominant firm structure;
        Oligopoly
Conglomerate form, 360–361
Conner Peripherals, 298
Conscious parallelism doctrine, 212
Consistency, organizational, 99–100
Consumer loyalty, incumbency
    advantage from, 226
Consumer preferences
    characteristics maps and, 157–161
    and product differentiation, 157–162
Contingency planning, 302
Continual improvement methods, 104
Contracts
    as entry barriers, 235
    explicit, 263
    relational, 256–257
Control Data Corporation (CDC),
    316
Coordination problem, 71–73, 74–75
    ARC analysis and, 89–90, 91
    corporate culture and, 88–89
    in incentives and rewards, 82–86
    organizational structure and, 79–82
    routinization and, 87, 374
    strategic alignment and, 96–97
    value creation and, 257–260
Corn Flakes, 160, 163, 165, 179, 180,
    182
Corporate direction, 377–378
Corporate strategy, 12–13
    business strategy versus, 351–352
    framework for, 356–357

Corporate strategy *(continued)*
   strategic spillovers, 354–356, 358,
      361–366
   strategy processes, 397–403
      role of general managers in,
         402–403
      for strategically independent
         businesses, 398–401
      for strategically interdependent
         businesses, 401–402
   *See also* Multibusiness company
Cost-quality frontier, 55–62
   framework for, 58–59
   to illustrate competitive advantage,
      59–62
   product quality and cost, 56–58
Cournot equilibrium. *See* Game theory
Creative destruction, 294
Creative process, 382
Credibility, in competition. *See* Game
      theory
Cross-functional teams, at Southwest
      Airlines, 68–69, 70–71, 97–99
Crown Cork & Seal, 332
Culture
   coordination problem and, 88–89
   defined, 76
   and exploitation/exploration, 115. *See
      also* Exploiters; Explorers
   incentive problem and, 89
   of Southwest Airlines, 69
Cumulative investment, as entry
      barrier, 222–226
Customer relationship, and positional
      advantage, 44
Customized components, 258–259


**D**
Daimler-Benz, 85, 339
Deadweight loss (DWL), 175
Dean Witter, 365–366
Decline stage, 286–287
*De facto* standards, 45, 326–327
*De jure* standards, 327

Dell Computer, 4–6, 12, 107, 254, 290
Demand-side increasing returns
      (DSIR), 228, 305–328, 386
   competition in markets with,
      311–317
      competitive strategies for building,
         315–317
      installed base and tipping, 311–315
   nature of, 305–306
   sources of, 306–310
      compatibility benefits, 306–308,
         317–318
      network benefits, 308–310
   standards-setting processes, 326–328
   systems of components, 317–321
      leveraging market position,
         318–321
      system compatibility, 317–318
   technology adoption, 321–326
      managing, 323–326
      nature of, 321–323
Digital Equipment Corporation
      (DEC), 5
Direct Satellite Broadcasting (DSB), 51
Disney Corporation, 24, 50, 354–357,
      358, 376
Distinctive competence, 47–48
Distribution channels, and positional
      advantage, 45
Diversification, 359–361, 366,
      368–369, 376
Divestiture strategy, 368*n*, 399
Divisional organization, 77, 78–79, 81,
      82–86
Dominant firm structure
   defined, 186
   market structure and firm behavior,
      154
   nature of, 151, 152–153, 209
   persistence of, 209–210
Dominion Engineering, 45
Double marginalization, 250–251
DSIR. *See* Demand-side increasing
      returns (DSIR)
DuPont, 78–79, 295

Durable productive assets, switching costs of, 227

**E**
Early adopters, 323
Eastman Kodak, 7, 186, 296–297
eBay, 230, 313, 314
Economies of scale, 23
  global efficiency and, 340–342
  incumbency advantage and, 217–222
  minimum efficient scale (MES), 220–222, 332–333
  in multibusiness company, 364
Economies of scope
  incumbency advantage from, 229–231
  in multibusiness company, 364
EDS, 153, 209, 367
Eisenhardt, Kathleen M., 401n
Eli Lilly, 332–333, 363
Elzinga, Kenneth K., 284, 285
Emergence stage, 278–282
EMI, 39–40, 280, 365
Entry barriers
  antitrust and, 236–237
  change and, 276
  cumulative investment, 222–226
  economies of scale, 217–222
  examples of, 138–140
  learning economies, 223–225
  nature of, 138, 216
  signaling, 235–236
  in Structure-Conduct-Performance (SCP) paradigm, 126–127
  theory of, 231–232
  in value chain analysis, 138–140, 142
  vertical foreclosure, 235
  *See also* Incumbency advantage
Essential facility, 211
European Union (EU), 213, 335
Evolutionary economics, 14, 15
Exit costs, 286–287
Experience goods, incumbency advantage from, 226–227
Explicit contracts, 263

Exploiters
  accountabilities in, 112–113
  ARC analysis of, 111–113
  centralized control of, 110–111
  exploration by, 114–116
  intentional process and, 397
  nature of, 94, 103–106
  organizational slack and, 109, 110
  tight coupling of, 108
Explorers
  ARC analysis of, 111–113
  autonomous processes and, 397
  decentralization of, 111
  exploitation by, 114–116
  globalization and, 333–334, 342–344
  hiring practices of, 112
  loose coupling of, 108–109
  nature of, 94, 103–106
  organizational slack and, 109, 110
Extensive form games. *See* Game theory
External environment, 43, 65
  business strategy evaluation in, 386–387
  defined, 2–3

**F**
FCB-Publicis, 80
Federation structure, 344–345
Financial capital, 367–369
Fine, Charles H., 278n, 291
Fiorina, Carly, as CEO of HP, 356
Firm
  concept of, 12–13
  performance of, 371–373
Firm behavior, nature of, 153–154
First-mover advantage, 6, 171, 198
Five Forces, 124–127
Fixed costs, 217–219
Flat organization, 79
Ford Motor Company, 146–147, 160–161, 171, 185, 207, 262, 274, 342–343, 361
Freeman, John, 14n

Fuji-Xerox, 302–304, 326
Functional organization, 77–78

**G**

Game theory, 405–426
  credibility, commitment, and
      flexibility, 416–421
  effect of repetition, 414–416
  Nash equilibrium and duopoly,
      410–414
  prisoners' dilemma, 406–410
  strategic behavior and asymmetric
      information, 422–425
Gap, The, 155–157, 172, 185
Gatekeepers, and positional advantage,
      45
Gates, Bill, 306, 315
General Electric (GE), 9–10, 40, 78–79,
      145, 368, 372, 375, 378, 399, 400
General manager
  and goals of strategic management,
      3–4
  impact of, 14–16
  nature of, 13
  role in corporate strategy process, 13,
      15–16, 402–403
General Motors (GM), 2, 6–7,
      160–161, 171, 206–207,
      254–257, 273–274, 299–301,
      345, 367
Geographic incumbency, and positional
      advantage, 45
Georgia-Pacific, 46, 47
Ghemawat, Pankaj, 2n, 48n
Ghoshal, Sumantra, 348n
Giveaways, 315–316
Global efficiency, 340–342
Globalization, 7, 329–349
  implications for managers, 330–332
  of industries and economies, 334–335
  organization structure in, 344–349
  and product differentiation, 167
  strategic challenges, 335–349
    global efficiency, 340–342

learning, 333–334, 342–344
local responsiveness, 336–340
organizing for, 344–349
strategic gains from, 332–334
Goals
  and business strategy, 20–21
  of strategic management, 3–4
Government protection and support,
      and positional advantage, 44–45
Grant, Robert M., 48, 48n
Grove, Andrew S., 288, 288n
Growth stage, 283–284

**H**

Hall, Bronwyn, 122, 123
Hamel, Gary, 52, 52n
Hamermesh, Richard, 9n
Hannan, Michael T., 14n, 282n, 286
Harrod's, 93
Hasselblad, 250
Henderson, Rebecca M., 297, 297n
Hewlett-Packard, 12, 79, 88, 297,
      299–301, 351, 356
Hidden action, 74. *See also* Game theory
Hidden information, 74. *See also* Game
      theory
Hirschman-Herfindahl Index (HHI),
      137
Hofstede, Geert H., 338
Honda, 171, 337, 394
Horizontal communication, 343–344
Horizontal differentiation, 161
Horizontal linkages, in organizational
      structure, 80–82, 343–344
Horizontal organization, of industry,
      287–292
Human capital, 369–371
Hurwicz, 139n

**I**

IBM, 50–51, 146, 147, 152–153, 166,
      210, 266–267, 280, 288, 295,
      316, 319, 324, 326

Incentive problem, 73–75
  ARC analysis and, 89–90, 91
  coordination problem and, 82–86
  culture and, 89
  routines and, 87–88
  strategic alignment and, 96–97
  value creation and, 260–263
Incumbency advantage, 138–140
  from consumer loyalty, 226
  from cumulative investment, 222–226
  from demand-side increasing returns,
      228
  nature of, 215–216
  through packing product space,
      232–235
  scale advantages, 217–222
  scope economies and, 229–231
  strategic creation of, 232–237
  from sunk costs, 229
  from switching costs, 227–228
  and uncertain product quality,
      226–227
  *See also* Entry barriers
Individualism-collectivism, 338–339
Industry analysis, 119–147
  competition in, 136–138, 139–140,
      142
  entry barriers in, 138–140
  example of, 133–136, 142–144
  framework, 127–144
  industry definition in, 144–147
  industry map in, 386–387
  organizing, 123–127
  performance effects of industry
      characteristics, 120–123
  Structure-Conduct-Performance
      (SCP) paradigm, 124–127
  value capture in, 136
  value creation in, 129–136
  vertical power in, 140–142
Industry definition, 144–147
Industry life cycle, 277–287
  decline, 286–287
  emergence, 278–282
  growth, 283–284

  maturity, 284–286
Industry structure, 287–294
  horizontal versus vertical, 287–292
  organizational implications of,
      292–294
Influence, 325, 374–375
Information
  diversification and, 369, 376
  in oligopoly, 188, 200–202
  routines for, 373–374
  signaling and, 200–202
  types of, 200
Innovation
  as entry barrier, 225–226
  recognizing value of, 343–344
Installed base, 45, 311–315
Intel, 153, 166, 288, 305, 311, 318
Intellectual property rights, 325–326
Intentional strategy process, 381,
      395–397
Interdependence
  nature of, 81–82
  and tight-coupling, 106–109
Interfirm agreements, 202–203, 213
Internal context, 43, 65
  business strategy evaluation in,
      385–386
  defined, 2–3
Internalization. *See* Globalization
Intervention, 375–377
Investment, as entry barrier, 222–226

**J**
Johnson & Johnson, 85, 375, 376–377

**K**
*Kaizen* method, 104
Keller, Greg, 160*n*
Kellogg's, 160, 165, 166, 237
Kirin, 336–337
Kmart, 93
Kodak, 7, 186, 296–297
Kreps, David M. 73*n*

**L**

Lamont, Owen, 81$n$
Lang, Larry H. P., 359$n$
Larson, Andrea, 262$n$
Lazear, 73$n$
Learning economies, 223–225
Leasing, 326
Liaison role, 80
Liggett & Meyers, 212
Limit pricing, 236
Line managers, in strategy process, 396
Litman, Barry, 329$n$
LL Bean, 46
Local adaptation, 345
Local responsiveness, 336–340
Location, switching costs of, 228
Locational advantage, 346–348, 349
Lockheed, 224
Logic
  and business strategy, 22–23
  logical incrementalism, 15
Loosely coupled organizations, 82, 106–109
Lotus, 325–326
Loyalty programs, switching costs of, 228

**M**

Management levels
  line managers, 396
  middle management, 396
  senior management, 83, 115, 382–383, 396
March, James, 94$n$, 104, 118, 118$n$, 296–297
Market position, leveraging, 318–321
Market segmentation, niche markets and, 163–165
Market share, and competition, 168–169
Market structure, nature of, 153–154
Market value to asset value, 121–123
Marks & Spencer, 44, 337
Mason, Edward S., 124$n$

Matsushita, 344–345
Maturity stage, 284–286
McDonald's, 58, 111
McGahan, Anita M., 122$n$, 160$n$
McKinsey and Co., 363–364, 399, 400
Merck, 46, 295, 364
Metcalfe's law, 308$n$
Microsoft, 128–129, 153, 166, 306, 314, 315, 318–319, 320–321, 324, 362, 389–390
Middle managers, in strategy process, 396
Miller, 159, 161
Minimum efficient scale (MES), 220–222, 332–333
Mintzberg, Henry, 13, 13$n$
Mission statement, 24–27
  example of, 25–26
  in strategic plans, 391
Mobility barriers, 171–172, 210
Monopoly
  market structure and firm behavior, 154
  nature of, 150–152, 173–176
  value capture in, 247–249
Mont Blanc, 56–57
Monteverde, Kirk, 274$n$
Montgomery, Cynthia A., 53, 53$n$, 360$n$
Morgan Stanley Dean Witter, 366
Motorola, 331
Multibusiness company, 351–379
  adding value, 358–361
  corporate direction, 377–378
  organization design, 371–377
  performance of diversified firms, 359–361
  resource allocation, 356–357, 367–371
  strategic spillovers, 354–356, 358, 361–366
  strategy process of, 397–403
  See also Corporate strategy
Murdoch, Rupert, 236

**N**

Nanus, Burt, 27, 27*n*

Nash equilibrium, 410–414

National culture
   individualism-collectivism, 338–339
   power distance, 338, 339

Natural monopoly, 51

Nelson, Richard, 15, 15*n*

Netscape, 315, 389–390

Network effects, 80, 228, 308–310

Nevo, Aviv, 158*n*

New United Motor Manufacturing Inc.
      (NUMMI), 256–257, 260

Niche markets
   and demand-side increasing returns,
      315, 316–317
   example of, 155–157
   market segments in, 163–165
   market structure and firm behavior,
      154
   nature of, 151, 152, 154–155, 178–183
   product differentiation and, 154–157

Nike, 44, 85, 335, 361

Noise, compensation and, 84

Nordstrom, 44

Norm of reciprocity, 88

North American Free Trade
      Agreement (NAFTA), 335

Northern Telecom, 185

Novo-Nordisk, 81, 332–333

Nucor, 122–123

NutraSweet, 112, 150, 383


**O**

Objectives
   performance, 10–12
   statement of, 382

Ohmae, Kenichi, 346

Oligopoly, 186–209
   actions in, 188, 189–197
   defined, 186
   information in, 188, 200–202
   market structure and firm behavior,
      154

nature of, 151, 153, 186–187
   players in, 187, 199–200
   repetition in, 188, 202–208
   timing in, 188, 197–199

OPEC cartel, 247

Open standard, 325

Opportunity analysis, 35–36

Opportunity cost of resources,
      129–130

Option value, 229

O'Reilly, Charles, 68*n*

Organizational ecology, 14

Organizational slack, 109–110

Organizational structure, 6–7, 76–82
   compensation and, 82–86
   coordination and, 79–82
   divisional organization, 77, 78–79,
      81, 82–86
   federated versus centralized,
      344–345
   flat organization, 79
   functional organization, 77–78
   in globalization, 344–349
   horizontal linkages in, 80–82,
      343–344
   structure of technology and, 297
   tall organization, 79

Organizational uncertainty, 280–281

Organization design, 65–92
   ARC analysis and, 75–90, 371–377
   architecture in, 75, 76–86, 89–90
   and competitive advantage, 65–67,
      93–118
   coordination problem, 71–73, 74–75,
      80–86, 89–90
   culture in, 76, 88–90
   incentive problem, 73–75, 82–86,
      89–90
   organizational consistency and,
      99–100
   routines in, 76, 86–88, 89–90
   at Southwest Airlines, 67–71
   strategic alignment and, 95
   and strategy process, 383

Organization learning, 105–106
  globalization and, 333–334,
    342–344
  learning economies, 223–225

**P**

Pacific Bell, 144–145
Packing the product space, 232–235
Pascale, Richard T., 394n
Patagonia, 11
Penetration pricing, 315–316
Penrose, Edith T., 53, 53n
PepsiCo, 85, 209, 210, 226, 254
Perceptual maps, 157–161
Perfect competition, nature of, 151,
    152, 176–178
Performance effects
  examples of, 120–121
  and market value to asset value,
    121–123
  nature of, 120
Performance objectives, 10–12
Periphery, 298–299
Pfeffer, Jeffrey, 68n
Philips, 334, 344
Pirating, 325–326
Players, in oligopoly, 187, 199–200
Porter, Michael E., 53, 60, 60n, 122n,
    124–127, 136, 346–348, 359,
    359n
Positional advantage, 41–46, 50–55, 66
  capability advantage versus, 41–43
  examples of, 44–46
  forms of, 43–44
  general characteristics of, 45–46
  relationship to capability advantage,
    51–55
  as sustainable competitive advantage,
    50–51
Positive feedback, from installed based,
    312–315
Potential industry earnings (PIE),
    129–144
  change and, 274–276

competition and, 136–138, 142
  determinants of, 130–133
  dividing, 136–144
  entry barriers and, 138–140, 142
  example of, 133–136
  incumbency advantage and, 216
  monopoly and, 173–176
  niche markets and, 178–183
  perfect competition and, 176–178
  in value creation and value capture,
    239–242
  vertical power and, 140–142
Power distance, 338, 339
Prahalad, C. K., 52, 52n
Predatory pricing, 211, 236–237,
    315–316
Price commitments, 326
Price discrimination, 175, 264–269
  antitrust restrictions on, 268–269
  bundling and, 267
  perfect, 265
  re-sale prevention and, 268
  time and, 267
  willingness to pay and, 265–267
Price fixing, 211–213
Procter & Gamble, 45–46, 85, 242,
    345, 364, 366
Product differentiation, 6, 137–138
  and competition, 165–169
  consumer preferences and, 157–162
  example of, 155–157
  horizontal, 161
  niche markets and, 154–157
  vertical, 161–162
Productivity, wages and, 341–342
Product positioning, 170–172
Profitability
  compensation and, 82–86
  performance effects of industry
    characteristics and, 120–123
Profit maximization, 11–12, 20–21,
    82
Promotional advantage, as entry
    barrier, 226
Public sector, 120, 327, 333

**Q**

Quality
    in cost-quality frontier, 55–62
    incumbency advantage and, 226–227
Quality circles, 104
Quantum, 298
Quigley, Joseph, 28*n*
Quinn, James Brian, 15, 15*n*


**R**

Rank Organization, 303
Ravenscraft, David J., 360*n*
Real options. *See* Game theory
Regional organization, 346
Reiss, Peter, 231, 232
Relational contracts, 256–257
Relationship-specific investments,
    258
Repetition, in oligopoly, 188, 202–208
Reputation, leveraging, 324. *See also*
    Game theory
Re-sale, preventing, 268
Resource allocation, 356–357, 367–371
    in corporate strategy process, 401
    financial capital, 367–369
    human capital, 369–371
    personnel evaluation and, 378
Ricoh, 303
R.J. Reynolds, 212, 358
RJR Nabisco, 212, 358
Robinson-Patman Act, 268–269
Rodrik, Dani, 342
Rolls Royce, 58
Ross, David, 213*n*
Rotemberg, Julio, 207*n*
Routines
    defined, 76
    for information and influence,
        373–375
    interfaces for, 87–88
    for intervention, 375–377
    nature of, 86–87
Rule of squares, 308*n*
Rumelt, Richard P., 122*n*

**S**

Saatchi and Saatchi, 120
Saloner, Garth, 101*n*, 207*n*
Samuel Adams, 159, 161
Saturn division (GM), 2, 160–161, 171,
    299
Scenario analysis, 301–302
Scherer, F. Michael, 213*n*, 360*n*
Schmalensee, Richard, 122*n*
Schumpeter, Joseph, 279, 279*n*, 294, 304
Schwinn, 291, 293
Scope of business, 21, 382
Scott Morton, Fiona, 213*n*
Screening. *See* Game theory
Seagate Technology, 298, 299
Secure Digital Music Initiative
    (SDMI), 326
Sega, 93
Self-enforcing agreements, 204
Senior management
    and business development function,
        115
    compensation and, 83
    and strategy process, 382–383, 396
Shapiro, Carl, 313*n*
Sherman Act, 211–213, 236–237
Shimano, 292
Signaling
    as entry barrier, 235–236
    nature of, 200–202. *See also* Game
        theory
Silicon Graphics, 101
Simple market transactions, 256–257
Sony Corporation, 46, 47, 49, 85, 101,
    325, 362–363
Southwest Airlines, 67–71, 73, 88–89,
    97–100, 387–388
Specialization, 77, 290, 293
Spectrum of competition, 150–154
    dominant firm, 151, 152–153, 154,
        209–210
    monopoly, 150–152, 154, 173–176,
        247–249
    niche markets, 151, 152, 154–157,
        163–165, 178–183, 315–317

Spectrum of competition (continued)
  oligopoly. See Oligopoly
  perfect competition, 151, 152,
    176–178
Sprint, 57
Standardization
  compatibility benefits of, 306–308
  de facto standards, 45, 326–327
  de jure standards, 327
  open standard, 325
  standards-setting process, 326–328
Standard Oil, 7
Status, and positional advantage, 45
Stern, Scott, 163n
Stevenson, Howard H., 48, 48n
Stigler, George, 290n
Strategic alignment, 95–101
  components of, 95–97
  other examples of, 101
  at Southwest Airlines, 97–100
Strategic alliances, 7–8
Strategic groups, niche markets and,
    163–165
Strategic management, 1–2
  goals of, 3–4
  nature of strategy and, 4
  role of business strategy and, 2–10
Strategic planning, 8–10
  problems of, 9–10
  strategic thinking versus, 8–10, 382
  in strategy process, 8–9, 15, 383,
    390–392
Strategic spillovers, 354–356, 358,
    361–366
  identifying and managing, 362–363
  sources of, 363–366
Strategic thinking
  requirements of, 12
  strategic planning versus, 8–10, 382
Strategic uncertainty, 281
Strategy process, 8–9, 381–403
  autonomous, 381, 395–397
  business strategy, 33–38, 383–390
  corporate strategy, 397–403
    role of general manager, 402–403

  for strategically independent
    businesses, 398–401
  for strategically interdependent
    businesses, 401–402
  evolution of strategy in, 389–390,
    393–397
  intentional, 381, 395–397
  principles of, 382–383
  selecting and communicating
    strategy, 388–389
  of Southwest Airlines, 67–71,
    387–388
  strategic change and, 36–38,
    271–304, 389–390
  strategic plans in, 8–10, 15, 382, 383,
    390–392
  strategy evaluation in, 35–36, 385–388
  strategy identification in, 34–35,
    384–385
Strategy statement, 28–32
  benefits of, 29–30
  example of, 31–32
  form and use of, 30–31
Structure-Conduct-Performance (SCP)
    paradigm, 124–127
Stulz, Rene M., 359n
Substitutes
  industry definition based on "close,"
    145–146
  Justice Department definition of,
    145–146
  nature of, 131–132
Sunk costs, incumbency advantage
    from, 229
Sun Microsystems, 326, 361
Sunrise Medical, charter of, 24–25
Supplier power, 245n
  bargaining with powerful buyers,
    251–254
  change and, 276
  in Structure-Conduct-Performance
    (SCP) paradigm, 126–127
  value capture and, 247–254
  in value chain analysis, 142, 243–244
  vertical power, 140–142

Sustainable competitive advantage, 48–51
Swatch, 335
Switching costs
   and demand-side increasing returns, 312–313, 317
   incumbency advantage from, 227
   sources of, 227–228
SWOT analysis, 35–36

**T**

Tall organization, 79
Task forces, 81
Teams, 81
Technological uncertainty, 280
Technology adoption, 321–326
   bandwagon effect, 322, 323
   early adopters, 323
   expectations, 323
   intermediate adopters, 323
   managing, 323–326
Teece, David, 274$n$
3Com, 358
360 degree evaluation, 84–85
3M Corporation, 7–8, 85, 105, 109, 112, 114, 383
Tightly coupled organizations, 82, 106–109
Time Warner, 235, 256
Timing, in oligopoly, 188, 197–199
Tipping, 311–315
Top-down approach, 16
Toyota, 171, 256–257, 260, 344–345
Training, switching costs of, 227
Trajtenberg, Manual, 39$n$, 163$n$
Transaction costs, 258
   switching costs of, 227–228, 312–313, 317
Transfer prices, 85
Transnational corporation, 348–349
Treaty of Rome, 213
Turner Broadcasting, 235, 256
Tushman, Michael L., 296$n$

**U**

Uncertainty
   in emerging markets, 278–282
   of product quality, 226–227
   scenario analysis and, 301–302
Unilever, 344
U.S. Steel, 7, 206, 211

**V**

Value
   adding, 358–361, 368–369, 383
   and competitive advantage, 39–40
Value-based corporate strategy, 369
Value capture, 244–255
   without buyer or supplier power, 245–247
   through dividing potential industry earnings (PIE), 136, 142–144
   in industry analysis, 136
   reducing power in other segments and, 254–255
   by single powerful supplier (or buyer), 247–249
   and value creation, 239–242
   when buyers and suppliers are powerful, 249–254
Value chain, 127–144
   buyer power in, 143, 244
   competition in, 136–138, 139–140, 142
   entry and incumbency advantage in, 138–140
   entry barriers in, 138–140, 142
   examples of, 128–129, 133–136, 139–140, 142–144, 242–243
   nature of, 127–128
   supplier power in, 142, 243–244
   value capture in, 136, 142–144
   value creation in, 129–136
   vertical power in, 140–142
Value creation, 255–263
   without buyer or supplier power, 246
   coordination problem in, 257–260
   example of, 133–136

incentive problem in, 260–263
potential industry earnings (PIE)
   and, 129–136, 274–276
with single monopolist, 248
and value capture, 239–242
Values statement, 26–27
Variable costs, 217
Varian, Hal, 313$n$
Variation, selection, and retention
   (VSR), 105–106, 345
Vertical communication, 343–344
Vertical differentiation, 161–162
Vertical foreclosure, 235
Vertical integration, to prevent re-sale,
   268
Vertical organization, of industry,
   287–292
Vertical power, in value chain analysis,
   140–142
Vision, 27, 391


W
Wages, productivity and, 341–342

Wal-Mart, 45, 102, 170–171, 227,
   241–242, 260
Walt Disney Corporation, 24, 50,
   354–356, 358, 376
Wayland, Rebecca E., 347
Welch, Jack, 11, 378
Wernerfeld, Birger, 53, 53$n$
Whinston, Michael, 139$n$
Wiersema, Fred, 68$n$
Winter, Sidney., 15$n$
World Trade Organization (WTO),
   334–335
World Wide Web, 310


X
Xerox Corporation, 8, 52, 85, 116,
   302–304


Z
Zilog, 305